READING CRITICALLY
WRITING WELL

A READER AND GUIDE

SEVENTH EDITION

READING CRITICALLY WRITING WELL

A READER AND GUIDE

Rise B. Axelrod
University of California, Riverside

Charles R. Cooper
University of California, San Diego

Alison M. Warriner
California State University, Hayward

BEDFORD/ST. MARTIN'S
Boston ◆ New York

For Bedford/St. Martin's

Senior Developmental Editor: John Elliott
Senior Production Editor: Harold Chester and Ryan Sullivan
Senior Production Supervisor: Nancy Myers
Senior Marketing Manager: Rachel M. Falk
Art Direction and Cover Design: Lucy Krikorian
Text Design: Wanda Kossak
Copy Editor: Wendy Polhemus-Annibell
Cover Art: Joan Gold, *Flourish,* © 2001. Courtesy of Lisa Harris Gallery.
Composition: Macmillan India Ltd.
Printing and Binding: R.R. Donnelley & Sons Company

President: Joan E. Feinberg
Editorial Director: Denise B. Wydra
Editor in Chief: Nancy Perry
Director of Marketing: Karen Melton Soeltz
Director of Editing, Design, and Production: Marcia Cohen
Managing Editor: Erica T. Appel

Acknowledgments

Natalie Angier. "Intolerance of Boyish Behavior." Originally titled "The Debilitating Malady Called Boyhood" from *The New York Times,* July 24, 1994. Copyright © 1994 by The New York Times Company. Reprinted by permission.

Beth L. Bailey. "Dating." From *Front Porch to Back Seat: Courtship in 20th Century America.* Copyright © 1988 by Beth L. Bailey. Reprinted with the permission of The Johns Hopkins University Press.

Acknowledgments and copyrights are continued at the back of the book on pages 761–63, which constitute an extension of the copyright page.

It is a violation of the law to reproduce these selections by any means whatsoever without the written permission of the copyright holder.

Preface

Read, read, read . . . Just like a carpenter who works as an apprentice and studies the master. Read!

—WILLIAM FAULKNER

I went back to the good nature books that I had read. And I analyzed them. I wrote outlines of whole books—outlines of chapters—so that I could see their structure. And I copied down their transitional sentences or their main sentences or their closing sentences or their lead sentences. I especially paid attention to how these writers made transitions between paragraphs and scenes.

— ANNIE DILLARD

In these quotations, the Nobel Prize–winning novelist William Faulkner and the Pulitzer Prize–winning essayist Annie Dillard tell us what many authors know intuitively—that reading critically helps writers learn to write well. Reading closely and critically also helps students become analytical thinkers.

Now in its seventh edition, *Reading Critically, Writing Well* helps students see the connection between reading closely and critically and writing thoughtfully and effectively. By using the book's approach, students learn how texts work rhetorically to achieve their purposes with particular readers. They also learn an array of strategies for critical reading and thinking—strategies that contribute to enhanced comprehension of a text, inspire active engagement with it, and stimulate analysis of the text's as well as the reader's own assumptions, values, and beliefs.

This book brings critical reading and writing together by engaging students in two fundamental ways of reading: reading for meaning and reading like a writer. While Reading for Meaning sections give students insight into how readers construct meanings from what they read, Reading like a Writer sections teach students how to construct their own texts rhetorically to influence their readers' understanding and critical response. The two strategies are introduced in Chapter 1, developed further at the beginning of each subsequent chapter, and applied to every reading selection throughout the text. Through continued use of these two critical reading strategies, students gain confidence in their ability to read with a critical eye and to write effectively in different rhetorical situations.

FEATURES

The special features of *Reading Critically, Writing Well* include:

Engaging Readings Demonstrating Eight Different Types of Real-World Writing

Reading Critically, Writing Well includes 58 readings—five or six published essays and two student essays in each assignment chapter (Chapters 2–9). Each of these chapters focuses on a specific type of writing that students will encounter during college or on the job, including four expository genres (autobiography, observation, reflection, and explanation of concepts) and four argumentative genres (evaluation, speculation about causes or effects, proposal to solve a problem, and position on a controversial issue). Chosen to stimulate lively class discussion and to illustrate a variety of writing strategies, the readings provide students with provocative perspectives on many important topics. You will find many tried and true essays by distinguished professional and academic writers such as Annie Dillard, John McPhee, Barbara Ehrenreich, Deborah Tannen, Stephen King, Amitai Etzioni, and Randall Kennedy.

Uniquely Thorough Instruction in the Reading-Writing Connection

Reading Critically, Writing Well teaches students how to analyze the content and craft of successful writing and then shows them how to apply what they have learned to their own writing. Each assignment chapter begins with a Guide to Reading and ends with a Guide to Writing, both tailored to the distinctive features of the chapter's genre. These guides provide an array of flexible activities designed to help students learn to read a specific kind of writing with a critical eye and write it with a clear purpose for their own readers. The Guide to Reading introduces the two overall strategies for critical reading—Reading for Meaning and Reading like a Writer—that frame the questions following each reading selection. The Guide to Writing scaffolds the composing process, using concepts students have learned in their Reading like a Writer activities. These major structural elements of the book provide guidance for students in moving from critical reading to effective writing.

In addition, Appendix 1, A Catalog of Critical Reading Strategies, explains and applies to Martin Luther King Jr.'s "Letter from Birmingham Jail" seventeen additional strategies for critical reading, from annotating and summarizing to exploring the significance of figurative language and judging the writer's credibility.

"Reading like a Writer" Activities That Teach Students to Read Rhetorically

The Reading like a Writer activities help students learn how to examine and assess the effectiveness of a writer's choices in light of the purpose and audience—that is, to read rhetorically. The Guide to Reading at the beginning of each chapter presents several Reading like a Writer activities that introduce the rhetorical strategies typical of the genre. Each subsequent essay in a chapter is followed by a Reading like a Writer activity inviting students to learn more about one of these strategies. Altogether, each chapter invites students to complete nine or ten focused rhetorical analyses of readings in the same genre.

Every Reading like a Writer activity directs students to a specific part of a reading—a few sentences or paragraphs—so that students lose no time wondering where to begin their analysis. Many activities show students the first step to take. Because they are focused and accessible, these activities make it possible for even the most inexperienced readers to complete them and engage in a serious program of rhetorical learning.

Guides to Writing That Support Students' Composing

As writing instructors, we know that students need help writing essays. To provide this support, each *Reading Critically, Writing Well* chapter concludes with a comprehensive Guide to Writing that escorts students through every stage of writing, from choosing a topic and gathering information and ideas to drafting and revising and then editing and proofreading an essay. In our experience, all students, from the most anxious to the most confident writers, benefit in some way from the Guides to Writing.

Grounded in research on composing as well as in genre and learning theory, each Guide to Writing scaffolds student learning about a genre, providing temporary support so that students can focus on one stage of writing at a time. In addition, it teaches students the kinds of questions they need to ask themselves as they write and helps them apply the rhetorical knowledge gleaned from reading to writing an essay in the genre. The Guide to Critical Reading in each chapter helps students engage in constructive peer critique of their classmates' writing.

Intensive Coverage of Strategies for Research and Documentation

The Guides to Writing and the comprehensive discussions of strategies for research and documentation in Appendix 2 provide students with clear, helpful guidelines for evaluating sources, integrating them with one's own writing, and citing them using the most current MLA and APA styles. With eight different genres, students have an opportunity to practice the full gamut of research strategies, from memory search to the field research methods of observation and interview to library and Internet research.

Activities That Ask Students to Reflect on Their Learning

Research has shown that when students reflect on their learning, they clarify their understanding and remember what they have learned longer. Reflecting also enables students to think critically about what they have learned and how they have learned it. *Reading Critically, Writing Well* now provides three opportunities for students to reflect on their learning and also to discuss what they have learned with others: Reflecting on Your Experience, Reviewing What Makes [the kind of essay] Effective, and Reflecting on What You Have Learned. These activities are placed at important transitions in each chapter, at points when looking back at what they have learned will help students move forward more productively.

NEW TO THIS EDITION

Important new features enhance the seventh edition:

Many Fascinating New and Topically Linked Readings

One-third of the reading selections—20 of 58—are new, written by award-winning writers such as Nancy Gibbs and Luis J. Rodriguez, social critics such as Saira Shah and Karen Kornbluh, and distinguished professors and researchers such as Howard Gardner, Vilayanur S. Ramachandran, and Edward M. Hubbard. There are two new student essays: an absorbing autobiographical account of shoplifting by Jean Brandt and a poetic observation of a glassmaker at work by Brenda Crow.

The new readings are sure to interest students and stimulate discussion. Some of them take up topics about which students will have much to say, such as Luis J. Rodriguez's autobiographical story about a fateful encounter with the police, Mark Edmundson's memoir of a teacher who changed his life, David Brooks's and Nancy Gibbs's reflections on contemporary childhood, and Daniel T. Gilbert and Timothy D. Wilson's explanation of the concept of miswanting. Several readings with illustrations—an explanation of the causes of synesthesia as well as evaluations of a fuel-cell prototype car and of the new Disney Concert Hall by renowned architect Frank Gehry—can be used to call students' attention to various aspects of visual rhetoric and to provide models for how students can use visuals in their own writing.

For the first time, each chapter includes at least one pair of essays or other pieces of writing that engage with each other, sometimes directly, on a topic. These topically linked readings—and the accompanying activity that focuses attention on the connections and differences between them—stimulate students to respond less passively and more critically to what they read. For example, students are asked to compare two essays debating gay marriage and two different versions of Brent Staples's reflections on how his mere presence as an African American man changes public space.

Expanded "Reading for Meaning" Activities to Strengthen Critical Thinking

Recent research indicates that students entering college have read less than previous generations of students and have gotten less out of their reading. For this reason, we have expanded the Reading for Meaning activities to provide more in-depth, explicit instruction. There are now three class-tested Reading for Meaning activities following each selection that give students more help in understanding and interpreting what they are reading.

The first activity, Read to Comprehend, helps students focus on an important aspect of the reading and summarize it. Students are also invited to think about word choice and to define any words they do not understand. The second activity, Read to Respond, engages students in exploring aspects of the reading that resonate for them or that stimulate strong reactions. The third activity, Read to Analyze Underlying Assumptions, leads students to think more critically about the cultural beliefs and values implicit in the reading's word choices and assertions. Students are also encouraged to examine the cultural bases for their own assumptions as readers. Each of these three Reading for Meaning activities concludes with a list of additional critical reading strategies from Appendix 1 that would most productively enhance the student's continued efforts to comprehend, respond to, or analyze the assumptions of the reading.

Depending on your students' needs and your priorities, you may want to use one, two, or all three of these Reading for Meaning activities. Using them on a regular basis will provide students with an array of critical reading and thinking skills they can use throughout their college career.

Stronger Coverage of Argument

In addition to four chapters on different kinds of argumentative writing, we have added two new critical reading strategies designed to help students sharpen their analytical and critical faculties for reading and writing argument:

- Recognizing Logical Fallacies explains some of the most common fallacies and provides examples of each one, while at the same time helping students understand the ambiguity and complexity often involved in specific instances of "fallacious" reasoning.

- Using a Toulmin Analysis gives a brief explanation of Stephen Toulmin's method for analyzing arguments and helps students see how it can be particularly useful in analyzing the assumptions that warrant or justify to a given audience a claim on the basis of certain kinds of evidence.

With these new activities, the Catalog of Critical Reading Strategies (Appendix 1) now includes six distinct strategies focused on argument, including Reflecting on Challenges to Your Beliefs and Values, Evaluating the Logic of an Argument, Recognizing Emotional Manipulation, and Judging the Writer's Credibility. They are all illustrated by Martin Luther King Jr.'s "Letter from Birmingham Jail." In the expanded Reading for Meaning apparatus following each reading, students are encouraged to apply these activities. Moreover, several of the linked readings in the proposal and position chapters help students see argument within a specific context and emphasize counterargument and refutation.

Specific Help for Drafting Effective Sentences in Each Genre

To provide students with practical help to increase their rhetorical prowess, we have introduced in every chapter a new section in the Guide to Writing, Considering a Useful Sentence Strategy, explaining and illustrating certain sentence patterns writers typically use when composing in that genre. For example, Chapter 2: Autobiography illustrates how autobiographers use participial phrases to show simultaneous actions, make an image more vivid, and relate what they were thinking or feeling at the time of an action. Similarly, Chapter 9: Position Paper shows how writers making an argument can concede the value of an opponent's criticism and then attempt to refute it immediately, either in the same sentence or in the one following.

Updated and Extended Help with Technology and Research

In recognition that many students now begin any writing assignment by going online, the first section of each Writing Guide, retitled "Invention and Research," now includes advice to help students make productive use of the Web in research for that specific genre. Topics range from searching for memorabilia for autobiographical writing to researching opposing views in argumentative essays. In addition, Appendix 2: Strategies for Research and Documentation, has been updated with the most current information on electronic research, more detail to help students understand how to paraphrase without inadvertently plagiarizing, and the latest guidelines for documenting sources in MLA and APA styles.

Expanded and Redesigned Instructor's Manual

The Instructor's Manual has been expanded and reorganized to offer instructors more practical advice on teaching each chapter's many reading and writing activities and to make the suggestions more easily accessible. In addition to providing strategies for using the activities in the book, we offer additional teaching material and ideas.

ACKNOWLEDGMENTS

We first want to thank our students and colleagues at the University of California, Riverside and the University of California, San Diego; California State University, Hayward and California State University, San Bernardino; and the University of Nevada, Reno who have taught us so much about reading, writing, and teaching. We are immensely indebted to Lawrence Barkley for his assistance with the Instructor's Manual.

We also owe a debt of gratitude to the many reviewers and questionnaire respondents who made suggestions for this revision. They include Mary Amato, Rider University; Terry Anderson, University of Wisconsin–Green Bay; John Bird, Winthrop University; Kristin Bivens, Western Illinois University; Christian Blum, Bryant and Stratton College; Deborah Borchers, Pueblo Community College; Sandra Clark, Anderson University; Lynn Fuller Clarkson, North Shore Community College; Jennifer Collins-Friederichs, Highline Community College; Paulette Goll, Case Western Reserve University; Stephen Hicks, Lock Haven University; Paul Johnson, Winona State University; Robert Johnson, Midwestern State University; Eleanor Latham, Central Oregon Community College; Leslie Lawrence, Tufts University; Martha Marinara, University of Central Florida; Karen Paley, Rhode Island College; Michael Pikus, Niagara County Community College; Kiki Leigh Rydell, Montana State University; Marty Salter, Iowa Central Community College; Michael Schroeder, Savannah State University; Sean Schultz, University of Wisconsin–Green Bay; Richard Sears, Indiana University; Stephen Smolen, Saddleback College; Wes Spratlin, Motlow State Community College; Linda van der Wal, Grand Canyon University; and Maribeth Winslow, Ivy Tech State College.

To the editorial, production, and marketing crew at Bedford/St. Martin's, we wish to convey our deepest appreciation. We want especially to thank our developmental editor, John Elliott, for his hard work, intelligence, generosity, and kindness. We also want to thank Nancy Perry and Joan Feinberg for their continued support and sound advice. We are grateful for Wendy Polhemus-Annibell's skillful copy editing, Harold Chester's and Ryan Sullivan's seamless coordination of the production process, and Laura King's careful editing of the Instructor's Manual. Thanks also to Sandy Schechter for her work on permissions and to Rachel Falk for her guidance in marketing.

Finally, Rise and Charles wish to express to Alison their profound gratitude for joining the team. Thanks so much for your intelligence, energy, and generosity. Alison dedicates this book with love to her husband, Jeremiah, touchstone and helpmate. Rise wishes to dedicate the book to her husband, Steven, and their son, Jeremiah, in appreciation for their enduring support and love.

Rise B. Axelrod
Charles R. Cooper
Alison M. Warriner

Contents

CHAPTER 9   Position Paper   571

Paired Readings

The first reading in each of the following pairs (or groups) is followed by an activity inviting students to compare and contrast the readings. In each pair or group, the page numbers in parentheses indicate the first pages of the readings; the page number at the end indicates the first page of the Comparing and Contrasting Related Readings activity.

READING CRITICALLY
WRITING WELL

A READER AND GUIDE

CHAPTER 1

Introduction

Reading Critically, Writing Well is designed to help prepare you for the special demands of learning in college, where all your reading should be critical reading—not only understanding what you read but also analyzing and evaluating it.

When you read a text critically, you alternate between two points of view: seeking to understand the text on its own terms and questioning the text's ideas and authority. Putting your questions aside even temporarily allows you to be open to new ideas. But reading critically requires that eventually you examine every idea—your own as well as those of others—skeptically.

Learning to read critically also helps you to write well. It leads you to a fuller understanding of the subject you plan to write about, enabling you to go beyond the obvious, to avoid superficiality and oversimplification. In addition, reading critically helps you anticipate what readers will expect and what questions they may have in mind as they read your writing.

Knowing your readers' expectations for the kind of essay you are writing helps you plan your essay with readers in mind. For example, if you are explaining an unfamiliar concept, you can assume your readers will expect concrete examples and comparisons to help them grasp the new and abstract idea. If you are arguing a position on a current issue, you know that readers will expect you not merely to assert your position but also to support it with facts, statistics, expert testimony, or other relevant evidence. In turn, knowing your readers' expectations will help you anticipate their questions. If you expect readers to accept certain of your ideas but to be skeptical about others, you can support with specific details, examples, or quotations those parts of your essay that present your most unfamiliar or controversial ideas.

Being able to anticipate how readers will respond does not mean that as a writer you always seek to please readers. In fact, good writing often challenges readers. But to challenge readers' assumptions, you need to know what they expect.

You will learn from the activities in this book that reading critically and writing well are intellectually demanding tasks that require your time and effort. Speed-reading may be the best strategy when you need to get the gist of an article or sort through a pile of possible sources. But when you need to understand new ideas or to evaluate complex arguments, when you are reading to prepare for class discussion or to write an essay, then you need to read more slowly and thoughtfully. Rereading is also essential.

The same principles apply to writing. Some kinds of writing can be dashed off in a single draft. The more practiced you are in a given kind of writing, the more efficient your writing process will be. If you write a lab report every week for a term, you should be able to write one rather quickly. If you know how to study for essay exams and have written them often, you should become quite adept at them. But when you need to do a kind of writing you have not mastered or to write about new and difficult material, then you will need more time to develop and organize your ideas.

Slowing down your reading and writing probably sounds like a bad idea to you right now, especially as you begin a new term and have just been told how much course work you will have to do. This book offers practical and efficient ways to meet this challenge by introducing basic strategies for reading critically and writing well.

■ Reading Critically

After you read each selection in *Reading Critically, Writing Well,* you will practice two basic strategies for reading critically: *reading for meaning* and *reading like a writer.* These strategies offer different but complementary ways of looking at a text.

When you read for meaning, you look at a text in terms of its ideas and information in order to understand and respond critically to what is being said. When you read like a writer, your focus shifts from meaning to rhetoric, from *what* is being communicated to *why* and *how* it is communicated. Although experienced readers may combine these two ways of reading—simultaneously reading for meaning and reading like a writer—we separate them here to give you an opportunity to refine your critical reading skills.

In Chapters 2 through 9, you will be asked to read a variety of essays in these two ways. Strategies such as summarizing, outlining, and evaluating the logic of an argument will be introduced to extend and deepen your repertoire of critical reading skills. Appendix 1 presents a complete catalog of these strategies.

READING FOR MEANING

When you read, your primary effort is to make the characters on the page or computer screen meaningful. But as you know from your experience as a reader, a text may be more meaningful or less so depending on your familiarity with the words that are used, your knowledge of the subject, and the kind of text or genre you are reading. If you have some knowledge about an issue currently being debated, for example, then an essay arguing for a position on that issue is likely to be relatively easy to read and full of meaning for you. If, however, you know nothing about the issue or the positions people have been taking on it, then the essay will probably be more difficult to read and less obviously meaningful.

Reading for meaning requires you to use your knowledge and experience to create meaning. You must bring to the text your knowledge about the subject and genre, your beliefs and values, your personal experience, as well as the historical and cultural contexts you share with others. Reading with this rich context helps you to see many possibilities for meaning in a text. Therefore, you will not be surprised that what you find meaningful in a given reading may overlap to some extent with what others find meaningful in the same reading, but also retain your own unique stamp.

As a reader, you are not a passive receptacle into which meaning is poured. Instead, as your eyes move across a text, you actively construct meaning from it, contributing your own relevant knowledge and point of view while also seeking to assimilate the text's new ideas and information. This highly significant and culturally important activity is what we mean by reading for meaning.

Annotating as you read is a powerful method for making sure you have something relevant to say about a given text. It helps concentrate your attention on the text's language and leaves you with a record of the insights, reactions, and questions that occurred to you in the process of reading for meaning. Annotating simply involves marking the page as you read. You note what you think is important in a reading, what you think it means, and what ideas and questions it raises for you. Annotating is easy to do. All it takes is a text you can write on and something to write with. Here are just a few ways to annotate a text:

- Highlight or underline key words and sentences.
- Bracket important passages.
- Connect related ideas with lines.
- Circle words to be defined.
- Outline the main ideas in the margin.
- Write brief comments and questions in the margin.

Some readers mark up the text extensively, while others mark only the parts they consider significant or problematic. What is important is not how you annotate or even how much you annotate, but *that* you annotate. The simple act of marking the page as you read makes it more likely that you will read closely and attentively. There is no right or wrong way to annotate. (For an example of annotating, see Appendix 1, pp. 649–54.)

After annotating, *exploratory writing* is a powerful way of developing your ideas about an essay. You will find that the very act of composing sentences leads you to clarify and extend your ideas, discovering new insights and raising new questions. The key to productive exploratory writing is to refrain from censoring yourself. Simply write at least a page. The goal at this stage is to allow ideas to flow freely.

We recommend, then, a two-step procedure: annotating as you read, followed by exploratory writing that develops meanings for a text. You can extend your understanding by adding a third step—conversing with others who have also read the essay. Your instructor will likely give you opportunities, whether in class or online, to discuss the reading with other students.

Previewing the Reading for Meaning Activities

A set of three Reading for Meaning activities follows each reading in the book: (1) *Read to Comprehend,* (2) *Read to Respond,* and (3) *Read to Analyze Underlying Assumptions.* Turn to pages 20–22 to see one of these sets of activities. As you read for meaning, you may use all of these activities or focus on one that seems most useful for a particular selection and your purpose for reading it. Your instructor may ask you to do the Reading for Meaning activities as homework or in class, individually or with others. You may do these activities in any order; but when done in the order they appear in, they lead you from a basic understanding of what the text says to an exploration of your reactions to it and finally to a deeper understanding of the beliefs and values on which the text and your reactions are based. Each of the activities ends with an invitation for you to apply one or more of the critical reading strategies that are explained and illustrated in Appendix 1.

Read to Comprehend

This activity helps you gain a fuller understanding of the reading. It often begins by asking you to locate the author's thesis statement or main point and rewrite it in your own words and then to define unfamiliar words. The activity ends with an invitation for you to expand your understanding by applying one or more of the critical reading strategies in Appendix 1 that are especially useful for increasing comprehension, such as outlining, summarizing, paraphrasing, and questioning to understand and remember.

Read to Respond

This activity helps you explore your reactions to the reading. It often begins by asking you to find a statement or passage that you have strong feelings about—perhaps because it resonates with your own experience, because you strongly agree or disagree with it, or because you question it or see it as contradicting other statements in the reading—and then to use exploratory writing to reflect on your reactions. The activity ends with an invitation for you to develop your response by applying one or more of the critical reading strategies in Appendix 1 that are especially useful for examining readers' responses, such as contextualizing, recognizing emotional manipulation, and judging the writer's credibility.

Read to Analyze Underlying Assumptions

This activity helps you probe the text more deeply in order to become aware of the reading's underlying assumptions as well as your own assumptions. Every text has subtexts—what we call assumptions. These assumptions always include those of the writer and may also include those of other people mentioned in the text. Likewise, every reader comes to the text with certain assumptions. All of these assumptions include values and beliefs that often are ingrained in culture and family tradition, ethnic and religious background, or language itself as it expresses cultural values, ideology, and philosophy. Although assumptions may be stated directly in a text, they are more often only implied; in the same way, a reader may not be consciously aware of the assumptions he or she brings to the text. To understand a text fully and to understand your own as well as other readers' responses to the text, you need to analyze and evaluate the underlying assumptions in the text and in your response to it. This activity helps you identify, analyze, and evaluate assumptions. It often begins by asking you to focus on the writer's word choices and use of examples or evidence and then to speculate about what has been left out. The activity ends with an invitation for you to probe assumptions more deeply by applying one or more of the critical reading strategies in Appendix 1 that are especially useful for analyzing and evaluating underlying assumptions, such as reflecting on challenges to your beliefs and values, exploring the significance of figurative language, looking for patterns of opposition, evaluating the logic of an argument, and performing a Toulmin analysis.

READING LIKE A WRITER

Reading like a writer shifts your focus from constructing meanings for a reading to analyzing and evaluating how its meanings are presented. Reading like a writer, you look closely at rhetoric—the ways writers make their ideas understandable and seek to influence readers.

To read rhetorically, you need to think about writing in terms of its purpose and audience. Writers make many choices when they write, choices that frequently depend on the writer's reason(s) for writing and the particular reader(s) being addressed. When you read like a writer, you examine the writer's choices and assess their effectiveness in light of the writer's purpose and audience. This kind of reading helps you make rhetorically effective choices in your own writing.

When you read like a writer, you follow the same simple procedure as you do for reading for meaning: annotating, followed by writing.

Previewing the Reading like a Writer Activities

A Reading like a Writer activity follows each selection in the book. Turn to page 22 to see one of these activities now. As you can see, each Reading like a Writer activity consists of one or two introductory paragraphs followed by two sections: *Analyze* and *Write*.

Analyze

The instructions in this section typically ask you to reread specific paragraphs in the reading and to underline or bracket certain words or sentences. These annotations, which you make as you read like a writer, focus on the characteristic textual features and rhetorical strategies of the genre—or type of writing—you are studying. Your aim is to use annotating as a way to begin analyzing the features and strategies typical of the genre and to begin evaluating how well they work in a particular reading.

Write

Here you are asked to write several sentences about what you discovered in analyzing and evaluating a reading's features and strategies in terms of how well they achieve the writer's purpose. Writing even a few sentences can help you develop your analysis and evaluation of a reading.

■ Writing Well

The following section introduces you to the essay-length writing you will do when you undertake the major assignments in Chapters 2 through 9 of *Reading Critically, Writing Well*. As you might guess, the briefer writing activities following every reading (Reading for Meaning and Reading like a Writer) prepare you to write your own full-length essay.

Before previewing the essay assignments, pause to think about your own writing experience in high school, college, or on the job.

THE WRITING ASSIGNMENTS

As you work through the assignments in Chapters 2 through 9 of *Reading Critically, Writing Well*, you will learn how to write the following genres or types of essays:

Autobiography (Chapter 2): telling readers about important events and people in your life

THINKING ABOUT YOUR PAST WRITING EXPERIENCE

1. *Recall* the last time you wrote something fairly difficult, long, or complicated. It may have been an assignment at school or at work, or it may have been something you initiated yourself. Do not choose something written under strict time limits, such as an in-class essay exam.

2. *Write* several sentences describing how you went about planning and writing. Begin by briefly explaining your purpose for writing and identifying your intended readers. *Note* any assumptions you made about your readers' knowledge of the subject or their expectations of your writing.

You can use one or more of the following questions if you need help remembering how you went about completing the writing. But do not restrict yourself to answering these questions. Write down whatever comes to mind as you think about your past writing experience.

- How long did it take before you started putting your ideas on paper?

- What kind of plan did you have? How did your plan evolve as you worked?

- What did you change as you were writing? What changes, if any, did you make after completing your first draft?

- What role did other people play in helping you develop your ideas and plans?

Observation (Chapter 3): presenting to readers your firsthand reports about intriguing places, people, and activities

Reflection (Chapter 4): exploring for readers the larger social implications of your experience or observation

Explaining concepts (Chapter 5): defining for readers the meaning and importance of key ideas

Evaluation (Chapter 6): arguing to convince readers that your judgment of a movie, book, performance, essay, noteworthy person, or other subject is justifiable

Speculation about causes or effects (Chapter 7): arguing to convince readers that it is plausible that some event, trend, or phenomenon resulted from certain causes or will result in certain effects

Proposal to solve a problem (Chapter 8): arguing to convince readers to accept or seriously consider your proposed solution to a problem

Position paper (Chapter 9): arguing to convince readers to accept or seriously consider your position on a controversial issue

Each of these writing assignments identifies a genre of writing done every day by countless writers. More than mere school writing exercises, they are real-world writing situations like those you will encounter in college and at work. Pause now to learn a bit more about these assignments.

Previewing the Writing Assignments

Look at the different writing genres that are represented in this book. On the second or third page of each assignment chapter (Chapters 2 through 9) is a brief set of Writing Situations. Read this section in all of the chapters to get a quick sense of the different kinds of writing. Then write several sentences responding to the following questions:

1. Which of these genres have you already written?

2. With which of these genres have you had the most experience? Where and when did you do this kind of writing? What was most challenging about writing it?

3. What other genres would you like to learn to write? Why do they interest you?

THE GUIDES TO WRITING

Following the Readings section of Chapters 2 through 9 in *Reading Critically, Writing Well,* a Guide to Writing helps you complete the writing assignment. These guides reflect the fact that writing is a process of discovery. As writers, we rarely if ever begin with a complete understanding of the subject. We put together some information and ideas, start writing, and let the writing lead us to understanding. While writing helps us achieve greater understanding, it also raises questions and unexpected complexities, which, in turn, can inspire more writing and, nearly always, generate further ideas and insights.

Experienced writers have learned to trust this fascinating discovery process because they know that writing is an unsurpassed way of thinking. Writing helps you discover, explore, develop, and refine your ideas in a way that cannot compare with sitting around and thinking about a subject. Because writing leaves a record of your thinking, it reduces the burden of remembering and allows you to direct all your energy toward solving the immediate problem. By rereading what you have written, you can figure out where you became derailed or recall points that you forgot were important or see new possibilities you did not notice before.

The Guide to Writing for each assignment leads you through the complex, creative process of discovery: Invention and Research, Drafting, Reading a Draft

Critically, Revising, and Editing and Proofreading. Because it helps to approach the first draft of an essay with some notes and other brief writings in hand, the first writing activity in each guide is called *invention*, a term used since classical Greek times to describe speakers' and writers' attempts to discover what they know and might say about a subject. Each Guide to Writing also includes advice about doing *research*, either to help you decide on a subject to write about or to learn more about your subject. Because *drafting* is most efficient and productive when you clarify your purpose and plan in advance, the Guide to Writing helps you set goals and organize your draft. Also, because nearly any draft can benefit from the advice of thoughtful readers, guidelines are included to help you and your classmates *read each other's drafts critically*. And because *revising* gives you the opportunity to refine your ideas and to make your writing communicate more clearly and effectively, each Guide to Writing includes suggestions for improving your draft. Finally, because you want your finished essay to conform to the conventions of grammar, mechanics, punctuation, spelling, and style, each guide concludes with advice on *editing and proofreading* your essay.

Before reading about the resources offered to support your invention and research, drafting, critical reading, revising, and editing and proofreading, take time to preview a Guide to Writing.

Previewing a Guide to Writing

Turn to one of the Guides to Writing toward the end of any writing assignment chapter. Skim the guide, reading the headings and the first paragraph in each major section to get an idea of what the guide offers.

Invention and Research

Invention begins with finding a subject to write about. The Considering Ideas for Your Own Writing section following each reading, together with the suggestions in the Guide to Writing, will help you list several possible subjects. This act of listing possibilities is itself inventive because one item often suggests the next, and as the list grows you come to understand your options better and can therefore more confidently choose a subject. In each chapter, you will find suggestions that will help you make a good choice and understand the implications of developing the subject you choose.

Because each writing situation makes unique demands on writers, the invention and research activities in each chapter differ. To see how, compare the activities under Invention and Research in two or three chapters—for example, in Chapter 2 on autobiography, Chapter 5 on explaining concepts, and Chapter 9 on arguing positions.

The immediate advantage of genre-specific invention is that it stimulates your thinking, getting you writing days before you begin drafting your essay. Although you will usually need no more than two hours to complete these invention and research activities, it is best to spread them over several days. As soon as you start writing the first few sentences about a subject, your mind goes to work on it, perhaps even offering ideas and insights when you are going about your daily activities, not consciously thinking about the subject. More invention writing will inspire more ideas. Your understanding of the subject will deepen and the possibilities will become more wide-ranging and subtle. An assignment that may have seemed daunting will become intellectually invigorating, and you will have pages of invention notes with which to launch your draft.

Drafting

After working on invention and research, you may be eager to begin drafting your essay. If, however, you are having difficulty making the transition from jotting down invention notes to writing a first draft, the Guide to Writing in each chapter will show you how to set achievable goals and devise a tentative plan that will ease the process of drafting. The guide's Drafting section offers several activities, including Setting Goals, Organizing Your Draft, and Considering a Useful Sentence Strategy. To set goals, you need to ask yourself questions about your purpose and audience, such as how to interest readers in your subject, describe a person vividly, or counterargue effectively. As you establish your goals, you will also be reminded of the strategies that you saw other writers in the chapter use to accomplish similar goals in their essays. Organizing Your Draft points out how the other writers in the chapter organize their essays and suggests that you make a scratch outline to develop a tentative plan for your own essay. Considering a Useful Sentence Strategy explains a specific grammatical structure or sentence pattern, one that writers have found especially helpful for that chapter's type of writing and that you may want to use as well, and provides examples from the chapter's readings.

Reading a Draft Critically

Your critical reading of a classmate's draft can be supportive and helpful because as a writer yourself you can give the kind of advice writers most need when they have written a draft but are unsure what is working and what needs improvement. In the case of revising a position paper, for example, writers may need advice on how to clarify the position, strengthen the argument, anticipate readers' objections, tighten the logic, and so on.

The Reading a Draft Critically section invites you to make practical use of all you have learned about reading a genre. It also invites you to try out your newly acquired expertise and even to show off a bit—all while doing a classmate a big favor. Part of the favor you provide is the written record of your critical reading that you give to your classmate, a record the classmate can refer to the next day or next week when revising his or her essay. You do yourself a favor as well. Like your classmate, you too will revise an essay in the same genre. As you read your classmate's essay critically, you will be reflecting intensely on your own just-completed draft. The more thoughtful and comprehensive your critical reading, the more likely you will be to discover ways to strengthen your own draft.

Revising

Revising offers the great opportunity of rethinking what you have written, given your purpose and your readers' needs and expectations. Assume you will want to make changes and add new material at this stage. Be prepared to cut sentences, move sentences, and reorder paragraphs. You provide the brainpower, and the computer provides the technology to make dramatic changes easy. The Revising section offers a range of suggestions for you to consider, along with the advice you received from your classmates and instructor.

Editing and Proofreading

Editing and proofreading are like taking a last look at yourself in the mirror before going out. You have given some thought to what you would wear and how you would look; now you check to make sure everything is the way you want it. When you write an essay, you spend a lot of time and energy planning, drafting, and revising; now you want to check to make sure that there are no glaring mistakes in grammar, punctuation, word choice, spelling, or matters of style. If you are unsure whether you have made a mistake or how to fix it, consult a writer's guidebook or handbook, another student, or your writing instructor.

Thinking about Your Learning

We know from research that if learning is not reviewed, reflected on, and consolidated, it soon fades and might not be available when new occasions arise for using or applying it. Therefore, in each assignment chapter, we provide two occasions for you to pause and reflect on what you have learned.

Reviewing What Makes Essays Effective

The first occasion for thinking about your learning comes after the last reading in the chapter. For example, in Chapter 9, Position Paper, this section is titled Reviewing What Makes Position Papers Effective. You are asked to choose one reading from the chapter that seemed to you a particularly good example of its genre, to reread it critically in light of all you have learned about the genre, and then to write a page or more justifying your choice. This activity enables you to review the characteristic features and rhetorical strategies of the genre you are about to write. Coming where it does, *before* the Guide to Writing, this activity helps you complete the transition from thinking like a reader to thinking like a writer.

Reflecting on What You Have Learned

This final occasion for thinking about your learning comes at the end of the chapter, where you are invited to describe what you are most pleased with in your final essay and to explain what contributed to this achievement. It reminds you that there is much you have learned and much to learn about writing—from reading others' work, from writing your own essays, and from collaborating with other writers.

2

Autobiography

Autobiography involves telling stories about key events in your life and describing people who played important roles in it. Whether writing about an exhilarating childhood game or a difficult relationship, you should evoke for readers a vivid impression to help them see what you saw, hear what you heard, and feel what you felt. To write autobiography, therefore, you need to revisit the past, immersing yourself in the sights, sounds, and other sensations of memory. You also need to think deeply about the meaning of your experience—why it was and still is significant to you. Thinking deeply about the significance of important events and people in your life can help you discover something about the forces within yourself and within society that have helped to shape who you are and what is important to you.

While writing about your own life can be both enjoyable and instructive, so too can reading about other people's lives. As readers, we often take pleasure in seeing reflections of our own experience in other people's autobiographical writing. We enjoy recognizing similarities between the people and the events we have known and those that we read about. But sometimes the differences can be far more thought-provoking. For example, we may see how certain conditions— such as whether we grew up in the suburbs or the city; whether we are male or female; whether we are of African, European, Asian, Middle Eastern, or mixed descent—can profoundly affect our lives and perspectives. Autobiography sometimes affirms our preconceptions, but it is most effective when it leads us to question our certainties, challenging us to see ourselves and others in a new light.

Whether you are reading or writing autobiography, it is important to remember that autobiography is public, not private. While it involves self-presentation and contributes to self-knowledge, it does not require writers to make unwanted self-disclosures. Autobiographers compose themselves for readers; they fashion a self in words, much as a novelist creates a character. As readers, we come to "know" the people we read about by the way they are portrayed. Consequently, when you write autobiography, you have to decide how to portray yourself. This decision depends on whom you expect to read your essay (your audience) and what you want to communicate to readers (your purpose).

As you work through this chapter, you will learn more about autobiography by reading several different examples of it. You will see that some autobiographical essays center on a single event that occurred over a brief period of hours or days, while other essays focus on a person who played a significant role in the writer's life. Whether you decide to tell a story about a remembered event or to write about another person, you will practice two of the most basic writing strategies—narration and description. As you will see in later chapters of this book, narration and description can play a role not only in autobiography but also in providing explanations and advancing arguments.

The readings in this chapter will help you learn a lot about autobiography. From the readings and from the ideas for writing that follow each reading, you will get ideas for your own autobiographical essay. As you read and write about the selections, keep in mind the following assignment, which sets out the goals for writing an autobiographical essay. To support your writing of this assignment, the chapter concludes with a Guide to Writing Autobiography.

THE WRITING ASSIGNMENT

Autobiography

Write an autobiographical essay about a significant event or person in your life. Choose the event or person with your readers in mind: The subject should be one that you feel comfortable presenting to others and that will lead readers to reflect on their own lives or on the differences between their personal experiences and your own. Present your experience dramatically and vividly so that readers can imagine what it was like for you. Through a careful choice of words and details, convey the meaning and importance in your life—the autobiographical significance—of this event or person.

WRITING SITUATIONS FOR AUTOBIOGRAPHY

You may think only scientists, novelists, politicians, movie stars, and other famous people write their autobiographies. But autobiographical writing is much more widespread, as the following examples indicate:

- As part of her college application, a high-school senior includes a brief autobiographical essay that conveys her reasons for wanting to study science and become a researcher. In the essay, she recalls what happened when she did her first scientific experiment on the nutritional effects of different breakfast cereals on mice.

- Asked to recall a significant early childhood memory for an assignment in a psychology class, a college student writes about a fishing trip he took as a nine-year-old. He reflects on the significance of the trip—it was the first trip he took alone with his father and it began a new stage in their relationship.

- As part of a workshop on management skills, a business executive writes about a person who influenced his ideas about leadership. As he explores his memory and feelings, he realizes that he mistook fear for admiration. He recognizes that he has been emulating the wrong model, an autocratic leader who got people to perform by intimidating them.

THINKING ABOUT YOUR EXPERIENCE WITH AUTOBIOGRAPHY

Before studying a type of writing, it is useful to spend some time thinking about what you already know about it. You have almost certainly told stories about events in your life and described memorable people you have known, even if you have not written down these stories. When you tell such stories, you are composing autobiography. You also may have written autobiographically for school assignments, for a college application, and in letters or emails to family and friends.

To reflect on your experience with autobiography, you might recall one particular story you told orally or in writing and then consider questions like these: What made you choose this event or person? What did you want your audience members to think and feel? How did they react to your story? What in your story caught their attention or seemed significant?

Reflect also on the autobiographical stories that have been told to you or that you have read or seen in films or on television. What made these stories interesting? What did you expect from these stories? What do you think others expect from the autobiographical stories you relate to them?

Write at least a page about your experience with autobiography.

A Guide to Reading Autobiography

This guide introduces you to autobiographical writing. By completing all the activities in it, you will prepare yourself to learn a great deal from the other readings in this chapter about how to read and write an autobiographical essay. The guide focuses on a brief but powerful piece of autobiography by Annie Dillard. You will read Dillard's autobiographical essay twice. First, you will read it for meaning, seeking to grasp the significance of the event for Dillard—what it meant to her both at the time she experienced it and years later when she wrote about it—as well as the meaning it holds for you. Then, you will reread the essay like a writer, analyzing the parts to see how Dillard crafts her essay and to learn the strategies she uses to make her autobiographical writing effective. These two activities—reading for meaning and reading like a writer—follow every reading in this chapter.

ANNIE DILLARD

An American Childhood

> *Annie Dillard (b. 1945) is a prolific writer whose first book,* Pilgrim at Tinker Creek *(1974), won the Pulitzer Prize for nonfiction writing. Since then, she has written meditations on nature and religion, including* For the Time Being *(1999); several collections of poetry, most recently* Mornings like This *(1996); a novel,* The Living *(1992); an account of her work as a writer,* The Writing Life *(1989); and an autobiography,* An American Childhood *(1987), from which the following reading is excerpted. Dillard also coedited* Modern American Memoirs *(1995), a collection of autobiographical works originally published between 1917 and 1992.*
>
> *"An American Childhood" relates an event that occurred one winter morning when the seven-year-old Dillard and a friend were chased relentlessly by an adult stranger at whom they had been throwing snowballs. Dillard admits that she was terrified at the time, and yet she asserts that she has "seldom been happier since."*
>
> *As you read, think about how this paradox helps you grasp the autobiographical significance of this experience for Dillard. Annotate anything that helps you appreciate the drama and significance of the event. Annotating involves writing on the text as you read—noting parts you think are important, identifying words or references you do not know, and writing comments and questions in the margin. (To learn more about annotating, see Appendix 1, pp. 648–54.)*

Some boys taught me to play football. This was fine sport. You thought up a new strategy for every play and whispered it to the others. You went out for a pass, fooling everyone. Best, you got to throw yourself mightily at someone's running legs. Either you brought him down or you hit the ground flat out on your chin, with your arms empty before you. It was all or nothing. If you hesitated in fear, you would miss and get hurt: you would take a hard fall while the kid got away, or you would get kicked in the face while the kid got away. But if you flung yourself wholeheartedly at the back of his knees—if you gathered and joined body and soul

1

and pointed them diving fearlessly—then you likely wouldn't get hurt, and you'd stop the ball. Your fate, and your team's score, depended on your concentration and courage. <u>Nothing girls did could compare with it.</u>

Boys welcomed me at baseball, too, for I had, through enthusiastic practice, what was weirdly known as a boy's arm. In winter, in the snow, there was neither baseball nor football, so the boys and I threw snowballs at passing cars. I got in trouble throwing snowballs, <u>and have seldom</u> been happier since.   2

On one weekday morning after Christmas, six inches of new snow had just fallen. We were standing up to our boot tops in snow on a front yard on trafficked Reynolds Street, waiting for cars. The cars traveled Reynolds Street slowly and evenly; they were targets all but wrapped in red ribbons, cream puffs. We couldn't miss.   3

I was seven; the boys were eight, nine, and ten. The oldest two Fahey boys were there—Mikey and Peter—polite blond boys who lived near me on Lloyd Street, and who already had four brothers and sisters. My parents approved Mikey and Peter Fahey. Chickie McBride was there, a tough kid, and Billy Paul and Mackie Kean too, from across Reynolds, where the boys grew up dark and furious, grew up skinny, knowing, and skilled. We had all drifted from our houses that morning looking for action, and had found it here on Reynolds Street.   4

It was cloudy but cold. The cars' tires laid behind them on the snowy street a complex trail of beige chunks like <u>crenellated</u> castle walls. I had stepped on some earlier; they squeaked. We could not have wished for more traffic. When a car came, we all popped it one. In the intervals between cars we reverted to the natural solitude of children.   5

I started making an iceball—a perfect iceball, from perfectly white snow, perfectly spherical, and squeezed perfectly translucent so no snow remained all the way through. (The Fahey boys and I considered it unfair actually to throw an iceball at somebody, but it had been known to happen.)   6

I had just embarked on the iceball project when we heard tire chains come clanking from afar. A black Buick was moving toward us down the street. We all spread out, banged together some regular snowballs, took aim, and, when the Buick drew nigh, fired.   7

A soft snowball hit the driver's windshield right before the driver's face. It made a smashed star with a hump in the middle.   8

Often, of course, we hit our target, but this time, the only time in all of life, the car pulled over and stopped. Its wide black door   9 opened; a man got out of it, running. He didn't even close the car door.

He ran after us, and we ran away from him, up the snowy Reynolds sidewalk. At the corner, I looked back; incredibly, he was still after us. He was in city clothes: a suit and tie, street shoes. Any normal adult would have quit, having sprung us into flight and made his point. This man was gaining on us. He was a thin man, all action. All of a sudden, we were running for our lives.

Wordless, we split up. We were on our turf; we could lose ourselves in the neighborhood backyards, everyone for himself. I paused and considered. Everyone had vanished except Mikey Fahey, who was just rounding the corner of a yellow brick house. Poor Mikey, I trailed him. The driver of the Buick sensibly picked the two of us to follow. The man apparently had all day.

He chased Mikey and me around the yellow house and up a backyard path we knew by heart: under a low tree, up a bank, through a hedge, down some snowy steps, and across the grocery store's delivery driveway. We smashed through a gap in another hedge, entered a scruffy backyard and ran around its back porch and tight between houses to Edgerton Avenue; we ran across Edgerton to an alley and up our own sliding woodpile to the Halls' front yard; he kept coming. We ran up Lloyd Street and wound through mazy backyards toward the steep hilltop at Willard and Lang.

He chased us silently, block after block. He chased us silently over picket fences, through thorny hedges, between houses, around garbage cans, and across streets. Every time I glanced back, choking for breath, I expected he would have quit. He must have been as breathless as we were. His jacket strained over his body. It was an immense discovery, pounding into my hot head with every sliding, joyous step, that this ordinary adult evidently knew what I thought only children who trained at football knew: that you have to fling yourself at what you're doing, you have to point yourself, forget yourself, aim, dive.

Mikey and I had nowhere to go, in our own neighborhood or out of it, but away from this man who was chasing us. He impelled us forward; we compelled him to follow our route. The air was cold; every breath tore my throat. We kept running, block after block; we kept improvising, backyard after backyard, running a frantic course and choosing it simultaneously, failing always to find small places or hard places to slow him down, and discovering always, exhilarated, dismayed, that only bare speed could save us—for he would never give up, this man—and we were losing speed.

He chased us through the backyard labyrinths of ten blocks   15
before he caught us by our jackets. He caught us and we all
stopped.

We three stood staggering, half blinded, coughing, in an obscure   16
hilltop backyard: a man in his twenties, a boy, a girl. He had released
our jackets, our pursuer, our captor, our hero: he knew we weren't
going anywhere. We all played by the rules. Mikey and I unzipped
our jackets. I pulled off my sopping mittens. Our tracks multiplied
in the backyard's new snow. We had been breaking new snow all
morning. We didn't look at each other. I was cherishing my excitement. The man's lower pants legs were wet; his cuffs were full of
snow, and there was a prow of snow beneath them on his shoes
and socks. Some trees bordered the little flat backyard, some messy
winter trees. There was no one around: a clearing in a grove, and
we the only players.

It was a long time before he could speak. I had some difficulty   17
at first recalling why we were there. My lips felt swollen; I couldn't
see out of the sides of my eyes; I kept coughing.

"You stupid kids," he began perfunctorily.   18

We listened perfunctorily indeed, if we listened at all, for the   19
chewing out was redundant, a mere formality, and beside the
point. The point was that he had chased us passionately without
giving up, and so he had caught us. Now he came down to earth. I
wanted the glory to last forever.

But how could the glory have lasted forever? We could have run   20
through every backyard in North America until we got to Panama.
But when he trapped us at the lip of the Panama Canal, what precisely could he have done to prolong the drama of the chase and
cap its glory? I brooded about this for the next few years. He could
only have fried Mikey Fahey and me in boiling oil, say, or dis-
membered us piecemeal, or staked us to anthills. None of which I
really wanted, and none of which any adult was likely to do, even
in the spirit of fun. He could only chew us out there in the Pana-
manian jungle, after months or years of exalting pursuit. He could
only begin, "You stupid kids," and continue in his ordinary Pittsburgh accent with his normal righteous anger and the usual common sense.

If in that snowy backyard the driver of the black Buick had cut   21
off our heads, Mikey's and mine, I would have died happy, for
nothing has required so much of me since as being chased all over
Pittsburgh in the middle of winter—running terrified, exhausted—
by this sainted, skinny, furious redheaded man who wished to
have a word with us. I don't know how he found his way back
to his car.

READING FOR MEANING

This section presents three activities that will help you reread Dillard's autobiographical essay with a critical eye. Done in sequence, these activities lead you from a basic understanding of the selection to a more personal response to it and finally to an analysis that deepens your understanding and critical thinking about what you are reading.

Read to Comprehend

Reread the selection, and write a few sentences briefly explaining what happened that winter morning when Dillard was seven years old. Also make a list of any words you do not understand—for example, *crenellated* (paragraph 5), *translucent* (6), *perfunctorily* (18), *righteous* (20). Look up their meanings in a dictionary to see which definition best fits the context.

To expand your understanding of this reading, you might use one or more of the following critical reading strategies that are explained and illustrated in Appendix 1: *outlining, summarizing, paraphrasing,* and *questioning to understand and remember.*

Read to Respond

Write several paragraphs exploring your initial thoughts and feelings about Dillard's autobiographical narrative. Focus on anything that stands out for you, perhaps because it resonates with your own experience or because you find a statement puzzling.

You might consider writing about

- how a particular scene—such as the iceballing (paragraphs 5–8) or confrontation (15–21) scene—contributes to your understanding of the event's significance for Dillard.

- why you think Dillard uses such words as "hero" (16) and "sainted" (21) to describe the man who chased her, even though she dismisses what he said when he finally caught her as "redundant, a mere formality, and beside the point" (19).

- how Dillard's experience reminds you of something you experienced.

To develop your response to Dillard's essay, you might use one or more of the following critical reading strategies that are explained and illustrated in Appendix 1: *contextualizing, recognizing emotional manipulation,* and *judging the writer's credibility.*

Read to Analyze Underlying Assumptions

Write several paragraphs exploring one or more of the assumptions, values, and beliefs underlying Dillard's autobiographical story. As you write, explain how the assumptions are reflected in the text, as well as what you now think of them (and perhaps of your own assumptions) after rereading the selection with a critical eye.

Notice that even when Dillard states her feelings and thoughts directly (such as in the opening paragraph, where she explains why football is a "fine sport"), readers have to analyze her word choices and examples to understand her values and beliefs—that is, her underlying assumptions. For example, what about the way she learned to play football makes it courageous? Why is "diving fearlessly" to tackle an opponent a good thing? Is it good in every situation or only in a sport? The Duke of Wellington famously said that the Battle of Waterloo, marking the final defeat of Napoleon, was won on the playing fields of Eton (a school in England). What he meant was that teaching children to play sports the way that Dillard learned to play football teaches them to become heroic and fearless soldiers.

Analyzing Dillard's assumptions, as we have begun to do here, would not necessarily lead you to conclude that Dillard is in favor of teaching children to become soldiers. But her use of words associated with war, courage, and heroism reveals a set of assumptions that would benefit from critical scrutiny. While most of us value courage and heroism, we seldom stop to think critically about why we hold these values or what they are based on. The purpose of analyzing underlying assumptions in a reading is to give us an opportunity to think critically about unexamined assumptions—the writer's and our own, many of which may be ingrained in our culture, our education, and even our language.

You might consider writing about

- Dillard's belief that "you have to fling yourself at what you're doing, you have to point yourself, forget yourself, aim, dive" (paragraph 13).

- the value system underlying Dillard's statement that she and the Fahey boys "considered it unfair actually to throw an iceball at somebody" (6).

- the values and beliefs underlying Dillard's proud assertion, "We all played by the rules" (16).

- the observation that "[n]othing girls did"—at least when Dillard was a child—"could compare with" the way the boys taught her to play football (1).

- why Dillard uses words like "joyous" (13) and "glory" (19) to describe the chase and words like "hero" (16) and "sainted" (21) to describe the stranger who chased her.

- what Dillard assumes when she refers to "the natural solitude of children" (5).

To probe assumptions more deeply, you might use one or more of the following critical reading strategies that are explained and illustrated in Appendix 1: *reflecting on challenges to your beliefs and values, exploring the significance of figurative language,* and *looking for patterns of opposition.*

READING LIKE A WRITER

This section leads you through an analysis of Dillard's autobiographical writing strategies: *narrating the story, presenting people, describing places,* and *conveying the autobiographical significance.* For each strategy you will be asked to reread and annotate part of Dillard's essay to see how she uses the strategy to accomplish her particular purpose.

When you study the selections later in this chapter, you will see how different autobiographers use these same strategies for different purposes. The Guide to Writing Autobiography near the end of the chapter suggests ways you can use these strategies in your own writing.

Narrating the Story

Whether focusing on a single event or a person, writers nearly always tell a story or several brief stories called *anecdotes*. Stories are so pervasive in our culture, indeed in most cultures, that we are all familiar with what makes a story effective. A well-told story draws readers in by arousing their curiosity and often keeps them reading by building suspense or drama, making them want to know what will happen next.

Storytellers use a variety of techniques to dramatize events. One way is to speed up the action and heighten the tension. This activity will help you see how Dillard uses active verbs and other verb forms to make her story dramatic.

Analyze

1. *Reread* paragraphs 12 and 13, underlining as many verbs and verbals as you can. Do not worry if you miss some. Verbals are verb forms that usually end in *ing,* as in "staggering" and "coughing" (paragraph 16), or *ed,* as in "blinded" (16) and "smashed" (8), or that begin with *to,* as in "to fling" and "to point" (13).

2. *Put a second line* under the verbs or verbals that name an action. For example, the verb "chased" in the following sentence names an action (double underline), whereas the verb "knew" does not name an action (single underline): "He <u>chased</u> Mikey and me around the yellow house and up a backyard path we <u>knew</u> by heart . . ." (12).

3. *Find* two or three sentences in which the action verbs and verbals help you imagine the drama of the chase.

Write

Write several sentences explaining what you have learned about Dillard's use of verbs and verbals to represent action and to make her narrative dramatic. *Use examples* from paragraphs 12 and 13 to support your explanation.

Presenting People

Autobiographers describe people by depicting what they look like, by letting readers hear how they speak, and by characterizing their behavior and personality. Often, one or two specific details about the way a person looks, dresses, talks, or acts will be sufficient to give readers a vivid impression of the person. As you will see when you read the essays later in this chapter by Mark Edmundson, Amy Wu, and Brad Benioff, even autobiographical essays that focus on a person rather than a single event tend to use only a few well-chosen details to present the person.

To see how Dillard presents people, let us look at the descriptions of the neighborhood boys in paragraph 4. Notice that she gives each boy a brief descriptive tag: "Mikey and Peter—polite blond boys who lived near me on Lloyd Street" and "Chickie McBride . . . a tough kid, and Billy Paul and Mackie Kean too, from across Reynolds, where the boys grew up dark and furious, grew up skinny, knowing, and skilled." The details "blond" and "skinny" create a visual image, whereas "polite," "tough," and "knowing" convey Dillard's characterizations or evaluations of the boys. These characterizations or evaluations contribute not only to the impression we get of each boy but also to our understanding of his significance in the writer's life. (As you will see later in the chapter, such characterizations are one way writers convey autobiographical significance.)

Analyze

1. In paragraphs 10, 16, and 21, *find* and *underline* words and phrases that visually describe the man. Also *put brackets around* words and phrases that characterize or evaluate the man.

2. *Look* at paragraph 18 and the last sentence of paragraph 20, where Dillard presents the man through dialogue. *Underline* the details used to describe how the man looks and sounds. Also *put brackets around* words and phrases used to characterize or evaluate what the man says and how he says it.

3. *Think about* how Dillard's presentation of the man in these five paragraphs helps you see him in your mind's eye and understand his role in the chase.

Write

Based on your analysis, *write* several sentences examining Dillard's use of descriptive details and characterizations to present the man. *Use examples* from the words and phrases you underlined and bracketed to support your ideas.

Describing Places

Whether autobiography centers on an event or a person, it nearly always includes some description of places. Writers make a remembered place vivid by naming memorable objects they want readers to see there and by detailing these objects. For examples of *naming* and *detailing,* look at paragraph 3, where Dillard describes what it looked like on that particular morning after Christmas. Notice that Dillard uses naming to point out the snow, Reynolds Street, and the cars. She also adds details that give information about these objects: "*six inches* of *new* snow," "*trafficked* Reynolds Street," "cars traveled . . . *slowly* and *evenly.*"

To make her description evocative as well as vivid, Dillard adds a third describing strategy: *comparing.* In paragraph 5, for example, she describes the trail made by car tires in the snow as being "like crenellated castle walls." The word *like* makes the comparison explicit and identifies it as a simile. Dillard also uses implicit comparisons, called metaphors, such as when she calls the cars "targets all but wrapped in red ribbons, cream puffs" (paragraph 3).

Analyze

1. *Examine* how Dillard uses naming and detailing to describe the "perfect iceball" in paragraph 6. What does she name it, and what details does she add to specify the qualities that make an iceball "perfect"?

2. Then *look closely* at the two comparisons in paragraphs 3 and 5. *Notice* also the following comparisons in other paragraphs: "smashed star" (8), "sprung us into flight" (10), "mazy backyards" (12), "every breath tore my throat" (14), and "backyard labyrinths" (15). Choose any single comparison—simile or metaphor—in the reading, and *think about* how it helps you imagine what the place was like for Dillard on that day.

Write

Write a few sentences explaining how Dillard uses the describing strategies of *naming, detailing,* and *comparing* to help you imagine what the places she presents seemed like during the chase. *Give at least one example* from the reading of each describing strategy.

Conveying the Autobiographical Significance

Autobiographers convey the significance of an event or a person in two ways: by *showing* and by *telling*. Through your analyses of how Dillard narrates the story, presents people, and describes places, you have looked at some of the ways she *shows* the event's significance. This activity focuses on what Dillard *tells* readers.

When Dillard writes in the opening paragraphs about boys teaching her to play football and baseball, she is telling why these experiences were memorable and important. Autobiographers usually tell both what they remember thinking and feeling *at the time* and what they think and feel now *as they write about the past.* Readers must infer from the ideas and the writer's choice of words whether a phrase or sentence conveys the writer's past or present perspective, remembered feelings and thoughts or current ones. For example, look at the following sentences from paragraph 1: "You thought up a new strategy for every play and whispered it to the others. You went out for a pass, fooling everyone." The words "whispered" and "fooling" suggest that here Dillard is trying to reconstruct a seven-year-old child's way of speaking and thinking. In contrast, when she tells us that football was a "fine sport" and what was fine about it—"Your fate, and your team's score, depended on your concentration and courage"—we can infer from words such as "fate," "concentration," and "courage" that Dillard is speaking from her present adult perspective, telling us what she may have sensed as a child but now can more fully understand and articulate.

To determine the autobiographical significance of the remembered event or person, then, readers need to pay attention to what Dillard tells about the significance—both her remembered feelings and thoughts and her present perspective.

Analyze

1. *Reread* paragraphs 19–21, where Dillard comments on the chase and the man's "chewing out." *Put brackets around* words and phrases that tell what the adult Dillard is thinking as she writes about this event from her past. For example, in the first sentence of paragraph 19, "perfunctorily," "redundant," and "a mere formality" may seem to you to be examples of adult language, rather than words a seven-year-old would use.

2. Then *underline* words and phrases in the same paragraphs that seem to convey thoughts and feelings that Dillard remembers from when she was a child.

Write

Write several sentences explaining what you have learned about the event's significance for Dillard. What does she tell readers about the thoughts and feelings she had as a child as well as the thoughts and feelings she has now as an adult look-ing back on the experience? *Quote* selected words and phrases from your under-lining and bracketing, indicating what identifies them as either remembered or present-perspective thoughts and feelings.

A SPECIAL READING STRATEGY

Comparing and Contrasting Related Readings: Dillard's "An American Childhood" and Rodriguez's "Always Running"

Comparing and contrasting related readings is a critical reading strat-egy useful both in reading for meaning and in reading like a writer. This strategy is particularly applicable when writers present similar subjects, as is the case in the autobiographical narratives in this chapter by Annie Dillard (p. 16) and Luis J. Rodriguez (p. 33). Both writers tell what hap-pened when they broke the rules and were chased by adults. In both instances, their transgressions are relatively minor; however, the chase is viewed very differently by each writer and its results also differ dramat-ically. To compare and contrast these two autobiographies, think about issues such as these:

- Compare these essays in terms of their cultural and historical con-texts. What seems to you to be most significant about the two versions of an American childhood represented in these essays?

- Compare how the two writers make their narratives dramatic. Com-pare the strategies Dillard uses in presenting the chase (paragraphs 11–14) with those Rodriguez uses (27–32). In addition to looking at the kinds of verbs each writer employs, you might also analyze how they construct sentences to push the action forward or slow it down. Notice also the length of the sentences and how much information the writers pack into sentences.

See Appendix 1 for detailed guidelines on using the comparing and contrasting related readings strategy.

■ Readings

SAIRA SHAH

Longing to Belong

Saira Shah (b. 1964) is a journalist and documentary film-maker. The daughter of an Afghan father and Indian mother, she was born and educated in England. After graduating from the School of Oriental and African Studies at London University, Shah began her career as a freelance journalist in the 1980s, reporting on the Afghan guerillas who were fighting the Soviet occupation; eventually she became a war correspondent for Britain's Channel 4 News. She is the recipient of the Courage under Fire and Television Journalist of the Year awards for her risky reporting on conflicts in some of the world's most troubled areas, including the Persian Gulf and Kosovo. She is best known in the United States for her undercover documentary films about the Taliban rule in Afghanistan, Beneath the Veil *(2001) and* Unholy War *(2002).*

"Longing to Belong," originally published in New York Times Magazine *in 2003, is adapted from Shah's autobiography* The Storyteller's Daughter *(2003), which relates her search to understand her father's homeland of Afghanistan. In this essay, Shah tells what happened when, at the age of seventeen, she visited her father's Afghan relatives living in Pakistan. As she explained in an interview, "I wanted this kind of romantic vision. This is the exile's condition, though, isn't it? If you grow up outside the place that you think of as your home, you want it to be impossibly marvelous. There is also the question of how Afghan I am. When I was growing up, I had this secret doubt—which I couldn't even admit to myself— that I was not at all an Afghan because I was born in Britain to a mixed family."*

As you read, think about Shah's search for her ethnic identity and the sense of cultural dislocation she experiences.

The day he disclosed his matrimonial ambitions for me, my uncle sat me at his right during lunch. This was a sign of special favor, as it allowed him to feed me choice tidbits from his own plate. It was by no means an unadulterated pleasure. He would often generously withdraw a half-chewed delicacy from his mouth and lovingly cram it into mine—an Afghan habit with which I have since tried to come to terms. It was his way of telling me that I was valued, part of the family.

My brother and sister, Tahir and Safia, and my elderly aunt Amina and I were all attending the wedding of my uncle's son.

Although my uncle's home was closer than I'd ever been, I was not yet inside Afghanistan. This branch of my family lived in Peshawar, Pakistan. On seeing two unmarried daughters in the company of a female chaperone, my uncle obviously concluded that we had been sent to be married. I was taken aback by the visceral longing I felt to be part of this world. I had never realized that I had been starved of anything. Now, at 17, I discovered that like a princess in a fairy tale, I had been cut off from my origins. This was the point in the tale where, simply by walking through a magical door, I could recover my gardens and palaces. If I allowed my uncle to arrange a marriage for me, I would belong.

Over the next few days, the man my family wished me to marry was introduced into the inner sanctum. He was a distant cousin. His luxuriant black mustache was generally considered to compensate for his lack of height. I was told breathlessly that he was a fighter pilot in the Pakistani Air Force. As an outsider, he wouldn't have been permitted to meet an unmarried girl. But as a relative, he had free run of the house. Whenever I appeared, a female cousin would fling a child into his arms. He'd pose with it, whiskers twitching, while the women cooed their admiration.   3

A huge cast of relatives had assembled to see my uncle's son marry. The wedding lasted nearly 14 days and ended with a reception. The bride and groom sat on an elevated stage to receive greetings. While the groom was permitted to laugh and chat, the bride was required to sit perfectly still, her eyes demurely lowered. I didn't see her move for four hours.   4

Watching this *tableau vivant* of a submissive Afghan bride, I knew that marriage would never be my easy route to the East. I could live in my father's mythological homeland only through the eyes of the storyteller. In my desire to experience the fairy tale, I had overlooked the staggeringly obvious: the storyteller was a man. If I wanted freedom, I would have to cut my own path. I began to understand why my uncle's wife had resorted to using religion to regain some control—at least in her own home. Her piety gave her license to impose her will on others.   5

My putative fiancé returned to Quetta, from where he sent a constant flow of lavish gifts. I was busy examining my hoard when my uncle's wife announced that he was on the phone. My intended was a favorite of hers; she had taken it upon herself to promote the match. As she handed me the receiver, he delivered a line culled straight from a Hindi movie: "We shall have a love-match, *ach-cha*?" Enough was enough. I slammed down the phone and went to find Aunt Amina. When she had heard me out, she said: "I'm glad that finally you've stopped this silly wild goose chase for your roots. I'll   6 have to extricate you from this mess. Wait here while I put on something more impressive." As a piece of Islamic one-upmanship, she returned wearing not one but three head scarves of different colors.

My uncle's wife was sitting on her prayer platform in the drawing room. Amina stormed in, scattering servants before her like chaff. "Your relative . . . ," was Amina's opening salvo, ". . . has been making obscene remarks to my niece." Her mouth opened, but before she could find her voice, Amina fired her heaviest guns: "Over the *telephone*!"

"How dare you!" her rival began.

It gave Amina exactly the opportunity she needed to move in for the kill. "What? Do you support this lewd conduct? Are we living in an American movie? Since when have young people of mixed sexes been permitted to speak to each other *on the telephone*? Let alone to talk—as I regret to inform you your nephew did—of love! Since when has love had anything to do with marriage? What a dangerous and absurd concept!"

My Peshawari aunt was not only outclassed; she was out-Islamed too. "My niece is a rose that hasn't been plucked," Amina said. "It is my task as her chaperone to ensure that this happy state of affairs continues. A match under such circumstances is quite out of the question. The engagement is off." My uncle's wife lost her battle for moral supremacy and, it seemed, her battle for sanity as well. In a gruff, slack-jawed way that I found unappealing, she made a sharp, inhuman sound that sounded almost like a bark.

READING FOR MEANING

This section presents three activities that will help you reread Shah's autobiographical essay with a critical eye. Done in sequence, these activities lead you from a basic understanding of the selection to a more personal response to it and finally to an analysis that deepens your understanding and critical thinking about what you are reading.

Read to Comprehend

Reread the selection, and write a few sentences briefly explaining what happened during Shah's visit with relatives in Pakistan. Also make a list of any words you do not understand—for example, *unadulterated* (paragraph 1), *tableau vivant* (5), *putative* (6). Look up their meanings in a dictionary to see which definition best fits the context.

To expand your understanding of this reading, you might use one or more of the following critical reading strategies that are explained and illustrated in

Appendix 1: *outlining, summarizing, paraphrasing,* and *questioning to understand and remember.*

Read to Respond

Write several paragraphs exploring your initial thoughts and feelings about Shah's autobiographical story. Focus on anything that stands out for you, perhaps because it resonates with your own experience or because you find a statement puzzling.

You might consider writing about

- Shah's "longing to belong."

- Shah's experience of new and different cultural traditions—perhaps in relation to your own experience.

- her uncle's assumption that Shah and her sister were sent to Pakistan "to be married" (paragraph 2).

- Shah's realization that "[i]f I wanted freedom, I would have to cut my own path" (5).

- the way her Aunt Amina gets Shah out of the predicament she was in (6–10).

To develop your response to Shah's essay, you might use one or more of the following critical reading strategies that are explained and illustrated in Appendix 1: *contextualizing, reflecting on challenges to your beliefs and values, recognizing emotional manipulation,* and *judging the writer's credibility.*

Read to Analyze Underlying Assumptions

Write several paragraphs exploring one or more of the assumptions, values, and beliefs underlying Shah's autobiographical essay. As you write, explain how the assumptions are reflected in the text, as well as what you now think of them (and perhaps of your own assumptions) after rereading the essay with a critical eye.

You might consider writing about

- Shah's and her uncle's different cultural values regarding his "Afghan habit" of feeding her from his plate or from his mouth (paragraph 1).

- Shah's beliefs that "like a princess in a fairy tale, I had been cut off from my origins" and that an arranged marriage was the way to restore her rightful place in the world (2).

- her relatives' assumptions about love, marriage, and the way men and women ought to behave—perhaps in relation to your own family's assumptions.

- Shah's idea that her "uncle's wife had resorted to using religion to regain some control" (5).

- the values implicit in the "battle" between Aunt Amina and Shah's Peshawari aunt for "moral supremacy" (10).

To probe assumptions more deeply, you might use one or more of the following critical reading strategies that are explained and illustrated in Appendix 1: *reflecting on challenges to your beliefs and values, exploring the significance of figurative language,* and *looking for patterns of opposition.*

READING LIKE A WRITER
CONVEYING AUTOBIOGRAPHICAL SIGNIFICANCE

Shah conveys the autobiographical significance of the event through a combination of showing and telling. She begins the essay with a vivid image of her uncle: "He would often generously withdraw a half-chewed delicacy from his mouth and lovingly cram it into mine." This image conveys dramatically how she felt at the time, especially to Western readers who, like her, are inclined to be repelled by this particular cultural practice. The choice of the word *cram,* because it implies force, conveys a sense not only of disgust but also of violation. Yet by modifying *cram* with the adverb *lovingly,* Shah makes clear the ambivalence of her feelings. When she calls her uncle's behavior "an Afghan habit," she suggests to her Western readers that it should be read not as a sign of domination but of love and acceptance. In effect, by taking food from his own mouth, he is extending to her his protection and treating her as if she were his own daughter.

Analyze

1. Shah uses a vivid image to convey her remembered feelings when she describes herself as "a princess in a fairy tale" (paragraph 2). *Reread* paragraphs 2–3 to see how she imagines this fairy tale and what she feels about the reality of her experience. *Underline* the words or phrases that show or tell you how Shah feels about the man with whom she has been matched.

2. *Reread* paragraphs 4–5 to see how the image of her uncle's son and his bride affect her fairy-tale fantasy. *Underline* words or phrases that show or tell how Shah feels about the role in which she has cast herself.

Write

Write several sentences explaining what you have learned about the autobiographical significance of this event for Shah. *Give two or three examples* from your underlining to support your explanation.

CONSIDERING IDEAS FOR YOUR OWN WRITING

Like Shah, consider writing about an event that you were looking forward to but that turned out differently than you had expected—perhaps a dreadful disappointment, a delightful surprise, or more likely a surprising combination of disappointment and delight. You might write about a time when you had thought you wanted something but then realized your desires were more complicated, when you were trying to fit in and discovered something about yourself or about the group to which you wanted to belong, or when you tried to conform to someone else's expectations for you or decided not to try to conform, but to rebel and go your own way. If, like Shah's, your experience involves a clash of cultures, you might write about that aspect of your experience and how it has affected you.

LUIS J. RODRIGUEZ

Always Running

> *Luis J. Rodriguez (b. 1954) is an award-winning writer who has published eight books, including the short story collection* The Republic of East L.A.: Stories *(2002), the children's book* It Doesn't Have to Be This Way: A Barrio Story *(1999), Poems across the Pavement (1989), the CD* My Name's Not Rodriguez *(2002), and the best-selling autobiography* Always Running: La Vida Loca, Gang Days in L.A. *(1993), from which this selection is excerpted. Among the many honors bestowed upon Rodriguez are the Chicago Sun-Times Book Award, a New York Times Notable Book Award, the Lila Wallace-Reader's Digest Writers' Award, and the Hispanic Heritage Award for Literature. Rodriguez also occasionally writes essays for* The Nation, Los Angeles Weekly, *and* Americas Review. *In addition to writing, Rodriguez has helped found several arts organizations in Chicago and Los Angeles and a nonprofit community group that works with gang members and other young people. If you want to learn more about Rodriguez, visit his official Web site at <http://www.luisjrodriguez.com>.*
>
> *In this excerpt from his autobiography, which he began writing when he was fifteen years old, Rodriguez tells what happened at the age of ten when he trespassed to play basketball in a school yard. As you read, put yourself in the young Rodriguez's place. Would you have climbed the fence? When you were a child, where could you go to play? If you were caught playing in a school yard after hours, would you run, as Rodriguez and his friend did?*

One evening dusk came early in South San Gabriel, with wind and cold spinning to earth. People who had been sitting on porches or on metal chairs near fold-up tables topped with cards and beer bottles collected their things to go inside. Others put on sweaters or jackets. A storm gathered beyond the trees.   1

Tino and I strolled past the stucco and wood-frame homes of the neighborhood consisting mostly of Mexicans with a sprinkling of poor white families (usually from Oklahoma, Arkansas and Texas). *Ranchera* music did battle with Country & Western songs as we continued toward the local elementary school, an oil-and-grime stained basketball under my arm.   2

We stopped in front of a chain-link fence which surrounded the school. An old brick building cast elongated shadows over a basketball court of concrete on the other side of the fence. Leaves and paper swirled in tiny tornadoes.   3

"Let's go over," Tino proposed.   4

I looked up and across the fence. A sign above us read: NO ONE ALLOWED AFTER 4:30 PM, BY ORDER OF THE LOS ANGELES COUNTY SHERIFF'S   5

DEPARTMENT. Tino turned toward me, shrugged his shoulders and gave me a who-cares look.

"Help me up, man, then throw the ball over."   6

I cupped my hands and lifted Tino up while the boy scaled the   7
fence, jumped over and landed on sneakered feet.

"Come on, Luis, let's go," Tino shouted from the other side.   8

I threw over the basketball, walked back a ways, then ran and   9
jumped on the fence, only to fall back. Although we were both
10 years old, I cut a shorter shadow.

"Forget you, man," Tino said. "I'm going to play without you."   10

"Wait!" I yelled, while walking further back. I crouched low to the   11
ground, then took off, jumped up and placed torn sneakers in the
steel mesh. I made it over with a big thud.

Wiping the grass and dirt from my pants, I casually walked up   12
to the ball on the ground, picked it up, and continued past Tino
toward the courts.

"Hey Tino, what are you waiting for?"   13

The gusts proved no obstacle for a half-court game of B-ball,   14
even as dark clouds smothered the sky.

Boy voices interspersed with ball cracking on asphalt. Tino's   15
lanky figure seemed to float across the court, as if he had wings
under his thin arms. Just then, a black-and-white squad car cruised
down the street. A searchlight sprayed across the school yard. The
vehicle slowed to a halt. The light shone toward the courts and
caught Tino in mid-flight of a lay-up.

The dribbling and laughter stopped.   16

"All right, this is the sheriff's," a voice commanded. Two deputies   17
stood by the fence, batons and flashlights in hand.

"Let's get out of here," Tino responded.   18

"What do you mean?" I countered. "Why don't we just stay   19
here?"

"You nuts! We trespassing, man," Tino replied. "When they get   20
a hold of us, they going to beat the crap out of us."

"Are you sure?"   21

"I know, believe me, I know."   22

"So where do we go?"   23

By then one of the deputies shouted back: "You boys get over   24
here by the fence—now!"

But Tino dropped the ball and ran. I heard the deputies yell for   25
Tino to stop. One of them began climbing the fence. I decided to
take off too.

It never stopped, this running. We were constant prey, and the   26
hunters soon became big blurs: the police, the gangs, the junkies, the
dudes on Garvey Boulevard who took our money, all smudged into
one. Sometimes they were teachers who jumped on us Mexicans as

if we were born with a hideous stain. We were always afraid. Always running.

Tino and I raced toward the dark boxes called classrooms. The 27 rooms lay there, hauntingly still without the voices of children, the commands of irate teachers or the clapping sounds of books as they were closed. The rooms were empty, forbidden places at night. We scurried around the structures toward a courtyard filled with benches next to the cafeteria building.

Tino hopped on a bench, then pulled himself over a high fence. 28 He walked a foot or two on top of it, stopped, and proceeded to climb over to the cafeteria's rooftop. I looked over my shoulder. The deputies weren't far behind, their guns drawn. I grabbed hold of the fence on the side of the cafeteria. I looked up and saw Tino's perspiring face over the roof's edge, his arm extended down toward me.

I tried to climb up, my feet dangling. But then a firm hand 29 seized a foot and pulled at it.

"They got me!" I yelled. 30

Tino looked below. A deputy spied the boy and called out: "Get 31 down here . . . you *greaser!*"

Tino straightened up and disappeared. I heard a flood of foot- 32 steps on the roof—then a crash. Soon an awful calm covered us.

"Tino!" I cried out. 33

A deputy restrained me as the other one climbed onto the roof. 34 He stopped at a skylight, jagged edges on one of its sides. Shining a flashlight inside the building, the officer spotted Tino's misshapen body on the floor, sprinkled over with shards of glass.

READING FOR MEANING

This section presents three activities that will help you reread with a critical eye the selection from Rodriguez's autobiography. Done in sequence, these activities lead you from a basic understanding of the selection to a more personal response to it and finally to an analysis that deepens your understanding and critical thinking about what you are reading.

Read to Comprehend

Reread the selection, and write a few sentences briefly explaining what happened when Rodriguez and his friend Tino tried to play basketball in the school yard. Also make a list of any words you do not understand—for example, *elongated* (paragraph 3), *lay-up* (15), *irate* (27). Look up their meanings in a dictionary to see which definition best fits the context.

To expand your understanding of this reading, you might use one or more of the following critical reading strategies that are explained and illustrated in

Appendix 1: *outlining, summarizing, paraphrasing,* and *questioning to understand and remember.*

Read to Respond

Write several paragraphs exploring your initial thoughts and feelings about Rodriguez's autobiographical story. Focus on anything that stands out for you, perhaps because it resonates with your own experience or because you find a statement puzzling.

You might consider writing about

- the shocking conclusion.
- the relationship between Rodriguez and Tino—perhaps reflecting on relationships you have had with friends.
- the sign posted on the school yard fence and the boys' reaction to it.
- the behavior of the police and of the boys when the police arrive.

To develop your response to Rodriguez's essay, you might use one or more of the following critical reading strategies that are explained and illustrated in Appendix 1: *contextualizing, reflecting on challenges to your beliefs and values, recognizing emotional manipulation,* and *judging the writer's credibility.*

Read to Analyze Underlying Assumptions

Write several paragraphs exploring one or more of the assumptions, values, and beliefs underlying Rodriguez's autobiographical story. As you write, explain how the assumptions are reflected in the text, as well as what you now think of them (and perhaps of your own assumptions) after rereading the selection with a critical eye.

You might consider writing about

- the assumptions underlying Tino's belief that the boys should run from the police: "We trespassing, man. . . . When they get a hold of us, they going to beat the crap out of us" (paragraph 20).
- the cultural values implicit in the officer's use of the word *"greaser"* (31).
- the assumptions underlying Rodriguez's assertion that the running "never stopped" (26).
- Rodriguez's assumptions about teachers' attitudes and values (implied in paragraphs 26 and 27).

To probe assumptions more deeply, you might use one or more of the following critical reading strategies that are explained and illustrated in Appendix 1: *reflecting on challenges to your beliefs and values, exploring the significance of figurative language,* and *looking for patterns of opposition.*

A SPECIAL READING STRATEGY

Contextualizing

Contextualizing is a special critical reading strategy. You can use it to read for meaning, to develop your analysis of the assumptions underlying "Always Running," and to compare your own assumptions with those of Rodriguez.

To contextualize an autobiographical essay like "Always Running," you need to explore the event's contexts:

- *When* the event occurred and how the historical moment influenced what happened: paragraph 9 indicates that the event occurred when Rodriguez was ten years old. According to Rodriguez's official Web site, he was born in 1954. So the event he is writing about occurred in 1964 or 1965. You could do further Internet research to learn what was happening during this historical period.

- *Where* the event occurred and how the location played a role: paragraph 1 identifies the location as "South San Gabriel," an area of Los Angeles, California. In paragraph 2, Rodriguez briefly describes the neighborhood. If you wanted to know more about this location during this period, you could read more of Rodriguez's autobiography or do further Internet research. If you do a Google search for "1960s Los Angeles ethnic," for example, you would learn about the area's ethnic makeup and political tensions, including the Watts riots of 1965.

- *Who* was involved and how the power relationships among those involved affected what happened: Rodriguez identifies himself and Tino as "Mexicans" (26). He does not identify the officers' ethnicity, but the fact that one of them calls Tino "you *greaser*" suggests his attitude toward people of Mexican descent and may help explain Tino's assumption that if he didn't run away, the police would beat him.

Appendix 1 (pp. 666–67) provides detailed guidelines on using contextualizing as a critical reading strategy.

READING LIKE A WRITER
PRESENTING PLACES AND PEOPLE

Autobiographers typically use a combination of *naming* and *detailing* along with *comparing* to present people and places. These descriptive strategies not only create vivid images that enable readers to imagine what the experience was like for the writer, but they also create a dominant impression that helps readers understand the autobiographical significance.

In paragraph 3, for example, Rodriguez describes the school yard this way:

> We stopped in front of a chain-link fence which surrounded the school. An old brick building cast elongated shadows over a basketball court of concrete on the other side of the fence. Leaves and paper swirled in tiny tornadoes.

Rodriguez names features such as the "fence," "building," and "basketball court" that he wants readers to notice about the scene. He also adds details to give readers information about these features. Descriptive details usually provide sensory information indicating what the place looks, sounds, smells, tastes, and/or feels like. Notice that Rodriguez chooses details like the "chain-link" of the fence, the "brick" of the building, and the "concrete" of the basketball court that give visual and tactile information. The brick and concrete suggest the hardness of these surfaces, an impression that is reinforced when we see how difficult it is for the young Rodriguez to get over the chain-link fence.

Rodriguez also uses comparison when he metaphorically describes the swirling leaves and papers as "tiny tornadoes." The word *tornadoes* reinforces other descriptive language in this selection. For example, the opening paragraph ends with a reference to a gathering storm, and the "gusts" and "dark clouds" of the gathering storm are mentioned again in paragraph 14. The storm is literal in that the weather actually is changing. But the storm is also figurative or symbolic—that is, it stands for the tragedy of Tino's death. It may also suggest the social upheaval that was building toward the cataclysm of the Watts riots.

Analyze

1. *Reread* the selection, underlining the naming, detailing, and comparing used to describe Tino's body language (paragraph 5), the ease with which he scales the fence (7), his body in motion as he plays basketball (15), his actions as he runs away (28), and finally his body fallen to the floor (34).

2. *Notice*, in paragraph 15, that Rodriguez describes Tino figuratively as if he were flying: seeming "to float across the court, as if he had wings." *Review* the descriptive language you have underlined to see where this image of Tino flying, or at least not being weighed down by gravity, is reinforced. *Contrast* this image of Tino with the way the young Rodriguez is described; in paragraphs 9–12, for example, Rodriguez struggles to scale the fence that Tino seems to climb so effortlessly.

Write

Write several sentences explaining what you have discovered about Rodriguez's description of Tino. What dominant impression do these images of

Tino suggest to you? How do they help you understand the significance of what happened? *Give two or three examples* from your underlining to support your explanation.

CONSIDERING IDEAS FOR YOUR OWN WRITING

In this autobiographical essay, Rodriguez writes about a traumatic event. If you have had the misfortune to experience something traumatic that you now feel comfortable sharing with your instructor and classmates, consider writing about it for this occasion. Instead of writing about something that turned out worse than you expected, you could also consider writing about something that turned out better or, at least, significantly different. Rodriguez's essay also suggests the possibility of writing about a time when you did something uncharacteristic or when you followed someone else's lead. You might also think about people—like Tino—whom you knew as a child or as an early adolescent and why those people were significant in your life.

MARK EDMUNDSON

The Teacher Who Opened My Mind

> *Mark Edmundson (b. 1952) writes essays about literature and contemporary culture for scholarly as well as popular publications, including* New York Times Magazine, Civilization, The Nation, *and* Harper's, *where he is a contributing editor. An English professor at the University of Virginia, Edmundson also has published several books, including* Nightmare on Main Street: Angels, Sado-Masochism, and the Culture of Gothic *(1997),* For Humanism *(2004), and* Teacher: The One Who Made the Difference *(2002).* Teacher, *a New York Times Notable Book of the Year, is an autobiography from which the following selection was adapted for the* UTNE *Reader, where it was published in 2003.*
>
> *After high school, Edmundson attended the University of Massachusetts at Amherst and Bennington College. Before returning to school to earn a doctorate in English at Yale, he spent several years driving a cab, working at rock shows, teaching at what he calls a "hippie school," and occasionally writing for the* Village Voice. *Commenting on the experience he writes about in "The Teacher Who Opened My Mind," Edmundson recalls: "It was a turning point in my life when a high school teacher looked up from his copy of* One Flew over the Cuckoo's Nest *and asked whether the protocols of the mental hospital, as Ken Kesey depicted them, might have had more than a little in common with the grinding protocols of our own high school. At that moment it became liberatingly clear to me that books have a capacity to criticize and challenge life as it is, and often to gesture toward something better."*
>
> *As you read, consider how Edmundson's narrative of his high-school experience compares with your own experience in high school and college.*

Frank Lears came to Medford High School with big plans for   1
his philosophy course. Together with a group of self-selected seniors, he was going to ponder the eternal questions: beauty, truth,
free will, fate, that sort of thing. The class would start out reading
The Story of Philosophy by Will Durant, then go on to Plato's dia-
logues, some Aristotle, Leibniz (a particular favorite of Lears'),
maybe just a little bit of Kant, then into a discussion of Bertrand
Russell's effort to clear the whole thing up with an injection of
clean scientific logic. Lears had just graduated from Harvard. All
of his intellectual aspirations were intact.

On the first day of class, we saw a short, slight man, with olive   2
skin—we thought he might be Mexican—wearing a skinny tie and
a moth-eaten suit with a paper clip fastened to the left lapel. He

had hunched shoulders and a droopy black mustache. Even when he strove for some dynamism, as he did that first day, explaining his plans for the course, he still had a melancholy presence. Having outlined the course, he turned away from us and began writing on the blackboard, in a script neater than any we would see from him again. It was a quotation from Nietzsche. He told us to get out our papers and pens and spend a couple of pages interpreting the quote "as a limbering-up exercise." I had never heard of Nietzsche. I had never read all the way through a book that was written for adults and that was not concerned exclusively with football.

The day before, I'd sat in the office of Mrs. Olmstead, the senior   3
guidance counselor, and been informed that I ranked 270th in a class of nearly 700. My prospects were not bright. We talked about Massachusetts Bay Community College, Salem State Teachers College; we discussed my working for the city of Medford—perhaps I'd start by collecting barrels, then graduate in time to a desk job (my father had some modest connections); I mentioned joining the Marines (I might have made it in time for the Cambodia invasion). Nothing was resolved.

As I was mumbling my way out the door, Mrs. Olmstead began   4
talking about a new teacher who was coming to the school, "someone we're especially proud to have." He was scheduled to teach philosophy. I didn't know what philosophy was, but I associated it with airy speculation, empty nothing; it seemed an agreeable enough way of wasting time.

So there I was in a well-lit room, wearing, no doubt, some sharp   5
back-to-school ensemble, pegged pants and sporty dice-in-the-back-alley shoes, mildly aching from two or three football-inflicted wounds, and pondering the Nietzsche quotation, which I could barely understand. I felt dumb as a rock, a sentiment with which I, at 17, had no little prior experience. But by putting the quotation on the board, Lears showed me that, in at least one department, his powers of comprehension were a few notches lower than mine. He had misunderstood Medford High School entirely.

The appearances had taken him in. No doubt he'd strolled   6
through the building on the day before students arrived; he'd seen desks, chalkboards, supply closets stocked full of paper and books, all the paraphernalia of education. He had seen these things and he'd believed that he was in a school, a place where people quested, by fits and starts, for the truth.

But I had acquired a few facts that Lears would not have been   7
primed to receive at Harvard, or at prep school, or at any of the other places where he had filled his hours. Medford High School,

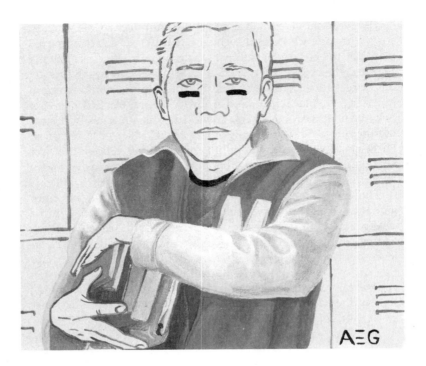

whatever its appearances, was not a school. It was a place where you learned to do—or were punished for failing in—a variety of exercises. The content of these exercises mattered not at all. What mattered was form, repetition, and form. You filled in the blanks, conjugated, declined, diagrammed, defined, outlined, summarized, recapitulated, positioned, graphed. It did not matter what: English, geometry, biology, history, all were the same. The process treated your mind as though it were a body part capable of learning a number of protocols, then repeating, repeating. If you'd done what you should have at Medford High, the transition into a factory, into an office, into the Marines would be something you'd barely notice; it would be painless.

Before Lears arrived, I never rebelled against the place, at least not openly. I didn't in part because I believed that Medford High was the only game there was. The factories where my father and uncles worked were extensions of the high school; the TV shows we watched were manufactured to fit the tastes for escape that such places form; the books we were assigned to read in class, *Ivanhoe, Silas Marner, The Good Earth,* of which I ingested about 50 pages each, could, as I saw it then, have been written by the English teachers, with their bland, babbling goodness

8

and suppressed hysterias (I've never had the wherewithal to check back into them). Small bursts of light came through in the Beethoven symphonies my father occasionally played at volume on our ancient stereo (the music sounded like it was coming in over a walkie-talkie) and the Motown tunes I heard on Boston's black radio station, WILD, but these sounds were not connected to any place or human possibility I knew about. So I checked out. I went low to the ground, despondent, suspicious, asleep in the outer self, barely conscious within.

This condition Frank Lears changed. That now, however imperfectly, I can say what's on my mind, and that I know what kind of life I hope for, I owe not to him alone, of course, but to many. Frank Lears pushed open the door to those others, though, other worlds, other minds. 9

For three months, Lears did his best with Will Durant and *The Story of Philosophy*. We barely gave him an inch. Dubby O'Day (Donald O'Day on his report cards and disciplinary citations) made enormous daisy chains out of the rubber bands he used to bind the advertising circulars he delivered on Saturday mornings or sat, his body tight with concentrated energy, inking in all of the *o*'s in the textbook. Tom Vincents pried tufts of grass off the soles of his soccer cleats; Michael de Leo and Tom Cappalano, wide receiver and quarterback for the Medford Mustangs (I blocked for them, sporadically), contemplated pass plays and the oncoming game with Newton, or Somerville, or Everett. Nora Balakanian was high school beautiful. Sandra Steinman, the school's only hippie—she wore wire-rim glasses and work boots and was, by her own choice, of no social consequence at all—conversed with Lears on subjects no one else cared about. 10

Lears thought well of himself. And we all wondered, if unspokenly, where this guy might have gotten his considerable lode of self-esteem. Teachers, as we could have told him, were losers out-and-out. And this one in particular wasn't strong or tough or worldly. He wore ridiculous clothes, old formal suits, and that weird paper clip in his lapel; he talked like a dictionary; his accent was over-cultivated, queer, absurd. Yet he thought highly of himself. And not much at all, it wasn't difficult to see, of us. He mocked us, and not always so genially, for never doing the reading, never knowing the answer, never having a thought in our heads. We were minor fools, his tone implied, for ignoring this chance to learn a little something before being fed live to what was waiting. For our part, we sat back, and waited to see what would turn up. 11

One day in mid-December or so, Lears walked in and told us to pass back our copies of *The Story of Philosophy*. Then he told us 12 that he had some other books for us to read but that we'd have to pay for them ourselves. Lears, it turned out, had asked no one's permission to do this; it just struck him as a good idea to try to get people who never picked up a book to do some reading by giving them work that might speak to their experience. At Medford High, this qualified as major educational innovation, real break-through thinking. And, of course, there were plenty of rules against using books that hadn't been approved by the school board. The books that Lears picked were on a theme, though I had no idea of that at the time. *The Stranger, One Flew Over the Cuckoo's Nest,* Freud's *Group Psychology and the Analysis of the Ego, Siddhartha:* The first three were about the oppressions of conformity (among other things), the last about the Buddha's serene, fierce rebellion against it. For the first few weeks, since virtually no one but Sandra would read a book at home, we simply sat in a circle and read the pages aloud in turn. Periodically, Lears would ask a question, and usually, in the beginning, it was he who would answer it or decide finally to let it drop. One day, when we were reading *The Stranger,* Lears asked us about solitude. What does it mean to be alone? Is it possible? What would it mean to be genuinely by oneself? Sandra Steinman raised her hand, no doubt ready to treat us to a description of Zen meditation and its capacity to melt the ego beyond solitude into pure nothingness. But Lears must have seen something ripple across Nora Balakanian's beautiful face. He gestured in her direction, though she hadn't volunteered.

Nora was a high school princess, whose autobiography, I'd have   13
guessed back then, would have translated into a graph peaking from prom to prom, with soft valleys of preparation in between. But what Nora did, in her teasing nasal voice, was to run through a litany of defenses against being alone. She mentioned listening to the radio and talking on the phone, then playing the songs and conversations over in her mind, and a myriad of other strategies, ending, perceptively enough, with our habit of blocking out the present by waiting for things to happen in the future. But Nora did not express herself with detachment. She said "I." "This is how I keep from being alone." "And why," asked Lears, "is it hard to be alone?" "Because," Nora answered, "I might start to think about things."

Nora had been, up until that point, one of the Elect, predes-   14
tined for all happiness; suddenly she had gone over to the terminally Lost. One of the great sources of grief for those who suffer inwardly is their belief that others exist who are perpetually and truly happy. From the ranks of the local happy few, Nora had just checked out, leaving some effective hints about those she'd left behind.

The book that mattered to me wasn't *The Stranger,* which had   15
gotten Nora going, or Freud's book on the herd instinct (when I
was writing my dissertation, a literary critical reading of Freud, my
working text of *Group Psychology* was, somehow, the one that had
belonged to Dubby O'Day, with the *o*'s colored in to about page 20),
but Kesey's *One Flew Over the Cuckoo's Nest.* It's a hard book for
me to read now, with its pumped-up, cartoon hero, Randall
Patrick McMurphy. But at the time it was all in all. I read it in a
lather, running through it in about 10 hours straight, then starting
in again almost immediately.

But that didn't happen right off. It was probably on the fifth day   16
of reading the book out loud in class that a chance remark Lears
made caught my attention, or what there was of it then to catch.
He said that prisons, hospitals, and schools were on a continuum,
controlling institutions with many of the same protocols and

objectives, and that Kesey, with his bitter portrait of the mental hospital, might be seen as commenting on all these places.

This idea, elementary as it was, smacked me with the force of revelation. Here was a writer who was not on the side of the teachers, who in fact detested them and their whole virtuous apparatus. That the book was in part crude and ugly I knew even at that time: Blacks in it are twisted sadists, the women castrators or sweet whores. But it was the anti-authoritarian part that swept me in; here was someone who found words—gorgeous, graffiti-sized, and apocalyptic—for what in me had been mere inchoate impulses.   17

Soon Lears started bringing things into class. Every Friday we got some music: I remember hearing Billie Holiday, Mozart, the Velvet Underground. He also showed us art books, read a poem from time to time, and brought in friends of his to explain themselves. A panel from Students for a Democratic Society appeared one day to discuss the Vietnam War with us. (Most of us were in favor.)   18

One February day, a group of black students burst into the room and announced that this was the anniversary of Malcolm X's death. Lears looked up mildly from his place in the circle and asked the foremost of them, "And when was he born, Malcolm Little?" The young man gave a date. Lears nodded and invited them to sit down. It was the first time I'd had an extended conversation about politics with blacks. More discussions followed and, though they didn't stop the ongoing racial guerrilla war at Medford High, they were something.   19

When the weather warmed up, the class occasionally went outside to sit on the grass and hold discussions there. This sometimes resulted in one or two of us nodding off, but Lears didn't much care; he had most of us most of the time now. He sat cross-legged, and laughed, and we answered the questions he asked, because what he thought mattered. It was a first, this outdoors business; no one at Medford High would have imagined doing it. One Thursday afternoon, just as we were wrapping up a discussion of Thoreau, Lears gave us a solemn, mischievous look, the sort of expression shrewd old rabbis are supposed to be expert in delivering, and said, "There's been some doubt expressed about our going outside." Then he told a story. Jingles McDermott, the feared school disciplinarian, had approached Lears in the faculty cafeteria as other teachers milled around. What would happen, McDermott asked Lears, if everyone held class outside?   20

Now this was familiar stuff to us all. McDermott's question came out of that grand conceptual bag that also contained lines like "Did you bring gum for everyone?" and "Would you like to share that   21 note with the whole class?" McDermott was trying to treat Lears like a student, like one of us—and in front of his colleagues.

McDermott did not know that Lears, however diminutive, thought himself something of a big deal and so would not have been prepared when Lears drew an easy breath and did what every high school kid would like to do when confronted with this sort of bullying. He didn't fight it, didn't stand on his dignity. He simply ran with it.   22

What if everyone held class outside on sunny days? Suppose that happened? And from there, Lears went on to draw a picture of life at Medford High School that had people outside on the vast lawn talking away about books and ideas and one thing and another, hanging out, being lazy, being absorbed, thinking hard from time to time, and reveling in the spring. It was Woodstock and Socrates' agora fused, and Lears spun it out for us, just as he had for McDermott. What if that happened, he asked us? How tragic would it be?   23

We went outside whenever we chose to after that. It was very odd: I had been at Medford High for three years and I had never seen McDermott lose a round. After class was over that day, Tom Cappalano, the quarterback, said, "You know, Lears can really be an asshole when he wants to be." In Medford, there were 50 intonations you could apply to the word "asshole." Spun right, the word constituted high praise.   24

That year of teaching was the last for Frank Lears. He got married, went to law school, and, I heard, eventually moved to Maine, where he could pursue a life a little akin to the one Thoreau, his longtime idol, managed to lead during his stay at Walden. I haven't seen Lears in about 25 years. But I do carry around with me the strong sense that the party, the outdoor extravaganza, he invited us to, me and Nora and Dubby and even Jingles McDermott, is still a live possibility. I had great teachers after Frank Lears, some of the world's most famous in fact, but I never met his equal. What I liked most about him, I suppose, was that for all the minor miracle of what he accomplished with us, he was no missionary: He served us but also himself. His goodness had some edge to it. He got what he wanted out of Medford High, which was a chance to affront his spiritual enemies, though with some generosity, and to make younger people care about the sorts of things he cared about, to pull them out of their parents' orbit and into his. All good teaching entails some kidnapping.   25

As well as some sorrow: Good teachers have many motivations, but I suspect that loneliness is often one of them. You need a small group, a coterie, to talk to; unable to find it in the larger world, you try to create it in the smaller sphere of a classroom. Lears, who   26 seemed at times a little lost in his life, a brilliant orphan, did something like that with us.

What Lears taught—or at least what I gleaned from him—is 27 that anything that's been successfully institutionalized, however rebellious it may seem or however virtuous, is stifling. What's called subversion only lasts for an instant in a school or a hospital or a home; it's quickly swept up to become part of the protocol, an element in "the way we do things around here." At the time, Kesey and Camus collided well enough with the dead protocols of Medford High, but now, for all I know, they fit in fine—alienation has become standard issue.

One pays for the kind of mental exhilaration that Lears initiated 28 in his students. One pays in self-doubt and isolation, in the suspicion that what seems to be true resistance is merely a perverse substitute for genuine talent, a cheap way of having something to say. Lears's path, so appealing in its first steps, separated me from my family, cut me loose from religion and popular faith, sent me adrift beyond the world bordered by TV and piety and common sense. One step down that road followed another, and now, at 50, I probably could not turn around if I wished to.

Still, the image I most often hit on when I think about Lears 29 glows brightly. It's late spring, a gloomy dead day. He's standing beside the beat-up phonograph at the back of the room with a record he's brought in by the Incredible String Band. I dislike the record and open my book, the *Autobiography of Malcolm X,* which has not been assigned in any class, and disappear into it. He cranks the music just a little louder. I keep reading. But then, curious, I raise my head. The racket of the String Band floods in. And there in the back of the room, Lears is dancing away. He's a terrible dancer, stiff and arrhythmic. Not until I saw Bob Dylan in concert did I ever see anyone dance so self-consciously. It struck me that this was probably the first time anyone had ever danced in this classroom. But here was Lears, bringing it off. It was like some strokes of light rendered by a painter for the first time, though with an unsteady enough hand. Lears had scored a benevolent victory over Medford High School. (You could say that he'd beaten them at their game, but really he'd shown them a new one.) He had a right to a little celebration.

READING FOR MEANING

This section presents three activities that will help you reread Edmundson's autobiographical essay with a critical eye. Done in sequence, these activities lead you from a basic understanding of the selection to a more personal response to

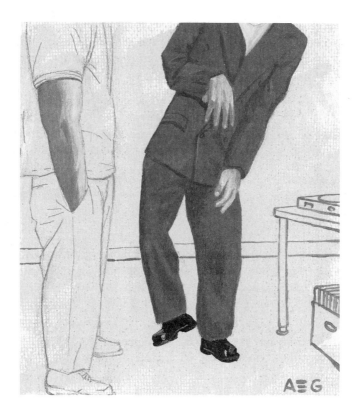

it and finally to an analysis that deepens your understanding and critical thinking about what you are reading.

Read to Comprehend

Reread the selection, and write a few sentences briefly explaining the influence that Edmundson's teacher, Frank Lears, had on him. Also make a list of any words you do not understand—for example, *dynamism* (paragraph 2), *despondent* (8), *anti-authoritarian* (17). Look up their meanings in a dictionary to see which definition best fits the context.

Notice that Edmundson drops several names, such as Plato, Aristotle, and Nietzsche. To understand the essay, you don't need to know much about these people other than that they are important philosophers. But if you are interested, look them up online at the Internet Encyclopedia of Philosophy (<http://www.iep.utm.edu>) or the Stanford Encyclopedia of Philosophy (<http://plato.stanford.edu/contents.html>).

To expand your understanding of this reading, you might use one or more of the following critical reading strategies that are explained and illustrated in Appendix 1: *outlining, summarizing, paraphrasing,* and *questioning to understand and remember.*

Read to Respond

Write several paragraphs exploring your initial thoughts and feelings about Edmundson's portrait of his high-school teacher. Focus on anything that stands out for you, perhaps because it resonates with your own experience or because you find a statement puzzling.

You might consider writing about

- the relationship between Edmundson and Lears—perhaps reflecting on relationships you have had with teachers.

- your own high-school or college experience in relation to Edmundson's experience of high school as "a place where you learned to do—or were punished for failing in—a variety of exercises. The content of these exercises mattered not at all. What mattered was form, repetition, and form" (paragraph 7).

- what Edmundson calls the "ongoing racial guerrilla war at Medford High"— perhaps in relation to racial and ethnic tensions in your own school experience (19).

- the way Lears handled the "bullying" of Jingles McDermott (20–24).

- what the drawings add to the effect of the essay or to your understanding of the young Edmundson and his relationship to Lears.

To develop your response to Edmundson's essay, you might use one or more of the following critical reading strategies that are explained and illustrated in Appendix 1: *contextualizing, reflecting on challenges to your beliefs and values, recognizing emotional manipulation,* and *judging the writer's credibility.*

Read to Analyze Underlying Assumptions

Write several paragraphs exploring one or more of the assumptions, values, and beliefs underlying Edmundson's autobiographical essay. As you write, explain how the assumptions are reflected in the text, as well as what you now think of them (and perhaps of your own assumptions) after rereading the selection with a critical eye.

You might consider writing about

- the young Edmundson's assumption that philosophy involves "airy speculation" and "an agreeable enough way of wasting time" (paragraph 4).

- the values and beliefs behind the contrast Edmundson makes between the schools Lears attended—such as "prep school" and "Harvard," "where people quested . . . for the truth"—and Medford High, where the mind was treated "as though it were a body part capable of learning a number of protocols, then repeating," and where "the transition into a factory, into an office, into the Marines would be something you'd barely notice" (6–7).

- Edmundson's assumptions about Nora Balakanian, before and after she speaks in class about how she keeps from "being alone" (12–14).

- the "revelation" Edmundson has after reading *One Flew over the Cuckoo's Nest* by Ken Kesey (15–17).

- the assumptions underlying the conclusions Edmundson draws from his experience with Lears: "that anything that's been successfully institutionalized, however rebellious it may seem or however virtuous, is stifling. What's called subversion only lasts an instant in a school or a hospital or a home" (27).

To probe assumptions more deeply, you might use one or more of the following critical reading strategies that are explained and illustrated in Appendix 1: *reflecting on challenges to your beliefs and values, exploring the significance of figurative language,* and *looking for patterns of opposition.*

READING LIKE A WRITER
PRESENTING A PERSON THROUGH ANECDOTES AND RECURRING ACTIVITIES

Autobiography uses narrative in various ways. Some autobiographies, like those by Annie Dillard, Luis J. Rodriguez, Saira Shah, and Jean Brandt, focus on a single memorable event that occurred within a few hours or days; whereas others, like those by Mark Edmundson, Amy Wu, and Brad Benioff, focus on a person with whom the writer had an important relationship. Autobiographies that focus on a person may use two narrating strategies: anecdotes and recurring activities. *Anecdotes* present experiences that are onetime occurrences. Like a snapshot, an anecdote catches the person at a particular place and time, giving the reader a sense of what the person did and said on that occasion, such as when someone tripped and dropped the cake at a birthday party. *Recurring activities,* in contrast, present experiences that are typical, that occur more than once, often on a regular basis with only a little variation over a period of time, such as several occasions when the same person tripped and dropped things, suggesting the person's clumsiness or nervousness. As you analyze Edmundson's use of anecdotes and recurring activities, you will see how they differ and what each contributes to the portrait of Frank Lears.

Analyze

1. *Reread* paragraphs 12–14, where Edmundson presents a recurring activity as well as an anecdote. As you read, mark the part where the recurring activity appears. Note the way Edmundson signals readers that he is narrating a recurring activity and not a onetime occurrence.

2. *Focus on* the anecdote that relates what happened when Lears called on Nora Balakanian. *Notice* how Edmundson signals to readers that this is a onetime occurrence and not a recurring activity.

Write

Write several sentences describing how the recurring activity and anecdote differ, pointing to specific ways Edmundson presents these experiences and helps readers understand them. Then *speculate about* what each of these narrating strategies contributes to Edmundson's portrait of Frank Lears.

CONSIDERING IDEAS FOR YOUR OWN WRITING

Like Edmundson, you might consider writing about a turning point in your schooling or the discovery of something that mattered to you—in the way that *One Flew over the Cuckoo's Nest* mattered to the young Edmundson. Perhaps there was an experience that helped you discover your intellectual or artistic potential, inspired your career aspirations, or made you decide not to pursue a particular interest or goal. Consider writing a before-and-after portrait of yourself that focuses on this experience. Another possibility is to write about someone in your life who, like Lears, served as a mentor, focusing on that person's special attributes or why you were susceptible to the person's influence at that particular moment in your life.

AMY WU

A Different Kind of Mother

Amy Wu (b. 1976) wrote this essay when she was seventeen years old, just before entering New York University, where she majored in history and journalism. Since then, she has worked for news organizations, for Internet companies, and as a freelance writer, publishing articles in the New York Times, Wired, Asian Week, *and other publications. In 1996–2001, Wu reported from Hong Kong. Now, she is on the staff of the* Monterey County Herald *in California. This essay was originally published in 1993 in* Chinese American Forum, *a quarterly magazine.*

As the title "A Different Kind of Mother" indicates, Wu wants readers to understand her special relationship with her mother. Notice, as you read, the cultural differences Wu points out between her "Chinese" mother and "American" friends' mothers. What significance do you think she wants readers to draw from these differences?

My best friend once asked me what it was like being brought up by a Chinese mother. Surprisingly, I could find no answer. I found myself describing my mother's beauty—the way my mother's hair was so silky and black, how her eyes were not small and squinty, but shaped like perfect almonds. How her lips and cheeks were bright red even if she put on no makeup.

Amy Wu and her mother.

But unlike my friends, who see my mother as a Chinese mother, I see my mother as simply "my" mother. The language between any mother and daughter is universal. Beyond the layers of arguments and rhetoric, and beyond the incidents of humiliation and misunderstandings, there is a love that unites every mother and daughter.

I am not blind, however, to the disciplinary differences between a culture from the west and a culture from the east. Unlike American mothers, who encourage their young children to speak whatever is on their mind, my mother told me to hold my tongue. Once, when I was 5 or 6, I interrupted my mother during a dinner with her friends and told her that I disliked the meal. My mother's eyes transformed from serene pools of blackness into stormy balls of fire. "Quiet!" she hissed, "do you not know that silent waters run deep?" She ordered me to turn my chair to the wall and think about what I had done. I remember throwing a red-faced tantrum before my mother's friends, pounding my fists into the rug, and throwing my utensils at the steaming dishes. Not only did I receive a harsh scolding, but a painful spanking. By the end of that evening, I had learned the first of many lessons. I learned to choose my words carefully before I opened my undisciplined mouth.

Whenever my friends and I strike up conversations about our mothers in the cafeteria or at slumber parties, I find myself telling them this story. Nevertheless, they respond to my story with straight and pale faces. "How," one of my friends asked, "can a mother be so cruel?" "You mean she beat you in front of other people?" another asked. My best friend told me that her mother disciplined her children wisely instead of abusing them. She sat them on her lap, patiently explaining what they had done wrong. She didn't believe in beating children into submission.

What my American friends cannot understand, however, is how my mother's lessons have become so embedded within me, while my friends have easily forgotten their mother's words. My mother's eyes are so powerful, her fists so strong, that somehow I cannot erase her words of advice. To this day, I choose my words carefully before I speak, unlike so many of my friends whose words spill out aimlessly when they open their mouths. My mother says that American girls are taught to squabble like chickens, but a Chinese girl is taught how to speak intelligently.

Only lately have I also discovered that Chinese mothers show their love in different ways. Ever since I was a little girl, my mother has spent hours cooking intricate dishes. I remember Friday evenings she would lay out the precious china her mother had given her as a wedding present—how she laid down the utensils and glasses so meticulously, how she made sure there was not a crease in the tablecloth.

She would spend the entire day steaming fish, baking ribs, cutting beef into thin strips, and rolling dough to make dumplings. In the evening, her work of labor and art would be unveiled. My father and I and a few Chinese neighbors and friends would be invited to feast on my mother's work of art.

I remember how silent my mother was as she watched her loved ones devour her labor of love. She would sit back, with a small smile on her face. She would nibble at the food in her dish while urging others to eat more, to take seconds, and thirds and fourths. "Eat, eat!" she would order me. I dared not tell her I was too full.

She would fill my bowl with mounds of rice and my dish with   9
endless vegetables, fish, and fried delicacies. A Chinese mother's love
flows from the time and energy she puts into forming a banquet. A
Chinese mother's love comes through her order to eat more.

My American friends laugh so hard that tears come out of their   10
eyes, when I tell them how my Chinese mother displays her love.
"So she wants you to get fat!" one screamed. They said that their
mothers showed love by hugging them tightly, buying them
clothes, and kissing them on the cheeks.

Deep inside, I know that my mother does show her love, except   11
she does it when she thinks I am asleep. Every so often, she will
tiptoe into my dark room, sit on the edge of my bed, and stroke
my hair. When I am awake, however, she is like a professor constantly hounding her prize student and expecting only the best.
All throughout my childhood, she drilled me on lessons of cleanliness and respect.

A few years ago at my Grandpa Du's 67th birthday party, I ran   12
up to my grandfather and planted a wet, juicy kiss on his right
cheek. To this day, I can easily remember the horrified looks on my
relatives' faces. My grandfather turned pale for a second and then
smiled meekly. He nodded his head and quickly sat down.

Later that evening, my mother cornered me against the wall.   13
"Do you not know that respect to elderly is to bow!" she screamed.
Her face turned bright purple. My excuses of "I didn't know . . ."
were lost in her powerful words.

From that day on, I bowed to anyone Chinese and older than I.   14
I have learned that respect for the elderly earns a young person a
different kind of respect. These days, my grandfather points to me
and tells my little cousins to follow my example. "She has been
taught well," he tells them.

It saddens me that my Chinese mother is so often misunderstood.   15
After she threw my friends out during my twelfth birthday party,
because they refused to take off their shoes, they saw her as a callous,
cruel animal. One of my friends went home and told her father that
I had an abusive mother. Her father even volunteered to call the child
welfare department. They never dared to step foot in my house again.

My mother has given me so many fine values and morals because   16
of her way of teaching me. I choose words carefully before I speak.
I am careful to speak and act toward the elderly a certain way. Without my mother's strong words and teachings, I believe that I would
be a rather undisciplined person who didn't value life greatly. I
would most likely have been spoiled and callous and ignorant. I
have also learned that there is more than one definition of love
between a mother and a daughter.

READING FOR MEANING

This section presents three activities that will help you reread Wu's autobiographical essay with a critical eye. Done in sequence, these activities lead you from a basic understanding of the selection to a more personal response to it and finally to an analysis that deepens your understanding and critical thinking about what you are reading.

Read to Comprehend

Reread the selection, and write a few sentences briefly explaining what Wu wants her readers to understand about her mother and their relationship. Also make a list of any words you do not understand—for example, *submission* (paragraph 4), *squabble* (5), *callous* (16). Look up their meanings in a dictionary to see which definition best fits the context.

To expand your understanding of this reading, you might use one or more of the following critical reading strategies that are explained and illustrated in Appendix 1: *outlining, summarizing, paraphrasing,* and *questioning to understand and remember.*

Read to Respond

Write several paragraphs exploring your initial thoughts and feelings about Wu's portrait of her mother. Focus on anything that stands out for you, perhaps because it resonates with your own experience or because you find a statement puzzling.

You might consider writing about

- how a particular scene—such as when Wu interrupted her mother (paragraph 3) or when she kissed her grandfather at his birthday party (12–14)—contributes to your understanding of the relationship between Wu and her mother, perhaps in relation to your own family customs.

- the characterization of Wu's mother as "abusive" (15), and your own response to Wu's mother's style of child-rearing.

- what the photograph adds to your understanding of Wu's relationship with her mother.

- the way Wu and her friends react to cultural differences in their families, perhaps in relation to your own experience.

To develop your response to Wu's essay, you might use one or more of the following critical reading strategies that are explained and illustrated in Appendix 1: *contextualizing, reflecting on challenges to your beliefs and values, recognizing emotional manipulation,* and *judging the writer's credibility.*

Read to Analyze Underlying Assumptions

Write several paragraphs exploring one or more of the assumptions, values, and beliefs underlying Wu's autobiographical essay. As you write, explain how the assumptions are reflected in the text, as well as what you now think of them (and perhaps of your own assumptions) after rereading the selection with a critical eye.

You might consider writing about

- what Wu assumes when she writes that the "language between any mother and daughter is universal" (paragraph 2) in relation to the contrasting ways Wu's mother and Wu's friends' mothers show their love.

- Wu's own assumptions and judgments about American child-rearing practices.

- Wu's judgments about her mother's child-rearing practices and expectations, perhaps in relation to the judgments of Wu's friends and their parents.

- the importance of ritual occasions, such as the banquets Wu's mother prepares for family and friends.

To probe assumptions more deeply, you might use one or more of the following critical reading strategies that are explained and illustrated in Appendix 1: *reflecting on challenges to your beliefs and values, exploring the significance of figurative language,* and *looking for patterns of opposition.*

READING LIKE A WRITER
PRESENTING A PERSON THROUGH DIALOGUE

Autobiographers often use dialogue to present people and to shed light on relationships. Dialogue reconstructs conversation, either through *direct quotation* to emphasize the speaker's choice of words or through *indirect quotation*— *paraphrasing* and *summarizing*—to focus on the substance of what was said instead of the precise words that were used. Effective dialogue gives readers an impression of the speaker's character or personality as well as how he or she relates to others. In this reading, Wu alternates between reporting two kinds of conversations, those she had about her mother with friends and those she had with her mother. This activity focuses on the conversations with her mother.

When writers compose dialogue, they usually include descriptive details depicting the speaker's tone of voice, facial expression, and hand gestures. For example, in paragraph 3, Wu describes her mother's physical reaction to her interruption with these details: "My mother's eyes transformed from serene pools of blackness into stormy balls of fire." And she characterizes her mother's response, "Quiet!," by describing her tone: "she hissed." These descriptive details convey the mood and emotion as well as the content of the conversation.

Analyze

1. *Reread* paragraphs 3, 8, and 13, where Wu uses dialogue to present her conversations with her mother. *Put brackets around* the dialogue—noting both the parts that are quoted and those that are paraphrased or summarized. Then *underline* any details that describe the speakers.

2. *Review* the bits of dialogue you bracketed and the details you underlined. *Single out* one or two examples that seem particularly effective in presenting Wu's mother and Wu's relationship with her.

Write

Write several sentences explaining what you have discovered about Wu's use of dialogue. From your annotations, *give two or three examples* to show how the quoted language and the details contribute to the dialogue's effectiveness.

CONSIDERING IDEAS FOR YOUR OWN WRITING

Autobiographers often write about people with whom they have close and somewhat complicated relationships. Like Wu, you might choose to present a person about whom you felt (and maybe still feel) strong and conflicting emotions, such as love, anger, disapproval, admiration, envy, disappointment, or hurt. Try to recall particular events or conversations with the person that you could use to help readers understand why the person aroused strong feelings or conflicting emotions in you. Another possibility is to write about a parent, a guardian, a counselor, a minister, or some other older person who influenced you deeply, for good or ill. Consider also someone who passed on to you a sense of your family history or culture.

BRAD BENIOFF

Rick

Brad Benioff was a first-year college student when he wrote the following essay for an assignment in his composition class. Like Mark Edmundson and Amy Wu in the two preceding selections, Benioff focuses his essay on a memorable person: his high-school water polo coach, Rick Rezinas.

As you read, notice how Benioff uses dialogue to dramatize his relationship with Rick.

I walked through the dawn chill, shivering as much from nervousness as from the cold. Steam curled up from the water in the pool and disappeared in the ocher morning light. Athletes spread themselves about on the deck, lazily stretching and whispering to each other as if the stillness were sacred. It was to be my first practice with the high school water polo team. I knew nothing about the game, but a friend had pushed me to play, arguing, "It's the most fun of any sport. Trust me." He had awakened me that morning long before daylight, forced me into a bathing suit, and driven me to the pool.

"Relax," he said. "Rick is the greatest of coaches. You'll like him. You'll have fun."

The mythical Rick. I had heard of him many times before. All the older players knew him by his first name and always spoke of him as a friend rather than a coach. He was a math teacher at our school, and his classes were very popular. Whenever class schedules came out, everyone hoped to be placed in Mr. Rezinas's class. He had been known to throw parties for the team or take them on weekend excursions skiing or backpacking. To be Rick's friend was to be part of an exclusive club, and I was being invited to join. And so I looked forward with nervous anticipation to meeting this man.

My friend walked me out to the pool deck and steered me toward a man standing beside the pool.

"Rick," announced my friend, "I'd like you to meet your newest player."

Rick was not a friendly looking man. He wore only swim trunks, and his short, powerful legs rose up to meet a bulging torso. His big belly was solid. His shoulders, as if to offset his front-heaviness, were thrown back, creating a deep crease of excess muscle from his sides around the small of his back, a crease like a huge frown. His arms were crossed, two medieval maces placed carefully on their racks, ready to be swung at any moment. His round cheeks and chin were darkened by traces of black whiskers. His hair was sparse. Huge, black, mirrored sunglasses replaced his eyes. Below his prominent nose was a thin, sinister mustache. I couldn't believe this menacing-looking man was the legendary jovial Rick.

He said nothing at first. In those moments of silence, I felt more inadequate than ever before in my life. My reflection in his glasses stared back at me, accusing me of being too skinny, too young, too stupid, too weak to be on his team. Where did I get the nerve to approach him with such a ridiculous body and ask to play water polo, a man's game? Finally, he broke the silence, having finished appraising my meager body. "We'll fatten him up," he growled.   7

Thus began a week of torture. For four hours a day, the coach stood beside the pool scowling down at me. I could do nothing right.   8

"No! No! No!" He shook his head in disgust. "Throw the damn ball with your whole arm! Get your goddamn elbow out of the water!"   9

Any failure on my part brought down his full wrath. He bellowed at my incompetence and punished me with pushups and wind sprints. Even when I was close to utter exhaustion, I found no sympathy. "What the hell are you doing on the wall?" he would bellow. "Coach . . . my side, it's cramped."   10

"Swim on it! If you can't take a little pain, then you don't play!" With this, he would push me off the wall.   11

He seemed to enjoy playing me against the older, stronger players. "Goddamn it, Brad! If someone elbows or hits you, don't look out at me and cry, 'It's not fair.' Push back! Don't be so weak!" I got elbowed around until it seemed that none of my internal organs was unscathed. He worked me until my muscles wouldn't respond, and then he demanded more.   12

"You're not trying! Push it!"   13

"Would you move? You're too slow! Swim!"   14

"Damn it! Get out and give me twenty!"   15

It took little time for me to hate both the game and the man who ruled it.   16

I reacted by working as hard as I could. I decided to deprive him of the pleasure of finding fault with me. I learned quickly and started playing as flawlessly as possible. I dispensed with looking tired, showing pain, or complaining of cramps. I pushed, hit, and elbowed back at the biggest of players. No matter how flawless or aggressive my performance, though, he would find fault and let me know it. He was never critical of other players. He would laugh and joke with the other players; but whenever he saw me, he frowned.   17

I decided to quit.   18

After a particularly demanding practice, I walked up to this tyrant. I tried to hold his gaze, but the black glasses forced me to look down. 19

"Coach Rezinas," I blurted, "I've decided that I don't want to play water polo." His scowl deepened. Then after a moment he said, "You can't quit. Not until after the first game." And he walked away. The dictator had issued his command. 20

There was no rule to keep me from quitting. Anger flushed through me. Somehow I would get revenge on this awful man. After the first game? Okay. I would play. I would show him what a valuable player I was. He would miss my talents when I quit. I worked myself up before the first game by imagining the hated face: the black glasses, the thin mustache, the open, snarling mouth. I was not surprised that he placed me in the starting lineup because I was certain he would take me out soon. I played furiously. The ball, the goal, the opposition, even the water seemed to be extensions of Rick, his face glaring from every angle, his words echoing loudly in my ears. Time and time again I would get the ball and, thinking of his tortures, fire it toward the goal with a strength to kill. I forgot that he might take me out. No defender could stand up to me. I would swim by them or over them. Anger and the need for vengeance gave me energy. I didn't notice the time slipping by, the quarters ending. 21

Then, the game ended. My teammates rushed out to me, congratulating and cheering me. I had scored five goals, a school record for one game, and shut out the other team with several key defensive plays. Now I could get revenge. Now I could quit. I stepped out of the pool prepared with the words I would spit into his face: "I QUIT!" 22

As I approached him, I stopped dead. He was smiling at me, his glasses off. He reached out with his right hand and shook mine with exuberance. 23

"I knew you had it in you! I knew it!" he laughed. 24

Through his laughter, I gained a new understanding of the man. He had pushed me to my fullest potential, tapping into the talent I may never have found in myself. He was responsible for the way I played that day. My glory was his. He never hated me. On the contrary, I was his apprentice, his favored pupil. He had brought out my best. Could I really hate someone who had done that much for me? He had done what he had promised: he had fattened me up mentally as well as physically. All this hit me in a second and left me completely confused. I tried to speak, but only managed to croak, "Coach . . . uh . . . I, uh. . . ." He cut me off with another burst of laughter. He still shook my hand. 25

"Call me Rick," he said. 26

READING FOR MEANING

This section presents three activities that will help you reread Benioff's autobiographical essay with a critical eye. Done in sequence, these activities lead you from a basic understanding of the selection to a more personal response to it and finally to an analysis that deepens your understanding and critical thinking about what you are reading.

Read to Comprehend

Reread the selection, and write a few sentences briefly explaining what you think Benioff wants readers to understand about Rick and why he was so important in Benioff's life. Also make a list of any words you do not understand—for example, *ocher* (paragraph 1), *mythical* (3), *unscathed* (12). Look up their meanings in a dictionary to see which definition best fits the context.

To expand your understanding of this reading, you might use one or more of the following critical reading strategies that are explained and illustrated in Appendix 1: *outlining, summarizing, paraphrasing,* and *questioning to understand and remember.*

Read to Respond

Write several paragraphs exploring your initial thoughts and feelings about Benioff's autobiographical essay about his relationship with Rick. Focus on anything that stands out for you, perhaps because it resonates with your own experience or because you find a statement puzzling.

You might consider writing about

- Rick's coaching style, perhaps comparing it with other styles of coaching or teaching with which you are familiar.

- Benioff's effort to deprive Rick of "the pleasure of finding fault" with him and the surprising fact that Rick found fault with him "[n]o matter how flawless or aggressive [his] performance" (paragraph 17).

- how being male or female may affect your response to Rick and to Benioff's attitudes toward Rick.

- high-school students' desire to be "Rick's friend" and thus "part of an exclusive club" (3), perhaps in relation to your experience with exclusive groups in high school or college.

To develop your response to Benioff's essay, you might use one or more of the following critical reading strategies that are explained and illustrated in Appendix 1: *contextualizing, reflecting on challenges to your beliefs and values, recognizing emotional manipulation,* and *judging the writer's credibility.*

Read to Analyze Underlying Assumptions

Write several paragraphs exploring one or more of the assumptions, values, and beliefs underlying Benioff's autobiographical essay. As you write, explain how the assumptions are reflected in the text, as well as what you now think of them (and perhaps of your own assumptions) after rereading the selection with a critical eye.

You might consider writing about

- Benioff's assumption that ultimately Rick, not Benioff, "was responsible for" Benioff's phenomenal performance in the game (paragraph 25).

- the values that led Benioff to see himself reflected in Rick's eyes as "too skinny, too young, too stupid, too weak" (7), perhaps in relation to your own ideas about how people develop a sense of self-esteem.

- the assumptions about masculinity underlying this essay.

- the assumptions about what one learns about oneself by playing competitive sports.

To probe assumptions more deeply, you might use one or more of the following critical reading strategies that are explained and illustrated in Appendix 1: *reflecting on challenges to your beliefs and values, exploring the significance of figurative language,* and *looking for patterns of opposition.*

READING LIKE A WRITER
DESCRIBING A PERSON THROUGH VISUAL DETAILS

Visual description enables readers to see the person and to get a sense of how that person appears to others. For example, providing vivid details of someone's facial features could show whether a person looks others directly in the eye or looks down on others. This activity will help you see how Benioff uses visual description to give readers a picture of Rick as well as an understanding of his significance to the writer.

Analyze

1. *Reread* paragraph 6, where Benioff describes Rick. *Notice* that the writer makes only two general statements characterizing Rick, in the first and last sentences of the paragraph. The remaining sentences in this paragraph offer visual details and images describing Rick's appearance. Because Rick is wearing only swim trunks and sunglasses, Benioff concentrates on the appearance of Rick's body.

2. *Underline* the parts of Rick's body that Benioff singles out, beginning with "legs" and "torso" in the second sentence. Then *put a wavy line* under each

visual detail Benioff uses to describe the parts of Rick's body, beginning with "short, powerful" and "bulging" in sentence 2.

3. *Put a star* by the two comparisons: a simile in sentence 4 (a simile makes an explicit comparison by using the word *like* or *as*), and a metaphor in sentence 5 (a metaphor implicitly compares two items by describing one in terms of the other).

Write

Write several sentences explaining the impression you get of Rick as seen through Benioff's eyes. *Quote* the visual details and comparisons that contribute most to this impression.

CONSIDERING IDEAS FOR YOUR OWN WRITING

Think about the coaches, teachers, employers, and other mentors who have influenced your life. Choose one of these people, and consider how you can describe what that person taught you and how he or she went about it. As a writer aiming to describe this individual's significance in your life, how would you reveal what you learned about the person and about yourself? Or as an alternative, you might consider someone with whom you have had continuing disagreements or conflicts, and then speculate on how you can describe your relationship with that person.

JEAN BRANDT

Calling Home

> *Jean Brandt wrote this essay as a first-year college student. In it, she tells about a memorable event that occurred when she was thirteen. Reflecting on how she felt at the time, Brandt writes, "I was afraid, embarrassed, worried, mad." As you read, look for places where these tumultuous and contradictory remembered feelings are expressed.*
>
> *The other readings in this chapter are followed by reading and writing activities. Following this reading, however, you are on your own to decide how to read for meaning and read like a writer.*

As we all piled into the car, I knew it was going to be a fabulous day. My grandmother was visiting for the holidays; and she and I, along with my older brother and sister, Louis and Susan, were setting off for a day of last-minute Christmas shopping. On the way to the mall, we sang Christmas carols, chattered, and laughed. With Christmas only two days away, we were caught up with holiday spirit. I felt light-headed and full of joy. I loved shopping— especially at Christmas.

The shopping center was swarming with frantic last-minute shoppers like ourselves. We went first to the General Store, my favorite. It carried mostly knickknacks and other useless items which nobody needs but buys anyway. I was thirteen years old at the time, and things like buttons and calendars and posters would catch my fancy. This day was no different. The object of my desire was a 75-cent Snoopy button. Snoopy was the latest. If you owned anything with the Peanuts on it, you were "in." But since I was supposed to be shopping for gifts for other people and not myself, I couldn't decide what to do. I went in search of my sister for her opinion. I pushed my way through throngs of people to the back of the store where I found Susan. I asked her if she thought I should buy the button. She said it was cute and if I wanted it to go ahead and buy it.

When I got back to the Snoopy section, I took one look at the lines at the cashiers and knew I didn't want to wait thirty minutes to buy an item worth less than one dollar. I walked back to the basket where I found the button and was about to drop it when suddenly, instead, I took a quick glance around, assured myself no one could see, and slipped the button into the pocket of my sweatshirt. I hesitated for a moment, but once the item was in my pocket, there was no turning back. I had never before stolen anything; but what was done was done. A few seconds later, my sister appeared and asked, "So, did you decide to buy the button?"

1

2

3

"No, I guess not." I hoped my voice didn't quaver. As we headed for the entrance, my heart began to race. I just had to get out of that store. Only a few more yards to go and I'd be safe. As we crossed the threshold, I heaved a sigh of relief. I was home free. I thought about how sly I had been and I felt proud of my accomplishment. 4

An unexpected tap on my shoulder startled me. I whirled around to find a middle-aged man, dressed in street clothes, flashing some type of badge and politely asking me to empty my pockets. Where did this man come from? How did he know? I was so sure that no one had seen me! On the verge of panicking, I told myself that all I had to do was give this man his button back, say I was sorry, and go on my way. After all, it was only a 75-cent item. 5

Next thing I knew, he was talking about calling the police and having me arrested and thrown in jail, as if he had just nabbed a professional thief instead of a terrified kid. I couldn't believe what he was saying. 6

"Jean, what's going on?" 7

The sound of my sister's voice eased the pressure a bit. She always managed to get me out of trouble. She would come through this time too. 8

"Excuse me. Are you a relative of this young girl?" 9

"Yes, I'm her sister. What's the problem?" 10

"Well, I just caught her shoplifting and I'm afraid I'll have to call the police." 11

"What did she take?" 12

"This button." 13

"A button? You are having a thirteen-year-old arrested for stealing a button?" 14

"I'm sorry, but she broke the law." 15

The man led us through the store and into an office, where we waited for the police officers to arrive. Susan had found my grandmother and brother, who, still shocked, didn't say a word. The thought of going to jail terrified me, not because of jail itself, but because of the encounter with my parents afterward. Not more than ten minutes later, two officers arrived and placed me under arrest. They said that I was to be taken to the station alone. Then, they handcuffed me and led me out of the store. I felt alone and scared. I had counted on my sister being with me, but now I had to muster up the courage to face this ordeal all by myself. 16

As the officers led me through the mall, I sensed a hundred pairs of eyes staring at me. My face flushed and I broke out in a sweat. Now everyone knew I was a criminal. In their eyes I was a juvenile delinquent, and thank God the cops were getting me off 17 the streets. The worst part was thinking my grandmother might be having the same thoughts. The humiliation at that moment was overwhelming. I felt like Hester Prynne being put on public display for everyone to ridicule.

That short walk through the mall seemed to take hours. But once   18
we reached the squad car, time raced by. I was read my rights and questioned. We were at the police station within minutes. Everything happened so fast I didn't have a chance to feel remorse for my crime. Instead, I viewed what was happening to me as if it were a movie. Being searched, although embarrassing, somehow seemed to be exciting. All the movies and television programs I had seen were actually coming to life. This is what it was really like. But why were criminals always portrayed as frightened and regretful? I was having fun. I thought I had nothing to fear—until I was allowed my one phone call. I was trembling as I dialed home. I didn't know what I was going to say to my parents, especially my mother.

"Hi, Dad, this is Jean."   19

"We've been waiting for you to call."   20

"Did Susie tell you what happened?"   21

"Yeah, but we haven't told your mother. I think you should tell   22
her what you did and where you are."

"You mean she doesn't even know where I am?"   23

"No, I want you to explain it to her."   24

There was a pause as he called my mother to the phone. For the   25
first time that night, I was close to tears. I wished I had never stolen that stupid pin. I wanted to give the phone to one of the officers because I was too ashamed to tell my mother the truth, but I had no choice.

"Jean, where are you?"   26

"I'm, umm, in jail."   27

"Why? What for?"   28

"Shoplifting."   29

"Oh no, Jean. Why? Why did you do it?"   30

"I don't know. No reason. I just did it."   31

"I don't understand. What did you take? Why did you do it? You   32
had plenty of money with you."

"I know but I just did it. I can't explain why. Mom, I'm sorry."   33

"I'm afraid sorry isn't enough. I'm horribly disappointed in you."   34

Long after we got off the phone, while I sat in an empty jail cell,   35
waiting for my parents to pick me up, I could still distinctly hear the disappointment and hurt in my mother's voice. I cried. The tears weren't for me but for her and the pain I had put her through. I felt like a terrible human being. I would rather have stayed in jail than confront my mom right then. I dreaded each passing minute

that brought our encounter closer. When the officer came to release me, I hesitated, actually not wanting to leave. We went to the front desk, where I had to sign a form to retrieve my belongings. I saw my parents a few yards away and my heart raced. A large knot formed in my stomach. I fought back the tears.

Not a word was spoken as we walked to the car. Slowly, I sank into the back seat anticipating the scolding. Expecting harsh tones, I was relieved to hear almost the opposite from my father. 36

"I'm not going to punish you, and I'll tell you why. Although I think what you did was wrong, I think what the police did was more wrong. There's no excuse for locking a thirteen-year-old behind bars. That doesn't mean I condone what you did, but I think you've been punished enough already." 37

As I looked from my father's eyes to my mother's, I knew this ordeal was over. Although it would never be forgotten, the incident was not mentioned again. 38

READING FOR MEANING

Reading for meaning involves three activities:

- reading to comprehend
- reading to respond
- reading to analyze underlying assumptions

Reread Brandt's essay, and then write a page or so explaining your understanding of its basic meaning or main point, a personal response you have to it, and what you see as one of its underlying assumptions.

READING LIKE A WRITER

Autobiographers focusing on a remembered event or person

- narrate the event or anecdotes.
- present people.
- present places.
- convey autobiographical significance.

Focus on one of these strategies in Brandt's story, and analyze it carefully through close rereading and annotating. Then write several sentences explaining what you have learned, giving specific examples from the reading to support your explanation. Add a few sentences evaluating how successfully Brandt uses the strategy to dramatize the experience for her readers.

REVIEWING WHAT MAKES AUTOBIOGRAPHY EFFECTIVE

In this chapter, you have been learning how to read autobiographical essays for meaning and how to read them like a writer. Before going on to write a piece of autobiography, pause here to review and contemplate what you have learned about the elements of effective autobiography.

Analyze

Choose one reading from this chapter that seems to you especially effective. Before rereading the selection, *jot down* one or two reasons you remember it as an example of good autobiographical writing.

Reread your chosen selection, adding further annotations about what makes it a particularly successful example of autobiography. *Consider* the selection's purpose and how well it achieves that purpose for its intended readers. (You can make an informed guess about the intended readers and their expectations by noting the publication source of the essay.) Then *focus* on how well the essay

- narrates the story.

- presents people.

- describes places.

- conveys the autobiographical significance.

You can review all of these basic features in the Guide to Reading Autobiography (p. 15).

Your instructor may ask you to complete this activity on your own or to work with a small group of other students who have chosen the same reading. If you work with others, allow enough time initially for all group members to reread the selection thoughtfully and to add their annotations. Then *discuss* as a group what makes the selection effective. *Take notes* on your discussion. One student in your group should then report to the class what the group has learned about the effectiveness of autobiographical writing. If you are working individually, write up what you have learned from your analysis.

Write

Write at least a page supporting your choice of this reading as an example of effective autobiographical writing. *Assume* that your readers— your instructor and classmates—have read the selection but will not remember many details about it. They also might not remember it as especially successful. Therefore, you will need to *refer* to details and specific parts of the essay as you explain how it works as autobiography and as you justify your evaluation of its effectiveness. You need not argue that it is the best reading in the chapter or that it is flawless, only that it is, in your view, a strong example of the genre.

■ A Guide to Writing Autobiography

The readings in this chapter have helped you learn a great deal about autobiographical writing. You have seen that some autobiographies tell dramatic stories, while others present vivid portraits of people who played a significant role in the writer's life. Whether the focus is on events or people, you have discovered that the overall purpose for writers of autobiography is to convey the significance—both the meaning and the importance—of their past experience. In so doing, autobiographers often present themselves as individuals affected by social and cultural influences.

As a reader of autobiography, you have examined how autobiographers convey through their writing drama and vividness as well as significance. But you may have also found that different readers interpret the significance of an autobiographical selection differently. In other words, you have seen how the meanings readers make are affected by their personal experience as well as their social and cultural contexts.

Having learned how autobiographers invest their writing with drama, vividness, and significance and how readers interpret and respond to autobiographical writing, you can now approach autobiography more confidently as a writer. You can more readily imagine the problems you must solve as a writer of autobiography, the materials and possibilities you have to work with, the choices and decisions you must make. This Guide to Writing offers detailed suggestions for writing autobiographical essays and resources to help you solve the special challenges this kind of writing presents.

INVENTION AND RESEARCH

The following activities will help you choose a memorable *event* or an important *person* to write about, recall details about your subject, and explore its significance in your life. Completing these activities will produce a record of remembered details and thoughts that will be invaluable as you draft your essay.

Choosing a Subject

Rather than limiting yourself to the first subject that comes to mind, take a few minutes to consider your options. By listing as many subjects as you can, you will have a variety of possible topics to choose from for your autobiographical essay. List the most promising subjects you can think of, beginning with any you listed for the Considering Ideas for Your Own Writing activities following the readings in this chapter. Here are some additional ideas to consider:

Events

- A difficult situation, such as when you had to make a tough choice, when someone you admired let you down (or you let someone else down), or when you struggled to learn or understand something

- An event that shaped you in a particular way or that revealed an aspect of your personality you had not seen before, such as your independence, insecurity, ambition, or jealousy

- An occasion when something did not turn out as you thought it would, such as when you expected to be criticized but were praised or ignored instead, or when you were convinced you would succeed but failed

- An event in which a single encounter with another person changed the way you view yourself, changed your ideas about how you fit into a particular group or community, or led you to consider seriously someone else's point of view

People

- Someone who helped you develop a previously unknown or undeveloped side of yourself

- Someone who led you to question assumptions or stereotypes you had about other people

- Someone who surprised or disappointed you

- Someone in a position of power over you, or someone over whom you had power

- Someone who made you feel you were part of a larger community or had something worthwhile to contribute, or, conversely, someone who made you feel alienated or like an outsider

Choose a subject that you feel comfortable sharing with your instructor and classmates. The subject also should be one that you want to try to remember in detail and to think about in terms of what it means to you. You may find the choice easy to make, or you may have several equally promising possibilities. In making a final choice, it may help to think about your readers and what you would want them to learn about you from reading about the event or person.

RESEARCHING YOUR SUBJECT ONLINE

The Web offers possible sites to help you write your autobiographical essay. Exploring Web sites where people write about their life experiences might inspire you by triggering memories of similar events and people in your own life. Moreover, the Web provides a rich repository of cultural and historical information, including photographs and music, that you might be able to use to prime your memory and create a richly detailed, multimedia text for your readers. As you search the Web, here are some possibilities to consider:

- Investigate sites such as <citystories.com> and <storypreservation.com> where people post brief stories about their lives.

- Search for sites featuring the people and places you are writing about, as well as sites of friends, family members, or others who have been important to you.

- Look for sites related to places or activities—such as neighborhoods, schools, workplaces, sports events, or films—that you associate with the person or event you are writing about.

Make notes of any ideas, memories, or insights suggested by your online research. Download any visuals you might consider including in your essay—such as pictures of people and places you may want to include. Also be sure to download or record the information necessary to cite any online sources you may want to refer to in your essay. See Appendix 2 for help in citing sources.

Developing Your Subject

The following activities will help you develop your subject by recalling actions that happened during the event or by telling anecdotes that reveal something about the person. These activities will also help you recall details of the place and people. Each activity takes only a few minutes but will help you produce a fuller, more focused draft.

Recalling the Event or Person.   *If you have chosen to write about an **event**, begin by writing for five minutes, simply telling what happened.* Do not worry about telling the story dramatically or even coherently.

*If you have chosen to write about a **person**, begin by listing anecdotes you could tell about the person.* Then choose one anecdote that reveals something important about the person or your relationship, and write for five minutes telling what happened.

Presenting Important People. *If you have chosen to write about a **person**, list aspects of the person's appearance and dress, ways of walking and gesturing, tone of voice and mannerisms—anything that would help readers see the person as you remember her or him.*

*If you have chosen to write about an **event**, recall other people who were involved, and write a brief description of each person.*

Reconstructing Dialogue. *Write a few lines of dialogue that you could use to convey something important about the event or to give readers an impression of the person you have chosen to write about.* You may use direct quotation, enclosing the words you remember being spoken in quotation marks, or you may use indirect quotation, paraphrasing and summarizing what was said. Try to re-create the give-and-take quality of normal conversation in the dialogue.

Describing Important Places. *Identify the place where the event happened or a place you associate with the person, and detail what you see in the scene as you visualize it.* Try to recall specific sensory details: size, shape, color, condition, and texture of the scene or memorable objects in it. Imagine the place from head-on and from the side, from a distance and from close-up.

Considering Visuals. *Consider whether visuals—photographs, postcards, ticket stubs—would strengthen your presentation of the event or person.* If you submit your essay electronically to other students and your instructor, or if you post it on a Web site, consider including photographs as well as snippets of film or sound or other memorabilia that might give readers a more vivid sense of the time, place, and people about which you are writing. Visual and audio materials are not at all a requirement of an effective autobiographical essay, as you can tell from the readings in this chapter, but they could add a new dimension to your writing. If you want to use photographs or recordings of people, though, be sure to request their permission.

Reflecting on Your Subject

The following activities will help you think about the significance of your subject by recalling your remembered feelings and thoughts as well as exploring your present perspective. The activities will also help you consider your purpose in writing about this subject and formulate a tentative thesis statement.

Recalling Your Feelings and Thoughts. *Write for a few minutes, trying to recall your thoughts and feelings when the event was occurring or when you knew the person.* What did you feel—in control or powerless, proud or embarrassed, vulnerable, detached, judgmental? How did you show or express your feelings? What did you want others to think of you at the time? What did you think of yourself? What were the immediate consequences for you personally?

Exploring Your Present Perspective. *Write for a few minutes, trying to express your present thoughts and feelings as you look back on the event or person.* How have your feelings changed? What insights do you now have? What does your present perspective reveal about what you were like at the time? Try looking at the event or person in broader, cultural or social terms. For example, consider whether you or anyone else upset gender expectations or felt out of place in some way.

Considering Your Purpose. *Write for several minutes exploring what you want your readers to understand about the significance of the event or person.* Use the following questions to help clarify your thoughts:

- What will writing about this event or person enable you to suggest about yourself as an individual? What will it let you suggest about the social and cultural forces that helped shape you—for example, how people exercise power over one another, how family and community values and attitudes have an impact on individuals, or how economic and social conditions influence our sense of self?

- What do you not understand fully about the event or relationship? What about it still puzzles you or seems contradictory? What do you feel ambivalent about?

- What about your subject do you expect will seem familiar to your readers? What do you think will surprise them, perhaps getting them to think in new ways or to question some of their assumptions and stereotypes?

Formulating a Tentative Thesis Statement. *Review what you wrote for Considering Your Purpose and add another two or three sentences that will help you convey to readers the significance of the event or person in your life.* Try to write sentences that do not just summarize what you have written, but that also extend your insights and reflections. These sentences may be contradictory because they express ambivalent feelings. They also must necessarily be partial and speculative because you may never understand fully the event's or person's significance.

Keep in mind that readers do not expect you to begin your essay with the kind of explicit introductory thesis statement typical of argumentative essays. None of the readings in this chapter offers to readers an explicit thesis statement explaining the significance of the event or person. Instead, the readings convey the significance by combining showing with telling in their narration of events and descriptions of people and places. And yet it is possible for readers to infer from each reading an implied thesis or impression of the significance. For example, some readers might decide that Dillard wants readers to think that what was most significant and memorable about the event was the way the man threw himself into the chase, showing that childlike enthusiasm sometimes can survive into adulthood. Other readers might focus on the idea that what was significant was that the man as well as the children "all played by the rules," and that when people play by the rules they act with honor and nobility (paragraph 16). If, like you, Dillard had tried to write a few sentences about the significance she hoped to convey in writing about this small but memorable event in her life, she might have written sentences like these.

Nearly all first attempts at stating a thesis are eventually revised once drafting gets under way. Writing the first draft helps autobiographers discover what they think and feel about their subject and find ways to convey its significance without ever spelling it out directly. Just because there is no explicit thesis statement in an autobiography does not mean that the essay lacks focus or fails to convey significance.

DRAFTING

The following guidelines will help you set goals for your draft, plan its organization, choose relevant details, think about a useful sentence strategy, and decide how to begin.

Setting Goals

Establishing goals for your draft before you begin writing will enable you to make decisions and work more confidently. Consider the following questions now, and keep them in mind as you draft. They will help you set goals for drafting as well as recall how the writers you have read in this chapter tried to achieve similar goals.

- *How can I present my subject vividly and memorably to readers?* Should I rely on dialogue to present people and relationships, as so many of the writers in this chapter do? Or should I concentrate on presenting action rather than dialogue, like Dillard and Rodriguez? Can I use visual or other sensory details, as Shah, Rodriguez, and Benioff do, to give readers a vivid impression of the person and place while also establishing the significance of my subject?

- *How can I help readers understand the meaning and importance of the event or person?* Can I build the suspense, as Dillard, Rodriguez, and Brandt do? Can I show how I changed, as Edmundson and Benioff do?

- *How can I avoid superficial or one-dimensional presentations of my experience and my relations with others?* Knowing that my readers will not expect easy answers about what makes the event or person significant, how can I satisfy their expectations for writing that has some depth and complexity? How might I employ one or more of the strategies illustrated by the writers I have read in this chapter—the paradox in Dillard's feeling both terror and pleasure as she is chased by the man in the black Buick; the contradictions Wu sets up in relating the cultural differences between her family and her friends' families; Benioff's love-hate relationship with his coach? What contradictions, paradoxes, or ironies exist in my own story?

Organizing Your Draft

With goals in mind, plan your draft by making a tentative outline. Although your plan may change as you write and revise your draft, outlining before you begin drafting can help you get organized. If you are uncertain about how to organize your material, review how some of the writers in this chapter organize their autobiographical essays.

For an *event,* outline the sequence of main actions, from the beginning to the end of the event.

For a *person,* outline the order of the recurring activities, or anecdotes you will use to present the person, interspersing relevant character traits, physical details, and dialogue.

Choosing Relevant Details

The invention and research activities helped you generate many details, probably more than you can use. To decide which details to include in your draft and which to leave out, consider how well each detail contributes to the overall impression you want to create. But before you discard any details that seem irrelevant, think again about what they might suggest about the significance of your subject. Sometimes, seemingly irrelevant details or ones that do not fit neatly can lead you to new insights.

Considering a Useful Sentence Strategy

As you draft your essay, you will need to present the details you have chosen in ways that help readers imagine the people, places, and events. One effective way to do so is to use sentences with participial phrases. These phrases begin with verb forms called participles: either present participles, ending in *ing* (*being, longing, grasping, drinking*), or past participles, usually ending in *ed, d, en, n,* or *t* (*baked, found, driven, torn, sent*). Participial phrases help you show simultaneous actions, make an action or image more specific or vivid, and relate what you were thinking or feeling at the time of an action.

- To show simultaneous actions:

  We kept running, block after block; we kept improvising, backyard after backyard, *running a frantic course* and *choosing it simultaneously, failing always to find small places or hard places to slow him down,* and *discovering always, exhilarated, dismayed, that only bare speed could save us*—for he would never give up, this man—and we were losing speed. (Dillard, paragraph 14)

I whirled around to find a middle-aged man, dressed in street clothes, *flashing some type of badge* and *politely asking me to empty my pockets.* (Brandt, paragraph 5)

- To make a previously mentioned action or image (shown here in bold type) more specific and vivid:

Shining a flashlight inside the building, the officer spotted **Tino's misshapen body on the floor**, *sprinkled over with shards of glass.* (Rodriguez, paragraph 34)

Amina stormed in, *scattering servants before her like chaff.* (Shah, paragraph 7)

I remember **throwing a red-faced tantrum** before my mother's friends, *pounding my fists into the rug, and throwing my utensils at the steaming dishes.* (Wu, paragraph 3)

- To relate what you were thinking or feeling at the time:

So there I was in a well-lit room, wearing, no doubt, some sharp back-to-school ensemble, pegged pants and sporty dice-in-the-back-alley shoes, mildly *aching from two or three football-inflicted wounds,* and *pondering the Nietzsche quotation, which I could barely understand.* (Edmundson, paragraph 5)

Slowly, I sank into the back seat *anticipating the scolding.* (Brandt, paragraph 36)

Participial phrases are not required for a successful autobiographical essay, yet they do provide writers an effective sentence option. For another sentence strategy that can strengthen your autobiographical writing, the use of speaker tags in sentences with dialogue, see page 152 in Chapter 3.

Writing the Beginning

In order to engage your readers' interest from the start, consider beginning with an arresting bit of dialogue (as Wu does) or a compelling graphic description (as Benioff and Rodriguez do), with a startling action (as Dillard does) or a vivid memory (as Shah does), or by creating a sense of expectation (as Brandt does). You might have to try two or three different beginnings before finding a promising way to start, but do not agonize for too long over the first sentence. Try out any possible beginning and see where it takes you.

READING A DRAFT CRITICALLY

Getting a critical reading of your draft will help you see how to improve it. Your instructor may schedule class time for reading drafts, or you may want to ask a classmate or a tutor in the writing center to read your draft. Ask your reader to use the following guidelines and to write out a response for you to consult during your revision.

Read for a First Impression

1. Read the draft without stopping to annotate or comment, and then write two or three sentences giving your general impression.

2. Identify one aspect of the draft that seems especially effective.

Read Again to Suggest Improvements

1. Recommend ways to make the narrative more dramatic and telling. For a draft presenting an *event:*

   - Point to any scenes where the action seems to drag or become confusing.

   - Suggest places where the drama might be intensified—by adding a close-up, using more active verbs, or shifting the placement of background information or descriptive detail, for example.

   - Indicate where dialogue could add drama to a confrontation scene.

   For a draft using anecdotes or recurring activities to present a *person:*

   - Note which anecdotes and recurring activities seem especially effective in illustrating something important about the person or the relationship.

   - Point to one weak anecdote or recurring activity and suggest how it could be made more effective, such as by adding graphic details and dialogue or by telling how it relates to the person's significance.

   - Indicate any passages where direct quotations could be more effectively presented indirectly, through paraphrase or summary, or by combining a striking quote with summary.

2. Indicate any areas where improving dull or weak description could more vividly or effectively convey the dominant impression of the essay.

   - Describe the impression you get from the writer's description of the event or person.

- Identify one or two passages where you think the description is especially vivid; for example, where the visual details and images help you picture the event or person.

- Point to any passages where the description could be made more vivid or where it seems to contradict the impression you get from other parts of the essay.

3. Suggest how the autobiographical significance could be developed.

- Briefly explain your understanding of the significance, indicating anything that puzzles or surprises you about the event or person.

- Note any word choice, contradiction, or irony—in the way people and places are described or in the way the story is told—that alerts you to a deeper meaning that the writer could develop.

- Point to any passages where the writer needs to clarify the historical, social, or cultural dimensions of the experience or relationship.

4. Suggest how the organizational plan could be improved. Consider the overall plan of the essay, perhaps by making a scratch outline (see Appendix 1, p. 659, for an example).

- For an *event,* indicate any passages where narrative transitions or verb tense markers are needed to make the story unfold more logically and clearly.

- For a *person,* suggest where topic sentences or transitions could be added or where the writer could more clearly indicate what impression of the person the anecdotes or recurring activities are intended to convey.

5. Evaluate the effectiveness of visuals.

- Look at any visuals in the essay, and tell the writer what they contribute to your understanding of the event or person.

- If any visuals do not seem relevant, or if there seem to be too many visuals, identify the ones that the writer could consider dropping, explaining your thinking.

- If a visual does not seem to be appropriately placed, suggest a better place for it.

REVISING

This section offers suggestions for revising your draft. Revising means reenvisioning your draft, trying to see it in a new way, given your purpose and readers, in order to develop a more engaging, coherent autobiography.

The biggest mistake you can make while revising is to focus initially on words or sentences. Instead, first try to see your draft as a whole in order to assess its likely impact on your readers. Think imaginatively and boldly about cutting unconvincing material, adding new material, and moving material around. Your computer makes even drastic revisions physically easy, but you still need to make the mental effort and decisions that will improve your draft.

You may have received help with this challenge from a classmate or tutor who gave your draft a critical reading. If so, keep this feedback in mind as you decide which parts of your draft need revising and what specific changes you could make. The following suggestions will help you solve problems and strengthen your essay.

To Make the Narrative More Dramatic and Telling

- If the story seems to meander and have no point, focus the action so that it builds up more directly toward the climax.

- Where the narrative drags or the tension slackens, try using more active verbs, more dialogue, or shorter sentences.

- Where background information or descriptive detail interrupts the drama or slows the pace, consider cutting or moving it.

- If the purpose of an anecdote or a recurring activity is not clear, make explicit what it illustrates.

- If the exact words in a conversation are not striking or important, use indirect instead of direct dialogue or combine the two, paraphrasing or summarizing most of what was said but quoting a memorable phrase or word.

To Present People Vividly

- Where more graphic description is needed, give visual details showing what the person looks like or how the person gestures. Consider using participial phrases to show simultaneous actions by the person or to make your descriptions more specific and vivid.

- If any detail seems inconsistent or contradictory, cut it or use it to develop the significance.

- If the description does not convey the impression you want it to convey, consider cutting some descriptive details and adding others, or rethinking the impression you want your writing to convey and the significance it suggests.

To Describe Places Vividly

- If any details about an important place do not fit together well and do not contribute to the dominant impression or reinforce the significance, omit them from the essay.

- Where readers cannot visualize the place, add more sensory detail. Consider using participial phrases to make the images you present of the place more specific and vivid.

- Where the description distracts from the action, cut or move the description.

- Where the point of view is confusing, consider simplifying it.

To Convey the Autobiographical Significance

- If readers may not understand the significance of the person or event, look for passages where you could convey it more directly. Consider using participial phrases to reveal what you were thinking or feeling as you interacted with the person or as the event occurred.

- If the significance seems too pat or simplistic, consider whether you could develop contradictions or allow for ambivalence.

- If readers may not understand the importance of the social, cultural, or historical context, consider giving background information to reveal its influence.

To Make the Organizational Plan More Effective

- If readers may be confused about what happened when, add transitions or verb tense markers.

- If readers may not see clearly how the anecdotes or recurring activities contribute to the portrait of the person, add forecasting statements or topic sentences to clarify what those elements demonstrate.

EDITING AND PROOFREADING

After you have revised your essay, be sure to spend some time checking for errors in usage, punctuation, and mechanics and considering matters of style. If you keep a list of errors you typically make, begin by checking your draft against this list. Ask someone else to proofread your essay before you print out a copy for your instructor or send it electronically.

From our research on student writing, we know that essays dealing with autobiographical subjects have a high percentage of errors in verb tense and punctuation.

You should proofread your narration for verb tense errors and your description for punctuation errors—such as comma splices and missing commas after introductory elements. Check a writer's handbook for help with these potential problems.

Autobiography

In this chapter, you have read critically several pieces of autobiography and have written one of your own. To better remember what you have learned, pause now to reflect on the reading and writing activities you completed in this chapter.

1. *Write* a page or so reflecting on what you have learned. *Begin* by describing what you are most pleased with in your essay. Then *explain* what you think contributed to your achievement. *Be specific* about this contribution.

   - If it was something you learned from the readings, *indicate* which readings and specifically what you learned from them.

   - If it came from your invention writing, *point out* the section or sections that helped you most.

   - If you got good advice from a critical reader, *explain* exactly how the person helped you—perhaps by helping you understand a particular problem in your draft or by adding a new dimension to your writing.

   - *Try to write* about your achievement in terms of what you have learned about the genre.

2. Now *reflect* more generally on how you tend to interpret autobiographical writing, your own as well as other writers'. *Consider* some of the following questions: In reading for meaning, do you tend to find yourself interpreting the significance of the event or person in terms of the writer's personal feelings, sense of self-esteem, or psychological well-being? Or do you more often think of significance in terms of larger social or economic influences—for example, whether the writer is male or female, rich or poor, suburban or urban, African American or Anglo? Where do you think you learned to interpret the significance of people's stories about themselves and their relationships—from your family, friends, television, school?

3

Observation

Certain kinds of writing are based on fresh observation or direct investigation. Travel writers, for example, profile places they have visited; naturalists describe phenomena they have observed undisturbed in nature. Investigative reporters or clinical psychologists write up interviews with individuals, while cultural anthropologists write ethnographies of groups they have studied in depth. Much of what we know about people and the world we learn from this kind of writing.

Writing about your own observations offers special challenges and rewards. It requires you to pay more attention than you normally do to everyday activities. You need to look with all your senses and give your curiosity free rein. Taking a questioning or inquiring stance will enable you to make discoveries in even the most mundane settings. In addition, it helps to take voluminous notes because you might not know what is significant until you begin to sort through the observations and quotations you have collected. That way, after the work of observing and interviewing is done, another kind of equally challenging and rewarding work can begin—making meaning of the bits and pieces you have gathered. Analyzing and synthesizing your notes, you interpret your subject, deciding what you want to tell your readers about it. These activities of close observation and careful notetaking, combined with thoughtful analysis and imaginative synthesis, form the basic strategies of researching and learning in many areas of college study.

When writing about your observations, you will have an immediate advantage if you choose a place, an activity, or a person that is new to readers. But even if the subject is familiar, you can still intrigue and inform readers by presenting it in a new light or by focusing on a specific aspect of the subject. By focusing on certain details, you not only help readers imagine what the place looks, sounds, and smells like or picture how the people dress, gesture, and talk, but you also create an impression that conveys your idea or interpretation of the subject.

The readings in this chapter will help you learn a lot about observational writing. From the readings and from the ideas for writing that follow each reading, you will get ideas for your own observational essay. As you read and write about the selections, keep in mind the following assignment, which sets out the goals for writing an observational essay. To support your writing of this assignment, the chapter concludes with a Guide to Writing Observational Essays.

THE WRITING ASSIGNMENT

Observation

Write an observational essay about an intriguing place, person, or activity in your community. Your essay may be a brief profile of an individual based on one or two interviews; a description of a place or activity observed once or twice; or a longer, more fully developed profile of a person, place, or activity based on observational visits and interviews conducted over several days. Observe your subject closely, and then present what you have learned in a way that both informs and engages readers.

WRITING SITUATIONS FOR OBSERVATIONAL ESSAYS

As we indicated earlier, many people—including travel writers, investigative reporters, clinical psychologists, and cultural anthropologists—write essays based on observations and interviews. In your other college courses, you may have an opportunity to write an observational essay like one of the following:

- For an art history course, a student writes about a local artist recently commissioned to paint outdoor murals for the city. The student visits the artist's studio and talks with him about the process of painting murals, large pictures painted on walls or the sides of buildings. The artist invites the student to spend the following day as a part of a team of local art students and neighborhood volunteers working on the mural under the artist's direction. This firsthand experience helps the student profile the artist, present some of the students, and give readers a clear impression of the process of collaboration involved in mural painting.

- For a journalism course, a student profiles a typical day in the life of an award-winning scientist. He spends a day observing the scientist at home and at work, and he then interviews colleagues, students, and family, as well as the scientist herself. Her daily life, he learns, is very much like that of other working mothers—a constant effort to balance the demands of her career against the needs of her family. He conveys this idea in his essay by alternating between details about the scientist's work and those about her family life.

- For a sociology class, a student writes about a controversial urban renewal project to replace decaying but repairable houses with a library and park. To learn about the history of the project, she reads newspaper reports and interviews people who helped plan the project as well as some neighborhood residents and activists who oppose it. She also tours the site with the project manager to see what is actually being done. In addition to presenting different points of view about the project, her essay describes the library and park in detail, including pictures of the neighborhood before the project and drawings of what it will look like afterward. She seeks to give the impression that the project manager has succeeded in winning neighborhood support and that most residents will be pleased with the completed project.

THINKING ABOUT YOUR EXPERIENCE WITH OBSERVATION

Before studying a type of writing, it is useful to spend some time thinking about what you already know about it. You may have written about your firsthand observations, describing what you saw or heard, for a school assignment or during a trip. If you haven't written observational essays or reports, you have certainly made them orally to friends and family.

To analyze your experience composing observational essays, you might recall one occasion when you reported your observations orally or in writing and then consider questions like these: Why were you communicating what you saw and heard to members of this particular audience? Did you make your report primarily to teach them something, to show that you had learned something yourself, to entertain them, or for some other reason? What did you choose to emphasize? Why?

Consider also observational reports you have read, heard, or seen on television. If you recall one such report in some detail, try to identify what made it interesting to you. What tone did the narrator adopt? What descriptive details, dialogue, or commentary stood out for you?

Write at least a page about your experience with observational writing.

■ A Guide to Reading Observational Essays

This guide introduces you to observational writing. By completing all of the activities in it, you will prepare yourself to learn a great deal from the other readings in this chapter about how to read and write an observational essay. The guide focuses on "Soup," an intriguing profile of Albert Yeganeh and his unique New York City restaurant, Soup Kitchen International. You will read this observational essay twice. First, you will read it for meaning, looking closely at the essay's content and ideas. Then, you will read the essay like a writer, analyzing its parts to see how the writer crafts the essay and to learn the strategies that make it vivid and informative. These two activities—reading for meaning and reading like a writer—follow every reading in this chapter.

THE NEW YORKER

Soup

"Soup" was published anonymously in a 1989 issue of the New Yorker, *a magazine read by many people across the country who enjoy cartoons, short stories, music and art reviews, political and social commentary, and profiles of people and places. The subject of this essay is Albert Yeganeh, the creative and demanding owner/chef of a small take-out restaurant that serves only soup. In 1995, Yeganeh's restaurant inspired an episode of the then-popular television program* Seinfeld.

The writer of "Soup" relies extensively on dialogue quoted from the interview to keep the focus on Yeganeh's personality and ideas. Readers can readily imagine the reporter interviewing Yeganeh, writing down soup names and ingredients, observing people in line, and even standing in line for a bowl of soup.

As you read, annotate anything that helps you imagine Yeganeh and his Soup Kitchen International.

When Albert Yeganeh says "Soup is my lifeblood," he means it. And when he says "I am extremely hard to please," he means that, too. Working like a demon alchemist in a tiny storefront kitchen at 259-A West Fifty-fifth Street, Mr. Yeganeh creates anywhere from eight to seventeen soups every weekday. His concoctions are so popular that a wait of half an hour at the lunchtime peak is not uncommon, although there are strict rules for conduct in line. But more on that later.

"I am psychologically kind of a health freak," Mr. Yeganeh said the other day, in a lisping staccato of Armenian origin. "And I

1

2

know that soup is the greatest meal in the world. It's very good for your digestive system. And I use only the best, the freshest ingredients. I am a perfectionist. When I make a clam soup, I use three different kinds of clams. Every other place uses canned clams. I'm called crazy. I am not crazy. People don't realize why I get so upset. It's because if the soup is not perfect and I'm still selling it, it's a torture. It's *my* soup, and that's why I'm so upset. First you clean and then you cook. I don't believe that ninety-nine per cent of the restaurants in New York know how to clean a tomato. I tell my crew to wash the parsley *eight* times. If they wash it five or six times, I scare them. I tell them they'll go to jail if there is sand in the parsley. One time, I found a mushroom on the floor, and I fired that guy who left it there." He spread his arms, and added, "This place is the only one like it in . . . in . . . the whole earth! One day, I hope to learn something from the other places, but so far I haven't. For example, the other day I went to a very fancy restaurant and had borscht. I had to send it back. It was *junk*. I could see all the chemicals in it. I never use chemicals. Last weekend, I had lobster bisque in Brooklyn, a very well-known place. It was *junk*. When I make a lobster bisque, I use a whole lobster. You know, I never advertise. I don't have to. All the big-shot chefs and the kings of the hotels come here to see what *I'm* doing."

As you approach Mr. Yeganeh's Soup Kitchen International   3
from a distance, the first thing you notice about it is the awning, which proclaims "Homemade Hot, Cold, Diet Soups." The second thing you notice is an aroma so delicious that it makes you want to take a bite out of the air. The third thing you notice, in front of the kitchen, is an electric signboard that flashes, saying, "Today's Soups . . . Chicken Vegetable . . . Mexican Beef Chili . . . Cream of Watercress . . . Italian Sausage . . . Clam Bisque . . . Beef Barley . . . Due to Cold Weather . . . For Most Efficient and Fastest Service the Line Must . . . Be Kept Moving . . . Please . . . Have Your Money . . . Ready . . . Pick the Soup of Your Choice . . . Move to Your Extreme . . . Left After Ordering."

"I am not prejudiced against color or religion," Mr. Yeganeh   4
told us, and he jabbed an index finger at the flashing sign. "Whoever follows that I treat very well. My regular customers don't say anything. They are very intelligent and well educated. They know I'm just trying to move the line. The New York cop is very smart— he sees everything but says nothing. But the young girl who wants to stop and tell you how nice you look and hold everyone up— *yah!*" He made a guillotining motion with his hand. "I tell you, I hate to work with the public. They treat me like a slave. My philosophy is: The customer is always wrong and I'm always right.

I raised my prices to try to get rid of some of these people, but it didn't work."

The other day, Mr. Yeganeh was dressed in chef's whites with orange smears across his chest, which may have been some of the carrot soup cooking in a huge pot on a little stove in one corner. A three-foot-long handheld mixer from France sat on the sink, looking like an overgrown gardening tool. Mr. Yeganeh spoke to two young helpers in a twisted Armenian-Spanish barrage, then said to us, "I have no overhead, no trained waitresses, and I have the cashier here." He pointed to himself theatrically. Beside the doorway, a glass case with fresh green celery, red and yellow peppers, and purple eggplant was topped by five big gray soup urns. According to a piece of cardboard taped to the door, you can buy Mr. Yeganeh's soups in three sizes, costing from four to fifteen dollars. The order of any well-behaved customer is accompanied by little waxpaper packets of bread, fresh vegetables (such as scallions and radishes), fresh fruit (such as cherries or an orange), a chocolate mint, and a plastic spoon. No coffee, tea, or other drinks are served. 5

"I get my recipes from books and theories and my own taste," Mr. Yeganeh said. "At home, I have several hundreds of books. When I do research, I find that I don't know anything. Like cabbage is a cancer fighter, and some fish is good for your heart but some is bad. Every day, I should have one sweet, one spicy, one cream, one vegetable soup—and they *must* change, they should always taste a little different." He added that he wasn't sure how extensive his repertoire was, but that it probably includes at least eighty soups, among them African peanut butter, Greek moussaka, hamburger, Reuben, B.L.T., asparagus and caviar, Japanese shrimp miso, chicken chili, Irish corned beef and cabbage, Swiss chocolate, French calf's brain, Korean beef ball, Italian shrimp and eggplant Parmesan, buffalo, ham and egg, short rib, Russian beef Stroganoff, turkey cacciatore, and Indian mulligatawny. "The chicken and the seafood are an addiction, and when I have French garlic soup I let people have only one small container each," he said. "The doctors and nurses love that one." 6

A lunch line of thirty people stretched down the block from Mr. Yeganeh's doorway. Behind a construction worker was a man in expensive leather, who was in front of a woman in a fur hat. Few people spoke. Most had their money out and their orders ready. 7

At the front of the line, a woman in a brown coat couldn't decide which soup to get and started to complain about the prices. 8

"You talk too much, dear," Mr. Yeganeh said, and motioned her to move to the left. "Next!" 9

"Just don't talk. Do what he says," a man huddled in a blue   10
parka warned.

"He's downright rude," said a blond woman in a blue coat.   11
"Even abusive. But you can't deny it, his soup is the best."

READING FOR MEANING

This section presents three activities that will help you reread the observational essay "Soup" with a critical eye. Done in sequence, these activities lead you from a basic understanding of the selection to a more personal response to it and finally to an analysis that deepens your understanding and critical thinking about what you are reading.

Read to Comprehend

Reread the selection, and write a few sentences describing Albert Yeganeh and the Soup Kitchen International. Also make a list of any words you do not understand—for example, *demon alchemist* (paragraph 1), *staccato* (2), *guillotining motion* (4). Look up their meanings in a dictionary to see which definition best fits the context.

To expand your understanding of this reading, you might use one or more of the following critical reading strategies that are explained and illustrated in Appendix 1: *outlining, summarizing, paraphrasing,* and *questioning to understand and remember.*

Read to Respond

Write several paragraphs exploring your initial thoughts and feelings about the observational essay "Soup." Focus on anything that stands out for you, perhaps because it resonates with your own experience or because you find a statement puzzling.

You might consider writing about

- Yeganeh's "strict rules for conduct" (paragraph 1) and his treatment of customers who complain (8–11).

- the kinds of soups Yeganeh serves, perhaps in relation to the restaurants you frequent.

- the way Yeganeh treats the staff at Soup Kitchen International.

- Yeganeh's business philosophy—"[t]he customer is always wrong" (4)— perhaps in relation to your own experience with other fast-food restaurants as a customer or employee.

To develop your response to "Soup," you might use one or more of the following critical reading strategies that are explained and illustrated in

Appendix 1: *contextualizing, reflecting on challenges to your beliefs and values, recognizing emotional manipulation,* and *judging the writer's credibility.*

Read to Analyze Underlying Assumptions

Write several paragraphs exploring one or more of the assumptions, values, and beliefs underlying the observational essay "Soup." As you write, explain how the assumptions are reflected in the text, as well as what you now think of them (and perhaps your own assumptions) after rereading the selection with a critical eye.

To analyze the underlying assumptions and values in observational writing, you need to look closely at what the writer chooses to emphasize about the subject as well as the connotations of the writer's word choices. Notice, for example, how this selection opens. The subject, Albert Yeganeh, is quoted twice describing himself, and after each quotation, the writer comments that Yeganeh means what he says (paragraph 1). These quotations are then summarized in the image of Yeganeh as "a demon alchemist," which is tantamount to calling him a mad scientist. An alchemist is a fabled chemist supposedly capable of transforming other metals into gold. Moreover, the word *demon* not only suggests frenetic activity but also implies that there is something satanic or devilish about Yeganeh, whose description of himself as "extremely hard to please" reinforces this idea. For someone to describe himself in these terms implies that the person is arrogant and unconcerned about what others think of him. The writer indicates at the end of the opening paragraph that we will learn more about this side of Yeganeh later in the essay. Analyzing the assumptions, as we have begun to do here, suggests that the writer thinks Yeganeh is crazy, perhaps a little sinister, but possibly also a magician of rare quality.

As a critical reader, then, you want to think about how Yeganeh represents himself, how the writer represents him, what these representations say about how each of them sees the world—and how you see the world after looking at it through their eyes. For example, most of us expect businesspeople to advertise themselves and their product by putting on a friendly face. But if you think of the way that Yeganeh and the writer see the reasons for his success and the way that another businessman, Donald Trump, represents himself as someone who loves to fire people on his popular television program *The Apprentice,* you might begin to wonder whether Americans are attracted by power and arrogance as much as—or perhaps more than—by friendliness and kindness. The purpose of analyzing underlying assumptions in a reading is to give us an opportunity to think critically about unexamined assumptions and values—the writer's as well as our own, many of which may be ingrained in our culture, our education, and even our language.

You might consider writing about

- what Yeganeh thinks of the work he does and its importance, and your sense of the writer's assumptions about these issues.

- the assumptions underlying Yeganeh's assertion that the soups "*must change, they should always taste a little different*" (paragraph 6).

- the values underlying Yeganeh's perfectionism or work ethic.

- the writer's assumptions in describing the different kinds of clothing worn by Yeganeh's customers (7–11).

- the writer's assumptions about the way Yeganeh treats his customers and workers.

To probe assumptions more deeply, you might use one or more of the following critical reading strategies that are explained and illustrated in Appendix 1: *reflecting on challenges to your beliefs and values, exploring the significance of figurative language,* and *looking for patterns of opposition.*

READING LIKE A WRITER

This section guides you through an analysis of the observational writing strategies illustrated in "Soup": *describing places and people, organizing the observations, engaging and informing readers,* and *conveying an impression of the subject.* For each strategy you will be asked to reread and annotate part of the essay to see how that particular strategy works in "Soup."

When you study the selections later in this chapter, you will see how different writers use these same strategies. The Guide to Writing Observational Essays near the end of the chapter suggests ways you can use these strategies in your own writing.

Describing Places and People

Observational writing, like autobiography (Chapter 2), succeeds by presenting the subject vividly and concretely. Writers of observation usually describe both places and people, although they may emphasize one over the other. Visual details usually predominate in an observational essay, but some writers complement these by describing sounds, smells, tastes, and even textures and temperatures.

Observational writers present people through visual details and action—how they look, how they dress, how they move, what they do. They also show how people talk and interact with one another, often including both direct quotations from their notes and paraphrases of what people have said. To gain a sense of an individual's personality, readers usually need only a few details indicating the person's tone of voice, facial expression, style of dress, or movements.

Analyze

1. *Reread* the description of Yeganeh and his establishment in paragraph 5, and *underline* all of the words and phrases used to describe them. To get started, *underline* the phrases "dressed in chef's whites" and "orange smears," which describe Yeganeh. Then *underline* "carrot" and "huge," which describe one of the soups and one of the utensils. Now *underline* the remaining words and phrases in paragraph 5 that describe Yeganeh and his soup kitchen. You will notice that the writer relies on visual details in this paragraph.

2. *Review* the visual details you underlined. *Single out* two or three that seem most vivid to you or that best help you imagine Soup Kitchen International as different from other fast-food places you have visited.

Write

Write several sentences explaining what you have discovered about the essay's use of visual details to present Yeganeh and his restaurant. From your annotations in paragraph 5, *give examples* of the details you find to be especially vivid or memorable. Then *explain* why they work so well for you.

Organizing the Observations

Observational writers typically present their subjects either narratively, as a more or less chronological story of their observations, or topically, as groups of related information the writer wants readers to know about the subject. "Soup" is a good example of topical organization. Some observational essays in this chapter are arranged narratively, as you will discover when you analyze John McPhee's observations of an outdoor farmers' market. While a narrative plan offers certain advantages—engaging readers and providing the drama of a good novel or movie—a topical plan keeps the focus firmly on the information.

Analyze

1. *Make a scratch outline* of "Soup," identifying the topics in the order in which they appear. *Notice* that some paragraphs have more than one topic; paragraph 2, for instance, raises several topics: the health benefits of soup, Yeganeh's perfectionism, his emphasis on cleanliness, and how his restaurant compares to others. (For an example of scratch outlining, see Appendix 1, p. 659.)

2. *Note* in your outline whether the source of the topic is the writer's interviews, the writer's firsthand observations, or both.

Write

Write several sentences commenting on what types of topics are presented, which sources they come from, and how effectively they are sequenced. Then *write a few more sentences* answering these questions: How does the sequence of topics contribute to or inhibit your growing understanding of Soup Kitchen International as you read through the essay? Which topics does the writer introduce and then drop? Which topics does he return to later?

Engaging and Informing Readers

Along with presenting their subjects vividly and organizing material effectively, observational writers strive both to engage or interest their readers and to inform them about the subject. Readers expect to learn something new from observational writing, and they anticipate savoring this learning experience. To accomplish these intertwined goals of engaging and informing readers, writers must pace the flow of information while engaging readers' interests. Strategies for engaging readers include beginning with an arresting image or statement, using active verbs, reporting unusual activities and events, and reporting revealing interview material.

Much of the information in observational writing tends to come from interviews and to be presented as quoted statements or conversations, as in "Soup." Information can also come from the writer's observations and background reading and may be quoted or summarized. Strategies for presenting information include identifying and defining new terms, listing, dividing into parts, classifying or grouping, and comparing or contrasting. A writer of observation needs to consider carefully what readers are likely to know about the subject as well as what will interest or even amuse them.

Analyze

1. *Skim the reading,* thinking about the pace of information. *Note* the overall quantity of the information, the different types of information, and whether the information comes at readers so fast they might be confused or so slow they might lose interest. *Put an "X"* in the margin by any information that seems to you to come too fast or too slow for readers who have never been to Soup Kitchen International.

2. *Skim the reading again,* this time looking for anything you think *New Yorker* readers, including yourself, might find engaging or amusing. *Put a checkmark* next to these spots.

Write

Write several sentences describing how the author of "Soup" informs and engages readers. *Cite examples* from your annotations. *Point out* what seems most and least successful about the pace of information and the attempts to engage readers.

Conveying an Impression of the Subject

Readers expect observational essays to convey a particular impression or interpretation of the subject. They want to know the writer's insight into the subject after having spent time observing the place and interviewing people.

To convey an impression, writers carefully select details of the place and people and put these details together in a particular way. They may also explicitly express an attitude toward the subject as well as an interpretation or evaluation of it, announcing these at the beginning, weaving them into the ongoing observations, or presenting them in the conclusion. More often, however, writers convey an impression by implication. The author of "Soup," for example, does not state an interpretation or evaluation directly but implies it through the quotes, the descriptive details, and the little drama presented at the end.

Analyze

1. *Underline* any words or phrases that suggest the author's attitudes toward or feelings about Yeganeh as a human being, cook, and businessman.

2. *Note in the margin* any interpretation or evaluation of Yeganeh and his way of doing business implied by what he says and does.

Write

Write several sentences identifying the overall impression you have of Yeganeh and his Soup Kitchen International. *Quote* two or three phrases or sentences from the essay that convey this impression most strongly, and *identify* briefly the attitude, interpretation, or evaluation you see in each phrase or sentence.

A SPECIAL READING STRATEGY

Comparing and Contrasting Related Readings: "Soup" and John Edge's "I'm Not Leaving Until I Eat This Thing"

Comparing and contrasting related readings is a special critical reading strategy useful both in reading for meaning and in reading like a writer. This strategy is particularly applicable when writers present similar subjects, as is the case in the observational essays in this chapter by the *New Yorker* writer (p. 86) and John T. Edge (p. 96). Both writers describe a business they observed and report on their interview with the business owner. In both instances, the business involves food products and their preparation; however, Edge adopts the role of participant-observer, whereas the author of "Soup" maintains a more "objective" distance. To compare and contrast these two observational essays, think about issues such as these:

- Compare these essays in terms of their cultural contexts. What seems to you to be most significant about the two business philosophies represented in these essays?

- Compare how the two writers organize the information derived from interview and observation. Highlight the places in each essay where information from interviews is quoted or summarized and places where information from direct observation is presented.

- Compare Edge's participant-observer role to the *New Yorker* writer's more distanced perspective. Note any places in "Soup" where you get a sense of the writer's point of view or judgment. What do the participant's observations add to Edge's essay?

See Appendix 1 for detailed guidelines on using the comparing and contrasting related readings strategy.

■ Readings

JOHN T. EDGE

I'm Not Leaving Until I Eat This Thing

> *John T. Edge (b. 1962) earned a master's degree in southern studies from the University of Mississippi and is director of the Southern Foodways Alliance at the university, where he coordinates an annual conference on southern food. Food writer for the national magazine* Oxford American, *he has also written for* Cooking Light, Food & Wine, *and* Gourmet. *His essays are regularly included in* Best Food Writing *anthologies, and he coedits cookbooks and travel guides, such as* Lonely Planet: New Orleans *(2003). He has published three books of his own:* A Gracious Plenty: Recipes and Recollections from the American South *(1999);* Southern Belly *(2000), a portrait of southern food told through profiles of people and places; and* Fried Chicken: An American Story *(2004).*
>
> *This reading first appeared in a 1999 issue of* Oxford American *(where the illustration on page 97 appeared) and was reprinted in 2000 in* Utne Reader. *Edge focuses his considerable observational writing skills on an unusual manufacturing business in a small Mississippi town—Farm Fresh Food Supplier. He introduces readers to the company's workers and its pig products, a best-seller being pickled pig lips, which are sometimes bottled in vivid patriotic and special-events colors. Unlike the author of the previous reading, Edge participates in his subject—not by joining in the activities at Farm Fresh, but by attempting to eat a pig lip at Jesse's Place, a nearby "juke" bar. You will see that the reading begins and ends with this personal experience.*
>
> *As you read, enjoy Edge's struggle to eat a pig lip, and pay attention to the information Edge offers about the history and manufacture of pickled pig lips at Farm Fresh.*

It's just past 4:00 on a Thursday afternoon in June at Jesse's   1
Place, a country juke 17 miles south of the Mississippi line and
three miles west of Amite, Louisiana. The air conditioner hacks
and spits forth torrents of Arctic air, but the heat of summer can't
be kept at bay. It seeps around the splintered doorjambs and set-
tles in, transforming the squat particleboard-plastered roadhouse
into a sauna. Slowly, the dank barroom fills with grease-smeared
mechanics from the truck stop up the road and farmers straight
from the fields, the soles of their brogans thick with dirt clods. A
few weary souls make their way over from the nearby sawmill. I sit

alone at the bar, one empty bottle of Bud in front of me, a second in my hand. I drain the beer, order a third, and stare down at the pink juice spreading outward from a crumpled foil pouch and onto the bar.

I'm not leaving until I eat this thing, I tell myself.

2

Half a mile down the road, behind a fence coiled with razor wire, Lionel Dufour, proprietor of Farm Fresh Food Supplier, is loading up the last truck of the day, wheeling case after case of pickled pork offal out of his cinder-block processing plant and into a semitrailer bound for Hattiesburg, Mississippi.

3

His crew packed lips today. Yesterday, it was pickled sausage; the day before that, pig feet. Tomorrow, it's pickled pig lips again. Lionel has been on the job since 2:45 in the morning, when he came in to light the boilers. Damon Landry, chief cook and maintenance man, came in at 4:30. By 7:30, the production line was at full tilt: six women in white smocks and blue bouffant caps, slicing ragged white fat from the lips, tossing the good parts in glass jars, the bad parts in barrels bound for the rendering plant. Across the aisle, filled jars clatter by on a conveyor belt as a worker tops them off with a Kool-Aid-red slurry of hot sauce, vinegar, salt, and food coloring. Around the corner, the jars are capped, affixed with a label, and stored in pasteboard boxes to await shipping.

4

Unlike most offal—euphemistically called "variety meats"—lips   5
belie their provenance. Brains, milky white and globular, look
like brains. Feet, the ghosts of their cloven hoofs protruding, look like
feet. Testicles look like, well, testicles. But lips are different. Loosed
from the snout, trimmed of their fat, and dyed a preternatural
pink, they look more like candy than like carrion.

At Farm Fresh, no swine root in an adjacent feedlot. No viscera-   6
strewn killing floor lurks just out of sight, down a darkened hall-
way. These pigs died long ago at some Midwestern abattoir. By the
time the lips arrive in Amite, they are, in essence, pig Popsicles,
50-pound blocks of offal and ice.

"Lips are all meat," Lionel told me earlier in the day. "No gris-   7
tle, no bone, no nothing. They're bar food, hot and vinegary, great
with a beer. Used to be the lips ended up in sausages, headcheese,
those sorts of things. A lot of them still do."

Lionel, a 50-year-old father of three with quick, intelligent eyes   8
set deep in a face the color of cordovan, is a veteran of nearly 40 years
in the pickled pig lips business. "I started out with my daddy when I
wasn't much more than 10," Lionel told me, his shy smile framed
by a coarse black mustache flecked with whispers of gray. "The
meatpacking business he owned had gone broke back when I was
6, and he was peddling out of the back of his car, selling dried
shrimp, napkins, straws, tubes of plastic cups, pig feet, pig lips,
whatever the bar owners needed. He sold to black bars, white bars,
sweet shops, snowball stands, you name it. We made the rounds
together after I got out of school, sometimes staying out till two or
three in the morning. I remember bringing my toy cars to this one
joint and racing them around the floor with the bar owner's son
while my daddy and his father did business."

For years after the demise of that first meatpacking company,   9
the Dufour family sold someone else's product. "We used to buy
lips from Dennis Di Salvo's company down in Belle Chasse," recalled
Lionel. "As far as I can tell, his mother was the one who came up
with the idea to pickle and pack lips back in the '50s, back when
she was working for a company called Three Little Pigs over in
Houma. But pretty soon, we were selling so many lips that we had
to almost beg Di Salvo's for product. That's when we started cooking up our own," he told me, gesturing toward the cast-iron kettle
that hangs from the rafters by the front door of the plant. "My
daddy started cooking lips in that very pot."

Lionel now cooks lips in 11 retrofitted milk tanks, dull   10
stainless-steel cauldrons shaped like oversized cradles. But little
else has changed. Though Lionel's father has passed away, Farm
Fresh remains a family-focused company. His wife, Kathy, keeps

the books. His daughter, Dana, a button-cute college student who has won numerous beauty titles, takes to the road in the summer, selling lips to convenience stores and wholesalers. Soon, after he graduates from business school, Lionel's younger son, Matt, will take over operations at the plant. And his older son, a veterinarian, lent his name to one of Farm Fresh's top sellers, Jason's Pickled Pig Lips.

"We do our best to corner the market on lips," Lionel told me, his voice tinged with bravado. "Sometimes they're hard to get from the packing houses. You gotta kill a lot of pigs to get enough lips to keep us going. I've got new customers calling every day; it's all I can do to keep up with demand, but I bust my ass to keep up. I do what I can for my family—and for my customers.   11

"When my customers tell me something," he continued, "just like when my daddy told me something, I listen. If my customers wanted me to dye the lips green, I'd ask, 'What shade?' As it is, every few years we'll do some red and some blue for the Fourth of July. This year we did jars full of Mardi Gras lips—half purple, half gold," Lionel recalled with a chuckle. "I guess we'd had a few beers when we came up with that one."   12

Meanwhile, back at Jesse's Place, I finish my third Bud, order my fourth. *Now,* I tell myself, my courage bolstered by booze, *I'm ready to eat a lip.*   13

They may have looked like candy in the plant, but in the barroom they're carrion once again. I poke and prod the six-inch arc of pink flesh, peering up from my reverie just in time to catch the barkeep's wife, Audrey, staring straight at me. She fixes me with a look just this side of pity and asks, "You gonna eat that thing or make love to it?"   14

Her nephew, Jerry, sidles up to a bar stool on my left. "A lot of people like 'em with chips," he says with a nod toward the pink juice pooling on the bar in front of me. I offer to buy him a lip, and Audrey fishes one from a jar behind the counter, wraps it in tinfoil, and places the whole affair on a paper towel in front of him.   15

I take stock of my own cowardice, and, following Jerry's lead, reach for a bag of potato chips, tear open the top with my teeth, and toss the quivering hunk of hog flesh into the shiny interior of the bag, slick with grease and dusted with salt. Vinegar vapors tickle my nostrils. I stifle a gag that rolls from the back of my throat, swallow hard, and pray that the urge to vomit passes.   16

With a smash of my hand, the potato chips are reduced to a pulp, and I feel the cold lump of the lip beneath my fist. I clasp the bag shut and shake it hard in an effort to ensure chip coverage in   17 all the nooks and crannies of the lip. The technique that Jerry uses—and I mimic—is not unlike that employed by home cooks mixing up a mess of Shake 'n Bake chicken.

I pull from the bag a coral crescent of meat now crusted with 18 blond bits of potato chips. When I chomp down, the soft flesh dissolves between my teeth. It tastes like a flaccid cracklin', unmistakably porcine, and not altogether bad. The chips help, providing texture where there was none. Slowly, my brow unfurrows, my stomach ceases its fluttering.

Sensing my relief, Jerry leans over and peers into my bag. "Kind 19 of look like Frosted Flakes, don't they?" he says, by way of describing the chips rapidly turning to mush in the pickling juice. I offer the bag to Jerry, order yet another beer, and turn to eye the pig feet floating in a murky jar by the cash register, their blunt tips bobbing up through a pasty white film.

READING FOR MEANING

This section presents three activities that will help you reread Edge's observational essay with a critical eye. Done in sequence, these activities lead you from a basic understanding of the selection to a more personal response to it and finally to an analysis that deepens your understanding and critical thinking about what you are reading.

Read to Comprehend

Reread the selection, and write a brief explanation of how Farm Fresh Food Supplier obtains and packs pig lips. Also make a list of any words you do not understand—for example, *offal* (3), *euphemistically* (5), *provenance* (5), *abattoir* (6). Look up their meanings in a dictionary to see which definition best fits the context.

To expand your understanding of this reading, you might use one or more of the following critical reading strategies that are explained and illustrated in Appendix 1: *outlining, summarizing, paraphrasing,* and *questioning to understand and remember.*

Read to Respond

Write several paragraphs exploring your initial thoughts and feelings about Edge's observational essay. Focus on anything that stands out for you, perhaps because it resonates with your own experience or because you find a statement puzzling.

You might consider writing about

- Edge's description of the production line at Farm Fresh Food Supplier (paragraph 4), perhaps in relation to your own work experience.

- Lionel Dufour's story about how he "made the rounds" with his father after school (8), perhaps in relation to your own experience learning from a relative or mentor.

- your reaction to Edge's attempt to eat the pig lip, possibly in relation to your own experience trying an unusual food.

- what the photograph adds to your understanding of and response to the essay.

To develop your response to Edge's essay, you might use one or more of the following critical reading strategies that are explained and illustrated in Appendix 1: *contextualizing, reflecting on challenges to your beliefs and values, recognizing emotional manipulation,* and *judging the writer's credibility.*

Read to Analyze Underlying Assumptions

Write several paragraphs exploring one or more of the assumptions, values, and beliefs underlying Edge's observational essay. As you write, explain how the assumptions are reflected in the text, as well as what you now think of them (and perhaps of your own assumptions) after rereading the selection with a critical eye.

You might consider writing about

- the assumptions about social class underlying Edge's description of Jesse's Place and its customers (paragraph 1), perhaps in relation to your own assumptions about people who like to eat pig lips or who frequent "country juke" places to eat and drink after work.

- Edge's values and assumptions as he describes the process of producing "variety meats" like pig lips (4–5).

- the values and beliefs behind Lionel Dufour's "family-focused" business and its products (7–12).

- the assumptions the barkeep's wife, Audrey, and her nephew, Jerry, seem to have about Edge's struggle to eat the lip.

To probe assumptions more deeply, you might use one or more of the following critical reading strategies that are explained and illustrated in Appendix 1: *reflecting on challenges to your beliefs and values, exploring the significance of figurative language,* and *looking for patterns of opposition.*

READING LIKE A WRITER
ENGAGING AND INFORMING READERS BY REPORTING PARTICIPATION

Readers of observational essays expect to be engaged or entertained as well as informed. Writers have many strategies available to them to engage readers, one effective strategy being to report a personal experience with the subject, either prior to writing about it or as a participant during the research on the subject. Consider that the unsigned writer of "Soup" never tells readers about his or her interest in soup or experience eating soup. The writer might have stayed in the line, placed an order, and then enjoyed one of Yeganeh's soups, later including among the observations just how the soup smelled and tasted. Perhaps the writer chose not to do so because he or she wanted to keep the focus on Yeganeh's encyclopedic knowledge of soup, high standards, and brusque treatment of customers. By contrast, John Edge sets out to learn about his subject by participating in it, attempting to eat a pig lip at the kind of bar in the South where pig lips are served. Edge frames—begins and ends—his observations of pig-lip packing and marketing with the relatively full story of his humorous attempt to eat one pig lip.

Analyze

1. *Reread* paragraphs 1, 2, and 13–19, where Edge tells the story of his attempt to eat a pig lip. *Notice* how he sets up the time and place, describes the bar, and locates himself in the bar. Then, in paragraphs 13–19, *notice* the roles of other characters in the story and the importance of reported conversation. *Underline* details that inform you about the appearance, texture, smell, and taste of the pig lip. (These strategies you may have learned about and used in your own essay in Chapter 2.)

2. *Reflect* on the relation of the bar story to the profile of Farm Fresh Food Supplier in paragraphs 3–12. *Make notes in the margin* about what you learn from the story about pig lips that you cannot find out from paragraphs 3–12. Also *note in the margin* any places in the story that influenced your engagement with or interest in the subject of pig lips.

Write

Write several sentences explaining what you have learned about the use of personal experience in reporting observations.

CONSIDERING IDEAS FOR YOUR OWN WRITING

Consider writing about a place that serves, produces, or sells something unusual, perhaps something that, like Edge, you could try yourself to discover more about for the purpose of informing and engaging your readers. If no such place comes to mind, you could browse the Yellow Pages of your local phone directory for ideas. One example is a company that produces or packages some special ethnic or regional food and/or a local cafe that serves it. There are many other possibilities: acupuncture clinic, caterer, novelty toy and balloon store, microbrewery, chain-saw dealer, boatbuilder, talent agency, ornamental iron manufacturer, bead store, manicure or nail salon, aquarium and pet fish supplier, auto-detailing shop, tattoo parlor, scrap-metal recycler, fly-fishing shop, handwriting analyst, dog- or cat-sitting service, photo restorer, burglar alarm installer, Christmas tree farm, wedding specialist, reweaving specialist, wig salon. You need not evaluate the quality of work at the place as part of your observational essay. Instead, keep the focus on informing readers about the service or product the place offers. Relating a personal experience with the service or product is a good idea but not a requirement of an observational essay.

VIRGINIA HOLMAN

Their First Patient

> *Virginia Holman (b. 1966) has written autobiography, observa-*
> *tional profiles, feature articles, and book reviews for such publications*
> *as* USA Today, Redbook, Self, *and the* Washington Post. *She received*
> *a master of fine arts degree from the University of North Carolina at*
> *Greensboro; worked as an editor as well as a creative writing teacher*
> *at public schools, community women's centers, and hospices; and is*
> *now Kenan visiting writer at UNC-Chapel Hill, where she is teaching*
> *and writing two novels. As the former writer-in-residence at Duke*
> *University Medical Center, Holman helped long-term pediatric*
> *patients and their families use writing as a tool to manage stress and*
> *facilitate healing. Holman is best known for her prize-winning auto-*
> *biography about her mother's mental illness,* Rescuing Patty Hearst:
> Memories from a Decade Gone Mad *(2003). In addition to the*
> *Pushcart Prize, Holman has received an Outstanding Literature*
> *Award from the National Alliance for the Mentally Ill and a Rosalynn*
> *Carter Fellowship in mental health journalism.*
>
> *In the observational essay "Their First Patient," originally pub-*
> *lished in the winter 2000 issue of* DoubleTake *magazine, Holman*
> *describes the experiences of first-year medical students in an anatomy*
> *course at Duke University Medical Center. As you read, notice how,*
> *like John T. Edge in the preceding selection, Holman adopts the role of*
> *participant-observer. Also think about what Holman's firsthand expe-*
> *rience contributes to her explanation of what medical students learn*
> *from dissecting a real human body.*

The gross anatomy laboratory at Duke University Medical Cen-   1
ter is a surprisingly cheery place. It's in a sub-basement room with
clean, white cinderblock walls. Lush fume-eating ferns and vines
thrive in the high glazed windows to the east. The fluorescent
lights overhead are bright and alarmingly clear—an effort perhaps
to banish the possibility of shadow?—and the empty metal tables
gleam. There are four bathtub-size sinks, each lined with three
spigots operated by foot pedals not unlike those found on a church
organ. Boxes filled with latex gloves and disposable plastic aprons
are stacked in the cabinets. A large pegboard mounted on the wall
is hung with common hardware: handsaws; bright blue, yellow,
and red plastic mallets; chisels. All carry the scars of use, but each
tool is clean and well maintained. This place—before the cadavers,
students, and teachers arrive—could almost be mistaken for a
commercial kitchen or the fanatically pristine woodworking shop
of an elderly neighbor.

Gross Anatomy is the essential and incomparable crucible of all   2
first-year medical students at Duke and every medical school. I'm
here not as a student but as an approved witness, writer, and perhaps, potential body donor.

Though I have never had the slightest qualm about giving up my   3
eyes or kidneys to some living soul who could use and benefit from
them, the idea of giving the rest of my body to Science, as the saying goes, seems a much murkier proposition. What, exactly, would
Science *do* with me? And would a gift of my entire mortal self be
appreciated and valued enough to offset my trepidation and that of
my surviving family? If I were dissected, what might become of my
parts once they had outlived their use to Science? For instance, would
my hand be dissected and studied by earnest future surgeons, or
would it merely wind up as part of a student's Halloween prank?
Could my body be buried or cremated after Science finished with it?
Or would my remains be unceremoniously tossed out in the orange
biohazard trash container?

In the eighteenth century, body donors and "anatomical gifts   4
programs" were unheard of. Medical students dissected the corpses
of executed criminals, stolen from fresh graves by "resurrection
men" who also trafficked in unclaimed corpses, left by family in hospitals or mental institutions. At Duke, students learn *only* from
donated bodies.

On the first day of Gross Anatomy, students assemble in a sleek   5
modern amphitheater replete with Internet portals and an individual microphone for each of the 120 students in attendance. A
group of anatomists and residents are also here to prepare the students for the emotionally grueling task ahead.

The first lecture is delivered by Dr. Matt Cartmill, a professor   6
with unkempt hair and silvered muttonchop whiskers and bifocals. He reminds the students that the bodies are now quite dead.

"D E A D," he writes on the board. The room is silent.   7

"Nothing will happen when you cut these bodies. They will not   8
cry out in pain. You will not be hurting these people." I find his
blunt reassurance comforting. He talks about the use of humor to
relieve the stress and tension during dissection and tells us that
we will all feel tempted at times to make jokes in lab about the bodies and the experience we're about to enter into. Then he pauses,
takes off his bifocals, and looks hard into the eyes of the students.
"It's tremendously disrespectful. So *don't* do it," he says. "Just don't
do it."

Several former anatomy students talk about the strong emo-   9
tions they felt when they dissected a fellow human. A psychologist
is on hand. The administrators of the anatomical gifts program at

Duke are there. Excerpts from family members' letters are read aloud.

Before we go to the lab, Dr. Daniel Schmitt, a youthful anatomy professor, clips a small portable microphone on his tie and energetically walks about the room as he lectures. "The bodies here wanted to be here—on your dissecting table. Why? So you could learn. This is an amazing gift. The donors knew that you would take them apart, that you would cut into them. So be respectful of them, but do not be shy. You do not honor these people unless you learn well. Don't blow this chance."

10

The first day in the gross anatomy lab is hands-on. The drowsy, antiseptic odor of human preservative fills each breath I take. The room thrums with the pulse of the ventilator fans. Several of the students don paper masks in an effort to block out the chemical smell, and I reach for one myself. Dr. Bill Hylander, a Biological Anthropology professor and anatomist, notices and laughs. "You get used to the smells here pretty fast. And the plants love the formaldehyde." Clearly, the seven-foot ficus adjacent to the teaching skeleton is hyper-fueled by such salubrious vapors.

11

"You might want to dress for the occasion," he observes as I shuck the clear plastic apron over my wool trousers and turtleneck. I notice that many of the students have changed into scrubs or sweats. "You're fine today, but things can get, well, messy." He offers up a wry smile and an unapologetic shrug. His lab coat, like all the formal white cloth jackets of the anatomy professors, has stains on the cuffs and instrument pockets—an indication of the involvement level that is expected.

12

The students at my table convene. We turn back the thick, crackling plastic sheet wound round the human shape laid out on our dissecting table. We begin familiarizing ourselves with the body we will spend the next two months dismantling and memorizing.

13

At our table, and at every table, there is an involuntary pause. Many students miss a breath. A lambent expression of shock plays upon the faces of the living. Nothing could ever prepare us for this moment: the cadaver before us is a person, a person dead. The cadavers are naked, and I am awed by the sturdy plain of skin that sweeps across each body. There's so *much* of it.

14

It startles me to see death and nakedness together, to see old age and nakedness together. I walk about the room to look at each table. Some bodies are only in their fifties, others are near-ancient at ninety-plus years. Age provides little indication of why one body appears robust or another frail. Occasionally there is sad evidence

15

of infirmity, a bedsore or a feeding tube, but during this first intimate look, the bodies refuse to yield much more information than
they would clothed and alive. I'm relieved there's no donor under
fifty. Already I feel as mortal as the day I gave birth. The students
here are over a decade younger than I am, and for some, this is
their first exposure to a dead body. I can't imagine what this is like
for them.

Tacked to the bulletin board, along with the lab schedule and   16
exam dates, is the cadaver list. There are twenty donors, and for
privacy's sake, the only information given is age and cause of
death. That doesn't stop the students' desire to know more about
the donors.

"I wish I knew her name." "I wonder what he did for a living."   17
"Is there any way to get more information about the donor?"

Daniel Schmitt explains that the students will not receive more   18
information about the cadavers, but that it is quite natural to wonder who these people were. He also reminds the students that there
will be a memorial service held in Duke Chapel at the conclusion
of the semester.

"Can we name the cadaver?" one student asks.   19

"Sure, if you find that helps. My personal view is that these peo- 20
ple already have names, but if you find it eases your mind, go
ahead." Our table decides against selecting a name.

The first task of the medical students is not to begin to dissect   21
the bodies but rather to protect them. We are instructed to wrap
the hands, feet, and face. These are dissected late in the course and
must be kept supple with a solution of formalin, glycerin, and pine
oil.

This moment between the living and the dead is remarkably   22
gentle. We wrap the donor's feet, one at a time, and ease them back
down on the table. The same with the hands. One student holds
the well manicured hand of the ninety-six-year-old woman at our
table while another winds the gauze around it. Then it is time to
wrap the head. The students study the faces of their cadavers.

One young man lets out a slight involuntary "Oh!"   23

"What?" I ask.   24

"Well, the cadaver is so real. Was so real," he corrects and pauses 25
again to regard the woman who lies before us. Indeed, evidence of
the individual before us is undeniable. Yet it is clear that the spark
of life is long gone. What remains is a mere fraction of a much
larger picture. The face of the woman on our table is quite elegant,
and I find its deep lines and furrows from a long life a comfort.
Her eyelids are open, but when I look into them I cannot find her
eyes.

"Was she an eye donor?" I ask Dr. Christine Wall, the anatomist who supervises our group and four other tables. Eyes are the only organs that body donors can give without compromising the integrity of the dissection process.   26

Chris comes over and leans her face uncomfortably near to the cadaver's. None of us at the table has dared get that close. "No. Her eyes are right here. Look."   27

I take a breath, bend over, and peer into the cadaver's face. Our donor's eyes are sunk deep within their sockets and are clouded gray like a seal's. Daniel Schmitt comes over. "We'll bring up her eyes and dissect them when we do the skull."   28

"Bring up the eyes?" I ask.   29

"When you fill them with water, the eyes rise up."   30

"Oh." I am finding this whole experience unsettling, and I also see fear on the faces of the students.   31

I raise the woman's head from the table while a student winds damp gauze around the woman's face. Her skull is heftier than I expected. I look to the other tables. One student absently pats his cadaver's hand. It's O.K., the gesture seems to say. I imagine this really serves to soothe him for the task ahead—the first cut.   32

Since the first dissection will be of the back, the seven of us struggle to turn the body from supine to prone. I notice around the room that some students try to protect the dignity of the cadavers. One table spreads paper towels across the buttocks of a man, while another arranges the plastic sheet to cover all but the dissection site. A student tucks the plastic under the exposed leg of a woman on his table, as if putting a child to bed.   33

We open *Grant's Dissector* and place it on the bookstand at the end of the table. The first incision is long, from the neck straight down the spine. The students at my table look at each other to decide who will brave it. The student who volunteers makes several attempts to fit a blade into her scalpel handle without much luck. Chris Wall comes over to help. "Like this." In two adept movements she secures the blade in the handle and then abruptly walks away.   34

"Students are often terrified to start cutting," she tells me later. "If I stay too long at a table before the students are acclimated to their cadaver, I'll start doing all their work—I never tire of dissecting. But it's important that they get comfortable touching the donors. Anatomy is best learned when it's applied."   35

The student takes a delicate hold on her scalpel, her fingers grasp midway down the shaft. Gingerly, she draws the scalpel down a length of spine. The blade is keen but the student must repeat the cut again, pressing harder, to cut all the way through the   36 skin and fat. Once the incision is made, another is drawn across the shoulder blades and yet another across the hips. The cuts look like the perforated doors on an Advent calendar.

On living tissue, blood would spring forth from an incision, but with these embalmed bodies, the flesh parted by the cuts merely affords us a clearer view into the small fissures. Now the students take turns at the tedious task of pulling and cutting the skin and fat away from the muscle underneath. The fat on our donor is bright yellow, cheesy-looking, and slick. We patiently "clear a field," as Chris Wall says, so that we will be able to see and identify the musculature of the back. It takes almost three hours to fully remove the skin and fat from the deep fascia—the thin pearlescent connective tissue shrink-wrapped around the internal body structures. Once these winglike flaps of skin are pulled away from the body, I can see the superficial muscles below. The cadaver finally resembles the pictures in our dissector, and we begin the process of identifying the structures we've exposed.

After the first lab, I go home and bathe. My clothes and hair smell like ham and formaldehyde. I pack overalls and a T-shirt for the next lab. Before I go to bed, I worry what I might dream that night. How will this experience affect me? Suddenly I am a bit unsteady. Can I really do this for the next two months?

In the following weeks I decide to try out A.D.A.M., the Animated Dissection of Anatomy for Medicine, a computer software program that will take me through a human dissection by clicks of a mouse. There are a number of such programs available—Netter's and Digital Anatomist are two other popular packages—and many students use them as tutorials.

Everything on A.D.A.M. is lucid. I can identify structures readily, but when I go to the lab and try to identify the same structures, I find the cadaver labyrinthine and confusing. Organs and veins are displaced by fat and look only vaguely like those in my dissector and in A.D.A.M.

One student holds up what seems like a white elastic band in our cadaver's leg.

"I can't find this ligament in our dissector."

Chris Wall comes over and takes a look. "That's the sciatic nerve," she says. "We tend not to think of nerves as being large and dissectable, but they can be."

"It's enormous," the students murmur and admire the thin bundle in its slippery myelin sheath.

Nothing in the body looks the way it does in A.D.A.M. or the dissector. The placement of the ovaries varies remarkably in each female donor. Occasionally nerves and veins take maverick pathways and show up in unexpected places.

The students who take Gross Anatomy quickly learn that the bodies of the donors, and those of their future patients, aren't fungible. A rosy, dense lung removed from one cadaver may be mottled and diseased in another. Hysterectomies leave some tables without reproductive organs. Tumors unknown to the donor are found. At one table, students cut and peel back the patellar tendon of the knee only to unexpectedly reveal a shiny titanium knee replacement. Students come over from other tables and we marvel at the surgeon's work and the presence of something manmade so deep inside a man. One student whistles—"That looks like something straight out of *The Terminator.*"   46

Daniel Schmitt and Matt Cartmill both extol the importance of the kinesthetic or tactile learning that dissection imparts: knowledge that can only be gained by the students' hands working on the bodies. After all, palpation is very much a part of a doctor's repertoire of skills.   47

Richard Brooks, one of the first-year medical students, says that though the software programs are adequate tutors, they can never give a full sense of a person or his parts. "For instance," he comments, "I could look at fat all day on A.D.A.M. but never understand without having had dissected a body that fat is heavy, that it's oily."   48

After we are through with the dissections, after we have removed and held the brain and lungs, bisected the skull and dissected the orbit of the eye, we replace the organs and wrap the bodies again so that they may be cremated whole. Some donors have requested that their remains be returned to family, others will have their ashes scattered at a special site in Duke Forest.   49

The memorial service, held in Duke Chapel, honors our most powerful teachers: the donors. There are over forty people seated in the section reserved for family. I cannot help but look at the first few pews and wonder if the family of the woman I helped dissect is present. In a way, we've already met.   50

Several students deliver short speeches and read poems of appreciation to the family members and teachers. They speak of their emotion upon first entering the anatomy lab and meeting the donors. Dr. Alison Weidner, Chief of the Division of Gynecological Services, thanks the family members. "We take this heavy responsibility very seriously. . . . It would be impossible to have these opportunities to learn without this marvelous and enormous sacrifice you and your loved ones have made."   51

Matt Cartmill delivers an eloquent speech on why dissection is   52
an essential part of each medical student's training. He succinctly
explains that "dissection teaches our hands" in ways books and
software programs cannot. "We are all built to a common plan, but
the details are always different. . . . This appreciation of human
uniqueness is also of crucial importance to the student physician;
and it, too, grows out of the practice of dissection."

It is Richard Brooks, however, who reminds me of the ultimate   53
importance of this experience. "I know," he confides to me, "that
I'll always think of the man we dissected as my first patient."

READING FOR MEANING

This section presents three activities that will help you reread Holman's
observational essay with a critical eye. Done in sequence, these activities lead you
from a basic understanding of the selection to a more personal response to it and
finally to an analysis that deepens your understanding and critical thinking about
what you are reading.

Read to Comprehend

Reread the selection, and write a few sentences briefly summarizing the
answers Holman gives to the questions she poses in paragraph 3. Indicate if she
fails to answer any of her own questions. Also make a list of any words you do
not understand—for example, *crucible* (paragraph 2), *salubrious* (11), *lambent*
(14), *fungible* (46). Look up their meanings in a dictionary to see which definition best fits the context.

To expand your understanding of this reading, you might use one or more
of the following critical reading strategies that are explained and illustrated in
Appendix 1: *outlining, summarizing, paraphrasing,* and *questioning to understand
and remember.*

Read to Respond

Write several paragraphs exploring your initial thoughts and feelings about
Holman's observational essay. Focus on anything that stands out for you, perhaps
because it resonates with your own experience or because you find a statement
puzzling.

You might consider writing about

- your response to Holman's description of the anatomy lab as "a surprisingly
  cheery place" that resembles "a commercial kitchen or [a] fanatically pristine
  woodworking shop" (paragraph 1).

- the reactions of Holman and the medical students as they first look at the dead body, wrap the hands and other extremities, and prepare for the first cut (14–33).

- the idea that "[s]tudents are often terrified to start cutting" (35), possibly in relation to your own experience dissecting an animal.

- your own familial, cultural, or religious attitudes about death and the proper handling of a dead body.

To develop your response to Holman's essay, you might use one or more of the following critical reading strategies that are explained and illustrated in Appendix 1: *contextualizing, reflecting on challenges to your beliefs and values, recognizing emotional manipulation,* and *judging the writer's credibility.*

Read to Analyze Underlying Assumptions

Write several paragraphs exploring one or more of the assumptions, values, and beliefs underlying Holman's observational essay. As you write, explain how the assumptions are reflected in the text, as well as what you now think of them (and perhaps of your own assumptions) after rereading the selection with a critical eye.

You might consider writing about

- the assumptions behind Holman's judgment that "Gross Anatomy is the essential and incomparable crucible of all first-year medical students" (paragraph 2).

- the assumptions that make Holman feel that donating her body to science is "a much murkier proposition" (3) than donating parts of her body to living recipients, perhaps in relation to your own feelings about being a body donor.

- the values implicit in Dr. Cartmill's injunction to the students not to make jokes, even though humor would help "to relieve the stress and tension during dissection" (8).

- the assumptions and values behind Daniel Schmitt's explanation (18–20) that it is "quite natural" for the students to want to know more about the cadavers, but that for "privacy's sake," they are only told the person's age and cause of death (16).

- the assumptions behind dissecting a real human body rather than relying on a computer program like A.D.A.M.

- the assumptions behind the need to combine "kinesthetic or tactile learning" with visual learning (47), perhaps in relation to Howard Gardner and Joseph Walter's explanation of "multiple intelligences" theory in Chapter 5 (p. 249).

To probe assumptions more deeply, you might use one or more of the following critical reading strategies that are explained and illustrated in Appendix 1: *reflecting on challenges to your beliefs and values, exploring the significance of figurative language,* and *looking for patterns of opposition.*

READING LIKE A WRITER
PRESENTING PLACES AND CREATING AN IMPRESSION

Observational writers often use descriptive language to give readers a vivid image of the place they visited and to create a strong impression. Sometimes the impression is made explicit, as when Holman begins her description of the gross anatomy laboratory by stating her impression of it as "a surprisingly cheery place" (paragraph 1). At other times, the impression is left for readers to infer from the writer's word choices and selection of images. Whether the impression is stated directly or implied, writers typically use a combination of naming, detailing, and comparing. These descriptive writing strategies are illustrated in this brief excerpt from paragraph 5:

> On the first day of Gross Anatomy, students assemble in a sleek modern amphitheater replete with Internet portals and an individual microphone for each of the 120 students in attendance.

Here Holman names such features as the "amphitheater," "portals," and "microphone" that she wants readers to notice about the scene. She also adds details to give readers information about these features: the amphitheater is described as "sleek" and "modern," and the fact that it is wired for the Internet and has "individual" microphones shows that it has the latest technology. This image of a cutting-edge learning environment is significant because the overall impression Holman makes in the essay is that the tactile experience of dissecting a human body cannot be replaced by even the most sophisticated computer program.

Analyze

1. *Reread* paragraph 1, highlighting the naming and detailing that Holman uses to describe the gross anatomy lab. Also *notice* the comparisons she makes at the end of the paragraph.

2. *Review* the descriptive language you have highlighted, noting whether Holman's word choices create an impression of the place as "surprisingly cheery" (1). Which words contribute to this impression, and which words, if any, suggest a different impression?

Write

Write several sentences explaining what you have discovered, through Holman's description, about the gross anatomy lab. What impression do these images suggest to you? How do they help you understand the significance of the place for Holman? *Give two or three examples* from your highlighting to support your explanation.

Comparing and Contrasting Related Readings: Virginia Holman's "Their First Patient" and Brian Cable's "The Last Stop"

Comparing and contrasting related readings is a special critical reading strategy useful both in reading for meaning and in reading like a writer. This strategy is particularly applicable when writers present similar subjects, as is the case in the observational essays in this chapter by Virginia Holman (p. 104) and Brian Cable (p. 133). Both writers observe places where people work with dead bodies, and they present firsthand information learned primarily from observations and interviews. However, their essays also differ in the role the writers adopt and in the meanings they derive from their research. To compare and contrast these two observational essays, think about issues such as these:

- Compare these essays in terms of how they represent cultural values—particularly scientific, religious, and commercial attitudes—toward death and the human body.

- Compare and contrast Holman's tone of reverence and Cable's tone of irreverence. What does humor contribute to Cable's essay? Do you think his use of humor appropriate and effective, especially in light of what Dr. Cartmill says in Holman's essay?

- Compare Holman's role of participant-observer to Cable's role of observer. How does being a participant affect Holman's credibility? What does Cable's essay gain from his adopting a more distanced, perhaps objective or ironic, position?

See Appendix 1 for detailed guidelines on using the comparing and contrasting related readings strategy.

CONSIDERING IDEAS FOR YOUR OWN WRITING

Leisure or educational activities that bring people together briefly for special training offer good material for observational essays. Given your time constraints for researching and writing the essay, consider choosing an activity or course that meets only a few times (one to five times is typical) on evenings or weekends. The offerings reflect people's diverse interests and differ somewhat from community to community: dog training, motorcycle riding, indoor climbing, skating, dancing, cooking, holiday decorating, stress reduction, conflict resolution, computer software training, public speaking, speed-reading. You can find these and other classes advertised in newspapers and listed in your college's extension-course catalog. Ask the instructor for permission to observe the class, and arrange to interview the instructor for a few minutes before or after class. Be bold in approaching two or three students to discover why they enrolled in the class and what they have to say about it. Take careful notes on your observations of at least one class meeting.

JOHN McPHEE

The New York Pickpocket Academy

John McPhee (b. 1931), a graduate of Princeton and Cambridge universities, lives in Princeton, New Jersey, where he occasionally teaches a writing workshop in the "literature of fact" at Princeton University. A staff writer for the New Yorker *and author of more than two dozen books, McPhee is highly regarded as a writer of profiles and observational essays in which he ingeniously integrates information from observations, interviews, and other research into engaging, readable prose. Readers marvel at the way he explains such complex subjects as experimental aircraft or modern physics and discovers the complexities of such ordinary subjects as bears or oranges. Among his books are* Oranges *(1967);* The Control of Nature *(1989);* Assembling California *(1993);* Annals of the Former World *(1998), for which he was awarded the Pulitzer Prize; and* The Founding Fish *(2002). He has been nominated on several occasions for the National Book Award in science, and he received the American Academy of Arts and Letters Award in literature.*

The following selection, from the collection of essays Giving Good Weight *(1979), is part of a longer profile of farmers who sell produce at open-air markets in New York City. The narrator of the story is McPhee himself, weighing and sacking produce, all the while looking beyond the zucchini and tomatoes for material that might interest readers.*

As you read, notice the many details McPhee provides about the people and the place: the vegetables and trucks and hats and colors and sounds of the market. Notice, too, the great variety of examples he presents of crime and honesty, some happening before his eyes and some told to him by people at the market.

Brooklyn, and the pickpocket in the burgundy jacket appears   1
just before noon. Melissa Mousseau recognizes him much as if
he were an old customer and points him out to Bob Lewis, who
follows him from truck to truck. Aware of Lewis, he leaves the
market. By two, he will have made another run. A woman with
deep-auburn hair and pale, nervous hands clumsily attracts the
attention of a customer whose large white purse she is rifling.
Until a moment ago, the customer was occupied with the choosing of apples and peppers, but now she shouts out, "Hey, what are
you doing? Your hand is in my purse. What are you doing?" The
auburn-haired woman not only has her hand in the purse but
most of her arm as well. She withdraws it, and with intense
absorption begins to finger the peppers. "How much are the peppers? Mister, give me some of these!" she says, looking up at me

with a gypsy's dark, starburst eyes. "Three pounds for a dollar," I tell her, with a swift glance around for Lewis or a cop. When I look back, the pickpocket is gone. Other faces have filled in—people unconcernedly examining the fruit. The woman with the white purse has returned her attention to the apples. She merely seems annoyed. Lewis once sent word around from truck to truck that we should regularly announce in loud voices that pickpockets were present in the market, but none of the farmers complied. Hodgson shrugged and said, "Why distract the customers?" Possibly Fifty-ninth Street is the New York Pickpocket Academy. Half a dozen scores have been made there in a day. I once looked up and saw a well-dressed gentleman under a gray fedora being kicked and kicked again by a man in a green polo shirt. He kicked him in the calves. He kicked him in the thighs. He kicked him in the gluteal bulge. He kicked him from the middle of the market out to the edge, and he kicked him into the street. "Get your ass out of here!" shouted the booter, redundantly. Turning back toward the market, he addressed the curious. "Pickpocket," he explained. The dip did not press charges.

People switch shopping carts from time to time. They make off with a loaded one and leave an empty cart behind. Crime on such levels is a part of the background here, something in the urban air, so many parts per million. The condition is accepted with a resignation that approaches nonchalance.

Most thievery is petty and is on the other side of the tables. As Rich describes it, "Brooklyn, Fifty-ninth Street, people rip off stuff everywhere. You just expect it. An old man comes along and puts a dozen eggs in a bag. Women choosing peaches steal one for every one they buy—a peach for me, a peach for you. What can you do? You stand there and watch. When they take too many, you complain. I watched a guy one day taking nectarines. He would put one in a plastic bag, then one in a pocket, then one in a pile on the ground. After he did that half a dozen times, he had me weigh the bag."

"This isn't England," Barry Benepe informed us once, "and a lot of people are pretty dishonest."

Now, in Brooklyn, a heavyset woman well past the middle of life is sobbing pitifully, flailing her arms in despair. She is sitting on a bench in the middle of the market. She is wearing a print dress, a wide-brimmed straw hat. Between sobs, she presents in a heavy Russian accent the reason for her distress. She was buying green beans from Don Keller, and when she was about to pay him she discovered that someone had opened her handbag—even while it was on her arm, she said—and had removed several books of food stamps, a telephone bill, and eighty dollars in cash. Lewis, in his daypack, stands over her and tells her he is sorry. He said, "This sort of thing will happen wherever there's a crowd."

Another customer breaks in to scold Lewis, saying, "This is the 6 biggest rip-off place in Brooklyn. Two of my friends were pick- pocketed here last week and I had to give them carfare home."

Lewis puts a hand on his forehead and, after a pensive moment, 7 says, "That was very kind of you."

The Russian woman is shrieking now. Lewis attends her like a 8 working dentist. "It's all right. It will be O.K. It may not be as bad as you think." He remarks that he would call the police if he thought there was something they could do.

Jeffrey Mack, eight years old, has been listening to all this, and 9 he now says, "I see a cop."

Jeffrey has an eye for cops that no one else seems to share. (A 10 squad car came here for him one morning and took him off to face a truant officer. Seeing his fright, a Pacific Street prostitute got into the car and rode with him.)

"Where, Jeffrey?" 11

"There," Jeffrey lifts an arm and points. 12

"Where?" 13

"There." He points again—at trucks, farmers, a falafel man. 14

"I don't see a policeman," Lewis says to him. "If you see one, Jef- 15 frey, go and get him."

Jeffrey goes, and comes back with an off-duty 78th Precinct cop 16 who is wearing a white apron and has been selling fruits and veg- etables in the market. The officer speaks sternly to the crying woman. "Your name?"

"Catherine Barta." 17

"Address?" 18

"Eighty-five Eastern Parkway." 19

Every Wednesday, she walks a mile or so to the Greenmarket. 20 She has lived in Brooklyn close to half her life, the rest of it in the Ukraine. Heading back to his vegetables, the officer observes that there is nothing he can do.

Out from behind her tables comes Joan Benack, the baker, of 21 Rocky Acres Farm, Milan, New York—a small woman with a high, thin voice. Leaving her tropical carrot bread, her zucchini bread, her anadama bread, her beer bread, she goes around with a bor- rowed hat collecting money from the farmers for Catherine Barta. Bills stuff that hat, size 7—the money of Alvina Frey and John Labanowski and Cleather Slade and Rich Hodgson and Bob Engle, who has seen it come and go. He was a broker for Merrill Lynch before the stock market imploded, and now he is a blond-bearded farmer in a basketball shirt selling apples that he grows in Clintondale, New York. Don Keller offers a dozen eggs, and one by one the farmers come out from their trucks to fill Mrs. Barta's shopping cart with beans and zucchini, apples, eggplants, tomatoes, peppers, and corn. As a result, her wails and sobs grow louder.

A man who gave Rich Hodgson a ten-dollar bill for a ninety-five-cent box of brown eggs asks Rich to give the ten back after Rich has handed him nine dollars and five cents, explaining that he has smaller bills that he wants to exchange for a twenty. Rich hands him the ten. Into Rich's palm he counts out five ones, a five, and the ten for a twenty and goes away satisfied, as he has every reason to be, having conned Rich out of nine dollars, five cents, and a box of brown eggs. Rich smiles at his foolishness, shrugs, and sells some cheese. If cash were equanimity, he would never lose a cent. One day, a gang of kids began taking Don Keller's vegetables and throwing them at the Hodgson truck. Anders Thueson threw an apple at the kids, who then picked up rocks. Thueson reached into the back of the truck and came up with a machete. While Hodgson told him to put it away, pant legs went up, switchblades came into view. Part of the gang bombarded the truck with debris from a nearby roof. Any indication of panic might have been disastrous. Hodgson packed deliberately, and drove away.

Todd Jameson, who comes in with his brother Dan from Farmingdale, New Jersey, weighed some squash one day, and put it in a brown bag. He set the package down while he weighed something else. Then, reaching for the squash, he picked up an identical bag that happened to contain fifty dollars in rolled coins. He handed it to the customer who had asked for the squash. Too late, Todd discovered the mistake. A couple of hours later, though, the customer—"I'll never forget him as long as I live, the white hair, the glasses, the ruddy face"—came back. He said, "Hey, this isn't squash. I didn't ask for money, I asked for squash." Whenever that man comes to market, the Jamesons give him a bag full of food. "You see, where I come from, that would never, never happen," Todd explains. "If I made a mistake like that in Farmingdale, no one—no one—would come back with fifty dollars' worth of change."

Dusk comes down without further crime in Brooklyn, and the farmers are packing to go. John Labanowski—short, compact, with a beer in his hand—is expounding on his day. "The white people are educating the colored on the use of beet greens," he reports. "A colored woman was telling me today, 'Cut the tops off,' and a white woman spoke up and said, 'Hold it,' and told the

22

23

24

colored woman, 'You're throwing the best part away.' They go on talking, and pretty soon the colored woman is saying, 'I'm seventy-three on Monday,' and the white says, 'I don't believe a word you say.' You want to know why I come in here? I come in here for fun. For profit, of course, but for relaxation, too. I like being here with these people. They say the city is a rat race, but they've got it backwards. The farm is what gets to be a rat race. You should come out and see what I—." He is interrupted by the reappearance in the market of Catherine Barta, who went home long ago and has now returned, her eyes hidden by her wide-brimmed hat, her shopping cart full beside her. On the kitchen table, at 85 Eastern Parkway, she found her telephone bill, her stamps, and her cash. She has come back to the farmers with their food and money.

READING FOR MEANING

This section presents three activities that will help you reread McPhee's observational essay with a critical eye. Done in sequence, these activities lead you from a basic understanding of the selection to a more personal response to it and finally to an analysis that deepens your understanding and critical thinking about what you are reading.

Read to Comprehend

Reread paragraphs 1–5 and 22, and jot down the types of crime McPhee observes at the farmer's market. Also make a list of any words you do not understand—for example, *rifling* (paragraph 1), *equanimity* (22), *expounding* (24). Look up their meanings in a dictionary to see which definition best fits the context.

To expand your understanding of this reading, you might use one or more of the following critical reading strategies that are explained and illustrated in Appendix 1: *outlining, summarizing, paraphrasing,* and *questioning to understand and remember.*

Read to Respond

Write several paragraphs exploring your initial thoughts and feelings about McPhee's observational essay. Focus on anything that stands out for you, perhaps because it resonates with your own experience or because you find a statement puzzling.

You might consider writing about

- what happens to Catherine Barta, and how the farmers at the market treat her, perhaps in relation to your own experience as a victim of crime.

- how the farmers reacted to Lewis's suggestion that they "should regularly announce in loud voices that pickpockets were present in the market" (paragraph 1), compared to how you would respond if you were a farmer or a shopper at the market.

- your response to the police officer's conclusion that "there is nothing he can do" (20).

- your response to Todd Jameson's story about the customer who returned the bag with fifty dollars in rolled coins (23).

To develop your response to McPhee's essay, you might use one or more of the following critical reading strategies that are explained and illustrated in Appendix 1: *contextualizing, reflecting on challenges to your beliefs and values, recognizing emotional manipulation,* and *judging the writer's credibility.*

Read to Analyze Underlying Assumptions

Write several paragraphs exploring one or more of the assumptions, values, and beliefs underlying McPhee's observational essay. As you write, explain how the assumptions are reflected in the text, as well as what you now think of them (and perhaps of your own assumptions) after rereading the selection with a critical eye.

You might consider writing about

- the assumptions underlying McPhee's assertion that "[c]rime on such levels is a part of the background here, something in the urban air" (paragraph 2), versus Todd Jameson's remark that no one in his hometown in New Jersey would return money received in error (23), perhaps in relation to your own assumptions about differences between cities and small towns or suburbs or in relation to conditions in the late 1970s, when McPhee was writing.

- the cultural assumption expressed by Barry Benepe: "This isn't England, . . . and a lot of people are pretty dishonest" (4), perhaps in relation to your own cultural assumptions about different nationalities or ethnicities.

- the assumptions and values behind John Labanowski's story of a white woman and a black woman disagreeing on the usefulness of beet greens (24).

- the values behind Rich Hodgson's reaction to his "foolishness" at being "conned . . . out of nine dollars, five cents, and a box of brown eggs" (22).

To probe assumptions more deeply, you might use one or more of the following critical reading strategies that are explained and illustrated in Appendix 1: *reflecting on challenges to your beliefs and values, exploring the significance of figurative language,* and *looking for patterns of opposition.*

READING LIKE A WRITER
ORGANIZING THE OBSERVATIONS

McPhee uses a narrative organization to present his observations chronologically, as they occur along a time line. His story begins "just before noon" (first sentence of paragraph 1) and ends as "dusk comes down" (first sentence of paragraph 24). To keep readers from getting confused about what is happening as the narrative moves along, McPhee uses narrative time markers. These markers include words and phrases that note the time of day (such as "noon" and "by two" in sentences 1 and 4 of paragraph 1) or indicate when something happened relative to when something else happened (such as "until a moment ago" and "but now" in sentence 6). This easy-to-follow chronological structure pushes readers along, keeping them on track as they are catapulted into the noisy, crowded world of the farmer's market.

For most of the essay, the narrative moves forward in time. But McPhee's narrative is not simple. He interweaves into his narrative of what happened that afternoon references to events that occurred at various points in the past. In the middle of paragraph 1, for example, the phrases "Lewis once sent word" and "I once looked up and saw" refer to events that occurred sometime before this particular afternoon. These references to earlier events give McPhee's narrative a thick fabric, enabling readers to imagine not only the swirl of activities occurring that afternoon but also what the market has been like on other occasions when McPhee was there observing the activity.

Analyze

1. *Skim* the selection, and *underline* the time markers, beginning with "just before noon" in the opening sentence of the essay.

2. *Note in the margin* which time markers refer to events that occurred that afternoon and which occurred in the past.

Write

Write several sentences describing how McPhee uses time markers to help readers understand which events occurred that afternoon and which occurred at other times. How effectively do the time markers keep you oriented? *Indicate* any passages in the essay where you are confused about when something happened.

Compare

To understand the difference between narrative and topical organization in observational writing, *compare* McPhee's narrative plan with the topical organization used in "Soup" (pp. 86–89). Given the subject and the writer's purpose in each essay, what advantages and disadvantages do you see in the type of organization chosen?

Write several sentences speculating about why each writer chose the particular organizational plan. Instead of working chronologically, could McPhee have organized the essay topically by the various types of crime he observes at the market, using anecdotes as examples of each type? Could the *New Yorker* writer have told the story of a typical day at the soup kitchen, weaving the various topics he discusses into the narrative of a day? *Consider* these alternatives, and *speculate about* why the writers might have chosen the plans they did.

CONSIDERING IDEAS FOR YOUR OWN WRITING

Public scenes crowded with people and action offer good material for observational essays. Crowds also present problems, mainly because of their size and scope: So many people are present and so much is happening at once that the observer may not be able to decide where to focus. Notice how McPhee solves this problem by remaining in one location, the stall where he is selling vegetables. The action takes place in one small area of a huge market, focusing on only a few people and events.

You could likewise find such a focus for an observational essay in some large public scene. Here are a few examples to start you thinking: the souvenir sellers or groundskeepers at a baseball game; a lifeguard station at a beach; an unusual store or restaurant at a shopping mall; one stall at a flea market; a small group of riders from the same club at a Harley-Davidson motorcycle reunion; one section of your college library; an ice-skating rink at a city park; a musician, vendor, or guard in a subway station. You need not seek to find some unexpected activity, like the pickpocketing at the Brooklyn farmer's market, but you could probably interest readers in the people and activities in one limited area of a public place— as a way of giving them a distinct impression of the large, complex public space.

AMANDA COYNE

The Long Good-Bye: Mother's Day in Federal Prison

Amanda Coyne (b. 1966), an award-winning staff writer for The Anchorage Press, *earned a master's degree in nonfiction writing from the University of Iowa. She wrote "The Long Good-Bye," her first piece of published writing, for the May 1997 issue of* Harper's, *a monthly magazine that publishes profiles of interesting people and places, autobiographical and reflective essays, and informative reports on current social and political issues.*

As Coyne explains in the essay, her observations are based on a one-day visit to a minimum security women's prison where her sister is incarcerated. She writes about her sister and other women in a similar situation to inform readers and to awaken their concern about the injustice of prison terms for people, especially girlfriends and wives, who aided drug dealers.

As you read, pay particular attention to Coyne's focus on two inmates, Jennifer (her sister) and Stephanie, and their relationships with their sons.

You can spot the convict-moms here in the visiting room by the way they hold and touch their children and by the single flower that is perched in front of them—a rose, a tulip, a daffodil. Many of these mothers have untied the bow that attaches the flower to its silver-and-red cellophane wrapper and are using one of the many empty soda cans at hand as a vase. They sit proudly before their flower-in-a-Coke-can, amid Hershey bar wrappers, half-eaten Ding Dongs, and empty paper coffee cups. Occasionally, a mother will pick up her present and bring it to her nose when one of the bearers of the single flower—her child—asks if she likes it. And the mother will respond the way that mothers always have and always will respond when presented with a gift on this day. "Oh, I just love it. It's perfect. I'll put it in the middle of my Bible." Or, "I'll put it on my desk, right next to your school picture." And always: "It's the best one here." 1

But most of what is being smelled today is the children themselves. While the other adults are plunking coins into the vending machines, the mothers take deep whiffs from the backs of their children's necks, or kiss and smell the backs of their knees, or take off their shoes and tickle their feet and then pull them close to their noses. They hold them tight and take in their own second scent—the scent assuring them that these are still their children and that they still belong to them. 2

The visitors are allowed to bring in pockets full of coins, and today that Mother's Day flower, and I know from previous visits to my older sister here at the Federal Prison Camp for women in Pekin, Illinois, that there is always an aberrant urge to gather immediately around the vending machines. The sandwiches are stale, the coffee weak, the candy bars the ones we always pass up in a convenience store. But after we hand the children over to their mothers, we gravitate toward those machines. Like milling in the kitchen at a party. We all do it, and nobody knows why. Polite conversation ensues around the microwave while the popcorn is popping and the processed-chicken sandwiches are being heated. We ask one another where we are from, how long a drive we had. An occasional whistle through the teeth, a shake of the head. "My, my, long way from home, huh?" "Staying at the Super 8 right up the road. Not a bad place." "Stayed at the Econo Lodge last time. Wasn't a good place at all." Never asking the questions we really want to ask: "What's she in for?" "How much time's she got left?" You never ask in the waiting room of a doctor's office either. Eventually, all of us—fathers, mothers, sisters, brothers, a few boyfriends, and very few husbands—return to the queen of the day, sitting at a fold-out table loaded with snacks, prepared for five or so hours of attempted normal conversation.

Most of the inmates are elaborately dressed, many in prison-crafted dresses and sweaters in bright blues and pinks. They wear meticulously applied makeup in corresponding hues, and their hair is replete with loops and curls—hair that only women with the time have the time for. Some of the better seamstresses have crocheted vests and purses to match their outfits. Although the world outside would never accuse these women of making haute-couture fashion statements, the fathers and the sons and the boyfriends and the very few husbands think they look beautiful, and they tell them so repeatedly. And I can imagine the hours spent preparing for this visit—hours of needles and hooks clicking over brightly colored yards of yarn. The hours of discussing, dissecting, and bragging about these visitors—especially the men. Hours spent in the other world behind the door where we're not allowed, sharing lipsticks and mascaras, and unraveling the occasional hair-tangled hot roller, and the brushing out and lifting and teasing . . . and the giggles that abruptly change into tears without warning—things that define any female-only world. Even, or especially, if that world is a female federal prison camp.

While my sister Jennifer is with her son in the playroom, an inmate's mother comes over to introduce herself to my younger sister, Charity, my brother, John, and me. She tells us about visiting her daughter in a higher-security prison before she was transferred here. The woman looks old and tired, and her shoulders sag under the weight of her recently acquired bitterness.

"Pit of fire," she says, shaking her head. "Like a pit of fire straight from hell. Never seen anything like it. Like something out of an old movie about prisons." Her voice is getting louder and she looks at each of us with pleading eyes. "My *daughter* was there. Don't even get me started on that place. Women die there." 6

John and Charity and I silently exchange glances. 7

"My daughter would come to the visiting room with a black eye and I'd think, 'All she did was sit in the car while her boyfriend ran into the house.' She didn't even touch the stuff. Never even handled it." 8

She continues to stare at us, each in turn. "Ten years. That boyfriend talked and he got three years. She didn't know anything. Had nothing to tell them. They gave her ten years. They called it conspiracy. Conspiracy? Aren't there real criminals out there?" She asks this with hands outstretched, waiting for an answer that none of us can give her. 9

The woman's daughter, the conspirator, is chasing her son through the maze of chairs and tables and through the other children. She's a twenty-four-year-old blonde, whom I'll call Stephanie, with Dorothy Hamill hair and matching dimples. She looks like any girl you might see in any shopping mall in middle America. She catches her chocolate-brown son and tickles him, and they laugh and trip and fall together onto the floor and laugh harder. 10

Had it not been for that wait in the car, this scene would be taking place at home, in a duplex Stephanie would rent while trying to finish her two-year degree in dental hygiene or respiratory therapy at the local community college. The duplex would be spotless, with a blown-up picture of her and her son over the couch and ceramic unicorns and horses occupying the shelves of the entertainment center. She would make sure that her son went to school every day with stylishly floppy pants, scrubbed teeth, and a good breakfast in his belly. Because of their difference in skin color, there would be occasional tension—caused by the strange looks from strangers, teachers, other mothers, and the bullies on the playground, who would chant after they knocked him down, "Your Momma's white, your Momma's white." But if she were home, their weekends and evenings would be spent together transcending those looks and healing those bruises. Now, however, their time is spent eating visiting-room junk food and his school days 11 are spent fighting the boys in the playground who chant, "Your Momma's in prison, your Momma's in prison."

He will be ten when his mother is released, the same age my nephew will be when his mother is let out. But Jennifer, my sister, was able to spend the first five years of Toby's life with him. Stephanie had Ellie after she was incarcerated. They let her hold him for eighteen hours, then sent her back to prison. She has done the "tour," and her son is a well-traveled six-year-old. He has spent weekends visiting his mother in prisons in Kentucky, Texas, Connecticut (the Pit of Fire), and now at last here, the camp—minimum security, Pekin, Illinois.

Ellie looks older than his age. But his shoulders do not droop like his grandmother's. On the contrary, his bitterness lifts them and his chin higher than a child's should be, and the childlike, wide-eyed curiosity has been replaced by defiance. You can see his emerging hostility as he and his mother play together. She tells him to pick up the toy that he threw, say, or to put the deck of cards away. His face turns sullen, but she persists. She takes him by the shoulders and looks him in the eye, and he uses one of his hands to swat at her. She grabs the hand and he swats with the other. Eventually, she pulls him toward her and smells the top of his head, and she picks up the cards or the toy herself. After all, it is Mother's Day and she sees him so rarely. But her acquiescence makes him angrier, and he stalks out of the playroom with his shoulders thrown back.

Toby, my brother and sister and I assure one another, will not have these resentments. He is better taken care of than most. He is living with relatives in Wisconsin. Good, solid, middle-class, churchgoing relatives. And when he visits us, his aunts and his uncle, we take him out for adventures where we walk down the alley of a city and pretend that we are being chased by the "bad guys." We buy him fast food, and his uncle, John, keeps him up well past his bedtime enthralling him with stories of the monkeys he met in India. A perfect mix, we try to convince one another. Until we take him to see his mother and on the drive back he asks the question that most confuses him, and no doubt all the other children who spend much of their lives in prison visiting rooms: "Is my Mommy a bad guy?" It is the question that most seriously disorders his five-year-old need to clearly separate right from wrong. And because our own need is perhaps just as great, it is the question that haunts us as well.

Now, however, the answer is relatively simple. In a few years, it won't be. In a few years we will have to explain mandatory minimums, and the war on drugs, and the murky conspiracy laws, and the enormous amount of money and time that federal agents pump into imprisoning low-level drug dealers and those who happen to be their friends and their lovers. In a few years he might have the reasoning skills to ask why so many armed robbers and rapists and child-molesters and, indeed, murderers are punished less severely than his mother. When he is older, we will somehow have to explain to him the difference between federal crimes, which don't allow for parole, and state crimes, which do. We will have to explain that his mother was taken from him for five years not because she was a drug dealer but because she made four phone calls for someone she loved.

But we also know it is vitally important that we explain all this 16
without betraying our bitterness. We understand the danger of abstract anger, of being disillusioned with your country, and, most of all, we do not want him to inherit that legacy. We would still like him to be raised as we were, with the idea that we live in the best country in the world with the best legal system in the world—a legal system carefully designed to be immune to political mood swings and public hysteria; a system that promises to fit the punishment to the crime. We want him to be a good citizen. We want him to have absolute faith that he lives in a fair country, a country that watches over and protects its most vulnerable citizens: its women and children.

So for now we simply say, "Toby, your mother isn't bad, she just 17
did a bad thing. Like when you put rocks in the lawn mower's gas tank. You weren't bad then, you just did a bad thing."

Once, after being given this weak explanation, he said, "I wish I 18
could have done something really bad, like my Mommy. So I could go to prison too and be with her."

It's now 3:00. Visiting ends at 3:30. The kids are getting cranky, 19
and the adults are both exhausted and wired from too many hours of conversation, too much coffee and candy. The fathers, mothers, sisters, brothers, and the few boyfriends, and the very few husbands are beginning to show signs of gathering the trash. The mothers of the infants are giving their heads one last whiff before tucking them and their paraphernalia into their respective carrying cases. The visitors meander toward the door, leaving the older children with their mothers for one last word. But the mothers never say what they want to say to their children. They say things like, "Do well in school," "Be nice to your sister," "Be good for Aunt Berry, or Grandma." They don't say, "I'm sorry I'm sorry I'm sorry. I love you more than anything else in the world and I think about you every minute and I worry about you with a pain that shoots straight to my heart, a pain so great I think I will just burst when I think of you alone, without me. I'm sorry."

We are standing in front of the double glass doors that lead to 20
the outside world. My older sister holds her son, rocking him
gently. They are both crying. We give her a look and she puts him
down. Charity and I grasp each of his small hands, and the four of
us walk through the doors. As we're walking out, my brother sings
one of his banana songs to Toby.

"Take me out to the—" and Toby yells out, "Banana store!" 21
"Buy me some—" 22
"Bananas!!" 23
"I don't care if I ever come back. For it's root, root, root for 24
the—"
"Monkey team!" 25

I turn back and see a line of women standing behind the glass 26
wall. Some of them are crying, but many simply stare with dazed
eyes. Stephanie is holding both of her son's hands in hers and
speaking urgently to him. He is struggling, and his head is twisting
violently back and forth. He frees one of his hands from her grasp,
balls up his fist, and punches her in the face. Then he walks with
purpose through the glass doors and out the exit. I look back at her.
She is still in a crouched position. She stares, unblinking, through
those doors. Her hands have left her face and are hanging on either
side of her. I look away, but before I do, I see drops of blood drip
from her nose, down her chin, and onto the shiny marble floor.

READING FOR MEANING

This section presents three activities that will help you reread Coyne's observational essay with a critical eye. Done in sequence, these activities lead you from a
basic understanding of the selection to a more personal response to it and finally
to an analysis that deepens your understanding and critical thinking about what
you are reading.

Read to Comprehend

Reread the selection, and write a few sentences briefly describing the two
inmates, Jennifer and Stephanie, and their relationships with their sons. Also
make a list of any words you do not understand—for example, *aberrant* (paragraph 3), *replete* (4), *acquiescence* (13), *paraphernalia* (19). Look up their meanings in a dictionary to see which definition best fits the context.

To expand your understanding of this reading, you might use one or more
of the following critical reading strategies that are explained and illustrated in
Appendix 1: *outlining, summarizing, paraphrasing,* and *questioning to understand
and remember.*

Read to Respond

Write several paragraphs exploring your initial thoughts and feelings about Coyne's observational essay. Focus on anything that stands out for you, perhaps because it resonates with your own experience or because you find a statement puzzling.

You might consider writing about

- the homey details used to describe the visiting room and the impressions they convey to you (paragraphs 1–4).

- your response to the story about the inmate who got ten years for waiting in the car while her boyfriend, who got three years, committed a crime (5–9).

- the fact that only "a few boyfriends, and very few husbands" visit the women inmates (3).

- Ellie's attitude and behavior toward Stephanie (13, 26).

- the idea that a person may be good even though his or her behavior may be bad (17), as Coyne believes is the case with her sister.

To develop your response to Coyne's essay, you might use one or more of the following critical reading strategies that are explained and illustrated in Appendix 1: *contextualizing, reflecting on challenges to your beliefs and values, recognizing emotional manipulation,* and *judging the writer's credibility.*

Read to Analyze Underlying Assumptions

Write several paragraphs exploring one or more of the assumptions, values, and beliefs underlying Coyne's observational essay. As you write, explain how the assumptions are reflected in the text, as well as what you now think of them (and perhaps of your own assumptions) after rereading the selection with a critical eye.

You might consider writing about

- the assumptions behind the mothers' habit of smelling their children (paragraph 2).

- the cultural assumptions behind Coyne's observations of Stephanie and her son.

- Coyne's assumption that, unlike Ellie, Toby will not resent his mother because he is living with "[g]ood, solid, middle-class, churchgoing relatives" (14).

- Coyne's assumptions about the fairness of the U.S. judicial and penal systems, perhaps in relation to your own experience or observation.

- why Coyne assumes "the mothers never say what they want to say to their children" (19).

To probe assumptions more deeply, you might use one or more of the following critical reading strategies that are explained and illustrated in Appendix 1: *reflecting on challenges to your beliefs and values, exploring the significance of figurative language,* and *looking for patterns of opposition.*

READING LIKE A WRITER
DESCRIBING PEOPLE

Writers of observational essays often focus their observations on people, alone or interacting with others. To present people, writers can choose from a repertoire of strategies. They may tell us how people look and dress, characterize their behavior or emotions, let us hear them talk, show them gesturing and moving, or compare them to other people. One of the most vividly described people in this reading is Ellie, Stephanie's six-year-old son. Coyne describes him mainly through his actions—his movements and gestures.

Analyze

1. *Reread* paragraphs 13 and 26, and *underline* the details that enable you to imagine Ellie. *Underline* details about his age, comparisons to other people, characterizations of his emotions, and details about his movements and gestures.

2. In the margin beside these paragraphs, *make notes* about the impression you get of Ellie and his relationship with his mother from the details you underlined.

Write

Write several sentences explaining how Coyne describes Ellie, giving examples from your annotations. *Add a few more sentences* identifying what you think is the most effective part of the description and explaining why you think it works so well.

CONSIDERING IDEAS FOR YOUR OWN WRITING

You might write about a public place where you can observe parents and children interacting, such as a neighborhood playground, a beach, a restaurant, or a toy store. Another possibility is to visit a place where people live in a communal setting, such as a hospital, a home for the elderly, or a halfway house. Alternatively, you might consider places where people see each other routinely but do not know each other very well; for example, a gym, a night course at the local community college, or a Little League baseball game.

A SPECIAL READING STRATEGY

Scratch Outlining

Outlining, especially *scratch outlining*, is an easy and surprisingly helpful strategy for reading critically. To outline a long and complicated essay like "The Long Good-Bye: Mother's Day in Federal Prison," you must distinguish between the essay's main ideas and its many supporting details and examples. Turn to pages 658–59 in Appendix 1 for detailed guidelines on scratch outlining.

BRIAN CABLE

The Last Stop

> Brian Cable wrote the following observational essay when he was
> a first-year college student. His observations are based on a onetime
> visit to a mortuary, or funeral home, a subject he views with both seri-
> ousness and humor. Hoping as he enters the mortuary not to end up
> as a participant that day, he records what he sees and interviews two
> key people, the funeral director and the embalmer. In reporting his
> observations, he seems equally concerned with the burial process—
> from the purchase of a casket to the display of the body—and the peo-
> ple who manage this process.
>
> As you read, notice how the writer presents the place and people
> and how he attempts to heighten readers' interest in the mortuary by
> considering it in the larger, social context of people's beliefs about
> death and burial.

Let us endeavor so to live that when we come to die even the undertaker
will be sorry.

—Mark Twain

Death is a subject largely ignored by the living. We don't discuss   1
it much, not as children (when Grandpa dies, he is said to be "going
away"), not as adults, not even as senior citizens. Throughout our
lives, death remains intensely private. The death of a loved one can
be very painful, partly because of the sense of loss, but also because
someone else's mortality reminds us all too vividly of our own.

Thus did I notice more than a few people avert their eyes as they   2
walked past the dusty-pink building that houses the Goodbody
Mortuaries. It looked a bit like a church—tall, with gothic arches
and stained glass—and somewhat like an apartment complex—
low, with many windows stamped out of red brick.

It wasn't at all what I had expected. I thought it would be more   3
like Forest Lawn, serene with lush green lawns and meticulously
groomed gardens, a place set apart from the hustle of day-to-day
life. Here instead was an odd pink structure set in the middle of a
business district. On top of the Goodbody Mortuaries sign was a
large electric clock. What the hell, I thought, mortuaries are concerned with time, too.

I was apprehensive as I climbed the stone steps to the entrance.   4
I feared rejection or, worse, an invitation to come and stay. The
door was massive, yet it swung open easily on well-oiled hinges.
"Come in," said the sign. "We're always open." Inside was a cool
and quiet reception room. Curtains were drawn against the outside glare, cutting the light down to a soft glow.

I found the funeral director in the main lobby, adjacent to the   5
reception room. Like most people, I had preconceptions about
what an undertaker looked like. Mr. Deaver fulfilled my expectations entirely. Tall and thin, he even had beady eyes and a bony
face. A low, slanted forehead gave way to a beaked nose. His skin,
scrubbed of all color, contrasted sharply with his jet black hair. He
was wearing a starched white shirt, gray pants, and black shoes.
Indeed, he looked like death on two legs.

He proved an amiable sort, however, and was easy to talk to. As   6
funeral director, Mr. Deaver ("call me Howard") was responsible
for a wide range of services. Goodbody Mortuaries, upon notifica-
tion of someone's death, will remove the remains from the hospital or home. They then prepare the body for viewing, whereupon
features distorted by illness or accident are restored to their natural
condition. The body is embalmed and then placed in a casket
selected by the family of the deceased. Services are held in one of
three chapels at the mortuary, and afterward the casket is placed in
a "visitation room," where family and friends can pay their last
respects. Goodbody also makes arrangements for the purchase of
a burial site and transports the body there for burial.

All this information Howard related in a well-practiced, profes-   7
sional manner. It was obvious he was used to explaining the
specifics of his profession. We sat alone in the lobby. His desk was
bone clean, no pencils or paper, nothing—just a telephone. He did
all his paperwork at home; as it turned out, he and his wife lived
right upstairs. The phone rang. As he listened, he bit his lips and
squeezed his Adam's apple somewhat nervously.

"I think we'll be able to get him in by Friday. No, no, the family   8
wants him cremated."

His tone was that of a broker conferring on the Dow Jones.   9
Directly behind him was a sign announcing "Visa and Master Charge
Welcome Here." It was tacked to the wall, right next to a crucifix.

"Some people have the idea that we are bereavement specialists,   10
that we can handle the emotional problems which follow a death:
Only a trained therapist can do that. We provide services for the
dead, not counseling for the living."

Physical comfort was the one thing they did provide for the liv-   11
ing. The lobby was modestly but comfortably furnished. There
were several couches, in colors ranging from earth brown to pastel
blue, and a coffee table in front of each one. On one table lay some
magazines and a vase of flowers. Another supported an aquarium.
Paintings of pastoral scenes hung on every wall. The lobby looked
more or less like that of an old hotel. Nothing seemed to match,
but it had a homey, lived-in look.

"The last time the Goodbodies decorated was in '59, I believe.   12
It still makes people feel welcome."

And so "Goodbody" was not a name made up to attract cus-   13
tomers but the owners' family name. The Goodbody family started
the business way back in 1915. Today, they do over five hundred
services a year.

"We're in *Ripley's Believe It or Not,* along with another funeral   14
home whose owners' names are Baggit and Sackit," Howard told
me, without cracking a smile.

I followed him through an arched doorway into a chapel that   15
smelled musty and old. The only illumination came from sunlight
filtered through a stained glass ceiling. Ahead of us lay a casket. I
could see that it contained a man dressed in a black suit. Wooden
benches ran on either side of an aisle that led to the body. I got no
closer. From the red roses across the dead man's chest, it was
apparent that services had already been held.

"It was a large service," remarked Howard. "Look at that casket—   16
a beautiful work of craftsmanship."

I guess it was. Death may be the great leveler, but one's coffin   17
quickly reestablishes one's status.

We passed into a bright, fluorescent-lit "display room." Inside   18
were thirty coffins, lids open, patiently awaiting inspection. Like
new cars on the showroom floor, they gleamed with high-gloss
finishes.

"We have models for every price range."   19

Indeed, there was a wide variety. They came in all colors and   20
various materials. Some were little more than cloth-covered cardboard boxes, others were made of wood, and a few were made of
steel, copper, or bronze. Prices started at $400 and averaged about
$1,800. Howard motioned toward the center of the room: "The
top of the line."

This was a solid bronze casket, its seams electronically welded   21
to resist corrosion. Moisture-proof and air-tight, it could be her-
metically sealed off from all outside elements. Its handles were
plated with 14-karat gold. The price: a cool $5,000.

A proper funeral remains a measure of respect for the deceased.   22
But it is expensive. In the United States the amount spent annually on funerals is about $2 billion. Among ceremonial expendi-
tures, funerals are second only to weddings. As a result, practices
are changing. Howard has been in this business for forty years.
He remembers a time when everyone was buried. Nowadays,
with burials costing $2,000 a shot, people often opt instead for
cremation—as Howard put it, "a cheap, quick, and easy means of dis-
posal." In some areas of the country, the cremation rate is now over

60 percent. Observing this trend, one might wonder whether burials are becoming obsolete. Do burials serve an important role in society?

For Tim, Goodbody's licensed mortician, the answer is very definitely yes. Burials will remain in common practice, according to the slender embalmer with the disarming smile, because they allow family and friends to view the deceased. Painful as it may be, such an experience brings home the finality of death. "Something deep within us demands a confrontation with death," Tim explained. "A last look assures us that the person we loved is, indeed, gone forever."

Apparently, we also need to be assured that the body will be laid to rest in comfort and peace. The average casket, with its inner-spring mattress and pleated satin lining, is surprisingly roomy and luxurious. Perhaps such an air of comfort makes it easier for the family to give up their loved one. In addition, the burial site fixes the deceased in the survivors' memory, like a new address. Cremation provides none of these comforts.

Tim started out as a clerk in a funeral home but then studied to become a mortician. "It was a profession I could live with," he told me with a sly grin. Mortuary science might be described as a cross between pre-med and cosmetology, with courses in anatomy and embalming as well as in restorative art.

Tim let me see the preparation, or embalming, room, a white-walled chamber about the size of an operating room. Against the wall was a large sink with elbow taps and a draining board. In the center of the room stood a table with equipment for preparing the arterial embalming fluid, which consists primarily of formaldehyde, a preservative, and phenol, a disinfectant. This mixture sanitizes and also gives better color to the skin. Facial features can then be "set" to achieve a restful expression. Missing eyes, ears, and even noses can be replaced.

I asked Tim if his job ever depressed him. He bridled at the question: "No, it doesn't depress me at all. I do what I can for people and take satisfaction in enabling relatives to see their loved ones as they were in life." He said that he felt people were becoming more aware of the public service his profession provides. Grade-school classes now visit funeral homes as often as they do police stations and museums. The mortician is no longer regarded as a minister of death.

Before leaving, I wanted to see a body up close. I thought I could be indifferent after all I had seen and heard, but I wasn't sure. Cautiously, I reached out and touched the skin. It felt cold and firm, not unlike clay. As I walked out, I felt glad to have satisfied my curiosity about dead bodies, but all too happy to let someone else handle them.

READING FOR MEANING

This section presents three activities that will help you reread Cable's observational essay with a critical eye. Done in sequence, these activities lead you from a basic understanding of the selection to a more personal response to it and finally to an analysis that deepens your understanding and critical thinking about what you are reading.

Read to Comprehend

Reread the selection, and write a few sentences briefly explaining what you learned about the activities that take place at a funeral home. Also make a list of any words you do not understand—for example, *mortality* (paragraph 1), *avert* (2), *pastoral* (11), *cosmetology* (25). Look up their meanings in a dictionary to see which definition best fits the context.

To expand your understanding of this reading, you might use one or more of the following critical reading strategies that are explained and illustrated in Appendix 1: *outlining, summarizing, paraphrasing,* and *questioning to understand and remember.*

Read to Respond

Write several paragraphs exploring one or more of the assumptions, values, and beliefs underlying Cable's observational essay. As you write, explain how the assumptions are reflected in the text, as well as what you now think of them (and perhaps of your own assumptions) after rereading the selection with a critical eye.

You might consider writing about

- your response to Cable's assertion that death is a subject we don't like to talk about "because someone else's mortality reminds us all too vividly of our own" (paragraph 1), perhaps in comparison to Tim's idea that "[s]omething deep within us demands a confrontation with death" (23).

- Cable's descriptions of Howard Deaver as having a "tone [like] that of a broker conferring on the Dow Jones" (9) and of coffins displayed "[l]ike new cars on the showroom floor" (18).

- Tim's claim that "[g]rade-school classes now visit funeral homes as often as they do police stations and museums" (27), perhaps in relation to the field trips you took in grade school.

- Cable's curiosity "about dead bodies" and what one feels like (28), in relation to your own firsthand experience of death.

To develop your response to Cable's essay, you might use one or more of the following critical reading strategies that are explained and illustrated in Appendix 1: *contextualizing, reflecting on challenges to your beliefs and values, recognizing emotional manipulation,* and *judging the writer's credibility.*

Read to Analyze Underlying Assumptions

Write several paragraphs exploring one or more of the assumptions, values, and beliefs underlying Cable's observational essay. As you write, explain how the assumptions are reflected in the text, as well as what you now think of them (and perhaps of your own assumptions) after rereading the selection with a critical eye.

You might consider writing about

- Cable's "preconceptions about what an undertaker looked like" (paragraph 5), in relation to stereotypical images of undertakers in fiction and the media.

- the assumptions behind Howard Deaver's statement that Goodbody Mortuaries "provide[s] services for the dead, not counseling for the living" (10).

- the assumptions and values underlying Cable's assertion that "[d]eath may be the great leveler, but one's coffin quickly reestablishes one's status" (17).

- your cultural, familial, and religious beliefs about death and burial (or cremation), compared with those expressed by Howard Deaver and Tim.

To probe assumptions more deeply, you might use one or more of the following critical reading strategies that are explained and illustrated in Appendix 1: *reflecting on challenges to your beliefs and values, exploring the significance of figurative language,* and *looking for patterns of opposition.*

READING LIKE A WRITER
CONVEYING AN IMPRESSION OF THE SUBJECT

Writers of observational essays are more than reporters. They do seek to inform readers about a subject, but they go further to convey to readers their impression of a subject. The impression is like an interpretation of the subject or an insight into it. Writers may create an impression in several ways: by revealing their attitude toward the place and people there, by stating their impression directly, or by implying an impression through the way they describe the subject. Readers may not find a sentence beginning "My impression is . . . ," but they will nevertheless get a distinct impression of the subject.

Analyze

1. *Underline* words and phrases in the essay that suggest Cable's attitudes toward or feelings about Goodbody Mortuaries. *Be selective;* in a successful essay, every detail reveals the author's attitude, but certain details will be especially revealing.

2. *Note in the margin* what your annotations seem to reveal about Cable's attitude toward his subject.

Write

Write several sentences explaining the impression you get about Goodbody Mortuaries, supporting your explanation with examples from the reading. Then *add a few sentences* evaluating how successful you think Cable is in conveying an impression of the funeral home.

CONSIDERING IDEAS FOR YOUR OWN WRITING

Think of places or activities about which you have strong preconceptions or with which you have had little or no experience, and yet have been curious about, or perhaps even put off by. Maybe in your neighborhood there is an upscale gym where you assume participants are interested primarily in posing for and competing with each other, a day-care center where you assume the teachers are idealistic and devoted to the children, a tattoo parlor where you assume all the clients are young, an acupuncture clinic where you doubt there is any scientific basis for the treatments, or a fast-food place where you expect that nearly all employees find their jobs onerous and unrewarding. Or perhaps on your campus there is a tutoring center where you assume tutors do students' work for them, a student counseling center where you have been led to believe that students are not treated with sympathy and understanding, or an office that seems to schedule campus events at times that make it difficult for commuter students to participate. Because many readers would likely share your preconceptions and curiosity, you would have a relatively easy time engaging their interest in the subject. How would you test your preconceptions through your observations and interviews? How might you use your preconceptions to capture readers' attention, as Cable does?

BRENDA CROW

The Dance with Glass

> *Brenda Crow wrote this observational essay when she was a first-year student at Front Range Community College, Larimer, in Fort Collins, Colorado. Crow describes in precise detail the materials and equipment that clutter Daggett Glass Studio. Perhaps most notable about her essay is the poetic way she narrates the process by which Dan Daggett creates his art. As you read, notice how Crow interweaves technical terms and definitions into her rhythmic narrative.*
>
> *The other readings in this chapter are followed by reading and writing activities. Following this reading, however, you are on your own to decide how to read for meaning and read like a writer.*

The door to one of the ovens is opened. Inside the light is intensely bright, glowing brighter than a volcano's lava. Four feet away, it feels as though going any closer would surely melt flesh from bone. Clear glass is being heated to a Day-Glo bright 2,150 degrees Fahrenheit. 1

The glassblower pushes one end of a five-foot-long stainless steel rod, called a *punty,* a couple of inches deep into the molten glass. He picks up the lump of molten glass and twirls the rod continuously as he closes the door of the oven and moves over to a metal worktable. He then lays the punty on to the tabletop and begins rolling the molten glass along the table's surface. "This is *mavering,*" he tells me. 2

On the right side of the table he has laid out three rows, each five inches long and a half-inch wide, of tiny, colored glass chips, poured from a collection of clear plastic bags and an odd assortment of coffee cans and Styrofoam cups that surround the table's edge. "*Frit,*" he says. 3

From oven, to table, to *glory hole,* a kiln-like oven with no door, the glassblower moves the molten glass. Glowing. Hot, hot, hot. The glassblower lays the punty on a small metal stand with two small rollers on the top. The opposite end of the punty is in the glory hole, reheating the glass. 4

"*Glory hole* got its name because that's where all the glory happens. That's where all the colors come together," he says. 5

The glassblower is constantly turning, always turning, and moving, always moving the punty inside the glory hole. Right to left, left to right. "*Flashing,*" he says. 6

Back to the table, more mavering. He then lays the liquid glass, which is suspended on the end of the punty, into the frit. He then lifts the punty, rotates it a half turn, and again lays the liquid glass 7 into the frit. He repeats the process yet again. He works quickly, the punty always moving, always spinning. Back to the glory hole, reheating the glass and melting the frit into the core of clear, molten glass. More mavering, again to the glory hole. Spinning, turning, spinning, rotating.

Quickly he lays the edge of the punty on one of the metal brackets, pushes it forward into the glory hole, slides in behind it, and sits with his back toward me. The pressed-wood bench he sits on sags slightly from his weight. He pulls the punty back, bringing the end with the molten glass closer to him. In swift, fluid movements, he lifts a wet, wooden block from one of the murky, water-filled, five-gallon buckets on either side of the bench. The blackened cup-shaped block on a long wooden handle has a section of the side cut away. With the punty resting on the bracket, he touches the glass with the cup-shaped block, steam rises, water hisses. He rounds the molten glass with it.

Up, off the bench, moving always moving, glory hole, more flashing, spinning, more spinning, back to the bench in fluid movement, this is the dance with glass. He lifts a pair of shears, places them an inch from the far end of the glass, and applies pressure. Turning, always turning the punty, slower now, pulling with the shears, extending the softened glass and causing a swirl pattern to form from the frit he had embedded into the clear glass moments earlier. Waiting now, gauging the temperature of the glass, he squeezes the shears harder, then pinches off a round piece of glass the size of a baseball. "Christmas ornament," states the glassblower.

A sign, in royal blue letters four feet by two feet on a white background to the left of the door on the old brick wall, reads, "Daggett Glass Studio—Hand Blown Art Glass." The studio is housed in an old, nondescript building in downtown Loveland, Colorado. The studio is somewhat cluttered, but a couple hundred beautiful and delicate pieces of blown and hand-shaped glass line the wall on my right. Some pieces are hanging from strands of nearly invisible fishing line; others sit on cloth-covered tables and display cases. The glass is in every shade of green, blue, red, purple, orange, and yellow and in every conceivable shape I can imagine. Vases; bowls; paperweights; perfume bottles; candy dishes; "witch balls," which, when hung in a window, are supposed to keep evil spirits at bay; Christmas ornaments; icicles; candy canes; fruit; and fish are on display. As are solid, dome-shaped pieces of clear glass with mother-of-pearl powder suspended in them, pieces the glassblower calls "Ice Fog," which he created one day as he was "playing."

The studio has one exposed brick wall, on which the glass is displayed. The other walls are paneled on the bottom one-third of the wall and painted white on the upper two-thirds. The ceiling is covered with old Victorian pressed tin tiles that have been painted a rust color. The floor is old and wooden, worn from the passage of many years and many feet. Heavy sheets of metal, which squeak when walked on and are joined together with what appears to be scuffed-up duct tape, cover the floor between the ovens and the worktables. The back of the studio is four-feet deep in clutter; I imagine only the owner knows what resides there. To my left are the ovens. The annealing oven is at 950 degrees. It holds finished pieces of glass and is set to cool at 60 degrees per hour in order to limit stress on the cooling glass. Glass cooled too quickly shatters. Beyond the annealing oven is the oven that holds the molten glass. Between the two, glowing bright yellow-orange, is the glory hole. Discarded pieces of worked glass line the floor under the annealing oven. Covered in dust that only partially obscures their beauty, they look like discarded jewels.

As I draw nearer, the man sitting behind the desk at the far end of the studio bounds out of his chair and strides toward me as he says hello. Dan Daggett is a tall, rotund man with a warm, friendly demeanor. He has pleasant brown eyes; curly, somewhat frizzy, brownish-gray hair, which he often runs his fingers through; and a graying mustache, which completely covers his upper lip. He is casually dressed in an untucked white T-shirt, khakis, and tennis shoes. I feel immediately comfortable in his studio and begin asking questions and commenting on the wonderful pieces of art glass he has created. Dan holds up one of his many multicolored, iridescent swirled glass icicles: "A woman from a magazine called me and asked if I would mind if they featured these in an article of fun things to buy. Would I *mind*? I would be delighted," he smiles.

From the glory hole, Dan grabs a *blowpipe,* a hollow punty. After he has picked up a dab of molten glass, mavered it, reheated it in the glory hole, mavered it again, picked up some frit—this time shards of flat dichoric glass, which is dark on one side and looks like metallic foil on the other—flashed it and mavered it yet again, he lifts the blowpipe and blows into the end. Because of the liquid state of the glass, Dan needs only to blow gently: "Not at all like blowing up a balloon," he says. I stand at the opposite end of the blowpipe and see the air bubble come into the molten glass and stay suspended there. He is quickly moving away, spinning always spinning the blowpipe, working the glass. Back to the glory hole, flashing more flashing, turning always turning.

Clear glass comes in a surprising form: small, chalky-looking pebbles that are then thrown into the oven. Clear glass is inexpensive,

"Twenty-eight cents a pound. It costs me as much to ship it as it does to buy the glass itself. Colored glass is more expensive. Red, especially, because gold is needed to produce the color," Dan says. He doesn't make his own colored glass because of the chemicals involved. Arsenic and cyanide are two he mentions. He purchases rods or canes of colored glass, which are solid tubes of varying circumferences, from Kugler, a company in Germany. "There is a wide variety of colors with varying amounts of transparency or opaqueness available," Dan informs me. "Some glass comes as twisted multi-colored canes called *latticino*."

Interesting effects are produced by layering different colors of liquid glass and by introducing colored glass by different methods. Adding salt to molten glass produces an iridescent quality on the finished piece's surface. "*Millefiori* is a type of floral-patterned cane glass," Dan tells me. "It was first made in Murano, an island not far from Venice, Italy. The methods used for making it were kept secret for over 400 years, by threat of death! Once an apprentice learned how to make *millefiori,* he had to stay on the island." These small canes, a quarter of an inch in diameter, are broken into three-eighth-inch pieces and added to the layers of molten glass.   15

As it turns out, Dan is somewhat of a storyteller, and I could have stayed for hours watching him work and listening to him talk. I comment to Dan that it is obvious he is a happy man. "I am blessed," he says. "I get to come here every day and play. Every night I go home and thank the Lord that I get to do what I do. I knew from the very first time I worked with glass that this was what I wanted to do for the rest of my life. I fell in love with it, the romance of it, the beauty of the colors, the immediacy of working with it." As he works, Dan shares stories rich in glass history: the story of Muhammad and his armies building a fire in the desert at night and discovering in the morning light that the heat had melted the sand into glass. Some say this event marks the discovery of glass. Or the story of a glassblower named John Booze who made bottles to store whiskey in.   16

Dan speaks of the loss of many old skills due to the lack of apprenticeships in today's workforce. On that note, Dan shares yet another story about an old glassblower from Niwot, Colorado, whose craft was making prosthetic glass eyes for people. The old craftsman bemoaned to Dan his regret at not being able to pass his skill on to anyone before he died.   17

"Duck!" my brain shouts, a split second after I hear the first sharp ping, followed by the sound of glass breaking and the sense of it shooting across the studio. I cannot locate the source, and I ask Dan what caused the noise. "As the small amount of glass that is left on the punty or blowpipe begins to cool, it shatters and pops   18 off, sending pieces shooting across the floor of the room," Dan informs me. While it is a startling occurrence, the second time it happens, running for cover seems a bit dramatic; instead, I stay seated and continue to watch Dan work his glass.

Dan is a craftsman, an artisan, and a teacher. As we speak of the classes he teaches, he tells me of high school students he is working with: "I was worried about working with high school kids, but it's been wonderful." Dan shows me a clay mask that has a resemblance to his face, mustache and all. "I came to work one morning, and this was on my desk," he says. "A student made it for me." The pride on his face and in his voice is no less brilliant than the shine on the multiple pieces of glass that are in front of us. Dan is touching lives not only by the beauty he creates but also by passing on the skills of his craft to others. He is an inspiration, a mentor. 19

READING FOR MEANING

Reading for meaning involves three activities:

- reading to comprehend
- reading to respond
- reading to analyze underlying assumptions

Reread Crow's essay, and then write a page or so explaining your understanding of its basic meaning or main point, a personal response you have to it, and what you see as one of its underlying assumptions.

READING LIKE A WRITER

Writers of observational essays

- describe places and people.
- organize or sequence the observations in a particular way.
- engage and inform readers.
- convey an impression of the subject.

Focus on one of these strategies in Crow's essay, and analyze it carefully through close rereading and annotating. Then write several sentences explaining what you have learned, giving specific examples from the reading to support your explanation. Add a few sentences evaluating how successfully Crow uses the strategy to help readers unfamiliar with glassmaking learn about the process.

REVIEWING WHAT MAKES OBSERVATIONAL ESSAYS EFFECTIVE

In this chapter, you have been learning how to read observational essays for meaning and how to read them like a writer. Before going on to write an observational essay, pause here to review and contemplate what you have learned about the elements of effective observational writing.

Analyze

Choose one reading from this chapter that seems to you especially effective. Before rereading the selection, *jot down* one or two reasons you remember it as an example of good observational writing.

Reread your chosen selection, adding further annotations about what makes it a particularly successful example of observation. *Consider* the selection's purpose and how well it achieves that purpose for its intended readers. (You can make an informed guess about the intended readers and their expectations by noting the publication source of the essay.) Then *focus* on how well the essay

- details places and people.

- organizes the observations.

- engages and informs readers.

- conveys an impression of its subject.

You can review all of these basic features in the Guide to Reading Observational Essays (p. 88).

Your instructor may ask you to complete this activity on your own or to work with a small group of other students who have chosen the same reading. If you work with others, allow enough time initially for all group members to reread the selection thoughtfully and to add their annotations. Then *discuss* as a group what makes the selection effective. *Take notes* on your discussion. One student in your group should then report to the class what the group has learned about the effectiveness of observational writing. If you are working individually, write up what you have learned from your analysis.

Write

Write at least a page supporting your choice of this reading as an example of effective observational writing. *Assume* that your readers—your instructor and classmates—have read the selection but will not remember many details about it. They also might not remember it as especially successful. Therefore, you will need to *refer* to details and specific parts of the essay as you explain how it works and as you justify your evaluation of its effectiveness. You need not argue that it is the best reading in the chapter or that it is flawless, only that it is, in your view, a strong example of the genre.

■ A Guide to Writing Observational Essays

The readings in this chapter have helped you learn a great deal about observational writing. You have seen that writers of observational essays present unfamiliar places and people. You have also seen that they collect large amounts of information and ideas from visits and interviews, which must be sorted, organized, and integrated into a readable draft. This Guide to Writing is designed to help you through the stages of invention and research, drafting, revising, and editing, as you gather the materials you will need and solve the problems you encounter as you write.

INVENTION AND RESEARCH

The following activities will help you choose a subject, research and reflect on your subject, plan and make observations, and decide on the impression you want your essay to convey to readers. Except for the visit or interview, each activity is easy to do and takes only a few minutes. If you can spread out the activities over several days, you will have adequate time to understand what you must do to present your subject in an engaging and informative way. Keep a written record of your invention work to use later when you draft and revise the essay.

Choosing a Subject

List the subjects you are interested in observing. To make the best possible choice and have alternatives in case the subject you choose requires too much time or is inaccessible, you should have a list of several possible subjects. You might already have a subject in mind, possibly one you listed for the Considering Ideas for Your Own Writing activities following the readings in this chapter. Here are some other suggestions that will help you think of possible topics:

People

- Anyone doing work that you might want to do—city council member, police officer, lab technician, computer programmer, attorney, salesperson
- Anyone with an unusual job or hobby—dog trainer, private detective, ham radio operator, race car driver, novelist
- A campus personality—coach, distinguished teacher, newspaper editor, oldest or youngest student
- Someone recently recognized for community service or achievement

Places

- Small-claims court, consumer fraud office, city planner's office

- Bodybuilding gym, weight-reduction clinic, martial arts school

- Hospital emergency room, campus health center, hospice, psychiatric unit

- Recycling center, airport control tower, theater, museum, sports arena

Activities

- Tutoring, registering voters, rehearsing for a play, repairing a car

- An unconventional sports event—dog's frisbee tournament, chess match, amateur wrestling or boxing meet, dogsledding, log sawing and splitting, ice-fishing contest, Olympics for people with disabilities

- A team practicing a sport or other activity (one you can observe as a curious outsider, not as an experienced participant)

- A community improvement project—graffiti cleaning, tree planting, house repairing, church painting, road or highway litter collecting

- Special courses—rock climbing, folk dancing, dog training, truck driving

Choose a subject about which you are genuinely curious—and one that you think will appeal to your readers. Keep in mind that the more unfamiliar the subject is for readers, the easier it will be for you to interest them in it. If you choose a subject familiar to readers, try to focus on some aspect of it likely to be truly informative, even surprising, to them. In choosing a subject, be sure to check on accessibility, requesting permission to visit one or more times to make detailed observations and to interview key people.

Researching Your Subject

The writing and research activities that follow will enable you to gather information and ideas about your subject.

Making a Schedule. *Set up a tentative schedule for your observational and interview visits.* Figure out first the amount of time you have to complete your essay. Then determine the scope of your project—a onetime observation, an interview with follow-up, or multiple observations and interviews. Decide what visits you will need to make, whom you will need to interview, and what library or Internet work you might want to do to get background information about your subject. Estimate the time necessary for each, knowing you might need to schedule more time than anticipated.

Make phone calls to schedule visits. When you write down your appointments, be sure to include names, addresses, phone numbers, dates and times, and

RESEARCHING YOUR SUBJECT ONLINE

One way to get a quick initial overview of the information available on the subject of your observational essay is to search for the subject online. Use Google <http://google.com> or Yahoo! Directory <http://dir.yahoo.com> to discover possible sources of information about the subject:

- For example, if you are writing about a beekeeper, you could get some useful background information to guide you in planning your interview by entering "bee keeping."

- If you are writing about a person, enter the full name to discover whether he or she has a personal Web site. If you are writing about a business or institution, the chances are even better that it offers a site. Either kind of site would orient and inform you prior to your interview or first visit.

Bookmark or keep a record of promising sites. After your interview with or visit to the subject, download any materials, including visuals, you might consider including in your own essay. If you find little or no information about your subject online, do not lose confidence in your choice. All of the information you need to develop your essay can come from your observations and interviews when you visit your subject.

any special arrangements you have made for each visit. (Consult the Field Research section in Appendix 2, pp. 699–704, for helpful guidelines on observing, interviewing, and taking notes.)

Exploring Readers' and Your Own Preconceptions.   *Write for several minutes about your readers' as well as your own assumptions and expectations.* For example, ask questions like these about your readers: Who are they? What are they likely to think about the subject? What would they want to know about it? Also reflect on yourself: Why do you want to research this subject? What do you expect to find out about it? What aspects of it do you expect to be interesting or entertaining?

Visiting a Place.   *During your visit, take notes on what you observe.* Do not try to impose order on your notes at this stage; simply record whatever you notice. Pay special attention to visual details and other kinds of details (sounds, smells) that you can draw on later to describe the place and people.

Interviewing a Person.   *Prepare for the interview by writing out some preliminary questions.* But do not be afraid of abandoning your script during the interview.

Listen carefully to what is said and ask follow-up questions. Take notes; if you like and your subject agrees, you may also tape-record the interview.

Gathering Information.   *If you do background reading, take careful notes and keep accurate bibliographic records of your sources.* Try to pick up relevant fliers, brochures, or reports at the place you observe. In addition, you might conduct research on the Internet or in your college library. (For more information, see the accompanying box, Researching Your Subject Online; also see the sections Library Research, pp. 705–16, and Internet Research, pp. 716–21, in Appendix 2.)

Reflecting on Your Subject

After you research your subject, consider your purpose for writing about it and formulate a tentative thesis statement.

Considering Your Purpose.   *Write for several minutes about the impression of the subject you want to convey to your readers.* As you write, try to answer this question: What makes this subject worth observing? Your answer to this question might change as you write, but a preliminary answer will give your writing a direction to follow, or what journalists commonly call an "angle" on the subject. This angle will help you choose what to include as well as what to emphasize in your draft. Use the following questions to help clarify the impression you want your essay to convey:

- What visual images or other sensory details of the subject stand out in your memory? Think about the feelings these images evoke in you. If they evoke contradictory feelings, consider how you could use them to convey to readers the complexity of your feelings about the place, people, or activities you observed.

- What is most surprising about your observations? Compare the preconceptions you listed earlier with what you actually saw or heard.

- What interests you most about the people you interviewed? Compare the direct observations you made about them with the indirect or secondhand information you gathered about them.

Formulating a Tentative Thesis Statement.   *Review what you wrote for Considering Your Purpose, and add two or three sentences that will bring into focus the impression you want to give readers about the person, place, or activity on which you are focusing.* This impression is based on an insight into, interpretation of, or idea about the person, place, or activity you have gained while observing it. Try to write sentences that do not summarize what you have already written but that express a deeper understanding of what impression you want to make on your readers.

Keep in mind that readers do not expect you to begin your observational essay with the kind of explicit thesis statement typical of argumentative essays.

None of the readings in this chapter offers to readers an explicit statement of the impression the writer hopes to convey about the subject. Instead, the writers convey an impression through the ways they describe their subjects, select information to share with readers, or narrate the story of their experiences with the subject. And yet it is possible for readers to infer from each reading an impression of the subject. For example, some readers are likely to come away from Virginia Holman's essay about the course in dissecting human bodies with the impression that for medical students, the cadaver they dissect truly is their "first patient," as the title and the last line of the essay state. But other readers might focus on the statement that begins the second paragraph: "Gross Anatomy is the essential and incomparable crucible of all first-year medical students." Or the main impression might be summarized in the idea that no software program can take the place of the invaluable "tactile learning . . . gained by the students' hands working on the bodies" (paragraph 47).

Nearly all first attempts to state an impression to be conveyed, to focus a jumble of notes and remembered observations, or to state a thesis are eventually revised once drafting gets under way. Writing the first draft helps writers of observational essays discover their main impression and find ways to convey that impression without ever stating it directly. Just because there is no explicit thesis statement in an observational essay does not mean that it lacks focus or fails to convey an impression of its subject.

Considering Visuals.   *Consider whether visuals—photographs you take, drawings you make, copies of revealing illustrative materials you picked up at the place observed—would strengthen your observational essay.* If you submit your essay electronically to other students and your instructor, or if you post it to a Web site, consider including snippets of your interviews or sounds from the place (if you make use of a tape recorder in your project) or your own digital photographs or video. Remember to ask permission to make visual or audio records: Some persons may be willing to be interviewed or share printed material but reluctant to allow photographs or recordings. Visual and audio materials are not at all a requirement of an effective observational essay, as you can tell from the readings in this chapter, but they could add a new dimension to your writing.

DRAFTING

The following guidelines will help you set goals for your draft, plan its organization, and think about a useful sentence strategy.

Setting Goals

Establishing goals for your draft before you begin writing will enable you to make decisions and work more confidently. Consider the following questions now, and keep them in mind as you draft. They will help you set goals for drafting as well as recall how the writers you have read in this chapter tried to achieve similar goals.

- *How can I help my readers imagine the subject?* In addition to describing visual details, as all of the authors in this chapter do, should I evoke other senses, in the way that Edge describes how a pig lip smells and tastes and what its unusual texture is? Should I characterize people by their clothes, facial expressions, and talk, as McPhee, Coyne, Crow, and Cable do? Should I use surprising metaphors or similes, as the author of "Soup" does in describing Yeganeh's "working like a demon alchemist" or as Holman does in comparing the gross anatomy laboratory to "a commercial kitchen or [a] fanatically pristine woodworking shop"?

- *How can I engage my readers?* Should I focus on dramatic interactions among people, as McPhee does? Should I begin with a vivid description, as Holman and Crow do? A poignant image, as Coyne does? A surprising statement, as in "Soup"? Personal experience with the subject, as Edge does? Humor, as Edge and Cable do?

- *How can I present and distribute the information so that readers do not become either bored or overwhelmed?* Should I present some information through reported conversation, as in "Soup"? Some as part of a personal experience story of participating in the subject, as McPhee and Edge do? Some from interviews, as Edge and Cable do? Some as observed visual and other details, as all the authors in this chapter do?

- *How should I organize my observations?* Should I organize them topically in groups of related information, as the author of "Soup" and Edge and Cable do? Or should I arrange them in a chronological narrative order, as McPhee, Holman, and Coyne do?

- *How can I convey the impression I want to leave with my readers?* Should I convey it explicitly, or should I try to convey an impression indirectly—by my choice of words, descriptive details, and the story, as all of the authors in this chapter do?

Organizing Your Draft

With your goals in mind, reread the notes you took about the place and people, and decide how to organize them—grouped into topics or put in chronological order. If you think a topical organization would work best, try grouping your observations and naming the topic of each group. If you think narrating what happened would help you organize your observations, make a time line and note where the information would go. You might want to try different kinds of outlines before settling on a plan and drafting your essay.

Writers who use a narrative structure usually follow a simple, straightforward chronology. Coyne, Holman, and Cable, for example, present activities observed over a limited period—a few hours or a few days—in the order in which they occurred. Writers may also punctuate their main narrative with additional events that occurred on other occasions: McPhee, for example, recounts what happened over a few hours at the Brooklyn farmer's market while also weaving in other stories about the market that took place at different times in the past. Coyne provides a lot of background information about the two families she juxtaposes.

Writers who organize their observations topically must limit the number of topics they cover. The author of "Soup," for example, focuses on Yeganeh's ideas about soup and his attitudes toward customers. Edge concentrates on the history and process of bottling and selling pig lips.

Considering a Useful Sentence Strategy

As you draft your essay, you will need to use speaker tags to present what people have said to you and others during your visits and interviews. Speaker tags are the words and phrases that identify who is speaking and characterize the person's tone, attitude, or appearance.

- Experienced writers rely mostly on general or all-purpose speaker tags, using forms of *say, tell,* and other neutral verbs.

  "Three pounds for a dollar," *I tell her.* (McPhee, paragraph 1)

  "It was a large service," *remarked Howard.* "Look at that casket—a beautiful work of craftsmanship." (Cable, paragraph 16)

- As you draft your essay, however, consider occasionally using specific or descriptive speaker tags that give readers help in imagining speakers' attitudes and personal styles or the circumstances in which they are speaking.

  "I am psychologically kind of a health freak," *Mr. Yeganeh said the other day, in a lisping staccato of Armenian origin.* ("Soup," paragraph 2)

  "I started out with my daddy when I wasn't much more than 10," *Lionel told me, his shy smile framed by a coarse black mustache flecked with whispers of gray.* (Edge, paragraph 8)

  "Pit of fire," *she says, shaking her head.* (Coyne, paragraph 6)

  He succinctly explains that "dissection teaches our hands" in ways books and software programs cannot. (Holman, paragraph 52)

  "Mister, give me some of these!" *she says, looking up at me with a gypsy's dark, starburst eyes.* (McPhee, paragraph 1)

  "You talk too much, dear," *Mr. Yeganeh said, and motioned her to move to the left.* "Next!" ("Soup," paragraph 9)

"Just don't talk. Do what he says," *a man huddled in a blue parka warned.* ("Soup," paragraph 10)

"We do our best to corner the market on lips," *Lionel told me, his voice tinged with bravado.* (Edge, paragraph 11)

One student whistles—"That looks like something straight out of *The Terminator*." (Holman, paragraph 46)

Readers expect to find speaker tags in dialogue. When a writer leaves out speaker tags—and breaks from the convention of indenting each new speaker's words—the effect can be striking, as in this example:

We ask one another where we are from, how long a drive we had. An occasional whistle through the teeth, a shake of the head. "My, my, long way from home, huh?" "Staying at the Super 8 right up the road. Not a bad place." "Stayed at the Econo Lodge last time. Wasn't a good place at all." Never asking the questions we really want to ask: "What's she in for?" "How much time's she got left?" (Coyne, paragraph 3)

Notice that even though Coyne does not think it is necessary to identify each speaker, she does give some of the flavor of the conversations by mentioning the whistles and head shakes that are part of them.

READING A DRAFT CRITICALLY

Getting a critical reading of your draft will help you see how to improve it. Your instructor may schedule class time for reading drafts, or you may want to ask a classmate or a tutor in the writing center to read your draft. Ask your reader to use the following guidelines and to write out a response for you to consult during your revision.

Read for a First Impression

1. Read the draft without stopping to annotate or comment, and then write two or three sentences giving your general impression.

2. Identify one aspect of the draft that seems particularly effective.

Read Again to Suggest Improvements

1. Suggest ways of making descriptions of places and people more vivid.

   - Find a description of a place, and suggest what details could be added to objects in the scene (location, size, color, and shape) or what sensory information (look, sound, smell, taste, and touch) could be included to help you picture the place.

- Find a description of a person, and indicate what else you would like to know about the person's dress, facial expression, tone of voice, and gestures.

- Find reported conversation, and note whether any of the quotes could be paraphrased or summarized without losing impact.

- Find passages where additional reported conversation could enhance the drama or help bring a person to life.

2. Recommend ways of making the organization clearer or more effective.

- If the essay is organized chronologically, look for passages where the narrative seems to wander pointlessly or leaves out important information. Also suggest cues that could be added to indicate time sequence *(initially, then, afterward)*.

- If the essay is organized topically, mark topics that get too much or too little attention, transitions between topics that need to be added or clarified, and topics that should be placed elsewhere.

- If the essay alternates narration with topical information, suggest where transitions could be made smoother or sequencing could be improved.

3. Suggest how the essay could be made more engaging and informative.

- If the essay seems boring or you feel overwhelmed by too much information, suggest how the information could alternate with vivid description or lively narration. Also consider whether any of the information could be cut or simplified.

- List any questions you still have about the subject.

4. Suggest ways to make the impression conveyed to you more focused and coherent.

- Tell the writer what impression you have of the subject.

- Point to key information that supports your impression, so that the writer knows how you arrived at it.

- Point to any information that makes you doubt or question your impression.

5. Evaluate the effectiveness of visuals.

- Look at any visuals in the essay, and tell the writer what they contribute to your impression of the subject and your understanding of the observations.

- If any visuals do not seem relevant, or if there seem to be too many visuals, identify the ones that the writer could consider dropping, explaining your thinking.

- If a visual does not seem to be appropriately placed, suggest a better place for it.

REVISING

This section offers suggestions for revising your draft. Revising means reenvisioning your draft, trying to see it in a new way, given your purpose and readers, in order to develop a more vivid, informative observational essay.

The biggest mistake you can make while revising is to focus initially on words or sentences. Instead, first try to see your draft as a whole in order to assess its likely impact on your readers. Think imaginatively and boldly about cutting unconvincing material, adding new material, and moving material around. Your computer makes even drastic revisions physically easy, but you still need to make the mental effort and decisions that will improve your draft.

You may have received help with this challenge from a classmate or tutor who gave your draft a critical reading. If so, keep this feedback in mind as you decide which parts of your draft need revising and what specific changes you could make. The following suggestions will help you solve problems and strengthen your essay.

To Make Your Description of Places and People More Vivid

- Cull your notes for additional details you could supply about people and objects in the scene.

- If your notes are sparse, consider revisiting the place to add to your visual observations, or try imagining yourself back at the place and write about what you see.

- Consider where you could add details about sounds, smells, or textures of objects.

- Identify where a simile or metaphor would enrich your description.

- Review reported conversations to make sure you directly quote only the language that conveys personality or essential information; paraphrase or summarize other conversations.

- Show people interacting with each other by talking, moving, or gesturing.

- Consider using more specific speaker tags to show how or in what circumstances people spoke.

To Make the Organization Clearer and More Effective

- If the essay is organized chronologically, keep the narrative focused and well-paced, adding time markers to clarify the sequence of events.

- If the essay is organized topically, make sure it moves smoothly from topic to topic, adding transitions where necessary.

- If the essay alternates narration with topical information, make sure the sequence is clear and easy to follow.

To Make the Essay More Engaging and Informative

- If the essay bores or overwhelms readers, cut information that is obvious or extraneous, and consider alternating blocks of information with descriptive or narrative materials.

- If readers have questions about the subject, try to answer them.

- If the essay seems abstract, provide specific definitions, examples, and details.

To Strengthen the Impression Your Essay Conveys

- If readers get an impression of the subject you did not expect, consider what may have given them that impression. You may need to add or cut material.

- If readers are unable to identify an impression, look for ways to make clearer the impression you want to convey.

EDITING AND PROOFREADING

After you have revised your essay, be sure to spend some time checking for errors in usage, punctuation, and mechanics and considering matters of style. If you keep a list of errors you typically make, begin by checking your draft against this list. Ask someone else to proofread your essay before you print out a copy for your instructor or send it electronically.

From our research on student writing, we know that observational essays tend to have errors in the use of quotation marks, when writers quote the exact words of people they have interviewed. Check a writer's handbook for help with this problem.

REFLECTING ON WHAT YOU HAVE LEARNED

Observation

In this chapter, you have read critically several observational essays and have written one of your own. To better remember what you have learned, pause now to reflect on the reading and writing activities you completed in this chapter.

1. *Write* a page or so assessing what you have learned. *Begin* by describing what you are most pleased with in your essay. Then *explain* what you think contributed to your achievement. *Be specific* about this contribution.

   - If it was something you learned from the readings, *indicate* which readings and specifically what you learned from them.

   - If it came from your invention writing, interviews, or observations, *point out* the parts that helped you most.

   - If you got good advice from a critical reader, *explain* exactly how the person helped you—perhaps by helping you understand a particular problem in your draft or by adding a new dimension to your writing.

   - *Try to write* about your achievement in terms of what you have learned about the genre.

2. Now *reflect* more generally on the genre of observational writing. Observational essays may seem impartial and objective, but they inevitably reflect the writer's interests, values, and other characteristics, such as gender and ethnicity or cultural heritage. For example, readers would expect a vegetarian to write a very different profile of a cattle ranch from one a beef lover would write. *Identify* a reading in the chapter where the writer's attitudes or characteristics seemed to influence the choice of subject, the observations, and the essay as a whole. *Explain* briefly how this influence is apparent to you. Then *consider* the following questions about your own project: How did your interests, values, or other characteristics influence your choice of subject, your observations, and your interactions with the people you interviewed? In your essay itself, how do these influences show through? If you tried to keep them hidden, *explain* briefly why. How could these influences be made more visible in your essay, and do you wish you had made them more visible? *Explain* why briefly.

4

Reflection

Like autobiographical and observational writing, reflective writing is based on the writer's personal experience. Reflective writers present something they did, saw, overheard, or read. They try to make their writing vivid so that the reader can imagine what they experienced. But unlike writers of autobiography and observation, their goal is not primarily to present their experience so that the reader can imagine it. Reflective writers, instead, present their experience in order to explore its possible meanings. They use events in their lives and people and places they have observed as the occasions or springboards for thinking about society—how people live and what people believe.

In this chapter, for example, one writer tells what happened one evening when he was taking a walk and he noticed a woman react to him with evident fear. This experience, and others like it, leads him to think about popular stereotypes concerning gender and race. Another writer notices how many helmets and other pieces of sports gear his daughter has accumulated. This observation makes him think about the kind of childhood that middle-class Americans experience today and how their activities help build character. Still another writer, who observed a spate of news reports on dysfunctional families, muses over the idea that families are not always the safe haven we like to think they are.

As you can see from these few examples, the subjects reflective essays explore are wide ranging. Reflective writers may think about social change with its many opportunities and challenges (changes in the family, in ways to perfect the body, and in the notion of community in the Internet age). They may examine cultural customs in our culturally diverse society (such as those related to eating, dating, and child-rearing). They may explore traditional virtues and vices (pride, jealousy, and compassion) or common hopes and fears (the desire for intimacy and the fear of it).

These subjects may seem far reaching, but writers of reflection have relatively modest goals. They do not attempt to exhaust their subjects, nor do they set themselves up as experts. They simply try out their ideas. One early meaning of the word *essay,* in fact, was "to try out." Reflective essays are exercises, experiments, simply opportunities to explore ideas informally and tentatively.

Reflective writing is enjoyable to write and read precisely because it is exploratory and creative. Reflective writing can be as stimulating as a lively conversation. It often surprises us with its insights and unlikely connections and encourages us to look in new ways at even the most familiar things, examining with a critical eye what we usually take for granted.

The readings in this chapter will help you learn a good deal about reflective writing. From the readings and from the suggestions for writing that follow each reading, you will get ideas for your own reflective essay. As you read and write about the selections, keep in mind the following assignment, which sets out the goals for writing a reflective essay. To support your writing of this assignment, the chapter concludes with a Guide to Writing Reflective Essays.

THE WRITING ASSIGNMENT

Reflection

Write a reflective essay based on something you experienced or observed. Describe this occasion vividly so that readers can understand what happened and will care about what you have to say about it. In reflecting on the particular occasion, make some general statements exploring its possible meanings or cultural significance. Consider what the occasion might imply about how people in our society behave toward one another, what they value, and what assumptions or stereotypes they may hold consciously or unconsciously. Think of reflective writing as a stimulating conversation in which you seek to expose—and perhaps question—your readers' attitudes and beliefs as well as your own.

WRITING SITUATIONS FOR REFLECTIVE ESSAYS

Writers use a wide range of particular occasions to launch their reflections. These occasions nearly always lead them to reflect on some aspect of contemporary culture, as the following examples indicate:

- A former football player writes a reflective essay for his college alumni magazine about his experience playing professional sports. He recounts a specific occasion when he sustained a serious injury but continued to play because he knew that playing with pain was regarded as a sign of manliness. As he reflects on what happened, he recalls that he first learned the custom of playing with pain from his father but that the lesson was reinforced later by coaches and other players. He wonders why boys playing sports are taught not to show pain but encouraged to show other feelings like aggression and competitiveness. Taking an anthropological view, he sees contemporary sports as equivalent to the kind of training Native American boys traditionally went through to become warriors. This comparison leads him to question whether sports training today prepares boys (and perhaps girls, too) for the kinds of roles they need to play in contemporary society.

- Writing for a political science course, a student reflects on her first experience voting in a presidential election. She begins by describing a recent conversation with friends about how people decide to vote for one presidential candidate over another. They agreed that most people they know seem to base their decisions on trivial, even bizarre, reasons, rather than on a candidate's experience, voting record in previous offices, character, or even campaign promises. For example, one friend knew someone who voted for a presidential candidate who reminded her of her grandfather, while another friend knew someone who voted against a candidate because he did not like the way the candidate dressed. The writer then reflects on the humorous as well as the serious implications of such voting decisions.

- A first-year college student, in an essay for his composition course, reflects on a performance of his high-school chorus that far surpassed the members' expectations. He describes their trip to the statewide competition and their anxious rehearsals before the performance and, during the competition, their unexpected feelings of confidence, their precision and control, and the exuberance of the performance. He considers factors that led to their success, such as fear of embarrassment, affection for their teacher, the excitement of a trip to the state capital, and the fact that they had rehearsed especially attentively for weeks because the music was so challenging and the competition so fierce. After considering possible reasons for their success, the writer concludes with some ideas about the special pleasures of success where cooperation and individual creativity are essential.

THINKING ABOUT YOUR EXPERIENCE WITH REFLECTION

Before studying a type of writing, it is useful to spend some time thinking about what you already know about it. You may have written about your reflections, exploring your ideas and reactions to things you have seen, heard, or read, in correspondence with friends or in writing for school.

To analyze your experience with reflections, you might recall a time when you communicated your reflections in writing or orally and then consider questions like these: What was the particular occasion that triggered your reflections? Was it something you observed firsthand, saw in a film, heard on the radio, or overheard on the street? Why did this particular occasion seem interesting or significant to you? Were you surprised by the ideas it stimulated?

Consider also reflections you have read, heard, or seen on television. If you recall someone else's reflections in some detail, try to identify what made them interesting to you. For example, were the ideas fascinating in themselves, were you intrigued by the person's take on things, or did something else account for your interest? What specific details do you recall? How did the specific details help you understand the more abstract ideas in the reflections?

Write at least a page about your experience with reflective writing.

■ A Guide to Reading Reflective Essays

This guide introduces you to reflective writing. By completing all the activities in it, you will prepare yourself to learn a great deal from the other readings in this chapter about how to read and write a reflective essay. The guide focuses on a brief but powerful piece of reflection by Brent Staples. You will read Staples's reflective essay twice. First, you will read it for meaning, seeking to understand Staples's experience, to follow his reflections, and to discover your own ideas about stereotyping and fear of others. Then, you will read the essay like a writer, analyzing the parts to see how Staples crafts his essay and to learn the strategies he uses to make his reflective writing effective. These two activities—reading for meaning and reading like a writer—follow every reading in this chapter.

BRENT STAPLES

Black Men and Public Space

Brent Staples (b. 1951) earned his Ph.D. in psychology from the University of Chicago and went on to become a journalist, writing for several magazines and newspapers, including the Chicago Sun-Times. *In 1985, he became assistant metropolitan editor of the* New York Times, *where he is now a member of the editorial board. His autobiography,* Parallel Time: Growing Up in Black and White *(1994), won the Anisfield Wolff Book Award.*

The following essay originally appeared in Ms. *magazine in 1986, under the title "Just Walk On By." Staples revised it slightly for publication in* Harper's *a year later under the present title. The particular occasion for Staples's reflections is an incident that occurred for the first time in the mid-1970s, when he discovered that his mere presence on the street late at night was enough to frighten a young white woman. Recalling this incident leads him to reflect on issues of race, gender, and class in the United States. (If you are interested in learning more about the issue of racial profiling that Staples brings up in this essay, be sure to read the selection by Randall Kennedy in Chapter 9, pp. 609–16.)*

As you read, think about why Staples chose the new title, "Black Men and Public Space."

My first victim was a woman—white, well dressed, probably in her early twenties. I came upon her late one evening on a deserted street in Hyde Park, a relatively affluent neighborhood in an otherwise mean, impoverished section of Chicago. As I swung onto the avenue behind her, there seemed to be a discreet, uninflammatory distance between us. Not so. She cast back a worried glance. To her, the youngish black man—a broad six feet two inches with a beard and billowing hair, both hands shoved into the pockets of a bulky military jacket—seemed menacingly close. After a few more quick glimpses, she picked up her pace and was soon running in earnest. Within seconds she disappeared into a cross street.

That was more than a decade ago, I was twenty-two years old, a graduate student newly arrived at the University of Chicago. It was in the echo of that terrified woman's footfalls that I first began to know the unwieldy inheritance I'd come into—the ability to alter public space in ugly ways. It was clear that she thought herself the quarry of a mugger, a rapist, or worse. Suffering a bout of insomnia, however, I was stalking sleep, not defenseless wayfarers. As a softy who is scarcely able to take a knife to a raw chicken—let alone hold one to a person's throat—I was surprised, embarrassed, and dismayed all at once. Her flight made me feel like an accomplice in tyranny. It also made it clear that I was indistinguishable from the muggers who occasionally seeped into the area from the surrounding ghetto. That first encounter, and those that followed, signified that a vast, unnerving gulf lay between nighttime pedestrians—particularly women—and me. And I soon gathered that being perceived as dangerous is a hazard in itself. I only needed to turn a corner into a dicey situation, or crowd some frightened, armed person in a foyer somewhere, or make an errant move after being pulled over by a policeman. Where fear and weapons meet—and they often do in urban America—there is always the possibility of death.

In that first year, my first away from my hometown, I was to become thoroughly familiar with the language of fear. At dark, shadowy intersections, I could cross in front of a car stopped at a traffic light and elicit the *thunk, thunk, thunk* of the driver—black, white, male, or female—hammering down the door locks. On less traveled streets after dark, I grew accustomed to but never comfortable with people crossing to the other side of the street rather than pass me. Then there were the standard unpleasantries with policemen, doormen, bouncers, cabdrivers, and others whose business it is to screen out troublesome individuals *before* there is any nastiness.

I moved to New York nearly two years ago and I have remained an avid night walker. In central Manhattan, the near-constant crowd cover minimizes tense one-on-one street encounters. Elsewhere—in SoHo, for example, where sidewalks are narrow and tightly spaced buildings shut out the sky—things can get very taut indeed.

After dark, on the warrenlike streets of Brooklyn where I live, I often see women who fear the worst from me. They seem to have set their faces on neutral, and with their purse straps strung across their chests bandolier-style, they forge ahead as though bracing themselves against being tackled. I understand, of course, that the danger they perceive is not a hallucination. Women are particularly vulnerable to street violence, and young black males are drastically overrepresented among the perpetrators of that violence. Yet these truths are no solace against the kind of alienation that comes of being ever the suspect, a fearsome entity with whom pedestrians avoid making eye contact.

It is not altogether clear to me how I reached the ripe old age of twenty-two without being conscious of the lethality nighttime pedestrians attributed to me. Perhaps it was because in Chester, Pennsylvania, the small, angry industrial town where I came of age in the 1960s, I was scarcely noticeable against a backdrop of gang warfare, street knifings, and murders. I grew up one of the good boys, had perhaps a half-dozen fistfights. In retrospect, my shyness of combat has clear sources.

As a boy, I saw countless tough guys locked away; I have since buried several, too. They were babies, really—a teenage cousin, a brother of twenty-two, a childhood friend in his mid-twenties—all gone down in episodes of bravado played out in the streets. I came to doubt the virtues of intimidation early on. I chose, perhaps unconsciously, to remain a shadow—timid, but a survivor.

The fearsomeness mistakenly attributed to me in public places often has a perilous flavor. The most frightening of these confusions occurred in the late 1970s and early 1980s, when I worked as a journalist in Chicago. One day, rushing into the office of a magazine I was writing for with a deadline story in hand, I was mistaken for a burglar. The office manager called security and, with an ad hoc posse, pursued me through the labyrinthine halls, nearly to my editor's door. I had no way of proving who I was. I could only move briskly toward the company of someone who knew me.   8

Another time I was on assignment for a local paper and killing time before an interview. I entered a jewelry store on the city's affluent Near North Side. The proprietor excused herself and returned with an enormous red Doberman pinscher straining at the end of a leash. She stood, the dog extended toward me, silent to my questions, her eyes bulging nearly out of her head. I took a cursory look around, nodded, and bade her good night.   9

Relatively speaking, however, I never fared as badly as another black male journalist. He went to nearby Waukegan, Illinois, a couple of summers ago to work on a story about a murderer who was born there. Mistaking the reporter for the killer, police officers hauled him from his car at gunpoint and but for his press credentials would probably have tried to book him. Such episodes are not uncommon. Black men trade tales like this all the time.   10

Over the years, I learned to smother the rage I felt at so often being taken for a criminal. Not to do so would surely have led to madness. I now take precautions to make myself less threatening. I move about with care, particularly late in the evening. I give a wide berth to nervous people on subway platforms during the wee hours, particularly when I have exchanged business clothes for jeans. If I happen to be entering a building behind some people who appear skittish, I may walk by, letting them clear the lobby before I return, so as not to seem to be following them. I have been calm and extremely congenial on those rare occasions when I've been pulled over by the police.   11

And on late-evening constitutionals I employ what has proved to be an excellent tension-reducing measure: I whistle melodies from Beethoven and Vivaldi and the more popular classical composers. Even steely New Yorkers hunching toward nighttime destinations seem to relax, and occasionally they even join in the tune. Virtually everybody seems to sense that a mugger wouldn't be warbling bright, sunny selections from Vivaldi's *Four Seasons*. It is my equivalent of the cowbell that hikers wear when they know they are in bear country.   12

READING FOR MEANING

This section presents three activities that will help you reread Staples's reflective essay with a critical eye. Done in sequence, these activities lead you from a basic understanding of the selection to a more personal response to it and finally to an analysis that deepens your understanding and critical thinking about what you are reading.

Read to Comprehend

Reread the selection, and write a few sentences explaining some of the ways Staples tries to alleviate people's fear of him and commenting on his feelings about these encounters. Also make a list of any words you do not understand—for example, *discreet* (paragraph 1), *unwieldy* (2), *avid* (4), *constitutionals* (12). Look up their meanings in a dictionary to see which definition best fits the context.

To expand your understanding of this reading, you might use one or more of the following critical reading strategies that are explained and illustrated in Appendix 1: *outlining, summarizing, paraphrasing,* and *questioning to understand and remember.*

Read to Respond

Write several paragraphs exploring your initial thoughts and feelings about Staples's reflective essay. Focus on anything that stands out for you, perhaps because it resonates with your own experience or because you find a statement puzzling.

You might consider writing about

- your response as a reader to Staples's opening words: "My first victim was a woman."

- Staples's reactions to being seen as threatening, perhaps in relation to how you think you would react if you were in his position.

- an experience you have had in which racial, gender, age, or other differences caused tension, comparing your experience with that of Staples or one of the people he encountered.

- whether in your experience the fear of strangers operates the same way in suburban or small-town public spaces as it does for Staples in an urban setting.

To develop your response to Staples's essay, you might use one or more of the following critical reading strategies that are explained and illustrated in Appendix 1: *contextualizing, reflecting on challenges to your beliefs and values, recognizing emotional manipulation,* and *judging the writer's credibility.*

Read to Analyze Underlying Assumptions

Write several paragraphs exploring one or more of the assumptions, values, and beliefs underlying Staples's reflective essay. As you write, explain how the assumptions are reflected in the text, as well as what you now think of them (and perhaps of your own assumptions) after rereading the selection with a critical eye.

Even though reflective writing directly presents the writer's feelings and thoughts, these may be more complex or less obvious than they appear at first. Looking closely at the choice of words and examples may give clues to any mixed feelings or assumptions that the writer implies rather than openly states. Staples, for example, uses the word "understand" to indicate that he does not blame the woman for being afraid (paragraph 5). He empathetically describes himself as he imagines she sees him: "To her, the youngish black man—a broad six feet two inches with a beard and billowing hair, both hands shoved into the pockets of a bulky military jacket—seemed menacingly close" (1). But by reading closely, we also see how angry Staples is at being misperceived, stereotyped, or what we call today racially profiled. The woman may sincerely think he is "menacingly close," but to him "there seemed to be a discreet, uninflammatory distance between" them (1). He describes his feelings as "surprised, embarrassed, and dismayed all at once" (2)—everything but angry. He even seems defensive when he describes his childhood timidity and the "precautions" he has taken as an adult to avoid both conflict and the possibility of being seen as a potential threat (11).

As a critical reader, you will want to think about what the writer only hints at or leaves unspoken as well as what is explicitly stated. Staples refers to his anger only once, in paragraph 11: "I learned to smother the rage I felt at so often being taken for a criminal. Not to do so would surely have led to madness." Notice that he acknowledges having felt angry, but says that he has conquered the feeling. His use of the word "madness" is interesting because it can be taken in two ways—as insanity and as anger. Smothering a feeling as strong as rage, particularly about an injustice such as the one Staples endures, surely could drive a person crazy as well as make him furious. Staples does not make the point, but the reader can infer that he thinks the fear with which black men are so often regarded reveals the insanity of a racist society. Staples may want readers to see him as a "softy" (2) who avoids conflict and tries to reduce "tension" in others as well as in himself (12). But his reflections may have the effect of enraging readers who share with him the sense of injustice. The purpose of analyzing underlying assumptions in a reading is to give us an opportunity to think critically about unexamined assumptions—the writer's and our own, many of which may be ingrained in our culture, our education, and even our language.

You might consider writing about

- Staples's assumption that he is himself endangered by the fear he engenders in people (paragraph 2).

- the values and beliefs underlying Staples's statement that there is a "kind of alienation that comes of being ever the suspect, a fearsome entity" (5).

- the cultural assumptions that make Staples's mere presence "alter public space in ugly ways" (2).

- the cultural assumptions that might explain why whistling Vivaldi melodies reduces strangers' fear of Staples.

To probe assumptions more deeply, you might use one or more of the following critical reading strategies that are explained and illustrated in Appendix 1: *reflecting on challenges to your beliefs and values, exploring the significance of figurative language,* and *looking for patterns of opposition.*

READING LIKE A WRITER

This section guides you through an analysis of Staples's reflective writing strategies: *presenting the particular occasion, developing the reflections, maintaining topical coherence,* and *engaging readers.* For each strategy you will be asked to reread and annotate part of Staples's essay to see how he uses the strategy in "Black Men and Public Space."

When you study the selections later in this chapter, you will see how different writers use these same strategies for different purposes. The Guide to Writing Reflective Essays near the end of the chapter suggests ways you can use these strategies in your own writing.

Presenting the Particular Occasion

Reflective writers present a particular occasion—something they experienced or observed—to introduce their general reflections. They may describe the occasion in detail, or they may sketch it out quickly. The key in either case is to present the occasion in a vivid and suggestive way that encourages readers to want to know more about the writer's thoughts. To succeed at presenting the occasion vividly, writers rely on the same narrating and describing strategies you practiced in Chapter 2 (Autobiography) and Chapter 3 (Observation).

Staples lets readers know from the word *first* in the introductory phrase ("My first victim") that what happened on this occasion happened again later. But he focuses in the opening paragraph on this first occasion, the one that started his reflections. Staples presents this first event in vivid detail, trying to give readers a sense of the surprise and anxiety he felt at the time. In addition to helping readers imagine what happened, Staples tries to present the event in a way that suggests the larger meanings he will develop in subsequent paragraphs. Looking closely at how he saw the woman and how she saw him helps readers understand his ideas about what happened.

Analyze

1. *Reread* the opening sentence of paragraph 1, where Staples describes the person he encountered. *Notice* that even before he identifies her by gender, he uses the word "victim" to name her. Then *underline* the details he gives to describe this person and the actions she takes.

2. Now *turn to* the places in paragraph 1 where Staples describes himself as the woman saw him. *Put brackets around* the names used to identify him, and *underline* the details used to describe him physically as well as the actions he takes.

3. *Review* the details you have underlined; then *choose* three or four details that you think help make this particular occasion especially vivid and dramatic.

Write

Write several sentences explaining what you have learned about how Staples uses this event to create a dramatic occasion that helps to introduce his reflections. *Support* your explanation with some of the details you singled out.

Developing the Reflections

While the particular occasion introduces the subject, the reflections explore the subject by developing the writer's ideas. For example, what occasions Staples's reflections is an event that occurred when his mere presence on the street frightened a woman into running away from him. He uses this particular event to introduce the general subject: fear resulting from racial stereotyping. As he explains, "It was in the echo of that terrified woman's footfalls that I first began to know the unwieldy inheritance I'd come into" (paragraph 2). Throughout the rest of the essay, Staples examines this "inheritance" from various angles, using a range of reflective writing strategies: He expresses his different feelings at being misperceived as a threat; he explains the effects of racial stereotyping, including the danger to himself; he gives examples of other occasions when people react to him with fear or hostility; and, finally, he lists the "precautions" he takes to make himself appear "less threatening" (11). These are just some of the strategies writers use to develop their reflections. This activity will help you see how Staples uses examples to illustrate and explain his ideas.

Analyze

1. *Look at* the opening sentence of paragraph 3, where Staples introduces the idea that there is a "language of fear." *Reread* the rest of the paragraph to see how the writer uses examples to help readers understand what he means.

2. Now *look at* paragraphs 11 and 12, where Staples writes about the "precautions" he takes to make himself seem "less threatening." *Mark* the examples, and *choose* one or two that you think work especially well to help readers understand what he means.

Write

Write several sentences explaining what you have learned about Staples's use of examples, pointing to the examples you think are especially effective.

Maintaining Topical Coherence

Reflective essays explore ideas on a subject by turning them this way and that, examining them first from one perspective and then from another, and sometimes piling up examples to illustrate the ideas. Such essays may seem rambling, with one idea or example added to another in a casual way. It is not always clear where the writer is going, and the essay may not seem to end conclusively. This apparently casual organization is deceptive, however, because in fact the reflective writer has arranged the parts carefully to give the appearance of a mind at work.

While each new idea or example may seem to turn the essay in an unexpected new direction, reflective writers use what we call *topical coherence* to make the parts of a reflective essay connect to the central subject. An important way of achieving topical coherence is to refer to the subject at various points in the essay by repeating certain key words or phrases associated with the subject. In the opening anecdote that presents the particular occasion, Staples dramatizes the woman's fear of him. He does not use the word "fear," however, until the end of paragraph 2. He then repeats that word twice: at the beginning of paragraph 3, in the phrase "language of fear," and at the beginning of paragraph 5. He also concludes the latter paragraph with a phrase that indicates how others, particularly women, see him: as "a fearsome entity." In addition, Staples uses several related words, such as "terrified" and "frightened" (paragraph 2) as well as "nervous" and "skittish" (11). By repeating the word "fear" and words related to it, Staples highlights the subject of his reflections.

Another way reflective writers achieve topical coherence is through carefully placed transitions. Staples, as you will see in this activity, uses time and place markers to introduce a series of examples illustrating the fear he engenders in others simply because of his race and gender.

Analyze

1. *Skim* paragraphs 2–4, 7–9, and 11, and *put brackets around* the time and place markers. *Begin* by bracketing the time marker "more than a decade

ago" and the place marker "at the University of Chicago" in the opening sentence of paragraph 2.

2. *Notice* how many different times and places Staples refers to with these markers.

Write

Write several sentences explaining how Staples uses time and place markers to help maintain topical coherence. *Support* your explanation with examples from the reading.

Engaging Readers

Readers of reflective essays, like readers of autobiographical and observational writing, expect writers to engage their interest. In fact, most readers have no pressing reason to read reflective writing. They choose to read an essay because something about it catches their eye—a familiar author's name, an intriguing title, an interesting graphic or drop quote. Journalists typically begin feature articles, ones that do not deal with "hard" news, with what they call a *hook*, designed to catch readers' attention. The particular occasion that opens many reflective essays often serves this purpose. Staples's opening phrase, "My first victim," certainly grabs attention.

But once "caught," readers have to be kept reading. One of the ways reflective writers keep readers engaged is by projecting an image of themselves—sometimes called the *writer's persona* or *voice*—that readers can identify with or at least find interesting. Staples, for example, uses the first-person pronouns *my* and *I* to present himself in his writing and to speak directly to readers. In paragraph 2, for example, he describes himself as "a softy" and explains how he felt when he realized that the woman was so frightened by him that she ran for her life. Like most reflective writers, Staples tries to make himself sympathetic to readers so that they will listen to what he has to say.

Analyze

1. *Reread* the essay looking for places where you get a sense of Staples as a person, and in the margin briefly *describe* the impression you get.

2. *Think about* what engages you or draws you into the essay.

Write

Write several sentences about the impressions you get of Staples from reading this essay, exploring how these impressions affect your interest in his ideas.

A SPECIAL READING STRATEGY

Comparing and Contrasting Related Readings: Brent Staples's "Black Men and Public Space" *and an excerpt from his autobiography,* Parallel Time

Comparing and contrasting related readings is a critical reading strategy useful both in reading for meaning and in reading like a writer. This strategy is particularly applicable when writers present similar subjects, as is the case in the two reflective readings by Brent Staples that are compared here. The first, "Black Men and Public Space," the essay you have just read, was first published in 1986. The second, the excerpt on pages 172–73 from Staples's autobiography *Parallel Time,* was published in 1994. Both readings deal with the same occasion—when Staples encountered his "first victim" (paragraph 1 in both). But you will notice that the details of this first encounter as well as Staples's reflections about it differ significantly in the two readings. As you read, notice what Staples keeps from the original and what he changes. To compare and contrast these two reflective readings, think about issues such as these:

- Compare these readings in terms of the way the particular occasion is described. What seems to you to be most significant about these two descriptions? Note, for example, the details about the location and the woman's appearance as well as how Staples describes his immediate reaction.

- Compare how Staples describes what he calls "the language of fear" in these readings (paragraph 3 in both). Highlight the places in each reading where the language of fear is described. In what ways is his description similar and different? How does he explain its causes?

- Compare these readings to see what Staples thinks and feels about the situation he finds himself in and what actions he decides to take. What are the main differences in his reactions? Speculate on why he decided to make so radical a revision of his earlier reflections in his autobiography published nearly a decade after his original essay was published. What do you think might have changed (in Staples's feelings, in the broader cultural climate, or in some other way) during that period that led Staples to share with readers his angry response rather than leaving readers with the image of himself he projects at the end of the original version?

See Appendix 1 for detailed guidelines on using the comparing and contrasting related readings strategy.

From *Parallel Time*

At night, I walked to the lakefront whenever the weather permitted. I was headed home from the lake when I took my first victim. It was late fall, and the wind was cutting. I was wearing my navy pea jacket, the collar turned up, my hands snug in the pockets. Dead leaves scuttled in shoals along the streets. I turned out of Blackstone Avenue and headed west on 57th Street, and there she was, a few yards ahead of me, dressed in business clothes and carrying a briefcase. She looked back at me once, then again, and picked up her pace. She looked back again and started to run. I stopped where I was and looked up at the surrounding windows. What did this look like to people peeking out through their blinds? I was out walking. But what if someone had thought they'd seen something they hadn't and called the police. I held back the urge to run. Instead, I walked south to The Midway, plunged into its darkness, and remained on The Midway until I reached the foot of my street. 1

I'd been a fool. I'd been walking the streets grinning good evening at people who were frightened to death of me. I did violence to them by just being. How had I missed this? I kept walking at night, but from then on I paid attention. 2

I became expert in the language of fear. Couples locked arms or reached for each other's hand when they saw me. Some crossed to the other side of the street. People who were carrying on conversations went mute and stared straight ahead, as though avoiding my eyes would save them. This reminded me of an old wives' tale: that rabid dogs didn't bite if you avoided their eyes. The determination to avoid my eyes made me invisible to classmates and professors whom I passed on the street. 3

It occurred to me for the first time that I was big. I was 6 feet 1½ inches tall, and my long hair made me look bigger. I weighed only 170 pounds. But the navy pea jacket that Brian had given me was broad at the shoulders, high at the collar, making me look bigger and more fearsome than I was. 4

I tried to be innocuous but didn't know how. The more I thought about how I moved, the less my body belonged to me; I became a false character riding along inside it. I began to avoid people. I turned out of my way into side streets to spare them the sense that they were being stalked. I let them clear the lobbies of buildings before I entered, so they wouldn't feel trapped. Out of nervousness I began to whistle and discovered I was good at it. My whistle was pure and sweet—and also in tune. On the street at night I whistled popular tunes from the Beatles and Vivaldi's *Four* 5

Seasons. The tension drained from people's bodies when they heard me. A few even smiled as they passed me in the dark.

Then I changed. I don't know why, but I remember when. I was 6 walking west on 57th Street, after dark, coming home from the lake. The man and the woman walking toward me were laughing and talking but clammed up when they saw me. The man touched the woman's elbow, guiding her toward the curb. Normally I'd have given way and begun to whistle, but not this time. This time I veered toward them and aimed myself so that they'd have to part to avoid walking into me. The man stiffened, threw back his head and assumed the stare: eyes dead ahead, mouth open. His face took on a bluish hue under the sodium vapor streetlamps. I suppressed the urge to scream into his face. Instead I glided between them, my shoulder nearly brushing his. A few steps beyond them I stopped and howled with laughter. I called this game Scatter the Pigeons.

Fifty-seventh Street was too well lit for the game to be much 7 fun; people didn't feel quite vulnerable enough. Along The Midway were heart-stopping strips of dark sidewalk, but these were so frightening that few people traveled them. The stretch of Blackstone between 57th and 55th provided better hunting. The block was long and lined with young trees that blocked out the streetlight and obscured the heads of people coming toward you.

One night I stooped beneath the branches and came up on the 8 other side, just as a couple was stepping from their car into their town house. The woman pulled her purse close with one hand and reached for her husband with the other. The two of them stood frozen as I bore down on them. I felt a surge of power: these people were mine; I could do with them as I wished. If I'd been younger with less to lose, I'd have robbed them, and it would have been easy. All I'd have to do was stand silently before them until they surrendered their money. I thundered, "Good evening!" into their bleached-out faces and cruised away laughing.

I held a special contempt for people who cowered in their cars 9 as they waited for the light to change at 57th and Woodlawn. The intersection was always deserted at night, except for a car or two stuck at the red. *Thunk! Thunk! Thunk!* They hammered down the door locks when I came into view. Once I had hustled across the street, head down, trying to seem harmless. Now I turned brazenly into the headlights and laughed. Once across, I paced the sidewalk, glaring until the light changed. They'd made me terrifying. Now I'd show them how terrifying I could be.

■ Readings

SUZANNE WINCKLER

A Savage Life

> *Suzanne Winckler (b. 1946) is a freelance writer. She has written several volumes in the* Smithsonian Guides to Natural America *series (including* The Plains States *[1998],* The Great Lakes States *[1998], and* The Heartland *[1997]) and has co-authored three books in the* Our Endangered Planet *series (on* Antarctica *[1992],* Population Growth *[1991], and* Soil *[1993]). In addition, her essays have been published in many newspapers and magazines, such as* Audubon, Atlantic Monthly, Kansas City Star, *and* New York Times Magazine, *in which "A Savage Life" appeared originally in 1999.*
>
> *Before you read Winckler's reflections on killing chickens, think about how distant most of us are from the processes of raising and butchering the food we eat and how that distance might affect our attitudes toward these activities.*

Every few years I butcher chickens with a friend named Chuck who lives near the farm my husband and I own in northern Minnesota. Chuck buys chicks and takes care of them for the 10 weeks it takes them to mature. I share in the feed costs, but my main contribution—for which I get an equal share of birds—is to help slaughter them.   1

One day last fall, Chuck, two other friends and I butchered 28 chickens. We worked without stopping from 10 A.M. to 6 P.M. By the time it was over we had decapitated, gutted, plucked, cleaned and swaddled each bird in plastic wrap for the freezer. We were exhausted and speckled with blood. For dinner that night we ate vegetables.   2

Butchering chickens is no fun, which is one reason I do it. It is the price I pay for being an omnivore and for eating other meat, like beef and pork, for which I have not yet determined a workable way to kill.   3

The first time I caught a chicken to chop its head off, I noticed, as I cradled it in my arms, that it had the heft and pliability of a newborn baby. This was alarming enough, but when I beheaded it, I was not prepared to be misted in blood or to watch it bounce on the ground. Headless chickens don't run around. They thrash with such force and seeming coordination that they sometimes turn back flips. When I first saw this, three things became clear to me.   4

I realized why cultures, ancient and contemporary, develop elaborate rituals for coping with the grisly experience of killing any sentient creature. I understood why so many people in my largely bloodless nation are alarmed at the thought of killing anything (except insects) even though they eat with relish meat other people process for them. I saw why a small subset of my contemporaries are so horrified by the thought of inflicting pain and causing death that they maintain people should never kill anything.

One risk I run in this self-imposed food-gathering exercise is leaving the impression, or perhaps even furtively feeling, that I am superior to the omnivores who leave the killing of their meat to someone else. I don't think I am. Slaughtering my own chickens is one of two opportunities (gardening is the other) where I can dispense with the layers of anonymous people between me and my food. I have no quarrel with them. I just don't know who they are. They are not part of my story.

Killing chickens provides narratives for gathering, cooking and sharing food in a way that buying a Styrofoam package of chicken breasts does not. I remember the weather on the days we have butchered our chickens, and the friends over the years who've come to help, who have included a surgical nurse, a cell biologist, a painter of faux interiors, a Minnesota state representative who is also a logger, a zoologist, a nurse with Head Start and a former Army medic who now runs the physical plant at a large hospital. I can measure the coming of age of my partner's two kids, who were tykes the first time we butchered chickens 10 years ago, and who this go-round were well into puberty with an array of pierced body parts.

My mother, who was born in 1907, belonged to the last generation for whom killing one's food was both a necessity and an ordinary event. Her family raised chickens for the purpose of eating them, and her father taught all his children to hunt. My survival does not depend on killing chickens, but in doing so I have found that it fortifies my connection to her. It also allows me to cast a tenuous filament back to my feral past. In 1914, Melvin Gilmore, an ethnobotanist, wrote, "In savage and barbarous life the occupation of first importance is the quest of food." Having butchered my own chickens, I now feel acquainted with the savage life.

As exhilarating as this may be, I do not thrill at the prospect of beheading chickens. Several days before the transaction, I circle around the idea of what my friends and I will be doing. On the assigned morning, we are slow to get going. There are knives and cleavers to sharpen, vats of water to be boiled in the sauna house, tables and chairs to set up, aprons and buckets to gather, an order of assembly to establish. In their own ritual progression, these preparations are a way to gear ourselves up. I feel my shoulders hunch and my focus is narrow. It is like putting on an invisible veil of resolve to do penance for a misdeed. I am too far gone in my rational Western head to appropriate the ritual of cultures for whom the bloody business of hunting was a matter of survival. But butchering chickens has permitted me to stand in the black night just outside the edge of their campfire, and from that prospect I have inherited the most important lesson of all in the task of killing meat: I have learned to say thank you and I'm sorry.

READING FOR MEANING

This section presents three activities that will help you reread Winckler's reflective essay with a critical eye. Done in sequence, these activities lead you from a basic understanding of the selection to a more personal response to it and finally to an analysis that deepens your understanding and critical thinking about what you are reading.

Read to Comprehend

Reread the selection, and write a brief summary of the three things that Winckler says became clear to her after the first time she beheaded a chicken. Also make a list of any words you do not understand—for example, *swaddled* (2), *pliability* (4), *furtively* (6), *penance* (9). Look up their meanings in a dictionary to see which definition best fits the context.

To expand your understanding of this reading, you might use one or more of the following critical reading strategies that are explained and illustrated in Appendix 1: *outlining, summarizing, paraphrasing,* and *questioning to understand and remember.*

Read to Respond

Write several paragraphs exploring your initial thoughts and feelings about Winckler's reflective essay. Focus on anything that stands out for you, perhaps because it resonates with your own experience or because you find a statement puzzling.

You might consider writing about

■your response to the vivid details Winckler gives in her descriptions of how to butcher a chicken (paragraph 2) and of what headless chickens do (4).

▪the different people who participate with Winckler in this ritual (7).

▪the ritual Winckler and her friends follow (9), perhaps relating it to rituals in which you participate.

▪how your own feelings about eating meat help you understand Winckler's choice to participate in this ritual.

To develop your response to Winckler's essay, you might use one or more of the following critical reading strategies that are explained and illustrated in Appendix 1: *contextualizing, reflecting on challenges to your beliefs and values, recognizing emotional manipulation,* and *judging the writer's credibility.*

Read to Analyze Underlying Assumptions

Write several paragraphs exploring one or more of the assumptions, values, and beliefs underlying Winckler's reflective essay. As you write, explain how the assumptions are reflected in the text, as well as what you now think of them (and perhaps of your own assumptions) after rereading the selection with a critical eye.

You might consider writing about

▪Winckler's assumption that she should pay a "price" (paragraph 3) or "do penance" (9) for eating meat, perhaps also speculating about why she does not just become a vegetarian.

▪the beliefs and values underlying the statement in the last sentence that "the most important lesson of all in the task of killing meat" is "to say thank you and I'm sorry."

▪the assumptions and values underlying Winckler's comparison of a chicken "cradled" in her arms to a "newborn baby" (4).

▪the values and beliefs implied in Winckler's statement in paragraph 7 that butchering chickens "provides narratives" that buying chicken does not provide.

▪the values and beliefs implied in Winckler's idea that butchering her own chickens connects her to her mother's generation and to her "feral past" (8).

To probe assumptions more deeply, you might want to use one or more of the following critical reading strategies that are explained and illustrated in Appendix 1: *reflecting on challenges to your beliefs and values, exploring the significance of figurative language,* and *looking for patterns of opposition.*

READING LIKE A WRITER
PRESENTING THE PARTICULAR OCCASION

Reflections are often triggered by a onetime event or observation. In the previous reading, for example, you saw how Brent Staples started thinking about his subject as a result of a particular event, and how he uses the time marker "late one evening" (paragraph 1) to let readers know this was a onetime event. Later in his essay, however, Staples refers to other occasions to make the point that what he became aware of on that particular night unhappily became a frequent occurrence. Similarly, Winckler begins her essay by referring to a recurring event, something she does "every few years." Then, in paragraph 2, she recounts a particular occasion signaled by the time marker "One day last fall." In paragraph 4, she recalls a second particular occasion, one that happened before the occasion narrated in the second paragraph. This activity will help you analyze the strategies Winckler uses to present these two particular occasions.

Analyze

1. *Look closely* at the occasion presented in paragraph 2. *Underline* the descriptive details and narrative actions Winckler uses to present what happened on this occasion.

2. Now *turn to* the event presented in paragraph 4. *Underline* the descriptive details and narrative actions Winckler uses here to present what happened.

3. *Review* the two events in paragraphs 2 and 4, and *choose* the one that you think makes the greatest impact on you as a reader.

Write

Write several sentences explaining how Winckler's descriptive details and narrative actions give the event you chose its impact. *Support* your explanation with examples from your annotations.

CONSIDERING IDEAS FOR YOUR OWN WRITING

Winckler's reflections may lead you to reflect on your own personal, familial, cultural, or religious traditions regarding food preparation and consumption. Consider any particular occasions you associate with certain kinds of foods. You also might consider reflecting on rituals more generally, such as the "rituals for coping" with painful or distasteful experiences that Winckler mentions in paragraph 5. You could reflect on the ways rituals are used to celebrate important occasions (such as drinking champagne on New Year's Eve), to signify a change in social status (a wedding or graduation), or to mark a significant stage in life (a bar mitzvah, confirmation, or other coming-of-age ceremony). Other subjects you could consider involve history and culture: Following Winckler's lead in calling her mother's "the last generation for whom killing one's food was both a necessity and an ordinary event" (paragraph 8), you could explore differences between your own and preceding generations. Alternatively, you could reflect on how people in the United States or in other countries maintain the kinds of traditions Winckler's mother grew up following.

NANCY GIBBS

Free the Children

Nancy Gibbs has degrees in history, politics, and philosophy from Yale and Oxford universities. She began her career as a journalist in 1985, when she joined Time *magazine, where she now writes news reports, feature articles, and essays as an editor-at-large, including* Time's *September 11 memorial issue and the award-winning cover stories "Teens, Sex and Value," "The Columbine Tapes," and "If You Want to Humble an Empire. . . ." As Ferris professor at Princeton University, Gibbs taught an advanced writing seminar on politics and the press. Among many other honors, she won the Luce Story of the Year Award and the Society of Professional Journalists Sigma Delta Chi Magazine Writing Award, both in 2002.*

"Free the Children" appeared in Time *in July 2003. As Gibbs explains at the beginning of the essay, her reflections are occasioned by her daughters' "playing hooky" from summer camp. Playing hooky is usually associated with school or work, so it is ironic to think that kids would want to play hooky from camp.*

Reflect on what playing hooky meant to you as a child and what it means to you now as an adult. As you read, think about what Gibbs values about summertime, perhaps in relation to what you most value about this or another time of the year.

My daughters are upstairs shrieking. And thumping. Nothing sounds broken, so I am leaving them alone to savor the outlaw feeling of playing hooky from the afternoon session of camp. They know absences don't count against them on some Permanent Record somewhere.

I long for them to have a whole summer that doesn't matter. When they can read for fun, even books that don't appear on the officially sanctioned summer reading list. When even the outfielders get to play first base sometimes because the game doesn't count. When they can ruin their brand-new sneakers because they found a great new creek. When a rule can be bent, if only to test its strength, and they can play all they want, without playing for keeps.

I want summer not to count because what happens as a result counts for so much. Maybe we adults idealize our own red-rover days, the hot afternoons spent playing games that required no coaches, eating foods that involved no nutrition, getting dirty in whole new ways and rarely glancing in the direction of a screen of any kind. Ask friends about the people and places that shaped them, and summer springs up quickly when they tell their story: their first kiss, first beer, first job that changed everything. The best summer moments were stretchy enough to carry us all through the year, which is why it's worth listening to all the warnings from social scientists about our Hurried Children who for the rest of the year wear their schedules like clothes that are too tight.

The experts have long charted the growing stress and disappearing downtime of modern children; now they say the trend extends across class and region. The combination of double shifts, shrinking vacations, fear of boredom and competitive instincts conspires to clog our kids' summer just as much as the rest of the year. Even camp isn't likely to be about s'mores and spud anymore: there is math camp and weight camp and leadership camp, as though summer were about perfecting ourselves, when in fact the opposite may be true.

That's because summer should be a season of grace—not of excuses but of exceptions, ice cream an hour before dinner just because it's so hot out, bedtimes missed in honor of meteor showers, weekdays and weekends that melt together because nothing feels like work. It's not just about relaxing; it's about rehearsing. All our efforts to guard and guide our children may just get in the way of the one thing they need most from us: to be deeply loved yet left alone so they can try a new skill, new slang, new style, new flip-flops. So they can trip a few times, make mistakes, cross them out, try again, with no one keeping score.

This may require some re-education, a kind of summer school   6
of play that teaches kids not to expect to be entertained every
moment, to adjust to days measured out not in periods or practices but in large clumps of opportunity called Morning and Afternoon. Go build a fort. Use every single art supply in the house to
make something big. Be bored and see where it takes you, because
the imagination's dusty wilderness is worth crossing if you want to
sculpt your soul.

Giving children some summer privacy and freedom takes nerve,   7
and not just because this is also precious time to be together as a
family. Last summer, the Amber Alert summer, who could take
their eyes off their kids in the front yard? When my 7-year-old was
half an hour late coming home one afternoon and the lifeguards
and counselors started asking me what she looked like, what she
was wearing, I couldn't get enough air in my lungs to tell them, the
fear was so strangling.

But when we finally found her, happily engrossed near Dead   8
Man's Cave catching frogs with a friend, I had to take a deep breath
and remember that maybe I had neglected to teach her to call
home if she was going to be late, because I had never needed to.
She is shuttled from school to playdate to soccer to chess, and only
in the summer does she control her own time and whereabouts at
all. Do I punish her for savoring liberty the first time she ever tasted
it? So we had a long talk while sitting under a tree before I grounded
her for a day.

We are bombarded with reasons to stay inside: we're afraid of   9
mosquitoes because of West Nile and grass because of pesticides
and sun because of cancer and sunscreen because of vitamin-D
deficiency. Ours is the generation that knows too much, including
what other kids are doing in the summer to get a head start in the
marathon that ends with a fat envelope from a top school. So apart
from the challenge of trusting our kids, there is the challenge of
trusting ourselves, steering by the stars of instinct and memory
rather than parent peer pressure or all those guidebooks on how
to raise a Successful Child.

I send my girls out to play in the hope that by summer's end I   10
will see the gifts that freedom brings. Kids seem four inches taller
in September than in June, whether they've grown any or not.
And the measuring stick is marked off in bruises healed and flags
captured, friends lost and found, goals achieved without anyone's help. I hope for the discipline not to discipline them too
much, because that's how I will learn how strong they have
become.

READING FOR MEANING

This section presents three activities that will help you reread Gibbs's reflective essay with a critical eye. Done in sequence, these activities lead you from a basic understanding of the selection to a more personal response to it and finally to an analysis that deepens your understanding and critical thinking about what you are reading.

Read to Comprehend

Reread the selection, and write a few sentences explaining what Gibbs thinks may be required of kids and their parents to make summer truly "a season of grace" (paragraph 5). Also make a list of any words you do not understand—for example, *sanctioned* (2), *grace* (5), *engrossed* (8). Look up their meanings in a dictionary to see which definition best fits the context.

To expand your understanding of this reading, you might use one or more of the following critical reading strategies that are explained and illustrated in Appendix 1: *outlining, summarizing, paraphrasing,* and *questioning to understand and remember.*

Read to Respond

Write several paragraphs exploring your initial thoughts and feelings about Gibbs's reflective essay. Focus on anything that stands out for you, perhaps because it resonates with your own experience or because you find a statement puzzling.

You might consider writing about

- your response to Gibbs's comment that she wants her children to "savor the outlaw feeling of playing hooky," perhaps in relation to your own experience of playing hooky from work, school, or something else (paragraph 1).

- the importance of summer in adults' stories "about the people and places that shaped them," perhaps in relation to your own stories (3).

- Gibbs's idea that children today may need "re-education . . . that teaches [them] not to expect to be entertained every moment" or to have their "days measured out" for them (6).

- your response to the trend indicating that children today are under more stress than children were in the past—in other words, that this generation has more stress than previous generations (4).

To develop your response to Gibbs's essay, you might use one or more of the following critical reading strategies that are explained and illustrated in Appendix 1: *contextualizing, reflecting on challenges to your beliefs and values, recognizing emotional manipulation,* and *judging the writer's credibility.*

Read to Analyze Underlying Assumptions

Write several paragraphs exploring one or more of the assumptions, values, and beliefs underlying Gibbs's reflective essay. As you write, explain how the assumptions are reflected in the text, as well as what you now think of them (and perhaps of your own assumptions) after rereading the selection with a critical eye.

You might consider writing about

- the beliefs and values that inspire people like Gibbs to "idealize our own red-rover days," perhaps in relation to your own nostalgia about childhood (paragraph 3).

- the values implicit in Gibbs's assertion that summer should not be about "perfecting ourselves" (4), in relation to your own values or those of your family.

- the value Gibbs places on freedom and the idea that what children need most from their parents is "to be deeply loved yet left alone" (5).

- the cultural assumptions behind the idea that today's parents need a lot of "nerve" to allow their children freedom (7).

- Gibbs's assumption that her children's summertime experience is like that of most American children today, perhaps in regard to social and economic class, ethnicity, or location.

To probe assumptions more deeply, you might use one or more of the following critical reading strategies that are explained and illustrated in Appendix 1: *reflecting on challenges to your beliefs and values, exploring the significance of figurative language,* and *looking for patterns of opposition.*

READING LIKE A WRITER

DEVELOPING THE REFLECTIONS THROUGH EXAMPLES

Writers rely on a number of essential strategies for developing their reflections, perhaps the most common one being illustration through example. Like Brent Staples, Gibbs relies on both brief and extended examples to illustrate and explain her ideas. In paragraph 3, for instance, she explains what she means by "red-rover days" through a series of brief examples: "the hot afternoons spent playing games that required no coaches, eating foods that involved no nutrition, getting dirty in whole new ways and rarely glancing in the direction of a screen of any kind." Notice that she does not define "red-rover days" but lets the examples convey her meaning. She also gives several examples rather than relying on only one. Moreover, Gibbs suggests what makes these activities examples of "red-rover days" when she repeats the word *no* in "required no coaches" and "involved no nutrition." These activities are not organized by adults, and they are not done because they are good for you or because you are supposed to do them. The last two examples—"getting dirty in whole new ways and rarely glancing in the direction of a screen of any kind"—extend the idea that red-rover days are meant to be liberating.

In addition, Gibbs uses an extended example, in paragraphs 7 and 8, to illustrate why "[g]iving children some summer privacy and freedom takes nerve." This extended example takes the form of an anecdote, a story about her seven-year-old daughter and what happened at a particular place and time.

Analyze

1. *Reread* paragraphs 2, 4, 5, and 6, and *note* in the margin all the places where Gibbs provides a series of brief examples.

2. *Underline* the general idea that each series of examples is meant to illustrate.

3. *Notice* the different ways the examples are presented grammatically— whether the series is preceded by a comma, colon, or period; whether each example is given its own sentence or is a phrase within a longer sentence.

Write

Write several sentences explaining what you have learned about how Gibbs uses brief examples to develop her reflections.

CONSIDERING IDEAS FOR YOUR OWN WRITING

Following Gibbs's lead, you might consider reflecting on a pattern of behavior you have noticed, perhaps one that indicates a change of some kind, or on your ideas about some aspect of childhood. For example, you might reflect on how children learn to amuse themselves, how people cope with their fears or anxieties, the "Hurried Children" phenomenon, the "outlaw feeling," the need for privacy, or the importance of freedom. Other possibilities for reflection include thinking about the kinds of play children are involved in today, such as organized sports and computer games.

A SPECIAL READING STRATEGY

Comparing and Contrasting Related Readings: Gibbs's "Free the Children" and Brooks's "The Merits of Meritocracy"

Comparing and contrasting related readings is a critical reading strategy useful both in reading for meaning and in reading like a writer. This strategy is particularly applicable when writers present similar subjects, as is the case in the reflective essays in this chapter by Nancy Gibbs (p. 180) and David Brooks (p. 193). Both writers reflect on childhood in contemporary America from the perspective of parents. To compare and contrast these two reflective essays, think about issues such as these:

- Compare these essays in terms of how they represent childhood in the United States today. Consider how the pictures of childhood they construct depend on such factors as economic class, ethnic background, and location.

- Compare Gibbs's attitude about the "Hurried Children" phenomenon (paragraph 3) with what Brooks calls "a busy childhood" (3).

- Compare the two writers' concern with children's moral development.

- Compare their views regarding the role of parents.

See Appendix 1 for detailed guidelines on using the comparing and contrasting related readings strategy.

BARBARA EHRENREICH

Are Families Dangerous?

Barbara Ehrenreich (b. 1941) earned her Ph.D. in biology but chose a career as a writer, explaining that her science background has helped her look at things both analytically and systematically. A prolific writer and researcher, Ehrenreich is the author of many books, including Fear of Falling: The Inner Life of the Middle Class *(1989),* The Worst Years of Our Lives: Irreverent Notes from a Decade of Greed *(1990),* Blood Rites: Origins and History of the Passions of War *(1997), and* Nickel and Dimed: On (Not) Getting By in America *(2001). Among numerous honors she has received are a National Magazine Award for Excellence in reporting, a Ford Foundation Award for humanistic perspectives on contemporary society, the Sidney Hillman Award for journalism, a Guggenheim Fellowship, and a John D. and Catherine T. MacArthur Foundation grant. Her essays have appeared in such journals and magazines as* American Scholar, Atlantic Monthly, *and* Harper's, *for which she is also a contributing editor. She writes a weekly column for* Time *magazine and the* Guardian, *a British newspaper.*

The following essay was published in Time *in 1994. The occasion for Ehrenreich's reflections is three well-publicized cases of family violence: Brothers Erik and Lyle Menendez, convicted of murdering their parents, claimed their parents abused them; Lorena Bobbitt cut off her husband's penis because he abused her; and O. J. Simpson abused his wife, Nicole, but was found not guilty of murdering her.*

As you read, notice how Ehrenreich weaves these cases in and out of her reflections about how dangerous, even deadly, some families can be. You will find yourself drawn into intense reflection about your own family and into evaluation of Ehrenreich's ideas.

A disturbing subtext runs through our recent media fixations. Parents abuse sons—allegedly at least, in the Menendez case—who in turn rise up and kill them. A husband torments a wife, who retaliates with a kitchen knife. Love turns into obsession, between the Simpsons anyway, and then perhaps into murderous rage: the family, in other words, becomes personal hell.

This accounts for at least part of our fascination with the Bobbitts and the Simpsons and the rest of them. We live in a culture that fetishes the family as the ideal unit of human community, the perfect container for our lusts and loves. Politicians of both parties are aggressively "pro-family," even abortion-rights bumper stickers proudly link "pro-family" and "pro-choice." Only with the occasional celebrity crime do we allow ourselves to think the nearly unthinkable: that the family may not be the ideal and perfect living

arrangement after all—that it can be a nest of pathology and a cradle of gruesome violence.

It's a scary thought, because the family is at the same time our   3
"haven in a heartless world." Theoretically, and sometimes actually,
the family nurtures warm, loving feelings, uncontaminated by
greed or power hunger. Within the family, and often only within
the family, individuals are loved "for themselves," whether or not
they are infirm, incontinent, infantile or eccentric. The strong
(adults and especially males) lie down peaceably with the small
and weak.

But consider the matter of wife battery. We managed to dodge   4
it in the Bobbitt case and downplay it as a force in Tonya Harding's
life. Thanks to O. J., though, we're caught up now in a mass
consciousness-raising session, grimly absorbing the fact that in
some areas domestic violence sends as many women to emergency
rooms as any other form of illness, injury or assault.

Still, we shrink from the obvious inference: for a woman, home   5
is, statistically speaking, the most dangerous place to be. Her worst
enemies and potential killers are not strangers but lovers, husbands and those who claimed to love her once. Similarly, for every
child like Polly Klaas who is killed by a deranged criminal on
parole, dozens are abused and murdered by their own relatives.
Home is all too often where the small and weak fear to lie down
and shut their eyes.

At some deep, queasy, Freudian level, we all know this. Even in   6
the ostensibly "functional," nonviolent family, where no one is
killed or maimed, feelings are routinely bruised and often twisted
out of shape. There is the slap or put-down that violates a child's
shaky sense of self, the cold, distracted stare that drives a spouse to
tears, the little digs and rivalries. At best, the family teaches the finest
things human beings can learn from one another—generosity and
love. But it is also, all too often, where we learn nasty things like
hate and rage and shame.

Americans act out their ambivalence about the family without   7
ever owning up to it. Millions adhere to creeds that are militantly
"pro-family." But at the same time millions flock to therapy groups
that offer to heal the "inner child" from damage inflicted by family
life. Legions of women band together to revive the self-esteem
they lost in supposedly loving relationships and to learn to love a
little less. We are all, it is often said, "in recovery." And from what?
Our families, in most cases.

There is a long and honorable tradition of "anti-family"   8
thought. The French philosopher Charles Fourier taught that the
family was a barrier to human progress; early feminists saw

a degrading parallel between marriage and prostitution. More recently, the renowned British anthropologist Edmund Leach stated that "far from being the basis of the good society, the family, with its narrow privacy and tawdry secrets, is the source of all discontents."

Communes proved harder to sustain than plain old couples, and the conservatism of the '80s crushed the last vestiges of life-style experimentation. Today even gays and lesbians are eager to get married and take up family life. Feminists have learned to couch their concerns as "family issues," and public figures would sooner advocate free cocaine on demand than criticize the family. Hence our unseemly interest in O. J. and Erik, Lyle and Lorena: they allow us, however gingerly, to break the silence on the hellish side of family life.

But the discussion needs to become a lot more open and forth-right. We may be stuck with the family—at least until someone invents a sustainable alternative—but the family, with its deep, impacted tensions and longings, can hardly be expected to be the moral foundation of everything else. In fact, many families could use a lot more outside interference in the form of counseling and policing, and some are so dangerously dysfunctional that they ought to be encouraged to disband right away. Even healthy families need outside sources of moral guidance to keep the internal tensions from imploding—and this means, at the very least, a public philosophy of gender equality and concern for child welfare. When, instead, the larger culture aggrandizes wife beaters, degrades women or nods approvingly at child slappers, the family gets a little more dangerous for everyone, and so, inevitably, does the larger world.

READING FOR MEANING

This section presents three activities that will help you reread Ehrenreich's reflective essay with a critical eye. Done in sequence, these activities lead you from a basic understanding of the selection to a more personal response to it and finally to an analysis that deepens your understanding and critical thinking about what you are reading.

Read to Comprehend

Reread the selection, and write a few sentences describing the dangers in families that Ehrenreich either implies or states directly. Also make a list of any words you do not understand—for example, *subtext* (paragraph 1), *fetishes* (2), *pathology* (2), *inference* (5). Look up their meanings in a dictionary to see which definition best fits the context.

To expand your understanding of this reading, you might use one or more of the following critical reading strategies that are explained and illustrated in Appendix 1: *outlining, summarizing, paraphrasing,* and *questioning to understand and remember.*

Read to Respond

Write several paragraphs exploring your initial thoughts and feelings about Ehrenreich's reflective essay. Focus on anything that stands out for you, perhaps because it resonates with your own experience or because you find a statement puzzling.

You might consider writing about

- the examples that open the essay and what they suggest to you about dysfunction in families.

- Ehrenreich's suggestion that our culture idealizes or "fetishes the family" (paragraph 2).

- the view of the family as "a nest of pathology" (2), where "feelings are routinely bruised" even in so-called "functional" families (6).

- the advice Ehrenreich gives in her conclusion about the need "to break the silence on the hellish side of family life" (9) and to develop "a public philosophy" beyond the family as a source of moral guidance (10).

- your experiences or observations of the best and the worst of family life, connecting them with Ehrenreich's reflections.

To develop your response to Ehrenreich's essay, you might use one or more of the following critical reading strategies that are explained and illustrated in Appendix 1: *contextualizing, reflecting on challenges to your beliefs and values, recognizing emotional manipulation,* and *judging the writer's credibility.*

Read to Analyze Underlying Assumptions

Write several paragraphs exploring one or more of the assumptions, values, and beliefs underlying Ehrenreich's reflective essay. As you write, explain how the assumptions are reflected in the text, as well as what you now think of them (and perhaps of your own assumptions) after rereading the essay with a critical eye.

You might consider writing about

- Ehrenreich's assumption that only "the occasional celebrity crime" allows us "to think the nearly unthinkable: that the family may not be the ideal and perfect living arrangement after all" (paragraph 2).

- the values and beliefs underlying the cultural need to see the family as "the ideal unit of human community" (2) and a " 'haven in a heartless world' " (3).

- the assumptions of early feminists about the family as compared to the experience of women today.

- why Ehrenreich assumes that "the family, with its deep, impacted tensions and longings, can hardly be expected to be the moral foundation of everything else" (10).

- Ehrenreich's assumption that "a public philosophy of gender equality and concern for child welfare" would help keep family tensions from "imploding" (10).

To probe assumptions more deeply, you might use one or more of the following critical reading strategies that are explained and illustrated in Appendix 1: *reflecting on challenges to your beliefs and values, exploring the significance of figurative language,* and *looking for patterns of opposition.*

READING LIKE A WRITER
ENGAGING READERS

Reflective writers use an array of strategies early in the essay to engage readers' interest. They often craft an attention-grabbing title—"A Savage Life," "Free the Children," or "Are Families Dangerous?"—and work to make their opening sentences intriguing. For example, Brent Staples opens his essay with a shocking confession ("My first victim was a woman"), and Wendy Lee begins with a mysterious statement ("When my friend told me that her father had once compared her to a banana, I stared at her blankly"). Reflective writers sometimes try to establish a tone or project a voice that will engage readers—by using humor or outrageous exaggeration, for instance.

Analyze

1. *Review* Ehrenreich's title, and *recall* its initial impact on you. How well did it engage your interest? What did you expect?

2. *Reread* the first two paragraphs, and *notice* the strategies Ehrenreich uses to interest readers, such as referring to family-related crimes that were heavily reported in the media and challenging the idealization of the family by politicians.

Write

Write several sentences explaining the strategies Ehrenreich uses to engage readers and how effective they are for you as a reader.

CONSIDERING IDEAS FOR YOUR OWN WRITING

Ehrenreich's essay suggests several different kinds of subjects you might consider. For example, she points out that families seldom live up to our idea of the perfect family. You could reflect on something else that falls short of expectations. Think of an experience you have had that was disappointing, such as a conflict with a friend, co-worker, or sibling; a job, class, or school that turned out to be less satisfying than you had hoped; a type of new technology that had great promise but was full of bugs. Ehrenreich mentions other subjects you could explore in your own reflective essay, such as "a child's shaky sense of self" (paragraph 6). Your own experience as a child might suggest a particular occasion you could use to reflect on how children develop a sense of individuality and self-worth. You could also explore your ideas of what an ideal society would be like and perhaps reflect on where your ideas about the ideal society come from.

DAVID BROOKS

The Merits of Meritocracy

David Brooks (b. 1961) graduated with a degree in history from the University of Chicago and now is a contributing editor at News-week *and the* Atlantic Monthly, *a senior editor at the* Weekly Stan-dard, *and a columnist for the* New York Times. *He has written two books,* Bobos in Paradise: The New Upper Class and How They Got There *(2000) and* On Paradise Drive: How We Live Now (and Always Have) in the Future Tense *(2004), and has edited the anthol-ogy* Backward and Upward: The New Conservative Writing *(1996). A widely respected spokesperson for politically conservative views, Brooks also regularly appears on* The NewsHour with Jim Lehrer *on PBS,* Late Edition *on CNN, and National Public Radio.*

In "The Merits of Meritocracy," which first appeared in the Atlantic Monthly *in 2002, Brooks reflects on the "busy childhood" of today's middle-class American children. What occasioned these reflec-tions, Brooks tells us in the opening paragraphs, is his observation of the many helmets and other sports-related gear in his garage. Think about the activities you were involved in as a child or the activities your own children or younger siblings are involved in today. As you read, notice how Brooks moves from his observations about children's activities to his reflections on the process of character building.*

My daughter is a four-helmet kid. She has a regular helmet she wears bike riding, pogo sticking, and when she borrows her older brother's skateboard. She has a pink batting helmet, which she wears during her Little League baseball games. She has a helmet for horseback-riding lessons, on Sundays. And she has a helmet for ice hockey, which she plays on Friday afternoons. (For hockey she also has an equipment bag large enough to hold several corpses.) My daughter's not even a jock (although she is something of a live wire). Her main interest is art, which she does in an after-school program on Tuesdays and at home on her own.

But it's her helmets that really got me thinking. They're generally scattered around the equipment racks in our garage, along with her brothers' helmet collections and all manner of sleds, mitts, scooters, bicycles, and balls, and they represent a certain sort of childhood— a childhood that has now become typical in middle-class America.

It's a busy childhood, filled with opportunities, activities, teams, coaches, and, inevitably, gear. It's a safety-conscious childhood, with ample adult supervision. And it is, I believe (at least I want to believe), a happy and fulfilling childhood that will prepare my daughter for a happy adult life.

This sort of childhood is different from the childhoods Americans have traditionally had. It's not an independent childhood, like Huck Finn's or the Bowery Boys'. Today's middle-class kids, by and large, don't live apart from adult society, free to explore and experiment and, through adventure and misadventure, teach themselves the important lessons of life. Nor is it a Horatio Alger childhood. Middle-class kids by definition haven't come from poverty and deprivation. Nor do they build self-discipline from having to work on a farm. If they hunger for success, it's not because they started at the bottom.

Today's mode of raising kids generates a lot of hand-wringing and anxiety, some of it on my part. We fear that kids are spoiled by the abundance and frenetic activity all around them. We fear that the world of suburban sprawl, Game Boys, Britney Spears CDs, and shopping malls will dull their moral senses. We fear that they are too deferential to authority, or that they are confronted with so many choices that they never have to make real commitments. Or we fear that they are skipping over childhood itself. The toy companies call this phenomenon "age compression": Kids who are ten no longer want toys that used to appeal to ten-year-olds. Now it is three-to-five-year-olds who go for Barbie dolls. By the time a girl is seven she wants to be a mini-adult.

But I've come to believe that our fears are overblown. The problem is that the way kids (and, for that matter, the rest of us) live is estranged from the formulaic ideas we have about building character. We assume that character is forged through hardship—economic deprivation, war, and so on—and that we who have had it easy, who have grown up in this past half century of peace and prosperity, must necessarily have weak or suspect souls.

It's true that we live amid plenty; even in time of war we are told to keep shopping. But today's kids have a way of life that entails its own character-building process, its own ethical system. They live in a world of almost crystalline meritocracy. Starting at birth, middle-class Americans are called on to master skills, do well in school, practice sports, excel in extracurricular activities, get into college, build their résumés, change careers, be good in bed, set up retirement plans, and so on. This is a way of life that emphasizes individual achievement, self-propulsion, perpetual improvement, and permanent exertion.

The prime ethical imperative for the meritocrat is self-fulfillment. The phrase sounds New Agey; it calls to mind a Zen vegan sitting on the beach at dawn contemplating his narcissism. But over the past several years the philosophers Charles Taylor, of McGill University, and Alan Gewirth, of the University of Chicago, have argued that a serious moral force is contained in the idea of self-fulfillment. Meritocrats may not necessarily be able to articulate this morality, but they live by it nonetheless.

It starts with the notion that we have a lifelong mission to realize our capacities. "It is a bringing of oneself to flourishing completion, an unfolding of what is strongest or best in oneself, so that it represents the successful culmination of one's aspirations or potentialities," Gewirth wrote in *Self-Fulfillment* (1998). The way we realize our potential is through our activities. By ceaselessly striving to improve at the things we enjoy, we come to define, enlarge, and attain our best selves. These activities are the bricks of our identities; if we didn't write or play baseball or cook or litigate (or whatever it is we do well), we would cease to be who we are. This is what Karl Marx was describing when he wrote, "Milton produced *Paradise Lost* as a silkworm produces silk, as the activation of his own nature."

In this mode of living, character isn't something one forges as a youth and then retains thereafter. Morality doesn't come to one in a single revelation or a grand moment of epiphany. Instead, virtue and character are achieved gradually and must be maintained through a relentless struggle for self-improvement. We are in an ongoing dialogue with our inadequacies, and we are happiest when we are most deeply engaged in overcoming them.

This is not a solitary process. Once ensconced in an activity, we find ourselves surrounded by mentors, coaches, teachers, colleagues, teammates, consultants, readers, and audience members. Society helps us in two ways. First, it gives us opportunities to participate in the things that will allow us to realize our capacities: Parents earnestly cast about for activities their children will love, and then spend their weekends driving them from one to another. Good schools have extracurricular offerings. Good companies and organizations allow their employees and members to explore new skills, and great nations have open, fluid societies—so that individuals can find their best avenues and go as far as their merit allows.

Second, society surrounds the individual with a web of instruction, encouragement, and recognition. The hunger for recognition is a great motivator for the meritocrat. People define themselves in part by the extent to which others praise and appreciate them. In traditional societies recognition was determined by birth, breeding, and social station, but in a purified meritocracy people have to win it through performance. Each person responds to signals from those around him, working hard at activities that win praise and abandoning those that don't. (America no doubt leads the world in trophy production per capita.) An individual's growth, then, is a joint project of the self and society.

In this joint project individuals not only improve their capacities; they also come to realize that they cannot fully succeed unless they make a contribution to the society that helped to shape them. A scientist may be good at science, but she won't feel fulfilled unless she has made important discoveries or innovations that help those around her. Few meritocrats are content to master pointless tasks.

Social contributions—giving back—flow easily and naturally from the meritocrat's life mission. Baseball players enjoy clinics where they share tips with younger players. Parents devote many hours to coaching, or they become teachers, managers, and mentors. In the best relationships what follows is a sort of love affair. Mentor and pupil work hard to help each other and to honor each other's effort. Most find that they glimpse their best selves while working with others on an arduous undertaking, whether it is staging a play, competing for a championship, or arguing a case in court.

The great moral contest for the meritocrat is not between good and evil or virtue and vice. Most meritocrats are prudent, so they don't commit terrible crimes or self-destructive follies. The great temptation is triviality. Society recognizes the fulfillment of noble capacities, but it also rewards shallow achievements. A person can be famous simply for being rich or good-looking. Sometimes it's the emptiest but splashiest activities that win the most attention. It can be easy to fall into a comfortable pattern of self-approval. Society seems to be rewarding you for what you are doing. Your salary goes up. You get promoted. You win bonuses. But you haven't tapped your capacities to the fullest.

Meritocrats therefore face a continual struggle to choose worthy opportunities over trivial ones. Charles Taylor argues that each of us has an intuitive ability to make what he calls "strong evaluations" of which aspirations are noblest. We do this, he believes, by tapping into any of a variety of moral frameworks, which have been handed down through time and which have "significance independent of us or our desires." It is necessary, then, to dig deep into what it means to be a Christian or a Jew or an American or a doctor. By this way of thinking, society's rebels had it all wrong when they tried to find self-fulfillment by breaking loose from tradition. Their rebellions created selves without roots or moral reference points. Burrowing down into an inherited tradition allows the meritocrat to strive upward.

For decades social critics have sold Americans short. All those books about the Organization Man, the culture of narcissism, the last man, and the flat, commercial materialism of American life underestimated the struggles and opportunities to build character that are embedded in the meritocratic system. The critics applied bygone codes to today's way of life. Inevitably, they have found kids, and us, wanting, and not in the areas where we truly are wanting (chief among these being that we don't sufficiently educate our children in the substance of the moral traditions they are inheriting—the history of Christianity, the history of Judaism, the history of America).

Today's kids live amid peace and prosperity, true. But theirs is not an easy life. Has there ever been a generation compelled to accomplish so much—to establish an identity, succeed in school, cope with technological change, maneuver through the world of group dating and diverse sexual orientation, and make daily decisions about everything from cell-phone rate plans to brands of sugar substitute? The meritocrat's life is radically open, but its very openness creates a series of choices and challenges that are demanding and subtle because they are never-ending and because they are embedded in the pattern of everyday life—rather than being faced, say, at one crucial, life-determining moment on the battlefield.

18

There is virtue in trying to articulate the codes we live by, open and diverse and sprawling as those codes may be. Perhaps if we can reach a reasonably accurate understanding of the moral landscape of our lives, we will be better able to achieve our dreams and guide our ethical debates—though we will no doubt still have need of protective headgear.

19

READING FOR MEANING

This section presents three activities that will help you reread Brooks's reflective essay with a critical eye. Done in sequence, these activities lead you from a basic understanding of the selection to a more personal response to it and finally to an analysis that deepens your understanding and critical thinking about what you are reading.

Read to Comprehend

Reread the selection, and write a few sentences briefly explaining what Brooks thinks is the main difference between the typical modern American childhood and the traditional American childhood. Also make a list of any words you do not understand—for example, *meritocracy* (title and paragraph 7), *frenetic* (5), *narcissism* (8), *epiphany* (10). Look up their meanings in a dictionary to see which definition best fits the context.

Notice that Brooks makes references to Horatio Alger (4), Britney Spears (5), and other examples of historical and contemporary popular culture. If you are unfamiliar with any of these references, use the Internet to look them up. What do Brooks's references contribute to his essay?

To expand your understanding of this reading, you might use one or more of the following critical reading strategies that are explained and illustrated in Appendix 1: *outlining, summarizing, paraphrasing,* and *questioning to understand and remember.*

Read to Respond

Write several paragraphs exploring your initial thoughts and feelings about Brooks's reflective essay. Focus on anything that stands out for you, perhaps because it resonates with your own experience or because you find a statement puzzling.

You might consider writing about

- Brooks's own children's activities (paragraphs 1 and 2), considering the activities you and your siblings or friends were involved in as children or that your own children are involved in now.

- your response to Brooks's description of the "sort of childhood" that he says is now typical of "[t]oday's middle-class kids" (4), perhaps considering the childhood of Americans who are not middle class and do not live in the suburbs.

- the kinds of fears parents have about raising kids (5).

- Gewirth's idea that "[t]he way we realize our potential" is by "ceaselessly striving to improve at the things we enjoy" (9).

- Brooks's ideas that "an individual's growth" should be seen as "a joint project of the self and society" (12) and that making a contribution to society should be part of the process of self-fulfillment (13).

To develop your response to Brooks's essay, you might use one or more of the following critical reading strategies that are explained and illustrated in Appendix 1: *contextualizing, reflecting on challenges to your beliefs and values, recognizing emotional manipulation,* and *judging the writer's credibility.*

Read to Analyze Underlying Assumptions

Write several paragraphs exploring one or more of the assumptions, values, and beliefs underlying Brooks's reflective essay. As you write, explain how the assumptions are reflected in the text, as well as what you now think of them (and perhaps of your own assumptions) after rereading the essay with a critical eye.

You might consider writing about

- Brooks's assumptions about what people think is lacking in the kind of busy middle-class childhood that his children experience.

- the traditional American values underlying images of a childhood like Huck Finn's or Horatio Alger's.

- the assumption that living in a meritocracy builds character.

- the value of self-fulfillment as "a serious moral force" (8).

- the value Brooks places on making a contribution to society, perhaps in relation to your own value system.

- the assumption that meritocrats need to find meaning in an inherited moral tradition like Christianity, Judaism, or Americanness.

To probe assumptions more deeply, you might use one or more of the following critical reading strategies that are explained and illustrated in Appendix 1: *reflecting on challenges to your beliefs and values, exploring the significance of figurative language,* and *looking for patterns of opposition.*

READING LIKE A WRITER
MAINTAINING TOPICAL COHERENCE

Because reflective essays are exploratory, often trying out several ideas, they may appear to be only loosely organized, following a "first I had this idea and then I had another idea" principle of organization. Yet readers seldom become confused because writers are careful to maintain topical coherence and to provide cues to help readers follow the writer's train of thought. One of the main ways writers establish logical coherence is by repeating a key word or phrase related to the essay's general subject. Recall that Brent Staples repeats the key word *fear* to help readers keep track of his reflections. Brooks also uses repetition in this way. But as you reread Brooks's essay, you will see that the key word for the general subject of his essay is introduced in the title and does not appear in the body of the essay until paragraph 7. This activity will help you analyze the way Brooks uses repetition of the word *meritocracy* and related words to help his readers keep track of his central subject.

You will also examine another kind of repetition that Brooks uses to maintain coherence, especially in the opening paragraphs of his essay: the repetition of an important word from one paragraph to the next. Look, for example, at his use of *helmets* in the first line of paragraph 2 to echo the topic introduced in paragraph 1, and of the word *childhood* in the last sentence of paragraph 2, the first lines of paragraph 3, and in paragraph 4. This activity will help you see how Brooks repeats certain words like links in a chain to make his paragraphs flow coherently from one to the other.

Analyze

1. *Skim* the essay, and *underline* each instance of the word *meritocracy* and related word forms (such as *meritocrat*).

2. *Reread* paragraphs 5–10, and *notice* which words are repeated in order to link together paragraphs 5–6 and paragraphs 7–10.

Write

Write several sentences explaining what you learned about Brooks's use of word repetition to maintain topical coherence and help readers follow his thinking.

A SPECIAL READING STRATEGY

Outlining

Outlining can be an especially useful strategy for reading long and wide-ranging reflective essays like Brooks's. You can make a simple scratch outline of the essay by restating the main idea of each paragraph. For help with outlining, see Appendix 1 (pp. 657–59).

CONSIDERING IDEAS FOR YOUR OWN WRITING

Brooks's essay suggests many subjects for reflection. As he points out in the last paragraph, "[t]here is virtue in trying to articulate the codes we live by." Consider exploring one of the codes you live by, a code you think people in general should live by, or one of the codes Brooks mentions, such as making a contribution to society. You might reflect on the social contributions college students can make, such as tutoring young children, aiding the elderly or infirm, or volunteering as a big brother or big sister.

Brooks's reflections about character building might lead you to think about your own ethical training. He writes about the importance of mentors and emphasizes that morality is developed over time, requiring "a relentless struggle for self-improvement" or "an ongoing dialogue with our inadequacies" (paragraph 10). You might reflect on a mentor who helped you develop an ethical system or on an occasion when you struggled to overcome a particular shortcoming.

WENDY LEE

Peeling Bananas

Wendy Lee wrote the following essay when she was a high-school student, and in 1993 it was published in Chinese American Forum, *a quarterly journal of news and opinion. In the essay, Lee reflects on growing up in America as the child of parents born in China. While she focuses mainly on going to school, her interest is larger: to discover how she can be American without losing the knowledge and experience of her Chinese heritage.*

As you read, reflect on how you might hold on to the special qualities of your family or ethnic group while at the same time becoming part of a larger regional or national community.

When my friend told me that her father had once compared her to a banana, I stared at her blankly. Then I realized that her father must have meant that outside she had the yellow skin of a Chinese, but inside she was white like an American. In other words, her appearance was Chinese, but her thoughts and values were American. Looking at my friend in her American clothes with her perfectly straight black hair and facial features so much like my own, I laughed. Her skin was no more yellow than mine.

In kindergarten, we colored paper dolls: red was for Indians, black for Afro-Americans, yellow was for Chinese. The dolls that we didn't color at all—the white ones—were left to be Americans. But the class wanted to know where were the green, blue or purple people? With the paper dolls, our well-meaning teacher intended to emphasize that everyone is basically the same, despite skin color. Secretly I wondered why the color of my skin wasn't the shade of my yellow Crayola. After we colored the dolls, we stamped each one with the same vacant, smiley face. The world, according to our teacher, is populated by happy, epidermically diverse people.

What does it mean to be a Chinese in an American school? One thing is to share a last name with a dozen other students, so that you invariably squirm when roll-call is taken. It means never believing that the fairy-tales the teacher read during story time could ever happen to you, because you don't have skin as white as snow or long golden hair. "You're Chinese?" I remember one classmate saying. "Oh, I *really* like Chinese food." In the depths of her over-friendly eyes I saw fried egg-rolls and chow mein. Once, for show-and-tell, a girl proudly told the class that one of her ancestors was in the picture of George Washington crossing the Delaware.

I promptly countered that by thinking to myself, "Well, my grandfather was Sun Yat-Sen's[1] physician, so THERE."

In my home, there is always a rather haphazard combination of the past and present. Next to the scrolls of black ink calligraphy on the dining room wall is a calendar depicting scenes from the midwest; underneath the stacked Chinese newspapers, the *L.A. Times*. In the refrigerator, next to the milk and butter, are tofu and bok choy from the weekly trips to the local Chinese supermarket. Spoons are used for soup, forks for salad, but chopsticks are reserved for the main course. I never noticed the disparity between my lifestyle and that of white Americans—until I began school. There, I became acquainted with children of strictly Caucasian heritage and was invited to their homes. Mentally I always compared the interiors of their homes to my own and to those of my mother's Chinese friends. What struck me was that their homes seemed to have no trace of their heritages at all. But nearly all Chinese-American homes retain aspects of the Chinese culture; aspects that reflect the yearning for returning home Chinese immigrants always have.

Chinese immigrants like my parents have an unwavering faith in China's potential to truly become the "middle kingdom," the literal translation of the Chinese words for China. They don't want their first-generation children to forget the way their ancestors lived. They don't want their children to forget that China has a heritage spanning thousands of years, while America has only a paltry two hundred. My mother used to tape Chinese characters over the words in our picture books. Ungratefully my sister and I tore them off because we were more interested in seeing how the story turned out. When she showed us her satin Chinese dresses, we were more interested in playing dress-up than in the stories behind the dresses; when she taught us how to use chopsticks, we were more concentrated on eating the Chinese delicacies she had prepared. (Incidentally, I still have to remind myself how to hold my chopsticks properly, though this may merely be a personal fault; I can't hold a pencil properly either.)

After those endless sessions with taped-over books and flashcards, my mother packed us off to Chinese School. There, we were to benefit from interaction with other Chinese-American children in the same predicament—unable to speak, read, or write Chinese nicely. There, we were supposed to make the same progress we made in our American schools. But in its own way, Chinese School is as

4

5

6

---

[1] *Sun Yat-Sen* (1866–1925): revolutionary leader of China and first president of the Chinese Republic (1911–1912). (*Ed.*)

much of a banana as are Chinese-Americans. A Chinese School day starts and ends with a bow to the teacher to show proper reverence. In the intervening three hours, the students keep one eye on the mysterious symbols of Chinese characters on the blackboard and the other on the clock. Their voices may be obediently reciting a lesson, but silently they are urging the minute hand to go faster. Chinese is taught through the American way, with workbooks and homework and tests. Without distinctive methods to make the experience memorable and worthwhile for its students, Chinese School, too, is in danger of becoming completely Americanized. Chinese-American kids, especially those in their teens, have become bewitched by the American ideal of obtaining a career that makes lots and lots of money. Their Chinese heritage probably doesn't play a big part in their futures. Many Chinese-Americans are even willing to shed their skins in favor of becoming completely American. Certainly it is easier to go forward and become completely American than to regress and become completely Chinese in America.

Sometimes I imagine what it would be like to go back to Taiwan or mainland China. Through eyes misty with romantic sentiment, I can look down a crooked, stone-paved street where a sea of black-haired and slanted-eyed people are bicycling in tandem. I see factories where people are hunch-backed over tables to manufacture plastic toys and American flags. I see fog-enshrouded mountains of Guilin, the yellow mud of Yangtze River, and the Great Wall of China snaking across the landscape as it does in the pages of a *National Geographic* magazine. When I look up at the moon, I don't see the pale, impersonal sphere that I see here in America. Instead, I see the plaintive face of Chang-Oh, the moon goddess. When I look up at the moon, I may miss my homeland like the famous poet Li Bai did in the poem that every Chinese School student can recite. But will that homeland be America or China?

When the crooked street is empty with no bicycles, I see a girl standing across from me on the other side of the street. I see mirrored in her the same perfectly straight black hair and facial features that my Chinese-American friend has, or the same that I have. We cannot communicate, for I only know pidgin Mandarin whereas she speaks fluent Cantonese, a dialect of southern China. Not only is the difference of language a barrier, but the differences in the way we were brought up and the way we live. Though we look the same, we actually are of different cultures, and I may cross the street into her world but only as a visitor. However, I also realize that as a hybrid of two cultures, I am unique, and perhaps that uniqueness should be preserved.

READING FOR MEANING

This section presents three activities that will help you reread Lee's reflective essay with a critical eye. Done in sequence, these activities lead you from a basic understanding of the selection to a more personal response to it and finally to an analysis that deepens your understanding and critical thinking about what you are reading.

Read to Comprehend

Reread the selection, and write a few sentences identifying the occasion for Lee's reflections and listing two or three experiences by which Lee remains aware of her Chinese ethnicity. Also make a list of any words you do not understand— for example, *epidermically* (paragraph 2), *disparity* (4), *paltry* (5), *reverence* (6). Look up their meanings in a dictionary to see which definition best fits the context.

To expand your understanding of this reading, you might use one or more of the following critical reading strategies that are explained and illustrated in Appendix 1: *outlining, summarizing, paraphrasing,* and *questioning to understand and remember.*

Read to Respond

Write several paragraphs exploring your initial thoughts and feelings about Lee's essay. Focus on anything that stands out for you, perhaps because it resonates with your own experience or because you find a statement puzzling.

You might consider writing about

- what calling someone a banana or an oreo implies.

- what Lee thinks of her kindergarten teacher's decision to have students color paper dolls, perhaps in connection to your own experience of "well-meaning" but misguided teachers (paragraph 2).

- your response to Lee's observation that the homes of her Caucasian friends "seemed to have no trace of their heritages at all" (4), perhaps in relation to signs of your ethnic heritage evident in your home.

- your personal experience of feeling different ethnically or in some other way, comparing it to Lee's experience.

To develop your response to Lee's essay, you might use one or more of the following critical reading strategies that are explained and illustrated in Appendix 1: *contextualizing, reflecting on challenges to your beliefs and values, recognizing emotional manipulation,* and *judging the writer's credibility.*

Read to Analyze Underlying Assumptions

Write several paragraphs exploring one or more of the assumptions, values, and beliefs underlying Lee's reflective essay. As you write, explain how the assumptions are reflected in the text, as well as what you now think of them (and perhaps of your own assumptions) after rereading the selection with a critical eye.

You might consider writing about

- the assumptions underlying Lee's statement that it was only when she began school that she "noticed the disparity between my lifestyle and that of white Americans" (paragraph 4).

- the values behind Lee's parents' desire that their children learn about their native country's history and traditions.

- the values and beliefs underlying the statement that "Chinese-American kids . . . have become bewitched by the American ideal of obtaining a career that makes lots and lots of money" (6).

- the assumptions Lee makes when she imagines "what it would be like to go back to Taiwan or mainland China" (7).

- what is implied in Lee's use of the word "hybrid" to describe her position in regard to American and Chinese cultures (8).

To probe assumptions more deeply, you might use one or more of the following critical reading strategies that are explained and illustrated in Appendix 1: *reflecting on challenges to your beliefs and values, exploring the significance of figurative language,* and *looking for patterns of opposition.*

READING LIKE A WRITER
DEVELOPING REFLECTIONS THROUGH COMPARISON AND CONTRAST

In reflective writing, insights and ideas are central; yet writers cannot merely list ideas, regardless of how fresh and daring their ideas might be. Instead, writers must work imaginatively to develop their ideas, to explain and elaborate them, to view them from one angle and then another. One well-established way to develop ideas is through comparison and contrast.

Analyze

1. *Review* the comparisons and contrasts in paragraphs 4, 6, and 8 of Lee's essay.

2. *Choose one* of these paragraphs to analyze more closely. What exactly is being compared or contrasted? *Underline* details that highlight the comparisons and contrasts.

Write

Write several sentences describing how Lee uses comparisons and contrasts to develop her ideas. From the one paragraph you chose to analyze, *identify* the terms (the items being compared) of the comparison or contrast and the ideas they enable Lee to develop.

CONSIDERING IDEAS FOR YOUR OWN WRITING

Consider reflecting on your own ethnicity, beginning your essay, like Lee does, with a concrete occasion. If you are among the "white Caucasians" Lee mentions, you may doubt that you have an ethnicity in the sense that Lee has one. Consider, however, that Asians do not comprise a single ethnicity. Among Asian Americans, there are many distinctly different ethnicities, as defined by their countries or regions of origin: Chinese, Japanese, Korean, Cambodian, Vietnamese, and Philippine, among others. "White Caucasians" also represent many national origins: German (still the single largest American immigrant group), Swedish, Russian, Polish, Irish, Italian, British, Greek, and French, to mention only a few. In all of these immigrant groups, as well as others, intermarriage and acculturation to whatever is uniquely American have blurred many of the original ethnic distinctions. Nevertheless, Lee's reflections remind us of the likelihood that in nearly every American family there remain remnants of one or more national or regional ethnicities. This idea for writing invites you to reflect on whatever meanings remain for you personally in your ethnic identities.

KATHERINE HAINES

Whose Body Is This?

> *Katherine Haines wrote this essay for an assignment in her first-year college composition course. As the title suggests, the writer reflects on her dismay and anger about American society's obsession with the perfect body—especially the perfect female body. As you read, note the many kinds of details Haines uses to develop her reflections.*
>
> *The other readings in this chapter are followed by reading and writing activities. Following this reading, however, you are on your own to decide how to read for meaning and read like a writer.*

"Hey Rox, what's up? Do you wanna go down to the pool with me? It's a gorgeous day." 1

"No thanks, you go ahead without me." 2

"What? Why don't you want to go? You've got the day off work, and what else are you going to do?" 3

"Well, I've got a bunch of stuff to do around the house . . . pay the bills, clean the bathroom, you know. Besides, I don't want to have to see myself in a bathing suit—I'm so fat." 4

Why do so many women seem obsessed with their weight and body shape? Are they really that unhappy and dissatisfied with themselves? Or are these women continually hearing from other people that their bodies are not acceptable? 5

In today's society, the expectations for women and their bodies are all too evident. Fashion, magazines, talk shows, "lite" and fat-free food in stores and restaurants, and diet centers are all daily reminders of these expectations. For instance, the latest fashions for women reveal more and more skin: shorts have become shorter, to the point of being scarcely larger than a pair of underpants, and the bustier, which covers only a little more skin than a bra, is making a comeback. These styles are only flattering on the slimmest of bodies, and many women who were previously happy with their bodies may emerge from the dressing room after a run-in with these styles and decide that it must be diet time again. Instead of coming to the realization that these clothes are unflattering for most women, how many women will simply look for different and more flattering styles, and how many women will end up heading for the gym to burn off some more calories or to the bookstore to buy the latest diet book? 6

When I was in junior high, about two-thirds of the girls I knew   7
were on diets. Everyone was obsessed with fitting into the smallest size miniskirt possible. One of my friends would eat a carrot
stick, a celery stick, and two rice cakes for lunch. Junior high (and
the onset of adolescence) seemed to be the beginning of the pressure for most women. It is at this age that appearance suddenly
becomes important. Especially for those girls who want to be "popular" and those who are cheerleaders or on the drill team. The
pressure is intense; some girls believe no one will like them or
accept them if they are "overweight," even by a pound or two. The
measures these girls will take to attain the body that they think
will make them acceptable are often debilitating and life threatening.

My sister was on the drill team in junior high. My sister wanted   8
to fit in with the right crowd—and my sister drove herself to the
edge of becoming anorexic. I watched as she came home from
school, having eaten nothing for breakfast and at lunch only a bag
of pretzels and an apple (and she didn't always finish that), and
began pacing the oriental carpet that was in our living room.
Around and around and around, without a break, from four
o'clock until dinnertime, which was usually at six or seven o'clock.
And then at dinner, she would take minute portions and only pick
at her food. After several months of this, she became much paler
and thinner, but not in any sort of attractive sense. Finally, after
catching a cold and having to stay in bed for three days because she
was so weak, she was forced to go to the doctor. The doctor said
she was suffering from malnourishment and was to stay in bed
until she regained some of her strength. He advised her to eat lots
of fruits and vegetables until the bruises all over her body had
healed (these were a result of vitamin deficiency). Although my
sister did not develop anorexia, it was frightening to see what she
had done to herself. She had little strength, and the bruises she had
made her look like an abused child.

This mania to lose weight and have the "ideal" body is not eas-   9
ily avoided in our society. It is created by television and magazines
as they flaunt their models and latest diet crazes in front of our
faces. And then there are the Nutri-System and Jenny Craig commercials, which show hideous "before" pictures and glamorous
"after" pictures and have smiling, happy people dancing around
and talking about how their lives have been transformed simply
because they have lost weight. This propaganda that happiness is
in large part based on having the "perfect" body shape is a message
that the media constantly sends to the public. No one seems to be
able to escape it.

My mother and father were even sucked in by this idea. One 10
evening, when I was in the fifth grade, I heard Mom and Dad calling me into the kitchen. Oh no, what had I done now? It was never
good news when you got summoned into the kitchen alone. As I
walked into the kitchen, Mom looked up at me with an anxious
expression; Dad was sitting at the head of the table with a pen in
hand and a yellow legal pad in front of him. They informed me
that I was going on a diet. A diet!? I wanted to scream at them, "I'm
only ten years old, why do I have to be on a diet?" I was so embarrassed, and I felt so guilty. Was I really fat? I guess so, I thought,
otherwise why would my parents do this to me?

It seems that this obsession with the perfect body and a woman's 11
appearance has grown to monumental heights. It is ironic, however,
that now many people feel that this problem is disappearing. People have begun to assume that women want to be thin because
they just want to be "healthy." But what has happened is that the
sickness slips in under the guise of wanting a "healthy" body.
The demand for thin bodies is anything but "healthy." How many
anorexics or bulimics have you seen that are healthy?

It is strange that women do not come out and object to society's 12
pressure to become thin. Or maybe women feel that they really
do want to be thin, and so go on dieting endlessly (they call it "eating sensibly"), thinking this is what they really want. I think if
these women carefully examined their reasons for wanting to lose
weight—and were not allowed to include reasons that relate to
society's demands, such as a weight chart, a questionnaire in a
magazine, a certain size in a pair of shorts, or even a scale—they
would find that they are being ruled by what society wants, not
what they want. So why do women not break free from these standards? Why do they not demand an end to being judged in such a
demeaning and senseless way?

Self-esteem plays a large part in determining whether women 13
succumb to the will of society or whether they are independent
and self-assured enough to make their own decisions. Lack of
self-esteem is one of the things the women's movement has had to
fight the hardest against. If women didn't think they were worthy,
then how could they even begin to fight for their own rights? The
same is true with the issue of body size. If women do not feel their
body is worthy, then how can they believe that it is okay to just let
it stay that way? Without self-esteem, women will be swayed by
society and will continue to make themselves unhappy by trying
to maintain whatever weight or body shape society is dictating for
them. It is ironic that many of the popular women's magazines—
Cosmopolitan, Mademoiselle, Glamour—often feature articles on

self-esteem and how essential it is and how to improve it, and then in the same issue give the latest diet tips. This mixed message will never give women the power they deserve over their bodies and will never enable them to make their own decisions about what type of body they want.

> "Rox, why do you think you're fat? You work out all the time, and you just bought that new suit. Why don't you just come down to the pool for a little while?"   14

> "No, I really don't want to. I feel so self-conscious with all those people around. It makes me want to run and put on a big, baggy dress so no one can tell what size I am!"   15

> "Ah, Rox, that's really sad. You have to learn to believe in yourself and your own judgment, not other people's."   16

READING FOR MEANING

Reading for meaning involves three activities:

- reading to comprehend
- reading to respond
- reading to analyze underlying assumptions

Reread Haines's essay, and then write a page or so explaining your understanding of its basic meaning or main point, a personal response you have to it, and what you see as one of its underlying assumptions.

READING LIKE A WRITER

Writers of reflective essays

- present the particular occasion.
- develop the reflections.
- maintain topical coherence.
- engage readers.

Focus on one of these strategies in Haines's essay, and analyze it carefully through close rereading and annotating. Then write several sentences explaining what you have learned, giving specific examples from the reading to support your explanation. Add a few sentences evaluating how successfully Haines uses the strategy to reflect on society's obsession with the perfect body.

REVIEWING WHAT MAKES REFLECTIVE ESSAYS EFFECTIVE

In this chapter, you have been learning how to read reflective essays for meaning and how to read them like a writer. Before going on to write a reflective essay, pause here to review and contemplate what you have learned about the elements of effective reflective essays.

Analyze

Choose one reading from this chapter that seems to you especially effective. Before rereading the selection, *jot down* one or two reasons you remember it as an example of good reflective writing.

Reread your chosen selection, adding further annotations about what makes it a particularly successful example of reflection. *Consider* the selection's purpose and how well it achieves that purpose for its intended readers. (You can make an informed guess about the intended readers and their expectations by noting the publication source of the essay.) Then *focus* on how well the essay

- presents the particular occasion.

- develops the reflections.

- maintains topical coherence.

- engages readers.

You can review all of these basic features in the Guide to Reading Reflective Essays (p. 161).

Your instructor may ask you to complete this activity on your own or to work with a small group of other students who have chosen the same reading. If you work with others, allow enough time initially for all group members to reread the selection thoughtfully and to add their annotations. Then *discuss* as a group what makes the selection effective. *Take notes* on your discussion. One student in your group should then report to the class what the group has learned about the effectiveness of reflective writing. If you are working individually, write up what you have learned from your analysis.

Write

Write at least a page supporting your choice of this reading as an example of effective reflective writing. *Assume* that your readers—your instructor and classmates—have read the selection but will not remember many details about it. They also might not remember it as especially successful. Therefore, you will need to *refer* to details and specific parts of the essay as you explain how it works and as you justify your evaluation of its effectiveness. You need not argue that it is the best reading in the chapter or that it is flawless, only that it is, in your view, a strong example of the genre.

■ A Guide to Writing Reflective Essays

The readings in this chapter have helped you learn a great deal about reflective writing. At its best, the reflective essay is interesting, lively, insightful, and engaging—much like good conversation—and it avoids sounding pretentious or preachy in its focus on basic human and social issues that concern us all. Writers of reflection are not reluctant to say what they think or to express their most personal observations.

As you develop your reflective essay, you can review the readings to see how other writers use various strategies to solve problems you might also encounter. This Guide to Writing is designed to help you through the various decisions you will need to make as you plan, draft, and revise your reflective essay.

INVENTION AND RESEARCH

The following activities will help you find a particular occasion and a general subject, test your choices, present the particular occasion, and develop your reflections. Taking some time now to consider a wide range of possibilities will pay off later when you draft your essay, giving you confidence in your choice of subject and in your ability to develop it effectively.

Finding a Particular Occasion and a General Subject

As the readings in this chapter illustrate, writers of reflection usually center their essays on one (or more than one) event or occasion. They connect this occasion to a subject they want to reflect on. In the process of invention, however, the choice of a particular occasion does not always come before the choice of a general subject. Sometimes writers set out to reflect on a general subject (such as envy or friendship) and must search for the right occasion (an image or anecdote) with which to particularize it.

Start by listing several possible occasions and the general subjects they suggest in a two-column chart, as shown in the following example:

Particular Occasions	*General Subjects*
I met someone covered by tattoos.	Body art or self-mutilation
I saw the film *Fight Club*.	Masculinity and male bonding
I am amazed by people's personal revelations on talk shows.	Desire for celebrity status
While shopping for clothes, I couldn't decide what to buy and let the sales person pressure me.	Indecisiveness and low self-esteem

For particular occasions, consider conversations you have had or overheard; memorable scenes you observed, read about, or saw in a movie or on television; and other incidents in your own or someone else's life that might lead you to reflect more generally. Then consider the general subjects suggested by the particular occasions—human qualities such as compassion, vanity, jealousy, and faithfulness; social customs for dating, eating, and working; abstract notions such as fate, free will, and imagination.

In making your chart, you will find that a single occasion might suggest several subjects and that a subject might be particularized by a variety of occasions. Each entry will surely suggest other possibilities for you to consider. Do not be concerned if your chart starts to look messy. A full and rich exploration of possible topics will give you confidence in the subject you finally choose and in your ability to write about it. If you have trouble getting started, review the Considering Ideas for Your Own Writing activities following the readings in this chapter. As further occasions and subjects occur to you over the next two or three days, add them to your chart.

RESEARCHING YOUR SUBJECT ONLINE

The Web offers a number of possible ways to help you write your reflective essay. A Web site might provide a particular occasion for your reflections, or you might see how other people use their experiences and observations as the occasion for their reflections. Reflective writing on various general subjects also can often be found on blogs. Once you have identified a general topic for your essay, you may be able to find sites with cultural and historical documents or photographs that stimulate your thinking or encourage you to create a multimedia text of your own. As you search the Web, here are some possibilities to consider:

- Find blog sites through <google.com>, <blogsearchengine.com>, <blogarama.com>, or other directories.

- Search for sites related to the general subject or particular occasion you are writing about.

Make notes of any ideas, memories, or insights suggested by your online research. Download any visuals you might consider using in your essay—such as pictures of people and places you may want to include. Also be sure to download or record the information necessary to cite any online sources you may want to refer to in your essay. See Appendix 2 for help in citing sources.

Testing Your Choices

Review your chart, and choose a particular occasion and a general subject you now think look promising. To test whether your choices will work, write for fifteen minutes or so, exploring your thoughts. Do not make any special demands on yourself to be profound or even coherent. Just write your ideas as they come to mind, letting one idea suggest another. Your aims are to determine whether you have enough to say about the occasion and subject and whether they hold your interest. If you discover that you do not have very much to say about the occasion or that you quickly lose interest in the subject, choose another set of possibilities and try again. It might take a few preliminary explorations to find the right occasion and subject.

Presenting the Particular Occasion

The following activities will help you recall details about the particular occasion for your reflection. Depending on the occasion you have decided to write about, choose Narrating an Event or Describing What You Observed.

Narrating an Event. *Write for five to ten minutes narrating what happened during the event.* Try to make your story vivid so that readers can imagine what it was like. Describe the people involved in the event—what they looked like, how they acted, what they said—and the place where it occurred.

Describing What You Observed. *Write for five or ten minutes describing what you observed.* Include as many details as you can recall so that your readers can imagine what you experienced.

Developing Your Reflections

To explore your ideas about the subject, try an invention activity called *cubing.* Based on the six sides of a cube, this activity leads you to turn over your subject as you would a cube, looking at it in six different ways. Complete the following activities in any order, writing for five minutes on each one. Your goal is to invent new ways of considering your subject.

Generalizing. *Consider what you have learned from the event or experience that will be the occasion for your reflections.* What ideas does it suggest to you? What does it suggest about people in general or about the society in which you live?

Giving Examples. *Illustrate your ideas with specific examples.* What examples would best help your readers understand your ideas?

Comparing and Contrasting.   *Think of a subject that could be compared with yours, and explore the similarities and the differences.*

Extending.   *Take your subject to its logical limits, and speculate about its implications.* Where does it lead?

Analyzing.   *Take apart your subject.* What is it made of? How are the parts related to one another? Are they all of equal importance?

Applying.   *Think about your subject in practical terms.* How can you use it or act on it? What difference would it make to you and to others?

Considering Your Purpose.   *Write for several minutes about your purpose for writing this essay.* As you write, try to answer the question: What do I want my readers to think about the subject after reading my essay? Your answer to this question may change as you write, but thinking about your purpose now may help you decide which of your ideas to include in the essay. Use the following questions to help clarify your purpose:

- Which of your ideas are most important to you? Why?

- How do your ideas relate to one another? If your ideas seem contradictory, consider how you could use the contradictions to convey to readers the complexity of your ideas and feelings on the subject.

- Which of your ideas do you think will most surprise your readers? Which are most likely to be familiar?

- Is the particular occasion for your reflections likely to resonate with your readers' experience and observation? If not, consider how you can make the particular occasion vivid or dramatic for readers.

Formulating a Tentative Thesis Statement.   *Review what you wrote for Considering Your Purpose and add another two or three sentences that will bring into focus your reflections.* What do they seem to be about? Try to write sentences that indicate what you think is most important or most interesting about the subject, what you want readers to understand from reading your essay.

Keep in mind that readers do not expect you to begin your reflective essay with the kind of thesis statement typical of an argumentative essay, which asserts an opinion the writer then goes on to support. None of the readings in this chapter begins with an explicit statement of the writer's main idea. They all begin with a particular occasion followed by ideas suggested by the occasion. Brent Staples, for example, follows the particular occasion with a general statement of his main idea: "It was in the echo of that terrified woman's footfalls that I first began to know the unwieldy inheritance I'd come into—the ability to alter public space in ugly ways" (paragraph 2). He then explores this rather abstract idea, indicating that his "unwieldy inheritance" is racial stereotyping and the fear it engenders in others. Similarly, Suzanne Winckler follows the particular occasion with the reflection that "Butchering chickens . . . is the price I pay for being an omnivore" (3). Barbara Ehrenreich also introduces her main idea after presenting the particular occasion: "We live in a culture that fetishes the family as the ideal unit of human community. . . . Only with the occasional celebrity crime do we allow ourselves to think the nearly unthinkable: that the family may not be the ideal and perfect living arrangement after all—that it can be a nest of pathology and a cradle of gruesome violence" (2).

As you explore your ideas and think about the particular occasion for your reflections, you can expect your ideas to change. The fun of writing a reflective essay is that you can share with readers your thinking process, taking them along for the ride.

Considering Visuals.   *Consider whether visuals—cartoons, photographs, drawings— would help readers understand and appreciate your reflections.* If you submit your essay electronically to other students and your instructor, or if you post it on a Web site, consider including photographs and snippets of film or sound. You could construct your own visuals, scan materials from books and magazines, or download them from the Internet. Visual and audio materials are not at all a requirement of an effective reflective essay, as you can tell from the readings in this chapter, but they could add a new dimension to your writing. If you want to use photographs or recordings of people, though, be sure to obtain their permission.

DRAFTING

The following guidelines will help you set goals for your draft, plan its organization, and think about a useful sentence strategy.

Setting Goals

Establishing goals for your draft before you begin writing will enable you to make decisions and work more confidently. Consider the following questions now, and keep them in mind as you draft. They will help you set goals for drafting as well as recall how the writers you have read in this chapter tried to achieve similar goals.

- *How can I present the particular occasion vividly and in a way that anticipates my reflections?* Should I narrate the event, like Staples does? Refer to shocking events in the news, like Ehrenreich? Create an imaginary dialogue, like Haines?

- *How can I best develop my reflections?* Should I include brief and extended examples, like all of the writers in this chapter do? Should I use comparisons and contrasts, like Brooks and Lee? Refer to authorities and history, like Ehrenreich and Brooks? Create an imaginary or conversational scene, like Lee and Haines?

- *How can I maintain topical coherence?* Like Winckler and Brooks, can I use topic sentences to make clear the connections between my ideas or insights and the examples that develop them? Can I use word repetition, like Ehrenreich and Brooks, to keep my readers on track as they follow the course of my reflections?

- *How can I engage and hold my readers' interest?* Should I reveal the human interest and social significance of my subject by opening my essay with a dramatic event, like Staples and Winckler do? Should I start with a personal observation, as Gibbs and Brooks do? A reminder of bizarre and troubling events in the news, like Ehrenreich? A familiar dialogue, like Haines? An ethnic stereotype, like Staples and Lee? Like all the writers in this chapter, should I reveal my personal commitment to the subject, and should I attempt to inspire my readers to think deeply about their own lives?

Organizing Your Draft

You might find it paradoxical to plan a type of essay that does not aim to reach conclusions or that seeks to give readers the impression that it is finding its way as it goes. And yet you have seen in the readings in this chapter that reflective essays, at least after they have been carefully revised with readers in mind, are usually easy to follow. Part of what makes a reflective essay easy to read is its topical coherence, such as the repetition of key words and phrases that keep the reader's focus on the subject that is being explored in the essay. Writers often develop coherence as they draft and revise their essays, but there are some ways in which planning can also help.

For example, one approach to planning is to begin with the particular occasion, outlining the sequence of events in a way that emphasizes the main point you want the occasion to make. After figuring out how you will present the particular occasion, you could choose one idea you want to develop in detail or list several ideas you think your essay will touch on, possibly indicating how each idea relates to the one that follows. Sometimes when writers go this far in planning, they are actually drafting segments of the essay, discovering a tentative plan as they write.

Another approach to planning begins with the ideas you want to discuss. You could consider various ways of sequencing your ideas. For example, you could start with an obvious idea, one you expect most readers would think of. Then, you could develop the idea in unexpected ways or build a train of ideas that leads in a surprising direction. Yet another approach is to pair ideas with examples and develop a sequence of pairs that explores different aspects of your subject or tries out different points of view on it.

Remember that the goal of planning is to discover what you want to say and a possible way of organizing your ideas. Planning a reflective essay can be especially challenging because the process of reflecting is itself a process of discovery: You won't really know what you want your essay to say until you've drafted and revised it. But if you think of planning simply as a way of getting started and remember that you will have a lot of opportunity to reorganize your ideas and develop them further, planning can become an extremely pleasurable and creative activity.

Considering a Useful Sentence Strategy

In addition to planning the sequence of your ideas and repeating key words and phrases, you can enhance the topical coherence of your reflective essay by using parallel grammatical structures to connect related ideas or examples. In the three sentences that make up paragraph 3 of Brooks's reflections on meritocracy, for example, notice how the beginning of each sentence (indicated in italics) uses not only similar language but also a similar structure:

> *It's a busy childhood,* filled with opportunities, activities, teams, coaches, and, inevitably, gear. *It's a safety-conscious childhood,* with ample adult supervision. *And it is,* I believe (at least I want to believe), *a happy and fulfilling childhood* that will prepare my daughter for a happy adult life.

Brooks uses virtually identical patterns ("It's a . . . childhood," "It's a . . . childhood," "And it is . . . a . . . childhood") to list the features that define the kind of American childhood he believes most middle-class suburban children experience today.

In the next paragraph, Brooks again uses parallelism, this time to list a series of features underscoring the difference between today's typical childhood and traditional ideas about an American childhood. In this case, the sentence structure shifts slightly each time, so that the beginning of the next sentence is similar but not completely parallel to the beginning of the previous one: "It's not an independent childhood. . . . Nor is it a Horatio Alger childhood. . . . Nor do they build self-discipline . . ." (paragraph 4). Then, in the following paragraph, Brooks returns to close parallelism by repeating the phrase "we fear" at the beginning of four sentences in a row, varying the sequence only in the last sentence by adding the conjunction "or" (5). This sequence serves to introduce a series of anxieties that modern middle-class suburban American parents have about their children.

Here are several similar uses of parallel form to signal related ideas or examples from other essays in this chapter:

> "I realized why . . . I understood why . . . I saw why . . ." (Winckler, paragraph 5)

> "When they can read for fun . . . When they can ruin their brand-new sneakers . . . When a rule can be bent . . ." (Gibbs, paragraph 2)

"We're afraid of mosquitoes because of . . . and grass because of . . . and sun because of . . . and sunscreen because of . . ." (Gibbs, paragraph 9)

"Millions . . . But at the same time millions . . . Legions . . ." (Ehrenreich, paragraph 7)

"The French philosopher . . . More recently, the renowned British anthropologist . . ." (Ehrenreich, paragraph 8)

"They don't want their first-generation children to forget. . . . They don't want their children to forget. . . ." (Lee, paragraph 5)

While there are many ways to signal that a group of ideas is related, writers of reflective essays tend to rely on parallel form because it is highly visible; readers notice it at a glance. Parallel form also creates a pleasant rhythm that engages readers and keeps them reading. Moreover, it is very flexible; the variations are endless. Clearly, parallelism is not required for a successful reflective essay, yet it provides you with an effective sentence option to try out in your own essay.

READING A DRAFT CRITICALLY

Getting a critical reading of your draft will help you see how to improve it. Your instructor may schedule class time for reading drafts, or you may want to ask a classmate or a tutor in the writing center to read your draft. Ask your reader to use the following guidelines and to write out a response for you to consult during your revision.

Read for a First Impression

1. Read the draft without stopping to annotate or comment, and then write two or three sentences giving your general impression.

2. Identify one aspect of the draft that seems especially effective.

Read Again to Suggest Improvements

1. Suggest ways of presenting the occasion more effectively.

   - Read the paragraphs that present the occasion for the reflections, and tell the writer if the occasion dominates the essay, taking up an unjustified amount of space, or if it needs more development.

   - Note whether this occasion suggests the significance or importance of the subject, and consider how well it prepares readers for the reflections by providing a context for them.

   - Tell the writer what in the occasion works well and what needs improvement.

2. Help the writer develop the reflections.

- Look for two or three ideas that strike you as especially interesting, insightful, or surprising, and tell the writer what interests you about them. Then, most important, suggest ways these ideas might be developed further through examples, comparisons or contrasts, social implications, connections to other ideas, and so on.

- Identify any ideas you find uninteresting, explaining briefly why you find them so.

3. Recommend ways to strengthen topical coherence.

- Skim the essay, looking for gaps between sentences and paragraphs, those places where the meaning does not carry forward smoothly. Mark each gap with a double slash (//), and try to recommend a way to make the meaning clear.

- Skim the essay again, looking for irrelevant or unnecessary material that disrupts coherence and diverts the reader's attention. Put brackets around this material, and explain to the writer why it seems to you irrelevant or unnecessary.

- Consider the essay as a sequence of sections. Ask yourself whether some of the sections could be moved to make the essay easier to follow. Circle any section that seems out of place, and draw an arrow to where it might be better located.

4. Suggest ways to further engage readers.

- Point out parts of the essay that draw you in, hold your interest, inspire you to think, challenge your attitudes or values, or keep you wanting to read to the end.

- Try to suggest ways the writer might engage readers more fully. Consider the essay in light of what is most engaging for you in the essays you have read in this chapter.

5. Evaluate the effectiveness of visuals.

- Look at any visuals in the essay, and tell the writer what they contribute to your understanding of the writer's reflections.

- If any visuals do not seem relevant, or if there seem to be too many visuals, identify the ones that the writer could consider dropping, explaining your thinking.

- If a visual does not seem to be appropriately placed, suggest a better place for it.

REVISING

This section offers suggestions for revising your draft. Revising means reenvisioning your draft, trying to see it in a new way, given your purpose and readers, in order to develop an engaging, coherent reflective essay.

The biggest mistake you can make while revising is to focus initially on words or sentences. Instead, first try to see your draft as a whole in order to assess its likely impact on your readers. Think imaginatively and boldly about cutting uninteresting material, adding new material, and moving material around. Your computer makes even drastic revisions physically easy, but you still need to make the mental effort and decisions that will improve your draft.

You may have received help with this challenge from a classmate or tutor who gave your draft a critical reading. If so, keep this feedback in mind as you decide which parts of your draft need revising and what specific changes you could make. The following suggestions will help you solve problems and strengthen your essay.

To Present the Particular Occasion More Effectively

- If the occasion for your reflections seems flat or too general and abstract, expand it with interesting details.

- If the occasion fails to illustrate the significance of your subject, revise it to do so.

- If the occasion seems not to anticipate the reflections that follow, revise it or come up with a new, more relevant occasion.

To Develop the Reflections More Fully

- If promising ideas are not yet fully developed, provide further examples, anecdotes, contrasts, and so on.

- If certain ideas now seem too predictable, drop them and try to come up with more insightful ideas.

- If your reflections do not move beyond personal associations, extend them into the social realm by commenting on their larger implications—what they mean for people in general.

To Strengthen Topical Coherence

- If there are distracting gaps between sentences or paragraphs, try to close them by revising sentences.

- If one section seems not to follow from the previous one, consider reordering the sequence of sections.

- If there are pairs or series of related ideas or examples, consider revising the items into parallel grammatical form.

To Better Engage Readers

- If your beginning—typically the presentation of the occasion—seems unlikely to draw readers in, make its event more dramatic, its comments less predictable, or its significance more pointed. If you cannot see how to make it more interesting, consider another beginning.

- If your reflections seem unlikely to lead readers to reflect on their own lives and their interactions with other people, try to carry your ideas further and to develop them in more varied ways.

EDITING AND PROOFREADING

After you have revised your essay, be sure to spend some time checking for errors in usage, punctuation, and mechanics and considering matters of style. If you keep a list of errors you typically make, begin by checking your draft against this list. Ask someone else to proofread your essay before you print out a copy for your instructor or send it electronically.

From our research on student writing, we know that essays reflecting on a particular occasion have a relatively high frequency of unnecessary shifts in verb tense and mood. Consult a writer's handbook for information on unnecessary verb shifts, and then edit your essay to correct any shifts that you find.

REFLECTING ON WHAT YOU HAVE LEARNED

Reflection

In this chapter, you have read critically several reflective essays and have written one of your own. To better remember what you have learned, pause now to reflect on the reading and writing activities you completed in this chapter.

1. *Write* a page or so reflecting on what you have learned. *Begin* by describing what you are most pleased with in your essay. Then *explain* what you think contributed to your achievement. *Be specific* about this contribution.

   - If it was something you learned from the readings, *indicate* which readings and specifically what you learned from them.

- If it came from your invention writing, *point out* the section or sections that helped you most.

- If you got good advice from a critical reader, *explain* exactly how the person helped you—perhaps by helping you understand a particular problem in your draft or by adding a new dimension to your writing.

- *Try to write* about your achievement in terms of what you have learned about the genre.

2. Now *reflect* more generally on reflective essays, a genre of writing that has been important for centuries and is still practiced in our society today. *Consider* some of the following questions: How comfortable do you feel relying on your own experience or observations as a basis for developing ideas about general subjects or for developing ideas about the way people are and the ways they interact? How comfortable are you with merely trying out your own personal ideas on a subject rather than researching it or interviewing people to collect their ideas? How comfortable is it to adopt a conversational rather than a formal tone? How would you explain your level of comfort? How might your gender or social class or ethnic group have influenced the ideas you came up with for your essay? What contribution might reflective essays make to our society that other genres cannot make?

CHAPTER 5

Explaining Concepts

Essays explaining concepts feature a kind of explanatory writing that is especially important for college students to understand. Each of the essays you will analyze in this chapter explains a single concept, such as *parthenogenesis* in biology, *multiple intelligences* in education, and *dating* in sociology. For your own explanatory essay, you will choose a concept from your current studies or special interests.

For you as a college student, a better understanding of how to read and write explanations of concepts is useful in several ways. It gives you strategies for critically reading the textbooks and other concept-centered material in your college courses. It helps give you confidence to write a common type of essay exam and paper assignment. And it acquaints you with the basic strategies or modes of development common to all types of explanatory writing: definition, classification or division, comparison and contrast, process narration, illustration, and causal explanation.

A *concept* is a major idea. Every field of study has its concepts: physics has quantum theory, subatomic particles, the Heisenberg principle; psychiatry has neurosis, schizophrenia, narcissism; composition has invention, heuristics, recursiveness; business management has corporate culture, micromanagement, and direct marketing; and music has harmony and counterpoint. Concepts include abstract ideas, phenomena, and processes. Concepts are central to the understanding of virtually every subject—we create concepts, name them, communicate them, and think with them.

As you work through this chapter, keep in mind that we learn a new concept by connecting it to what we have previously learned. Good explanatory writing, therefore, must be incremental, adding bit by bit to the reader's knowledge. Explanatory writing goes wrong when the flow of new information is either too fast or too slow for the intended readers, when the information is too difficult or too simple, or when the writing is digressive or just plain dull.

The readings in this chapter will help you see what makes explanatory writing interesting and informative. From the readings and from the ideas for writing that follow each reading, you will get ideas for writing your own essay about a concept. As you read and write about the selections, keep in mind the following assignment, which sets out the goals for writing an essay explaining a concept. To support your writing of this assignment, the chapter concludes with a Guide to Writing Essays Explaining Concepts.

THE WRITING ASSIGNMENT

Explaining Concepts

Choose a concept that interests you enough to study further. Write an essay explaining the concept. Consider carefully what your readers already know about the concept and how your essay can add to their knowledge.

WRITING SITUATIONS FOR ESSAYS EXPLAINING CONCEPTS

Writing that explains concepts is familiar in college and professional life, as the following examples show:

- For a presentation at the annual convention of the American Medical Association, an anesthesiologist writes a report on the concept of *awareness during surgery*. He presents evidence that patients under anesthesia, as in hypnosis, can hear, and he reviews research demonstrating that they can perceive and carry out instructions that speed their recovery. He describes briefly how he applies the concept in his own work: how he prepares patients before surgery, what he tells them while they are under anesthesia, and what happens as they recover.

- A business reporter for a newspaper writes an article about *virtual reality*. She describes the lifelike, three-dimensional experience created by wearing gloves and video goggles wired to a computer. To help readers understand this new concept, she contrasts it with television. For investors, she describes which corporations have shown an interest in the commercial possibilities of virtual reality.

- As part of a group assignment, a college student at a summer biology camp in the Sierra Nevada mountains reads about the condition of mammals at birth. She discovers the distinction between infant mammals that are *altricial* (born nude and helpless within a protective nest) and those that are *precocial* (born well-formed with eyes open and ears erect). In her part of a group report, she develops this contrast point by point, giving many examples of specific mammals but focusing in detail on altricial mice and precocial porcupines. Domestic cats, she points out, are an intermediate example—born with some fur but with eyes and ears closed.

THINKING ABOUT YOUR EXPERIENCE WITH EXPLANATORY WRITING

Before studying a type of writing, it is useful to spend some time thinking about what you already know about it. In school, you have undoubtedly written numerous explanations of concepts for exams and papers. In and out of school, you have probably also had extensive experience explaining concepts to friends and family.

To analyze your experience with explanations, you might recall an occasion when you tried to explain a concept to others. It may have been memorable because you were trying to explain something you cared about or because you had a hard time getting your audience to understand. Try to recall the situation, what you were trying to explain, why it was important, and what difficulties you were able to anticipate. What strategies did you use? For example, did you think of examples to make your explanation more understandable or compare your subject to something more familiar?

Consider also explanations you have heard or read in school, on the Internet, on television, or elsewhere. Think of one explanation that you thought was especially successful. Looking back on it, do you think this particular explanation worked well because it was so clear or well organized, because it used examples or images to make the information vivid, or for some other reason or combination of reasons?

Write at least a page about your experience with explanatory writing.

■ A Guide to Reading Essays Explaining Concepts

This guide introduces you to explanatory writing. By completing all of the activities in it, you will prepare yourself to learn a great deal from the other readings in this chapter about how to read and write an essay explaining a concept. The guide focuses on an engaging essay by the science writer David Quammen, "Is Sex Necessary? Virgin Birth and Opportunism in the Garden." You will read Quammen's essay twice. First, you will read it for meaning, looking closely at its content and ideas. Then, you will reread the essay like a writer, analyzing the parts to see how Quammen crafts his essay and to learn the range of strategies he employs to make his concept explanation effective. These two activities—reading for meaning and reading like a writer—follow every reading in this chapter.

DAVID QUAMMEN

Is Sex Necessary? Virgin Birth and Opportunism in the Garden

David Quammen (b. 1948), a novelist and nature writer, writes a column and is editor-at-large for the magazine Outside *and has published articles in* Smithsonian Magazine, Audubon, Esquire, Rolling Stone, *and* Harper's. *His books include the novel* The Soul of Viktor Tronko *(1987) and an edited collection (with Burkhard Bilger) of outstanding writing in his specialties,* The Best American Science and Nature Writing 2000 *(2000). Several collections of his own writing have also been published, including* Natural Acts: A Sidelong View of Science and Nature *(1985),* Wild Thoughts from Wild Places *(1998),* Boilerplate Rhino: Nature in the Eye of the Beholder *(2000), and* Monster of God: The Man-Eating Predator in the Jungles of History and the Mind *(2003).*

The readers of Outside *have special interests in nature, outdoor recreation, and the environment, but few have advanced training in ecology or biology. In this essay, originally published as a column in* Outside *and reprinted in* Natural Acts, *Quammen gives us a nonscientist's introduction to parthenogenesis—not only to the facts of it but also to its significance in nature.*

As you read, annotate anything that helps you understand the concept of parthenogenesis. Notice also Quammen's attempts to amuse as well as inform, and think about how his playfulness might help or get in the way of readers' understanding of the concept.

Birds do it, bees do it, goes the tune. But the songsters, as usual, would mislead us with drastic oversimplifications. The full truth happens to be more eccentrically nonlibidinous: Sometimes they *don't* do it, those very creatures, and get the same results anyway. Bees of all species, for instance, are notable to geneticists precisely for their ability to produce offspring while doing *without*. Likewise at least one variety of bird—the Beltsville Small White turkey, a domestic dinnertable model out of Beltsville, Maryland—has achieved scientific renown for a similar feat. What we are talking about here is celibate motherhood, procreation without copulation, a phenomenon that goes by the technical name *parthenogenesis*. Translated from the Greek roots: virgin birth.

1

And you don't have to be Catholic to believe in this one.   2

Miraculous as it may seem, parthenogenesis is actually rather   3
common throughout nature, practiced regularly or intermittently
by at least some species within almost every group of animals except
(for reasons still unknown) dragonflies and mammals. Reproduction by virgin females has been discovered among reptiles, birds,
fishes, amphibians, crustaceans, mollusks, ticks, the jellyfish clan,
flatworms, roundworms, segmented worms; and among insects
(notwithstanding those unrelentingly sexy dragonflies) it is especially favored. The order *Hymenoptera*, including all bees and
wasps, is uniformly parthenogenetic in the manner by which males
are produced: Every male honeybee is born without any genetic
contribution from a father. Among the beetles, there are thirty-five
different forms of parthenogenetic weevil. The African weaver ant
employs parthenogenesis, as do twenty-three species of fruit fly
and at least one kind of roach. The gall midge *Miastor* is notorious
for the exceptionally bizarre and grisly scenario that allows its
fatherless young to see daylight: *Miastor* daughters cannibalize the
mother from inside, with ruthless impatience, until her hollowed-
out skin splits open like the door of an overcrowded nursery. But the
foremost practitioners of virgin birth—their elaborate and versatile
proficiency unmatched in the animal kingdom—are undoubtedly
the aphids.

Now no sensible reader of even this can be expected, I realize,   4
to care faintly about aphid biology *qua* aphid biology. That's just
asking too much. But there's a larger rationale for dragging you
aphidward. The life cycle of these little nebbishy sap-sucking
insects, the very same that infest rose bushes and house plants, not
only exemplifies *how* parthenogenetic reproduction is done; it also
very clearly shows *why*.

First the biographical facts. A typical aphid, which feeds entirely   5
on plant juices tapped off from the vascular system of young
leaves, spends winter dormant and protected, as an egg. The egg is
attached near a bud site on the new growth of a poplar tree. In
March, when the tree sap has begun to rise and the buds have
begun to burgeon, an aphid hatchling appears, plugging its sharp
snout (like a mosquito's) into the tree's tenderest plumbing. This
solitary individual aphid will be, necessarily, a wingless female. If
she is lucky, she will become sole founder of a vast aphid population. Having sucked enough poplar sap to reach maturity, she
produces—by *live birth* now, and without benefit of a mate—
daughters identical to herself. These wingless daughters also plug
into the tree's flow of sap, and they also produce further wingless
daughters, until sometime in late May, when that particular branch

of that particular tree can support no more thirsty aphids. Suddenly there is a change: The next generation of daughters are born with wings. They fly off in search of a better situation.

One such aviatrix lands on an herbaceous plant—say a young climbing bean in some human's garden—and the pattern repeats. She plugs into the sap ducts on the underside of a new leaf, commences feasting destructively, and delivers by parthenogenesis a great brood of wingless daughters. The daughters beget more daughters, those daughters beget still more, and so on, until the poor bean plant is encrusted with a solid mob of these fat little elbowing greedy sisters. Then again, neatly triggered by the crowded conditions, a generation of daughters are born with wings. Away they fly, looking for prospects, and one of them lights on, say, a sugar beet. (The switch from bean to beet is fine, because our species of typical aphid is not inordinately choosy.) The sugar beet before long is covered, sucked upon mercilessly, victimized by a horde of mothers and nieces and granddaughters. Still not a single male aphid has appeared anywhere in the chain.

The lurching from one plant to another continues; the alternation between wingless and winged daughters continues. But in September, with fresh tender plant growth increasingly hard to find, there is another change.

Flying daughters are born who have a different destiny: They wing back to the poplar tree, where they give birth to a crop of wingless females that are unlike any so far. These latest girls know the meaning of sex! Meanwhile, at long last, the starving survivors back on that final bedraggled sugar beet have brought forth a generation of males. The males have wings. They take to the air in quest of poplar trees and first love. *Et voilà.* The mated females lay eggs that will wait out the winter near bud sites on that poplar tree, and the circle is thus completed. One single aphid hatching—call her the *fundatrix*—in this way can give rise in the course of a year, from her own ovaries exclusively, to roughly a zillion aphids.

Well and good, you say. A zillion aphids. But what is the point of it?

The point, for aphids as for most other parthenogenetic animals, is (1) exceptionally fast reproduction that allows (2) maximal exploitation of temporary resource abundance and unstable environmental conditions, while (3) facilitating the successful colonization of unfamiliar habitats. In other words the aphid, like the gall midge and the weaver ant and the rest of their fellow parthenogens, is by its evolved character a galloping opportunist.

This is a term of science, not of abuse. Population ecologists make an illuminating distinction between what they label *equilibrium* and *opportunistic* species. According to William Birky and John Gilbert, from a paper in the journal *American Zoologist*: "Equilibrium species, exemplified by many vertebrates, maintain relatively constant population sizes, in part by being adapted to reproduce, at least slowly, in most of the environmental conditions which they meet. Opportunistic species, on the other hand, show extreme population fluctuations; they are adapted to reproduce only in a relatively narrow range of conditions, but make up for this by reproducing extremely rapidly in favorable circumstances. At least in some cases, opportunistic organisms can also be categorized as colonizing organisms." Birky and Gilbert also emphasize that "The potential for rapid reproduction is the essential evolutionary ticket for entry into the opportunistic lifestyle."

And parthenogenesis, in turn, is the greatest time-saving gimmick in the history of animal reproduction. No hours or days are wasted while a female looks for a mate; no minutes lost to the act of mating itself. The female aphid attains sexual maturity and, bang, she becomes automatically pregnant. No waiting, no courtship, no fooling around. She delivers her brood of daughters, they grow to puberty and, zap, another generation immediately.... The time saved to parthenogenetic species may seem trivial, but it is not. It adds up dizzyingly: In the same time taken by a sexually reproducing insect to complete three generations for a total of 1,200 offspring, an aphid (assuming the *same* time required for each female to mature, and the *same* number of progeny in each litter), squandering no time on courtship or sex, will progress through six generations for an extended family of 318,000,000. 12

Even this isn't speedy enough for some restless opportunists. That matricidal gall midge *Miastor*, whose larvae feed on fleeting eruptions of fungus under the bark of trees, has developed a startling way to cut further time from the cycle of procreation. Far from waiting for a mate, *Miastor* does not even wait for maturity. When food is abundant, it is the *larva*, not the adult female fly, who is eaten alive from inside by her own daughters. And as those voracious daughters burst free of the husk that was their mother, each of them already contains further larval daughters taking shape ominously within its own ovaries. While the food lasts, while opportunity endures, no *Miastor* female can live to adulthood without dying of motherhood. 13

The implicit principle behind all this nonsexual reproduction, all this hurry, is simple: Don't argue with success. Don't tamper with a genetic blueprint that works. Unmated female aphids, and 14 gall midges, pass on their own gene patterns virtually unaltered (except for the occasional mutation) to their daughters. Sexual reproduction on the other hand, constitutes, by its essence, genetic tampering. The whole purpose of joining sperm with egg is to shuffle the genes of both parents and come up with a new combination that might perhaps be more advantageous. Give the kid something neither Mom nor Pop ever had. Parthenogenetic species, during their hurried phases at least, dispense with this genetic shuffle. They stick stubbornly to the gene pattern that seems to be working. They produce (with certain complicated exceptions) natural clones of themselves.

But what they gain thereby in reproductive rate, in great explosions of population, they give up in flexibility. They minimize their genetic options. They lessen their chances of adapting to unforeseen changes of circumstance. 15

Which is why more than one biologist has drawn the same conclusion as M. J. D. White: "Parthenogenetic forms seem to be frequently successful in the particular ecological niche which they occupy, but sooner or later the inherent disadvantages of their genetic system must be expected to lead to a lack of adaptability, followed by eventual extinction, or perhaps in some cases by a return to sexuality." 16

So it *is* necessary, at least intermittently (once a year, for the aphids, whether they need it or not), this thing called sex. As of course you and I knew it must be. Otherwise surely, by now, we mammals and dragonflies would have come up with something more dignified. 17

READING FOR MEANING

This section presents three activities that will help you reread Quammen's explanatory essay with a critical eye. Done in sequence, these activities lead you from a basic understanding of the selection to a more personal response to it and finally to an analysis that deepens your understanding and critical thinking about what you are reading.

Read to Comprehend

Reread the selection, and write a few sentences explaining the concept *parthenogenesis* and its significance. Also make a list of any words you do not understand—for example, *opportunism* (in the title), *nonlibidinous* (paragraph 1), *qua* (4), *matricidal* (13). Look up their meanings in a dictionary to see which definition best fits the context.

To expand your understanding of this reading, you might use one or more of the following critical reading strategies that are explained and illustrated in Appendix 1: *outlining, summarizing, paraphrasing,* and *questioning to understand and remember.*

Read to Respond

Write several paragraphs exploring your initial thoughts and feelings about Quammen's explanatory essay. Focus on anything that stands out for you, perhaps because it resonates with your own experience or because you find a statement puzzling.

You might consider writing about

- the essay's title.

- your response to Quammen's assumption that his readers are uninterested in "aphid biology *qua* aphid biology" (paragraph 4).

- Quammen's joke about not having "to be Catholic to believe in this one" (2).

- the grisly description of the reproductive behavior of the gall midge *Miastor* (3).

- the notion that parthenogenetic reproduction may be effective for opportunistic species, but that even they need to reproduce sexually once in a while to refresh the gene pool (14–17).

To develop your response to Quammen's essay, you might use one or more of the following critical reading strategies that are explained and illustrated in Appendix 1: *contextualizing, recognizing emotional manipulation,* and *judging the writer's credibility.*

Read to Analyze Underlying Assumptions

Write several paragraphs exploring one or more of the assumptions, values, and beliefs underlying Quammen's explanation of parthenogenesis. As you write, explain how the assumptions are reflected in the text, as well as what you now think of them (and perhaps of your own assumptions) after rereading the selection with a critical eye.

Even though explanatory writing attempts to be clear and direct, analyzing a writer's word choices, examples, and comparisons often reveals assumptions that may only be suggested. Quammen, for example, plays with our assumption that because we are at the top of the evolutionary ladder, our method of procreation is the best from an evolutionary perspective. The opening lyrics *"Birds do it, bees do it,"* from the witty Cole Porter song "Let's Do It (Let's Fall in Love)," express the assumption that all species follow our lead or wish they did. To get us to think more critically about evolution, Quammen deflates our species pride by pointing out that other animal species not only use different methods, but also that their methods may be better than ours or at least enable them to adapt extraordinarily effectively to their habitats. At the start of paragraph 12, he makes this comparison to human sexual reproduction explicit:

> And parthenogenesis, in turn, is the greatest time-saving gimmick in the history of animal reproduction. No hours or days are wasted while a female looks for a mate; no minutes lost to the act of mating itself. . . . No waiting, no courtship, no fooling around.

Saving time may not seem important to humans in this context, but Quammen wants us to understand how important speed in reproducing is to the survival of species living in conditions of significant environmental variation. By comparing aphid and human reproduction, he helps readers understand how evolution works.

As a critical reader, you will want to think about how a writer's choices reveal assumptions and values, as well as how they may have an unlooked-for effect on readers. Quammen helps us become aware of and question our own narrow perspective on the world. Analyzing underlying assumptions in a reading gives us an opportunity to think critically about unexamined assumptions—the writer's and our own, many of which may be ingrained in our culture, our education, and even our language.

You might consider writing about

- the beliefs and values underlying Quammen's statement that "no sensible reader . . . can be expected . . . to care faintly about aphid biology *qua* aphid biology" (paragraph 4).

- the assumptions behind Quammen's assertion that readers might think being called "a galloping opportunist" could be "a term of . . . abuse" (10 and 11).

- Birky and Gilbert's classification of species according to the kind of environmental conditions to which they have to adapt (11).

- the idea that sexual reproduction "constitutes, by its essence, genetic tampering"—possibly in light of the ongoing debate about genetic engineering and cloning (14).

To probe assumptions more deeply, you might use one or more of the following critical reading strategies that are explained and illustrated in Appendix 1: *reflecting on challenges to your beliefs and values, exploring the significance of figurative language*, and *looking for patterns of opposition*.

READING LIKE A WRITER

This section guides you through an analysis of Quammen's explanatory writing strategies: *devising a readable plan, using appropriate explanatory strategies, integrating sources smoothly*, and *engaging readers' interest*. For each strategy you will be asked to reread and annotate part of Quammen's essay to see how he uses the strategy in "Is Sex Necessary?"

When you study the selections later in this chapter, you will see how different writers use these same strategies. The Guide to Writing Essays Explaining Concepts near the end of the chapter suggests ways you can use these strategies in your own writing.

Devising a Readable Plan

Experienced writers of explanation know that readers often have a hard time making their way through new and difficult material and sometimes give up in frustration. Writers who want to avoid this scenario construct a reader-friendly plan by dividing the information into clearly distinguishable topics. They also give readers road signs—forecasting statements, topic sentences, transitions, and summaries—to guide them through the explanation.

Writers often provide a forecasting statement early in the essay to let readers know where they are heading. Forecasting statements can also appear at the beginnings of major sections of the essay. Topic sentences announce each segment of information as it comes up, transitions (such as *in contrast* and *another*) relate what is coming to what came before, and summaries remind readers what has been explained already. Quammen effectively deploys all of these strategies.

Analyze

1. *Underline* the last sentence in paragraph 4, the first sentence in paragraph 5, all of the sentences in paragraph 9, and the first sentence in paragraph 10.

2. *Consider* these the key sentences in Quammen's effort to devise a readable plan and make that plan unmistakably clear to readers. *Make notes* in the margin by these sentences about how they forecast, announce topics, make transitions, and offer brief summaries. (These strategies are defined in the preceding paragraph.)

Write

Write several sentences, explaining how Quammen makes use of forecasting statements, transitions, brief summaries, and topic sentences to reveal his overall plan to readers. *Give examples* from the reading to support your explanation. Then, considering yourself among Quammen's intended readers, *write a few more sentences* evaluating how successful the writer's efforts are for you.

Using Appropriate Explanatory Strategies

When writers organize and present information, they rely on strategies we call the building blocks of explanatory essays: defining, classifying or dividing, comparing and contrasting, narrating a process, illustrating, and reporting causes or effects. The strategies a writer chooses are determined by the topics covered, the kinds of information available, and the writer's assessment of readers' knowledge about the concept. Following are brief descriptions of the writing strategies that are particularly useful in explaining concepts:

Defining: briefly stating the meaning of the concept or any other word likely to be unfamiliar to readers

Classifying or dividing: grouping related information about a concept into two or more separate groups and labeling each group, or dividing a concept into parts to consider each part separately

Comparing and contrasting: pointing out how the concept is similar to and different from a related concept

Narrating a process: presenting procedures or a sequence of steps as they unfold over time to show the concept in practice

Illustrating: giving examples, relating anecdotes, listing facts and details, and quoting sources to help readers understand a concept

Reporting causes or effects: identifying the known causes or effects related to a concept

Quammen makes good use of all these fundamentally important explanatory strategies: defining in paragraphs 1, 8, and 11; classifying in paragraphs 10 and 11; comparing and contrasting in paragraphs 11–14 (as well as establishing the analogy between insects and humans that runs through the essay); narrating a process in paragraphs 5–8; illustrating in paragraph 3; and reporting known effects in paragraphs 12–14.

Analyze

1. *Review* Quammen's use of each explanatory strategy described in the preceding paragraph, and *select one* to analyze more closely.

2. *Make notes* in the margin about how Quammen uses that one strategy and what special contribution it makes to your understanding of parthenogenesis within the context of the whole reading.

Write

Write several sentences explaining how the strategy you have analyzed works in this essay to help readers understand parthenogenesis.

Integrating Sources Smoothly

In addition to drawing on personal knowledge and fresh observations, writers often do additional research about the concepts they are trying to explain. Doing research in the library and on the Internet, writers immediately confront the ethical responsibility to their readers of locating relevant sources, evaluating them critically, and representing them without distortion. You will find advice on meeting this responsibility in Appendix 2 (pp. 725–60).

Developing an explanation sentence by sentence on the page or the screen, writers confront a different challenge in using sources: how to integrate source material smoothly into their own sentences and to cite the sources of those materials accurately, sometimes using formal citation styles that point readers to a full description of each source in a list of works cited at the end of the essay.

How writers cite or refer to research sources depends on the writing situation they find themselves in. Certain formal situations, such as college assignments or scholarly publications, have prescribed rules for citing sources. As a student, you may be expected to cite your sources formally because your writing will be judged in part by what you have read and how you have used your reading. For more informal writing occasions—newspaper and magazine articles, for example—readers do not expect writers to include page references or publication information, only to identify their sources. In this chapter's readings, all the writers except Quammen and Deborah Tannen cite their sources formally.

Writers may quote, summarize, or paraphrase their sources: quoting when they want to capture the exact wording of the original source; summarizing to convey only the gist or main points; and paraphrasing when they want to include most of the details in some part of the original. Whether they quote, summarize, or paraphrase, writers try to integrate source material smoothly into their writing. For example, they deliberately vary the way they introduce borrowed material, avoiding repetition of the same signal phrases (*X said, as Y put it*) or sentence pattern (a *that* clause, use of the colon).

Analyze

1. *Look closely* at paragraphs 11 and 16, where Quammen quotes sources directly.

2. *Put brackets* ([ ]) *around* the signal phrase or key part of a sentence pattern that he uses to introduce each quotation, noticing how he integrates the quotation into his sentence.

Write

Write a few sentences describing how Quammen introduces and integrates quotations into his writing. *Give examples* from your annotations in paragraphs 11 and 16.

Engaging Readers' Interest

Most people read explanations of concepts because they are helpful for work or school. Readers do not generally expect the writing to entertain, but simply to inform. Nevertheless, explanations that keep readers engaged with lively writing are usually appreciated. Writers explaining concepts may engage readers' interest in a variety of ways. For example, they may remind readers of what they already know about the concept. They may show readers a new way of using a familiar concept or dramatize that the concept has greater importance than readers had realized. They can connect the concept, sometimes through metaphor or analogy, to common human experiences. They may present the concept in a humorous way to convince readers that learning about a concept can be painless or even pleasurable.

Quammen relies on many of these strategies to engage his readers' interest. Keep in mind that his original readers could either read or skip his column. Those who enjoyed and learned from his earlier columns would be more likely to try out the first few paragraphs of this one, but Quammen could not count on their having any special interest in parthenogenesis. He has to try to generate that interest—and rather quickly, in the first few sentences or paragraphs.

Analyze

Reread paragraphs 1–4, and *note in the margin* the various ways Quammen reaches out to interest readers in his subject.

Write

Write several sentences explaining how Quammen attempts to engage his readers' interest in parthenogenesis. To support your explanation, *give examples* from your annotations in paragraphs 1–4. What parts seem most effective to you? Least effective?

A SPECIAL READING STRATEGY

Comparing and Contrasting Related Readings: Quammen's "Is Sex Necessary?" and Curtis and Barnes's "Parthenogenesis"

Comparing and contrasting related readings is a critical reading strategy useful both in reading for meaning and in reading like a writer. This strategy is particularly applicable when writers present similar subjects, as is the case in the concept explanation by David Quammen (p. 227) and the following excerpt from a biology textbook by Helena Curtis and N. Sue Barnes. As you read the textbook explanation of parthenogenesis and compare it to Quammen's explanation, consider the following issues:

- Compare these two explanations in terms of how well they help you understand parthenogenesis—how it works, how widespread it is, and what its benefits are.

- Compare the use of technical terms and sources in the two explanations, considering the purpose and readers for each publication.

- Compare the use of examples, especially that of the gall midge (paragraph 3 in Quammen and paragraph 4 in Curtis and Barnes).

- Compare how the explanations attempt to engage readers' interest.

See Appendix 1 for detailed guidelines on using the comparing and contrasting related readings strategy.

HELENA CURTIS AND N. SUE BARNES

Parthenogenesis

Another form of asexual reproduction is parthenogenesis, the development of an organism from an unfertilized egg. In species in which the male gamete determines the sex of the offspring, parthenogenesis always results in all female offspring. Hence, it is far more efficient than sexual reproduction. If . . . houseflies . . . reproduced parthenogenetically, each female would have . . . twice as many female young in every generation, and the population would [be] 358×10^{12} at the end of seven generations.

Parthenogenesis in plants lacks the advantage of the parental support system supplied by vegetative growth, which is traded off for the possibilities of larger numbers and, usually, wider dispersal of the young. Dandelions reproduce parthenogenetically. They form conspicuous flowers and also some functionless pollen grains, which may be taken as evidence that the present asexual species of dandelions evolved from sexual ones. As a consequence of parthenogenetic reproduction, dandelions growing in a single locality often consist of several different populations, each composed of genetically identical individuals. Otto Solbrig compared two such populations of dandelions growing together in various localities near Ann Arbor, Michigan. One genotype, genotype D, outperformed the other under all environmental conditions, both in the number of plants that survived and in their total dry weight. On the other hand, genotype A always produced more seeds and produced them earlier, so it always got a head start whenever a newly disturbed area became available for occupation.

Completely asexual species are also found among small invertebrates—some rotifers, for example—as well as among plants. Recently, several species of fish, lizards, and frogs have been found that apparently reproduce only parthenogenetically. Many other organisms alternate sexual and asexual phases. Freshwater *Daphnia*, for instance, multiply by parthenogenesis when the plankton on which they feed is abundant. Then, in response to some environmental cue, they start producing both males and females. Typically, the asexual phase occurs when conditions are favorable for rapid local growth, and the sexual phase when the population is facing a less certain future and less homogeneous conditions. 3

Among the organisms that alternate sexual and asexual phases is the fungus-eating gall midge, which should perhaps be awarded the prize for precocious development among multicellular animals. These small flies, which are found on mushroom beds, can reproduce sexually. However, when abundant food is available, a female can produce parthenogenetic eggs, which are retained inside her body. The larvae develop inside the mother, devour her tissues, and, completely skipping the usual metamorphosis, emerge with eggs inside their own tissues. Within two days, larvae emerge from these eggs, devour their own mother, and are soon devoured in turn. Eventually, in response to some environmental signal, the parthenogenetic cycle is broken, and the females produce normal males and females that fly off in search of new mushrooms. 4

■ Readings

DEBORAH TANNEN

Marked Women

Deborah Tannen (b. 1945), who holds the title of University Professor in Linguistics at Georgetown University, has written more than twenty books and scores of articles. Although she does write technical works in linguistics, she also writes for a more general audience on the ways that language reflects the society in which it develops, particularly the society's attitudes about gender. Both her 1986 book, That's Not What I Meant!: How Conversational Style Makes or Breaks Your Relations with Others, *and her 1990 book,* You Just Don't Understand: Women and Men in Conversation, *were best-sellers. Her most recent books include* The Argument Culture: Moving from Debate to Dialogue *(1998) and* I Only Say This Because I Love You: Talking to Your Parents, Partner, Sibs, and Kids When You're All Adults *(2002). In addition, Tannen writes poetry, plays, and reflective essays.*

In the following selection, originally published in the New York Times Magazine *in 1993, Tannen explains the concept of markedness, a "staple of linguistic theory." Linguistics—the study of language as a system for making meaning—has given birth to a new discipline called* semiology, *the study of any system for making meaning. Tannen's essay embodies this shift, as it starts with a verbal principle (the marking of words) and applies it to the visual world (the marking of hairstyle and clothing). As you read the opening paragraphs, notice how Tannen unpacks the meaning of what various conference participants are wearing.*

Some years ago I was at a small working conference of four   1
women and eight men. Instead of concentrating on the discussion
I found myself looking at the three other women at the table,
thinking how each had a different style and how each style was
coherent.

One woman had dark brown hair in a classic style, a cross   2
between Cleopatra and Plain Jane. The severity of her straight hair
was softened by wavy bangs and ends that turned under. Because
she was beautiful, the effect was more Cleopatra than plain.

The second woman was older, full of dignity and composure.   3
Her hair was cut in a fashionable style that left her with only one
eye, thanks to a side part that let a curtain of hair fall across half
her face. As she looked down to read her prepared paper, the hair

robbed her of bifocal vision and created a barrier between her and the listeners.

The third woman's hair was wild, a frosted blond avalanche falling over and beyond her shoulders. When she spoke she frequently tossed her head, calling attention to her hair and away from her lecture.

Then there was makeup. The first woman wore facial cover that made her skin smooth and pale, a black line under each eye and mascara that darkened already dark lashes. The second wore only a light gloss on her lips and a hint of shadow on her eyes. The third had blue bands under her eyes, dark blue shadow, mascara, bright red lipstick and rouge; her fingernails flashed red.

I considered the clothes each woman had worn during the three days of the conference: In the first case, man-tailored suits in primary colors with solid-color blouses. In the second, casual but stylish black T-shirts, a floppy collarless jacket and baggy slacks or a skirt in neutral colors. The third wore a sexy jump suit; tight sleeveless jersey and tight yellow slacks; a dress with gaping armholes and an indulged tendency to fall off one shoulder.

Shoes? No. 1 wore string sandals with medium heels; No. 2, sensible, comfortable walking shoes; No. 3, pumps with spike heels. You can fill in the jewelry, scarves, shawls, sweaters—or lack of them.

As I amused myself finding coherence in these styles, I suddenly wondered why I was scrutinizing only the women. I scanned the eight men at the table. And then I knew why I wasn't studying them. The men's styles were unmarked.

The term "marked" is a staple of linguistic theory. It refers to the way language alters the base meaning of a word by adding a linguistic particle that has no meaning on its own. The unmarked form of a word carries the meaning that goes without saying— what you think of when you're not thinking anything special.

The unmarked tense of verbs in English is the present—for example, *visit*. To indicate past, you mark the verb by adding *ed* to yield *visited*. For future, you add a word: *will visit*. Nouns are presumed to be singular until marked for plural, typically by adding *s* or *es*, so *visit* becomes *visits* and *dish* becomes *dishes*.

The unmarked forms of most English words also convey "male." Being male is the unmarked case. Endings like *ess* and *ette* mark words as "female." Unfortunately, they also tend to mark them for frivolousness. Would you feel safe entrusting your life to a doctorette? Alfre Woodard, who was an Oscar nominee for best supporting actress, says she identifies herself as an actor because "actresses worry about eyelashes and cellulite, and women who are actors worry about the characters we are playing." Gender markers pick up extra meanings that reflect common association with the female gender: not quite serious, often sexual.

Each of the women at the conference had to make decisions about hair, clothing, makeup and accessories, and each decision carried meaning. Every style available to us was marked. The men in our group had made decisions, too, but the range from which they chose was incomparably narrower. Men can choose styles that are marked, but they don't have to, and in this group none did. Unlike the women, they had the option of being unmarked.   12

Take the men's hair styles. There was no marine crew cut or oily longish hair falling into eyes, no asymmetrical, two-tiered construction to swirl over a bald top. One man was unabashedly bald; the others had hair of standard length, parted on one side, in natural shades of brown or gray or graying. Their hair obstructed no views, left little to toss or push back or run fingers through and, consequently, needed and attracted no attention. A few men had beards. In a business setting, beards might be marked. In this academic gathering, they weren't.   13

There could have been a cowboy shirt with string tie or a three-piece suit or a necklaced hippie in jeans. But there wasn't. All eight men wore brown or blue slacks and nondescript shirts of light colors. No man wore sandals or boots; their shoes were dark, closed, comfortable, and flat. In short, unmarked.   14

Although no man wore makeup, you couldn't say the men didn't wear makeup in the sense that you could say a woman didn't wear makeup. For men, no makeup is unmarked.   15

I asked myself what style we women could have adopted that would have been unmarked, like the men's. The answer was none. There is no unmarked woman.   16

There is no woman's hair style that can be called standard, that says nothing about her. The range of women's hair styles is staggering, but a woman whose hair has no particular style is perceived as not caring about how she looks, which can disqualify her from many positions, and will subtly diminish her as a person in the eyes of some.   17

Women must choose between attractive shoes and comfortable shoes. When our group made an unexpected trek, the woman who wore flat, laced shoes arrived first. Last to arrive was the woman in spike heels, shoes in hand and a handful of men around her.   18

If a woman's clothing is tight or revealing (in other words, sexy), it sends a message—an intended one of wanting to be attractive, but also a possibly unintended one of availability. If her clothes are   19 not sexy, that too sends a message, lent meaning by the knowledge that they could have been. There are thousands of cosmetic products from which women can choose and myriad ways of applying them. Yet no makeup at all is anything but unmarked. Some men see it as a hostile refusal to please them.

Women can't even fill out a form without telling stories about themselves. Most forms give four titles to choose from. "Mr." carries no meaning other than that the respondent is male. But a woman who checks "Mrs." or "Miss" communicates not only whether she has been married but also whether she has conservative tastes in forms of address—and probably other conservative values as well. Checking "Ms." declines to let on about marriage (checking "Mr." declines nothing since nothing was asked), but it also marks her as either liberated or rebellious, depending on the observer's attitudes and assumptions.

I sometimes try to duck these variously marked choices by giving my title as "Dr."—and in so doing risk marking myself as either uppity (hence sarcastic responses like "Excuse *me!*") or an overachiever (hence reactions of congratulatory surprise like "Good for you!").

All married women's surnames are marked. If a woman takes her husband's name, she announces to the world that she is married and has traditional values. To some it will indicate that she is less herself, more identified by her husband's identity. If she does not take her husband's name, this too is marked, seen as worthy of comment: She has *done* something; she has "kept her own name." A man is never said to have "kept his own name" because it never occurs to anyone that he might have given it up. For him using his own name is unmarked.

A married woman who wants to have her cake and eat it too may use her surname plus his, with or without a hyphen. But this too announces her marital status and often results in a tongue-tying string. In a list (Harvey O'Donovan, Jonathan Feldman, Stephanie Woodbury McGillicutty), the woman's multiple name stands out. It is marked.

I have never been inclined toward biological explanations of gender differences in language, but I was intrigued to see Ralph Fasold bring biological phenomena to bear on the question of linguistic marking in his book *The Sociolinguistics of Language*. Fasold stresses that language and culture are particularly unfair in treating women as the marked case because biologically it is the male that is marked. While two X chromosomes make a female, two Y chromosomes make nothing. Like the linguistic markers *s,*

20

21

22

23

24

es, or *ess*, the Y chromosome doesn't "mean" anything unless it is attached to a root form—an X chromosome.

Developing this idea elsewhere Fasold points out that girls are born with full female bodies, while boys are born with modified female bodies. He invites men who doubt this to lift up their shirts and contemplate why they have nipples.

In his book, Fasold notes "a wide range of facts which demonstrates that female is the unmarked sex." For example, he observes that there are a few species that produce only females, like the whiptail lizard. Thanks to parthenogenesis, they have no trouble having as many daughters as they like. There are no species, however, that produce only males. This is no surprise, since any such species would become extinct in its first generation.

Fasold is also intrigued by species that produce individuals not involved in reproduction, like honeybees and leaf-cutter ants. Reproduction is handled by the queen and a relatively few males; the workers are sterile females. "Since they do not reproduce," Fasold said, "there is no reason for them to be one sex or the other, so they default, so to speak, to female."

Fasold ends his discussion of these matters by pointing out that if language reflected biology, grammar books would direct us to use "she" to include males and females and "he" only for specifically male referents. But they don't. They tell us that "he" means "he or she," and that "she" is used only if the referent is specifically female. This use of "he" as the sex-indefinite pronoun is an innovation introduced into English by grammarians in the eighteenth and nineteenth centuries, according to Peter Mühlhäusler and Rom Harré in *Pronouns and People*. From at least about 1500, the correct sex-indefinite pronoun was "they," as it still is in casual spoken English. In other words, the female was declared by grammarians to be the marked case.

Writing this article may mark me not as a writer, not as a linguist, not as an analyst of human behavior, but as a feminist—which will have positive or negative, but in any case powerful, connotations for readers. Yet I doubt that anyone reading Ralph Fasold's book would put that label on him.

I discovered the markedness inherent in the very topic of gender after writing a book on differences in conversational style based on geographical region, ethnicity, class, age, and gender. When I was interviewed, the vast majority of journalists wanted to talk about the differences between women and men. While I thought I was simply describing what I observed—something I had learned to do as a researcher—merely mentioning women and men marked me as a feminist for some.

When I wrote a book devoted to gender differences in ways of   31
speaking, I sent the manuscript to five male colleagues, asking
them to alert me to any interpretation, phrasing, or wording that
might seem unfairly negative toward men. Even so, when the book
came out, I encountered responses like that of the television talk
show host who, after interviewing me, turned to the audience and
asked if they thought I was male-bashing.

Leaping upon a poor fellow who affably nodded in agree-   32
ment, she made him stand and asked, "Did what she said accurately describe you?" "Oh, yes," he answered. "That's me exactly."
"And what she said about women—does that sound like your
wife?" "Oh, yes," he responded. "That's her exactly." "Then why
do you think she's male-bashing?" He answered, with disarming
honesty, "Because she's a woman and she's saying things about
men."

To say anything about women and men without marking   33
oneself as either feminist or anti-feminist, male-basher or apologist for men seems as impossible for a woman as trying to get
dressed in the morning without inviting interpretations of her
character.

Sitting at the conference table musing on these matters, I felt   34
sad to think that we women didn't have the freedom to be unmarked
that the men sitting next to us had. Some days you just want to get
dressed and go about your business. But if you're a woman, you
can't, because there is no unmarked woman.

READING FOR MEANING

This section presents three activities that will help you reread Tannen's
explanatory essay with a critical eye. Done in sequence, these activities lead you
from a basic understanding of the selection to a more personal response to it and
finally to an analysis that deepens your understanding and critical thinking about
what you are reading.

Read to Comprehend

Reread the selection, and write a few sentences identifying a few examples of
markedness from Tannen's essay and explaining how they help you understand the
concept and its significance. Also make a list of any words you do not understand—
for example, *composure* (paragraph 3), *referents* (28), *inherent* (30), *disarming* (32).
Look up their meanings in a dictionary to see which definition best fits the
context.

To expand your understanding of this reading, you might use one or more
of the following critical reading strategies that are explained and illustrated in

Appendix 1: *outlining, summarizing, paraphrasing,* and *questioning to understand and remember.*

Read to Respond

Write several paragraphs exploring your initial thoughts and feelings about Tannen's explanatory essay. Focus on anything that stands out for you, perhaps because it resonates with your own experience or because you find a statement puzzling.

You might consider writing about

- the idea that men have a choice of whether to be marked or unmarked but women are always marked no matter what they do, perhaps in relation to your own experience.

- the personal style that each of the three women described in paragraphs 1–8 created, perhaps in relation to your own efforts to create your own style.

- your response to the assertion that how a choice like checking "Ms." on a form is understood depends on the interpreter's "attitudes and assumptions" (paragraph 20), considering what might influence such attitudes and assumptions.

- your view of Tannen in light of her assertion that "this article may mark me not as a writer, not as a linguist, not as an analyst of human behavior, but as a feminist—which will have positive or negative, but in any case powerful, connotations for readers" (29).

To develop your response to Tannen's essay, you might use one or more of the following critical reading strategies that are explained and illustrated in Appendix 1: *contextualizing, recognizing emotional manipulation,* and *judging the writer's credibility.*

Read to Analyze Underlying Assumptions

Write several paragraphs exploring one or more of the assumptions, values, and beliefs underlying Tannen's essay. As you write, explain how the assumptions are reflected in the text, as well as what you now think of them (and perhaps of your own assumptions) after rereading the selection with a critical eye.

You might consider writing about

- cultural assumptions about the connection between markers and stereotypes—perhaps in relation to markers you can think of for ethnicity, age, social class, income level, or anything else.

- the assumptions and values implied by Tannen's examples of what a marked style in hair and clothes might look like for men.

- the assumptions about context in marking that are suggested by this example: "In a business setting, beards might be marked. In this academic gathering, they weren't" (paragraph 13).

- the values and beliefs behind Tannen's observation that when the "group made an unexpected trek," the woman with high heels arrived last with "a handful of men around her" (18).

- the assumptions underlying Tannen's claim that "[t]o say anything about women and men without marking oneself as either feminist or anti-feminist, male-basher or apologist for men seems as impossible for a woman as trying to get dressed in the morning without inviting interpretations of her character" (33)—perhaps considering whether this generalization applies to you and your classmates.

To probe assumptions more deeply, you might use one or more of the following critical reading strategies that are explained and illustrated in Appendix 1: *reflecting on challenges to your beliefs and values, exploring the significance of figurative language*, and *looking for patterns of opposition*.

READING LIKE A WRITER
ENGAGING READERS' INTEREST

Explanatory writing aimed at nonspecialist readers usually makes an effort to engage those readers' interest in the information offered. David Quammen, for example, writing for a popular magazine, exerts himself to be engaging, even entertaining. Also writing for a magazine read by an educated but nonspecialist audience, Tannen likewise attempts to engage and hold her readers' interest. Like Quammen, she weaves these attempts to engage readers into the flow of information. While they are not separate from the information—for information itself, even dryly presented, can interest readers—direct attempts to engage are nevertheless a recognizable feature of Tannen's explanatory essay. For example, she opens the essay in an inviting way, with several intriguing descriptions, which later serve as examples of the concept. In addition, she adopts an informal conversational tone by using the first-person pronoun *I*, and she comments on her own thinking process.

Analyze

1. *Reread* paragraphs 1–8, and *look for* places where you are aware of Tannen's tone or voice.

2. *Skim* the rest of the essay, focusing on paragraphs 13–16, 21, 24, and 29–34, where Tannen uses the first-person *I* or other conversational devices, such as "Take the men's hair styles" as an opener for paragraph 13. *Make notes* about these devices and their effect on you as a reader.

Write

Write several sentences describing Tannen's tone and some of the strategies she uses to create it. *Give examples* from the reading to illustrate your analysis.

CONSIDERING IDEAS FOR YOUR OWN WRITING

If you are taking a course concerned with language and society, you might want to learn about and then explain another linguistic concept, such as semantics, language acquisition, connotation, or discourse community; or a semiotic concept, such as signification, code, iconography, ideology, or popular culture. Related fields with interesting concepts to learn and write about are gender studies and sociology. Gender studies is concerned with such concepts as gender, femininity, masculinity, identity formation, objectification, intersubjectivity, nonsexist language, androgyny, domesticity, patriarchy, and the construction of desire. Sociology studies group dynamics and social patterns using such concepts as socialization, the family, role model, community, cohort, social stratification, positivism, dysfunctional families, and status.

HOWARD GARDNER AND JOSEPH WALTERS

A Rounded Version: The Theory of Multiple Intelligences

Howard Gardner (b. 1943), an educational psychologist, is the John H. and Elisabeth A. Hobbs Professor of Cognition and Education at Harvard University's Graduate School of Education. He also holds adjunct positions as professor of psychology at Harvard and professor of neurology at Boston University School of Medicine and serves as co-director of several research groups, including Project Zero at Harvard's Graduate School of Education, which has investigated the development of learning processes since 1967. The recipient of numerous honors, including eighteen honorary degrees and a MacArthur Prize Fellowship, Gardner is the author of nineteen books. They include Frames of Mind (1983), his first full-length statement of the theory of multiple intelligences; Intelligence Reframed: Multiple Intelligences for the Twenty-first Century (1999), which updates his theory to include multimedia and technological intelligence; The Unschooled Mind: How Children Think and How Schools Should Teach (1991), which introduced the idea of learning styles; and Good Work: When Excellence and Ethics Meet (2001).

The following selection, written with Joseph Walters, first appeared as a chapter in Gardner's book Multiple Intelligences: The Theory in Practice (1993). A specialist in research and evaluation, Walters worked with Gardner for years at Project Zero; he is now the director of the Collaborative Learning Environments Online (CLEO) Initiative and the director of research for the Testbed for Telecollaboration. With other members of the Project Zero team, Walters coauthored Portfolio Practices: Thinking through the Assessment of Children's Work (1997). He also has written many articles and book chapters, including, with Gardner, "Children as Reflective Practioners: Bringing Metacognition to the Classroom" (1994).

In "A Rounded Version: The Theory of Multiple Intelligences," Gardner and Walters make clear that the concept of multiple intelligences is founded on research into neurological and brain damage, research that reveals the correlations between sites in the brain and certain kinds of intelligence. As they point out, such research finds a "biological proclivity" to different kinds of problem solving, therefore making multiple intelligences appear to be "universal" or cross-cultural. But notice that they also emphasize the importance of "cultural nurturing" in the development of different intelligences. As you read, think about the kinds of intelligence that are valued and encouraged in your family and community culture as well as the kinds that are devalued and discouraged.

Two eleven-year-old children are taking a test of "intelligence." They sit at their desks laboring over the meanings of different words, the interpretation of graphs, and the solutions to arithmetic problems. They record their answers by filling in small circles on a single piece of paper. Later these completed answer sheets are scored objectively: the number of right answers is converted into a standardized score that compares the individual child with a population of children of similar age.

The teachers of these children review the different scores. They notice that one of the children has performed at a superior level; on all sections of the test, she answered more questions correctly than did her peers. In fact, her score is similar to that of children three to four years older. The other child's performance is average— his scores reflect those of other children his age.

A subtle change in expectations surrounds the review of these test scores. Teachers begin to expect the first child to do quite well during her formal schooling, whereas the second should have only moderate success. Indeed these predictions come true. In other words, the test taken by the eleven-year-olds serves as a reliable predictor of their later performance in school.

How does this happen? One explanation involves our free use of the word "intelligence": the child with the greater "intelligence" has the ability to solve problems, to find the answers to specific questions, and to learn new material quickly and efficiently. These skills in turn play a central role in school success. In this view, "intelligence" is a singular faculty that is brought to bear in any problem-solving situation. Since schooling deals largely with solving problems of various sorts, predicting this capacity in young children predicts their future success in school.

"Intelligence," from this point of view, is a general ability that is found in varying degrees in all individuals. It is the key to success in solving problems. This ability can be measured reliably with standardized pencil-and-paper tests that, in turn, predict future success in school.

What happens after school is completed? Consider the two individuals in the example. Looking further down the road, we find that the "average" student has become a highly successful mechanical engineer who has risen to a position of prominence in both the professional community of engineers as well as in civic groups in his community. His success is no fluke—he is considered by all to be a talented individual. The "superior" student, on the other hand, has had little success in her chosen career as a writer; after repeated rejections by publishers, she has taken up a middle management position in a bank. While certainly not a "failure," she is considered by her peers to be quite "ordinary" in her adult accomplishments. So what happened?

This fabricated example is based on the facts of intelligence testing. IQ tests predict school performance with considerable accuracy, but they are only an indifferent predictor of performance in a profession after formal schooling.[1] Furthermore, even as IQ tests measure only logical or logical-linguistic capacities, in this society we are nearly "brain-washed" to restrict the notion of intelligence to the capacities used in solving logical and linguistic problems.

To introduce an alternative point of view, undertake the following "thought experiment." Suspend the usual judgment of what constitutes intelligence and let your thoughts run freely over the capabilities of humans—perhaps those that would be picked out by the proverbial Martian visitor. In this exercise, you are drawn to the brilliant chess player, the world-class violinist, and the champion athlete; such outstanding performers deserve special consideration. Under this experiment, a quite different view of *intelligence* emerges. Are the chess player, violinist, and athlete "intelligent" in these pursuits? If they are, then why do our tests of "intelligence" fail to identify them? If they are not "intelligent," what allows them to achieve such astounding feats? In general, why does the contemporary construct "intelligence" fail to explain large areas of human endeavor?

In this chapter we approach these problems through the theory of multiple intelligences (MI). As the name indicates, we believe that human cognitive competence is better described in terms of a set of abilities, talents, or mental skills, which we call "intelligences." All normal individuals possess each of these skills to some extent; individuals differ in the degree of skill and in the nature of their combination. We believe this theory of intelligence may be more humane and more veridical than alternative views of intelligence and that it more adequately reflects the data of human "intelligent" behavior. Such a theory has important educational implications, including ones for curriculum development.

WHAT CONSTITUTES AN INTELLIGENCE?

The question of the optimal definition of intelligence looms large in our inquiry. Indeed, it is at the level of this definition that the theory of multiple intelligences diverges from traditional points of view. In a traditional view, intelligence is defined operationally as

[1] Jencks, C. (1972). *Inequality*. New York: Basic Books.

the ability to answer items on tests of intelligence. The inference from the test scores to some underlying ability is supported by statistical techniques that compare responses of subjects at different ages; the apparent correlation of these test scores across ages and across different tests corroborates the notion that the general faculty of intelligence, g, does not change much with age or with training or experience. It is an inborn attribute or faculty of the individual.

Multiple intelligences theory, on the other hand, pluralizes the traditional concept. An intelligence entails the ability to solve problems or fashion products that are of consequence in a particular cultural setting or community. The problem-solving skill allows one to approach a situation in which a goal is to be obtained and to locate the appropriate route to that goal. The creation of a *cultural product* is crucial to such functions as capturing and transmitting knowledge or expressing one's views or feelings. The problems to be solved range from creating an end for a story to anticipating a mating move in chess to repairing a quilt. Products range from scientific theories to musical compositions to successful political campaigns. 11

MI theory is framed in light of the biological origins of each problem-solving skill. Only those skills that are universal to the human species are treated. Even so, the biological proclivity to participate in a particular form of problem solving must also be coupled with the cultural nurturing of that domain. For example, language, a universal skill, may manifest itself particularly as writing in one culture, as oratory in another culture, and as the secret language of anagrams in a third. 12

Given the desire of selecting intelligences that are rooted in biology, and that are valued in one or more cultural settings, how does one actually identify an "intelligence"? In coming up with our list, we consulted evidence from several different sources: knowledge about normal development and development in gifted individuals; information about the breakdown of cognitive skills under conditions of brain damage; studies of exceptional populations, including prodigies, idiots savants, and autistic children; data about the evolution of cognition over the millennia; cross-cultural accounts of cognition; psychometric studies, including examinations of correlations among tests; and psychological training studies, particularly measures of transfer and generalization across tasks. Only those candidate intelligences that satisfied all or a majority of the criteria were selected as bona fide intelligences. A more complete discussion of each of these criteria for an "intelligence" and the seven intelligences that have been proposed so far, 13 is found in *Frames of Mind.*[2] This book also considers how the theory might be disproven and compares it to competing theories of intelligence.

In addition to satisfying the aforementioned criteria, each intelligence must have an identifiable core operation or set of operations. As a neutrally based computational system, each intelligence is activated or "triggered" by certain kinds of internally or externally presented information. For example, one core of musical intelligence is the sensitivity to pitch relations, whereas one core of linguistic intelligence is the sensitivity to phonological features.

An intelligence must also be susceptible to encoding in a symbol system—a culturally contrived system of meaning, which captures and conveys important forms of information. Language, picturing, and mathematics are but three nearly worldwide symbol systems that are necessary for human survival and productivity. The relationship of a candidate intelligence to a human symbol system is no accident. In fact, the existence of a core computational capacity anticipates the existence of a symbol system that exploits that capacity. While it may be possible for an intelligence to proceed without an accompanying symbol system, a primary characteristic of human intelligence may well be its gravitation toward such an embodiment.

THE SEVEN INTELLIGENCES

Having sketched the characteristics and criteria of an intelligence, we turn now to a brief consideration of each of the seven intelligences. We begin each sketch with a thumbnail biography of a person who demonstrates an unusual facility with that intelligence. These biographies illustrate some of the abilities that are central to the fluent operation of a given intelligence. Although each biography illustrates a particular intelligence, we do not wish to imply that in adulthood intelligences operate in isolation. Indeed, except for abnormal individuals, intelligences always work in concert, and any sophisticated adult role will involve a melding of several of them. Following each biography we survey the various sources of data that support each candidate as an "intelligence."

Musical Intelligence

When he was three years old, Yehudi Menuhin was smuggled into the San Francisco Orchestra concerts by his parents.

[2] Gardner, H. (1983). *Frames of mind: The theory of multiple intelligences.* New York: Basic Books.

The sound of Louis Persinger's violin so entranced the youngster that he insisted on a violin for his birthday and Louis Persinger as his teacher. He got both. By the time he was ten years old, Menuhin was an international performer.[3]

Violinist Yehudi Menuhin's musical intelligence manifested itself even before he had touched a violin or received any musical training. His powerful reaction to that particular sound and his rapid progress on the instrument suggest that he was biologically prepared in some way for that endeavor. In this way evidence from child prodigies supports our claim that there is a biological link to a particular intelligence. Other special populations, such as autistic children who can play a musical instrument beautifully but who cannot speak, underscore the independence of musical intelligence.   17

A brief consideration of the evidence suggests that musical skill passes the other tests for an intelligence. For example, certain parts of the brain play important roles in perception and production of music. These areas are characteristically located in the right hemisphere, although musical skill is not as clearly "localized," or located in a specifiable area, as language. Although the particular susceptibility of musical ability to brain damage depends on the degree of training and other individual differences, there is clear evidence for "amusia" or loss of musical ability.   18

Music apparently played an important unifying role in Stone Age (Paleolithic) societies. Birdsong provides a link to other species. Evidence from various cultures supports the notion that music is a universal faculty. Studies of infant development suggest that there is a "raw" computational ability in early childhood. Finally, musical notation provides an accessible and lucid symbol system.   19

In short, evidence to support the interpretation of musical ability as an "intelligence" comes from many different sources. Even though musical skill is not typically considered an intellectual skill like mathematics, it qualifies under our criteria. By definition it deserves consideration; and in view of the data, its inclusion is empirically justified.   20

Bodily-Kinesthetic Intelligence

Fifteen-year-old Babe Ruth played third base. During one game his team's pitcher was doing very poorly and Babe loudly criticized him from third base. Brother Mathias, the coach, called out, "Ruth, if you know so much about it, YOU pitch!" Babe was surprised and embarrassed because he had

[3] Menuhin, Y. (1977). *Unfinished journey*. New York: Knopf.

never pitched before, but Brother Mathias insisted. Ruth said later that at the very moment he took the pitcher's mound, he KNEW he was supposed to be a pitcher and that it was "natural" for him to strike people out. Indeed, he went on to become a great major league pitcher (and, of course, attained legendary status as a hitter).[4]

Like Menuhin, Babe Ruth was a child prodigy who recognized his "instrument" immediately upon his first exposure to it. This recognition occurred in advance of formal training. 21

Control of bodily movement is, of course, localized in the motor cortex, with each hemisphere dominant or controlling bodily movements on the contra-lateral side. In right-handers, the dominance for such movement is ordinarily found in the left hemisphere. The ability to perform movements when directed to do so can be impaired even in individuals who can perform the same movements reflexively or on a nonvoluntary basis. The existence of specific *apraxia* constitutes one line of evidence for a bodily-kinesthetic intelligence. 22

The evolution of specialized body movements is of obvious advantage to the species, and in humans this adaptation is extended through the use of tools. Body movement undergoes a clearly defined developmental schedule in children. And there is little question of its universality across cultures. Thus it appears that bodily-kinesthetic "knowledge" satisfies many of the criteria for an intelligence. 23

The consideration of bodily-kinesthetic knowledge as "problem solving" may be less intuitive. Certainly carrying out a mime sequence or hitting a tennis ball is not solving a mathematical equation. And yet, the ability to use one's body to express an emotion (as in a dance), to play a game (as in a sport), or to create a new product (as in devising an invention) is evidence of the cognitive features of body usage. The specific computations required to solve a particular bodily-kinesthetic *problem*, hitting a tennis ball, are summarized by Tim Gallwey: 24

> At the moment the ball leaves the server's racket, the brain calculates approximately where it will land and where the racket will intercept it. This calculation includes the initial velocity of the ball, combined with an input for the progressive decrease in velocity and the effect of wind and after

---

[4] Connor, A. (1982). *Voices from Cooperstown*. New York: Collier. (Based on a quotation taken from *The Babe Ruth story*, Babe Ruth and Bob Considine. New York: Dutton, 1948.)

the bounce of the ball. Simultaneously, muscle orders are given: not just once, but constantly with refined and updated information. The muscles must cooperate. A movement of the feet occurs, the racket is taken back, the face of the racket kept at a constant angle. Contact is made at a precise point that depends on whether the order was given to hit down the line or cross-court, an order not given until after a split-second analysis of the movement and balance of the opponent.

To return an average serve, you have about one second to do this. To hit the ball at all is remarkable and yet not uncommon. The truth is that everyone who inhabits a human body possesses a remarkable creation.[5]

Logical-Mathematical Intelligence

In 1983 Barbara McClintock won the Nobel Prize in medicine or physiology for her work in microbiology. Her intellectual powers of deduction and observation illustrate one form of logical-mathematical intelligence that is often labeled "scientific thinking." One incident is particularly illuminating. While a researcher at Cornell in the 1920s McClintock was faced one day with a problem: while *theory* predicted 50-percent pollen sterility in corn, her research assistant (in the "field") was finding plants that were only 25- to 30-percent sterile. Disturbed by this discrepancy, McClintock left the cornfield and returned to her office where she sat for half an hour, thinking:

> Suddenly I jumped up and ran back to the (corn) field. At the top of the field (the others were still at the bottom) I shouted "Eureka, I have it! I know what the 30% sterility is!" . . . They asked me to prove it. I sat down with a paper bag and a pencil and I started from scratch, which I had not done at all in my laboratory. It had all been done so fast; the answer came and I ran. Now I worked it out step by step—it was an intricate series of steps—and I came out with [the same result]. [They] looked at the material and it was exactly as I'd said it was; it worked out exactly as I had diagrammed it. Now, why did I know, without having done it on paper? Why was I so sure?[6]

---

[5] Gallwey, T. (1976). *Inner tennis.* New York: Random House.

[6] Keller, E. (1983). *A feeling for the organism* (p. 104). Salt Lake City: W. H. Freeman.

This anecdote illustrates two essential facts of the logical-mathematical intelligence. First, in the gifted individual, the process of problem solving is often remarkably rapid—the successful scientist copes with many variables at once and creates numerous hypotheses that are each evaluated and then accepted or rejected in turn.

The anecdote also underscores the *nonverbal* nature of the intelligence. A solution to a problem can be constructed *before* it is articulated. In fact, the solution process may be totally invisible, even to the problem solver. This need not imply, however, that discoveries of this sort—the familiar "Aha!" phenomenon—are mysterious, intuitive, or unpredictable. The fact that it happens more frequently to some people (perhaps Nobel Prize winners) suggests the opposite. We interpret this as the work of logical-mathematical intelligence.

Along with the companion skill of language, logical-mathematical reasoning provides the principal basis for IQ tests. This form of intelligence has been heavily investigated by traditional psychologists, and it is the archetype of "raw intelligence" or the problem-solving faculty that purportedly cuts across domains. It is perhaps ironic, then, that the actual mechanism by which one arrives at a solution to a logical-mathematical problem is not as yet properly understood.

This intelligence is supported by our empirical criteria as well. Certain areas of the brain are more prominent in mathematical calculation than others. There are idiots savants who perform great feats of calculation even though they remain tragically deficient in most other areas. Child prodigies in mathematics abound. The development of this intelligence in children has been carefully documented by Jean Piaget and other psychologists.

Linguistic Intelligence

At the age of ten, T. S. Eliot created a magazine called *Fireside* to which he was the sole contributor. In a three-day period during his winter vacation, he created eight complete issues. Each one included poems, adventure stories, a gossip column, and humor. Some of this material survives and it displays the talent of the poet.[7]

As with the logical intelligence, calling linguistic skill an "intelligence" is consistent with the stance of traditional psychology.

---

[7] Soldo, J. (1982). Jovial juvenilia: T. S. Eliot's first magazine. *Biography*, 5, 25–37.

26

27

28

29

30

Linguistic intelligence also passes our empirical tests. For instance, a specific area of the brain, called "Broca's Area," is responsible for the production of grammatical sentences. A person with damage to this area can understand words and sentences quite well but has difficulty putting words together in anything other than the simplest of sentences. At the same time, other thought processes may be entirely unaffected.

The gift of language is universal, and its development in children   31
is strikingly constant across cultures. Even in deaf populations where a manual sign language is not explicitly taught, children will often "invent" their own manual language and use it surreptitiously! We thus see how an intelligence may operate independently of a specific input modality or output channel.

Spatial Intelligence

Navigation around the Caroline Islands in the South Seas is accomplished without instruments. The position of the stars, as viewed from various islands, the weather patterns, and water color are the only sign posts: Each journey is broken into a series of segments; and the navigator learns the position of the stars within each of these segments. During the actual trip the navigator must envision mentally a reference island as it passes under a particular star and from that he computes the number of segments completed, the proportion of the trip remaining, and any corrections in heading that are required. The navigator cannot *see* the islands as he sails along; instead he maps their locations in his mental "picture" of the journey.[8]

Spatial problem solving is required for navigation and in the   32
use of the notational system of maps. Other kinds of spatial problem solving are brought to bear in visualizing an object seen from a different angle and in playing chess. The visual arts also employ this intelligence in the use of space.

Evidence from brain research is clear and persuasive. Just as the   33
left hemisphere has, over the course of evolution, been selected as the site of linguistic processing in right-handed persons, the right hemisphere proves to be the site most crucial for spatial processing. Damage to the right posterior regions causes impairment of the ability to find one's way around a site, to recognize faces or scenes, or to notice fine details.

[8] Gardner, H. (1983). *Frames of mind: The theory of multiple intelligences.* New York: Basic Books.

Patients with damage specific to regions of the right hemisphere   34
will attempt to compensate for their spacial deficits with linguistic
strategies. They will try to reason aloud, to challenge the task, or even
make up answers. But such nonspatial strategies are rarely successful.

Blind populations provide an illustration of the distinction   35
between the spatial intelligence and visual perception. A blind person can recognize shapes by an indirect method: running a hand
along the object translates into length of time of movement, which
in turn is translated into the size of the object. For the blind person,
the perceptual system of the tactile modality parallels the visual
modality in the seeing person. The analogy between the spatial
reasoning of the blind and the linguistic reasoning of the deaf is
notable.

There are few child prodigies among visual artists, but there are   36
idiots savants such as Nadia.[9] Despite a condition of severe autism,
this preschool child made drawings of the most remarkable repre-
sentational accuracy and finesse.

Interpersonal Intelligence

With little formal training in special education and nearly blind   37
herself, Anne Sullivan began the intimidating task of instructing a
blind and deaf seven-year-old Helen Keller. Sullivan's efforts at
communication were complicated by the child's emotional struggle with the world around her. At their first meal together, this
scene occurred:

> Annie did not allow Helen to put her hand into Annie's plate
> and take what she wanted, as she had been accustomed to do
> with her family. It became a test of wills—hand thrust into
> plate, hand firmly put aside. The family, much upset, left the
> dining room. Annie locked the door and proceeded to eat
> her breakfast while Helen lay on the floor kicking and
> screaming, pushing and pulling at Annie's chair. [After half
> an hour] Helen went around the table looking for her family.
> She discovered no one else was there and that bewildered
> her. Finally, she sat down and began to eat her breakfast, but
> with her hands. Annie gave her a spoon. Down on the floor
> it clattered, and the contest of wills began anew.[10]

---

[9] Selfe, L. (1977). *Nadia: A case of extraordinary drawing in an autistic child.*
New York: Academic Press.

[10] Lash, J. (1980). *Helen and teacher: The story of Helen Keller and Anne Sullivan Macy* (p. 52). New York: Delacorte.

Anne Sullivan sensitively responded to the child's behavior. She wrote home: "The greatest problem I shall have to solve is how to discipline and control her without breaking her spirit. I shall go rather slowly at first and try to win her love."

In fact, the first "miracle" occurred two weeks later, well before the famous incident at the pumphouse. Annie had taken Helen to a small cottage near the family's house, where they could live alone. After seven days together, Helen's personality suddenly underwent a profound change—the therapy had worked:

> My heart is singing with joy this morning. A miracle has happened! The wild little creature of two weeks ago has been transformed into a gentle child.[11]

It was just two weeks after this that the first breakthrough in Helen's grasp of language occurred; and from that point on, she progressed with incredible speed. The key to the miracle of language was Anne Sullivan's insight into the *person* of Helen Keller.

Interpersonal intelligence builds on a core capacity to notice distinctions among others; in particular, contrasts in their moods, temperaments, motivations, and intentions. In more advanced forms, this intelligence permits a skilled adult to read the intentions and desires of others, even when these have been hidden. This skill appears in a highly sophisticated form in religious or political leaders, teachers, therapists, and parents. The Helen Keller–Anne Sullivan story suggests that this interpersonal intelligence does not depend on language.

All indices in brain research suggest that the frontal lobes play a prominent role in interpersonal knowledge. Damage in this area can cause profound personality changes while leaving other forms of problem solving unharmed—a person is often "not the same person" after such an injury.

Alzheimer's disease, a form of presenile dementia, appears to attack posterior brain zones with a special ferocity, leaving spatial, logical, and linguistic computations severely impaired. Yet, Alzheimer's patients will often remain well groomed, socially proper, and continually apologetic for their errors. In contrast, Pick's disease, another variety of presenile dementia that is more frontally oriented, entails a rapid loss of social graces.

Biological evidence for interpersonal intelligence encompasses two additional factors often cited as unique to humans. One factor is the prolonged childhood of primates, including the close attachment to the mother. In those cases where the mother is

[11] Lash (p. 54).

removed from early development, normal interpersonal development is in serious jeopardy. The second factor is the relative importance in humans of social interaction. Skills such as hunting, tracking, and killing in prehistoric societies required participation and cooperation of large numbers of people. The need for group cohesion, leadership, organization, and solidarity follows naturally from this.

Intrapersonal Intelligence

In an essay called "A Sketch of the Past," written almost as a diary entry, Virginia Woolf discusses the "cotton wool of existence"—the various mundane events of life. She contrasts this "cotton wool" with three specific and poignant memories from her childhood: a fight with her brother, seeing a particular flower in the garden, and hearing of the suicide of a past visitor: 45

> These are three instances of exceptional moments. I often tell them over, or rather they come to the surface unexpectedly. But now for the first time I have written them down, and I realize something that I have never realized before. Two of these moments ended in a state of despair. The other ended, on the contrary, in a state of satisfaction.
>
> The sense of horror (in hearing of the suicide) held me powerless. But in the case of the flower, I found a reason; and was thus able to deal with the sensation. I was not powerless.
>
> Though I still have the peculiarity that I receive these sudden shocks, they are now always welcome; after the first surprise, I always feel instantly that they are particularly valuable. And so I go on to suppose that the shock-receiving capacity is what makes me a writer. I hazard the explanation that a shock is at once in my case followed by the desire to explain it. I feel that I have had a blow; but it is not, as I thought as a child, simply a blow from an enemy hidden behind the cotton wool of daily life; it is or will become a revelation of some order; it is a token of some real thing behind appearances; and I make it real by putting it into words.[12]

This quotation vividly illustrates the intrapersonal intelligence—   46
knowledge of the internal aspects of a person: access to one's own feeling life, one's range of emotions, the capacity to effect discriminations among these emotions and eventually to label them and

[12] Woolf, V. (1976). *Moments of being* (pp. 69–70). Sussex: The University Press.

to draw upon them as a means of understanding and guiding one's own behavior. A person with good intrapersonal intelligence has a viable and effective model of himself or herself. Since this intelligence is the most private, it requires evidence from language, music, or some other more expressive form of intelligence if the observer is to detect it at work. In the above quotation, for example, linguistic intelligence is drawn upon to convey intrapersonal knowledge; it embodies the interaction of intelligences, a common phenomenon to which we will return later.

We see the familiar criteria at work in the intrapersonal intelligence. As with the interpersonal intelligence, the frontal lobes play a central role in personality change. Injury to the lower area of the frontal lobes is likely to produce irritability or euphoria; while injury to the higher regions is more likely to produce indifference, listlessness, slowness, and apathy—a kind of depressive personality. In such "frontal-lobe" individuals, the other cognitive functions often remain preserved. In contrast, among aphasics who have recovered sufficiently to describe their experiences, we find consistent testimony: while there may have been a diminution of general alertness and considerable depression about the condition, the individual in no way felt himself to be a different person. He recognized his own needs, wants, and desires and tried as best he could to achieve them. 47

The autistic child is a prototypical example of an individual with impaired intrapersonal intelligence; indeed, the child may not even be able to refer to himself. At the same time, such children often exhibit remarkable abilities in the musical, computational, spatial, or mechanical realms. 48

Evolutionary evidence for an intrapersonal faculty is more difficult to come by, but we might speculate that the capacity to transcend the satisfaction of instinctual drives is relevant. This becomes increasingly important in a species not perennially involved in the struggle for survival. 49

In sum, then, both interpersonal and intrapersonal faculties pass the tests of an intelligence. They both feature problem-solving endeavors with significance for the individual and the species. Interpersonal intelligence allows one to understand and work with others; intrapersonal intelligence allows one to understand and work with oneself. In the individual's sense of self, one encounters a melding of inter- and intrapersonal components. Indeed, the sense of self emerges as one of the most marvelous of human inventions— a symbol that represents all kinds of information about a person and that is at the same time an invention that all individuals construct for themselves. 50

SUMMARY: THE UNIQUE CONTRIBUTIONS
OF THE THEORY

As human beings, we all have a repertoire of skills for solving   51
different kinds of problems. Our investigation has begun, therefore, with a consideration of these problems, the contexts they are
found in, and the culturally significant products that are the outcome. We have not approached "intelligence" as a reified human
faculty that is brought to bear in literally any problem setting;
rather, we have begun with the problems that humans *solve* and
worked back to the "intelligences" that must be responsible.

Evidence from brain research, human development, evolution,   52
and cross-cultural comparisons was brought to bear in our search
for the relevant human intelligences: a candidate was included only
if reasonable evidence to support its membership was found across
these diverse fields. Again, this tack differs from the traditional one:
since no candidate faculty is *necessarily* an intelligence, we could
choose on a motivated basis. In the traditional approach to "intelligence," there is no opportunity for this type of empirical decision.

We have also determined that these multiple human faculties,   53
the intelligences, are to a significant extent *independent*. For example, research with brain-damaged adults repeatedly demonstrates
that particular faculties can be lost while others are spared. This
independence of intelligences implies that a particularly high level
of ability in one intelligence, say mathematics, does not require a
similarly high level in another intelligence, like language or music.
This independence of intelligences contrasts sharply with traditional measures of IQ that find high correlations among test scores.
We speculate that the usual correlations among subtests of IQ tests
come about because all of these tasks in fact measure the ability to
respond rapidly to items of a logical-mathematical or linguistic
sort; we believe that these correlations would be substantially
reduced if one were to survey in a contextually appropriate way
the full range of human problem-solving skills.

Until now, we have supported the fiction that adult roles depend   54
largely on the flowering of a single intelligence. In fact, however,
nearly every cultural role of any degree of sophistication requires
a combination of intelligences. Thus, even an apparently straightforward role, like playing the violin, transcends a reliance on simple musical intelligence. To become a successful violinist requires
bodily-kinesthetic dexterity and the interpersonal skills of relating
to an audience and, in a different way, choosing a manager; quite
possibly it involves an intrapersonal intelligence as well. Dance
requires skills in bodily-kinesthetic, musical, interpersonal, and

spatial intelligences in varying degrees. Politics requires an interpersonal skill, a linguistic facility, and perhaps some logical aptitude. Inasmuch as nearly every cultural role requires several intelligences, it becomes important to consider individuals as a collection of aptitudes rather than as having a singular problem-solving faculty that can be measured directly through pencil-and-paper tests. Even given a relatively small number of such intelligences, the diversity of human ability is created through the differences in these profiles. In fact, it may well be that the "total is greater than the sum of the parts." An individual may not be particularly gifted in any intelligence; and yet, because of a particular combination or blend of skills, he or she may be able to fill some niche uniquely well. Thus it is of paramount importance to assess the particular combination of skills that may earmark an individual for a certain vocational or avocational niche.

READING FOR MEANING

This section presents three activities that will help you reread Gardner and Walters's explanatory essay with a critical eye. Done in sequence, these activities lead you from a basic understanding of the selection to a more personal response to it and finally to an analysis that deepens your understanding and critical thinking about what you are reading.

Read to Comprehend

Reread the selection, and write a few sentences explaining the concept of multiple intelligences. Begin by listing the "criteria" that Gardner and Walters use to select the seven intelligences (paragraphs 11–15). Also make a list of any words you do not understand—for example, *fabricated* (paragraph 7), *veridical* (9), *correlation* (10), *surreptitiously* (31), *intrapersonal* (46). Look up their meanings in a dictionary to see which definition best fits the context.

To expand your understanding of this reading, you might use one or more of the following critical reading strategies that are explained and illustrated in Appendix 1: *outlining, summarizing, paraphrasing*, and *questioning to understand and remember*.

Read to Respond

Write several paragraphs exploring your initial thoughts and feelings about Gardner and Walters's explanatory essay. Focus on anything that stands out for you, perhaps because it resonates with your own experience or because you find a statement puzzling.

You might consider writing about

- your response to the notion of multiple intelligences and to the claim that logical-mathematical and linguistic intelligence—the kinds measured by IQ tests—are not the only valued intelligences in American culture today.

- your experience with one of the less traditional kinds of intelligence.

- your response to the anecdote that opens the selection, perhaps in relation to your observation of teachers' expectations surrounding test scores (paragraphs 1–6).

- the kind of intelligence nurtured most in your cultural tradition, in relation to what Gardner and Walters say about the need for cultural nurturing of intelligence.

- any other kinds of intelligence that you think should be included, perhaps in relation to your own experience.

To develop your response to Gardner and Walters's essay, you might use one or more of the following critical reading strategies that are explained and illustrated in Appendix 1: *contextualizing, recognizing emotional manipulation,* and *judging the writer's credibility.*

Read to Analyze Underlying Assumptions

Write several paragraphs exploring one or more of the assumptions, values, and beliefs underlying Gardner and Walters's explanation of multiple intelligences. As you write, explain how the assumptions are reflected in the text, as well as what you now think of them (and perhaps of your own assumptions) after rereading the selection with a critical eye.

You might consider writing about

- the values and beliefs underlying the "traditional view" of intelligence (paragraph 10).

- the belief that the theory of multiple intelligences "may be more humane and more veridical than alternative views of intelligence" (9).

- the idea that intelligence is not simply a "biological proclivity" (12) or an "inborn attribute or faculty of the individual" (10), but something that "must also be coupled with . . . cultural nurturing" (12).

- the importance of language or a "symbol system" to intelligence (15).

- the values and beliefs behind any one of the multiple intelligences that Gardner and Walters list, perhaps in relation to your own assumptions about that kind of intelligence.

To probe assumptions more deeply, you might use one or more of the following critical reading strategies that are explained and illustrated in Appendix 1: *reflecting on challenges to your beliefs and values, exploring the significance of figurative language,* and *looking for patterns of opposition.*

READING LIKE A WRITER
EXPLAINING THROUGH CLASSIFICATION AND ILLUSTRATION

Because concepts are abstractions, mental rather than physical realities, they can be hard to grasp. Writers often use classification and illustration to make an abstract concept easier for readers to understand. As you will see, Gardner and Walters use these two strategies in tandem to explain the concept of multiple intelligences.

Classification helps readers understand a broad general concept by breaking it down into smaller, more manageable categories of information. In explaining parthenogenesis, for example, Quammen uses a two-part classification—the ecological distinction between equilibrium and opportunistic species—to explain how parthenogenesis is evolutionarily advantageous (paragraph 11). Similarly, Gardner and Walters use a seven-part classification system to explain multiple intelligences.

Examples—in the form of anecdotes, descriptive details, and specific facts and figures—provide concrete images that help readers grasp or visualize concepts. Writers explaining concepts usually give several brief examples and sometimes include an extended example. In his essay explaining parthenogenesis, Quammen cites several examples of parthenogenetic species (paragraphs 1 and 3) and develops over several paragraphs the example of the aphid (4–8) so that readers can understand fully what is involved in the process of parthenogenesis. Gardner and Walters open their essay with an extended hypothetical example, or what they call a "fabricated example" (7). They present the example in paragraphs 1–3 and analyze it in the following paragraphs (4–7). This activity invites you to look at how Gardner and Walters combine classification and illustration.

Analyze

1. *Look closely* at paragraph 16, where Gardner and Walters forecast their discussion of the seven categories of intelligence. One common problem with classification is that categories can overlap. How do Gardner and Walters anticipate this problem in paragraph 16?

2. *Choose* one category or type of intelligence to analyze closely, and *note* how Gardner and Walters use an example to illustrate that category. How effective is this strategy of illustrating each kind of intelligence with its own example? What are the strengths and weaknesses of this strategy?

Write

Write several sentences explaining the benefits and shortcomings of using the strategies of classification and illustration to explain the concept of multiple intelligences. *Cite examples* from the selection for the category of intelligence you analyzed closely.

CONSIDERING IDEAS FOR YOUR OWN WRITING

Like Gardner and Walters, you might write about the concept of intelligence, perhaps even define a kind of intelligence they leave out. You could research intelligence testing for a historical explanation of IQ scores or testing. You might also consider explaining a related concept: problem-solving skills, aptitude, talent, empiricism, autism, or spatial reasoning.

BETH L. BAILEY

Dating

Beth L. Bailey (b. 1957) is professor in American studies at the University of New Mexico, where she holds the prestigious title of Regents Lecturer. She has also taught at Barnard College and at the University of Indonesia. A historian, she has written several scholarly books on nineteenth- and twentieth-century American culture, including Sex in the Heartland *(1999) and* A History of Our Time *(2003). She has also edited, with David Farber,* The Columbia Guide to America in the 1960s *(2001) and* America in the Seventies *(2004). "Dating" comes from Bailey's first book,* From Front Porch to Back Seat: Courtship in Twentieth-Century America *(1988).*

Bailey tells us that she first became interested in studying courtship attitudes and behavior when, as a college senior, she appeared on a television talk show to defend co-ed dorms, which were then relatively new and controversial. She was surprised when many people in the audience objected to co-ed dorms not on moral grounds, but out of fear that too much intimacy between young men and women would hasten "the dissolution of the dating system and the death of romance."

Before you read Bailey's historical explanation of dating, think about the attitudes and behavior of people your own age in regard to courtship and romance.

One day, the 1920s story goes, a young man asked a city girl if he might call on her (Black, 1924, p. 340). We know nothing else about the man or the girl—only that, when he arrived, she had her hat on. Not much of a story to us, but any American born before 1910 would have gotten the punch line. "She had her hat on": those five words were rich in meaning to early twentieth-century Americans. The hat signaled that she expected to leave the house. He came on a "call," expecting to be received in her family's parlor, to talk, to meet her mother, perhaps to have some refreshments or to listen to her play the piano. She expected a "date," to be taken "out" somewhere and entertained. He ended up spending four weeks' savings fulfilling her expectations.

In the early twentieth century this new style of courtship, dating, had begun to supplant the old. Born primarily of the limits and opportunities of urban life, dating had almost completely replaced the old system of calling by the mid-1920s—and, in so doing, had transformed American courtship. Dating moved courtship into the public world, relocating it from family parlors and community events to restaurants, theaters, and dance halls. At the same time, it removed couples from the implied supervision of the private sphere—from the watchful eyes of family and local community—to the anonymity of the public sphere. Courtship among strangers offered couples new freedom. But access to the public world of the city required money. One had to buy entertainment, or even access to a place to sit and talk. Money—men's money—became the basis of the dating system and, thus, of courtship. This new dating system, as it shifted courtship from the private to the public sphere and increasingly centered around money, fundamentally altered the balance of power between men and women in courtship.

The transition from calling to dating was as complete as it was fundamental. By the 1950s and 1960s, social scientists who studied American courtship found it necessary to remind the American public that dating was a "recent American innovation and not a traditional or universal custom" (Cavin, as cited in "Some," 1961, p. 125). Some of the many commentators who wrote about courtship believed dating was the best thing that had ever happened to relations between the sexes; others blamed the dating system for all the problems of American youth and American marriage. But virtually everyone portrayed the system dating replaced as infinitely simpler, sweeter, more innocent, and more graceful. Hardheaded social scientists waxed sentimental about the "horse-and-buggy days," when a young man's offer of a ride home from church was tantamount to a proposal and when young men came calling in the evenings and courtship took place safely within the warm bosom of the family. "The courtship which grew out of the sturdy social roots [of the nineteenth century]" one author wrote, "comes through to us for what it was—a gracious ritual, with clearly defined roles for man and woman, in which everyone knew the measured music and the steps" (Moss, 1963, p. 151).

Certainly a less idealized version of this model of courtship had existed in America, but it was not this model that dating was supplanting. Although only about 45 percent of Americans lived in urban areas by 1910, few of them were so untouched by the sweeping changes of the late nineteenth century that they could live that dream of rural simplicity. Conventions of courtship at that time were not set by simple yeoman farmers and their families but by the rising middle class, often in imitation of the ways of "society." ...

The call itself was a complicated event. A myriad of rules governed everything: the proper amount of time between invitation and visit (a fortnight or less); whether or not refreshments should be served (not if one belonged to a fashionable or semi-fashionable circle, but outside of "smart" groups in cities like New York and Boston, girls *might* serve iced drinks with little cakes or tiny cups of coffee or hot chocolate and sandwiches); chaperonage (the first call must be made on daughter and mother, but excessive chaperonage would indicate to the man that his attentions were unwelcome); appropriate topics of conversation (the man's interests, but never too personal); how leave should be taken (on no account should the woman "accompany [her caller] to the door nor stand talking while he struggles into his coat") ("Lady," 1904, p. 255).

Each of these "measured steps," as the mid-twentieth century   6
author nostalgically called them, was a test of suitability, breeding, and background. Advice columns and etiquette books empha-sized that these were the manners of any "well-bred" person—and conversely implied that deviations revealed a lack of breeding. However, around the turn of the century, many people who did lack this narrow "breeding" aspired to politeness. Advice columns in women's magazines regularly printed questions from "Country Girl" and "Ignoramus" on the fine points of calling etiquette. Young men must have felt the pressure of girls' expectations, for they wrote to the same advisers with questions about calling. In 1907, *Harper's Bazaar* ran a major article titled "Etiquette for Men," explaining the ins and outs of the calling system (Hall, 1907, pp. 1095–97). In the first decade of the twentieth century, this rigid system of calling was the convention not only of the "respectable" but also of those who aspired to respectability.

At the same time, however, the new system of dating was   7
emerging. By the mid-1910s, the word *date* had entered the vocab-ulary of the middle-class public. In 1914, the *Ladies' Home Journal,* a bastion of middle-class respectability, used the term (safely enclosed in quotation marks but with no explanation of its mean-ing) several times. The word was always spoken by that exotica, the college sorority girl—a character marginal in her exoticness but nevertheless a solid product of the middle class. "One beautiful evening of the spring term," one such article begins, "when I was a college girl of eighteen, the boy whom, because of his popularity in every phase of college life, I had been proud gradually to allow the monopoly of my 'dates,' took me unexpectedly into his arms. As he kissed me impetuously I was glad, from the bottom of my heart, for the training of that mother who had taught me to hold myself aloof from all personal familiarities of boys and men" ("How," 1914, p. 9).

Sugarcoated with a tribute to motherhood and virtue, the   8
dates—and the kiss—were unmistakably presented for a middle-class audience. By 1924, ten years later, when the story of the unfor-tunate young man who went to call on the city girl was current, dating had essentially replaced calling in middle-class culture.

The knowing smiles of the story's listeners had probably started with the word *call*—and not every hearer would have been sympathetic to the man's plight. By 1924, he really should have known better. . . .

Dating, which to the privileged and protected would seem a   9
system of increased freedom and possibility, stemmed originally from the lack of opportunities. Calling, or even just visiting, was not a practicable system for young people whose families lived crowded into one or two rooms. For even the more established or independent working-class girls, the parlor and the piano often simply didn't exist. Some "factory girls" struggled to find a way to receive callers. The *Ladies' Home Journal* approvingly reported the case of six girls, workers in a box factory, who had formed a club and pooled part of their wages to pay the "janitress of a tenement house" to let them use her front room two evenings a week. It had a piano. One of the girls explained their system: "We ask the boys to come when they like and spend the evening. We haven't any place at home to see them, and I hate seeing them on the street" (Preston, 1907, p. 31).

Many other working girls, however, couldn't have done this   10
even had they wanted to. They had no extra wages to pool, or they had no notions of middle-class respectability. Some, especially girls of ethnic families, were kept secluded—chaperoned according to the customs of the old country. But many others fled the squalor, drabness, and crowdedness of their homes to seek amusement and intimacy elsewhere. And a "good time" increasingly became identified with public places and commercial amusements, making young women whose wages would not even cover the necessities of life dependent on men's "treats" (Peiss, 1986, pp. 75, 51–52). Still, many poor and working-class couples did not so much escape from the home as they were pushed from it.

These couples courted on the streets, sometimes at cheap dance   11
halls or eventually at the movies. These were not respectable places, and women could enter them only so far as they, themselves, were not considered respectable. Respectable young women did, of course, enter the public world, but their excursions into the public were cushioned. Public courtship of middle-class and upper-class youth was at least *supposed* to be chaperoned; those with money and social position went to private dances with carefully controlled guest lists, to theater parties where they were a private group within the public. As rebels would soon complain, the supervision of society made the private parlor seem almost free by contrast. Women who were not respectable did have relative freedom of action—but the trade-off was not necessarily a happy one for them.

The negative factors were important, but dating rose equally from   12
the possibilities offered by urban life. Privileged youth, as Lewis
Erenberg shows in his study of New York nightlife, came to see the
possibility of privacy in the anonymous public, in the excitement
and freedom the city offered (1981, pp. 60–87, 139–42). They looked
to lower-class models of freedom—to those beyond the constraints
of respectability. As a society girl informed the readers of the *Ladies'*
Home Journal in 1914: "Nowadays it is considered 'smart' to go to the
low order of dance halls, and not only be a looker-on, but also to
dance among all sorts and conditions of men and women. . . .
Nowadays when we enter a restaurant and dance place it is hard to
know who is who" ("A Girl," 1914, p. 7). In 1907, the same magazine
had warned unmarried women never to go alone to a "public restaurant" with any man, even a relative. There was no impropriety in the
act, the adviser had conceded, but it still "lays [women] open to
misunderstanding and to being classed with women of undesirable
reputation by the strangers present" (Kingsland, May 1907, p. 48).
Rebellious and adventurous young people sought that confusion,
and the gradual loosening of proprieties they engendered helped to
change courtship. Young men and women went out into the world
together, enjoying a new kind of companionship and the intimacy of
a new kind of freedom from adult supervision.

The new freedom that led to dating came from other sources as   13
well. Many more serious (and certainly respectable) young women
were taking advantage of opportunities to enter the public world—
going to college, taking jobs, entering and creating new urban professions. Women who belonged to the public world by day began to
demand fuller access to the public world in general. . . .

Between 1890 and 1925, dating—in practice and in name—had   14
gradually, almost imperceptibly, become a universal custom in America. By the 1930s it had transcended its origins: Middle America associated dating with neither upper-class rebellion nor the urban lower
classes. The rise of dating was usually explained, quite simply, by the
invention of the automobile. Cars had given youth mobility and
privacy, and so had brought about the system. This explanation—
perhaps not consciously but definitely not coincidentally—revised
history. The automobile certainly contributed to the rise of dating as
a *national* practice, especially in rural and suburban areas, but it was
simply accelerating and extending a process already well under way.
Once its origins were located firmly in Middle America, however,
and not in the extremes of urban upper- and lower-class life, dating
had become an American institution.

Dating not only transformed the outward modes and conven-   15
tions of American courtship, it also changed the distribution of

control and power in courtship. One change was generational: the dating system lessened parental control and gave young men and women more freedom. The dating system also shifted power from women to men. Calling, either as a simple visit or as the elaborate late nineteenth-century ritual, gave women a large portion of control. First of all, courtship took place within the girl's home—in women's "sphere," as it was called in the nineteenth century—or at entertainments largely devised and presided over by women. Dating moved courtship out of the home and into man's sphere—the world outside the home. Female controls and conventions lost much of their power outside women's sphere. And while many of the conventions of female propriety were restrictive and repressive, they had allowed women (young women and their mothers) a great deal of immediate control over courtship. The transfer of spheres thoroughly undercut that control.

Second, in the calling system, the woman took the initiative.   16
Etiquette books and columns were adamant on that point: it was the "girl's privilege" to ask a young man to call. Furthermore, it was highly improper for the man to take the initiative. In 1909 a young man wrote to the *Ladies' Home Journal* adviser asking, "May I call upon a young woman whom I greatly admire, although she had not given me the permission? Would she be flattered at my eagerness, even to the setting aside of conventions, or would she think me impertinent?" Mrs. Kingsland replied: "I think that you would risk her just displeasure and frustrate your object of finding favor with her." Softening the prohibition, she then suggested an invitation might be secured through a mutual friend (Kingsland, 1909, p. 58). . . .

Contrast these strictures with advice on dating etiquette from   17
the 1940s and 1950s: An advice book for men and women warns that "girls who [try] to usurp the right of boys to choose their own dates" will "ruin a good dating career. . . . Fair or not, it is the way of life. From the Stone Age, when men chased and captured their women, comes the yen of a boy to do the pursuing. You will control your impatience, therefore, and respect the time-honored custom of boys to take the first step" (Richmond, 1958, p. 11). . . .

This absolute reversal of roles almost necessarily accompanied   18
courtship's move from woman's sphere to man's sphere. Although the convention-setters commended the custom of woman's initiative because it allowed greater exclusivity (it might be "difficult for a girl to refuse the permission to call, no matter how unwelcome or unsuitable an acquaintance of the man might be"), the custom was based on a broader principle of etiquette (Hart and Brown, 1944, p. 89). The host or hostess issued any invitation; the guest

did not invite himself or herself. An invitation to call was an invitation to visit in a woman's home.

An invitation to go out on a date, on the other hand, was an invitation into man's world—not simply because dating took place in the public sphere (commonly defined as belonging to men), though that was part of it, but because dating moved courtship into the world of the economy. Money—men's money—was at the center of the dating system. Thus, on two counts, men became the hosts and assumed the control that came with that position.

There was some confusion caused by this reversal of initiative, especially during the twenty years or so when going out and calling coexisted as systems. (The unfortunate young man in the apocryphal story, for example, had asked the city girl if he might call on her, so perhaps she was conventionally correct to assume he meant to play the host.) Confusions generally were sorted out around the issue of money. One young woman, "Henrietta L.," wrote to the *Ladies' Home Journal* to inquire whether a girl might "suggest to a friend going to any entertainment or place of amusement where there will be any expense to the young man." The reply: "Never, under any circumstances." The adviser explained that the invitation to go out must "always" come from the man, for he was the one "responsible for the expense" (Kingsland, Oct. 1907, p. 60). This same adviser insisted that the woman must "always" invite the man to call; clearly she realized that money was the central issue.

The centrality of money in dating had serious implications for courtship. Not only did money shift control and initiative to men by making them the "hosts," it led contemporaries to see dating as a system of exchange best understood through economic analogies or as an economic system pure and simple. Of course, people did recognize in marriage a similar economic dimension—the man undertakes to support his wife in exchange for her filling various roles important to him—but marriage was a permanent relationship. Dating was situational, with no long-term commitments implied, and when a man, in a highly visible ritual, spent money on a woman in public, it seemed much more clearly an economic act.

In fact, the term *date* was associated with the direct economic exchange of prostitution at an early time. A prostitute called "Maimie," in letters written to a middle-class benefactor/friend in the late nineteenth century, described how men made "dates" with her (Peiss, 1986, p. 54). And a former waitress turned prostitute described the process to the Illinois Senate Committee on Vice this way: "You wait on a man and he smiles at you. You see a chance to get a tip and you smile back. Next day he returns and you try harder than ever to please him. Then right away he wants to make a date, and offer you money and presents if you'll be a good fellow and go out with him" (Rosen, 1982, p. 151). These men, quite clearly, were buying sexual favors—but the occasion of the exchange was called a "date."

Courtship in America had always turned somewhat on money (or background). A poor clerk or stockyards worker would not have called upon the daughter of a well-off family, and men were expected to be economically secure before they married. But in the dating system money entered directly into the relationship between a man and a woman as the symbolic currency of exchange in even casual dating. 23

Dating, like prostitution, made access to women directly dependent on money. . . . In dating, though, the exchange was less direct and less clear than in prostitution. One author, in 1924, made sense of it this way. In dating, he reasoned, a man is responsible for all expenses. The woman is responsible for nothing—she contributes only her company. Of course, the man contributes his company, too, but since he must "add money to balance the bargain" his company must be worth less than hers. Thus, according to this economic understanding, she is selling her company to him. In his eyes, dating didn't even involve an exchange; it was a direct purchase. The moral "subtleties" of a woman's position in dating, the author concluded, were complicated even further by the fact that young men, "discovering that she must be bought, [like] to buy her when [they happen] to have the money" (Black, 1924, p. 342). 24

Yet another young man, the same year, publicly called a halt to such "promiscuous buying." Writing anonymously (for good reason) in *American Magazine*, the author declared a "one-man buyer's strike." This man estimated that, as a "buyer of feminine companionship" for the previous five years, he had "invested" about $20 a week—a grand total of over $5,000. Finally, he wrote, he had realized that "there is a point at which any commodity—even such a delightful commodity as feminine companionship—costs more than it is worth" ("Too-high," 1924, pp. 27, 145–50). The commodity he had bought with his $5,000 had been priced beyond its "real value" and he had had enough. This man said "enough" not out of principle, not because he rejected the implications of the economic model of courtship, but because he felt he wasn't receiving value for money. 25

In . . . these economic analyses, the men are complaining about the new dating system, lamenting the passing of the mythic good old days when "a man without a quarter in his pocket could call on 26 a girl and not be embarrassed," the days before a woman had to be "bought" ("Too-high," 1924, pp. 145–50). In recognizing so clearly the economic model on which dating operated, they also clearly saw that the model was a bad one—in purely economic terms. The exchange was not equitable; the commodity was overpriced. Men were operating at a loss.

Here, however, they didn't understand their model completely. 27 True, the equation (male companionship plus money equals female companionship) was imbalanced. But what men were buying in the dating system was not just female companionship, not just entertainment—but power. Money purchased obligation; money purchased inequality; money purchased control.

The conventions that grew up to govern dating codified women's 28 inequality and ratified men's power. Men asked women out; women were condemned as "aggressive" if they expressed interest in a man too directly. Men paid for everything, but often with the implica-tion that women "owed" sexual favors in return. The dating system required men always to assume control, and women to act as men's dependents.

Yet women were not without power in the system, and they 29 were willing to contest men with their "feminine" power. Much of the public discourse on courtship in twentieth-century America was concerned with this contestation. Thousands of sources chron-icled the struggles of, and between, men and women—struggles mediated by the "experts" and arbiters of convention—to create a balance of power, to gain or retain control of the dating system. These struggles, played out most clearly in the fields of sex, science, and etiquette, made ever more explicit the complicated relations between men and women in a changing society.

References

A Girl. (1914, July). Believe me. *Ladies' Home Journal*, 7.
Black, A. (1924, August). Is the young person coming back? *Harper's*, 340, 342.
Erenberg, L. (1981). *Steppin' out*. Westport, Conn.: Greenwood Press.
Hall, F. H. (1907, November). Etiquette for men. *Harper's Bazaar*, 1095–97.
Hart, S., & Brown, L. (1944). *How to get your man and hold him*. New York: New Power Publications.
How may a girl know? (1914, January). *Ladies' Home Journal*, 9.
Kingsland. (1907, May). *Ladies' Home Journal*, 48.
————. (1907, October). *Ladies' Home Journal*, 60.
————. (1909, May). *Ladies' Home Journal*, 58.
Lady from Philadelphia. (1904, February). *Ladies' Home Journal*, 255.
Moss, A. (1963, April). Whatever happened to courtship? *Mademoiselle*, 151.
Peiss, K. (1986). *Cheap amusements: Working women and leisure in turn-of-the-century New York*. Philadelphia: Temple University Press.

Preston, A. (1907, February). After business hours—what? *Ladies' Home Journal*, 31.

Richmond, C. (1958). *Handbook of dating*. Philadelphia: Westminster Press.

Rosen, R. (1982). *The lost sisterhood: Prostitution in America, 1900–1918*. Baltimore: Johns Hopkins University Press, 1982.

Some expert opinions on dating. (1961, August). *McCall's*, 125.

Too-high cost of courting. (1924, September). *American Magazine*, 27, 145–50.

READING FOR MEANING

This section presents three activities that will help you reread Bailey's explanatory essay with a critical eye. Done in sequence, these activities lead you from a basic understanding of the selection to a more personal response to it and finally to an analysis that deepens your understanding and critical thinking about what you are reading.

Read to Comprehend

Reread the selection, and write a few sentences about the differences between calling and dating as explained in Bailey's essay. Also make a list of any words you do not understand—for example, *supplant* (paragraph 2), *chaperonage* (5), *propriety* (15), *arbiters* (29). Look up their meanings in a dictionary to see which definition best fits the context.

To expand your understanding of this reading, you might use one or more of the following critical reading strategies that are explained and illustrated in Appendix 1: *outlining, summarizing, paraphrasing,* and *questioning to understand and remember.*

Read to Respond

Write several paragraphs exploring your initial thoughts and feelings about Bailey's explanatory essay. Focus on anything that stands out for you, perhaps because it resonates with your own experience or because you find a statement puzzling.

You might consider writing about

- the contrasts between the dating system in the early decades of the twentieth century (as described by Bailey) and the courtship system you know today, connecting your contrasts to specific features of the early system.

- the role of advice columns and etiquette books in the past compared to today.

- the identification of a "good time" with "public places and commercial amusements" (paragraphs 10 and 11), perhaps in relation to your own view of what constitutes a good time.

- the "centrality of money in dating" (21).

To develop your response to Bailey's essay, you might use one or more of the following critical reading strategies that are explained and illustrated in Appendix 1: *contextualizing, recognizing emotional manipulation,* and *judging the writer's credibility.*

Read to Analyze Underlying Assumptions

Write several paragraphs exploring one or more of the assumptions, values, and beliefs underlying Bailey's explanatory essay. As you write, explain how the assumptions are reflected in the text, as well as what you now think of them (and perhaps of your own assumptions) after rereading the selection with a critical eye.

You might consider writing about

- the cultural assumptions that underlie the difference between calling and dating, perhaps in relation to differences in social class, ethnicity, or anything else.

- Bailey's assumptions about the role of location (urban, rural, or suburban) in relation to the conventions of dating.

- the values and beliefs surrounding the changing attitudes toward respectability or propriety, perhaps in relation to the attitudes of your family and friends.

- the assumptions about men's and women's spheres.

- the assumptions underlying the connection between money and power in dating.

To probe assumptions more deeply, you might use one or more of the following critical reading strategies that are explained and illustrated in Appendix 1: *reflecting on challenges to your beliefs and values, exploring the significance of figurative language,* and *looking for patterns of opposition.*

READING LIKE A WRITER
EXPLAINING THROUGH COMPARISON/CONTRAST

One of the best ways of explaining something new is to relate it, through comparison or contrast, to something that is familiar or well known. A *comparison* points out similarities between items; a *contrast* points out differences. Sometimes writers use both comparison and contrast; sometimes they use only one or the other. Bailey uses comparison and contrast a little differently. She is not explaining something new to readers by relating it to something already known to them. Instead, she is explaining something already known—dating—by relating it to something that is unknown to most readers—calling, an earlier type of courtship. Since she is studying dating as a sociologist, this historical perspective enables her to consider the changing relationship between men and women and what it tells us about changing social and cultural expectations and practices.

Analyze

1. *Reread* paragraphs 15–19, and *put a line* under the sentences that assert the points of the contrast Bailey develops in these paragraphs. To get started, *underline* the first and last sentences in paragraph 15. Except for paragraph 17, you will find one or two sentences in the other paragraphs that assert the points.

2. *Examine closely* the other sentences to discover how Bailey develops or illustrates each of the points of the contrast between calling and dating.

Write

Write several sentences reporting what you have learned about how Bailey develops the contrast between calling and dating. *Give examples* from paragraphs 15–19 to support your explanation. *Write a few more sentences* evaluating how informative you find Bailey's contrast given your own knowledge of dating. What parts are least and most informative? What makes the most informative part so successful?

CONSIDERING IDEAS FOR YOUR OWN WRITING

Like Bailey, you might choose a concept that tells something about current or historical social values, behaviors, or attitudes. To look at changing attitudes toward immigration and assimilation, for example, you could write about the concept of the melting pot and the alternatives that have been suggested. Some related concepts you might consider are multiculturalism, race, ethnicity, masculinity or femininity, heterosexuality or homosexuality, and affirmative action.

DANIEL T. GILBERT AND TIMOTHY D. WILSON

Miswanting: Some Problems in the Forecasting of Future Affective States

Daniel T. Gilbert is a psychology professor at Harvard University and the director of Harvard's Social Cognition and Emotion Lab. Timothy D. Wilson is the Sherrell J. Aston Professor of Psychology at the University of Virginia. In addition to the work they have published together, the authors have written many articles and books with others and on their own, including Wilson's Social Psychology *(2001) and* Strangers to Ourselves *(2004) and Gilbert's* Handbook of Social Psychology *(1998),* Psychology *(2004), and* Stumbling on Happiness *(2004). As a graduate student, Gilbert published several science fiction stories in* Asimov's Science Fiction, Amazing Stories, *and other well-known publications. Both he and Wilson have won awards for teaching excellence as well as various other honors.*

Gilbert and Wilson frequently collaborate on their research in affective forecasting, the ability to predict how people will react emotionally to future events. The following explanation of the concept miswanting, *originally published in a collection of essays entitled* Thinking and Feeling: The Role of Affect in Social Cognition *(1999), is part of their affective forecasting research project. In an interview, Gilbert explained what intrigues him about this research:*

> *On the one hand, once basic needs are met, further wealth doesn't seem to predict further happiness. So the relationship between money and happiness is complicated, and definitely not linear. If it were linear, then billionaires would be a thousand times happier than millionaires, who would be a hundred times happier than professors. That clearly isn't the case. On the other hand, social relationships are a powerful predictor of happiness—much more so than money is. Happy people have extensive social networks and good relationships with the people in those networks. What's interesting to me is that while money is weakly and complexly correlated with happiness, and social relationships are strongly and simply correlated with happiness, most of us spend most of our time trying to be happy by pursuing wealth. Why?*

Before reading the essay, think about what would make you happy. Then, as you read, consider whether you would or would not stick to your prediction—and why.

It would not be better if things happened to men just as they want.
　　　　　　　　　　　　　　—Heraclitus, *Fragments* (500 B.C.)

INTRODUCTION

Like and *want* are among the first things children learn to say, and once they learn to say them, they never stop. Liking has to do with how a thing makes us feel, and wanting is, simply enough, a prediction of liking. When we say, "I like this doughnut," we are letting others know that the doughnut currently under consumption is making us feel a bit better than before. When we say, "I want a doughnut," we are making an abbreviated statement whose extended translation is something like, "Right now I'm not feeling quite as good as I might be, and I think fried dough will fix that." Statements about wanting tend to be statements about those things that we believe will influence our sense of well-being, satisfaction, happiness, and contentment. Hence, when we say we want something, we are more or less promising that we will like it when we get it.

But promises are easier to make than to keep, and sometimes we get what we say we want and feel entirely unhappy about it. We order a cheeseburger only to find that it looks and smells precisely as cheeseburgers always look and smell, and despite that fact, we have absolutely no interest in eating it. We are perplexed and embarrassed by such mistakes and can only offer cunning explanations such as, "I guess I didn't really want a cheeseburger after all." Dining companions often consider such accounts inadequate. "If you didn't *want* the damned thing, then why did you *get* it?" they may ask, at which point we are usually forced to admit the truth, which is that we just do not know. We only know that it looks exactly like what we said we wanted, we are not going to eat it, and the waiter is not amused.

Although we tend to think of unhappiness as something that happens to us when we do not get what we want, much unhappiness is actually of the cheeseburger variety and has less to do with not getting what we want, and more to do with not wanting what we like. When wanting and liking are uncoordinated in this way we may say that a person has *miswanted*. The word sounds odd at first, but if wanting is indeed a prediction of liking, then it, like any prediction, can be wrong. When the things we want to happen do not improve our happiness, and when the things we want not to happen do, it seems fair to say that we have wanted badly. Why should this happen to people as clever and handsome as us?

THE FUNDAMENTALS OF MISWANTING

In a perfect world, wanting would cause trying, trying would   4
cause getting, getting would cause liking, and this chapter would
be missing all the words. Ours is apparently not such a place. How
is it possible to get what we want and yet not like what we get? At
least three problems bedevil our attempts to want well.

Imagining the Wrong Event

The fundamental problem, of course, is that the events we imag-   5
ine when we are in the midst of a really good want are not precisely
the events we experience when we are at the tail end of a really disappointing get. For instance, most of us are skeptical when we hear
movie stars describe how relentless adoration can be a source of suffering, or when terminally ill patients insist that a dreaded disease
has given their lives deeper meaning. We feel certain that we would
be delighted in the first instance and devastated in the second
because most of us have no idea what stardom or terminal illness
actually entails. When we think of "adoring fans," we tend to envision a cheering throng of admirers calling us back for an encore performance rather than a slightly demented autograph hound peeping
through our bedroom window at midnight. When we think of "terminal illness," we tend to envision ourselves wasting away in a hospital bed, connected to machines by plugs and tubes, rather than
planting flowers in the hospice garden, surrounded by those we love.
Terminal illness is not an event, but a class of events, and each member of the class unfolds in a different way. How much we like an
event depends mightily on the details of its unfolding. When the
imagined cheeseburger (a half-pound of prime aged beef) is not the
experienced cheeseburger (three ounces of rubbery soy), it seems
inevitable that our wanting and our liking will be poorly matched.

Given how varied a class of events can be, we might expect peo-   6
ple prudently to refrain from directing their wants toward classes ("I
don't know if I want a cheeseburger") and direct them instead
toward particular, well-understood members of the class ("However, I know I don't want *that* cheeseburger"). Research suggests that
people are not always so prudent, and that when asked to make predictions about future events, they tend to imagine a particular event
while making little provision for the possibility that the particular
event they are imagining may not necessarily be the particular event
they will be experiencing (Dunning, Griffin, Milojkovic, & Ross,
1990; Griffin, Dunning, & Ross, 1990; Griffin & Ross, 1991; Lord,
Lepper, & Mackie, 1984; Robinson, Keltner, Ward, & Ross, 1995).
When our spouse asks us to attend "a party" on Friday night, we

instantly imagine a particular kind of party (e.g., a cocktail party in the penthouse of a downtown hotel with waiters in black ties carrying silver trays of hors d'oeuvres past a slightly bored harpist) and then estimate our reaction to that imagined event (e.g., yawn). We generally fail to consider how many different members constitute the class (e.g., birthday parties, orgies, wakes) and how different our reactions would be to each. So we tell our spouse that we would rather skip the party, our spouse naturally drags us along anyhow, and we have a truly marvelous time. Why? Because the party involves cheap beer and hula hoops rather than classical music and seaweed crackers. It is precisely our style, and we like what we previously did not want because the event we experienced (and liked) was not the event we imagined (and wanted to avoid).

Using the Wrong Theory

If imagining the wrong event were the sole cause of miswanting, then we would only miswant objects and experiences when the details of their unfolding were unknown to us. The fact is, people often want—and then fail to like—objects and experiences whose details they know quite well. Even when we know precisely the kind of party our spouse is hauling us to, or precisely the kind of cheeseburger this particular restaurant serves, we may still be surprised to find that we enjoy it a great deal more or less than we had anticipated. For example, Read and Loewenstein (1995) asked subjects to plan a menu by deciding which of several snacks they would eat when they returned to the laboratory on each of three consecutive Mondays (cf. Simonson 1990). Subjects tended to order a mixed plate that included instances of their favorite snack ("I'll have a Snickers bar on the first two Mondays"), as well as instances of their next favorite ("And tortilla chips on the third Monday"). Alas, when it actually came time to eat the snacks, subjects were not so pleased on the day when they arrived at the laboratory only to find themselves faced with a snack that was . . . well, not their favorite. Their disappointment was perfectly understandable. We *should* be disappointed when we do not get what we like most, and the only thing that seems hard to understand is why subjects wanted something that they knew perfectly well they did not like perfectly well?

Apparently, subjects in this study believed that variety is the spice of life—and in this case, they were wrong (cf. Kahneman & Snell, 1992). A Snickers with every meal is indeed a dull prospect for anyone, but a Snickers once a week is just about right. As such, Snickers lovers are made *less* happy—and not *more* happy—when their weekly Snickers is replaced by a less desirable treat. Because subjects in this study had erroneous theories about their own need for variety over time, they miswanted tortilla chips when they planned their menu. The moral of this ripping yarn about snack foods is that even when people have a perfect idea of what an event will entail (i.e., tortilla chips are deep-fried corn pancakes covered with salt—period), they may still have imperfect ideas about themselves and thus may make imperfect predictions about how they will react to the event. People who can imagine sun, surf, sand, and daiquiris in exquisite detail may still be surprised when their desert island vacation turns out to be a bust—not because they imagined *this* island and ended up on *that* one, but simply because they did not realize how much they require daily structure, intellectual stimulation, or regular infusions of Pop Tarts. Highbrows fall asleep at the ballet, pacifists find themselves strangely excited by a glimpse of world class wrestling, and tough guys in leather jackets are occasionally caught making clucking sounds by the duck pond. To the extent that we have incorrect theories about who we are, we may also have incorrect beliefs about what we will like.

Misinterpreting Feelings

If we could imagine events exactly as they were actually to unfold, and if we had complete and accurate knowledge of our relevant tastes and attitudes, could we necessarily avoid miswanting? Unfortunately not. When we imagine a future event, we normally have an affective reaction to its mental representation (imagining one's spouse happily entwined with the mail carrier usually illustrates this fact convincingly), and we naturally take this affective reaction to the mental representation of the event as a proxy for the affective reaction we might have to the event itself. If the mere thought of a mate's infidelity makes us feel slightly nauseous, then we have every reason to suppose that the real thing would end in an upchuck. Our affective reactions to imaginary events are, in a sense, experiential previews of our affective reactions to the events themselves, and they figure prominently in our predictions of future liking. Few of us need to consult a cookbook to know that we should avoid any event involving liver and maple syrup. That funny feeling right *here* is information enough (see Forgas, 1995; Schwarz & Clore, 1983; Schwarz, 1990). 9

Wantings, then, are based on three ingredients: the particular details that we imagine when we consider a future event, our beliefs about the ways in which people like us are likely to react to such events, and the "gut reactions" we experience when we imagine the event. Just as the first two of these ingredients can lead us to miswant, so too can the third. How so? The crux of the problem is that the feelings we experience when we imagine a future event are not necessarily or solely caused by that act of imagination. We may feel 10 enormously excited when we contemplate spending next Sunday at the circus, and thus we may drop buckets of money on ringside tickets without realizing that the good news we received about our aging uncle's miraculous recovery from psoriasis just moments before we purchased our ticket has contaminated our affective reaction to the thought of dancing elephants (Wilson & Brekke, 1994). Come Sunday, we may find ourselves bored to tears beneath the big top, wondering why we paid good money to see a herd of clowns in a little car. Our miswanting in this case would not have been a result of having imagined the wrong event ("Oh, I was thinking of a flea circus") nor of having had a false conception of ourselves ("Why did I think I liked men in floppy shoes?"). Rather, we would have miswanted because when we initially thought about the circus we felt excited, and we took that fact as information about the circus rather than as information about Uncle Frank's remission. Feelings do not say where they came from, and thus it is all too easy for us to attribute them to the wrong source.

Experimental demonstrations of this home truth abound. People may mistakenly believe that their lives are empty when, in fact, their gloomy mood is a consequence of rain (Schwarz & Clore, 1983); they may mistakenly believe that a person is attractive when, in fact, their pounding pulse is being caused by the swaying of a suspension bridge (Dutton & Aron, 1974); and so on. Because we cannot always tell if the feelings we are having as we imagine an event are being caused solely by that imagining, we may use these feelings as proxies for future liking, and hence, miswant. . . .

11

MISWANTING OVER TIME

What do spaghetti, cheeseburgers, marshmallow cookies, tortilla chips, and Snickers bars have in common? They are objects that can be wanted today and liked tomorrow, but once that liking occurs, they quickly become a trivial bit of personal history that only our thighs remember. Each of these objects can be experienced, but none of these experiences has enduring emotional consequences, and thus none provides an opportunity for us to think about how people might want or miswant in the long run. When we want a bite of pecan pie or a warm shower or a sexy kiss, it is not because we think these things will change us in some significant way, but because we think they will be perfectly lovely for as long as they last. On the other hand, when we want a promotion or a wedding or a college degree, it is not so much because we believe these things will improve our lives at the moment we attain them, but because we think they will provide emotional rewards that will persist long enough to repay the effort we spent in their pursuit. Significant

12

events are supposed to have significant emotional consequences, and the duration of these consequences matters a lot.

If it is difficult to know whether we will be happy 15 minutes after eating a bite of spaghetti, it is all the more difficult to know whether we will be happy 15 months after a divorce or 15 years after a marriage. Gilbert, Pinel, Wilson, Blumberg, and Wheatley (1998) have suggested that people tend to overestimate the duration of their emotional reactions to future events—especially negative events—and that this can lead them to miswant in the long term. For example, Gilbert et al. (1998) asked assistant professors to predict how happy they would be in general a few years after achieving or failing to achieve tenure at their current university, and they also measured the general happiness of those former assistant professors who had or had not achieved tenure at the same institution. Although assistant professors believed that the tenure decision would dramatically influence their general happiness for many years to come (and hence desperately wanted tenure), the former assistant professors who had not achieved tenure were no less happy than the former assistant professors who had. Similarly, Gilbert et al. (1998) asked voters in a gubernatorial election to predict how happy they would generally be a month after an election. Voters believed that they would be significantly happier a month after the election if their candidate won than if their candidate lost. As it turned out, a month after the election, the losers and winners were just as happy as they had been before the election (see Brickman, Coates, & Janoff-Bulman, 1978; Taylor, 1983; 1996; Wortman & Silver, 1989).

Do not misunderstand: Those assistant professors who were promoted and those voters whose candidate triumphed were surely happier about the event, and were surely happier for some time after the event, than were those who lost their jobs or who backed the incumbent governor, who lost hers. But after just a little while—a much littler while than the assistant professors and voters had themselves predicted—the emotional traces of these events had evaporated (see Suh, Diener, & Fujita, 1996). What might cause people to overestimate the enduring emotional impact of such events?

Focalism: The Invisible Future

When asked how we might feel a year after losing our left hand, we tend to imagine the immediate emotional impact of this calamity ("No more clapping, no more shoe tying—I'd be sad"). What we do *not* do is go on to calculate the impact of the dental appointments, foreign films, job promotions, freak snowstorms, and Snickers bars that will inevitably fill the year that follows our unhanding. Rather, we naturally focus on the event whose emotional impact we are trying to gauge and then make some provision for the passage of time ("I guess a year later I'd be a little less sad"). But how we will feel in general a year after losing a hand, and how we will feel *about* losing a hand a year after the loss, are not the same thing. Predicting the latter may be relatively simple, but predicting the former requires that we estimate the combined impact of the focal event and all the nonfocal events that follow it. Put another way, our general happiness some time after an event is influenced by just two things: (a) the event, and (b) everything else. If we estimate that happiness by considering only the event, then we are ignoring some of the most powerful determinants of our future well-being (see Loewenstein & Schkade, in press; Schkade & Kahneman, 1997).

Wilson, Wheatley, Meyers, Gilbert, and Axsom (1998) demonstrated how focalism (the failure to consider the consequences of nonfocal events when making predictions about the ultimate affective impact of focal events) can give rise to the durability bias and hence promote miswanting. College students were asked to predict their happiness the day after their football team won or lost an important game. Some students were also asked to complete a "future diary" in which they listed the events that they thought would occur in the 3 days after the game. Those students who completed the diary, and who were thus most likely to consider the impact of future nonfocal events when making their predictions, made less extreme predictions about their general happiness—predictions that turned out to be more accurate when their overall happiness was measured the day after the game. 16

It seems that merely considering the emotional impact of an event can lead us to overestimate that impact, simply because we do not also consider other impactful events as well. Focalism is an especially vexing problem because avoiding it seems to require that we do the impossible, namely, consider the impact of *every* event before estimating the impact of *any* event. If we think of happiness as a general state that is determined by innumerable events, it does indeed seem likely that no single event will have the power to influence our general happiness for very long. Indeed, those events that seem to make a big difference (e.g., moving to a new country) tend to be those that give rise to many other events, which suggests that the ramifications of an event—that is, the sheer number of experiences it alters—may be the best predictor of its ultimate emotional impact. Although few parents would believe it, the death of a spouse may have more impact than the death of a child, simply because the former produces more changes in one's life than does the latter (see Lehman et al., 1993). In any 17 case, it seems quite clear that focusing on an event can cause us to overestimate the duration of its influence on our happiness, and, hence, to miswant.

Immune Neglect: The Invisible Shield

Many shrewd observers of the human condition have remarked on people's extraordinary ability to change the way they feel simply by changing the way they think. When circumstances threaten our psychological well-being, we execute an assortment of cognitive strategies, tactics, and maneuvers that are designed to prevent, limit, or repair the damage (e.g., Festinger, 1957; Freud, 1937; Steele, 1988; Taylor & Brown, 1988; Vaillant, 1993; Westen, 1994). These maneuvers usually have two properties. First, they work like a charm, enabling all of us to be well above average in all the ways that count. Second and more important, we tend not to know we are executing them, and what looks like rationalization to the giggling onlooker feels very much like rational reasoning to us. Taken together, the mechanisms that protect the sources of our psychological well-being (e.g., our sense of competence, integrity, and worth) in the face of assault constitute a psychological immune system that seems to be both powerful and invisible to the person it serves.

If our happiness is, in fact, defended by an invisible shield, then it is easy to see why we overestimate our vulnerability to the slings and arrows of outrageous fortune. Recall that voters in the Gilbert et al. (1988) study overestimated the duration of their emotional reactions to their candidate's electoral triumph or defeat. Interestingly, voters in that study were also asked to predict how their opinions of the candidates would change once one was elected, and their answers may tell us something about why they overestimated the durability of their emotions. Although voters flatly denied that the outcome of the election would change their opinions of the candidates by even a hair, a month after the election, those voters whose candidate had lost had experienced an unforeseen transformation: Although the new governor had yet to take office, had yet to perform an official act, and had yet to make a substantive speech, those who had voted against him had a significantly higher opinion of him than they had had a month earlier. It seems that those voters overestimated the duration of their disappointment because they did not realize that once they were stuck with a governor whom they had not wanted, their psychological immune systems would help them locate 16 new reasons to like him anyway.

Gilbert et al. (1998) provided direct experimental evidence of immune neglect: the tendency for people to fail to consider how readily their psychological immune systems will vitiate their despair.

18

19

20

Students were given the opportunity to apply for an exciting and lucrative position as an ice-cream taster in a model business. The application process included answering several questions before a video camera while judges watched from another room. The situation was arranged such that if students were rejected, their psychological immune systems would have much more work to do in one condition than the other. Specifically, students in the "difficult rationalization" condition were shown a number of highly relevant questions and were told that while answering these questions they would be observed by a panel of judges, who would then vote on the student's appropriateness for the job. Unless the judges unanimously disapproved of the student, he or she would be offered the job. In the "easy rationalization" condition, students were shown a number of largely irrelevant questions and were told that while answering these questions they would be observed by a single judge who would solely determine whether or not they were offered the job. Students in each condition predicted how they would feel if they were rejected, and how they would feel 10 minutes later. All participants then answered the relevant or irrelevant questions before the video camera and were promptly rejected. Their happiness was measured immediately following the rejection and then again 10 minutes later.

As the top part of Figure [1] shows, the students believed they would be much less happy immediately following rejection than they actually turned out to be. But as the bottom part of Figure [1] shows, the more interesting effect occurred 10 minutes later. Not only were all the students happier than they expected to be 10 minutes after being rejected, but they were happier when they had been rejected by a solo judge who had heard them answer irrelevant questions than when they had been rejected by a panel of judges who had heard them answer irrelevant questions. This difference reveals the work of the psychological immune system, which should have found it easier to heal the wounds of rejection in the easy rationalization condition ("One guy doesn't think I'm competent. So what? Maybe I look like his ex-roommate, or maybe he's biased against Southerners, or maybe he just didn't have enough information to go on") than in the difficult rationalization condition ("An entire group of judges agreed on the basis of adequate information that I'm not smart enough to taste ice cream? Yikes!"). The important point is that the students did not *anticipate* this difference, which suggests that when they looked into their emotional futures, they saw only the pain of rejection. What they did not consider was the ease or difficulty with which their psychological immune systems would dispatch their malaise.

21

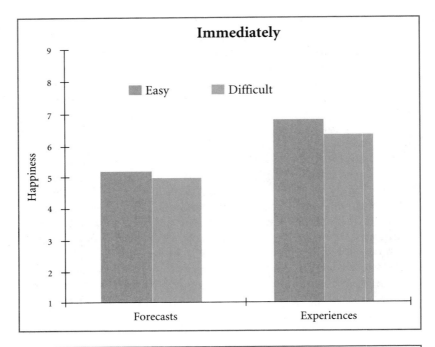

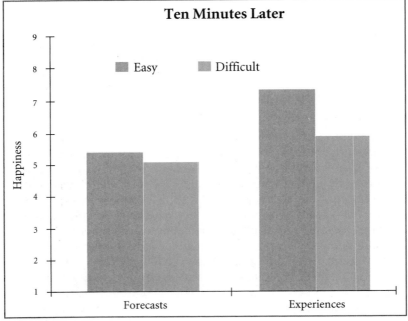

FIGURE [1]. Predicted and actual happiness after rejection.

Immune neglect can have important interpersonal conse-   22
quences too. For example, few of us would expect to come undone
if an irritated motorist shouted a few choice words about our
parentage as we crossed against the light, but we might well expect
to be shocked and dismayed if a good friend did the same. We
expect an insulting remark from a stranger to be less painful than
an insulting remark from a friend, and thus we might naturally
expect the former to have less enduring emotional consequences
than the latter. Gilbert and Lieberman (1998) asked pairs of college students to evaluate each other's personalities on the basis of
brief autobiographies in which they had explicitly been asked to
describe some embarrassing incidents. Some students were told
that they would work together as a team later in the experiment
("partners") and others were told that they would never meet
("strangers"). The students were asked to predict how they would
feel a few minutes after finding out that the other student had read
their autobiography and given them a very negative evaluation,
and indeed, they predicted that they would feel worse if the negative evaluation came from their partner than from a stranger. In
fact, the students were considerably *happier* after receiving a negative evaluation from their partner than from a stranger, and they
even forgave their partners more readily than they forgave
strangers. Why should this have happened?

Once again, the invisibility of the psychological immune system   23
seems to explain these paradoxical results. Most of us find it rather
uncomfortable to interact with people we do not like, and so we
are highly motivated to like those with whom we must interact
(Darley & Berscheid, 1967). Our psychological immune systems
work much harder to help us find ways to forgive our partner's
transgressions ("My partner probably didn't realize that the
embarrassing incident I wrote about in my autobiography was a
unique occurrence, and now that I think of it, I'd probably
have made the same negative evaluation myself if I were in the
same position") than to forgive the transgressions of strangers.
The insulted students' psychological immune systems did what
they were designed to do by enabling them to feel happy about
working with someone who had evaluated them negatively. What
is interesting, of course, is that the students were unable to predict
this outcome just 10 minutes before it happened. Like most of
us, they blithely predicted that a big pain would last longer than a
little one, unaware that big pains often evoke remedies that little
pains do not. Broken legs hurt so much that they cry out to be
fixed, whereas trick knees are often allowed to go on hurting for a
lifetime.

Immune neglect can cause us to miswant by causing us to fear   24
and avoid outcomes that will not, in the long run, hinder our happiness. But one ironic consequence of the failure to anticipate the
operation of the psychological immune system is that we may
inadvertently do things that impair its operation, thereby undermining our own hidden talent for happiness. For example, if given
the opportunity to shop at a store that allows customers to return
merchandise for any reason and another store at which all sales
are final, most of us would patronize the first rather than the
second—and we might even be willing to pay a bit more just so we
could have the luxury of changing our minds later on. We firmly
believe that bridges ought to be there for crossing and recrossing,
and our aversion to burning them is probably wise in many
respects. But if keeping one's options open is wise in many respects,
it is not wise in all respects, because open options have the unfortunate consequence of paralyzing the psychological immune system.
As dissonance theorists have long noted, it is the firm commitment
to a single course of action that most effectively triggers attempts to
justify it.

Gilbert and Jenkins (1998) gave college students a short course   25
in black-and-white photography. The students took photographs
of their favorite people and places on campus and were then
taught how to develop their photographs. After students had
printed their two favorite photographs, they were asked to donate
one of them to the experimenter's "photography project." Some
students were told that the donated photograph would be mailed
to England that evening, whereas others were told that the photograph would not be mailed for 5 days. Students in this latter condition were told that if they changed their minds about which
photograph to keep after they made the donation, they could swap
the chosen for the donated photograph anytime before it was
mailed. When the students' happiness with their photographs was
measured 2 days later, those whose decisions were reversible did
not like the chosen photograph as much as did those students
whose decisions were irreversible. This makes sense inasmuch as
these students were probably still in the process of deciding which
photograph they would keep, and thus they did not yet have a final
outcome with which their psychological immune systems could
help them feel happy. But interestingly, 9 days later, the irreversible
deciders were *still* happier with their photographs than were the
reversible deciders—despite the fact that the reversible deciders'
"swapping opportunity" had expired days ago and their unchosen
photograph was irrevocably winging its way across the Atlantic. It
seems that merely having had a brief opportunity to change their

minds prevented reversible deciders from *ever* exercising their hidden talent for happiness.

All of this work on immune neglect leads to one conclusion: Our tendency to neglect the operation of the immune system when anticipating the future can have unhappy consequences. We often want one thing so much more than another that we willingly incur enormous costs in our attempts to avoid the unwanted event. We may spend little time with our children and neglect our hobbies while putting in long hours at the office because we are convinced that keeping our current job will be better than being forced to find a new one. What we fail to realize is that while the thing we wanted to experience is in some ways better than the thing we wanted to avoid, it is probably worse in others, and should we fail to achieve what we wanted, our psychological immune systems will quickly help us locate the ways in which the thing we got was better than the thing we were aiming for. As the man who narrowly missed the opportunity to franchise the first McDonalds restaurant (and hence narrowly missed the opportunity to become a billionaire) noted many decades later, "I believe it turned out for the best" (Van Gelder, 1997). If we do indeed have a greater talent for happiness than we recognize, then our ignorance of this talent may cause us to pay a steeper price for future experiences than we should.

26

CONCLUSIONS

The naïve psychology of happiness is simple: We want, we try, we get, we like. And then, with the help of television commercials, we want some more. Wants are underwritten by our beliefs about the relation between getting and liking, and in this sense they are prescriptions for action. They tell us what to do with our time by telling us what to aim for and what to avoid, and we allow ourselves to be steered by them because we trust that they are, by and large, correct. Most of us feel certain that if we could experience all the events and only the events we want to experience, happiness would inevitably follow.

27

The research discussed in this chapter suggests that there are at least two flaws in the naïve analysis of happiness. First, our wants are, like any other prediction, susceptible to error. We may misconstrue events, misunderstand ourselves, misinterpret our feelings— and any of these mistakes can be a cause of miswanting. In short, things do not always feel the way we expect them to feel. Second, even if we could predict how much we would like an event when it happened, we might still be unable to predict how that event would affect us in the long run. One reason is that our general happiness

28

is influenced by a multitude of events. It is impossible to consider all of these influences every time we consider one of them, of course, but unless we do just that, we have little hope of correctly predicting the future states that are their conjoint products. A second reason why we have trouble predicting the enduring emotional consequences of an event is that liking does not *follow* from getting so much as it *accommodates* it. Although our initial emotional reaction to an event is usually based on those properties of the event that caused us to aim for it or avoid it in the first place, once a particular outcome is achieved, we have an uncanny ability to reconstrue it in terms of its most sanguine properties. Because we do not recognize how easily we can reconstrue events in this way, we anticipate more enduring reactions than we often have.

"In the world there are only two tragedies," wrote Oscar Wilde (1893). "One is not getting what one wants, and the other is getting it." We all chuckle and nod knowingly when we hear this clever quip, but not one of us believes it for a moment. Rather, our chuckling and nodding are licensed by a serene certainty that the things we run after will, in fact, bring us far greater happiness than the things we run from. The research discussed in this chapter does not suggest that all ends are emotionally equivalent or that all desires are misdirected. Rather, it merely suggests that if we could know the future, we still might not know how much we would like it when we got there. The psychological mechanisms that keep us from this knowledge are many, and a better understanding of them seems well worth wanting.

References

Brickman, P., Coates, D., & Janoff-Bulman, R. J. (1978). Lottery winners and accident victims: Is happiness relative? *Journal of Personality and Social Psychology, 36,* 917–927.

Darley, J. M., & Berscheid, E. (1967). Increased liking caused by the anticipation of interpersonal contact. *Human Relations, 10,* 29–40.

Dunning, D., Griffin, D. W., Milojkovic, J., & Ross, L. (1990). The overconfidence effect in social prediction. *Journal of Personality and Social Psychology, 58,* 568–581.

Dutton, D. G., & Aron, A. P. (1974). Some evidence for heightened sexual attraction under conditions of high anxiety. *Journal of Personality and Social Psychology, 30,* 510–517.

Festinger, L. (1957). *A theory of cognitive dissonance.* Stanford, CA: Stanford University Press.

Forgas, J. P. (1995). Mood and judgment: The affect infusion model (AIM). *Psychological Bulletin, 117,* 39–66.

Freud, A. (1937). *The ego and the mechanisms of defense.* London: Hogarth Press.

Gilbert, D. T., Gill, M., & Wilson, T. D. (1998). *How do we know what we will like? The informational basis of affective forecasting.* Unpublished manuscript, Harvard University.

Gilbert, D. T., & Jenkins, J. (1998). *Effects of decision reversibility on satisfaction.* Unpublished data, Harvard University.

Gilbert, D. T., & Lieberman, M. (1998). *Factors influencing forgiveness of an interpersonal transgression.* Unpublished data, Harvard University.

Gilbert, D. T., Pinel, E., Wilson, T. D., Blumberg, S., & Wheatley, T. (1998). Immune neglect: A source of durability bias in affective forecasting. *Journal of Personality and Social Psychology, 75,* 617–638.

Griffin, D. W., Dunning, D., & Ross, L. (1990). The role of construal processes in over-confident predictions about the self and others. *Journal of Personality and Social Psychology, 59,* 1128–1139.

Griffin, D. W., & Ross, L. (1991). Subjective construal, social inference, and human misunderstanding. In M. Zanna (Ed.), *Advances in experimental social psychology* (Vol. 24, pp. 319–356). New York: Academic Press.

Kahneman, D., & Snell, J. (1992). Predicting a change in taste: Do people know what they will like? *Journal of Behavioral Decision Making, 5,* 187–200.

Lehman, D. R., Davis, C. G., Delongis, A., Wortman, C. B., Bluck, S., Mandel, D. R., & Ellard, J. H. (1993). Positive and negative life changes following bereavement and their relations to adjustment. *Journal of Social and Clinical Psychology, 12,* 90–112.

Loewenstein, G., & Schkade, D. (in press). Wouldn't it be nice?: Predicting future feelings. In E. Diener, N. Schwartz, & D. Kahneman (Eds.), *Hedonic psychology: Scientific approaches to enjoyment, suffering, and well-being.* New York: Russell Sage Foundation Press.

Lord, C. G., Lepper, M. R., & Mackie, D. (1984). Attitude prototypes as determinants of attitude-behavior consistency. *Journal of Personality and Social Psychology, 46,* 1254–1266.

Read, D., & Loewenstein, G. (1995). Diversification bias: Explaining the discrepancy in variety seeking between combined and separated choices. *Journal of Experimental Psychology: Applied, 1,* 34–49.

Robinson, R. J., Keltner, D., Ward, A., & Ross, L. (1995). Actual versus assumed differences in construal: "Naive realism" in intergroup perception and conflict. *Journal of Personality and Social Psychology, 68,* 404–417.

Schwarz, N. (1990). Feelings as information: Informational and motivational functions of affective states. In E. T. H. R. Sorrentino (Ed.), *Handbook of motivation and cognition: Foundations of social behavior* (Vol. 2, pp. 527–561). New York: Guilford Press.

Schwarz, N., & Clore, G. L. (1983). Mood, misattribution, and judgments of well-being: Informative and directive functions of affective states. *Journal of Personality and Social Psychology, 45,* 513–523.

Schkade, D. A., & Kahneman, D. (1997). *Would you be happy if you lived in California? A focusing illusion in judgments of well-being.* Unpublished manuscript, University of Texas, Austin.

Simonson, I. (1990). The effect of purchase quantity and timing on variety seeking behavior. *Journal of Marketing Research, 32,* 150–162.

Steele, C. M. (1988). The psychology of self-affirmation: Sustaining the integrity of self. In L. Berkowitz (Ed.), *Advances in experimental social psychology* (Vol. 21, pp. 261–302). New York: Academic Press.

Suh, E., Diener, E., & Fujita, F. (1996). Events and subjective well-being: Only recent events matter. *Journal of Personality and Social Psychology, 70,* 1091–1102.

Taylor, S. E. (1983). Adjustment to threatening events: A theory of cognitive adaptation. *American Psychologist, 38*, 1161–1173.

Taylor, S. E., & Brown, J. D. (1988). Illusion and well-being: A social-psychological perspective on mental health. *Psychological Bulletin, 103*, 193–210.

Taylor, S. E., & Armor, D. A. (1996). Positive illusions and coping with adversity. *Journal of Personality, 64*, 873–898.

Vaillant, G. (1993). *The wisdom of the ego*. Cambridge: Harvard University Press.

Van Gelder, L. (1996, January 7). Remembering the road not taken. *The New York Times*, p. F 7.

Westen, D. (1994). Toward an integrative model of affect regulation: Applications to social psychological research. *Journal of Personality, 62*, 641–667.

Wilde, O. (1893). *Lady Windermere's fan: A play about a good woman*. London: Mathews & Lane.

Wilson, T. D., & Brekke, N. (1994). Mental contamination and mental correction: Unwanted influences on judgments and evaluations. *Psychological Bulletin, 116*, 117–142.

Wilson, T. D., Lisle, D., Schooler, J., Hodges, S. D., Klaaren, K. J., & LaFleur, S. J. (1993). Introspecting about reasons can reduce post-choice satisfaction. *Personality and Social Psychology Bulletin, 19*, 331–339.

Wilson, T. D., Wheatley, T., Meyers, J., Gilbert, D. T., & Axsom, D. (1998). *Focalism: A source of durability bias in affective forecasting*. Unpublished manuscript, University of Virginia.

Wortman, C. B., & Silver, R. C. (1989). The myths of coping with loss. *Journal of Consulting and Clinical Psychology, 57*, 349–357.

READING FOR MEANING

This section presents three activities that will help you reread Gilbert and Wilson's explanatory essay with a critical eye. Done in sequence, these activities lead you from a basic understanding of the selection to a more personal response to it and finally to an analysis that deepens your understanding and critical thinking about what you are reading.

Read to Comprehend

Reread the selection, and write a few sentences explaining the concept of miswanting and its significance. Also make a list of any words you do not understand— for example, *affective* (in the title), *experiential* (paragraph 9), *paradoxical* (23), *reconstrue* (28). Look up their meanings in a dictionary to see which definition best fits the context.

To expand your understanding of this reading, you might use one or more of the following critical reading strategies that are explained and illustrated in Appendix 1: *outlining, summarizing, paraphrasing,* and *questioning to understand and remember.*

Read to Respond

Write several paragraphs exploring your initial thoughts and feelings about Gilbert and Wilson's explanatory essay. Focus on anything that stands out for you, perhaps because it resonates with your own experience or because you find a statement puzzling.

You might consider writing about

- your reaction to the authors' assertion that "[a]lthough we tend to think of unhappiness as something that happens to us when we do not get what we want, much unhappiness is actually of the cheeseburger variety and has less to do with not getting what we want, and more to do with not wanting what we like" (paragraph 3).

- the idea that "[f]eelings do not say where they came from, and thus it is all too easy for us to attribute them to the wrong source" (10).

- the claim that "what looks like rationalization to the giggling onlooker feels very much like rational reasoning to us" (18).

- your reaction to the research that "open options," like being able to return purchases to a store for any reason or having time to change your mind as in the photography experiment, can make you unhappy (24–25).

- your response to any of the examples in the essay, perhaps in relation to examples from your own experience.

To develop your response to Gilbert and Wilson's essay, you might use one or more of the following critical reading strategies that are explained and illustrated in Appendix 1: *contextualizing, recognizing emotional manipulation,* and *judging the writer's credibility.*

Read to Analyze Underlying Assumptions

Write several paragraphs exploring one or more of the assumptions, values, and beliefs underlying Gilbert and Wilson's explanation of the concept *miswanting*. As you write, explain how the assumptions are reflected in the text, as well as what you now think of them (and perhaps of your own assumptions) after rereading the selection with a critical eye.

You might consider writing about

- the beliefs and values underlying the surprising complaints made by celebrities and the surprising sense of meaning expressed by terminally ill patients (paragraph 5).

- the assumptions underlying the difference between "directing" one's "wants toward classes" or "toward particular, well-understood members of the class" (6), or the cultural assumptions and values underlying Gilbert and Wilson's example of this phenomenon.

- the assumptions underlying Gilbert's research on immune neglect (18–26).

- the notions that "we have an uncanny ability to reconstrue" or rationalize events, but that "we do not recognize how easily we can reconstrue events" (28).

To probe assumptions more deeply, you might use one or more of the following critical reading strategies that are explained and illustrated in Appendix 1: *reflecting on challenges to your beliefs and values, exploring the significance of figurative language,* and *looking for patterns of opposition.*

READING LIKE A WRITER
DEVISING A READABLE PLAN

Think of a readable plan as fundamentally a logical, interrelated sequence of topics. One topic or main idea follows the preceding topic in a way that makes sense to readers. In addition, as you may have noticed in analyzing David Quammen's explanatory essay about parthenogenesis, readers appreciate when the sequence of topics is visibly cued by forecasting statements, topic sentences, transitions, and brief summaries. We see all of these cueing devices in Gilbert and Wilson's essay, which also makes use of rhetorical questions and of headings and subheadings to clearly label the topic of the paragraphs that follow. These important cueing strategies can do nothing to rescue an illogical sequence of topics, however. That is, they can only point out logical connections; they cannot *create* such connections. You can learn more about how writers devise readable plans by outlining their essays.

Analyze

1. *Skim* the essay, and *notice* how the headings and subheadings present the topics in a logical sequence. *Make an outline* of this system of heads and subheads.

2. *Examine* Gilbert and Wilson's use of rhetorical questions in paragraphs 3, 4, 7, 12, 14, and 22. *Make notes* about where these questions are placed in the paragraph and where their answers appear.

3. *Point to* any places where the writers forecast the topics that come next and summarize what came before.

Write

Write several sentences describing the main strategies Gilbert and Wilson use to construct a readable plan for their essay.

CONSIDERING IDEAS FOR YOUR OWN WRITING

Gilbert and Wilson's explanation of miswanting includes other concepts you might consider explaining, such as happiness, need or desire, gut reaction, psychological well-being, and rationalization. Or you might consider concepts in other subjects you are studying: acculturation, ethnocentrism, and kinship in anthropology; social construction of identity, socialization, and stratification in sociology; torque, aerodynamics, and ergonomics in automotive design; and nanotechnology, stem-cell research, and genetic engineering in biology.

LINH KIEU NGO

Cannibalism: It Still Exists

> *Linh Kieu Ngo wrote this essay when he was a first-year college student. In it, he explains a concept of importance in anthropology and of wide general interest—cannibalism, the eating of human flesh by other humans. Most Americans may know about survival cannibalism, but few may know about the importance historically of dietary and ritual cannibalism. Ngo explains all of these types in his essay.*
>
> *Before you read, think about any examples of survival cannibalism you may have read about.*

Fifty-five Vietnamese refugees fled to Malaysia on a small fishing boat to escape communist rule in their country following the Vietnam War. During their escape attempt, the captain was shot by the coast guard. The boat and its passengers managed to outrun the coast guard to the open sea, but they had lost the only person who knew the way to Malaysia, the captain.

The men onboard tried to navigate the boat, but after a week fuel ran out and they drifted farther out to sea. Their supply of food and water was gone; people were starving, and some of the elderly were near death. The men managed to produce a small amount of drinking water by boiling salt water, using dispensable wood from the boat to create a small fire near the stern. They also tried to fish, but had little success.

A month went by, and the old and weak died. At first, the crew threw the dead overboard, but later, out of desperation, the crew turned to human flesh as a source of food. Some people vomited as they attempted to eat it, while others refused to resort to cannibalism and see the bodies of their loved ones sacrificed for food. Those who did not eat died of starvation, and their bodies in turn became food for others. Human flesh was cut out, washed in salt water, and hung to dry for preservation. The liquids inside the cranium were eaten to quench thirst. The livers, kidneys, heart, stomach, and intestines were boiled and eaten.

Five months passed before a whaling vessel discovered the drifting boat, looking like a graveyard of bones. There was only one survivor.

Cannibalism, the act of human beings eating human flesh (Sagan 2), has a long history and continues to hold interest and create controversy. Many books and research reports offer examples of cannibalism, but a few scholars have questioned whether cannibalism was ever practiced anywhere, except in cases of ensuring survival in times of famine or isolation (Askenasy 43–54).

Recently, some scholars have tried to understand why people in the West have been so eager to attribute cannibalism to non-westerners (Barker, Hulme, and Iversen). Cannibalism has long been a part of American popular culture. For example, Mark Twain's "Cannibalism in the Cars" tells a humorous story about cannibalism by well-to-do travelers on a train stranded in a snow-storm, and cannibalism is still a popular subject for jokes ("Cannibal Jokes").

If we assume there is some reality to the reports about canni-   6
balism, how can we best understand this concept? Cannibalism can be broken down into two main categories: exocannibalism, the eating of outsiders or foreigners, and endocannibalism, the eating of members of one's own social group (Shipman 70). Within these categories are several functional types of cannibalism, three of the most common being survival cannibalism, dietary cannibalism, and religious and ritual cannibalism.

Survival cannibalism occurs when people trapped without food   7
have to decide "whether to starve or eat fellow humans" (Shipman 70). In the case of the Vietnamese refugees, the crew and passengers on the boat ate human flesh to stay alive. They did not kill people to get human flesh for nourishment, but instead waited until the people had died. Even after human carcasses were sacrificed as food, the boat people ate only enough to survive. Another case of survival cannibalism occurred in 1945, when General Douglas MacArthur's forces cut supply lines to Japanese troops stationed in the Pacific Islands. In one incident, Japanese troops were reported to have sacrificed the Arapesh people of northeastern New Guinea for food in order to avoid death by starvation (Tuzin 63). The most famous example of survival cannibalism in American history comes from the diaries, letters, and interviews of survivors of the California-bound Donner Party, who in the winter of 1846 were snowbound in the Sierra Nevada Mountains for five months. Thirty-five of eighty-seven adults and children died, and some of them were eaten (Hart 116–17; Johnson).

Unlike survival cannibalism, in which human flesh is eaten as a   8
last resort after a person has died, in dietary cannibalism, humans are purchased or trapped for food and then eaten as a part of a culture's traditions. In addition, survival cannibalism often involves people eating other people of the same origins, whereas dietary cannibalism usually involves people eating foreigners.

In the Miyanmin society of the west Sepik interior of Papua,   9
New Guinea, villagers do not value human flesh over that of pigs or marsupials because human flesh is part of their diet (Poole 17). The Miyanmin people observe no differences in "gender, kinship,

ritual status, and bodily substance"; they eat anyone, even their own dead. In this respect, then, they practice both endocannibalism and exocannibalism; and to ensure a constant supply of human flesh for food, they raid neighboring tribes and drag their victims back to their village to be eaten (Poole 11). Perhaps, in the history of this society, there was at one time a shortage of wild game to be hunted for food, and because people were more plentiful than fish, deer, rabbits, pigs, or cows, survival cannibalism was adopted as a last resort. Then, as their culture developed, the Miyanmin may have retained the practice of dietary cannibalism, which has endured as a part of their culture.

Similar to the Miyanmin, the people of the Leopard and Alligator societies in South America eat human flesh as part of their cultural tradition. Practicing dietary exocannibalism, the Leopard people hunt in groups, with one member wearing the skin of a leopard to conceal the face. They ambush their victims in the forest and carry their victims back to their village to be eaten. The Alligator people also hunt in groups, but they hide themselves under a canoelike submarine that resembles an alligator, then swim close to a fisherman's or trader's canoe to overturn it and catch their victims (MacCormack 54). 10

Religious or ritual cannibalism is different from survival and dietary cannibalism in that it has a ceremonial purpose rather than one of nourishment. Sometimes only a single victim is sacrificed in a ritual, while at other times many are sacrificed. For example, the Bangala tribe of the Congo River in central Africa honors a deceased chief or leader by purchasing, sacrificing, and feasting on slaves (Sagan 53). The number of slaves sacrificed is determined by how highly the tribe members revered the deceased leader. 11

Ritual cannibalism among South American Indians often serves as revenge for the dead. Like the Bangalas, some South American tribes kill their victims to be served as part of funeral rituals, with human sacrifices denoting that the deceased was held in high honor. Also like the Bangalas, these tribes use outsiders as victims. Unlike the Bangalas, however, the Indians sacrifice only one victim instead of many in a single ritual. For example, when a warrior of a tribe is killed in battle, the family of the warrior forces a victim to take the identity of the warrior. The family adorns the victim with the deceased warrior's belongings and may even force him to marry the deceased warrior's wives. But once the family believes the victim has assumed the spiritual identity of the deceased warrior, the family kills him. The children in the tribe soak their hands in the victim's blood to symbolize their revenge of the warrior's 12 death. Elderly women from the tribe drink the victim's blood and then cut up his body for roasting and eating (Sagan 53–54). By sacrificing a victim, the people of the tribe believe that the death of the warrior has been avenged and the soul of the deceased can rest in peace.

In the villages of certain African tribes, only a small part of a dead body is used in ritual cannibalism. In these tribes, where the childbearing capacity of women is highly valued, women are obligated to eat small, raw fragments of genital parts during fertility rites. Elders of the tribe supervise this ritual to ensure that the women will be fertile. In the Bimin-Kuskusmin tribe, for instance, a widow eats a small, raw fragment of flesh from the penis of her deceased husband in order to enhance her future fertility and reproductive capacity. Similarly, a widower may eat a raw fragment of flesh from his deceased wife's vagina along with a piece of her bone marrow; by eating her flesh, he hopes to strengthen the fertility capacity of his daughters borne by his dead wife, and by eating her bone marrow, he honors her reproductive capacity. Also, when an elder woman of the village who has shown great reproductive capacity dies, her uterus and the interior parts of her vagina are eaten by other women who hope to further benefit from her reproductive power (Poole 16–17). 13

Members of developed societies in general practice none of these forms of cannibalism, with the occasional exception of survival cannibalism when the only alternative is starvation. It is possible, however, that our distant-past ancestors were cannibals who through the eons turned away from the practice. We are, after all, descended from the same ancestors as the Miyanmin, the Alligator, and the Leopard people, and survival cannibalism shows that people are capable of eating human flesh when they have no other choice. 14

Works Cited

Askenasy, Hans. *Cannibalism: From Sacrifice to Survival*. Amherst, NY: Prometheus, 1994.

Barker, Francis, Peter Hulme, and Margaret Iversen, eds. *Cannibalism and the New World*. Cambridge: Cambridge UP, 1998.

Brown, Paula, and Donald Tuzin, eds. *The Ethnography of Cannibalism*. Washington: Society of Psychological Anthropology, 1983.

"Cannibal Jokes." *The Loonie Bin of Jokes*. 22 Sept. 1999 <http://www.looniebin.mb.ca/cannibal.html>.

Hart, James D. *A Companion to California*. Berkeley: U of California P, 1987.

Johnson, Kristin. "New Light on the Donner Party." 28 Sept. 1999 <http://www.metrogourmet.com/crossroads.KJhome.htm>.

MacCormack, Carol. "Human Leopard and Crocodile." Brown and Tuzin 54–55.

Poole, Fitz John Porter. "Cannibals, Tricksters, and Witches." Brown and Tuzin 11, 16–17.

Sagan, Eli. *Cannibalism*. New York: Harper, 1976.

Shipman, Pat. "The Myths and Perturbing Realities of Cannibalism." *Discover* Mar. 1987: 70+.

Tuzin, Donald. "Cannibalism and Arapesh Cosmology." Brown and Tuzin 61–63.

Twain, Mark. "Cannibalism in the Cars." *The Complete Short Stories of Mark Twain.* Ed. Charles Neider. New York: Doubleday, 1957. 9–16.

READING FOR MEANING

This section presents three activities that will help you reread Ngo's explanatory essay with a critical eye. Done in sequence, these activities lead you from a basic understanding of the selection to a more personal response to it and finally to an analysis that deepens your understanding and critical thinking about what you are reading.

Read to Comprehend

Reread the selection, and write a few sentences briefly explaining the different types of cannibalism, according to Ngo. Also make a list of any words you do not understand—for example, *resort* (verb, paragraph 3), *last resort* (8), *kinship* (9), *eons* (14). Look up their meanings in a dictionary to see which definition best fits the context.

To expand your understanding of this reading, you might use one or more of the following critical reading strategies that are explained and illustrated in Appendix 1: *outlining, summarizing, paraphrasing,* and *questioning to understand and remember.*

Read to Respond

Write several paragraphs exploring your initial thoughts and feelings about Ngo's explanatory essay. Focus on anything that stands out for you, perhaps because it resonates with your own experience or because you find a statement puzzling.

You might consider writing about

- your response to the anecdotes about the Vietnamese refugees (paragraphs 1–4) and the Donner Party in California (7).

- your response to the idea that cannibalism may be performed for ceremonial or ritual purposes.

- whether you think you would resort to cannibalism in order to survive.

To develop your response to Ngo's essay, you might use one or more of the following critical reading strategies that are explained and illustrated in Appendix 1: *contextualizing, recognizing emotional manipulation,* and *judging the writer's credibility.*

Read to Analyze Underlying Assumptions

Write several paragraphs exploring one or more of the assumptions, values, and beliefs underlying Ngo's explanatory essay. As you write, explain how the assumptions are reflected in the text, as well as what you now think of them (and perhaps of your own assumptions) after rereading the selection with a critical eye.

You might consider writing about

- the cultural assumptions underlying Ngo's observation that "some scholars have tried to understand why people in the West have been so eager to attribute cannibalism to non-westerners" (paragraph 5), perhaps in relation to your own assumptions about people who are different in some way.

- the particular assumptions about the body and death that make some people unable, even in the most extreme conditions, to eat dead bodies.

- the values and beliefs underlying the differences among survival, dietary, and religious cannibalism.

- the assumptions underlying Ngo's comment that "a few scholars have questioned whether cannibalism was ever practiced anywhere, except in cases of ensuring survival in times of famine or isolation" (5).

To probe assumptions more deeply, you might use one or more of the following critical reading strategies that are explained and illustrated in Appendix 1: *reflecting on challenges to your beliefs and values, exploring the significance of figurative language,* and *looking for patterns of opposition.*

READING LIKE A WRITER
INTEGRATING SOURCES SMOOTHLY

When writers explain concepts to their readers, they nearly always rely in part on information gleaned from sources in a library or on the Internet. When they do so, they must acknowledge these sources. Within their essays, writers must find ways to integrate smoothly into their own sentences the information borrowed from each source and to acknowledge or cite each source. When you analyzed David Quammen's essay, you learned that writers rely on certain signal phrases and sentence structures to integrate quoted materials smoothly into their essays. Sometimes, however, writers do not quote a source but instead summarize or paraphase it. (See Appendix 1, pp. 660–63, for examples of summarizing and paraphrasing.) When they do so, they may acknowledge the source of the summarized or paraphrased material through signal phrases or special sentence structures, or they may use a formal style of parenthetical citation. Ngo relies on both these strategies. (Ngo's parenthetical citations refer to sources in the works-cited list at the end of his essay.)

Analyze

1. In paragraphs 7 and 9, *notice* how Ngo sets up a sentence to integrate the quoted phrases.

2. *Put a checkmark* in the margin by each instance of parenthetical citation in paragraphs 5, 6, and 9–13. *Notice* where these citations are located in Ngo's sentences and the different forms they take.

3. *Make notes* in the margin about similarities and differences you observe in Ngo's use of parenthetical citations.

Write

Write a few sentences explaining how Ngo integrates quoted phrases into his sentences and makes use of parenthetical citations. *Illustrate* your explanation with examples from the reading.

CONSIDERING IDEAS FOR YOUR OWN WRITING

Consider writing about some other well-established human taboo or practice, such as ostracism, incest, pedophilia, murder, circumcision, celibacy or virginity, caste systems, a particular religion's dietary restrictions, adultery, stealing, gourmandism, or divorce.

A SPECIAL READING STRATEGY

Summarizing

Summarizing, a potent reading-for-meaning strategy, is also a kind of writing you will encounter in your college classes and on the job. By rereading Ngo's essay on cannibalism with an eye toward finding its main ideas, you can do the groundwork for writing a summary of it. Taking the time to write a summary will help you remember what you have read and could help you explain to others the important ideas in Ngo's essay. For detailed guidelines on writing an extended summary, see Appendix 1 (pp. 000–00).

LYN GUTIERREZ

Music Therapy

> Lyn Gutierrez wrote this essay when she was a first-year college student. In it she presents an alternative form of healing—music therapy—from a variety of perspectives: by tracing its historical development, by providing institutional and individual definitions, by explaining a music therapist's training, by detailing when and how music therapy is used, and by outlining a music therapy session. Gutierrez builds logically on each piece of information until she has provided readers a comprehensive view of her subject.
>
> The other readings in this chapter are followed by reading and writing activities. Following this reading, however, you are on your own to decide how to read for meaning and read like a writer.

Why do department stores play music for their customers? Why does the dentist let patients pick music to listen to while in the chair? Why do companies have music playing for the callers waiting on hold? Why do most people listen to music while driving? The answer is simple: music is therapeutic—it can relax, rejuvenate, calm, and energize.

During and after World War I and World War II, musicians visited veterans hospitals around the country in an effort to lift the spirits of patients suffering from physical and emotional trauma. The performers would sing, dance, play instruments, and perform skits. Doctors noticed positive physical and emotional patient responses to the music; it wasn't long before these facilities were hiring musicians to perform on a regular basis. In 1944, Michigan State University offered the first formal degree in music therapy. The desire to expand the use of music therapy resulted in the formation of the National Association for Music Therapy (NAMT) in 1950. Twenty-one years later, in 1971, the American Association for Music Therapy (AAMT) was established. In 1998, NAMT joined forces with AAMT to form the American Music Therapy Association (AMTA). Today, AMTA boasts 5,000 members.

AMTA defines music therapy as "the prescribed use of music by a qualified person to effect positive changes in the psychological, physical, cognitive, or social functioning of individuals with health or educational problems" ("Frequently Asked Questions"). Bruce Martin, a registered and board-certified music therapist working in Vancouver, Washington, defines music therapy as "an arts therapy which has been used to help people withstand pain and provide relaxation and recreation. It is used in every stage of human development, from birth through death. Music therapy is used to maintain, restore, or increase a person's social, physical, or mental well-being" ("Sound Therapy Works"). Whether derived from an institutional definition or a personal one, the primary goal of music therapy is clearly to promote well-being.

But a music therapist does not simply decide one day to pick up   4
a guitar and visit a hospital. A music therapist must complete an approved college curriculum,[1] including courses in anatomy, psychology, sociology, biology, special education, and music history and theory. Once the student has earned a degree in music therapy and has completed an internship, he or she may become either a registered music therapist (RMT) or a certified music therapist (CMT). The music therapist may then elect to participate in a national board examination to become certified by the Certification Board for Music Therapists. Once board certified, the music therapist may choose to practice in nursing homes, schools, institutions, hospitals, hospices, correctional facilities, drug and alcohol rehabilitation centers, community mental health centers, or agencies assisting developmentally disabled persons, or he or she may decide to go into private practice.

Within the institutions listed in the previous paragraph, music   5
therapy has been used in various ways; for example, music therapy has been used in general hospitals to relieve pain in conjunction with anesthesia or pain medication, promote physical rehabilitation, and counteract apprehension or fear. Nursing homes use music therapy with elderly persons "to increase or maintain their level of physical, mental, and social/emotional functioning" ("Frequently Asked Questions"). Schools will also hire music therapists to provide music therapy services that are listed on the Individualized Education Plan for mainstreamed special learners. And in psychiatric facilities, music therapy is used to allow individuals "to explore personal feelings, make positive changes in mood and emotional states, have a sense of control over life through successful experiences, practice problem solving, and resolve conflicts leading to stronger family and peer relationships" ("Frequently Asked Questions").

Regardless of the settings in which they work, music therapists   6
follow certain standards of practice, have a number of non-musical goals, and may use a variety of musical tools in an effort to restore a patient's or group's physical, psychological, and/or emotional health. In any field that strives to be ethical and professional, standards of practice help define professionalism. This is no less true of music therapists. Among those practices a music therapist should engage in are (1) individualized assessments for each client;

(2) recommendations for or against treatment based on the assessment; (3) written, time-specific goals and objectives for each client; (4) a written treatment plan specifying music-therapy strategies and techniques that will be used to address the goals and objectives; (5) regular music-therapy sessions, with strategies and techniques chosen on the basis of the assessment and goals; (6) regular reevaluation of the effectiveness of the interventions being used; (7) written documentation; and (8) dismissal of the client from music therapy when the services are no longer necessary or appropriate (Brunk and Coleman).

Beyond embracing the profession's standards of practice, a music therapist will identify specific non-musical goals applicable to the patient with whom the therapist is working. Such non-musical goals may include "improving communication skills, decreasing inappropriate behavior, improving academic and motor skills, increasing attention span, strengthening social and leisure skills, pain management and stress reduction. Music therapy can also help individuals on their journey of self-growth and understanding" (Lindberg).

Music therapists may also use their instruments—their musical tools—in a number of therapeutic ways. For example, they may encourage a person to express feelings and emotions through music. Therapists believe that teaching a person to write music or play an instrument can be an emotional release and improve basic motor skills. Therapists also believe that listening to a song can relieve stress, counteract depression, and increase pain tolerance; singing can improve verbal skills, express emotions, and increase social skills; and banging on a drum can relieve tension and improve hand-eye coordination. Therapists advocate music for counteracting anxiety and fear, relieving tension and pain during the birthing process, and relaxing patients before and after surgery.

Once at work, there is no typical session for a music therapist. The therapist must evaluate each client and the results of each session with the clients' needs in mind. Improving a person's musical abilities is not the primary goal of music therapy. There are no specific steps to follow, as every person and each circumstance is different. A therapist must draw on his or her own education in and experience with music therapy to encourage the development of the person. For example, in conducting a group session on relaxation through awareness and communication, two additional music therapists may be involved—one to guide the initial exploration and participate in the primary musical movement, and one to improvise for the second musical movement and the relaxation. The first musical movement, using energetic, rhythmic music, acts as a warm-up in which everyone participates. The therapists encourage everyone, especially new members to the session, to stand, since once the music starts, individuals may not have the courage to rise and move about. The second musical movement is improvised atonally—to avoid any musical associations—in response to the patients' associations to a specific stimulus. The music therapist will usually allow the individual who is least able to express him- or herself physically or verbally to choose the stimulus (which may vary among tactile stimuli, visual stimuli, symbols, or even quotations) so that the person feels he or she has invested in the session. When each member of the session has shared some association to the stimulus, the playing therapist improvises music—arrhythmically and atonally—to consciously reflect the ideas and feelings expressed by the group, or to echo unexpressed, unverbalized feelings within the group. During the remainder of the session, the lead therapist works with patients, ultimately guiding them through a series of relaxation exercises (Priestley 78–81).

In 1966, twenty-two years after Michigan State University offered the first formal degree in music therapy, Juliette Alvin wrote, "Music therapy has become a more or less recognized ancillary therapy and a remedial means [of addressing patient ailments]. . . . [A] number of physicians, psychologists, educationalists and musicians are taking an interest in the subject" (104). And even today, while music therapists claim that their work improves the overall health of a patient and "[w]hile there is a broad literature covering the application of music therapy as reported in the medical press, there is an absence of valid clinical research material from which substantive conclusions may be drawn" (Aldridge 83). But this does not mean we should dismiss music therapy as a valid medical alternative. For while there are few cross-cultural studies supporting the claims of music therapists, within the field of nursing—where much of the research has been developed—music is recognized as an additional and useful therapeutic procedure (Aldridge 84).

10

Society is constantly looking for new and innovative ways to assist people in improving their way of life and bettering their physical and emotional circumstances. Music therapists believe that they offer an effective alternative to conventional medicine.

11

Note

1. A list of institutions offering degrees in music therapy may be found at <http://www.musictherapy.org/Career/Schools.html>.

Works Cited

Aldridge, David. *Music Therapy Research and the Practice of Medicine.* Bristol, PA: Jessica Kingsley Publishers, 1996.

Alvin, Juliette. *Music Therapy.* New York: Humanities P, 1966.

Brunk, Betsey, and Kathleen Coleman. "Medical Music Therapy." 1997. 2 Mar. 1999 <http://home.att.net/~preludetherapy/medic.html>.

————. "What to Expect from a Music Therapist." 1997. 2 Mar. 1999 <http://home.att.net/~preludetherapy/mtbc.html>.

"Frequently Asked Questions about Music Therapy." 1999. American Music Therapy Association. 1 Jan. 1999 <http://www.musictherapy.org/faqs.html>.

Lindberg, Katherine. "Music Therapy Info Link." 8 Apr. 1997. 2 Mar. 1999 <http://members.aol.com/kathysl/questions.html>.

Priestley, Mary. *Music Therapy in Action.* New York: St. Martin's Press. 1975.

"Sound Therapy Works." 1997. 2 Mar. 1999 <http://www.pacifier.com/~stwmt/stw.html>.

READING FOR MEANING

Reading for meaning involves three activities:

- reading to comprehend
- reading to respond
- reading to analyze underlying assumptions

Reread Gutierrez's essay, and then write a page or so explaining your understanding of its basic meaning or main point, a personal response you have to it, and what you see as one of its underlying assumptions.

READING LIKE A WRITER

Writers of essays explaining concepts

- devise a readable plan.
- use appropriate explanatory strategies.
- integrate sources smoothly into the writing.
- engage readers' interest.

Focus on one of these strategies in Gutierrez's essay, and analyze it carefully through close rereading and annotating. Then write several sentences explaining what you have learned, giving specific examples from the reading to illustrate your explanation. Add a few sentences evaluating how successfully Gutierrez uses the strategy to explain music therapy.

REVIEWING WHAT MAKES ESSAYS EXPLAINING CONCEPTS EFFECTIVE

In this chapter, you have been learning how to read essays explaining concepts for meaning and how to read them like a writer. Before going on to write an essay explaining a concept, pause here to review and contemplate what you have learned about the elements of effective concept explanations.

Analyze

Choose one reading from this chapter that seems to you especially effective. Before rereading the selection, *jot down* one or two reasons you remember it as an example of good concept explanation.

Reread your chosen selection, adding further annotations about what makes it a particularly successful example of concept explanation. *Consider* the selection's purpose and how well it achieves that purpose for its intended readers. (You can make an informed guess about the intended readers and their expectations by noting the publication source of the essay.) Then *focus* on how well the essay

- devises a readable plan.

- uses appropriate explanatory strategies.

- integrates sources smoothly into the writing.

- engages readers' interest.

You can review all of these basic features in the Guide to Reading Essays Explaining Concepts (p. 226).

Your instructor may ask you to complete this activity on your own or to work with a small group of other students who have chosen the same reading. If you work with others, allow enough time initially for all group members to reread the selection thoughtfully and to add their annotations. Then *discuss* as a group what makes the selection effective. *Take notes* on your discussion. One student in your group should then report to the class what the group has learned about the effectiveness of essays explaining concepts. If you are working individually, write up what you have learned from your analysis.

Write

Write at least a page, justifying your choice of this reading as an example of effective concept explanation. *Assume* that your readers— your instructor and classmates—have read the selection but will not remember many details about it. They also might not remember it as especially successful. Therefore, you will need to *refer* to details and specific parts of the essay as you explain how it works and as you justify your evaluation of its effectiveness. You need not argue that it is the best reading in the chapter or that it is flawless, only that it is, in your view, a strong example of the genre.

■ A Guide to Writing Essays Explaining Concepts

The readings in this chapter have helped you learn a great deal about essays explaining concepts. The readings also have helped you understand new concepts and learn more about concepts with which you are already familiar. Now that you have seen how writers use explanatory strategies that are appropriate for their readers, anticipating what their readers are likely to know, you can approach this type of writing confidently. This Guide to Writing will help you at every stage in the process of composing an essay explaining a concept—from choosing a concept and organizing your explanatory strategies to evaluating and revising your draft.

INVENTION AND RESEARCH

The following activities will help you choose a concept, consider what your readers need to know, explore what you already know, and gather and sort through your information.

Choosing a Concept

List different concepts you could explain, and then choose the one that interests you and would be likely to interest your readers. To make the best choice and have alternatives in case the first choice does not work out, you should have a full list of possibilities. You might already have a concept in mind, possibly one suggested to you by the Considering Ideas for Your Own Writing activities following the readings in this chapter. Pause now to review the dozens of suggested concepts in those activities. Here are some other concepts from various fields of study for you to consider:

- *Literature:* representation, figurative language, canon, postcolonialism, modernism, irony, epic

- *Philosophy:* Platonic forms, causality, syllogism, existentialism, nihilism, logical positivism, determinism, phenomenology

- *Business management:* autonomous work group, quality circle, management by objectives, zero-based budgeting, benchmarking, focus group

- *Psychology:* phobia, narcissism, fetish, emotional intelligence, divergent/convergent thinking, behaviorism, Jungian archetype

- *Government:* one person/one vote, minority rights, federalism, communism, theocracy, popular consent, exclusionary rule, political machine, political action committee

- *Biology:* photosynthesis, ecosystem, plasmolysis, phagocytosis, DNA, species, punctuated evolution, homozygosity, diffusion

- *Art:* composition, cubism, iconography, Pop Art, conceptual art, performance art, graffiti, Dadaism, surrealism, expressionism

- *Math:* Mobius transformation, boundedness, null space, eigenvalue, complex numbers, integral, exponent, polynomial, factoring, Pythagorean theorem, continuity, derivative, infinity

- *Physical sciences:* gravity, mass, weight, energy, quantum theory, law of definite proportions, osmotic pressure, first law of thermodynamics, entropy, free energy, fusion

- *Public health:* alcoholism, epidemic, vaccination, drug abuse, contraception, prenatal care, AIDS education

- *Environmental studies:* acid rain, recycling, ozone depletion, sewage treatment, toxic waste, endangered species

- *Sports psychology:* Ringelman effect, leadership, cohesiveness, competitiveness, anxiety management, aggression, visualization, runner's high

- *Law:* arbitration, strike, minimum wage, liability, reasonable doubt, sexual harassment, nondisclosure agreement, assumption of evidence

- *Meteorology:* jet stream, hydrologic cycle, El Niño, Coriolis effect, Chinook or Santa Ana wind, standard time system, tsunami

- *Nutrition and health:* vegetarianism, bulimia, diabetes, food allergy, aerobic exercise, obesity, Maillard reaction

Choose a promising concept to explore, one that interests you and that you think would interest your readers. You might not know very much about the concept now, but the guidelines that follow will help you learn more about it so that you can explain it to others.

Analyzing Your Readers

Write for a few minutes, analyzing your potential readers. Begin by identifying your readers and what you want them to know. Even if you are writing only for your instructor, you should consider what he or she knows about your concept. Ask yourself the following questions to stimulate your thinking: What might my potential readers already know about the concept or about the field of study to which it applies? What new, useful, or interesting information about the concept could I provide for them? What questions might they ask?

Researching the Concept

Even if you know quite a bit about the concept, you may want to do additional library or Internet research or consult an expert. Before you begin, check with your instructor for special requirements, such as submitting photocopies of your written sources or using a particular documentation style.

Exploring What You Already Know about the Concept.   *Write for a few minutes about the concept to discover what you know about it.* Pose any questions you now have about the concept and try to answer questions you expect your readers would have.

Finding Information at the Library or on the Internet.   *Learn more about your concept by finding sources, taking notes on or making copies of relevant material, and keeping a working bibliography.* Before embarking on research, review any materials you already have at hand that explain your concept. If you are considering a concept from one of your courses, find explanatory material in your textbook and lecture notes. (See Appendix 2, Strategies for Research and Documentation, for detailed guidance on finding information at a library and on the Internet.)

RESEARCHING YOUR SUBJECT ONLINE

One way to get a quick initial overview of the information available on a concept is to conduct an online search. You can do this in several ways:

- Enter the name of your concept in a search tool such as Google <http://google.com> to discover possible sources of information about the concept.

- Check an online encyclopedia in the field to which the concept belongs. Here are a few specialized encyclopedias that may be helpful:

  Encyclopedia of Psychology <http://www.psychology.org>

  The Internet Encyclopedia of Philosophy <http://www.utm.edu/research/iep>

  Webopedia <http://webopedia.com>

Bookmark or keep a record of promising sites so that when you focus your search, you will know where to look. Download any materials, including visuals, that you might consider including in your essay.

Consulting Experts. *Identify one or more people knowledgeable about the concept or the field of study in which it is used, and request information from them.* If you are writing about a concept from a course, consult the professor, teaching assistant, or other students. If the concept relates to your job, consider asking your supervisor. If it relates to a subject you have encountered on television, in the newspaper, or on the Internet, you might email the author or post a query at a relevant Web site. Consulting experts can answer your questions as well as lead you to other sources—Web sites, chatrooms, articles, and books.

Focusing Your Explanation. *With your own knowledge of the concept and that of your readers in mind, consider how you might focus your explanation.* Determine how the information you have gathered so far could be divided. For example, if you were writing about the concept of schizophrenia, you might focus on the history of its diagnosis and treatment, its symptoms, its effects on families, the current debate about its causes, or the current preferred methods of treatment. If you were writing a book, you might want to cover all these aspects of the concept, but in a relatively brief essay you can focus on only one or two of them.

Confirming Your Focus. *Choose a focus for your explanation, and write several sentences justifying the focus you have chosen.* Why do you think this focus will appeal to your readers? What interests you about it? Do you have enough information to plan and draft your explanation? Do you know where you can find any additional information you need?

Formulating a Working Thesis. *Draft a thesis statement.* A working thesis—as opposed to a final, revised thesis—will help you begin drafting your essay purposefully. The thesis in an essay explaining a concept simply announces the concept and focus of the explanation. Here are three examples from the readings.

- "What we are talking about here is celibate motherhood, procreation without copulation, a phenomenon that goes by the technical name *parthenogenesis.* Translated from the Greek roots: virgin birth" (Quammen, paragraph 1).

- "Each of the women at the conference had to make decisions about hair, clothing, makeup and accessories, and each decision carried meaning. Every style available to us was marked. The men in our group had made decisions, too, but the range from which they chose was incomparably narrower. Men can choose styles that are marked, but they don't have to, and in this group none did. Unlike the women, they had the option of being unmarked" (Tannen, paragraph 12).

- "Cannibalism can be broken down into two main categories: exocannibalism, the eating of outsiders or foreigners, and endocannibalism, the eating of members of one's own social group (Shipman 70). Within these categories are several functional types of cannibalism, three of the most common being survival cannibalism, dietary cannibalism, and religious and ritual cannibalism" (Ngo, paragraph 6).

Notice that Ngo's thesis statement not only announces the concept, but also forecasts the main topics he will take up in the essay. Forecasts, though not required, can be helpful to readers, especially when the concept is unfamiliar or the explanation is complicated.

Considering Visuals.   *Consider whether visuals—tables, graphs, drawings, photographs—would make your explanation clearer.* You could construct your own visuals; download materials from the Internet; copy images from print sources like books, magazines, and newspapers; or scan into your essay visuals from books and magazines. Visuals are not at all a requirement of an essay explaining a concept, as you can tell from the readings in this chapter, but they could add a new dimension to your writing.

DRAFTING

The following guidelines will help you set goals for your draft, plan its organization, and think about a useful sentence strategy.

Setting Goals

Establishing goals for your draft before you begin writing will enable you to make decisions and work more confidently. Consider the following questions now, and keep them in mind as you draft. They will help you set goals for drafting as well as recall how the writers you have read in this chapter tried to achieve similar goals.

- *How can I begin engagingly so as to capture my readers' attention?* Should I try to be amusing, like Quammen? Should I begin with an anecdote, as Tannen, Bailey, and Ngo do, or with a scenario or "fabricated example," as Gardner and Walters do? Should I begin with a fact and an example to illustrate it, as Gilbert and Wilson do? Should I, like Gutierrez, begin by asking rhetorical questions?

- *How can I orient readers so they do not get confused?* Should I provide an explicit forecasting statement, as Ngo does? Should I add transitions to help readers see how the parts of my essay relate to one another, as Ngo and Bailey do? Should I use rhetorical questions and summary statements, as Quammen does? Or should I use all of these cueing devices, together with headings and subheadings, as Gardner and Walters as well as Gilbert and Wilson do?

- *How should I conclude my explanation?* Should I frame the essay by echoing the opening at the end, as Quammen and Tannen do? Should I summarize my explanation and discuss the implications, as Gardner and Walters, Gilbert and Wilson, and Ngo do?

Organizing Your Draft

With goals in mind, make a tentative outline of the topics you now think you want to cover as you give readers information about the concept. You might want to make two or three different outlines before choosing the one that looks most promising. Try to introduce new material in stages, so that readers' understanding of the concept builds slowly but steadily. Keep in mind that an essay explaining a concept is made up of four basic parts:

1. An attempt to engage readers' interest in the explanation

2. The thesis statement, announcing the concept and the way it will be focused and perhaps also forecasting the sequence of topics

3. An orientation to the concept, which may include a description or definition of it

4. The information about the concept, organized around a series of topics that reflect how the information has been divided up

An attempt to gain readers' interest could take as little space as two or three sentences or as much as four or five paragraphs. The thesis statement and orientation are usually quite brief, sometimes only a few sentences. One topic may require one or several paragraphs, and there can be few or many topics, depending on how the information has been divided up.

Consider tentative any outline you do before you begin drafting. Never be a slave to an outline. As you draft, you will usually see ways to improve on your original plan. Be ready to revise your outline, shift parts around, or drop or add parts as you draft.

Considering a Useful Sentence Strategy

As you draft your essay, you will need to identify people, introduce terms, and present details to help readers understand the concept you are explaining. One way to accomplish these goals is to use sentences with appositives. An appositive is made up of a group of words, usually based on a noun or a pronoun, that identifies or gives more information about another noun or pronoun just preceding it. Appositives come in many forms and may be introduced by a comma, dash, or parenthesis, as shown in these examples (the appositives appear in bold type):

this new style of courtship, **dating,** . . . (Bailey, paragraph 2)

demonstrated how focalism (**the failure to consider the consequences of nonfocal events when making predictions about the ultimate affective impact of focal events**) can . . . (Gilbert and Wilson, paragraph 16)

One single aphid hatching—**call her the *fundatrix*—** ... (Quammen, paragraph 8)

All of this chapter's readings use appositives. Writers explaining concepts rely on appositives because they serve many different purposes, as shown in the following examples.

- To identify a thing or person and establish a source's authority:

  In 1914, the *Ladies' Home Journal,* **a bastion of middle-class respectability,** used ... (Bailey, paragraph 7)

  Bruce Martin, **a registered and board-certified music therapist working in Vancouver, Washington,** defines ... (Gutierrez, paragraph 3)

- To introduce and define a new term:

  What we are talking about here is celibate motherhood, procreation without copulation, **a phenomenon that goes by the technical name *parthenogenesis*.** (Quammen, paragraph 1)

- To give examples or more specific information:

  The third woman's hair was wild, **a frosted blonde avalanche falling over and beyond her shoulders**. (Tannen, paragraph 4)

  True, the equation **(male companionship plus money equals female companionship)** was imbalanced. (Bailey, paragraph 27)

Appositives accomplish these and other purposes efficiently by enabling the writer to put related bits of information next to each other in the same sentence, thereby merging two potential sentences into one or shrinking a potential clause to a phrase. For example, Ngo uses an appositive in this sentence:

Cannibalism, **the act of human beings eating human flesh,** ... has a long history and continues to hold interest and create controversy. (Ngo, paragraph 5)

But he could have conveyed the same information in either of the following sentences:

Cannibalism can be defined as the act of human beings eating human flesh. It has a long history and continues to hold interest and create controversy.

Cannibalism, which can be defined as the act of human beings eating human flesh, has a long history and continues to hold interest and create controversy.

Both of these versions are readable and clear. By using an appositive, however, Ngo saves four or five words, subordinates the definition of cannibalism to his main idea about history and controversy, and yet locates the definition exactly where readers need to see it, right after the word being defined.

In addition to using appositives, you can strengthen your concept explanation with other kinds of sentence strategies. For example, you may want to review the information in Chapter 6 on sentences that express comparison and contrast (p. 392).

READING A DRAFT CRITICALLY

Getting a critical reading of your draft will help you see how to improve it. Your instructor may schedule class time for reading drafts, or you may want to ask a classmate or a tutor in the writing center to read your draft. Ask your reader to use the following guidelines and to write out a response for you to consult during your revision.

Read for a First Impression

1. Read the draft without stopping to annotate or comment, and then write two or three sentences giving your general impression.

2. Identify one aspect of the draft that seems particularly effective.

Read Again to Suggest Improvements

1. Consider whether the concept is clearly explained and focused.

   - Restate briefly what you understand the concept to mean, indicating if you have any uncertainty or confusion about its meaning.

   - Identify the focus of the explanation and assess whether the focus seems appropriate, too broad, or too narrow for the intended readers.

   - If you can, suggest another, possibly more interesting, way to focus the explanation.

2. Recommend ways of making the organization clearer or more effective.

   - Indicate whether a forecasting statement, topic sentences, or transitions could be added or improved.

   - Point to any place where you become confused or do not know how something relates to what went before.

   - Comment on whether the conclusion gives you a sense of closure or leaves you hanging.

3. Consider whether the content is appropriate for the intended readers.

   - Point to any place where the information might seem too obvious to readers or too elementary for them.

   - Circle any terms that the writer should define or define more clearly, as well as any that the writer has defined but you do not think need to be defined.

   - Think of unanswered questions readers might have about the concept. Try to suggest additional information that should be included.

   - Recommend new strategies the writer could usefully adopt: comparing the concept to a concept more familiar to readers, dividing some of the information into smaller or larger topics, reporting known causes or effects of the concept, giving further facts or examples, or narrating how a part of the concept actually works. Explain how the writer could make use of the strategy.

4. Assess whether quotations are integrated smoothly and acknowledged properly.

   - Point to any place where a quotation is not smoothly integrated into the writer's sentence and offer a revision.

   - Indicate any quotations that would have been just as effective if put in the writer's own words.

   - If sources are not acknowledged correctly, remind the writer to consult Appendix 2.

   - If you can, suggest other sources the writer might consult.

5. Evaluate the effectiveness of visuals.

   - Look at any visuals in the essay, and tell the writer what they contribute to your understanding of the concept explanation.

   - If any visuals do not seem relevant, or if there seem to be too many visuals, identify the ones that the writer could consider dropping, explaining your thinking.

   - If a visual does not seem appropriately placed, suggest a better place for it.

REVISING

This section offers suggestions for revising your draft. Revising means reenvisioning your draft, trying to see it in a new way, given your purpose and readers, in order to develop a more lively, engaging, and informative essay explaining a concept.

The biggest mistake you can make while revising is to focus initially on words or sentences. Instead, first try to see your draft as a whole in order to assess its likely impact on your readers. Think imaginatively and boldly about cutting unconvincing material, adding new material, and moving material around. Your computer makes even drastic revisions physically easy, but you still need to make the mental effort and decisions that will improve your draft.

You may have received help with this challenge from a classmate or tutor who gave your draft a critical reading. If so, keep this feedback in mind as you decide which parts of your draft need revising and what specific changes you could make. The following suggestions will help you solve problems and strengthen your essay.

To Make the Concept Clearer and More Focused

- If readers are confused or uncertain about the concept's meaning, try defining it more precisely or giving concrete examples. Consider using an appositive to introduce and define new terms or give specific details.

- If the focus seems too broad, concentrate on one aspect of the concept and explain it in greater depth.

- If the concept seems too narrow, go back to your invention and research notes and look for a larger or more significant aspect of it to focus on.

To Improve the Organization

- If readers have difficulty following the essay, improve the forecasting at the beginning of the essay by listing the topics in the order they will appear.

- If there are places where the topic gets blurred from one sentence or paragraph to the next, make the connections between the sentences or paragraphs clearer.

- If the essay seems to lose steam before it comes to a conclusion, consider again what you want readers to learn from your essay.

- If the essay is long and complicated, consider using headings and subheadings to orient readers.

To Strengthen the Explanatory Strategies

- If the content seems thin, consider whether you could add any other explanatory strategies or develop more fully the ones you are using already.

- If some of the words you use are new to most readers, take the time to define them now, perhaps explaining how they relate to more familiar terms or adding analogies and examples to make them less abstract. Consider using an appositive for your definition.

- If the way you have divided or categorized the information is unusual or unclear, write a sentence or two making explicit what you are doing and why.

- If the concept seems vague to readers, try comparing it to something familiar or applying it to a real-world experience.

To Integrate Quotations Smoothly and Acknowledge Sources Properly

- If any quotations are not smoothly integrated into the text, add appropriate signal phrases or rewrite the sentences.

- If your critical reader has identified a quotation that could just as effectively be described in your own words, try paraphrasing or summarizing the quote.

- If your sources are not acknowledged properly, check Appendix 2 for the correct citation form. Consider using an appositive to identify your source and establish its authority.

EDITING AND PROOFREADING

After you have revised your essay, be sure to spend some time checking for errors in usage, punctuation, and mechanics and considering matters of style. If you keep a list of errors you typically make, begin by checking your draft against this list. Ask someone else to proofread your essay before you print out a copy for your instructor or send it electronically.

From our research on student writing, we know that essays explaining concepts tend to have errors in essential or nonessential clauses beginning with *who, which,* or *that,* as well as errors in the use of commas to set off phrases that interrupt the flow of the sentence. Check a writer's handbook for help with these potential problems.

REFLECTING ON WHAT YOU HAVE LEARNED

Explaining Concepts

In this chapter, you have read critically several essays explaining concepts and have written one of your own. To better remember what you have learned, pause now to reflect on the reading and writing activities you completed in this chapter.

1. *Write* a page or so reflecting on what you have learned. *Begin* by describing what you are most pleased with in your essay. Then

explain what you think contributed to your achievement. *Be specific* about this contribution.

- If it was something you learned from the readings, *indicate* which readings and specifically what you learned from them.

- If it came from your invention writing, *point out* the section or sections that helped you most.

- If you got good advice from a critical reader, *explain* exactly how the person helped you—perhaps by helping you understand a particular problem in your draft or by adding a new dimension to your writing.

- *Try to write* about your achievement in terms of what you have learned about the genre.

2. Now *reflect* more generally on explaining concepts, a genre of writing that plays an important role in education and in our society. *Consider* that concept explanations attempt to present their information as uncontested truths. *Reflect* on your own essay, and *write* answers to the following questions: When you were doing research on the concept, did you discover that some of the information was being challenged by experts? If so, what were the grounds for this challenge? Did you at any point think that your readers might question any of the information you were presenting? How did you decide what information might seem new or surprising to readers? Did you feel comfortable in your roles as the selector and giver of knowledge? *Describe* how you felt in these roles.

CHAPTER **6**

Evaluation

We make evaluations every day, stating judgments about such things as food, clothes, books, classes, teachers, political candidates, television programs, performers, and films. Most of our everyday judgments simply express our personal preference—"I liked it" or "I didn't like it." But as soon as someone asks "Why?" we realize that evaluation goes beyond individual taste.

If you want others to take your judgment seriously, you have to give reasons for it. Instead of merely asserting that "*Traffic* was fantastic," you might say that the acting in the film was extraordinarily powerful and that its documentary style was appropriate for its subject—drug trafficking, or the smuggling of drugs from Mexico and their distribution and use in the United States.

For readers to find your judgment and reasons convincing, they must recognize that your reasons are appropriate standards for evaluating a movie. An inappropriate reason for the judgment "*Traffic* is a great thriller" would be that the seats in the theater were comfortable. The comfort of the seats may contribute on one occasion to your enjoyment of the theater experience (and, indeed, would be an appropriate reason for judging the quality of a movie theater), but such a reason has nothing to do with the quality of a particular film.

For reasons to be considered appropriate, they must reflect the values or standards typically used in evaluating the kind of thing under consideration, such as a film or a car. The standards you would use for evaluating a film obviously differ from those you would use for evaluating a car. Acting, musical score, and story are common standards for judging films. Handling, safety, and styling are some of the standards used for judging cars.

Readers expect writers of evaluations both to offer appropriate reasons and to support their reasons. If one of your reasons for liking the BMW 330i sports sedan is its quick acceleration, you could cite the *Consumer Reports* road-test results (0 to 60 mph in 6.6 seconds) as evidence. (Statistical support like this, of course, makes sense only when the rate is compared with the acceleration rates of other comparable cars.) Similarly, if one of your reasons for liking *Traffic* is the series of short dramatic scenes featuring soap-opera style close-ups of the actors, you could give examples of several of these short scenes. You might describe the scene where a key witness is poisoned by his room-delivery breakfast on the day he is to testify against a drug lord or the scene where the wealthy father finds his drug-addicted daughter in a hotel room with a man who has paid her for sex. Support is important because it deals in specifics, showing exactly what value terms like *dramatic* and *close-up* mean to you.

As you can see, evaluation of the kind you will read and write in this chapter is intellectually rigorous. In college, you will have many opportunities to write evaluations. You may be asked to critique a book or a journal article, judge a scientific hypothesis against the results of an experiment, assess the value of conflicting interpretations of a historical event or a short story, or evaluate a class you have taken. You will also undoubtedly read evaluative writing in your courses and be tested on what you have read.

Written evaluations will almost certainly play an important part in your work life as well. On the job, you will probably be evaluated periodically and may have to evaluate people whom you supervise. It is also likely that you will be asked your opinion of various plans or proposals under consideration, and your ability to make reasonable, well-supported evaluations will affect your chances for promotion.

As the word *evaluation* suggests, evaluative arguments are basically about values, about what each of us thinks is important. Reading and writing evaluations will help you understand your own values as well as those of others. You will learn that when your basic values conflict with your readers' values, you may not be able to convince readers to accept a judgment different from their own. In such cases, you will usually want to try to bridge the difference by showing respect for their concerns despite your disagreement with them or to clarify the areas of agreement and disagreement.

The readings in this chapter will help you learn a good deal about evaluative writing. From the readings and from the ideas for writing that follow each reading, you will get ideas for your own evaluative essay. As you read and write about the selections, keep in mind the following assignment, which sets out the goals for writing an evaluative essay. To support your writing of this assignment, the chapter concludes with a Guide to Writing Evaluations.

Evaluation

Choose a subject that you can both evaluate and make a confident judgment about. Write an essay evaluating this subject. State your judgment clearly, and back it up with reasons and support. Describe the subject for readers unfamiliar with it, and give them a context for understanding it. Your purpose is to convince readers that your judgment is informed and based on generally accepted standards for this kind of subject.

WRITING SITUATIONS FOR EVALUATIONS

Following are a few examples to suggest the range of situations that may call for evaluative writing, including academic and work-related situations:

- For a conference on innovation in education, an elementary schoolteacher evaluates *Schoolhouse Rock,* an animated television series developed in the 1970s and reinvented in several new formats: books, CD-ROM learning games, and CDs. She praises the original series as an entertaining way of presenting information, giving two reasons the series remains an effective teaching tool: Witty lyrics and catchy tunes make the information memorable, and cartoonlike visuals make the lessons pleasurable. She supports each reason by showing and discussing videotaped examples of popular *Schoolhouse Rock* segments, such as "Conjunction Junction," "We the People," and "Three Is a Magic Number." She ends by expressing her hope that teachers and developers of educational multimedia will learn from the example of *Schoolhouse Rock.*

- A supervisor reviews the work of a probationary employee. She judges the employee's performance as being adequate overall but still needing improvement in several key areas, particularly completing projects on time and communicating clearly with others. To support her judgment, she describes several problems that the employee has had over the six-month probationary period.

- An older brother, a college junior, sends an email message to his younger brother, a high-school senior who is trying to decide which college to attend. Because the older brother attends one of the colleges being considered and has friends at another, he feels competent to offer advice. He centers his message on the question of what standards to use in evaluating colleges. He argues that if playing football is the primary goal, then college number one is the clear choice. But if having the opportunity to work in an award-winning scientist's genetics lab is more important, then the second college is the better choice.

THINKING ABOUT YOUR EXPERIENCE WITH EVALUATIONS

Before studying a type of writing, it is useful to spend some time thinking about what you already know about it. You may have discussed with friends or family why a particular movie or diet is good or bad, successful or unsuccessful. You might have written evaluative essays for school about a literary text, a theatrical performance, or a scientific report.

To analyze your experience with evaluations, try to recall a time when you were evaluating—orally or in writing—something you had seen, heard, read, or tried, such as a movie, performance, CD, book, magazine, restaurant, television show, video game, computer software, or concept. What were your criteria for evaluation—the standards upon which you based your judgments? Who was your audience for your argument? What did you hope to achieve with your evaluation? What interested you about your topic or made you think it was significant? Was your judgment all positive or all negative, or a mixture?

Also consider the evaluations you have read, heard, or seen on television. If you recall one of them in some detail, try to identify what made it interesting. Was it the subject, or did the author perhaps present ideas new to you? How did the author make the evaluation convincing? Did it contain illuminating details or an unusual point of view?

Write at least a page about your experience with evaluations.

■ A Guide to Reading Evaluations

This guide introduces you to evaluative writing. By completing all the activities in it, you will prepare yourself to learn a great deal from the other readings in this chapter about how to read and write an evaluative essay. The guide focuses on "Working at McDonald's," a well-known essay by Amitai Etzioni, a sociologist and one of the founders of the communitarian movement, which advocates that people value group traditions no more than they value national unity. You will read Etzioni's evaluative essay twice. First, you will read it for meaning, looking closely at its content and ideas. Then, you will reread the essay like a writer, analyzing the parts to see how Etzioni crafts his essay and to learn the strategies he uses to make the evaluation informative and convincing. These two activities—reading for meaning and reading like a writer—follow every reading in this chapter.

AMITAI ETZIONI

Working at McDonald's

Amitai Etzioni (b. 1929), who teaches sociology at George Washington University, has written numerous articles and books reflecting his commitment to a communitarian agenda, including Spirit of Community: Rights, Responsibilities, and the Communitarian Agenda *(1993),* The New Golden Rule: Morality and Community in a Democratic Society *(1998),* Civic Repentance *(1999), and* The Limits of Privacy *(1999). He is also the founder of the* Responsive Community, *a journal.*

The following essay was originally published in 1986 in the Miami Herald, *a major newspaper that circulates in South Florida. The original headnote identifies Etzioni as the father of five sons, including three teenagers, and points out that his son Dari helped Etzioni write this essay—although it does not say what Dari contributed.*

Before you read, think about the part-time jobs you held during high school—not just summer jobs but those you worked during the months when school was in session. Recall the pleasures and disappointments of these jobs. In particular, think about what you learned that might have made you a better student and prepared you for college. Perhaps you worked at a fast-food restaurant. If not, you have probably been in many such places and have observed students working there.

Annotate the essay as you read and as you complete the activities following the selection. For an illustration of the strategies and benefits of annotating, see Appendix 1, pages 648–54.

McDonald's is bad for your kids. I do not mean the flat patties and the white-flour buns; I refer to the jobs teen-agers undertake, mass-producing these choice items. 1

As many as two-thirds of America's high school juniors and seniors now hold down part-time paying jobs, according to studies. Many of these are in fast-food chains, of which McDonald's is the pioneer, trend-setter, and symbol. 2

At first, such jobs may seem right out of the Founding Fathers' educational manual for how to bring up self-reliant, work-ethic-driven, productive youngsters. But in fact, these jobs undermine school attendance and involvement, impart few skills that will be useful in later life, and simultaneously skew the values of teen-agers—especially their ideas about the worth of a dollar. 3

It has been a longstanding American tradition that youngsters ought to get paying jobs. In folklore, few pursuits are more deeply revered than the newspaper route and the sidewalk lemonade stand. Here the youngsters are to learn how sweet are the fruits of labor and self-discipline (papers are delivered early in the morning, 4 rain or shine), and the ways of trade (if you price your lemonade too high or too low . . .).

Roy Rogers, Baskin Robbins, Kentucky Fried Chicken, *et al.*, may at first seem nothing but a vast extension of the lemonade stand. They provide very large numbers of teen jobs, provide regular employment, pay quite well compared to many other teen jobs, and, in the modern equivalent of toiling over a hot stove, test one's stamina.   5

Closer examination, however, finds the McDonald's kind of job highly uneducational in several ways. Far from providing opportunities for entrepreneurship (the lemonade stand) or self-discipline, self-supervision, and self-scheduling (the paper route), most teen jobs these days are highly structured—what social scientists call "highly routinized."   6

True, you still have to have the gumption to get yourself over to the hamburger stand, but once you don the prescribed uniform, your task is spelled out in minute detail. The franchise prescribes the shape of the coffee cups; the weight, size, shape, and color of the patties; and the texture of the napkins (if any). Fresh coffee is to be made every eight minutes. And so on. There is no room for initiative, creativity, or even elementary rearrangements. These are breeding grounds for robots working for yesterday's assembly lines, not tomorrow's high-tech posts.   7

There are very few studies of the matter. One of the few is a 1984 study by Ivan Charper and Bryan Shore Fraser. The study relies mainly on what teen-agers write in response to questionnaires rather than actual observations of fast-food jobs. The authors argue that the employees develop many skills such as how to operate a food-preparation machine and a cash register. However, little attention is paid to how long it takes to acquire such a skill, or what its significance is.   8

What does it matter if you spend 20 minutes to learn to use a cash register, and then—"operate" it? What skill have you acquired? It is a long way from learning to work with a lathe or carpenter tools in the olden days or to program computers in the modern age.   9

A 1980 study by A. V. Harrell and P. W. Wirtz found that, among those students who worked at least 25 hours per week while in school, their unemployment rate four years later was half of that of seniors who did not work. This is an impressive statistic. It must be seen, though, together with the finding that many who begin as part-time employees in fast-food chains drop out of high school and are gobbled up in the world of low-skill jobs.   10

Some say that while these jobs are rather unsuited for college-bound, white, middle-class youngsters, they are "ideal" for lower-class, "non-academic," minority youngsters. Indeed, minorities are   11 "over-represented" in these jobs (21 percent of fast-food employ-ees). While it is true that these places provide income, work, and even some training to such youngsters, they also tend to perpetuate their disadvantaged status. They provide no career ladders, few marketable skills, and undermine school attendance and involvement.

The hours are often long. Among those 14 to 17, a third of fast-food employees (including some school dropouts) labor more than 30 hours per week, according to the Charper-Fraser study. Only 20 percent work 15 hours or less. The rest: between 15 to 30 hours. [12]

Often the stores close late, and after closing one must clean up and tally up. In affluent Montgomery County, Md., where child labor would not seem to be a widespread economic necessity, 24 percent of the seniors at one high school in 1985 worked as much as five to seven days a week; 27 percent, three to five. There is just no way such amounts of work will not interfere with school work, especially homework. In an informal survey published in the most recent yearbook of the high school, 58 percent of the seniors acknowledged that their jobs interfere with their school work. [13]

The Charper-Fraser study sees merit in learning teamwork and working under supervision. The authors have a point here. However, it must be noted that such learning is not automatically educational or wholesome. For example, much of the supervision in fast-food places leans toward teaching one the wrong kinds of compliance: blind obedience, or shared alienation with the "boss." [14]

Supervision is often both tight and woefully inappropriate. Today, fast-food chains and other such places of work (record shops, bowling alleys) keep costs down by having teens supervise teens with often no adult on the premises. [15]

There is no father or mother figure with which to identify, to emulate, to provide a role model and guidance. The work-culture varies from one place to another: Sometimes it is a tightly run shop (must keep the cash registers ringing); sometimes a rather loose pot party interrupted by customers. However, only rarely is there a master to learn from, or much worth learning. Indeed, far from being places where solid adult work values are being transmitted, these are places where all too often delinquent teen values dominate. Typically, when my son Oren was dishing out ice cream for Baskin Robbins in upper Manhattan, his fellow teen-workers considered him a sucker for not helping himself to the till. Most youngsters felt they were entitled to $50 severance "pay" on their last day on the job. [16]

The pay, oddly, is the part of the teen work-world that is most difficult to evaluate. The lemonade stand or paper route money was for your allowance. In the old days, apprentices learning a trade from a master contributed most, if not all of their income to their [17]

parents' household. Today, the teen pay may be low by adult standards, but it is often, especially in the middle class, spent largely or
wholly by the teens. That is, the youngsters live free at home ("after
all, they are high school kids") and are left with very substantial
sums of money.

Where this money goes is not quite clear. Some use it to support   18
themselves, especially among the poor. More middle-class kids set
some money aside to help pay for college, or save it for a major
purchase—often a car. But large amounts seem to flow to pay for
an early introduction into the most trite aspects of American con-
sumerism: flimsy punk clothes, trinkets, and whatever else is the
last fast-moving teen craze.

One may say that this is only fair and square; they are being good   19
American consumers and spend their money on what turns them
on. At least, a cynic might add, these funds do not go into illicit
drugs and booze. On the other hand, an educator might bemoan
that these young, yet unformed individuals, so early in life are driven to buy objects of no intrinsic educational, cultural, or social
merit, learn so quickly the dubious merit of keeping up with the
Joneses in ever-changing fads, promoted by mass merchandising.

Many teens find the instant reward of money, and the youth   20
status symbols it buys, much more alluring than credits in calcu-
lus courses, European history, or foreign languages. No wonder
quite a few would rather skip school—and certainly homework—
and instead work longer at a Burger King. Thus, most teen work
these days is not providing early lessons in work ethic; it fosters
escape from school and responsibilities, quick gratification, and a
short cut to the consumeristic aspects of adult life.

Thus, parents should look at teen employment not as automat-   21
ically educational. It is an activity—like sports—that can be turned
into an educational opportunity. But it can also easily be abused.
Youngsters must learn to balance the quest for income with the
needs to keep growing and pursue other endeavors that do not pay
off instantly—above all education.

Go back to school.   22

READING FOR MEANING

This section presents three activities that will help you reread Etzioni's essay
with a critical eye. Done in sequence, these activities lead you from a basic understanding of the selection to a more personal response to it and finally to an analysis that deepens your understanding and critical thinking about what you are
reading.

Read to Comprehend

Reread the selection, and write a few sentences briefly explaining Etzioni's claim about part-time jobs for kids, along with a few of the reasons he gives to support it. What is Etzioni evaluating in this article? Also make a list of any words you do not understand—for example, *skew* (paragraph 3), *entrepreneurship* (6), *apprentices* (17). Look up their meanings in a dictionary to see which definition best fits the context.

To expand your understanding of this reading, you might use one or more of the following critical reading strategies that are explained and illustrated in Appendix 1: *outlining, summarizing, paraphrasing*, and *questioning to understand and remember*.

Read to Respond

Write several paragraphs exploring your initial thoughts and feelings about Etzioni's evaluation. Focus on anything that stands out for you, perhaps because it resonates with your own experience or because you find a statement puzzling. You might consider writing about

- Etzioni's claim that the kinds of jobs he is evaluating in this article are bad for minority youngsters because such jobs "tend to perpetuate their disadvantaged status" (paragraph 11).

- how and why Etzioni addresses the opinions of those who might disagree with him, such as where he points out that students who work while in school are more often employed four years later (10), where he notes that one might view these part-time workers as good American consumers (19), or where he compares part-time work to sports (21).

- whether Etzioni's judgment of part-time jobs such as those at fast-food enterprises reminds you of your own jobs during the summer or school year. What would Etzioni have thought of your jobs? What do you think of them, having read this article?

To develop your response to Etzioni's essay, you might use one or more of the following critical reading strategies that are explained and illustrated in Appendix 1: *contextualizing, recognizing emotional manipulation*, and *judging the writer's credibility*.

Read to Analyze Underlying Assumptions

Write several paragraphs exploring one or more of the assumptions, values, and beliefs underlying Etzioni's evaluative essay. As you write, explain how the assumptions are reflected in the text, as well as what you now think of them (and perhaps of your own assumptions) after rereading the selection with a critical eye.

Notice that even when Etzioni clearly states his opinion and the reasons for it, readers need to pay close attention to the words and examples he uses and to think about how these reflect certain values upon which he is basing his judgment. As early as paragraph 3, he asserts that "these jobs undermine school attendance and involvement, impart few skills that will be useful in later life, and simultaneously skew the values of teen-agers—especially their ideas about the worth of a dollar." Already a careful reader can see several of the author's values emerging from these reasons that he gives to support his claim: Why does he think attendance and involvement in school are more important than part-time work? What does he believe a part-time job should prepare you to do—and why? What kind of value do you think he places on the dollar? As you read the article, see if you can find key words and phrases that illuminate the values Etzioni thinks are important, looking particularly at the reasons he uses to support his claim. For example, he criticizes fast-food franchises for spelling out tasks and not allowing "room for initiative, creativity, or even elementary rearrangements" (7). What does this language say about Etzioni's judgment of how part-time work should prepare someone for the future? And do you share his assumptions, or does thinking about his make you aware of how different your own attitudes and beliefs are? The purpose of analyzing underlying assumptions in a reading is to give us an opportunity to think critically about unexamined assumptions—especially the writer's and our own—many of which may be ingrained in our culture, our education, and even our language.

You might consider writing about

- the values underlying Etzioni's assertion that "the McDonald's kind of job [is] highly uneducational in several ways. . . . [M]ost teen jobs these days are highly structured—what social scientists call 'highly routinized'" (paragraph 6).

- the value system underlying Etzioni's comparison of the skill required to use a cash register to the skill of working with a lathe or carpenter tools or of programming computers (9).

- the values embodied in the theme of the lemonade stand and the newspaper route (4–6 and 17).

- the values underlying Etzioni's observation that in the workplaces he is discussing, "[t]here is no father or mother figure with which to identify, to emulate, to provide a role model and guidance" (16).

- what Etzioni is assuming when he says "[o]ne may say that this is only fair and square; they are being good American consumers and spend their money on what turns them on" (19).

- why Etzioni claims that "these jobs . . . skew the values of teen-agers—especially their ideas about the worth of a dollar" (3).

To probe assumptions more deeply, you might use one or more of the following critical reading strategies that are explained and illustrated in Appendix 1:

reflecting on challenges to your beliefs and values, evaluating the logic of an argument, and *judging the writer's credibility.*

READING LIKE A WRITER

This section leads you through an analysis of Etzioni's evaluative writing strategies: *presenting the subject, asserting an overall judgment, giving reasons and support, counterarguing,* and *establishing credibility.* For each strategy, you will be asked to reread and annotate part of Etzioni's essay to see how he uses the strategy in "Working at McDonald's."

When you study the selections later in this chapter, you will see how different writers use these same strategies. The Guide to Writing Evaluations near the end of the chapter suggests ways you can use these strategies in your own writing.

Presenting the Subject

Writers must present the subject so readers know what is being judged. Writers can simply name the subject, but usually they describe it in some detail. A film reviewer, for example, might identify the actors, describe the characters they play, and tell some of the plot. As a critical reader, you may notice that the language used to present the subject also may serve to evaluate it. Therefore, you should look closely at how the subject is presented. Note where the writer's information about the subject comes from, whether the information is reliable, and whether anything important seems to have been left out.

Analyze

1. *Reread* paragraphs 5–7, 9, 12, 15, and 16, and *underline* the factual details that describe the people who work at fast-food restaurants and what they do. *Ask* yourself the following question as you analyze how Etzioni presents the subject: Where does the writer seem to get his information—from firsthand observation, from conversation with others, or by reading published research?

2. Based on your own knowledge of fast-food jobs, *point to* the details in these paragraphs that you accept as valid as well as to details you think are inaccurate or only partially true. Finally, *consider* whether any information you know about fast-food jobs is missing from Etzioni's presentation of work at fast-food places.

Write

Write several sentences discussing how Etzioni presents the subject to his intended audience—education-minded adults, particularly parents of high-school students—and *give examples* from the reading. Then *write a few more sentences* evaluating Etzioni's presentation of the subject in terms of accuracy and completeness.

Asserting an Overall Judgment

A writer's overall judgment of the subject is the main point of an evaluative essay, asserting that the subject is good or bad, or better or worse, than something comparable. Although readers expect a definitive judgment, they also appreciate a balanced one that acknowledges, for example, some good qualities of a subject judged overall to be bad. Evaluations usually explicitly state the judgment up front in the form of a thesis and may restate it in different ways throughout the essay.

Analyze

1. *Reread* paragraphs 3 and 20–21, where Etzioni states his overall judgment, and *consider* whether you find his statements clear.

2. *Decide* whether Etzioni changes his initial judgment in any way when he restates it in somewhat different language at the end of the essay. *Consider* why he restates his judgment.

Write

Write a few sentences describing and evaluating Etzioni's assertion of his overall judgment.

Giving Reasons and Support

Any evaluative argument must explain and justify the writer's judgment. To be convincing, the reasons given must be recognized by readers as appropriate for evaluating the type of subject under consideration. That is, the reasons must reflect the values or standards of judgment that people typically use in similar situations. The reasons also must be supported by relevant examples, quotations, facts, statistics, or personal anecdotes. This support may come from the writer's own knowledge or experience, from that of other people, and from published materials.

Analyze

1. Etzioni names three principal reasons for his judgment in the final sentence of paragraph 3. *Underline* these reasons, and then *consider* the appropriateness of each one given Etzioni's intended readers—the largely middle-class adult subscribers to the *Miami Herald*. Why do you think they would or would not likely accept each reason as appropriate for evaluating part-time jobs for

teenagers? What objections, if any, might a critical reader have to Etzioni's reasoning?

2. One reason Etzioni gives to clarify his view that working at McDonald's is "bad" for students is that the jobs "impart few skills that will be useful in later life" (paragraph 3). Etzioni then attempts to support (to argue for) this reason in paragraphs 4–9. *Reread* these paragraphs noticing the kinds of support Etzioni relies on.

3. *Evaluate* how well Etzioni supports his argument in paragraphs 4–9. Why do you think his readers will or will not find the argument convincing? Which supporting details might they find most convincing? Least convincing?

Write

Write several sentences reporting what you have learned about how Etzioni uses reasons and support as an evaluative writing strategy in his essay. *Give examples* (from paragraphs 4–9) of the type of support he provides for the "imparting few skills" reason. *Write a few more sentences* explaining how convincing you think his readers will find this support.

Counterarguing

To gain credibility with their readers, writers often anticipate that some readers may resist their judgments, reasons, or support. This strategy, called *counterarguing,* involves responding to or countering readers' likely questions or objections. For example, some parents with children in high school may question Etzioni's reasons for damning an easily available source of income. A relatively poor family, for instance, might firmly oppose his judgment, seeing part-time work at McDonald's as good for high-school students who must buy their own clothes and pay for their entertainment. Other parents may object to Etzioni's comparing a fast-food job unfavorably to a job selling lemonade or delivering newspapers.

Etzioni certainly is aware that some readers have questions and objections in mind. These objections do not cause him to waver in his own judgment, as you have seen, but they do persuade him to anticipate readers' likely questions and objections and to respond to them by counterarguing. There are two basic ways to counterargue: A writer can *refute* readers' objections, arguing that they are simply wrong, or *accommodate* objections, acknowledging that they are justified but do not irreparably damage the writer's reasoning. Etzioni uses both refutation and accommodation in his counterarguments.

Analyze

1. *Reread* paragraphs 8–11, 14, and 19, where Etzioni brings up either a reader's likely objection or an alternative judgment about the worth of part-time

work. (Some alternative judgments are attributed to researchers, rather than readers, though it is likely some readers would have similar ideas.) *Underline* the alternative judgment or objection in each of these paragraphs.

2. *Choose* any two of these counterarguments, and then *look closely* at Etzioni's strategy. *Decide* first whether he refutes or accommodates the objection or alternative judgment. Then *note* how he goes about doing so.

3. *Evaluate* whether Etzioni's counterarguments are likely to convince skeptical readers to accept his views.

Write

Write several sentences identifying the objections and alternative judgments against which Etzioni counterargues. *Describe* his counterarguments, and *evaluate* how persuasive they are likely to be with his intended audience.

Establishing Credibility

The success of an evaluation depends to a large extent on readers' confidence in the writer's judgment as well as their willingness to recognize and acknowledge the writer's credibility or authority. Evaluative writers usually try to establish their credibility by showing (1) they know a lot about the subject and (2) their judgment is based on valid values and standards. Biographical information can play a role in establishing a writer's authority by providing facts about his or her educational and professional accomplishments. It is the essay itself, however, that usually tells readers what the writer knows about the subject and from where that knowledge comes.

Analyze

1. Quickly *reread* the biographical headnote and the entire essay. As you do so, *put a checkmark* next to any passages where you believe readers would find Etzioni especially credible or trustworthy, and *place a question mark* next to any passages where you think they might question his credibility.

2. *Look over* the passages you marked, then *underline* the words and bits of information that contribute to your evaluation of Etzioni's credibility with his readers.

Write

Write several sentences summarizing your analysis of Etzioni's credibility with his intended audience—parents with children in high school. *Give examples* from both the headnote and the essay to support your analysis.

■ Readings

BRAD LEMLEY

Stop Driving with Your Feet

> *Brad Lemley (b. 1943) is a journalist who has written for many magazines, journals, and newspapers, especially those that focus on science, such as* Discover *and* Science World, *and on unusual approaches to psychology and medicine. (For example, he has written about synesthesia, the topic of an essay that appears on page 436 in Chapter 7.) As a woodworker, he has published in* This Old House *and coauthored* Thos. Moser: Artistry in Wood *(2002) with cabinetmaker Thomas Moser. Lemley also races cars.*
>
> *In this essay, originally published in* Discover *in 2003, Lemley evaluates a new and potentially revolutionary type of car, the Hy-wire. A General Motors product, the Hy-wire is powered by hydrogen fuel cells and controlled completely by electrical impulses running through wires rather than by the usual kinds of mechanical connections. Notice that in contrast to Amitai Etzioni in the previous essay, Lemley is using or participating in what he is evaluating rather than just observing it as an outsider. At one point, he remarks that he is "a pain at these drive-the-concept car events," implying that he has done this sort of participant-evaluation before.*
>
> *As you read, think about your own experience with driving cars as well as your feelings about environmental issues. Would you be interested in buying a hybrid car if it cost the same as other cars? What values do you share with Lemley? Where do your values differ?*

I am driving a car that costs $5 million. I am heading toward a concrete barrier at 45 miles per hour. I can't find the brake pedal. Not good.

But a moment before I wreck one of the most expensive cars in the world, I recall that nothing about this vehicle resembles the various clunkers, hot rods, and suburban wagons I've piloted for 32 years. I can't find the brake pedal because there are no pedals. The throttle and brake are built into the steering grips: twist to accelerate, squeeze to stop. There are no mirrors, no clutch, no stick to shift, no dashboard—not much, really, but four seats and a few simple controls. The interior is as cool and spare as a Finnish loft.

I am driving the Hy-wire, General Motors's big-bet concept car, powered by hydrogen fuel cells, and as I squeeze the handlebar and avert disaster, I find myself warming up to the thing.

Automobiles have not changed much in 100 years. The "three-box" configuration has remained essentially static since the Hupmobile: engine compartment, cab, and trunk, propelled by a gasoline-powered internal combustion engine and controlled by mechanical linkages. Even as the world's automakers inch toward incorporating hydrogen and fuel cells into their vehicles, old-style thinking reigns. Typically, manufacturers pop in a fuel-cell system where the engine used to be and install a compressed-hydrogen tank in the trunk, where the fuel tank used to be, and call it good. I have driven three such cars—one each from Toyota, Honda, and Ford—and can report that the experience is almost identical to piloting each company's gas-engine counterparts. In other words, *zzzzzzz*. Is the future just a Civic with lousy trunk space?

Fortunately, GM took a different tack. "We asked, 'What would we do if we invented the automobile from scratch today, given today's technology and today's global challenges?' " says J. Byron McCormick, executive director of GM fuel-cell activities. The response was the AUTOnomy, introduced at the Detroit Auto Show in January last year. It consisted of a six-inch-thick wheeled platform (dubbed the skateboard) into which engineers squeezed the fuel-cell stack, compressed-hydrogen tanks, system controls, heat exchangers, front and rear crush zones, and inside-the-wheel electric motors—all topped by a sleek roadster shell. The idea was that all the car's controls would be "by wire," meaning that steering, brakes, throttle, everything would be controlled by electrical pulses coursing through wires instead of the conventional mélange of mechanical linkages.

But the AUTOnomy was just a prototype that wasn't drivable. Its successor, the Hy-wire, which made its debut at the Paris Auto Show last September, really is roadworthy. So recently I tooled around in this amazing car in the wet, empty parking lot of RFK Stadium in Washington, D.C.

The fact that it runs on hydrogen has gotten the most attention, but making, storing, and transporting that gas in sufficient quantities to run the world's automobiles has a dubious future. Establishing a hydrogen infrastructure depends on an unpredictable mix of technological innovation, consumer acceptance, and government incentives. No one knows when, how, or if those planets will align.

But almost everyone has missed the real innovation of the Hy-wire. It's not about fuel cells or hydrogen; it's about drive-by-wire.

After climbing into the streamlined silver-gray sedan, the first thing I noticed was that everything is adjustable. The steering console, known as the driver-control unit, slides back and forth

HY-POWER STEERING The Hy-wire's X-drive control grips, which flank a rearview video monitor, can slide on rails for instant conversion to left- or right-hand drive. The grips are electronically linked to two motors, which direct the front wheels via rack-and-pinion steering gears. "Obviously, you don't want your steering motor to fail. That's why we have two," says Nicholas Zielinski, the drive-by-wire program manager for General Motors.

on rails, as do all of the seats. Switching from left- to right-side drive—a mechanic's nightmare—can be done in seconds with a gentle push.

The next revelation was a refreshing sense of emptiness. Without   10
a box housing an engine, or a steering-wheel column, or another box comprising a trunk, the automakers were free to take glass panes right down to the bottom of the car's snout and back end. That means the driver can see the road directly in front of and in back of the car. The most tragic of car accidents—running over an unseen toddler crawling near the front or back wheels—could become history with this car. Minimalism also rules the controls: Hy-wire development engineer Jeff Wolak, sitting next to me in the front passenger seat, started the car by pressing a single power button, creating a soft whir as the fuel cells kicked in. There are just four push-button power train settings: park, neutral, drive, and reverse.

The real fun was driving entirely by hand, and it was surpris-   11
ingly easy to master. "Reaction time is quicker with your hands than with your feet," says Nicholas Zielinski, manager for GM's drive-by-wire program. "Picking up your foot, moving it over, and putting it on the pedal just can't compete." Zielinski says today's teenagers, raised on a steady diet of video games, will most likely embrace hands-only driving, but their aging parents probably won't. No problem: A drive-by-wire car could accommodate both. "It's pretty easy to make a vehicle that works either way—a gas pedal pops out of the floor or retracts if you don't want it," he says. "You could even possibly have a steering wheel on some vehicles

HY-VISIBILITY   The front end of the Hy-wire features two windshields: a large, conventional upper pane for distance and a small pane mounted in the snout for viewing objects within roughly two feet of the bumper. Side visibility is impressive, too, because engineers eliminated the post between the front and rear doors. More than 30 patents protect the vehicle's innovations. Credit for the car's name goes to 14-year-old Aleksei Dachyshyn, son of a GM executive, who aimed to capture the car's two key technologies: hydrogen fuel and by-wire controls.

and a joystick on others; it's incredibly flexible." And the single skateboard chassis can also accommodate dozens of different bodies: pickup, van, sedan, even odd arrangements such as driver-out-front in a Plexiglas bubble. Swapping bodies simply requires battening down 10 connection points and plugging the control wire into a single port in the skateboard.

I found acceleration sluggish but acceptable. The fuel-cell stack, roughly the size of a PC tower, powers a transversely mounted brushless DC motor that pumps out 60 kilowatts; by contrast, the hydrogen-fuel-cell Toyota I drove last year had an 80-kilowatt motor. So I cranked the grip all the way around.

I am a pain at these drive-the-concept-car events; I like to go fast, which makes company representatives blanch. "You might want to avoid the puddles," said Wolak politely but firmly as I

HY-CONCEPT The Hy-wire's 11-inch-thick aluminum "skateboard" platform incorporates three high-pressure hydrogen tanks made of carbon composite, 200 single fuel cells connected in series as a stack, and a three-phase asynchronous electric motor with integrated power electronics. Popping on a new body takes only a few minutes. The sedan shell could easily be exchanged for, say, a pickup truck shell. This easy interchangeability will benefit GM as well as the public, says Timothy Vail, director of distributed generation solutions. "Today, GM has 68 models of car on 50 different platforms. If we could produce maybe three skateboard platforms—small, medium, and large—that would lower our structural costs." The company could then concentrate on making a wide variety of specialized body shells to serve niche markets, Vail says.

zoomed through a huge one (the electric controllers and harness connections on this prototype aren't sealed, he explained patiently). Fine. So I went for a couple of hard turns. No problem. I found the car extraordinarily stable, as well it might be, with most of its 4,180-pound weight concentrated in the bottom of the vehicle. Flipping a Hy-wire would take real initiative.

Instead of rearview mirrors that would cause wind drag, the Hy-wire uses rear-facing cameras to beam video to a couple of high-resolution screens inside the cab. It also features low-rolling-resistance tires and regenerative braking, both designed to maximize fuel efficiency. Company officials were forthright about the challenge of range in hydrogen vehicles. "We are trying to get to 300 miles; now we are a little south of 200," says Timothy Vail, director of distributed generation solutions, part of GM's fuel-cell activities group. One way GM is looking to get there is to double the compressed-hydrogen tank's pressure from 5,000 to 10,000 pounds per square inch.

14

Meanwhile, the blessings of drive-by-wire are already visiting American cars. "Throttle-by-wire is here in production vehicles—many of our vehicles have no mechanical linkage between the gas pedal and the engine," says Zielinski, noting that this allows a computerized controller to smooth acceleration and improve mileage. Some General Motors pickups and sport-utility vehicles also use optional steer-by-wire on their rear wheels to improve the turning radius.

15

"We're learning," adds Zielinski. "And we're applying what we learn."

16

No one can say where this education will lead. None of the other large automakers seems to think skateboards are inevitable, and they may be right. Dismal sales for GM's EV1 electric car, introduced in 1996, taught the company that "consumers would not buy a vehicle that did not fit their needs, no matter how advanced, no matter how environmentally sensitive," says Beth Lowery, GM's vice president of environment and energy. The Hy-wire and its descendants will need to be affordable, safe, easy to refuel, and generally nonthreatening, or they will most likely lose out to conservatively designed hydrogen cars from other companies—assuming mass-market hydrogen cars happen at all.

17

On the other hand, Americans have a long history of embracing genuinely useful automotive innovations, and the Hy-wire definitely has its charms. Back home, stomping the creaky throttle of my aging Camry, I found I missed that twist-grip.

18

READING FOR MEANING

This section presents three activities that will help you reread Lemley's evaluative essay with a critical eye. Done in sequence, these activities lead you from a basic understanding of the selection to a more personal response to it and finally to an analysis that deepens your understanding and critical thinking about what you are reading.

Read to Comprehend

Reread the selection, and write a few sentences briefly explaining why Lemley believes the Hy-wire might be the car of the future. Also make a list of any words you do not understand—for example, *mélange* (paragraph 5), *infrastructure* (7), *chassis* (11), *regenerative* (14). Look up their meanings in a dictionary to see which definition best fits the context.

To expand your understanding of this reading, you might use one or more of the following critical reading strategies that are explained and illustrated in Appendix 1: *annotating, outlining,* and *questioning to understand and remember.*

Read to Respond

Write several paragraphs exploring your initial thoughts and feelings about "Stop Driving with Your Feet." Focus on anything that stands out for you, perhaps because it resonates with your own experience or because you find a statement puzzling.

You might consider writing about

- the problems with traditional cars, and how the Hy-wire would or would not solve those problems.

- Lemley's use of technical terms and jargon, perhaps in the context of how technical you would expect an evaluation of this subject to be.

- Lemley's personal reaction to the Hy-wire.

- how the illustrations and captions do or do not help you understand the Hy-wire.

To develop your response to Lemley's essay, you might use one or more of the following critical reading strategies that are explained and illustrated in Appendix 1: *contextualizing, looking for patterns of opposition,* and *evaluating the logic of an argument.*

Read to Analyze Underlying Assumptions

Write several paragraphs exploring one or more of the assumptions, values, and beliefs underlying Lemley's evaluative essay. As you write, explain how the assumptions are reflected in the text, as well as what you now think of them (and perhaps of your own assumptions) after rereading the selection with a critical eye.

You might consider writing about

- the values underlying Lemley's comment that the Hy-wire "really is roadworthy" (paragraph 6), perhaps in relation to what "roadworthy" means to you.

- Lemley's assumption that the fact that "[a]utomobiles have not changed much in 100 years" (4) makes them boring—as opposed to the assumption that if something remains unchanged over a long period of time, then perhaps it is working very well.

- the assumptions about car manufacturers reflected in Lemley's assertion that he is "a pain at these drive-the-concept-car events" (13).

To probe assumptions more deeply, you might use one or more of the following critical reading strategies that are explained and illustrated in Appendix 1: *reflecting on challenges to your beliefs and values, exploring the significance of figurative language,* and *looking for patterns of opposition.*

READING LIKE A WRITER
PRESENTING THE SUBJECT

The subject must be clearly identified if readers are to know what is being evaluated. Therefore, writers of evaluative essays usually begin by naming and describing their subject. As they go on to argue for and support their judgment of the subject, they may give further information about it. Evaluators need provide only enough information to give readers a context for the judgment. However, certain kinds of evaluations—such as book, television, music, and movie reviews—usually require more information than other kinds because reviewers have to assume that readers will be unfamiliar with the subject and will be reading, in part, to learn more about it. Most people are familiar with the subject of cars, but not with hybrid cars, so in reviewing the Hy-wire, Lemley must present a history of traditional cars and a description of the new car as well as present its outstanding features and drawbacks. He also needs to present the criteria for judging all of these elements.

Analyze

1. *Reread* paragraphs 3–8, and *underline* the phrases that give you information about cars. *Label* the information as "old" for traditional cars or "new" for hybrid cars.

2. Then *reread* the rest of the essay, and *circle* words that provide further description of the new Hy-wire car. *Contrast* the way information is presented in these paragraphs with the way it is presented in paragraphs 3–8.

Write

Write several sentences explaining how Lemley presents his subject to readers who are unfamiliar with it. *Give examples* from the reading to illustrate your explanation. Then *write one or two more sentences* evaluating how successful you think Lemley's presentation of the subject is for his readers, especially his strategy of being a test-driver for the new vehicle.

CONSIDERING IDEAS FOR YOUR OWN WRITING

Consider evaluating something that involves new technology or innovations in a field, as Lemley has done with hybrid cars. For example, recent innovations in architecture include houses where interior walls have been replaced with electronic fields that can shield a room from view or, with a flick of a switch, allow the room to be seen. You could also write about innovations in landscaping, in museum displays, in music, in art, in computers, or in theaters or other performance spaces. For such an evaluation, you could choose something that is completely accessible to you and with which you are familiar, or you could do some research to educate yourself. Whatever you choose, you should be able to see or hear it more than once because you will notice many more features a second or third time around.

LEIGH CHRISTY

Gehry's Disney Concert Hall

Leigh Christy, born (1973) and raised in Akron, Ohio, studied architecture at the University of Michigan and the University of California, Berkeley. She worked for architectural firms in Akron, New York City, and San Francisco before moving to Los Angeles, where she is now a designer/project architect with the firm John Friedman/Alice Kim Architects. Christy's projects include a loft renovation in Manhattan, a new housing project in San Francisco, and an elementary school addition in Los Angeles. Until putting together her thesis in her final semester of graduate school, she had never considered writing professionally. Since then, however, she has published several architectural reviews and informational pieces.

The following review was first published in December 2003 in Architecture Week <www.architectureweek.com>, *an online journal for architects and other readers interested in architectural design. In it, Christy reviews the newly opened Walt Disney Concert Hall in Los Angeles, designed by the internationally renowned architect Frank Gehry. She evaluates not only the hall's architecture but also its acoustics, landscaping, and setting.*

As you read, think about whether you have ever considered architecture as something that could be formally evaluated. When you look at a building, statue, park, garden, or other human-made structure and think "I like that" or "I don't like that," on what do you base your judgment? What criteria and values help you make such judgments?

Crowning Bunker Hill in downtown Los Angeles, the stainless steel curves of the Walt Disney Concert Hall (WDCH) by Frank Gehry shine in the Southern California sun. They shine in quick flashes glimpsed through nondescript high-rises, throwing fortuitous reflections among the shadows. The taller forms stretch up and out toward the city, while the lower forms bend down toward passersby.

The building is a stunning piece of architecture, ripe for metaphoric interpretations ranging from blooming flower to sailing ship. The main auditorium, designed by Yasuhisa Toyota of Nagata Acoustics, is being lauded for its acoustic quality. The building's very existence is a miracle of logistics and perseverance. But in the long run, the success of the WDCH will depend on what happens when its shiny novelty wears off.

EXPECTATIONS

Though largely funded privately, the $274 million WDCH is owned by the County of Los Angeles. It has been heralded as

Two views of the exterior of the Walt Disney Concert Hall from Grand Avenue, Los Angeles.

a symbol of the area's diversity and egalitarian qualities, a testament to the city's cultural arrival, and the "crown jewel" of a $1.2 billion civic redevelopment project planned for the area.

This is Frank Gehry's first major public commission in his home-town and his most anticipated project since the Guggenheim Muse-um in Bilbao. Local officials hope that the WDCH will have a "Bilbao effect" of economic rejuvenation on a much-derided downtown.   4

Whether this hope will pan out remains to be seen. In the meantime, the county and one of the occupants, the Los Angeles Philharmonic, are pulling out all the stops to make the inaugural season a success, with massive publicity efforts and three opening galas. The WDCH will likely be the defining achievement for L.A. Philharmonic music director Esa-Pekka Salonen, as well as for the responsible local officials.   5

The project took 16 years to complete, required over 30,000 architectural drawings, and cost roughly twice the originally bud-geted amount. The question on everyone's mind seems to be: is it worth it?   6

INTIMACY AND INCLUSION

In addition to the philharmonic, the 293,000-square-foot (27,000-square-meter) WDCH is also the new home for the Los Angeles Master Chorale and the Roy and Edna Disney/Cal Arts Theater. At the building's center, both literally and figuratively, sits the 2,265-seat main auditorium.   7

According to Gehry, the WDCH was designed from the inside out. The most important issues were that "the musicians could come on stage, feel at home, and hear each other" and that "the orchestra and the audience would have an intimate connection with each other." He sought to create a "synergy" through intimacy and inclusion.   8

Intimate it is. Though essentially a rectangle, one would never   9
know it to sit inside the sculpted Douglas fir and cedar auditorium. Swooping concave walls of staggered wood panels hold ter-
raced seating in the "vineyard" layout made famous in the Berlin
Philharmonic. The audience surrounds the stage, which is elevated
slightly higher than the adjacent orchestra seats. The hall feels
smaller and cozier than the number of seats might indicate.

Protesting the usual concert hall elitism, Salonen and Gehry   10
included no private boxes. While ticket prices may inhibit some
potential audience members, exclusive seating will not. Indeed,
there does not seem to be a bad seat in the house. Each location is
visually and acoustically unique.

A billowing wood ceiling hangs lightly over the space, strategi-   11
cally placed to achieve the early sound reflection that acoustician
Toyota deemed so important. The warm wood, the molded forms,
and the resultant vibrancy of sound combine to create the perception of being inside a living creature. The music is its pulse.

As some visiting performers have noted, the only drawback is   12
that the creature makes noises of its own. A dropped program, a
closing door, or a simple cough becomes part of the symphony in
this acoustically energetic hall. (Kiosks dispensing complimentary
cough drops have been added recently to the lobbies.) But this
seems a small price to pay for the ability to hear an individual flute
within the larger orchestra.

CONTROLLING CHAOS

Stepping outside the womb of the auditorium, the WDCH also   13
houses an underground parking garage, preconcert foyer, green

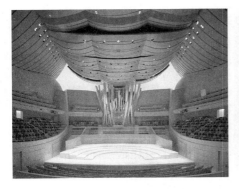

The stage and pipe organ in the main auditorium *(left)*, and the auditorium as seen from the organ *(right)*.

The entry lobby features curving walls, skylights, and columns of Douglas fir resembling tree branches.

room and support spaces, two outdoor amphitheaters, and California's smallest state park on the 3.6-acre (1.5-hectare) site.

Gehry, a self-proclaimed control freak, stated that he continually strives to "control chaos and relate that to the urban world" and that he "loves pulling these chaotic forces together." This inevitably causes some collisions at the boundaries. The resulting in-between spaces are both the most engaging and the most awkward of the project.   14

The middle zone between the central box of the auditorium and the spreading curves of the exterior walls holds many opportunities to nestle smaller spaces. The interior BP Hall (preconcert foyer) and the exterior W. M. Keck Foundation Children's Amphitheater are two inviting examples of such molded spaces. Both are swelling extensions of circulation paths, carved out of recesses in the walls, with comfortable yet reverential proportions.   15

The BP Hall mimics the finishes of the main auditorium but elegantly substitutes acoustical wood panels for the Douglas fir. Undulating walls reach up to the roof, drawing light from one of the building's four large skylights. Here is one of the few places where one can simultaneously experience the warmth of the interior paneling, the strength of the steel structure, and the California sunlight. This area, for preconcert gatherings and small performances, is one of the most intriguing of the project.   16

A public garden wraps around the western and southern sides of the site.

Open daily to the public, the entry lobby and adjacent restau-   17
rant, cafe, and gift shop—the latter three interiors designed by
local architect Hagy Belzberg of Belzberg Architects—greet the
city by spilling out onto Grand Avenue through a large expanse of
transparent doors and windows.

Numerous video screens and an overhead sound system con-   18
nect the open lobby with the orchestra during both performances
and rehearsals. Acting as the conduit between the city and the
symphony, the entry lobby bustles with energy day and night.

Many of the other lobbies and passages in the middle zone,   19
however, simply feel like odd-angled leftover spaces hiding potential sectional wonders. The lack of clear organization may be egalitarian, but the control of chaos slips a bit here.

The exterior in-betweens, on the other hand, are extraordinary.   20
The public garden wraps around the western and southern sides of
the site, providing panoramic views of the city while maintaining
a sense of enclosure.

The site is filled with a variety of trees, shrubs, and perennials—   21
all selected to ensure that something will be in bloom year-round.
Meanwhile, the curved exterior corridors circumscribing the
building create unique spatial experiences reminiscent of Richard
Serra sculptures.

REVERBERATIONS

Handprints of curious visitors are already beginning to mute   22
the shine of the steel, the orchestra has begun to adjust to the viva-
cious auditorium, and press attention is waning. But the question
remains: is it worth it?

As architecture, the stainless steel exterior forms a stunning   23
organic sculpture set on a deftly planned base of public spaces. As
a concert hall, the rich wood interior allows musicians and listeners to dwell inside an instrument of exquisite craftsmanship. As a
civic symbol, its very existence is a testament to the commitment
of local planners and developers.

Even if the neighborhood never meets the city's utopian expec-   24
tations, and despite the smattering of awkward spaces and outrageous floral fabrics, the answer remains a resounding yes. To dwell
on those secondary issues would be to miss a more important
sensory adventure.

READING FOR MEANING

This section presents three activities that will help you reread Christy's evaluative essay with a critical eye. Done in sequence, these activities lead you from a
basic understanding of the selection to a more personal response to it and finally
to an analysis that deepens your understanding and critical thinking about what
you are reading.

Read to Comprehend

Reread the selection, and write a few sentences briefly explaining the characteristics of the new Walt Disney Concert Hall that make it, according to
Christy, "worth it" (paragraphs 6 and 22). Also make a list of any words you do
not understand—for example, *nondescript* (paragraph 1), *fortuitous* (1), *lauded* (2),
logistics (2), *billowing* (11). Look up their meanings in a dictionary to see which
definition best fits the context.

To expand your understanding of this reading, you might use one or more of
the following critical reading strategies that are explained and illustrated in
Appendix 1: *previewing, paraphrasing,* or *questioning to understand and remember.*

Read to Respond

Write several paragraphs exploring your initial thoughts and feelings about
"Gehry's Disney Concert Hall." Focus on anything that stands out for you, perhaps because it resonates with your own experience or because you find a statement puzzling.

You might consider writing about

- your reaction to the writer's focus on architecture.

- your own experience with performance spaces or with buildings that are
  integrated into a neighborhood or park system, and how your experience
  affects your reaction to Christy's evaluation.

- the city planners' hopes for the "Bilbao effect" (paragraph 4), in which another project by architect Frank Gehry, the Guggenheim Museum, transformed a small city (Bilbao) in northern Spain into a thriving tourist destination.

- Christy's description of the main auditorium as a "living creature" (11).

- how the photographs and captions enhance (or why they do not enhance) Christy's text.

To develop your response to Christy's evaluation, you might use one or both of the following critical reading strategies that are explained and illustrated in Appendix 1: *contextualizing* and *exploring the significance of figurative language.*

Read to Analyze Underlying Assumptions

Write several paragraphs exploring one or more of the assumptions, values, and beliefs underlying Christy's evaluation. As you write, explain how the assumptions are reflected in the text, as well as what you now think of them (and perhaps of your own assumptions) after rereading the selection with a critical eye.
You might consider writing about

- the values and assumptions of those who herald the hall "as a symbol of the area's diversity and egalitarian qualities, a testament to the city's cultural arrival, and the 'crown jewel' of a . . . civic redevelopment project" (paragraph 3).

- what the headings for some of the sections imply about the values of the architect, and how these are shown in the review.

- what Christy assumes about her readers when she describes the different woods on the inside of the hall and the different landscaping on the outside.

- how Christy feels about the use of light, especially in paragraph 16.

To probe assumptions more deeply, you might use one or both of the following critical reading strategies that are explained and illustrated in Appendix 1: *judging the writer's credibility* and *performing a Toulmin analysis.*

READING LIKE A WRITER
ESTABLISHING CREDIBILITY

Establishing credibility is particularly important for writers of evaluations because they want the reader to accept the validity of their judgments. To make a sound judgment, writers should demonstrate that they are knowledgeable about the subject and that their values and standards are accepted by others in the field. Readers can learn about the writer's credibility from bio-graphical information that accompanies the text, from the reputation of the publication where it appeared or the publisher or group that published it, and from information within the text that testifies to the knowledge and values of the writer.

Analyze

1. *Reread* paragraphs 2, 4, 5, 8, 10, 14, 15, 17, and 21. *Underline* the names of the people Christy mentions, and *add a brief phrase* about who they are.

2. *Reread* paragraphs 3, 7, 13, and 23. *Note* the additional "insider" information Christy provides.

Write

Write several sentences analyzing how Christy establishes her credibility as a reviewer of architecture. *Give examples* from the reading. Then *write a few more sentences* analyzing her credibility as a reviewer of the Walt Disney Concert Hall.

CONSIDERING IDEAS FOR YOUR OWN WRITING

Christy's evaluation of the Walt Disney Concert Hall suggests the possibility of evaluating architectural or landscape structures in your surroundings. For example, you might evaluate a distinctive building, a local or regional park, a bike or running trail, or a golf course or stadium, considering its history, archi-tectural features, and urban, suburban, or rural setting. How could you interest your readers in the features of your subject, whether architecture or landscape? For what reasons would you praise or criticize its features? You could support these reasons convincingly only if you have considerable experience with what you are evaluating, so you should choose something with which you are famil-iar. Even so, you may have to do some research to deepen your knowledge of the subject.

Alternatively, you could consider evaluating music in any of its many forms, such as a CD, a movie score, the music of a TV program, a Broadway (or off-Broadway) show, or another kind of show like *Riverdance* or *Cirque du Soleil*. Or you could evaluate the technology that brings you music, such as a sound system, an iPod or similar digital storage system, or a satellite radio system for an auto-mobile. You could also evaluate a particular performance, such as by a conduc-tor, an orchestra, or a musician on stage.

TY BURR

King *Has Pageantry, Purpose, but It's Not Quite the Greatest Show on Middle-Earth*

Ty Burr (b. 1957), a film critic for the Boston Globe *since 2002, has also worked for* Entertainment Weekly *as chief video critic and also covered film, music, theater, books, and the Internet. After studying film at Dartmouth College and New York University, he began his career at Home Box Office in the 1980s, serving as an in-house "film evaluator" and helping to put Corey Haim's films on Cinemax. Burr has written two books,* The Hundred Greatest Stars of All Time *(1998) and* The Hundred Greatest Movies of All Time *(1999), as well as numerous articles on film and other subjects for the* New York Times, Spin, *and the* Boston Phoenix, *among other publications.*

The following review of The Lord of the Rings: The Return of the King *was published in the* Boston Globe *just before the movie's release in 2003. Like the two previous films in the trilogy that Burr mentions, it is based on the book trilogy* The Lord of the Rings *by J. R. R. Tolkien, a fantasy about an imaginary world that was first published in the 1950s. Burr seems to assume that his audience is at least somewhat familiar with the book trilogy, since he mentions the author in the last paragraph using only his last name, as well as with the two previous parts of the film trilogy. It is clear that Burr himself has seen the two previous movies in the series and judges* King *based on his opinion of them as well as on its own merit.*

As you read, notice how Burr, even though he thinks highly of producer Peter Jackson's newest movie, tempers his judgment by pointing out some of the drawbacks that he finds disappointing. If you have seen any of the films in the Lord of the Rings *trilogy, compare Burr's judgments to your own.*

Maybe it's just hobbit fatigue. 1

The Lord of the Rings: The Return of the King delivers on all the 2
mighty expectations Peter Jackson created in *The Fellowship of the Ring* and *The Two Towers*. Armies clash, towers crash, Middle-earth is made free once more. Yet where many viewers staggered out of *Towers* last year in a daze of exaltation, *Return* may leave one overwhelmed and exhausted. Hopes have been awfully high—unfairly high—for this crowning chapter, and a lot of us have been devoutly wishing for a grand slam. Only in that context can an inside-the-park home run be viewed with faint disappointment.

Make no mistake: *The Return of the King* unfurls with the sprawl- 3
ing pageantry of the first two installments, movies in which Jackson

reclaimed the fantasy epic as a source of headlong astonishment. Tolkien purists will find plenty to fault with the collapsing, collating, and streamlining that has been done to the book, but with one exception—the missing passages in which Aragorn (Viggo Mortensen) truly becomes a king out of legend—*King* is a shapelier movie for it. Those audiences who don't have halberds to grind and who possess rear ends of steel and a taste for declamatory heroics will find themselves rewarded.

The Two Towers began with that stunner of a sequence in which Gandalf battled the Balrog all the way down to the roots of the mountains. *The Return of the King* opens with a smaller back story: the moment in which a hobbitlike creature named Smeagol (Andy Serkis) sees his friend pull a gold ring out of a river and kills him for it. Through a series of graceful, unforgiving cuts, we see Smeagol degenerate over the centuries into Gollum, bringing us into the film's present and leaving Gollum, Frodo (Elijah Wood), and Sam (Sean Astin) at the edge of Mordor.

The Fellowship is fully scattered, and the uncommitted viewer probably needs a score card to keep track. Very well. Now that the armies of men have won the day at Helm's Deep and Treebeard's Ents have brought down Saruman's tower, Gandalf (Ian McKellen) and Pippin (Billy Boyd) ride to the city of Minas Tirith in Gondor to warn the surly steward Denethor (John Noble) of the approach of Sauron's orcs. Merry (Dominic Monaghan) stays behind in Rohan while King Theoden (Bernard Hill) and Eomer (Karl Urban) put their country back in order and Eowyn (Miranda Otto) makes puppy-eyes at Aragorn. Legolas (Orlando Bloom) and Gimli (John Rhys-Davies) hang about with little to do, a problem in the book that's exacerbated in the movie (the Dwarf in particular is limited to comic relief, as though Buddy Hackett had been brought on and handed a battle-ax).

That's the chessboard before Jackson starts moving his pieces around, and there is, in fact, something dutiful about the way *King* marches to its inexorable Mount Doom. If *Fellowship* established the world of Middle-earth and the stakes at play, and *Towers* brought the story out of the Shire and onto the endless fields of battle, the final film thunders toward its resolution without looking to either side. The sense of purpose is impressive, but all that solemnity begins to pall over the backstretch.

Jackson does pause to give us wonders, but just barely. The sequence in which the beacon fires from Gondor to Rohan are lit—across hundreds of miles, from snowy peak to peak—plays like Maxfield Parrish on steroids, and Aragorn's foray along the

4

5

6

7

Paths of the Dead culminates in a meeting with a ghost army that flickers like a nightmare aurora borealis.

Minas Tirith itself is a gasp-inducing CGI invention: a ziggurat jutting onto the plains like a massive stone ship. Sam and Frodo's adventures in Shelob's Lair (carried over from the second novel) play out with skittery monster-movie dread, and if the battle of the Pelennor Fields, with its giant elephants clomping through the action, strikes some as reminiscent of *The Empire Strikes Back*, Jackson has directed the scene with the clarity of a battle map.

The human dimension is what goes missing amid all the illuminated heroism. Not that Tolkien cared two crumpets for psychology, but there was a measure of classic tragedy in Denethor's attempts to drag surviving son Faramir (David Wenham) down with him to hopelessness and death, and that's been reduced to a Lifetime movie moment here. Doubly so for the strained relationship between elven Arwen (Liv Tyler) and her father, Elrond (Hugo Weaving), and triply so for Aragorn's coming into his sense of kingship.

Humanity is accorded mostly to the hobbits, and mostly because Frodo and Sam have nothing to do but suffer on the long road to the Cracks of Doom. There isn't a bad performance anywhere in these films, but Elijah Wood comes out of *The Lord of the Rings* with extra laurels, so wearily and sorrowfully does the actor carry the growing weight of his character's mission. Many are wounded in *The Return of the King* but only Frodo is truly scarred, and only in him are you struck by the cost of what is lost.

There are signs of haste in some of the special effects in *King*, and there's also the sense that the director just doesn't want to let go: Even without the events in the book's penultimate "Scouring of the Shire" chapter, the film's final scenes feel like a road that does, in fact, go on forever. You can't blame Jackson, since the trilogy represents both the realization of a long-held dream and possibly the apex of his career: If *King* isn't everything I'd hoped, the filmmaker still deserves an Oscar for the combination of artistry and orneriness it took to get the entire project made.

Still, how do you follow a thing like this? Jackson will next tackle a remake of *King Kong*, but he has announced future plans to film *The Hobbit*—no word yet on *The Silmarillion* or *Farmer Giles of Ham*. Clearly, the man strides through Tolkien's world with great joy. Yet what I felt when the lights came up at the end of this visionary, titanic, relentless experience was something different: a strange relief that it was, at last, over.

READING FOR MEANING

This section presents three activities that will help you reread Burr's film review with a critical eye. Done in sequence, these activities lead you from a basic understanding of the selection to a more personal response to it and finally to an analysis that deepens your understanding and critical thinking about what you are reading.

Read to Comprehend

Reread the selection, and write a few sentences briefly explaining the strong and weak points of *The Lord of the Rings: The Return of the King,* according to Burr. Also make a list of any words you do not understand—for example, *declamatory* (paragraph 3), *laurels* (10), *penultimate* (11). Look up their meanings in a dictionary to see which definition best fits the context.

To expand your understanding of this reading, you might use one or more of the following critical reading strategies that are explained and illustrated in Appendix 1: *outlining, summarizing,* and *contextualizing.*

Read to Respond

Write several paragraphs exploring your initial thoughts and feelings about Burr's film review. Focus on anything that stands out for you, perhaps because it resonates with your own experience or because you find a statement puzzling.

You might consider writing about

- what Burr means when he says that the "human dimension is what goes missing amid all the illuminated heroism" (paragraph 9).

- why Burr starts his essay with the one-sentence paragraph "Maybe it's just hobbit fatigue."

- why Burr includes two full paragraphs (4 and 5) of background information.

- Burr's use of figurative language, such as the grand slam/home run (2) and the chessboard (6).

- your opinion of *The Lord of the Rings: The Return of the King,* as compared with Burr's evaluation.

- how easy or difficult it is to follow Burr's review if you have not read *The Lord of the Rings* or seen the earlier films based on the books.

To develop your response to Burr's evaluation, you might use one or both of the following critical reading strategies that are explained and illustrated in Appendix 1: *contextualizing* and *exploring the significance of figurative language.*

Read to Analyze Underlying Assumptions

Write several paragraphs exploring one or more of the assumptions, values, and beliefs underlying Burr's film review. As you write, explain how the assumptions are reflected in the text, as well as what you now think of them (and perhaps of your own assumptions) after rereading the selection with a critical eye.

You might consider writing about

- the values reflected in the comment that "the filmmaker . . . deserves an Oscar for the combination of artistry and orneriness it took to get the entire project made" (paragraph 11).

- what Burr wishes for when he mentions that some of the characters "hang about with little to do, a problem in the book that's exacerbated in the movie" (5).

- what Burr seems to value in acting, as he describes it in paragraph 10.

- the meaning of the examples Burr uses to illustrate his "faint disappointment" (2).

To probe assumptions more deeply, you might use one or more of the following critical reading strategies that are explained and illustrated in Appendix 1: *reflecting on challenges to your beliefs and values, exploring the significance of figurative language,* and *looking for patterns of opposition.*

READING LIKE A WRITER
ASSERTING AN OVERALL JUDGMENT BY USING FIGURATIVE LANGUAGE

Writers of evaluations must assert an overall judgment about the subject, although sometimes the judgment is implied rather than stated explicitly. Often the judgment is not all positive or all negative—in fact, many overall judgments are balanced, as the writer finds both good and bad elements in whatever is being evaluated. Usually the writer will assert the overall judgment near the beginning of the evaluation, in the form of a thesis statement, and then refer to it in various ways later on.

One common way to express an overall judgment is by comparing the subject to another subject of the same kind or to something else entirely, using figurative language. Throughout his review, Burr uses figurative language to illustrate his overall judgment of *The Lord of the Rings: The Return of the King.* In his second paragraph, he notes that hopes have been high for a "grand slam" conclusion to the *Lord of the Rings* trilogy but that *The Return of the King* provides only "an inside-the-park home run." The effect of this figurative language—an analogy to baseball, in this case—is to help readers understand that in Burr's opinion the movie is very, very good (a home run), but even so, it falls short of being the best (a grand slam). Even the title, with "It's Not Quite the Greatest

Show on Middle-Earth," is an allusion to *The Greatest Show on Earth,* a movie from the 1950s that was highly touted. Often comparing one thing to another in this way makes it easier for readers to understand the values and beliefs of the writer and the overall judgment that the writer is making about the subject.

Analyze

1. *Reread* paragraphs 1–3, 5, 6, and 11. *Underline* each example of figurative language you can find.

2. *Notice* the effect this figurative language has on your understanding of Burr's overall judgment of the movie.

Write

Write several sentences explaining how figurative language both illuminates Burr's overall judgment of the film and colors your own perception of it.

CONSIDERING IDEAS FOR YOUR OWN WRITING

Consider writing an evaluation of a film, television show, or other visual or media event. You could review another movie produced by Peter Jackson, movies in this genre, or movies in any other genre that you find appealing. Try to choose a genre with which you are already familiar; your evaluation will be richer because of your greater knowledge. Movies are often divided into genres, such as action, drama, comedy, adventure, fantasy, thriller, docudrama, and so on; there are also subgenres, such as Japanese anime (animation) films. Remember that you do not have to write an all-positive or all-negative evaluation; a mixed review can be just as valuable to readers.

A SPECIAL READING STRATEGY

Comparing and Contrasting Related Readings: Burr's and Berardinelli's Reviews of The Lord of the Rings: The Return of the King

Comparing and contrasting related readings is a critical reading strategy useful both in reading for meaning and in reading like a writer. This strategy is particularly applicable when writers present similar or identical subjects, as is the case in the movie reviews in this chapter by

Ty Burr (p. 358) and James Berardinelli (p. 365). Both writers offer highly favorable evaluations of *The Lord of the Rings: The Return of the King*, but they focus on different aspects of the film and come to different conclusions about its merits. To compare and contrast these two reviews, think about issues such as these:

- Compare Burr's mostly positive but mixed assessment of the film with Berardinelli's enthusiastic, even extravagant endorsement. What are the reasons for the difference? Are the two reviewers not giving the same importance to certain elements of the movie? Are their values and beliefs different?

- Compare the placement of the paragraphs each author devotes to Tolkien's readers, the movie viewers who will care whether the movie version follows the book. Does the difference in placement suggest a difference in how important the authors consider this aspect of the movie to be? Why or why not?

See Appendix 1 for detailed guidelines on using the comparing and contrasting related readings strategy.

JAMES BERARDINELLI

Review of The Lord of the Rings: The Return of the King

> *James Berardinelli (b. 1967) has an unusual background for a film critic in that he earned both bachelor's and master's degrees in electrical engineering and still makes his living in that field. As a child, he did not attend many movies, but he became interested in film in college, and, now that he is a reviewer, he sees over two hundred theatrical releases each year.*
>
> *Berardinelli's review of* The Lord of the Rings: The Return of the King *originally appeared in 2003 on his Web site at <http://movie -reviews.colossus.net/movies/l/lotr3.html>, one of the most highly respected sites for online film criticism. He has published an encyclopedia of his reviews,* ReelViews: The Ultimate Guide to the Best Modern Movies on DVD and Video *(2003), and has written for the* Chicago Sun-Times, Playboy.com, *and other Internet journals.*
>
> *As you read, think about the kinds of movies you like and how your preferences influence your judgments about any movie you see. Also think about whether or how much reviews influence your decision about whether to see a movie and how you react to it. Do you trust any particular reviewers (or sources of reviews) more than others? If so, why?*

According to the calendar, Christmas is December 25. According to the movie release schedule, it's December 17. There can be no greater gift for a movie lover than the one bestowed upon audiences by Peter Jackson, whose *The Lord of the Rings: The Return of the King* is not only the best movie of 2003, but the crowning cinematic achievement of the past several years. In fact, labeling this as a "movie" is almost an injustice. This is an experience of epic scope and grandeur, amazing emotional power, and relentless momentum. 1

One could be forgiven for initially approaching *The Return of the King* with a little trepidation. As good as the first two films, *The Fellowship of the Ring* and *The Two Towers,* are (in either their theatrical or extended DVD versions), movie history is littered with occasions when trilogy conclusions have crashed and burned. *Return of the Jedi. Godfather III. The Matrix Revolutions.* And so on . . . Yet, with *The Return of the King,* Jackson has done more than just bucked the trend. Not only is this motion picture an entirely worthy conclusion to the landmark trilogy, but it's better than its predecessors. Somehow, Jackson has managed to synthesize what worked in *The Fellowship of the Ring* and *The Two Towers,* 2 while siphoning off the less successful elements. The result is amazing. Taken as a whole, there is nothing out there today that can come close to comparing to *The Lord of the Rings.*

As with *The Two Towers,* some form of previous knowledge of *The Lord of the Rings* is necessary. However, with the earlier chapters readily available on DVD, anyone with the desire can be prepared. *The Return of the King* opens where *The Two Towers* ended, with hobbits Frodo (Elijah Wood) and Sam (Sean Astin) and the creature Gollum (Andy Serkis) approaching the dark land of Mordor. Meanwhile, the company of Gandalf the wizard (Ian McKellen), Aragorn the ranger (Viggo Mortensen), Legolas the elf (Orlando Bloom), and Gimli the dwarf (John Rhys-Davies) reunite with their hobbit friends Pippin (Billy Boyd) and Merry (Dominic Monaghan) in the wake of the battle of Isengard. From there, the film follows two branches. The first tracks Frodo's progress as the increasingly haunted and weary ringbearer attempts to make his way to Mount Doom. Along the way, he is burdened by betrayal and paranoia, and must face a deadly giant spider called Shelob. Meanwhile, Gandalf and Pippin head to the city of Minas Tirith to warn them against a coming invasion, while Aragorn prepares to announce himself as Isildur's heir, the returned king of Gondor.

The slowest portions of *The Return of the King* occur early in the proceedings, as Jackson re-establishes the characters. From there, it's a slow, steady buildup to a rousing climax. The experience is so immersive that I found myself in the middle of the Battle of the Pelennor Fields along with the heroes, rooting for them—even though I knew how things were going to turn out! Along the way, there are moments of genuine pathos that draw a tear from the eye; times of triumph that cause the heart to soar; instances of overwhelming tension that cause the adrenaline to surge; and images of spectacle that make the jaw drop. The pace is unflagging—once Jackson has us, he doesn't let go. When the movie was over, I couldn't believe that 3-1/4 hours had passed.

Although it's unfair to characterize the film as a collection of great moments—the character arcs and overall narrative are too strong for that—it is nevertheless impossible to deny the power of many individual scenes. One of Jackson's most notable contributions is that he directs the film with the intention that certain instances will raise nape hairs. It's the "wow" factor, and it is frequently repeated. Gene Siskel once argued that a great film needs three memorable scenes to go along with no bad ones. *The Return of the King* exceeds that criteria by a considerable amount.

I can think of three key reasons why this film is stronger than   6
the earlier chapters. The first is that this is the conclusion—the
resolution we have eagerly awaited for what seems like more than
two years. The second is that Jackson, like Tolkien, saved the best
for last. As impressive as the Battle of Helm's Deep was, it is
dwarfed by the Siege of Minas Tirith and the Battle of the Pelennor Fields. And Frodo's struggles have become magnified. Jackson
views elements of the hobbit's travails as operatic (witness the
choral aspects of Howard Shore's score). Finally, there's the simple
fact that we have gotten to know the characters. By now, they have
been with us for two years and six hours of screen time (over seven
if you count the DVD special editions).

For those who despise truncated endings, Jackson has a treat in   7
store. *The Return of the King* ends with a 20-minute epilogue that
chronicles events after the War of the Ring, going as much as four
years into the future and tying up nearly every possible loose end.
The film concludes on exactly the same note as the book (in fact,
with the same line), and, while the final chapter of the trilogy is
as satisfying as it could possibly be, there's still a vague sense of
melancholy when "The End" appears on the screen, because it
means that these adventures are over.

Tolkien purists will be as disgruntled with *The Return of the*   8
King as they were with *The Fellowship of the Ring* and *The Two*
Towers, but this isn't made for them. This is Tolkien's saga as filtered through Jackson's fertile imagination, not some dry, slavishly
faithful adaptation (although it is probably as true to the books in
both spirit and narrative as any movie version could be). If you
want rigorous adherence to the text, wait for the next *Harry Potter*
movie. It's hard to fault the director for many of his choices. There
are some omissions in *The Return of the King*. A couple—Saruman's
death at the hands of Wormtongue and the Houses of Healing—
were cut due to time constraints, but will appear on the DVD.
Another, "The Scouring of the Shire," was not filmed. While that
may be a viable way to end the book, it is too anticlimactic for a
movie, and, as such, is better excised.

The acting shines through more in *The Return of the King* than   9
in the other films. Elijah Wood is excellent as Frodo, a shell of the
cheerful hobbit he once was. Sean Astin transforms Sam into a
fierce knight protector, defending his master against the treacher-
ous Gollum, the terrifying Shelob, and the forces of Mordor. Viggo
Mortensen gives Aragorn his fullest opportunity to be seen as a
three-dimensional hero. Newcomer John Noble, as Denethor, the
Protector of Gondor, displays madness laced with cunning. Orlando Bloom and John Rhys-Davies have less to do, but provide us

with a little comedic banter as well as some more serious moments. Miranda Otto's Eowyn is as sharp and fierce as any man, and far better looking. Billy Boyd and Dominic Monaghan are given a chance to flesh out Pippin and Merry. Cate Blanchett, Liv Tyler, Hugo Weaving, and Ian Holm all make brief appearances.

But the two I must single out are Ian McKellen and Andy Serkis. For the first time, Gandalf is on screen for a significant portion of time (rather than somewhere in the distance fighting a balrog, trapped by Saruman, or rounding up the Riders of Rohan). McKellen presents the wizard as a man of great wisdom, little patience, and incomparable battle skill. Using a sword and staff instead of magic, Gandalf proceeds to kick butt big-time. In fantasy mythology, Gandalf is second only to Merlin when it comes to famous sorcerers. On screen, McKellen's wizard is second to none.   10

For most of the film, Serkis is heard but only partially seen—Gollum is a computer-generated creature that gets its cues from Serkis' body movements. (Although there is one flashback in which Serkis plays the pre-corrupted Smeagol.) The subtlety of Gollum's movements and expressions is so astonishing that it's difficult to believe this isn't a real creature. Serkis deserves a lion's share of the credit, since Gollum is as much his creation as it is that of the animators. Although a long shot, Serkis is deserving of some sort of awards credit.   11

Expectedly, the special effects set a new standard. The CGI [computer-generated imagery] participants of the major battles look more like real combatants than cartoonish computer creations. The locations, set design, and costumes are without flaw. By building many of the elaborate locales, Jackson achieves a sense of verisimilitude that he might not have attained by relying more heavily on computers. And composer Howard Shore's score is perfectly wed to the visuals, being alternately bombastic and delicate, as circumstances dictate.   12

Leaving Middle Earth, Jackson is now headed for Skull Island and a remake of *King Kong* that already has me excited. He has not ruled out a return to this fantasy world—he would like to make *The Hobbit* with some of the same actors, if the complicated rights issues surrounding the prequel can be straightened out. In the meantime, he has given us a trilogy of films to savor and remember. *The Lord of the Rings* will go down in cinematic lore as a milestone. It has legitimatized fantasy like no other production and has shown that it is possible for studio executives to realize huge gains when taking huge risks. (Had *The Lord of the Rings* failed, New Line Cinema would have gone down with it.) History will show   13 the importance of *The Lord of the Rings*. The present illustrates its broad appeal and undeniable critical and commercial success. For many, the release of *The Return of the King* is the event of the year. And this is one time when the product is good enough to weather the storm of hype. This ring is golden.

READING FOR MEANING

This section presents three activities that will help you reread Berardinelli's film review with a critical eye. Done in sequence, these activities lead you from a basic understanding of the selection to a more personal response to it and finally to an analysis that deepens your understanding and critical thinking about what you are reading.

Read to Comprehend

Reread the selection, and write a few sentences briefly explaining the reasons Berardinelli gives for his judgment that *The Lord of the Rings: The Return of the King* "is not only the best movie of 2003, but the crowning cinematic achievement of the past several years" (paragraph 1). Also make a list of any words you do not understand—for example, *trepidation* (paragraph 2), *siphoning off* (2), *immersive* (4), *verisimilitude* (12). Look up their meanings in a dictionary to see which definition best fits the context.

To expand your understanding of this reading, you might use one or more of the following critical reading strategies that are explained and illustrated in Appendix 1: *outlining, synthesizing,* and *contextualizing.*

Read to Respond

Write several paragraphs exploring your initial thoughts and feelings about Berardinelli's film review. Focus on anything that stands out for you, perhaps because it resonates with your own experience or because you find a statement puzzling.

You might consider writing about

- the reasons Berardinelli offers for believing this third film in the trilogy "is stronger than the earlier" ones (paragraph 6).

- the vocabulary Berardinelli uses to describe the movie, such as the patterns in his use of adjectives.

- the writer's tone of unqualified praise for every aspect of the movie.

- your own response to the film, compared to Berardinelli's.

To develop your response to Berardinelli's film review, you might use one or more of the following critical reading strategies that are explained and illustrated in Appendix 1: *exploring the significance of figurative language, evaluating the logic of an argument,* and *comparing and contrasting related readings.*

Read to Analyze Underlying Assumptions

Write several paragraphs exploring one or more of the assumptions, values, and beliefs underlying Berardinelli's film review. As you write, explain how the assumptions are reflected in the text, as well as what you now think of them (and perhaps of your own assumptions) after rereading the selection with a critical eye.

You might consider writing about

- what Berardinelli means when he says the experience of watching this movie is "immersive" (paragraph 4).

- why the writer points out that the movie is "not some dry, slavishly faithful adaptation" of Tolkien's book (8).

- the kind of acting Berardinelli seems to value (9–11).

To probe assumptions more deeply, you might use one or more of the following critical reading strategies that are explained and illustrated in Appendix 1: *reflecting on challenges to your beliefs and values, exploring the significance of figurative language, recognizing emotional manipulation,* and *comparing and contrasting related readings.*

READING LIKE A WRITER
GIVING REASONS AND SUPPORT

At the center of every evaluation are the writer's reasons for making a judgment and the support for those reasons. The reasons should be appropriate for evaluating the subject, and they should be convincing to readers. Furthermore, the reasons should be visible: You do not want readers to miss them. As a writer, you make reasons visible by cueing them strongly—for example, by putting them at the beginnings of paragraphs. Berardinelli offers several reasons to support the high opinion he has of *The Lord of the Rings: The Return of the King,* and he attempts to support each reason.

Analyze

1. *Underline* the reasons Berardinelli gives in paragraph 1 for reviewing *The Lord of the Rings: The Return of the King* so positively. *Look* at the last sentence in particular.

2. *Notice* how, in the following paragraphs, Berardinelli tries to support (to argue for) each of the reasons you have identified.

3. *Consider* whether Berardinelli's reasons are likely to seem appropriate and believable to his readers. Then *decide* whether you think the support he offers is convincing. What do you find most and least convincing about the reasons and support he offers?

Write

Write several sentences explaining what you have learned about how Berardinelli uses reasons and support to justify his evaluation of *The Lord of the Rings: The Return of the King. Give examples* from the reading. Then *write a few more sentences* evaluating how successfully Berardinelli supports his judgment.

CONSIDERING IDEAS FOR YOUR OWN WRITING

You could compare and contrast the two reviews of *The Lord of the Rings: The Return of the King* by Berardinelli and Burr, or you could read other reviews of the film and compare those to one or both of these reviews. Or you could write an evaluation of one of these reviews, judging it on the criteria established in this chapter for a successful evaluation, or even write your own review of this or another movie you are—or could become—knowledgeable about. Alternatively, you could write an evaluation of another kind of text—not a movie, but a book, a magazine or journal that has a clearly defined audience (such as *Car and Driver* or *Seventeen*), or an advertisement.

CHRISTINE ROMANO

"Children Need to Play, Not Compete," by Jessica Statsky: An Evaluation

> *Christine Romano wrote the following essay when she was a first-year college student. In it she evaluates a position paper written by another student, Jessica Statsky's "Children Need to Play, Not Compete," which appears in Chapter 9 of this book (pp. 627–31). Romano focuses not on the writing strategies or basic features of this position paper but rather on its logic—on whether the argument is likely to convince the intended readers. She evaluates the logic of the argument according to the standards presented in Appendix 1 (pp. 675–79). You might want to review these standards before you read Romano's evaluation. Also, if you have not read Statsky's essay, you might want to do so now, thinking about what seems most and least convincing to you about her argument that competitive sports can be harmful to young children.*

Parents of young children have a lot to worry about and to hope for. In "Children Need to Play, Not Compete," Jessica Statsky appeals to their worries and hopes in order to convince them that organized competitive sports may harm their children physically and psychologically. Statsky states her thesis clearly and fully forecasts the reasons she will offer to justify her position: Besides causing physical and psychological harm, competitive sports discourage young people from becoming players and fans when they are older and inevitably put parents' needs and fantasies ahead of children's welfare. Statsky also carefully defines her key terms. By *sports,* for example, she means to include both contact and non-contact sports that emphasize competition. The sports may be organized locally at schools or summer sports camps or nationally, as in the examples of Peewee Football and Little League Baseball. She is concerned only with children six to twelve years of age.

In this essay, I will evaluate the logic of Statsky's argument, considering whether the support for her thesis is appropriate, believable, consistent, and complete. While her logic *is* appropriate, believable, and consistent, her argument also has weaknesses: it seems incomplete because it neglects to anticipate parents' predictable questions and objections, and because it fails to support certain parts fully.

Statsky provides appropriate support for her thesis. Throughout her essay, she relies for support on different kinds of information (she cites twelve separate sources, including books, newspapers,

1

2

3

and Web sites). Her quotations, examples, and statistics all support the reasons she believes competitive sports are bad for children. For example, in paragraph 3, Statsky offers the reason that "overly competitive sports" may damage children's growing bodies and that contact sports, in particular, may be especially hazardous. She supports this reason by paraphrasing Koppett that muscle strain or even lifelong injury may result when a twelve-year-old throws curve balls. She then quotes Tutko on the dangers of tackle football. The opinions of both experts are obviously appropriate. They are relevant to her reason, and we can easily imagine that they would worry many parents.

Not only is Statsky's support appropriate but it is also believable. Statsky quotes or summarizes authorities to support her argument in paragraphs 3–6, 8, 9, and 11. The question is whether readers would find these authorities believable or credible. Since Statsky relies almost entirely on authorities to support her argument, readers must believe these authorities for her argument to succeed. I have not read Statsky's sources, but I think there are good reasons to consider them authoritative. First of all, the newspaper authors she quotes write for two of America's most respected newspapers, the *New York Times* and the *Los Angeles Times*. These newspapers are read across the country by political leaders and financial experts and by people interested in the arts and popular culture. Both have sports reporters who not only report on sports events but also take a critical look at sports issues. In addition, both newspapers have reporters who specialize in children's health and education. Second, Statsky gives background information about the authorities she quotes, information intended to increase the person's believability in the eyes of parents of young children. In paragraph 3, she tells readers that Thomas Tutko is "a psychology professor at San Jose State University and coauthor of the book *Winning Is Everything and Other American Myths.*" In paragraph 5, she announces that Martin Rablovsky is "a former sports editor for the *New York Times*," and she notes that he has watched children play organized sports for many years. Third, she quotes from three Web sites—the official Little League site, the site of the National Association of Sports Officials, and the Parentsknow.com database. Parents are likely to accept the authority of the Little League site and be interested in what other parents and sports officials have to say.

In addition to quoting authorities, Statsky relies on examples and anecdotes to support the reasons for her position. If examples and anecdotes are to be believable, they must seem representative to readers, not bizarre or highly unusual or completely unpredictable.

Readers can imagine a similar event happening elsewhere. For anecdotes to be believable, they should, in addition, be specific and true to life. All of Statsky's examples and anecdotes fulfill these requirements, and her readers would find them believable. For example, early in her argument, in paragraph 4, Statsky reasons that fear of being hurt greatly reduces children's enjoyment of contact sports. The anecdote comes from Tosches's investigative report on Peewee Football as does the quotation by the mother of an eight-year-old player who says that the children become frightened and pretend to be injured in order to stay out of the game. In the anecdote, a seven-year-old makes himself vomit to avoid playing. Because these echo the familiar "I feel bad" or "I'm sick" excuse children give when they do not want to go somewhere (especially school) or do something, most parents would find them believable. They could easily imagine their own children pretending to be hurt or ill if they were fearful or depressed. The anecdote is also specific. Tosches reports what the boy said and did and what the coach said and did.

Other examples provide support for all the major reasons   6
Statsky gives for her position:

- That competitive sports pose psychological dangers—children becoming serious and unplayful when the game starts (paragraph 5)

- That adults' desire to win puts children at risk—parents fighting each other at a Peewee Football game, a coach setting fire to an opposing team's jersey, and the fatal beating of a man supervising a hockey game by the unhappy parent of a player (paragraph 8)

- That organized sports should emphasize cooperation and individual performance instead of winning—a coach banning scoring but finding that parents would not support him and a New York City basketball league in which all children play an equal amount of time and scoring is easier (paragraph 11)

All of these examples are appropriate to the reasons they support. They are also believable. Together, they help Statsky achieve her purpose of convincing parents that organized, competitive sports may be bad for their children and that there are alternatives.

If readers are to find an argument logical and convincing, it   7
must be consistent and complete. While there are no inconsistencies or contradictions in Statsky's argument, it is seriously incomplete because it neglects to support fully one of its reasons, it fails to anticipate many predictable questions parents would have, and it pays too little attention to noncontact competitive team sports.

The most obvious example of thin support comes in paragraph 11, where Statsky asserts that many parents are ready for children's team sports that emphasize cooperation and individual performance. Yet the example of a Little League official who failed to win parents' approval to ban scores raises serious questions about just how many parents are ready to embrace noncompetitive sports teams. The other support, a brief description of City Sports for Kids in New York City, is very convincing but will only be logically compelling to those parents who are already inclined to agree with Statsky's position. Parents inclined to disagree with Statsky would need additional evidence. Most parents know that big cities receive special federal funding for evening, weekend, and summer recreation. Brief descriptions of six or eight noncompetitive teams in a variety of sports in cities, rural areas, suburban neighborhoods—some funded publicly, some funded privately—would be more likely to convince skeptics. Statsky is guilty here of failing to accept the burden of proof, a logical fallacy.

Statsky's argument is also incomplete in that it fails to anticipate certain objections and questions that some parents, especially those she most wants to convince, are almost sure to raise. In the first sentences of paragraphs 6, 9, and 10, Statsky does show that she is thinking about her readers' questions. She does not go nearly far enough, however, to have a chance of influencing two types of readers: those who themselves are or were fans of and participants in competitive sports and those who want their six- to twelve-year-old children involved in mainstream sports programs despite the risks, especially the national programs that have a certain prestige. Such parents might feel that competitive team sports for young children create a sense of community with a shared purpose, build character through self-sacrifice and commitment to the group, teach children to face their fears early and learn how to deal with them through the support of coaches and team members, and introduce children to the principles of social cooperation and collaboration. Some parents are likely to believe and to know from personal experience that coaches who burn opposing teams' jerseys on the pitching mound before the game starts are the exception, not the rule. Some young children idolize teachers and coaches, and team practice and games are the brightest moments in their lives. Statsky seems not to have considered these reasonable possibilities, and as a result her argument lacks a compelling logic it might have had. By acknowledging that she was aware of many of these objections—and perhaps even accommodating more of them in her own argument, as she does in paragraph 10, while refuting other objections—she would have strengthened her argument.

8

Finally, Statsky's argument is incomplete because she over-   9
looks examples of noncontact team sports. Track, swimming, and
tennis are good examples that some readers would certainly think
of. Some elementary schools compete in track meets. Public and
private clubs and recreational programs organize competitive
swimming and tennis competitions. In these sports, individual
performance is the focus. No one gets trampled. Children exert
themselves only as much as they are able to. Yet individual performances are scored, and a team score is derived. Because Statsky
fails to mention any of these obvious possibilities, her argument is
weakened.

The logic of Statsky's argument, then, has both strengths and   10
weaknesses. The support she offers is appropriate, believable, and
consistent. The major weakness is incompleteness—she fails to
anticipate more fully the likely objections of a wide range of readers.
Her logic would prevent parents who enjoy and advocate competitive sports from taking her argument seriously. Such parents and
their children have probably had positive experiences with team
sports, and these experiences would lead them to believe that the
gains are worth whatever risks may be involved. Many probably
think that the risks Statsky points out can be avoided by careful
monitoring. For those parents inclined to agree with her, Statsky's
logic is likely to seem sound and complete. An argument that successfully confirms readers' beliefs is certainly valid, and Statsky succeeds admirably at this kind of argument. Because she does not offer
compelling counterarguments to the legitimate objections of those
inclined not to agree with her, however, her success is limited.

READING FOR MEANING

This section presents three activities that will help you reread Romano's
evaluation with a critical eye. Done in sequence, these activities lead you from a
basic understanding of the selection to a more personal response to it and finally
to an analysis that deepens your understanding and critical thinking about what
you are reading.

Read to Comprehend

Reread the selection, and write a few sentences briefly explaining the
strengths and weaknesses of Statsky's argument, according to Romano. Also
make a list of any words you do not understand—such as *credible* (paragraph 4),
anecdotes (5), *representative* (5), *skeptics* (7). Look up their meanings in a dictionary to see which definition best fits the context.

To expand your understanding of this reading, you might use one or more of the following critical reading strategies that are explained and illustrated in Appendix 1: *annotating, paraphrasing,* and *synthesizing.*

Read to Respond

Write several paragraphs exploring your initial thoughts and feelings about Romano's evaluation. Focus on anything that stands out for you, perhaps because it resonates with your own experience or because you find a statement puzzling.

You might consider writing about

- why Romano finds Statsky's argument believable (paragraphs 4–6).

- some of the reasons Romano finds Statsky's argument to be incomplete.

- further reasons explaining why parents of six- to twelve-year-old children might find Statsky's argument incomplete.

- your own experience as a member of an organized sports team for children of the same age group, comparing or contrasting it with what Romano finds believable or incomplete in Statsky's argument.

To develop your response to Romano's evaluation, you might use one or more of the following critical reading strategies that are explained and illustrated in Appendix 1: *contextualizing, looking for patterns of opposition,* and *evaluating the logic of an argument.*

Read to Analyze Underlying Assumptions

Write several paragraphs exploring one or more of the assumptions, values, and beliefs underlying Romano's evaluation. As you write, explain how the assumptions are reflected in the text, as well as what you now think of them (and perhaps of your own assumptions) after rereading the selection with a critical eye.

You might consider writing about

- Romano's assumptions about why many parents want to involve their children in "mainstream sports programs" (paragraph 8).

- how much Romano believes must be included in Statsky's argument for it to be "complete."

- the elements of a logical argument that Romano believes Statsky explores successfully.

- Romano's assumptions about the sources Statsky uses.

To probe assumptions more deeply, you might use one or more of the following critical reading strategies that are explained and illustrated in

Appendix 1: *reflecting on challenges to your beliefs and values, evaluating the logic of an argument,* and *judging the writer's credibility.*

READING LIKE A WRITER
COUNTERARGUING

Romano clearly admires Statsky's argument, yet she also sees that it is not perfect. Ty Burr takes a similar approach to evaluating his subject. Like Romano, he goes beyond his first reaction to his subject in order to consider it critically; that is, with some distance and skepticism. This stance enables each writer to counterargue—to offer a balanced evaluation by expressing reservations about a subject the writer admires. While Romano must have admired Statsky's argument when she first read it—and she does express that admiration at length—she is not blind to its gaps or weaknesses. Consequently, she is able to offer a balanced evaluation of it by both arguing for its apparent strengths and counterarguing weaknesses that some readers would probably see. In counterarguing, Romano tries to convince readers that the weaknesses are real and that they compromise Statsky's evaluation. Romano may have discovered these weaknesses on her own, without thinking about her readers—other students in her writing class and her instructor, all of whom would have read Statsky's essay—but upon reflection she likely realized that some of her readers would share her reservations about the essay and might have considered her naive if she had not brought them up.

Analyze

1. *Reread* paragraphs 7–9, and then *underline* the one sentence in each paragraph that most concisely states a weakness Romano finds in Statsky's evaluation.

2. *Consider* how Romano goes about supporting her counterargument in these paragraphs. *Make notes* in the margin about how many and what kinds of examples she offers.

3. *Evaluate* how successful Romano is in convincing readers that Statsky's argument has major weaknesses. What seems most and least convincing in her counterargument?

Write

Write several sentences reporting on what you have learned about how Romano counterargues weaknesses in Statsky's position paper on children's competitive sports teams. How does Romano bring up the weaknesses, and how does she counterargue? *Add a few more sentences* evaluating how convincing her counterargument is likely to be for her intended readers.

CONSIDERING IDEAS FOR YOUR OWN WRITING

List several texts you would consider evaluating. For example, you might include in your list an essay from one of the chapters in this book. If you choose an argument from Chapters 6 through 9, you could evaluate its logic (as Romano does), emotional appeals, or credibility, relying on the guidelines in Appendix 1 (pp. 675–79). You might prefer to evaluate a children's book you read when you were younger or one you now read to your own children, a magazine for people interested in computers or cars (or another topic), or a scholarly article you read for a research paper. You need not limit yourself to texts written on paper; also consider a Web site or an article from the online magazine *Slate* or *Salon*. Choose one possibility from your list, and see whether you can come up with three or four reasons for why you find it a strong or weak text.

SCOTT HYDER

Poltergeist: *It Knows What Scares You*

> *Scott Hyder wrote this movie review for his first-year writing class. Like all reviewers, he cannot assume readers have seen the subject of his review:* Poltergeist, *a movie released in 1982. But he probably assumes that they have seen other horror movies like it. As you read the review, think about how Hyder attempts to hold your interest in a movie you might not have seen in a theater or on video.*
>
> *The other readings in this chapter are followed by reading and writing activities. Following this reading, however, you are on your own to decide how to read for meaning and read like a writer.*

You are an eight-year-old boy all tucked in for the night. Your little sister is sleeping in the bed next to you. Suddenly, you hear a crash of thunder, and through the window, you can see the big, old, growling tree in the lightning. It seems to be, well, to be making faces at you! But, you are a big boy. Nothing scares *you*. Nothing at—BANG! WHOOSH! The tree comes to life as it tumbles through the window, grabbing you with its pulsating, hairy roots from your bed. As you scream for Mommy, the closet door slowly opens and an invisible, windlike presence kidnaps your sister. Your nice, cozy dreamhouse turns into a living hell. Watch out! "They're hee-re!"

In June 1982, producer-director-writer Steven Spielberg defined "horror" with a new word: *Poltergeist*. At first and final glance, *Poltergeist* is simply a riveting demonstration of a movie's power to terrify. It creates honest thrills within the confines of a PG rating, reaching for shock effects and the forced suspension of disbelief throughout the movie. Spielberg wrote the story, coproduced it, and supervised the final editing. The directing credit goes to Tobe Hooper, best known for his cult shocker *The Texas Chainsaw Massacre,* which probably explains *Poltergeist*'s violence and slight crudeness.

Nevertheless, *Poltergeist* cannot be classified in the same horror category with such movies as *A Nightmare on Elm Street,* where a deformed psychotic slashes his victims with razor-edged fingernails. Unlike most horror flicks, *Poltergeist* works! Its success is due to excellent characters, music, and special effects—and to the fact that the story stays within the bounds of believability.

The movie takes place in a suburban housing tract. Steve (Craig T. Nelson) and Diane (JoBeth Williams) Freeling have just purchased a new home when their adorable five-year-old daughter, Carol Anne (Heather O'Rourke), awakes to odd voices coming from the snowy TV screen that Steve falls asleep in front of during the late movie. She calls them the "TV people," and with the help of special-effects producer George Lucas and his Industrial Light and Magic, these people abduct little Carol Anne, provoking turbulence and misery for this once-happy family.

A mere synopsis simply cannot give a real feeling for the story. As Steve Freeling says to the parapsychologists who have come to see the house, "You have to see it to believe it." Each character possesses a unique personality, which contributes to the overall feeling the audience has for the story. The characters are represented to be as normal and American as bologna sandwiches—Dad sells houses, Mom sings along to TV jingles. Spielberg likes these characters, illustrating their go-with-the-flow resilience. When things get suddenly hectic toward the climax, these people can display their fear and anger as well as summon their inner strengths. This is particularly evident when Tangina, the parapsychologist the Freelings hire, instructs Diane to lie to her daughter in order to lure Carol Anne into the light and save her.

"Tell her to go into the light," Tangina instructs. "Tell her that *you* are in the light!"

"No," Diane replies with betrayed emotions.

Tangina immediately puts everything into the proper perspective. "You can't choose between life and death when we're dealing with what's in between! Now tell her before it's too late!"

Such scenes clearly illustrate that Spielberg's characters are, in a sense, the ordinary heroes of the movies.

A horror movie, however, cannot rely on terror, anger, and disbelief to hold its audience for two hours. Something needs to accompany these emotions, equally expressing the full extent of the characters' fear and anger. Music composer Jerry Goldsmith contributes his share of eeriness with his Academy Award-winning soundtrack. The basic theme is a lullaby (entitled "Carol Anne's Theme") that soothes the watcher, providing a cheerful, childlike innocence to the picture. The inverse is the ghost music that accompanies the abduction of Carol Anne and forces our stomachs to writhe. The music brings a straining, vibrating tone that is responsible for 60 percent of the audience's terror. When the clown doll's hand wraps around Robbie's (Oliver Robins) neck, the sudden blaring of Goldsmith's orchestra is what makes viewers swallow their stomachs. Without it, the scene would never slap our face or give our necks a backward whiplash. Goldsmith matches the actions and emotions of the characters with the corresponding instrumental music, enabling the audience to parallel its feelings with those delivered on the screen.

If a horror movie has a well-developed plot with superior actors 11
and an excellent score to accompany their emotions, then it should
be a sure winner at the box office, right? Looking back at such
movies as *Rosemary's Baby, The Exorcist,* and the original *Psycho*
one would obviously agree. *Poltergeist,* however, doesn't stop here.
It goes even further by providing its audience with a special treat.
With the help of *Star Wars* creator George Lucas, Spielberg and
Hooper whip up a dazzling show of light and magic. There's an
eerie parade of poltergeists in chiffons of light marching down the
Freelings' staircase to the climactic scene as a huge, bright, nuclear-
colored mouth strives to suck the Freeling children into their closet.
Hooper's familiarity with film violence surfaces in a grotesque
scene in which one of the parapsychologists hallucinates that he is
tearing his face. Such shocking, hair-raising scenes as this make a
huge contribution to horrifying the audience. Many horror films
never achieve such reactions. *Poltergeist's* precise timing with such
effects makes it completely unpredictable as far as what is to come.
From the first sign of a ghostlike hand jumping out of the TV to
the staggering scene of dead bodies popping out of the half-dug
swimming pool, the special-effects team draws every bit of energy
out of the audience members, dazzling them and forcing them to
believe in the horror on the screen.

There have been many movies that possess superior ratings in 12
all of the above. Such movies as John Carpenter's *The Thing* and
David Cronenberg's *Scanners* won raves for superior acting, background music, and special effects. Why was *Poltergeist* accepted at
the box office more than other such movies? Every movie is forced
to set up boundaries of believability through certain actions and
concepts, and at one point these boundaries will be accepted by
the viewer. In *Indiana Jones and the Temple of Doom,* Spielberg distinguished boundaries within which Indiana Jones defined his
heroic stunts. Spielberg, however, unfortunately crossed his
boundaries during a scene in which Indiana Jones jumps from one
track to another with a moving train cart. From previous observations of Indiana Jones's capabilities, viewers are unable to accept
this, nodding their heads with a "give me a break" expression.

In *Poltergeist,* Spielberg and Hooper remain within their estab- 13
lished boundaries. Unlike most horror movies that have unfeasible
killers who are incapable of dying or monsters that pop out of
people's stomachs, *Poltergeist* focuses on the supernatural—a subject with *very wide* boundaries. Because of our lack of knowledge
in the area, we are "at the mercy of the writers and directors," as
Alfred Hitchcock phrased it. The boundaries can be greater than
most horror movies because of *Poltergeist's* subject matter. The

characters' disbelief of their surroundings encourages the audience to accept what is in front of them. Hence, *Poltergeist* successfully stays within its limits, taking them to their maximum, but luring the audience to believe the characters' situation.

Poltergeist reflects a lot of the fears that most of us grow up with: seeing scary shadows from the light in your closet, making sure your feet are not dangling over the bed, forming scary images of the objects in your room. As Spielberg's *E. T.* reminisces about our childhood dreams, *Poltergeist* surfaces our childhood nightmares. With its characters, music, and special effects, and its clearly distinguished boundaries of belief, *Poltergeist* is able to capture its audience with its unique thrills, allowing viewers to link their most inner-locked fears to those on the screen. *Poltergeist:* It knows what scares you! 14

READING FOR MEANING

Reading for meaning involves three activities:

- reading to comprehend

- reading to respond

- reading to analyze underlying assumptions

Reread Hyder's essay, and then write a page or so explaining your understanding of its basic meaning or main point, a personal response you have to it, and what you see as one of its underlying assumptions.

READING LIKE A WRITER

Writers of evaluative essays

- present the subject.

- assert an overall judgment.

- give reasons and support.

- counterargue.

- establish credibility.

Focus on one of these strategies in Hyder's essay, and analyze it carefully through close rereading and annotating. Then write several sentences explaining what you have learned, giving specific examples from the reading to support your explanation. Add a few sentences evaluating how successfully Hyder uses the strategy to evaluate *Poltergeist*.

REVIEWING WHAT MAKES EVALUATIONS EFFECTIVE

In this chapter, you have been learning how to read evaluative essays for meaning and how to read them like a writer. Before going on to write an evaluation of your own, pause here to review and contemplate what you have learned about the elements of effective evaluations.

Analyze

Choose one reading from this chapter that seems to you especially effective. Before rereading the selection, *jot down* one or two reasons you remember it as an example of good evaluative writing.

Reread your chosen selection, adding further annotations about what makes it a particularly successful example of evaluation. *Consider* the selection's purpose and how well it achieves that purpose for its intended readers. (You can make an informed guess about the intended readers and their expectations by noting the publication source of the essay.) Then *focus* on how well the essay

- presents the subject.

- asserts an overall judgment.

- gives reasons and support.

- counterargues.

- establishes credibility.

You can review all of these basic features in the Guide to Reading Evaluations (p. 329).

Your instructor may ask you to complete this activity on your own or to work with a small group of other students who have chosen the same reading. If you work with others, allow enough time initially for all group members to reread the selection thoughtfully and to add their annotations. Then *discuss* as a group what makes the essay effective. *Take notes* on your discussion. One student in your group should then report to the class what the group has learned about the effectiveness of evaluative writing. If you are working individually, write up what you have learned from your analysis.

Write

Write at least a page supporting your choice of this reading as an example of effective evaluative writing. *Assume* that your readers—your instructor and classmates—have read the selection but will not remember many details about it. They also might not remember it as especially successful. Therefore, you will need to *refer* to details and specific parts of the reading as you explain how it works and as you justify your evaluation of its effectiveness. You need not argue that it is the best essay in the chapter or that it is flawless, only that it is, in your view, a strong example of the genre.

■ A Guide to Writing Evaluations

The readings in this chapter have helped you learn a great deal about evaluative writing. Now that you have seen how writers of evaluations argue to support their assertions, you are in a good position to approach this type of writing confidently. As you develop your essay, you can review the readings to see how other writers use various strategies to solve the problems you face in your own writing.

This Guide to Writing is designed to assist you in writing an evaluation. Here you will find activities to help you choose a subject and discover what to say about it, organize your ideas and draft the essay, read the draft critically, revise the draft to strengthen your argument, and edit and proofread the essay to improve its readability.

INVENTION AND RESEARCH

Invention is a process of discovery and planning by which you generate something to say. The following activities will help you choose a subject and develop your evaluation of it. A few minutes spent on each writing activity will improve your chances of producing a detailed and convincing first draft.

Choosing a Subject

Begin by looking over the subjects suggested in the Considering Ideas for Your Own Writing activities in this chapter. The selections suggest several different subjects you could write about. Arts and entertainment products are popular subjects for review: fashion, sports, television programs, films, magazines, books, restaurants, and video games. Technology, since it changes so quickly, is also a source of many possible subjects: new hardware and software, new procedures, and laws. There are countless other possibilities, such as public figures, businesses, educational programs, and types of equipment (cars, sporting gear).

To find a subject, list specific examples in several of the following categories. Although you may be inclined to pick the first idea that comes to mind, try to make your list of possible subjects as long as you can. This will ensure that you have a variety of subjects from which to choose and will encourage you to think of unique subjects.

- A film or group of films by a single director or actor
- A hit song or music CD
- A live or videotaped concert or theatrical performance
- A magazine or newspaper

- A book (perhaps one—either fiction or nonfiction—that you have recently read for one of your classes)

- A club or organized activity—dance instruction, camping or hiking trip, college sports programs, debate group—or a subject (like Etzioni's) that is generally viewed positively but that your experience leads you to evaluate more negatively (or, alternatively, a subject generally viewed negatively that your experience leads you to evaluate more positively)

- A contemporary political movement (perhaps evaluating the movement's methods as well as its goals and achievements)

- A proposed or existing law

- A noteworthy person—someone in the news or a local professional, such as a teacher, doctor, social worker, auto mechanic, or minister (perhaps using your personal experience with the local figure to strengthen your evaluation)

- An artist, a writer, or his or her works

- A local business or businessperson

- Particular brands of machines or equipment with which you are familiar (perhaps comparing a "superior" to an "inferior" brand to make your evaluation more authoritative)

- One of the essays in this book (evaluating it as a strong or weak example of its type) or two essays (arguing that one is better than the other)

After you have a list of possible subjects, consider the following questions as you make your final selection:

- *Do I already know enough about this subject, or can I get the information I need in time?* If, for instance, you decide to review a film, you should be able to see it soon. If you choose to evaluate a brand of machine or equipment, you should already be somewhat familiar with it or have time to learn enough about it to be able to write with some authority.

- *Do I already have a settled judgment about this subject?* It is always easier to write about a subject that you think you can judge confidently, although it is conceivable that you could change your mind as you write. If you choose a subject about which you feel indifferent, you may experience difficulty devising an argument to support your judgment. The more sure you are of your judgment, the more persuasive your evaluation is likely to be.

Developing Your Argument

The writing and research activities that follow will enable you to explore your subject, analyze your readers, and begin developing your evaluation.

Exploring Your Subject.   *To find out what you already know about the subject, list the main things you now know about it and then make notes about how you will go about becoming familiar enough with your subject to write about it like an expert or insider.* You may know little or much about your subject, and you may feel uncertain how to learn more about it. For now, discover what you do know.

Analyzing Your Readers.   *Make notes about your readers.* Who exactly are your readers? They may be your classmates, or you may want—or be asked by your instructor—to write for another audience. You could write for the general public, as most of the writers in this chapter seem to be doing. Or you could write for a more narrow audience: parents ready to purchase a new child's learning game, advanced users of email or some other technology, or viewers who have seen (or who have never seen) several other films by the director of the film you are reviewing. How much will your readers know about your subject and others of its type? How can you describe your readers' attitudes and opinions about the subject? What standards might they use to judge a subject like yours?

Considering Your Judgment.   *Make a list of the good and bad qualities of your subject.* Then decide whether your judgment will be positive or negative. You can certainly acknowledge both the good and bad qualities in your essay, but your judgment should not be ambivalent throughout. In a movie review, for example, you must ultimately decide whether you do or do not recommend that your readers try to see the film. If your list leaves you feeling genuinely ambivalent, you might want to trust the processes of learning and writing about your subject to help you decide whether you want to praise or criticize it. Another option, of course, is to choose a different subject to evaluate.

If you can judge your subject now, *write a sentence or two asserting your judgment.* At the end of these activities, you will have an opportunity to revise this assertion.

Testing Your Choice.   *Pause now to decide whether you have chosen a subject about which you may be able to make a convincing evaluative argument.* At this point, you should be very familiar with your subject—you have viewed the movie again, reread the essay, listened to the music CD, attended another concert, reexamined a machine or piece of equipment, or consumed another meal at the restaurant. It is important that you be able to continue studying your subject as you complete these invention activities and, later, as you draft and revise your essay: The more intimate your knowledge of the subject, the more details you can bring to bear to support your evaluation. If your interest in the subject is growing and you feel increasingly confident about your judgment of it, you have probably made a good choice. If you have not made progress in experiencing and understanding your subject and do not see how you can do so right away, it is probably wise for you to choose another subject.

Listing Reasons.   *List all the reasons you might give to persuade your readers of your judgment of the subject.* Reasons answer the question, "Everything considered, why do you evaluate this subject positively [or negatively]?" Write down all the reasons you can think of.

Then look over your list to consider which reasons you feel are the most important and which would be most convincing to your readers, given the generally accepted standards for evaluating this type of subject. *Put an asterisk by these convincing reasons.*

Consider this list only a starting point. Continue to revise it as you learn more about your subject. A preliminary list of reasons gives you a head start on planning your essay.

Finding Support for Your Reasons.   *Make notes about how to support your most promising reasons.* For support, most evaluations rely largely on details and examples from the subject itself. For that reason, you will have to reexamine the subject closely even if you know it quite well. Depending on the subject, evaluations may also make use of facts, quotations from experts, statistics, or the writer's personal experience.

Work back and forth between your list of reasons and notes for support. The reasons list will remind you of the support you need and help you discover which reasons have substance. The credibility of your argument will depend to a large extent on the amount of specific, relevant support you can bring to your argument.

Anticipating Readers' Alternative Judgments, Questions, and Objections.   *List a few questions your particular readers would likely want to ask you or objections they might have to your argument. Write for a few minutes responding to at least two of these questions or objections.* Now that you can begin to see how your argument might shape up, assume that some of your particular readers would judge your subject differently from the way you do. Remember that your responses—your counterargument—could simply acknowledge the disagreements, accommodate readers' views by conceding certain points, or refute readers' arguments as uninformed or mistaken.

RESEARCHING YOUR SUBJECT ONLINE

One way to learn more about judgments of your subject that differ from your own judgment is to search for reviews or evaluations of your subject online. You may even decide to incorporate quotations from or references to alternative judgments as part of your counterargument, although you need not do so in order to write a successful evaluation. Enter the name of your subject—movie title, restaurant name, compact disc title, title of a proposed law, name of a candidate for public office—in a search engine such as Google <www.google.com> or Yahoo! Directory <http://dir.yahoo.com>. (Sometimes you can narrow the search usefully by including the keyword *review* as well.) Of course, not all subjects are conveniently searchable online, and some subjects—a local concert, a college sports event, a campus student service, a neighborhood program—will likely not have been reviewed by anyone but you.

Bookmark or keep a record of promising sites. Download any materials you might wish to cite in your evaluation, making sure you have all the information necessary to document the source.

Considering Visuals. *Consider whether visuals—screen shots, photographs, or drawings—would help you present your subject more effectively to readers or strengthen your evaluation of it.* If you submit your essay electronically to other students and your instructor, or if you post it on a Web site, consider including photographs as well as snippets of film or sound or other memorabilia that might give readers a more vivid sense of your subject. Visual and audio materials are not at all a requirement of an effective evaluative argument, as you can tell from the readings in this chapter, but they could add a new dimension to your writing. If you want to use photographs or recordings of people, though, be sure to obtain their permission.

Considering Your Purpose. *Write for a few minutes exploring your purpose for writing an evaluative essay.* The following questions may help you think about your purpose:

- What do I want my readers to believe or do after they read my essay?

- How can I connect to their experience with my subject (or subjects like it)? How can I interest them in a subject that is outside their experience?

- Can I assume that readers will share my standards for judging the subject, or must I explain and justify the standards?

- How can I offer a balanced evaluation that will enhance my credibility with readers?

Formulating a Working Thesis. *Draft a thesis statement.* A working thesis—as opposed to a final, revised thesis—will help you begin drafting your essay purposefully. The thesis statement in an evaluative essay is simply a concise assertion of your overall judgment. Here are two examples from the readings:

- "There can be no greater gift for a movie lover than the one bestowed upon audiences by Peter Jackson, whose *The Lord of the Rings: The Return of the King* is not only the best movie of 2003, but the crowning cinematic achievement of the past several years. In fact, labeling this as a 'movie' is almost an injustice. This is an experience of epic scope and grandeur, amazing emotional power, and relentless momentum" (Berardinelli, paragraph 1).

- "Unlike most horror flicks, *Poltergeist* works! Its success is due to excellent characters, music, and special effects—and to the fact that the story stays within the bounds of believability" (Hyder, paragraph 3).

Notice that there is no ambivalence in these statements. They are clear, assertive, and unmistakably positive in their judgments. (An assertive judgment does not preclude a writer's later acknowledging problems or weaknesses in a subject judged positively or anticipating readers' likely reservations about the evaluation.) Also notice that both thesis statements forecast the major reasons for the judgment, the reasons that are at the heart of the evaluation. Forecasts are not required, but readers often find them helpful.

DRAFTING

The following guidelines will help you set goals for your draft, plan its organization, and think about a useful sentence strategy.

Setting Goals

Establishing goals for your draft before you begin writing will enable you to make decisions and work more confidently. Consider the following questions now, and keep them in mind as you draft. They will help you set goals for drafting as well as recall how the writers you have read in this chapter tried to achieve similar goals.

- *What is my primary purpose in writing this evaluation?* What do I want to accomplish with my evaluation? Is my primary purpose to make a recommendation, as Berardinelli and Hyder do? Do I want to celebrate my subject, as Lemley, Hyder, and Christy do, or expose its flaws, as Etzioni does? Do I want to strive for a carefully balanced evaluation, as Burr and Romano do?

- *How can I present the subject so that I can inform and interest my readers in it?* How much experience evaluating a subject of this kind can I expect my readers to have? Must I provide a full context for my subject, as Burr and Berardinelli do, or describe it in a general way, as Hyder does? Can I assume familiarity with it, as does Etzioni? Will readers share my standards, as Hyder seems to assume his readers do, or will I need to explain or define some of my standards, as Lemley does? Can I present my subject by showing myself as an engaged user of it, as Lemley does?

- *How can I assert my judgment effectively?* How can I construct a clear, unambiguous thesis statement like those in all of the readings in this chapter?

Should I assert my judgment in the first sentence and reassert it at the end of my evaluation, as Etzioni does? Or should I first describe my subject or provide a context for evaluating it, as Lemley, Christy, Burr, and Berardinelli do?

- *How can I give convincing reasons and adequate support for my reasons?* How can I ensure that the reasons I offer to justify my judgment will seem appropriate and convincing to my readers? Should I forecast my reasons, as Etzioni, Romano, and Hyder do? For my subject, will I offer a wide range of types of support, as Etzioni does? How can I gather an adequate amount of support for my reasons, as do all of the writers in this chapter? Should I rely on comparisons to support my reasoning, as Lemley and Hyder do?

- *How can I anticipate readers' reservations?* Should I pointedly anticipate my readers' likely reservations, objections, and questions, as Etzioni, Lemley, and Romano do?

- *How can I establish credibility with my readers?* Should I feature my personal experience with the subject, as Lemley, Burr, and Berardinelli do? Or should I demonstrate my expertise with the subject by making comparisons with similar subjects, as Christy does?

Organizing Your Draft

With goals in mind and invention notes at hand, you are ready to make a first outline of your draft. Review the list of reasons you have developed. Tentatively select from that list the reasons you think will most effectively convince your readers of the plausibility of your judgment. Then decide how you will sequence these reasons. Some writers prefer to save their most telling reason or reasons for the end, whereas others try to group the reasons logically (for example, the technical reasons in a movie review). Still other writers like to begin with reasons based on standards of judgment familiar to their readers. Whatever sequence you decide on for your reasons, make sure it will strike your readers as a logical or step-by-step sequence.

Considering a Useful Sentence Strategy

As you draft your evaluative essay, you may want to compare or contrast your subject with similar subjects to establish your authority with readers. In addition, you are likely to want to balance your evaluation by criticizing one or more aspects of the subject if you generally praise it or by praising one or more aspects of it if you generally criticize it. To do so, you will need to use sentences that express comparisons or contrasts, specifically ones that contrast criticism with praise and vice versa.

Use sentences comparing or contrasting your subject with similar subjects to help convince readers that you are knowledgeable about the kind of subject you are evaluating. These sentences often make use of key comparative terms, such as *more, less, most, least, as, than, like, unlike, similar,* and *dissimilar,* as the readings in this chapter illustrate.

> Nevertheless, *Poltergeist* cannot be classified in the same horror category with such movies **as** *A Nightmare on Elm Street,* where a deformed psychotic slashes his victims with razor-edged fingernails. **Unlike** most horror flicks, *Poltergeist* works! (Hyder, paragraph 3)

In these sentences, Hyder indicates his knowledge about other horror films and compares one unfavorably to *Poltergeist.*

> I have driven three such cars—one each from Toyota, Honda, and Ford—and can report that the experience is almost **identical to** piloting each company's gas-engine counterparts. (Lemley, paragraph 4)

In this sentence Lemley compares hybrid and conventional cars, showing he has experience with both.

> "Reaction time is **quicker** with your hands **than** with your feet," says Nicholas Zielinski, manager for GM's drive-by-wire program. "Picking up your foot, moving it over, and putting it on the pedal just can't compete." (Lemley, paragraph 11)

Lemley compares an essential feature of the Hywire car—driving with your hands—to the way we drive cars now, with our feet, making the point that the new car is superior to current cars. Note that even though he does not use the comparative term *more,* he implies it with the comparative word *quicker.*

> Some say that **while** these jobs are rather unsuited for college-bound, white, middle-class youngsters, they are "ideal" for lower-class, "non-academic," minority youngsters. (Etzioni, paragraph 11)

Here Etzioni compares what some people say about the suitability of after-school jobs for a particular economic class of students. He does not use a specific comparative term, but the structure of his sentence, using *while* to set up the contrast, prepares the reader for the upcoming comparison.

> This is Tolkien's saga as filtered through Jackson's fertile imagination, **not** some dry, slavishly faithful adaptation (although it is probably as true to the books in both spirit and narrative as any movie version could be). (Berardinelli, paragraph 8)

In this sentence Berardinelli contrasts the adaptation of the movie from the book in *The Lord of the Rings: The Return of the King* to the adaptation from *Harry Potter*—unfavorably. He shows that he is knowledgeable about other movies based on books.

You can increase your authority with readers by using sentences expressing comparison or contrast to balance criticism and praise. The sentence strategies are similar for introducing criticism followed by praise and introducing praise followed by criticism, strategies we refer to in this chapter as *counterargument*. In general, these strategies rely on words expressing contrast—*but, although, however, while,* and *yet*—to set up the shift between the two responses.

- Praise followed by criticism:

> *The Lord of the Rings: The Return of the King* delivers on all the mighty expectations Peter Jackson created in *The Fellowship of the Ring* and *The Two Towers*. Armies clash, towers crash, Middle-earth is made free once more. **Yet** where many viewers staggered out of *Towers* last year in a daze of exaltation, *Return* may leave one overwhelmed and exhausted. (Burr, paragraph 2)

> The sense of purpose is impressive, **but** all that solemnity begins to pall over the backstretch. (Burr, paragraph 6)

> **While** it is true that these places provide income, work, and even some training to such youngsters, they also tend to perpetuate their disadvantaged status. (Etzioni, paragraph 11)

> Statsky does show that she is thinking about her readers' questions. She does not go nearly far enough, **however**, to have a chance of influencing two types of readers. (Romano, paragraph 8)

- Criticism followed by praise:

> If *King* isn't everything I'd hoped, the filmmaker still deserves an Oscar for the combination of artistry and orneriness it took to get the entire project made. (Burr, paragraph 11)

In addition to using sentences that make comparisons or contrasts with other subjects and sentences that balance criticism and praise, you can strengthen your evaluation with other kinds of sentences as well. You may want to look at the information about using appositives (pp. 319–21) and sentences that combine concession and refutation (pp. 639–40).

READING A DRAFT CRITICALLY

Getting a critical reading of your draft will help you see how to improve it. Your instructor may schedule class time for reading drafts, or you may want to ask a classmate or a tutor in the writing center to read your draft. Ask your reader to use the following guidelines and to write out a response for you to consult during your revision.

Read for a First Impression

1. Read the draft without stopping to annotate or comment, and then write two or three sentences giving your general impression.

2. Identify one aspect of the draft that seems especially effective.

Read Again to Suggest Improvements

1. Recommend ways to strengthen the presentation of the subject.

   - Locate the places in the draft where the subject is described. The description might be spread out over several paragraphs, serving both to identify the subject and to provide support for the argument. Point to any areas where you do not understand what is being said or where you need more detail or explanation.

   - If you are surprised by the way the writer has presented the subject, briefly explain your expectations for reading about this particular subject or subjects of this kind.

   - Indicate whether any of the information given about the subject seems unnecessary.

   - Finally and most important, raise questions wherever information about the subject seems unconvincing, inaccurate, or only partially true.

2. Suggest ways to strengthen the thesis statement.

   - Find and underline the statement of the writer's overall judgment in the draft. If you cannot find a clear thesis, let the writer know.

   - If you find several restatements of the thesis, examine them closely for consistency. Look specifically at the value terms the writer uses to see whether they are unclear or waffling.

3. Recommend ways to strengthen the supporting reasons.

   - Highlight the reasons you find in the essay. The reasons in an evaluation may take the form of judgments of the subject's qualities, judgments that in turn need to be explained and supported. Look closely at any reasons that seem problematic, and briefly explain what bothers you. Be as specific and constructive as you can, suggesting what the writer might do to solve the problem. For example, if a reason seems inappropriate, indicate what other kind of reason you would expect a writer to use when evaluating this subject.

   - Look for instances of faulty logic. Note whether the writer's argument is based on personal tastes rather than on generally accepted standards of judgment. Point out any areas where you detect *either/or* reasoning (that is, seeing only the good or only the bad qualities) and weak or misleading comparisons.

4. Suggest ways to extend and improve the counterargument.

- Locate places where the writer anticipates readers' questions, objections, and reservations about the reasons and support. Consider whether these anticipations seem cursory or adequate, logical or questionable, considerate or dismissive. Point to specific problems you see, and suggest possible revisions.

- Look for areas where the writer anticipates readers' alternative judgments of the subject (that is, where readers may value the subject for different reasons or judge the subject in a different way). Note whether the writer addresses readers' alternative judgments responsibly and accurately and responds to them fairly.

- If the writer does not counterargue, consider where doing so might be appropriate. Help the writer anticipate any reservations and alternative judgments that have been overlooked, providing advice on how to respond to them. Keep in mind that the writer may choose to accommodate *or* refute readers' reservations or alternative judgments.

5. Suggest ways to strengthen the credibility of both the writer and the writer's judgment.

- Ignoring whether you agree or disagree with the writer's judgment on the subject, point to any places in the essay where you do not trust the writer's credibility. For instance, look for areas where the writer seems insufficiently knowledgeable, where the examples seem unconvincing or distorted, or where the writer is being unfair, perhaps criticizing a minor point unnecessarily or emphasizing something beyond the control of the subject's producers.

- Let the writer know whether you think the judgment is sound or based on some idiosyncratic, trivial, or other inappropriate standard of judgment.

6. Suggest how the organizational plan might be improved.

- Consider the overall plan of the draft, perhaps by making a scratch outline. (Scratch outlining is illustrated in Appendix 1, p. 659.) Decide whether the sequence of reasons and counterarguments is logical or whether you can suggest rearrangements to improve it.

- Indicate where new or better transitions might help identify different steps in the argument and keep readers on track.

7. Evaluate the effectiveness of visuals.

- Look at any visuals in the essay, and tell the writer what they contribute to your understanding of the evaluation.

- If any visuals do not seem relevant, or if there seem to be too many visuals, identify the ones that the writer could consider dropping, explaining your thinking.

- If a visual does not seem appropriately placed, suggest a better place for it.

REVISING

This section offers suggestions for revising your draft. Revising means reenvisioning your draft, trying to see it in a new way, given your purpose and readers, in order to develop a better-argued evaluation.

The biggest mistake you can make while revising is to focus initially on words or sentences. Instead, first try to see your draft as a whole in order to assess its likely impact on your readers. To improve readability and strengthen your argument, think imaginatively and boldly about cutting unconvincing material, adding new material, and moving material around. Your computer makes even drastic revisions physically easy, but you still need to make the mental effort and decisions that will improve your draft.

You may have received help with this challenge from a classmate or tutor who gave your draft a critical reading. If so, keep this feedback in mind as you decide which parts of your draft need revising and what specific changes you could make. The following suggestions will help you solve problems and strengthen your essay.

To Present the Subject More Effectively

- If more specific information about the subject is needed, review your invention writing to see whether you have forgotten details you could now add to the draft. Or do some further invention work to generate and add new information.

- If critical readers have asked specific questions, consider whether you need to answer those questions in your revision.

- If you have included information that readers regard as unnecessary or redundant, consider cutting it.

- If any of the information strikes readers as inaccurate or only partially true, reconsider its accuracy and completeness and then make any necessary changes to reassure readers.

- Consider comparing or contrasting your subject with similar subjects to highlight its features.

To Clarify the Overall Judgment

- If your overall judgment is not stated explicitly or clearly, state it more obviously.

- If readers think your restatements of the judgment are contradictory, reread them with a critical eye and, if you agree, make them more consistent.

- If readers think your judgment is unemphatic or waffling, reconsider the value terms you use.

- If your essay discusses both the good and the bad qualities of the subject, be sure that your thesis statement is compatible with what you say about the subject in the essay.

To Strengthen the Reasons and Support

- If a reason seems inappropriate to readers, consider how you might better convince them that the reason is appropriate (for example, that it is used often by others or that it is based on widely shared and valid standards of judgment).

- If readers do not fully understand how a particular reason applies to the subject, make your thinking more explicit.

- If the connection between a reason and its support seems vague or weak, explain why you think the support is relevant.

- Most important, if you have not fully supported your reasons with many examples from your subject, collect further examples by revisiting your subject (revisit the Web site, see the movie again, reread the text, play the computer game again, and so forth).

To Strengthen the Counterargument

- If you have not anticipated readers' likely questions, objections, or reservations, revise to accommodate or refute them.

- If you have not anticipated alternative judgments that are likely for your particular audience, revise to respond to them.

- If any counterargument seems to attack your readers rather than their ideas, revise it to focus on the ideas.

To Make the Organizational Plan More Effective

- If readers express confusion over your plan, consider a different sequence for your reasons, or forecast your plan more explicitly by giving clear signals like transitions and topic sentences to distinguish the stages of your argument.

- If readers point to gaps in your argument, close the gaps by making connections explicit.

- If readers find your conclusion abrupt or less than helpful, try restating your judgment or summarizing your argument.

To Enhance Credibility

- If readers question your knowledge of the subject or your authority to evaluate it, reassure them by discussing the subject in greater depth and detail and comparing it to other subjects of the same kind.

- If the standards you choose to emphasize seem minor to readers, explain why you think they are important.

- If readers think your essay is too one-sided, consider whether there is any quality of the subject you could either praise or criticize. Consider using sentences that contrast criticism with praise and vice versa.

EDITING AND PROOFREADING

After you have revised your essay, be sure to spend some time checking for errors in usage, punctuation, and mechanics and considering matters of style. If you keep a list of errors you typically make, begin by checking your draft against this list. Ask someone else to proofread your essay before you print out a copy for your instructor or send it electronically.

From our research on student writing, we know that evaluative essays have frequent problems in sentences that set up comparisons. The comparisons can be incomplete, illogical, or unclear. Edit carefully any sentences that set up comparisons between your subject and others. Check a writer's handbook for help with making all comparisons complete, logical, and clear.

REFLECTING ON WHAT YOU HAVE LEARNED

Evaluation

In this chapter, you have read critically several evaluative essays and have written one of your own. To better remember what you have learned, pause now to reflect on the reading and writing activities you completed in this chapter.

1. *Write* a page or so reflecting on what you have learned. *Begin* by describing what you are most pleased with in your essay. Then *explain* what you think contributed to your achievement. *Be specific* about this contribution.

   - If it was something you learned from the readings, *indicate* which readings and specifically what you learned from them.

   - If it came from your invention writing, *point out* the section or sections that helped you most.

   - If you got good advice from a critical reader, *explain* exactly how the person helped you—perhaps by helping you understand a particular problem in your draft or by adding a new dimension to your writing.

   - *Try to write* about your achievement in terms of what you have learned about the genre.

2. Now *reflect* more generally on evaluative essays, a genre of writing that plays an important role in education and in many other areas of life and work in the United States. *Consider* some of the following questions: How confident do you feel about asserting a judgment and supporting it? How comfortable are you playing the role of judge and jury on the subject? How do your personal preferences and values influence your judgment? How might your gender, ethnicity, religious beliefs, age, or social class influence your ideas about the subject? What contribution might evaluative essays make to our society that other genres cannot make?

CHAPTER 7

Speculating about Causes or Effects

When something surprising occurs, we automatically look to the past and ask, "Why did that happen?" Whether we want to understand it, to make it happen again, or to find a way to prevent its recurrence, we need to speculate about what *caused* it.

Or our focus may shift from cause to *effect,* from "Why did that happen?" to "What is going to happen?" Anticipating possible effects can be useful in planning and decision making.

In many cases, questions about causes and effects are relatively easy to answer. Through personal experience or scientific experimentation, we know what causes some things to happen and what effects they will have. For example, scientists have discovered that the HIV virus causes AIDS, and we all know its potential deadly effects. We cannot be completely certain, however, what causes the virus to develop into AIDS in particular individuals or what long-term effects AIDS will have on society. In these situations, the best we can do is make educated guesses. In this chapter, you will read and write speculative essays about causes and effects that cannot be known for certain.

This kind of speculative cause or effect writing is published every day. A political analyst conjectures about the cause of the outcome of the 2004 presidential election. An economist suggests some likely effects of the Iraq war on the U.S. economy. A sportswriter speculates about why the Pacific Ten nearly always defeats the Big Ten in the Rose Bowl.

Speculation about causes or effects also plays an important role in government, business, and education. To give credit where it is due, a mayor asks the police commission to report on why complaints by African Americans and Latinos against the police have decreased recently. A salesperson writes a memo to the district sales manager explaining why a local advertising campaign may have failed to increase sales of Chevrolet Corvettes. Before proposing changes in the math curriculum, a school principal appoints a committee to investigate the causes of falling math test scores at the school.

Cause or effect speculation is equally important in college study. For example, you might read a history essay in which a noted scholar evaluates other scholars' proposed causes of the Civil War in order to argue for a never-before-considered cause. (If the essay merely summarizes other scholars' proposed causes, the historian would be reporting established information, not speculating about new possibilities.) Or you might encounter a sociological report conjecturing about a recent increase in marriages among the elderly. The writer may not know for certain why this trend exists but could conjecture about its possible causes—and then argue with relevant facts, statistics, or anecdotes to support the conjectures.

Writing an essay in which you speculate about causes or effects involves some of the most challenging problem-solving and decision-making situations a writer can experience. You will test your powers of reasoning and creativity as you search out hidden, underlying causes or speculate about effects that are surprising yet plausible. You will continue to develop a sensitivity to your readers' knowledge and attitudes, anticipating their objections and discovering ways to convince them to take your speculations seriously.

The readings in this chapter will help you see what makes arguments about causes or effects convincing. From the readings and from the ideas for writing that follow each reading, you will get ideas for your own essay speculating about causes or effects. As you read and write about the selections, keep in mind the following assignment, which sets out the goals for writing an essay speculating about causes or effects. To support your writing of this assignment, the chapter concludes with a Guide to Writing Essays Speculating about Causes or Effects.

THE WRITING ASSIGNMENT

Speculating about Causes or Effects

Choose a subject—an event, a phenomenon, or a trend—that invites you to speculate about its causes or effects: why it may have happened or what its effects may be. Write an essay arguing for your proposed causes or effects. Essays about causes look to the past to ponder why something happened, whereas essays about effects guess what is likely to happen in the future. Whether you choose to write about causes or effects, you need to do two things: (1) Establish the existence and significance of the subject, and (2) convince readers that the causes or effects you propose are plausible.

WRITING SITUATIONS FOR ESSAYS SPECULATING ABOUT CAUSES OR EFFECTS

The following examples suggest further the kinds of causal arguments writers typically make:

- A science writer notes that relatively few women get advanced degrees in science and speculates that social conditioning may be the major cause. To support her causal argument, she cites research on the way boys and girls are treated differently in early childhood. She also gives examples to attempt to show that the social pressure to conform to female role expectations may discourage junior-high-school girls from doing well in math and science. She acknowledges that other as-yet-unrecognized causes may contribute as well.

- A student writes in the school newspaper about the rising number of pregnancies among high-school students. Interviews with pregnant students lead her to speculate that the chief cause of the trend is a new requirement that parents must give written consent for minors to get birth-control devices at the local clinic. She explains that many students fail to get birth-control information, let alone devices, because of this regulation. She reports that her interviews do not support alternative explanations that young women have babies to give meaning to their lives, gain status among their peers, or live on their own supported by public assistance.

- A psychology student writes about the effects—positive and negative—of extensive video-game playing among preteens. Based on his own experience and observation, he suggests that video games may improve children's hand-eye coordination, as well as their ability to concentrate on a single task. He speculates that, on the negative side, some children's grades may suffer as a result of spending too much time playing video games.

THINKING ABOUT YOUR EXPERIENCE WITH CAUSE OR EFFECT WRITING

Before studying a type of writing, it is useful to spend some time thinking about what you already know about it. You may have discussed with friends or family members why a certain phenomenon, event, or trend occurred, in which case you were trying to figure out the causes. Or you may have discussed what a phenomenon, event, or trend might lead to or result in, in which case you were speculating about effects. In school, you may have written essays examining the causes, say, of a scientific phenomenon such as the extinction of the dinosaurs or the effects of a social trend such as an increase in interracial marriage.

To analyze your experience with cause or effect arguments, try to recall times when you were arguing—orally or in writing—for the reasons you think something happened or the effects that would result from some event, phenomenon, or trend that concerned you. What triggered your speculations? Who was your audience for your argument? What did you hope to achieve with your speculations? What interested you about this issue or made you think it was significant? Did you choose to address the causes, the effects, or both?

Consider also the cause or effect arguments you have read, heard, or seen on television. If you recall someone else's argument in some detail, try to identify what made it interesting to you. Was it the subject, or did the author perhaps present ideas new to you? How did the author make the argument for causes or effects convincing? Were you intrigued by illuminating details or an unusual point of view?

Write at least a page about your experience with cause or effect arguments.

■ A Guide to Reading Essays Speculating about Causes or Effects

This guide introduces you to written texts that speculate about causes or effects. By completing all of the activities in it, you will prepare yourself to learn a great deal from the other readings in this chapter about how to read and write a speculative essay. The guide makes use of "Why We Crave Horror Movies," a well-known essay by the novelist and screenwriter Stephen King. You will read King's essay twice. First, you will read it for meaning, looking closely at the content and ideas. Then, you will read the essay like a writer, analyzing the parts to see how King crafts his essay and to learn the strategies he uses to make his speculative writing convincing. These two activities—reading for meaning and reading like a writer—follow every reading in this chapter.

STEPHEN KING

Why We Crave Horror Movies

Stephen King (b. 1947) is internationally known for his best-selling horror novels, such as Carrie *(1974),* The Shining *(1977),*

Misery (1987), Bag of Bones (1998), and Dreamcatcher (2001). He
also has published a number of short story collections, the serial nov-
els The Green Mile *(1996–2000) and* The Dark Tower *(1982–2004),*
and On Writing: A Memoir of the Craft *(2001). Many of his novels*
have been made into movies, and recently some of his works have been
dramatized on television (Salem's Lot, Riding the Bullet).

The following selection originally appeared in Playboy *magazine*
in 1981. As King's title indicates, the essay attempts to explain
the causes for a common phenomenon: most people's liking—even
craving—for horror movies. Before you read, think about the horror
movie that you remember best and consider why it appeals to you.
How old were you when you first saw it? What was most terrifying
about it? How did you talk about it at the time, and how do you
remember it now?

As you read, test King's argument about the appeal of horror
movies against your own experience. On first reading, how convinc-
ing do you find his causal speculations?

I think that we're all mentally ill; those of us outside the asylums   1
only hide it a little better—and maybe not all that much better,
after all. We've all known people who talk to themselves, people
who sometimes squinch their faces into horrible grimaces when
they believe no one is watching, people who have some hysterical
fear—of snakes, the dark, the tight place, the long drop . . . and, of
course, those final worms and grubs that are waiting so patiently
underground.

When we pay our four or five bucks and seat ourselves at tenth-   2
row center in a theater showing a horror movie, we are daring the
nightmare.

Why? Some of the reasons are simple and obvious. To show that   3
we can, that we are not afraid, that we can ride this roller coaster.
Which is not to say that a really good horror movie may not surprise a scream out of us at some point, the way we may scream
when the roller coaster twists through a complete 360 or plows
through a lake at the bottom of the drop. And horror movies, like
roller coasters, have always been the special province of the young;
by the time one turns 40 or 50, one's appetite for double twists or
360-degree loops may be considerably depleted.

We also go to re-establish our feelings of essential normality;   4
the horror movie is innately conservative, even reactionary. Freda
Jackson as the horrible melting woman in *Die, Monster, Die!* confirms for us that no matter how far we may be removed from the
beauty of a Robert Redford or a Diana Ross, we are still light-years
from true ugliness.

And we go to have fun.   5

Ah, but this is where the ground starts to slope away, isn't it? Because this is a very peculiar sort of fun, indeed. The fun comes from seeing others menaced—sometimes killed. One critic has suggested that if pro football has become the voyeur's version of combat, then the horror film has become the modern version of the public lynching.

It is true that the mythic, "fairy-tale" horror film intends to take away the shades of gray. . . . It urges us to put away our more civilized and adult penchant for analysis and to become children again, seeing things in pure blacks and whites. It may be that horror movies provide psychic relief on this level because this invitation to lapse into simplicity, irrationality, and even outright madness is extended so rarely. We are told we may allow our emotions a free rein . . . or no rein at all.

If we are all insane, then sanity becomes a matter of degree. If your insanity leads you to carve up women like Jack the Ripper or the Cleveland Torso Murderer, we clap you away in the funny farm (but neither of those two amateur-night surgeons was ever caught, heh-heh-heh); if, on the other hand, your insanity leads you only to talk to yourself when you're under stress or to pick your nose on your morning bus, then you are left alone to go about your business . . . though it is doubtful that you will ever be invited to the best parties.

The potential lyncher is in almost all of us (excluding saints, past and present; but then, most saints have been crazy in their own ways), and every now and then, he has to be let loose to scream and roll around in the grass. Our emotions and our fears form their own body, and we recognize that it demands its own exercise to maintain proper muscle tone. Certain of these emotional muscles are accepted—even exalted—in civilized society; they are, of course, the emotions that tend to maintain the status quo of civilization itself. Love, friendship, loyalty, kindness—these are all the emotions that we applaud, emotions that have been immortalized in the couplets of Hallmark cards and in the verses (I don't dare call it poetry) of Leonard Nimoy.

When we exhibit these emotions, society showers us with positive reinforcement; we learn this even before we get out of diapers. When, as children, we hug our rotten little puke of a sister and give her a kiss, all the aunts and uncles smile and twit and cry, "Isn't he the sweetest little thing?" Such coveted treats as chocolate-covered graham crackers often follow. But if we deliberately slam the rotten little puke of a sister's fingers in the door, sanctions follow— angry remonstrance from parents, aunts, and uncles; instead of a chocolate-covered graham cracker, a spanking.

But anticivilization emotions don't go away, and they demand 11 periodic exercise. We have such "sick" jokes as, "What's the difference between a truckload of bowling balls and a truckload of dead babies?" (You can't unload a truckload of bowling balls with a pitchfork . . . a joke, by the way, that I heard originally from a ten-year-old.) Such a joke may surprise a laugh or a grin out of us even as we recoil, a possibility that confirms the thesis: If we share a brotherhood of man, then we also share an insanity of man. None of which is intended as a defense of either the sick joke or insanity but merely as an explanation of why the best horror films, like the best fairy tales, manage to be reactionary, anarchistic, and revolutionary all at the same time.

The mythic horror movie, like the sick joke, has a dirty job to 12 do. It deliberately appeals to all that is worst in us. It is morbidity unchained, our most base instincts let free, our nastiest fantasies realized . . . and it all happens, fittingly enough, in the dark. For those reasons, good liberals often shy away from horror films. For myself, I like to see the most aggressive of them—*Dawn of the Dead,* for instance—as lifting a trap door in the civilized forebrain and throwing a basket of raw meat to the hungry alligators swimming around in that subterranean river beneath.

Why bother? Because it keeps them from getting out, man. It 13 keeps them down there and me up here. It was Lennon and McCartney who said that all you need is love, and I would agree with that.

As long as you keep the gators fed. 14

READING FOR MEANING

This section presents three activities that will help you reread King's causal argument with a critical eye. Done in sequence, these activities lead you from a basic understanding of the selection to a more personal response to it and finally to an analysis that deepens your understanding and critical thinking about what you are reading.

Read to Comprehend

Reread the selection, and write a few sentences briefly explaining the reasons King gives for why people crave horror movies. Also make a list of any words you do not understand—for example, *innately* (paragraph 4), *penchant* (7), *psychic relief* (7), *anarchistic* (11). Look up their meanings in a dictionary to see which definition best fits the context.

To expand your understanding of this reading, you might use one or more of the following critical reading strategies that are explained and illustrated in

Appendix 1: *annotating, outlining, summarizing,* and *questioning to understand and remember.*

Read to Respond

Write several paragraphs exploring your initial thoughts and feelings about King's causal argument essay. Focus on anything that stands out for you, perhaps because it resonates with your own experience or because you find a statement puzzling.

You might consider writing about

- why King writes "[i]f we are all insane, then sanity becomes a matter of degree" (paragraph 8).

- the difference between pro-civilization and "anticivilization" emotions as King presents them in paragraphs 10–13, indicating what you think about his distinction between these two kinds of emotions.

- your own experience and feelings about horror novels or films.

To develop your response to King's essay, you might use one or more of the following critical reading strategies that are explained and illustrated in Appendix 1: *contextualizing, reflecting on challenges to your beliefs and values, recognizing emotional manipulation,* and *judging the writer's credibility.*

Read to Analyze Underlying Assumptions

Write several paragraphs exploring one or more of the assumptions, values, and beliefs underlying King's causal argument. As you write, explain how the assumptions are reflected in the text, as well as what you now think of them (and perhaps of your own assumptions) after rereading the selection with a critical eye.

Notice, for example, that even though King never mentions the "subconscious," he seems to believe there is something in us that embodies "our emotions and our fears" and "demands its own exercise to maintain proper muscle tone" (paragraph 9). He calls on our post-Freudian assumption that there is a subconscious part of our minds to explain why we crave horror movies. Notice also how King uses figurative language—similes and metaphors—to make these abstract ideas vivid. Similes and metaphors take words literally associated with one object or idea and apply them to another one in order to make the second object or idea more dramatic and enrich meaning. But these comparisons often have connotations—that is, they carry emotional associations—reflecting values and beliefs that are not as obvious as if these values and beliefs were expressed directly. For example, is the subconscious mind really like the physical body in that it requires "exercise to maintain proper muscle tone"? Or are the two things really not very similar at all, and we as readers are just being swept along by the power of the writer's metaphor? The purpose of analyzing underlying assumptions in what we read is to give us an opportunity to think critically about unexamined assumptions and values—especially the writer's and our own—many of which may be ingrained in our culture, our education, and even our language.

You might consider writing about

- the writer's assumptions about children and young people reflected in his assertions that "horror movies . . . have always been the special province of the young" (paragraph 3) and that we go to see them "to have fun" (5) and "to put away our more civilized and adult penchant for analysis and to become children again" (7).

- King's assumptions that the horror movie "has a dirty job to do," which is that it "deliberately appeals to all that is worst in us" (12).

- the values and beliefs underlying King's claim that "all you need is love" so "long as you keep the gators fed" (13 and 14).

- the values and beliefs underlying King's assertion that "the horror movie is innately conservative, even reactionary" (4), that we watch such movies to "re-establish our feelings of essential normality" (4), and that "good liberals often shy away from" them (12).

To probe assumptions more deeply, you might use one or more of the following critical reading strategies that are explained and illustrated in Appendix 1: *reflecting on challenges to your beliefs and values, exploring the significance of figurative language, recognizing emotional manipulation,* and *judging the writer's credibility.*

READING LIKE A WRITER

This section guides you through an analysis of King's argumentative strategies: *presenting the subject, making a cause or effect argument, counterarguing,* and *establishing credibility.* For each strategy you will be asked to reread and annotate part of King's essay to see how King uses the strategy in "Why We Crave Horror Movies."

When you study the selections later in this chapter, you will see how different writers use the same strategies to make causal arguments or speculate about effects. The Guide to Writing Essays Speculating about Causes or Effects near the end of the chapter suggests ways you can use these strategies in your own writing.

Presenting the Subject

In presenting the subject of an essay speculating about causes or effects, the writer must be sure that readers will recognize and understand the subject. In some writing situations, the writer can safely assume that readers will already know a great deal about a familiar subject; in this case, the writer can simply identify the subject and immediately begin the speculations about its causes or effects. In many other cases, however, writers must present an unfamiliar subject in enough detail for readers to understand it fully. On occasion, writers may even need to convince readers that their subject is important and worth speculating about.

When writers decide they need to prove that the trend or phenomenon they are writing about exists, they may describe it in great detail, give examples, offer factual evidence, cite statistics, or quote statements by authorities. To establish the importance of the trend or phenomenon, writers may show that it involves a large number of people or has great importance to certain people.

Analyze

1. How does King present horror movies as a particular movie genre? *Skim* the essay to see which horror movies he mentions by title. Are the few examples he cites sufficient? Do you think readers need to have seen the movies he mentions to get the point? What does King seem to assume about his readers' experiences with horror films?

2. *Consider* how King establishes the importance of his subject. *Underline* one or two comments King makes about the subject that are likely to increase his readers' curiosity about why people crave horror movies.

Write

Write several sentences explaining how King presents his subject.

Making a Cause or Effect Argument

At the heart of an essay speculating about causes or effects is an argument. The argument is made up of at least two parts: the proposed causes or effects, and the reasoning and support for each cause or effect. In addition, the writer may anticipate readers' objections or questions, a strategy we take up in the next section on counterargument. In analyzing King's argument, we will look at some of the causes he proposes and how he supports them.

Writers speculating about causes or effects rarely consider only one possibility. They know that most puzzling phenomena (like people's attraction to horror movies) have multiple possible causes. However, they also know that it would be foolish to try to identify every possible cause. Writers must therefore be selective if they hope to make a convincing argument. The best arguments avoid the obvious. They offer new and imaginative ways of thinking—either proposing causes or effects that will surprise readers or arguing for familiar causes or effects in new ways.

Writers support their arguments with various kinds of evidence: facts, statistical correlations, personal anecdotes, testimony of authorities, examples, and analogies. In this activity, we focus on King's use of analogies.

Analyze

1. *Reread* paragraphs 3 and 12, and *identify* the analogy in each paragraph. An analogy is a special form of comparison in which one part of the comparison is used to explain the other. In arguing by analogy, the writer reasons that if two situations are alike, their causes will also be similar.

2. *Think about* how well the comparisons in paragraphs 3 and 12 hold up. For example, you may be able to use your personal experience to test whether watching a horror movie is much like riding a roller coaster. *Ask yourself* in what ways the two are alike—and different. Are they more alike than different? Also *consider* how you are or are not like a hungry alligator when you watch a horror movie.

Write

Describe and *evaluate* King's support-by-analogy in paragraphs 3 and 12. *Explain* the parts of each analogy—the two separate things being compared. *Evaluate* how well each analogy works logically. In what ways are the two things being compared actually alike? Also *evaluate* what the two analogies contribute to King's causal argument. How is the essay strengthened by them?

Counterarguing

When causes or effects cannot be known for certain, there is bound to be disagreement. Consequently, writers try to anticipate possible objections and alternative causes or effects readers might put forward. Writers bring these objections and alternatives directly into their essays and then either refute (argue against) them or find a way to accommodate them in the argument.

Analyze

1. King anticipates a possible objection from readers when he poses the question "Why bother?" in paragraph 13. *Reread* paragraphs 11 and 12 to understand the context in which King anticipates the need to pose that question. *Notice* his direct answer to the question in paragraph 13.

2. *Think about* the effectiveness of King's counterargument. *Consider* whether it satisfactorily answers the objection.

Write

Write a few sentences explaining why you think King asks the question at this point in his argument. *Consider* whether some of King's readers would ask themselves this question. *Evaluate* how satisfied they would be with King's response.

Establishing Credibility

Because cause or effect writing is highly speculative, its effectiveness depends in large part on whether readers trust the writer. Readers sometimes use information about the writer's professional and personal accomplishments in forming their judgments about the writer's credibility. The most important information, however, comes from the writing itself, specifically how writers argue for their own proposed causes or effects, as well as how they handle readers' objections.

Writers seek to establish their credibility with readers by making their reasoning clear and logical, their evidence relevant and trustworthy, and their handling of objections fair and balanced. They try to be authoritative (knowledgeable) without appearing authoritarian (opinionated and dogmatic).

Analyze

1. *Reread* the headnote that precedes King's essay, and *reflect on* what his *Playboy* readers might have already known about him. King is more widely known now than he was when "Why We Crave Horror Movies" was published in 1981, but his readers at that time would likely have heard of him.

2. With King's readers in mind, *skim* the essay in order to decide whether the reasoning is clear and logical and the examples and analogies relevant and trustworthy. *Notice* that King's reasoning is psychological: He argues that mental and emotional needs explain why some people crave horror films. Therefore, you, along with King's intended readers, can evaluate King's credibility in light of your own personal experience—your understanding of the role horror novels and films play in your own life. On the basis of your own experience and your evaluation of the logic and consistency of King's argument, *decide* whether you think most readers would consider him a credible writer on the subject of horror films.

Write

Write several sentences describing the impression readers might get of King from reading both the headnote and his essay on horror films. What might make them trust or distrust what he says about his subject?

■ Readings

NATALIE ANGIER

Intolerance of Boyish Behavior

> *One of America's preeminent science writers, Natalie Angier (b. 1958) won a Pulitzer Prize in 1991 for her reports on various scientific topics published in the* New York Times, *where she has worked as a reporter since 1990, specializing in biology and medicine. Angier has also published articles in magazines, including* Discovery, Time, *and the* Atlantic, *and has taught in New York University's Graduate Program in Science and Environmental Reporting. Her 1988 book,* Natural Obsessions: The Search for the Oncogene, *won the Lewis Thomas Award for excellence in writing about the life sciences. Her most recent books are* Natural Obsessions: Striving to Unlock the Deepest Secrets of the Cancer Cell *(1999) and* Woman, an Intimate Geography *(2000). She also edited* The Best American Science and Nature Writing *(2002).*
>
> *The following selection appeared in the* New York Times *in 1994. The* Times *is a major newspaper in the New York City region; but because people living in dozens of mid- to large-sized American cities can have it delivered to their homes daily, the* Times *has wide national influence. Politicians, academics, and other journalists give it special attention. Journalists such as Angier who write about scientific topics for newspapers and magazines do not assume that readers have a high level of scientific training; they write for a broad audience, including college students interested in ideas and issues.*
>
> *In this reading Angier seeks to explain the increasing intolerance by teachers, parents, counselors, and therapists of certain kinds of behavior that have been labeled "boyish." Angier speculates about the causes of a trend—an increase or decrease in something over time. Unexpected or alarming social trends—such as the increasing use of medication with boys for behavior that was previously tolerated or overlooked—especially invite causal speculation. You will notice that Angier is careful to demonstrate that there is in fact an increasing intolerance of boyish behavior.*
>
> *As you read, think about your own experience as a sibling, as a friend of other young children, as a student in elementary school, or perhaps even as a parent of a boy with "boyish" behavior. Does Angier convince you that most boys are more rambunctious than most girls? Do you believe that many teachers and parents now see this as a big problem? Consider also how plausible you find Angier's proposed causes for the growing intolerance of boyish behavior.*

Until quite recently, the plain-spun tautology "boys will be boys" summed up everything parents needed to know about their Y-chromosome bundles. Boys will be very noisy and obnoxious. Boys will tear around the house and break heirlooms. They will transform any object longer than it is wide into a laser weapon with eight settings from stun to vaporize. They will swagger and brag and fib and not do their homework and leave their dirty underwear on the bathroom floor.

But they will also be . . . boys. They will be adventurous and brave. When they fall down, they'll get up, give a cavalier spit to the side, and try again. Tom Sawyer may have been a slob, a truant and a hedonist; he may have picked fights with strangers for no apparent reason; but he was also resourceful, spirited and deliciously clever. Huckleberry Finn was an illiterate outcast, but as a long-term rafting companion he had no peer.

Today, the world is no longer safe for boys. A boy being a shade too boyish risks finding himself under the scrutiny of parents, teachers, guidance counselors, child therapists—all of them on watch for the early glimmerings of a medical syndrome, a bona fide behavioral disorder. Does the boy disregard authority, make snide comments in class, push other kids around and play hooky? Maybe he has a conduct disorder. Is he fidgety, impulsive, disruptive, easily bored? Perhaps he is suffering from attention-deficit hyperactivity disorder, or ADHD, the disease of the hour and the most frequently diagnosed behavioral disorder of childhood. Does he prefer computer games and goofing off to homework? He might have dyslexia or another learning disorder.

"There is now an attempt to pathologize what was once considered the normal range of behavior of boys," said Melvin Konner of the departments of anthropology and psychiatry at Emory University in Atlanta. "Today, Tom Sawyer and Huckleberry Finn surely would have been diagnosed with both conduct disorder and ADHD." And both, perhaps, would have been put on Ritalin, the drug of choice for treating attention-deficit disorder.

To be fair, many children do have genuine medical problems like ADHD, and they benefit enormously from the proper treatment. Psychiatrists insist that they work very carefully to distinguish between the merely rambunctious child, and the kid who has a serious, organic disorder that is disrupting his life and putting him at risk for all the demons of adulthood: drug addiction, shiftlessness, underemployment, criminality and the like.

At the same time, some doctors and social critics cannot help but notice that so many of the childhood syndromes now being diagnosed in record numbers affect far more boys than girls.

Attention-deficit disorder, said to afflict 5 percent of all children, is thought to be about three to four times more common in boys than girls. Dyslexia is thought to be about four times more prevalent in boys than girls; and boys practically have the patent on conduct disorders. What is more, most of the traits that brand a child as a potential syndromeur just happen to be traits associated with young males: aggression, rowdiness, restlessness, loud-mouthedness, rebelliousness. None of these characteristics is exclusive to the male sex, of course—for the ultimate display of aggressive intensity, try watching a group of city girls engaged in a serious game of jump-rope—but boys more often will make a spectacle of themselves. And these days, the audience isn't smiling at the show.

"People are more sensitized to certain extremes of boyishness,"   7
said Dr. John Ratey, a psychiatrist at Harvard Medical School. "It's not as acceptable to be the class clown. You can't cut up. You won't be given slack anymore." Woe to the boy who combines misconduct with rotten grades; he is the likeliest of all to fall under professional observation. "If rowdiness and lack of performance go together, you see the button being pushed much quicker than ever before," he said, particularly in schools where high academic performance is demanded.

Lest males of all ages feel unfairly picked upon, researchers   8
point out that boys may be diagnosed with behavioral syndromes and disorders more often than girls for a very good reason: their brains may be more vulnerable. As a boy is developing in the womb, the male hormones released by his tiny testes accelerate the maturation of his brain, locking a lot of the wiring in place early on; a girl's hormonal bath keeps her brain supple far longer. The result is that the infant male brain is a bit less flexible, less able to repair itself after slight injury that might come, for example, during the arduous trek down the birth canal. Hence, boys may well suffer disproportionately from behavioral disorders for reasons unrelated to cultural expectations.

However, biological insights can only go so far in explaining   9
why American boyhood is coming to be seen as a state of protodisease. After all, the brains of boys in other countries also were exposed to testosterone in utero, yet non-American doctors are highly unlikely to diagnose a wild boy as having a conduct disorder or ADHD.

"British psychiatrists require a very severe form of hyperactivity   10
before they'll see it as a problem," said Dr. Paul R. McHugh, chairman and director of psychiatry at the Johns Hopkins School of Medicine in Baltimore. "Unless a child is so clearly disturbed that he goes at it until he falls asleep in an inappropriate place like

a wastebasket or a drawer, and then wakes up and starts it all over again, he won't be put on medication." Partly as a result of this sharp difference in attitudes, the use of Ritalin-like medications has remained fairly stable in Britain, while pharmaceutical companies here have bumped up production by 250 percent since 1991.

Perhaps part of the reason why boyish behavior is suspect these days is Americans' obsessive fear of crime. "We're all really terrified of violence," said Dr. Edward Hallowell, a child psychiatrist at Harvard. "Groups of people who have trouble containing aggression come under suspicion." And what group has more trouble containing aggression than males under the age of 21? Such suspiciousness is not helped by the fact that the rate of violent crime has climbed most steeply among the young, and that everybody seems to own a gun or know where to steal one. Sure, it's perfectly natural for boys to roll around in the dirt fighting and punching and kicking; but toss a firearm into the equation, and suddenly no level of aggression looks healthy.

Another cause for the intolerance of boyish behavior is the current school system. It is more group-oriented than ever before, leaving little room for the jokester, the tough, the tortured individualist. American children are said to be excessively coddled and undisciplined, yet in fact they spend less time than their European or Japanese counterparts at recess, where kids can burn off the manic energy they've stored up while trapped in the classroom. Because boys have a somewhat higher average metabolism than do girls, they are likely to become more fidgety when forced to sit still and study.

The climate is not likely to improve for the world's Sawyers or Finns or James Deans or any other excessively colorful and unruly specimens of boyhood. Charlotte Tomaino, a clinical neuropsychologist in White Plains, notes that the road to success in this life has gotten increasingly narrow in recent years. "The person who used to have greater latitude in doing one thing and moving onto another suddenly is the person who can't hold a job," she said. "We define success as what you produce, how well you compete, how well you keep up with the tremendous cognitive and technical demands put upon you." The person who will thrive is not the restless version of a human tectonic plate, but the one who can sit still, concentrate and do his job for the 10, 12, 14 hours a day required.

A generation or two ago, a guy with a learning disability—or an ornery temperament—could drop out of school, pick up a trade and become, say, the best bridge builder in town. Now, if a guy cannot at the very least manage to finish college, the surging, roaring, indifferent Mississippi of the world's economy is likely to take his little raft, and break it into bits.

READING FOR MEANING

This section presents three activities that will help you reread Angier's causal argument with a critical eye. Done in sequence, these activities lead you from a basic understanding of the selection to a more personal response to it and finally to an analysis that deepens your understanding and critical thinking about what you are reading.

Read to Comprehend

Reread the selection, and write a few sentences briefly explaining the causes Angier gives for the rise in intolerance of boyish behavior. Also make a list of any words you do not understand—for example, *bona fide* (paragraph 3), *pathologize* (4), *syndromeur* (6), *syndromes* (8), *trek* (8). Look up their meanings in a dictionary to see which definition best fits the context.

To expand your understanding of this reading, you might use one or both of the following critical reading strategies that are explained and illustrated in Appendix 1: *outlining* and *contextualizing*.

Read to Respond

Write several paragraphs exploring your initial thoughts and feelings about Angier's causal argument. Focus on anything that stands out for you, perhaps because it resonates with your own experience or because you find a statement puzzling.

You might consider writing about

- why Angier incorporates examples from Mark Twain's novels *The Adventures of Tom Sawyer* and *The Adventures of Huckleberry Finn,* and how her use of them contributes to your understanding of the essay.

- Angier's assertion that "it's perfectly natural for boys to roll around in the dirt fighting and punching and kicking" (paragraph 11).

- a time when you experienced, expressed, or observed intolerance of boyish behavior, connecting your experience to ideas or examples in Angier's essay.

- the extent to which your own experience and observation supports Angier's proposed causes in paragraphs 11–14.

- how the World Wide Web and other information technologies that have come into wide use since Angier's article was published might affect her argument.

To develop your response to Angier's essay, you might use one or more of the following critical reading strategies that are explained and illustrated in Appendix 1: *contextualizing, recognizing emotional manipulation,* and *judging the writer's credibility.*

Read to Analyze Underlying Assumptions

Write several paragraphs exploring one or more of the assumptions, values, and beliefs underlying Angier's causal argument. As you write, explain how the assumptions are reflected in the text, as well as what you now think of them (and perhaps of your own assumptions) after rereading the selection with a critical eye.

You might consider writing about

- Angier's own assumptions about boyish behavior, as reflected, for instance, in the first two paragraphs.

- the assumptions underlying the causal explanations Angier writes about in paragraphs 11–13.

- the values and beliefs underlying the language Angier uses to describe boys, especially the adjectives in paragraphs 1, 2, and 6 and language such as the following: "merely rambunctious" (5), "misconduct" (7), "Americans' obsessive fear of crime" (11), "trapped in the classroom" (12), "the restless version of a human tectonic plate" (13).

To probe assumptions more deeply, you might use one or more of the following critical reading strategies that are explained and illustrated in Appendix 1: *reflecting on challenges to your beliefs and values, exploring the significance of figurative language,* and *recognizing emotional manipulation.*

READING LIKE A WRITER
COUNTERARGUING

Writers speculating about causes must work imaginatively and persistently to support their proposed causes, using all the relevant resources available to them—quoting authorities, citing statistics and research findings, comparing and contrasting, posing rhetorical questions, offering literary allusions, and crafting metaphors, among others. (Angier uses all of the resources in this list.) In addition to supporting their proposed causes, writers usually do more. Because they aim to convince particular readers of the plausibility of their causal argument, writers try to be keenly aware that at every point in the argument their readers will have questions, objections, and other causes in mind. Anticipating and responding to these questions, objections, and alternative causes is known as *counterarguing.*

As readers work their way through a causal argument, nearly all of them will think of questions they would like to ask the writer; or they will resist or object to certain aspects of the support, such as the way the writer uses facts or statistics, relies on an authority, sets up an analogy, or presents an example or personal experience. Readers may doubt whether the support is appropriate, believable, or consistent with the other support provided by the writer. They may come to believe that the writer relies too much on emotional appeals and too little on reason.

Readers may also resist or reject the writer's proposed causes, or they may believe that other causes better explain the trend. Experienced writers anticipate all of these predictable concerns. Just as imaginatively as they argue for their proposed causes, writers attempt to answer readers' questions, react to their objections, and evaluate their preferred causes. When you write your essay about causes or effects, anticipating and responding to your readers' concerns will be one of the most challenging and interesting parts of constructing your argument.

Analyze

1. Angier counterargues in at least three places in her causal argument: paragraphs 5, 6, and 8. *Reread* these paragraphs, and *identify* and *underline* the three main objections that Angier anticipates her readers will have to her argument. For example, in the first sentence of paragraph 5, she anticipates readers' likely objection that some boys do have medical problems requiring treatment.

2. *Examine closely* how Angier counterargues readers' objections and questions. For the three objections or questions you identified in paragraphs 5, 6, and 8, *notice* the kinds of support she relies on to argue against each objection. *Decide* whether the support is similar or different among the three cases.

Write

Write several sentences reporting what you have learned about how Angier anticipates her readers' objections. Specifically, in each case, how does she support her counterargument? How appropriate do you, as one of her intended readers, find her support? How believable do you find it?

A SPECIAL READING STRATEGY

Comparing and Contrasting Related Readings: Angier's "Intolerance of Boyish Behavior" and Konner's "Why the Reckless Survive"

Comparing and contrasting related readings is a special critical reading strategy useful both in reading for meaning and in reading like a writer. This strategy is particularly applicable when writers present similar subjects, as is the case in the causal arguments in this chapter by Natalie Angier (p. 413) and Melvin Konner (p. 422). Both authors are scientists who are writing about connections between science and human behavior and trying to establish the causes for behavior that is unfair (in Angier's view) or odd (in Konner's view). To compare and contrast these two writers' causal arguments, think about issues such as these:

- Compare how the authors first establish that a problem exists and that it is worthy of investigation. Why is it important to spend several paragraphs establishing the problem? What strategies does each author use to investigate and document the problem?

- Compare how the authors speculate about the causes for the problem. What scientific data do they use? How do they support their speculations? How do they conclude?

- Speculate about how Konner would explain, with his theory of why humans are reckless, the behavior of boys as established by Angier.

See Appendix 1 for detailed guidelines on using the comparing and contrasting related readings strategy.

A SPECIAL READING STRATEGY

Evaluating the Logic of an Argument

To evaluate the logic of an argument speculating about causes, ask yourself three basic questions:

- How appropriate is the support for each cause being speculated about?

- How believable is the support?

- How consistent and complete is the overall argument?

Such an evaluation requires a comprehensive and thoughtful critical reading, but your efforts will help you understand more fully what makes a causal argument successful. To evaluate the logic of Angier's argument, follow the guidelines in Appendix 1 (pp. 675–79). There you will find definitions and explanations as well as an illustration based on an excerpt from a famous essay by Martin Luther King Jr. (the excerpt appears on pp. 649–54).

CONSIDERING IDEAS FOR YOUR OWN WRITING

Think about other groups or categories of people you have the opportunity to observe, and try to identify trends or changes in aspects of their behavior. For example, does it seem to you that girls or women are increasingly interested in math and science or in participating in team sports? If you have been working for a few years, have you noticed that employees have become more docile and more eager to please management? If you have young children, does it seem to you that day-care workers have become increasingly professional?

Select one group whose behavior is changing, and consider how you would convince readers that the behavior is in fact changing—increasing or decreasing over time. What kind of evidence would you need to gather in the library or on the Internet to corroborate your personal impressions? As a writer speculating about a behavioral change, consider how you would come up with some possible causes for the trend.

MELVIN KONNER

Why the Reckless Survive

Melvin Konner (b. 1946) is Samuel Candler Dobbs Professor of Anthropology and associate professor of psychiatry and neurology at Emory University. He earned both a Ph.D. in biological anthropology from Harvard University and an M.D. from Harvard Medical School and spent two years doing fieldwork among the Kalahari San (Bushmen) of Africa, studying infant development and the mechanism by which hormones prevent conception in breast-feeding women. Lately Konner has been an advocate of a single-payer system of national health insurance and has testified twice at U.S. Senate hearings.

The following essay was first published in Konner's book Why the Reckless Survive—and Other Secrets of Human Nature *(1990). In addition to this collection, Konner has written, among other books,* The Tangled Wing: Biological Constraints on the Human Spirit *(1982), which was nominated for an American Book Award in science;* Childhood *(1991); and* Medicine at the Crossroads: The Crisis in Health Care *(1993).*

In this essay, Konner explores why so many people engage in behaviors that to others carry unacceptable physical, financial, or other kinds of risks—such as not wearing seat belts, riding motorcycles, eating unhealthy food, or playing the lottery. He points out that while few people take the most extreme kinds of risks, almost everyone decides, consciously or not, to accept some risks that outside observers would see as irrational or foolish. And he looks to humans' remote evolutionary past for an explanation. As you read the essay, notice how Konner's professional and academic qualifications as a physician and anthropologist are reinforced by the sources he chooses to support his argument about the causes of "reckless" human behavior.

In a recent election Massachusetts rescinded its seat-belt law. As a result some hundreds of citizens of that commonwealth have in the past year gone slamming into windshields instead of getting a pain in the neck from the shoulder belt. Quite a few are unnecessarily brain-damaged or dead. Such laws in fact make a difference. Americans in general use seat belts at a rate of about 20 percent; but in Texas, where failure to wear one can cost you not only your life but also fifty dollars, nearly seven people in ten wear them habitually—a fivefold increase since the law was passed in 1985. Having lived in Massachusetts for fifteen years, I considered it—wrongly, perhaps—the most sensible state in the union, so I was rather amazed by its recent collective decision.

But I shouldn't have been. All I needed to do was to look at my own behavior. I have, while coauthoring a book on health, sat at

1

2

my word processor at three A.M. guzzling coffee and gobbling Oreo cookies by the dozen, pecking solemnly away about our need to take better care of ourselves. I could almost feel the fat from the cookies sinking into the arteries of my brain, the coffee laying the groundwork for future cardiac arrhythmias.

Why can't we follow our own advice, or others', even when we know it's right? Is it the heedless child in us, or the perverse, destructive teenager, or only the antiauthoritarian, freedom-loving adult that says, *I will do as I please, thank you*? Or could it be that there is something inevitable—even something good—about the taking of all these chances? 3

People don't think clearly about risk. This is no mere insult, but a conclusion that emerges from attempts by behavioral scientists to understand how people make decisions. In part these studies were sparked by the unprecedented demand for risk reduction that has emerged in recent years. How many cases of cancer do people consider acceptable nationally as a result of the widespread use of a food additive or an industrial chemical? None. How many accidents or near-accidents at nuclear power plants? None. How many airline crashes per decade? Basically, none. 4

We may consider the change good: doesn't it reflect a healthy increase in awareness of real risks? But consider that this is the same American public that, after years of education, wears seat belts at the rate of 20 percent and has reduced its cigarette smoking only somewhat. The widespread success of lotteries alone shows that people do not think or act rationally, even in their own self-interest. 5

So we ignore some risks and overestimate others. The conundrum for an evolutionist is simple. Natural selection should have relentlessly culled systematic biases in decision making, producing a rational organism that hews to the order of real cost-benefit analysis—an organism that behaves efficiently to minimize those ratios. How can evolution, with its supposedly relentless winnowing out of error, have preserved this bewildering array of dangerous habits? 6

We are highly sensitive to certain dangers. A Harris poll conducted in 1980 showed that 78 percent of the American public (as opposed to roughly half of business and government leaders) thought that risks in general were greater than they had been twenty years before. The greatest perceived risks were in the areas of crime and personal safety, international and domestic political stability, energy sources, and "the chemicals we use." Comfortable majorities of the general public (but only small minorities of the 7 leadership groups) agreed with the statements "Society has only perceived the tip of the iceberg with regard to the risks associated with modern technology" and "Unless technological development is restrained, the overall safety of society will be jeopardized significantly in the next twenty years."

But the logic of our concerns is problematic. People are willing to pay indirectly large sums of money to reduce the risk of a nuclear accident or a cancer death from a chemical to levels they consider acceptably low. But they will not pay a much smaller amount for air bags in automobiles, that, inflating on impact, will save many more lives; and they will not stop smoking, although this risk-reducing measure would actually save money, both immediately and in the long term.

Apparently, irrational factors are at work. But before we consider them, and why we may be subject to them, it is worth looking at the realities of risk. John Urquhart and Klaus Heilmann, both physicians, have reviewed some of these realities in their book *Riskwatch: The Odds of Life.* There is a genuine hierarchy of danger. For example, the number of deaths linked to cigarette smoking in the United States is equivalent to three jumbo jets full of passengers crashing daily, day in and day out. We have fifty thousand traffic fatalities a year—almost the number of deaths we suffered during our entire involvement in Vietnam. Half involve drunk drivers, and a large proportion would be prevented by seat belts or air bags.

Yet neither of these sources of risk evokes the interest—indeed the fear—shown in response to possible nuclear accidents, or to toxic-shock syndrome caused by tampons, or even to homicide, all (for most of us) trivial risks by comparison to smoking or driving. If you tremble when you strap yourself into the seat of an airliner, you ought to really shudder when you climb onto your bicycle, since that is much more dangerous as a regular activity. As for homicide, the people most afraid of it are the ones least likely to be victimized. And the millions of women who stopped taking birth-control pills because of the risk of death from stroke did so in response to an annual probability of dying equal to about one fourth their routine risk of death in an automobile.

Urquhart and Heilmann deal with this quirkiness in our response to risk by developing a Safety-Degree Scale analogous to the Richter scale for earthquake severity. The units are logarithms of the cohort size necessary for one death to occur. Thus lightning, which kills fewer than one person per million exposed, has a safety degree of more than six, while motorcycling, which kills one in a thousand, has a safety degree of three; motorcycling is three orders of magnitude more dangerous. But they aren't perceived in that relation. In general, people will accept one to two orders of magnitude more danger in voluntary risks than they will in involuntary ones. And that is only one aspect of the quirkiness. Risks that result in many deaths at once will be perceived as worse than probabilistically equal risks that kill in a more distributed way. And any bad outcome that is reported unexpectedly—especially if its shock value is exploited—increases fear.

Chronic departures from rationality have been the subject of a major line of thought in economics, in which the most distinguished name is Herbert Simon's. Simon, a winner of the Nobel Memorial prize in economics, has for years criticized and occasionally ridiculed the economic decision theory known as subjective expected utility, or SEU. According to this classic approach, individuals face their life choices with full knowledge of the probability and value of all possible outcomes, and furthermore they possess an unambiguous value scale to measure utility—in plain English, they know a great deal, in advance, about the consequences of their choices, and, more important, they know what they want. In the real world, Simon points out, no such knowledge exists. Whether in the choices of executives or in those of consumers, knowledge is imperfect and values (at least to some extent) indeterminate and mercurial.

A similar point was demonstrated in laboratory experiments by psychologists Amos Tversky and Daniel Kahnemann, in which people are shown to be rather feeble in their abilities to choose among various outcomes. They are readily confused by differences in the language in which a problem is posed. In one study, Tversky and Kahnemann asked physicians to choose among possible programs to combat a hypothetical disease that was on the verge of killing six hundred people. The physicians favored a program guaranteed to save *two hundred lives* over one that had a one-third probability of saving everyone and a two-thirds probability of saving no one. Yet a second group of physicians favored the riskier program over one described as resulting in exactly *four hundred deaths*. They were, of course, rejecting the same alternative the previous group had chosen. The only difference was that it was now being described in terms of victims rather than survivors. Human decision making is rife with such framing errors, and analyzing them has become a cottage industry.

At least equally interesting is a new psychological view—advanced by Lola Lopes among others—that certain "errors" may not be errors at all. Lottery players can be shown to be irrational by multiplying the prize by the probability of winning, and comparing that

12

13

14

number to the cost of the ticket. But that does not take into account the subjective value placed on becoming rich, or the fact that this may be someone's only chance for that outcome. Nor, of course, does it consider the thrill of playing.

But another aspect of this behavior clearly is irrational: people—especially, but not only, compulsive gamblers—have unrealistically high expectations of winning. On the average, in the larger game of life, they also have unrealistically high expectations of protection against losing. Linda Perloff and others have shown that people—average people—think that they will live longer than average, that they will have fewer diseases than average, and even that their marriages will last longer than average. Since average people are likely to have average rates of disease, death, and divorce, they are (in these studies) underestimating their risks—a tendency Lionel Tiger has summarized as a ubiquitous, biologically based human propensity to unwarranted optimism.   15

While these results fit well with the prevalence of risky behavior, they seem to contradict the findings about people's *overestimate* of the risk of violent crime, or terrorist attacks, or airline crashes, or nuclear-plant accidents. Part of this is resolvable by reference to the principle that risks beyond our control are more frightening than those we consider ourselves in charge of. So we drink and drive, and buckle the seat belt behind us, and light up another cigarette, on the strength of the illusion that to *these* risks at least, we are invulnerable; and we cancel the trip to Europe on the one-in-a-million chance of a . . . terrorist attack.   16

Three patterns, then, emerge in our misestimates. First, we prefer voluntary risks to involuntary ones—or, put another way, risks that we feel we have some control over to those that we feel we don't. By the way we drive and react to cues on the road, we think, we reduce our risk to such a low level that seat belts add little protection. But in the case of the terrorist attack or the nuclear-plant accident, we feel we have no handle on the risks. (We seem especially to resent and fear risks that are imposed on us by others, especially if for their own benefit. If I want to smoke myself to death, we seem to say, it's my own business; but if some company is trying to put something over on me with asbestos or nerve gas, I'll be furious.)   17

Second, we prefer familiar risks to strange ones. The homicide during a mugging, or the airliner hijacked in Athens, or the nerve gas leaking from an armed forces train, get our attention and so loom much larger in our calculations than they should in terms of real risk. Third, deaths that come in bunches—the jumbo-jet crash of the disaster movie—are more frightening than those that come in a steady trickle, even though the latter may add up to more risk   18 when the counting is done. This principle may be related in some way to the common framing error in which people in Tversky and Kahnemann's studies will act more strongly to prevent two hundred deaths in six hundred people than they will to guarantee four hundred survivors from the same group. Framing the risk in terms of death rather than survival biases judgment.

But there is yet another, more interesting complication. "The general public," "average people," "human" rational or irrational behavior—these categories obscure the simple fact that people differ in these matters. [19]

Average people knowingly push their cholesterol levels upward, but only a third pay essentially no attention to doctors' orders when it comes to modifying their behavior (smoking, or eating a risky diet) in the setting of an established illness worsened by that behavior. Average people leave their seat belts unbuckled, but only some people ride motorcycles, and fewer still race or do stunts with them. Average people play lotteries, friendly poker, and church bingo, but an estimated one to four million Americans are pathological gamblers, relentlessly destroying their lives and the lives of those close to them by compulsively taking outrageous financial risks. [20]

Psychologists have only begun to address these individual differences, but several different lines of research suggest that there is such a thing as a risk-taking or sensation-seeking personality. For example, studies of alcohol, tobacco, and caffeine abuse have found these three forms of excess to be correlated, and also to be related to various other measures of risk taking. [21]

For many years psychologist Marvin Zuckerman, of the University of Delaware, and his colleagues have been using the Sensation Seeking Scale, a questionnaire designed to address these issues directly. Empirically, the questions fall along four dimensions: *thrill and adventure seeking*, related to interest in physical risk taking, as in sky-diving and mountain climbing; *experience seeking*, reflecting a wider disposition to try new things, in art, music, travel, friendship, or even drugs; *disinhibition*, the hedonistic pursuit of pleasure through activities like social drinking, partying, sex, and gambling; and *boredom susceptibility*, an aversion to routine work and dull people. [22]

At least the first three of these factors have held up in many samples, of both sexes and various ages, in England and America, but there are systematic differences. Males always exceed females, and sensation seeking in general declines in both sexes with age. There is strongly suggestive evidence of a genetic predisposition: 233 pairs of identical twins had a correlation of 0.60 in sensation [23] seeking, while 138 nonidentical twin pairs had a corresponding correlation of only 0.21.

More interesting than these conventional calculations is a series of studies showing that sensation seeking, as measured by the questionnaire, has significant physiological correlates. For example, heart-rate change in reaction to novelty is greater in sensation-seekers, as is brain-wave response to increasingly intense stimulation. The activity of monoamine oxidase (MAO), an enzyme that breaks down certain neurotransmitters (the chemicals that transmit signals between brain cells), is another correlate. Sensation seekers have less MAO activity, suggesting that neurotransmitters that might be viewed as stimulants may persist longer in their brains. Finally, the sex hormones, testosterone and estrogen, show higher levels in sensation seekers. 24

But in addition this paper-and-pencil test score correlates with real behavior. High scores engage in more frequent, more promiscuous, and more unusual sex; consume more drugs, alcohol, cigarettes, and even spicy food; volunteer more for experiments and other unusual activities; gamble more; and court more physical danger. In the realm of the abnormal, the measure is correlated with hypomania, and in the realm of the criminal, with psychopathy. 25

In other words, something measured by this test has both biological and practical significance. Furthermore, independent studies by Frank Farley and his colleagues at the University of Wisconsin, using a different instrument and a somewhat distinct measure they call thrill seeking, have confirmed and extended these findings. For example, in prison populations fighting and escape attempts are higher in those who score high on thrill seeking. But Farley also emphasizes positive outcomes—a well-established correlation between sensation seeking and the extraverted personality underscores the possibility that some such people are well primed for leadership. 26

We can now return to the main question: how could all this irrationality have been left untouched by natural selection? Herbert Simon, in an accessible, even lyrical, summary of his thought, the 1983 book *Reason in Human Affairs,* surprised some of us in anthropology and biology who are more or less constantly railing against the un-Darwinian musings of social scientists. He shows a quite incisive understanding of Darwin's theories and of very recent significant refinements of them. 27

But my own anthropological heart was most warmed by passages such as this one: "If this [situation] is not wholly descriptive of the world we live in today . . . it certainly describes the world in which human rationality evolved: the world of the cavemen's ancestors, 28 and of the cavemen themselves. In that world . . . periodically action had to be taken to deal with hunger, or to flee danger, or to secure protection against the coming winter. Rationality could focus on dealing with one or a few problems at a time. . . ." The appeal to the world of our ancestors, the hunters and gatherers, is as explicit as I could wish. As Simon recognizes, this is the world in which our rationality, limited as it is, evolved. It could not be much better now than it needed to be then, because less perfect rationality would not have been selected against; and we, the descendants of those hunters and gatherers, would have inherited their imperfections.

The result is what Simon calls "bounded rationality"—a seat- 29 of-the-pants, day-by-day sort of problem solving that, far from pretending to assess all possible outcomes against a clear spectrum of values, attempts no more than to get by. "Putting out fires" is another way of describing it; and it follows directly from the concept of economic behavior that made Simon famous: "satisficing," the notion that people are just trying to solve the problem at hand in a way that is "good enough"—his practical answer to those too-optimistic constructions of economists, "maximizing" and "optimizing."

Simon has perceived that the basic human environment did not 30 call for optimal decision making, in the modern risk-benefit sense of the phrase; thus our imperfection, this "bounded rationality." But this does not explain the systematic departures from rationality—the preference for "controllable" or familiar rather than "uncontrollable" or strange risks, or the particular fear attached to large disasters. And it does not explain, especially, the sense of invulnerability of risk takers. Certain kinds of recklessness are easy to handle by looking at the specific evolutionary provenance of certain motives. Kristin Luker, a sociologist at the University of California at San Diego, studied contraceptive risk taking and uncovered what often seemed an unconscious desire for a baby. It is no challenge to reconcile this with evolutionary theory; a Darwinian couple ought to take such risks right and left. Sexual indiscretions in general could be covered by a similar line of argument: sexy sensation seekers perpetuate their genes. Slightly more interesting are the specific risks involved in certain human culinary preferences. We overdo it on fats and sweets because our ancestors were rewarded for such excesses with that inch of insulation needed to carry them through shortages. Death by atherosclerosis may be a pervasive threat today, but for most of the past three million years it was a consummation devoutly to be wished.

But we are still far from the comprehensive explanation of reck- 31 lessness we need. For this we must look to the darker side of human nature, as expressed in that same ancestral environment. Martin Daly and Margo Wilson, both psychologists at McMaster University in Ontario, explore this matter directly in a book called *Homicide*. Although their analysis is restricted to only one highly dramatic form of risk taking, it is paradigmatic of the problem.

Homicides occur in all human societies, and a frequent cause is   32 a quarrel over something seemingly trivial—an insult, a misunderstanding, a disagreement about a fact neither combatant cares about. Of course, these conflicts are never *really* trivial; they are about status and honor—which in practical terms means whether and how much you can be pushed around. And on this will depend your access to food, land, women (the participants are almost always male)—in short, most of what matters in life and in natural selection. In societies where heads are hunted or coups counted, the process is more formalized, but the principle is similar.

If you simulate, as Daly and Wilson do, a series of fights in   33 which individuals with different risk propensities—low, medium, and high—encounter each other, the high-risk individuals invariably have the highest mortality. But any assumption that winning increases Darwinian fitness—virtually certain to be correct in most environments—leads to predominance of high- or medium-risk individuals. Their candles burn at both ends, but they leave more genes.

The underlying assumption is that the environment is a dan-   34 gerous one, but this assumption is sensible. The environments of our ancestors must have been full of danger. "Nothing ventured, nothing gained" must have been a cardinal rule; and yet venturing meant exposure to grave risk: fire, heights, cold, hunger, predators, human enemies. And all this risk has to be seen against a background of mortality from causes outside of human control— especially disease. With an average life expectancy at birth of thirty years, with a constant high probability of dying from pneumonia or malaria—the marginal utility, in economic terms, of strict avoidance of danger would have been much lower than it is now, perhaps negligible. In Oscar Lewis's studies of the Mexican "culture of poverty" and in Eliot Liebow's studies of poor black streetcorner men, the point is clearly made: the failure of such people to plan for the future is not irrational—they live for the day because they know that they have no future.

To die, in Darwinian terms, is not to lose the game. Individuals   35 risk or sacrifice their lives for their kin. Sacrifice for offspring is ubiquitous in the animal world, and the examples of maternal defense of the young in mammals and male death in the act of copulation in insects have become familiar. But great risks are taken and sacrifices made for other relatives as well. Consider the evisceration of the worker honeybee in the act of stinging an intruder and the alarm call of a bird or ground squirrel, calling the predator's attention to itself while warning its relatives. During our own evolution small, kin-based groups might have gained much from having a minority of reckless sensation seekers in the ranks—people who wouldn't hesitate to snatch a child from a pack of wild dogs or to fight an approaching grass fire with a counterfire.

In any case, both sensation seekers and people in general should have taken their risks selectively. They may have found it advantageous to take risks with the seemingly controllable and familiar, even while exaggerating the risk of the unknown, and hedging it around with all sorts of taboo and ritual. It is difficult to imagine a successful encounter with a volcano, but an early human would have had at least a fighting chance against a lion. And we, their descendants, fear toxic nuclear waste but leave our seat belts unbuckled.

Why can't we adjust our personal behavior to our modern middle-class spectrum of risks? Because we are just not built to cut it that finely. We are not designed for perfectly rational calculations, or to calibrate such relatively unimpressive risks. For many of us, life seems compromised by such calculations; they too have a cost—in effort, in freedom, in self-image, in fun. And the fun is not incidental. It is evolution's way of telling us what we were designed for.

Sensation seeking fulfills two of the three cardinal criteria for evolution by natural selection: it varies in the population, and the varieties are to some extent inheritable. In any situation in which the varieties give rise in addition to different numbers of offspring, evolution will occur. The notion that riskier types, because they suffer higher mortality, must slowly disappear is certainly wrong for many environments, and it may still be wrong even for ours.

Ideally, of course, one would want a human organism that could take the risks that—despite the dangers—enhance fitness, and leave aside the risks that don't. But life and evolution are not that perfect. The result of the vastly long evolutionary balancing act is a most imperfect organism. The various forms of personal risk taking often hang together; you probably can't be the sort of person who makes sure to maintain perfectly safe and healthy habits, and yet reflexively take the risks needed to ensure survival and reproductive success in the basic human environment. If you are designed, emotionally, for survival and reproduction, then you are not designed for perfect safety.

So when my father buckles his seat belt behind him, and my brother keeps on smoking, and my friend rides her motorcycle to work every day, it isn't because, or only because, they somewhat underestimate the risks. My father wants the full sense of competence and freedom that he has always had in driving, since long before seat belts were dreamed of. My brother wants the sense of calm that comes out of the cigarette. My friend wants to hear the roar of the Harley and feel the wind in her hair. And they want the risk, because risk taking, for them, is part of being alive.   40

As for me, when I avoid those risks, I feel safe and virtuous but perhaps a little cramped. And I suspect that, like many people who watch their diet carefully—despite the lapses—and exercise more or less scrupulously and buckle up religiously, I am a little obsessed with immortality, with the prospect of controlling that which cannot be controlled. I know I am doing the sensible thing— my behavior matches, most of the time, the spectrum of real probabilities. But against what scale of value? I sometimes think that the more reckless among us may have something to teach the careful about the sort of immortality that comes from living fully every day.   41

READING FOR MEANING

This section presents three activities that will help you reread Konner's causal argument with a critical eye. Done in sequence, these activities lead you from a basic understanding of the selection to a more personal response to it and finally to an analysis that deepens your understanding and critical thinking about what you are reading.

Read to Comprehend

Reread the selection, and write a few sentences briefly explaining both the primary reasons Konner gives to explain why humans engage in reckless behavior and how the writer reconciles this reckless behavior with evolutionists' belief that species will engage only in behavior that perpetuates the species. Also make a list of any words you do not understand—for example, *conundrum* (paragraph 6), *ubiquitous* (15), *propensity* (15), *predisposition* (23), *correlates* (24), *provenance* (30), *paradigmatic* (31). Look up their meanings in a dictionary to see which definition best fits the context.

To expand your understanding of this reading, you might use one or more of the following critical reading strategies that are explained and illustrated in Appendix 1: *annotating, previewing, outlining,* and *summarizing.*

Read to Respond

Write several paragraphs exploring your initial thoughts and feelings about Konner's causal argument. Focus on anything that stands out for you, perhaps because it resonates with your own experience or because you find a statement puzzling.

You might consider writing about

- your opinion of the "risky" behaviors Konner examines in his essay.

- your reaction to the research Konner cites in support of his argument.

- your response to the final sentence of the essay.

- your own risky behaviors, and how you feel about them now that you've read this essay.

To develop your response to Konner's essay, you might use one or both of the following critical reading strategies that are explained and illustrated in Appendix 1: *questioning to understand and remember* and *recognizing emotional manipulation.*

Read to Analyze Underlying Assumptions

Write several paragraphs exploring one or more of the assumptions, values, and beliefs underlying Konner's causal argument. As you write, explain how the assumptions are reflected in the text, as well as what you now think of them (and perhaps of your own assumptions) after rereading the selection with a critical eye.

You might consider writing about

- what Konner assumes about his readers' knowledge of Darwin's theory of natural selection and about their beliefs and values regarding this theory (paragraphs 6 and 27–39).

- the belief underlying the statement that "[t]o die, in Darwinian terms, is not to lose the game" (35).

- Konner's assumption that recklessness can be explained in terms of the conditions in which early humans lived.

- the assumption that death is the most feared and the worst outcome of risky behaviors, considering what other outcomes might be particularly undesirable.

- Konner's questioning of the assumption that people would not play the lottery if they understood rationally how little chance they had of winning (14), perhaps also considering other risky activities with possible outcomes so desirable they outweigh the dangers.

To probe assumptions more deeply, you might use one or more of the following critical reading strategies that are explained and illustrated in Appendix 1: *evaluating the logic of an argument, performing a Toulmin analysis,* and *judging the writer's credibility.*

READING LIKE A WRITER
MAKING THE CONNECTION BETWEEN THE SUBJECT AND THE CAUSES

Writers of causal arguments need to present their causes so the reader can see the logical connection between the event, phenomenon, or trend and the writer's speculations about what caused it. Konner begins his essay with anecdotes that illustrate a phenomenon: People (including Konner himself) engage in reckless behavior even when they know it could kill them. He then poses three questions in paragraph 3. The first summarizes the phenomenon and poses the central question of its cause: "Why can't we follow our own advice, or others', even when we know it's right?" The second suggests some possible causes, and the third sets out the cause he eventually argues for: "Or could it be that there is something inevitable—even something good—about the taking of all these chances?"

To answer his questions, Konner first examines the seeming irrationality of human behavior, especially in light of Charles Darwin's theory of natural selection, which refers to the mechanism whereby certain traits that enable organisms, like human beings, to adapt to their environment and therefore to live long enough to reproduce are passed on to future generations. Not until paragraph 31, once he has established varying causes of "irrational" behavior, does he turn to specifically examining causes of recklessness. As you examine Konner's presentation of the causes of reckless behavior, you will see how thoroughly he explains and supports his reasoning.

Analyze

1. *Reread* paragraphs 1–30, and *make notes* about the different fields from which Konner draws his sources to explain the irrationality of human behavior when it comes to risk-taking. For example, in the first few paragraphs he refers to research by behavioral scientists, to a Harris poll, and to a book by two physicians. *Find* other references, and *note* what they say about irrational behavior.

2. *List* Konner's sources, and *summarize* what they contribute to Konner's argument.

3. Then *reread* the rest of the essay, and *consider* how Konner explains the "darker side of human nature" (31).

Write

Write several sentences explaining how Konner presents the causes for the two different sections of his essay, the causes of irrationality (paragraphs 1–30) and the causes of reckless behavior (31–41). How convinced are you by Konner's argument? What other possibilities might he have considered?

CONSIDERING IDEAS FOR YOUR OWN WRITING

Konner's essay may suggest to you several ideas for your own essay speculating about causes, such as what might cause groups of people to do something or to behave in some way: What causes some people to stay in or drop out of college, devote themselves to strenuous exercise programs, abuse their spouses, join cults or gangs, become vegetarians, or listen to talk radio? You should be able to think of many other examples.

VILAYANUR S. RAMACHANDRAN AND
EDWARD M. HUBBARD

Hearing Colors, Tasting Shapes

Vilayanur S. Ramachandran (b. 1951) directs the Center for Brain and Cognition at the University of California at San Diego (UCSD) and is adjunct professor at the Salk Institute for Biological Studies. Originally trained as a physician, he later obtained a doctorate from Cambridge University. He has published in such popular scientific magazines as Nature *and* Science *as well as in academic science journals. Edward M. Hubbard (b. 1972) is a graduate student in the departments of psychology and cognitive science at UCSD. Ramachandran and Hubbard collaborate on studies of synesthesia, the blending of perceptions from different senses, such as sight and sound. The following essay about synesthesia was first published in 2003 in* Scientific American, *a journal popular with both scientists and general readers interested in science.*

As you read, think about how the authors first consider others' psychological explanations of the causes of synesthesia before carefully showing how their own experiments establish to their satisfaction that synesthesia is a physical condition likely caused by cross-wiring in the brain. Notice also their speculations about the possible effects of synesthesia, especially on creativity and the development of language in humans. Included with the essay are two "sidebars" published along with it, one that answers common questions about synesthesia and another that explains how it could have led to the creation of language.

When Matthew Blakeslee shapes hamburger patties with his hands, he experiences a vivid bitter taste in his mouth. Esmerelda Jones (a pseudonym) sees blue when she listens to the note C sharp played on the piano; other notes evoke different hues—so much so that the piano keys are actually color-coded, making it easier for her to remember and play musical scales. And when Jeff Coleman looks at printed black numbers, he sees them in color, each a different hue. Blakeslee, Jones and Coleman are among a handful of otherwise normal people who have synesthesia. They experience the ordinary world in extraordinary ways and seem to inhabit a mysterious no-man's-land between fantasy and reality. For them the senses—touch, taste, hearing, vision and smell—get mixed up instead of remaining separate.

Modern scientists have known about synesthesia since 1880, when Francis Galton, a cousin of Charles Darwin, published a paper in *Nature* on the phenomenon. But most have brushed it aside as fakery, an artifact of drug use (LSD and mescaline can

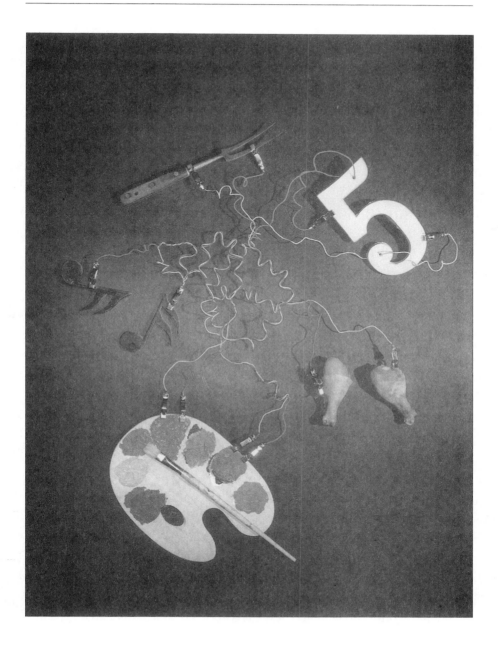

produce similar effects) or a mere curiosity. About four years ago, however, we and others began to uncover brain processes that could account for synesthesia. Along the way, we also found new clues to some of the most mysterious aspects of the human mind, such as the emergence of abstract thought, metaphor and perhaps even language.

A common explanation of synesthesia is that the affected people are simply experiencing childhood memories and associations. Maybe a person had played with refrigerator magnets as a child and the number 5 was red and 6 was green. This theory does not answer why only some people retain such vivid sensory memories, however. You might *think* of cold when you look at a picture of an ice cube, but you probably do not feel cold, no matter how many encounters you may have had with ice and snow during your youth. 3

Another prevalent idea is that synesthetes are merely being metaphorical when they describe the note C flat as "red" or say that chicken tastes "pointy"—just as you and I might speak of a "loud" shirt or "sharp" cheddar cheese. Our ordinary language is replete with such sense-related metaphors, and perhaps synesthetes are just especially gifted in this regard. 4

We began trying to find out whether synesthesia is a genuine sensory experience in 1999. This deceptively simple question had plagued researchers in this field for decades. One natural approach is to start by asking the subjects outright: "Is this just a memory, or do you actually see the color as if it were right in front of you?" When we tried asking this question, we did not get very far. Some subjects did respond, "Oh, I see it perfectly clearly." But a more frequent reaction was, "I kind of see it, kind of don't" or "No, it is not like a memory. I see the number as being clearly red but I also *know* it isn't; it's black. So it must be a memory, I guess." 5

To determine whether an effect is truly perceptual, psychologists often use a simple test called pop-out or segregation. If you look at a set of tilted lines scattered amid a forest of vertical lines, the tilted lines stand out. Indeed, you can instantly segregate them from the background and group them mentally to form, for example, a separate triangular shape. Similarly, if most of a background's elements were green dots and you were told to look for red targets, the reds would pop out. On the other hand, a set of black 2's scattered among 5's of the same color almost blend in [see the illustration on p. 439]. It is hard to discern the 2's without engaging in an item-by-item inspection of numbers, even though any individual number is just as clearly different from its neighbors as a tilted line is from a straight line. We thus 6

COLOR-CODED WORLD

In a test of visual-segregation capabilities, synesthetes who link a specific hue with a given number can instantly see an embedded pattern in an image with black numbers scattered on a white page. Whereas a person with normal perception must undertake a digit-by-digit search to pick out, in this example, 2's amid 5's *(left)*, the triangle-shaped group of 2's pops out for a synesthete *(right)*.

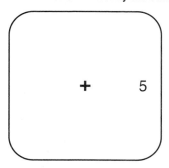

"Invisible" numbers show up for synesthetes in a perceptual test. When a person stares at a central object, here a plus sign, a single digit off to one side is easy to see with peripheral vision *(left)*. But if the number is surrounded by others *(right)*, it appears blurry—invisible—to the average person. In contrast, a synesthete could deduce the central number by the color it evokes.

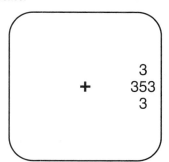

may conclude that only certain primitive, or elementary, features, such as color and line orientation, can provide a basis for grouping. More complex perceptual tokens, such as numbers, cannot do so.

We wondered what would happen if we showed the mixed numbers to synesthetes who experience, for instance, red when they see

7

a 5 and green with a 2. We arranged the 2's so that they formed a triangle. If synesthesia were a genuine sensory effect, our subjects should easily see the triangle because for them, the numbers would look colored.

When we conducted pop-out tests with volunteers, the answer was crystal clear. Unlike normal subjects, synesthetes correctly reported the shape formed by groups of numbers up to 90 percent of the time (exactly as nonsynesthetes do when the numbers actually have different colors). This result proves that the induced colors are genuinely sensory and that synesthetes are not just making things up. It is impossible for them to fake their success. In another striking example, we asked a synesthete who sees 5 tinged red to watch a computer display. He could not tell when we surreptitiously added an actual red hue to the white number unless the red was sufficiently intense; he could instantly spot a real green added to the 5.

8

VISUAL PROCESSING

Confirmation that synesthesia is real brings up the question, Why do some people experience this weird phenomenon? Our experiments lead us to favor the idea that synesthetes are experiencing the result of some kind of cross wiring in the brain. This basic concept was initially proposed about 100 years ago, but we have now identified where in the brain and how such cross wiring might occur.

9

An understanding of the neurobiological factors at work requires some familiarity with how the brain processes visual information [see the illustration on p. 441]. After light reflected from a scene hits the cones (color receptors) in the eye, neural signals from the retina travel to area 17, in the occipital lobe at the back of the brain. There the image is processed further within local clusters, or blobs, into such simple attributes as color, motion, form and depth. Afterward, information about these separate features is sent forward and distributed to several far-flung regions in the temporal and parietal lobes. In the case of color, the information goes to area V4 in the fusiform gyrus of the temporal lobe. From there it travels to areas that lie farther up in the hierarchy of color centers, including a region near a patch of cortex called the TPO (for the junction of the temporal, parietal and occipital lobes). These higher areas may be concerned with more sophisticated aspects of color processing. For example, leaves look as green at dusk as they do at midday, even though the mix of wavelengths reflected from the leaves is very different.

10

MINGLED SIGNALS

In one of the most common forms of synesthesia, looking at a number evokes a specific hue. This apparently occurs because brain areas that normally do not interact when processing numbers or colors do activate each other in synesthetes.

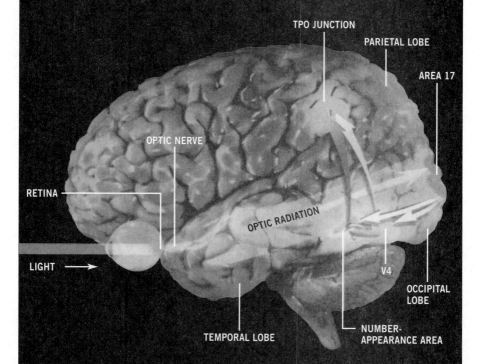

Neural signals from the retina travel via optic radiation to area 17, in the rear of the brain, where they are broken into simple shared attributes such as color, form, motion and depth.

Color information continues on to V4, near where the visual appearance of numbers is also represented—and thus is a site for cross-linking between the color and number areas *(vertical arrows)*.

Ultimately, color proceeds "higher," to an area near the TPO (for *t*emporal, *p*arietal, *o*ccipital lobes) junction, which may perform more sophisticated color processing. Similarly, a later stage of numerical computation occurs in the angular gyrus, a part of the TPO concerned with the concepts of sequence and quantity. This could explain synesthesia in people who link colors with abstract numerical sequences, like days of the week.

Numerical computation, too, seems to happen in stages. An   11
early step also takes place in the fusiform gyrus, where the actual
shapes of numbers are represented, and a later one occurs in the
angular gyrus, a part of the TPO that is concerned with numerical
concepts such as ordinality (sequence) and cardinality (quantity).
(When the angular gyrus is damaged by a stroke or a tumor, the
patient can still identify numbers but can no longer divide or sub-
tract. Multiplication often survives because it is learned by rote.) In
addition, brain-imaging studies in humans strongly hint that visually presented letters of the alphabet or numbers (graphemes) activate cells in the fusiform gyrus, whereas the sounds of the syllables
(phonemes) are processed higher up, once again in the general
vicinity of the TPO.

Because both colors and numbers are processed initially in the   12
fusiform gyrus and subsequently near the angular gyrus, we sus-
pected that number-color synesthesia might be caused by cross
wiring between V4 and the number-appearance area (both within
the fusiform) or between the higher color area and the number-
concept area (both in the TPO). Other, more exotic forms of
the condition might result from similar cross wiring of different
sensory-processing regions. That the hearing center in the temporal
lobes is also close to the higher brain area that receives color signals from V4 could explain sound-color synesthesia. Similarly,
Matthew Blakeslee's tasting of touch might occur because of cross
wiring between the taste cortex in a region called the insula and an
adjacent cortex representing touch by the hands.

Assuming that neural cross wiring does lie at the root of synes-   13
thesia, why does it happen? We know that it runs in families, so it
has a genetic component. Perhaps a mutation causes connections
to emerge between brain areas that are usually segregated. Or
maybe the mutation leads to defective pruning of preexisting connections between areas that are normally connected only sparsely.
If the mutation were to be expressed (that is, to exert its effects) in
some brain areas but not others, this patchiness might explain why
some synesthetes conflate colors and numbers whereas others see
colors when they hear phonemes or musical notes. People who
have one type of synesthesia are more likely to have another, which
adds weight to this idea.

Although we initially thought in terms of physical cross wiring,   14
we have come to realize that the same effect could occur if the
wiring—the number of connections between regions—was fine
but the balance of chemicals traveling between regions was skewed.
So we now speak in terms of cross activation. For instance, neighboring brain regions often inhibit one another's activity, which

serves to minimize cross talk. A chemical imbalance of some kind that reduces such inhibition—for example, by blocking the action of an inhibitory neurotransmitter or failing to produce an inhibitor—would also cause activity in one area to elicit activity in a neighbor. Such cross activation could, in theory, also occur between widely separated areas, which would account for some of the less common forms of synesthesia.

Support for cross activation comes from other experiments, some of which also help to explain the varied forms synesthesia can take. One takes advantage of a visual phenomenon known as crowding [see the illustration on p. 439]. If you stare at a small plus sign in an image that also has a number 5 off to one side, you will find that it is easy to discern that number, even though you are not looking at it directly. But if we now surround the 5 with four other numbers, such as 3's, then you can no longer identify it. It looks out of focus. Volunteers who perceive normally are no more successful at identifying this number than mere chance. That is not because things get fuzzy in the periphery of vision. After all, you could see the 5 perfectly clearly when it wasn't surrounded by 3's. You cannot identify it now because of limited attentional resources. The flanking 3's somehow distract your attention away from the central 5 and prevent you from seeing it. 15

A big surprise came when we gave the same test to two synesthetes. They looked at the display and made remarks like, "I cannot see the middle number. It's fuzzy but it looks red, so I guess it must be a 5." Even though the middle number did not consciously register, it seems that the brain was nonetheless processing it somewhere. Synesthetes could then use this color to deduce intellectually what the number was. If our theory is right, this finding implies that the number is processed in the fusiform gyrus and evokes the appropriate color *before* the stage at which the crowding effect occurs in the brain; paradoxically, the result is that even an "invisible" number can produce synesthesia. 16

Another finding we made also supports this conclusion. When we reduced the contrast between the number and the background, the synesthetic color became weaker until, at low contrast, subjects saw no color at all, even though the number was perfectly visible. Whereas the crowding experiment shows that an invisible number can elicit color, the contrast experiment conversely indicates that viewing a number does not guarantee seeing a color. Perhaps low-contrast numbers activate cells in the fusiform adequately for conscious perception of the number but not enough to cross-activate the color cells in V4. 17

Finally, we found that if we showed synesthetes Roman numerals, a V, say, they saw no color—which suggests that it is not the numerical *concept* of a number, in this case 5, but the grapheme's visual appearance that drives the color. This observation, too, implicates cross activation within the fusiform gyrus itself in number-color synesthesia, because that structure is mainly involved in analyzing the visual shape, not the high-level meaning of the number. One intriguing twist: Imagine an image with a large 5 made up of little 3's; you can see either the "forest" (the 5) or focus minutely on the "trees" (the 3's). Two synesthete subjects reported that they saw the color switch, depending on their focus. This test implies that even though synesthesia can arise as a result of the visual appearance alone—not the high-level concept—the manner in which the visual input is categorized, based on attention, is also critical. [18]

But as we began to recruit other volunteers, it soon became obvious that not all synesthetes who colorize their world are alike. In some, even days of the week or months of the year elicit colors. Monday might be green, Wednesday pink, and December yellow. [19]

The only thing that days of the week, months and numbers have in common is the concept of numerical sequence, or ordinality. For certain synesthetes, perhaps it is the abstract concept of numerical sequence that drives the color, rather than the visual appearance of the number. Could it be that in these individuals, the cross wiring occurs between the angular gyrus and the higher color area near the TPO instead of between areas in the fusiform? If so, that interaction would explain why even abstract number representations, or the *idea* of the numbers elicited by days of the week or months, will strongly evoke specific colors. In other words, depending on where in the brain the mutant gene is expressed, it can result in different types of the condition—"higher" synesthesia, driven by numerical concept, or "lower" synesthesia, produced by visual appearance alone. Similarly, in some lower forms, the visual appearance of a letter might generate color, whereas in higher forms it is the *sound,* or phoneme, summoned by that letter; phonemes are represented near the TPO. . . . [20]

A WAY WITH METAPHOR

Our insights into the neurological basis of synesthesia could help explain some of the creativity of painters, poets and novelists. According to one study, the condition is seven times as common in creative people as in the general population. [21]

COMMON QUESTIONS

Are there different types of synesthesia?
Science counts about 50. The condition runs in families and may be more common in women and creative people; perhaps one person in 200 has synesthesia. In the most prevalent type, looking at numbers or listening to tones evokes colors. In one rare kind, each letter is associated with the male or female sex—an example of the brain's tendency to split the world into binary categories.

If a synesthete associates a color with a single letter or number, what happens if he looks at a pair of letters, such as "ea," or double digits, as in "25"?
He sees colors that correspond with the individual letters and numbers. If the letters or numbers are too close physically, however, they may cancel each other out (color disappears) or, if the two happen to elicit the same color, enhance each other.

Does it matter whether letters are uppercase or lowercase?
In general, no. But people have sometimes described seeing less saturated color in lowercase letters, or the lowercase letters may appear shiny or even patchy.

How do entire words look?
Often the color of the first letter spreads across the word; even silent letters, such as the "p" in "psalm," cause this effect.

What if the synesthete is multilingual?
One language can have colored graphemes, but a second (or additional others) may not, perhaps because separate tongues are represented in different brain regions.

What about when the person mentally pictures a letter or number?
Imagining can evoke a stronger color than looking at a real one. Perhaps that exercise activates the same brain areas as does viewing real colors—but because no competing signals from a real number are coming from the retina, the imagined one creates a stronger synesthetic color.

Does synesthesia improve memory?
It can. The late Russian neurologist Aleksandr R. Luria described a mnemonist who had remarkable recall because all five of his senses were linked. Even having two linked senses may help.

One skill that many creative people share is a facility for using metaphor ("It is the east, and Juliet is the sun"). It is as if their brains are set up to make links between seemingly unrelated domains—such as the sun and a beautiful young woman. In other words, just

22

as synesthesia involves making arbitrary links between seemingly unrelated perceptual entities such as colors and numbers, metaphor involves making links between seemingly unrelated conceptual realms. Perhaps this is not just a coincidence.

Numerous high-level concepts are probably anchored in specific brain regions, or maps. If you think about it, there is nothing more abstract than a number, and yet it is represented, as we have seen, in a relatively small brain region, the angular gyrus. Let us say that the mutation we believe brings about synesthesia causes excess communication among different brain maps—small patches of cortex that represent specific perceptual entities, such as sharpness or curviness of shapes or, in the case of color maps, hues. Depending on where and how widely in the brain the trait was expressed, it could lead to both synesthesia and to a propensity toward linking seemingly unrelated concepts and ideas—in short, creativity. This would explain why the apparently useless synesthesia gene has survived in the population.

In addition to clarifying why artists might be prone to experiencing synesthesia, our research suggests that we all have some capacity for it and that this trait may have set the stage for the evolution of abstraction—an ability at which humans excel. The TPO (and the angular gyrus within it), which plays a part in the condition, is normally involved in cross-modal synthesis. It is the brain region where information from touch, hearing and vision is thought to flow together to enable the construction of high-level perceptions. For example, a cat is fluffy (touch), it meows and purrs (hearing), it has a certain appearance (vision) and odor (smell), all of which are derived simultaneously by the memory of a cat or the sound of the word "cat."

Could it be that the angular gyrus—which is disproportionately larger in humans compared with that in apes and monkeys—evolved originally for cross-modal associations but then became co-opted for other, more abstract functions such as metaphors? Consider two drawings, originally designed by psychologist Wolfgang Köhler. One looks like an inkblot and the other, a jagged piece of shattered glass [see the illustrations on p. 447]. When we ask, "Which of these is a 'bouba,' and which is a 'kiki'?" 98 percent of people pick the inkblot as a bouba and the other one as a kiki. Perhaps that is because the gentle curves of the amoeba-like figure metaphorically mimic the gentle undulations of the sound "bouba" as represented in the hearing centers in the brain as well as the gradual inflection of the lips as they produce the curved "boobaa" sound. In contrast, the waveform of the sound "kiki" and the sharp

23

24

25

THE PUZZLE OF LANGUAGE

Imagine a band of ancestral hominids about to invent language. Clearly, they did not begin by having a leader say, "Hey, look at this—let's call it a banana. All of you say after me, *ba-na-na.*" Undoubtedly, though, the group had a set of capacities that prepared the ground for systematic verbal communication. Our studies of the neurobiological basis of synesthesia suggest that a facility for metaphor—for seeing deep links between superficially dissimilar and unrelated things—provided a key seed for the eventual emergence of language.

Humans have a built-in bias to associate certain sounds with particular visual shapes, which could well have been important in getting hominids started on a shared vocabulary. In addition, specific brain areas that process visual shapes of objects, letters and numbers, and word sounds can activate each other even in non-synesthetes, causing people to expect, say, jagged shapes to have harsh-sounding names.

Two other types of neural connections support our idea. First, the sensory areas for visual shapes and for hearing in the back of the brain can cross-activate specific motor areas in the front of the brain that participate in speech. A sharp visual inflection or a harsh sound induces the motor control area for speech to produce an equally sudden inflection of the tongue on the palate. (Or consider

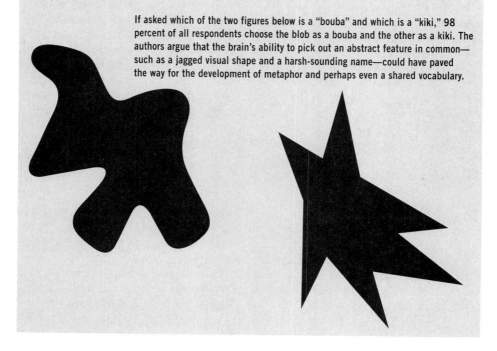

If asked which of the two figures below is a "bouba" and which is a "kiki," 98 percent of all respondents choose the blob as a bouba and the other as a kiki. The authors argue that the brain's ability to pick out an abstract feature in common—such as a jagged visual shape and a harsh-sounding name—could have paved the way for the development of metaphor and perhaps even a shared vocabulary.

the spoken words "diminutive," "teeny-weeny" and "*un peu,*" which involve pursing the lips to mimic the small size of the object.) The brain seems to possess pre-existing rules for translating what we see and hear into mouth motions that reflect those inputs.

Second, a kind of spillover of signals occurs between two nearby motor areas: those that control the sequence of muscle movements required for hand gestures and those for the mouth. We call this effect "synkinesia." As Charles Darwin pointed out, when we cut paper with scissors, our jaws may clench and unclench unconsciously as if to echo the hand movements. Many linguists do not like the theory that manual gesturing could have set the stage for vocal language, but we believe that synkinesia suggests that they may be wrong.

Assume that our ancestral hominids communicated mainly through emotional grunts, groans, howls and shrieks, which are known to be produced by the right hemisphere and an area in the frontal lobes concerned with emotion. Later the hominids developed a rudimentary gestural system that became gradually more elaborate and sophisticated; it is easy to imagine how the hand movement for pulling someone toward you might have progressed to a "come hither" wave. If such gestures were translated through synkinesia into movements of the mouth and face muscles, and if emotional guttural utterances were channeled through these mouth and tongue movements, the result could have been the first spoken words.

How would we import syntax, the rules for using words and phrases in language, into this scheme? We believe that the evolution of tool use by hominids may have played an important role. For example, the tool-building sequence—first shape the hammer's head, then attach it to a handle, then chop the meat— resembles the embedding of clauses within larger sentences. Following the lead of psychologist Patricia Greenfield of the University of California at Los Angeles, we propose that frontal brain areas that evolved for subassembly in tool use may later have been co-opted for a completely novel function—joining words into phrases and sentences.

Not every subtle feature of modern language is explained by such schemes, but we suspect that these elements were critical for setting in motion the events that culminated in modern language.

inflection of the tongue on the palate mimic the sudden changes in the jagged visual shape. The only thing these two kiki features have in common is the abstract property of jaggedness that is extracted somewhere in the vicinity of the TPO, probably in the angular gyrus. (We recently found that people with damage to the angular gyrus lose the bouba-kiki effect—they cannot match the shape with the correct sound.) In a sense, perhaps we are all closet synesthetes.

So the angular gyrus performs a very elementary type of   26
abstraction—extracting the common denominator from a set of
strikingly dissimilar entities. We do not know how exactly it does
this job. But once the ability to engage in cross-modal abstraction
emerged, it might have paved the way for the more complex types
of abstraction. The opportunistic takeover of one function for a
different one is common in evolution. For example, bones in the
ear used for hearing in mammals evolved from the back of the
jawbone in reptiles. Beyond metaphor and abstract thinking,
cross-modal abstraction might even have provided seeds for language [see the box on pp. 447–48].

When we began our research on synesthesia, we had no inkling   27
of where it would take us. Little did we suspect that this eerie phenomenon, long regarded as a mere curiosity, might offer a window
into the nature of thought.

More to Explore

The Man Who Tasted Shapes. R. E. Cytowic. MIT Press, 1993.

Synaesthesia: Classic and Contemporary Readings. S. Baron-Cohen and J. E. Harrison.
Blackwell, 1997.

"Psychophysical Investigations into the Neural Basis of Synaesthesia." V. S. Ramachandran and E. M. Hubbard in *Proceedings of the Royal Society of London,* B, Vol. 268,
pages 979–983; 2001.

"Synaesthesia: A Window into Perception, Thought and Language." V. S. Ramachandran and E. M. Hubbard in *Journal of Consciousness Studies,* Vol. 8, No. 12, pages
3–34; 2001.

"Synaesthetic Photisms Influence Visual Perception." D. Smilek, M. J. Dixon, C. Cud-
ahy and M. Merikle in *Journal of Cognitive Neuroscience,* Vol. 13, No. 7, pages
930–936; 2001.

"Functional Magnetic Resonance Imaging of Synesthesia: Activation of V4/V8
by Spoken Words." J. A. Nunn, L. J. Gregory, M. Brammer, S. C. R. Williams,
D. M. Parslow, M. J. Morgan, R. G. Morris, E. T. Bullmore, S. Baron-Cohen and
J. A. Gray in *Nature Neuroscience,* Vol. 5, pages 371–375; 2002.

For more on synesthesia, visit www.sciam.com/ontheweb.

READING FOR MEANING

This section presents three activities that will help you reread Ramachandran
and Hubbard's cause-and-effect argument with a critical eye. Done in sequence,
these activities lead you from a basic understanding of the selection to a more
personal response to it and finally to an analysis that deepens your understanding
and critical thinking about what you are reading.

Read to Comprehend

Reread the selection, and write a few sentences briefly explaining synesthesia and the causes and effects of it that Ramachandran and Hubbard discuss. Also make a list of any words you do not understand—for example, *replete* (paragraph 4), *phenomenon* (9), *neurobiological* (10), *mutation* (13). Look up their meanings in a dictionary to see which definition best fits the context.

To expand your understanding of this reading, you might use one or more of the following critical reading strategies that are explained and illustrated in Appendix 1: *previewing, outlining, summarizing, paraphrasing,* and *questioning to understand and remember.*

Read to Respond

Write several paragraphs exploring your initial responses to "Hearing Colors, Tasting Shapes." Focus on anything that stands out for you, perhaps because it resonates with your own experience or because you find a statement puzzling.

You might consider writing about

- the effect of the scientific jargon used by the authors, in light of how familiar you are with the terms they use and whether you become familiar with the terms as they are used repeatedly throughout the essay.

- how the visuals help clarify the information provided in the text.

- which causes and effects of synesthesia seem most plausible to you—and why.

- your own experience (or that of someone you know) with synesthesia.

To develop your response to "Hearing Colors, Tasting Shapes," you might use one or both of the following critical reading strategies that are explained and illustrated in Appendix 1: *questioning to understand and remember* and *judging the writer's credibility.*

Read to Analyze Underlying Assumptions

Write several paragraphs exploring one or more of the assumptions, values, and beliefs underlying "Hearing Colors, Tasting Shapes." As you write, explain how the assumptions are reflected in the text, as well as what you now think of them (and perhaps of your own assumptions) after rereading the selection with a critical eye.

You might consider writing about

- the reasons the authors tell the story of their research, narrating the events of their discoveries.

- what the authors' speculations about the causes and effects of synesthesia reveal about their assumptions about scientific research and human thought processes.

- the theory or belief underlying the authors' explanation of "why the apparently useless synesthesia gene has survived in the population" (paragraph 23).

To probe assumptions more deeply, you might use one or more of the following critical reading strategies that are explained and illustrated in Appendix 1: *reflecting on challenges to your beliefs and values, evaluating the logic of an argument,* and *judging the writer's credibility.*

READING LIKE A WRITER
PRESENTING THE SUBJECT

When writers speculate about the causes of a phenomenon, they must define or describe the phenomenon for readers. Readers must be assured that the phenomenon actually exists. Furthermore, readers are more likely to be engaged by the speculations if they can recognize or be convinced that the phenomenon is important to them personally or that it has some larger significance. In some writing situations, writers may safely assume readers are thoroughly familiar with the phenomenon and therefore need little more than a mention of it. In most situations, however, writers know that readers will require a relatively full presentation of the subject. Because synesthesia is not a commonly known phenomenon, the authors must carefully define it; they also must show that they have considered seriously previously speculated causes and effects of synesthesia before they present their own causes and effects.

Analyze

1. *Reread* paragraphs 1–8. *Notice* the sources the authors use to define synesthesia and its history, as well as the questions they ask to find out more about the phenomenon and its genuineness.

2. *Reread* the sidebar entitled "The Puzzle of Language." *Notice* how the authors speculate on a topic of interest to most people: how language came about.

Write

Write several sentences explaining how Ramachandran and Hubbard present their subject. Then *add a few more sentences* evaluating how successfully they do so. What sources and details in paragraphs 1–8 and in the sidebar seem most helpful to readers? What, if anything, seems to be missing from their presentation? Where are they most successful in declaring or suggesting the importance of their subject?

CONSIDERING IDEAS FOR YOUR OWN WRITING

Ramachandran and Hubbard speculate about a phenomenon that has, until their and others' recent research, been unexplained or explained unconvincingly. They explore both the possible causes and possible effects of their phenomenon. In your essay, you will need to explore *only* causes *or* effects, but you could choose a phenomenon or trend that is puzzling to you. This could be something you've noticed in your daily life or a scientific phenomenon that you think has not been fully explained yet. For example, you could speculate about the causes of traffic patterns that lead to unusual congestion where you live, about the effects of a change in policies for student loans, or about why your college decided to discontinue a sports team. If you have noticed or know about a scientific phenomenon, such as changes in wildflower patterns in your part of the country or an increase in the population of feral cats in your city, you could explore the causes for that change.

JONATHAN KOZOL

The Human Cost of an Illiterate Society

A well-known critic of American schools, Jonathan Kozol (b. 1936) was in the forefront of educational reformers during the 1970s and 1980s. He has taught in the Boston and Newton, Massachusetts, public schools, as well as at Yale University and the University of Massachusetts at Amherst. Kozol's books include Death at an Early Age *(1967), for which he won the National Book Award;* On Being a Teacher *(1981);* Illiterate America *(1985);* Amazing Grace: The Lives of Children and the Conscience of a Nation *(1985);* Savage Inequalities: Children in America's Schools *(1991);* Blueprint for a Democratic Education *(1992); and* Ordinary Resurrections: Children in the Years of Hope *(2000).*

The following selection is from Illiterate America, *a comprehensive study of the nature, causes, and effects of illiteracy. The book is intended for a broad readership. Certainly, you are among Kozol's intended readers. In this chapter from the book, Kozol speculates about the human consequences of illiteracy, outlining the limitations and dangers in the lives of adults who cannot read or write. Elsewhere in the book, Kozol conjectures about the causes of illiteracy, but here he concentrates on the effects of the phenomenon, speculating about what life is like for illiterates. He adopts this strategy to argue that the human costs of the problem pose a moral dilemma for our country.*

As you read, decide whether Kozol convinces you that illiteracy is not just a social problem but also a special danger to democracy.

PRECAUTIONS. READ BEFORE USING.
Poison: Contains sodium hydroxide (caustic soda-lye).
Corrosive: Causes severe eye and skin damage, may cause blindness.
Harmful or fatal if swallowed.
If swallowed, give large quantities of milk or water.
Do not induce vomiting.
Important: Keep water out of can at all times to prevent contents from violently erupting. . . .

—WARNING ON A CAN OF DRANO

Questions of literacy, in Socrates' belief, must at length be judged as matters of morality. Socrates could not have had in mind the moral compromise peculiar to a nation like our own. Some of our Founding Fathers did, however, have this question in their minds. One of the wisest of those Founding Fathers [James Madison] recognized the special dangers that illiteracy would pose to basic equity in the political construction that he helped to shape:

A· people who mean to be their own governors must arm   2
themselves with the power knowledge gives. A popular
government without popular information or the means of
acquiring it, is but a prologue to a farce or a tragedy, or perhaps both.

Tragedy looms larger than farce in the United States today. Illit-   3
erate citizens seldom vote. Those who do are forced to cast a vote
of questionable worth. They cannot make informed decisions
based on serious print information. Sometimes they can be alerted
to their interests by aggressive voter education. More frequently,
they vote for a face, a smile, or a style, not for a mind or character
or body of beliefs.

The number of illiterate adults exceeds by 16 million the entire   4
vote cast for the winner in the 1980 presidential contest. If even
one third of all illiterates could vote, and read enough and do sufficient math to vote in their self-interest, Ronald Reagan would
not likely have been chosen president. There is, of course, no way
to know for sure. We do know this: Democracy is a mendacious
term when used by those who are prepared to countenance the
forced exclusion of one third of our electorate. So long as 60 million people are denied significant participation, the government is
neither of, nor for, nor by, the people. It is a government, at best,
of those two thirds whose wealth, skin color, or parental privilege
allows them opportunity to profit from the provocation and
instruction of the written word.

The undermining of democracy in the United States is one   5
"expense" that sensitive Americans can easily deplore because it
represents a contradiction that endangers citizens of all political
positions. The human price is not so obvious at first.

Illiterates cannot read the menu in a restaurant.   6

They cannot read the cost of items on the menu in the *window*   7
of the restaurant before they enter.

Illiterates cannot read the letters that their children bring home   8
from their teachers. They cannot study school department circulars that tell them of the courses that their children must be taking
if they hope to pass the SAT exams. They cannot help with homework. They cannot write a letter to the teacher. They are afraid to
visit in the classroom. They do not want to humiliate their child or
themselves.

Illiterates cannot read instructions on a bottle of prescription   9
medicine. They cannot find out when a medicine is past the year
of safe consumption; nor can they read of allergenic risks, warnings
to diabetics, or the potential sedative effect of certain kinds of

nonprescription pills. They cannot observe preventive health care admonitions. They cannot read about "the seven warning signs of cancer" or the indications of blood-sugar fluctuations or the risks of eating certain foods that aggravate the likelihood of cardiac arrest.

Illiterates live, in more than literal ways, an uninsured existence. They cannot understand the written details on a health insurance form. They cannot read the waivers that they sign preceding surgical procedures. Several women I have known in Boston have entered a slum hospital with the intention of obtaining a tubal ligation and have emerged a few days later after having been subjected to a hysterectomy. Unaware of their rights, incognizant of jargon, intimidated by the unfamiliar air of fear and atmosphere of ether that so many of us find oppressive in the confines even of the most attractive and expensive medical facilities, they have signed their names to documents they could not read and which nobody, in the hectic situation that prevails so often in those overcrowded hospitals that serve the urban poor, had even bothered to explain.

10

Even the roof above one's head, the gas or other fuel for heating that protects the residents of northern city slums against the threat of illness in the winter months become uncertain guarantees. Illiterates cannot read the lease that they must sign to live in an apartment which, too often, they cannot afford. They cannot manage check accounts and therefore seldom pay for anything by mail. Hours and entire days of difficult travel (and the cost of bus or other public transit) must be added to the real cost of whatever they consume. Loss of interest on the check accounts they do not have, and could not manage if they did, must be regarded as another of the excess costs paid by the citizen who is excluded from the common instruments of commerce in a numerate society.

11

"I couldn't understand the bills," a woman in Washington, D.C., reports, "and then I couldn't write the checks to pay them. We signed things we didn't know what they were."

12

Illiterates cannot read the notices that they receive from welfare offices or from the IRS. They must depend on word-of-mouth instruction from the welfare worker—or from other persons whom they have good reason to mistrust. They do not know what rights they have, what deadlines and requirements they face, what options they might choose to exercise. They are half-citizens. Their rights exist in print but not in fact.

13

Illiterates cannot look up numbers in a telephone directory. Even if they can find the names of friends, few possess the sorting skills to make use of the yellow pages; categories are bewildering and trade names are beyond decoding capabilities for millions of nonreaders. Even the emergency numbers listed on the first page

14

of the phone book—"Ambulance," "Police," and "Fire"—are too frequently beyond the recognition of nonreaders.

Many illiterates cannot read the admonition on a pack of cigarettes. Neither the Surgeon General's warning nor its reproduction on the package can alert them to the risks. Although most people learn by word of mouth that smoking is related to a number of grave physical disorders, they do not get the chance to read the detailed stories which can document this danger with the vividness that turns concern into determination to resist. They can see the handsome cowboy or the slim Virginia lady lighting up a filter cigarette; they cannot heed the words that tell them that this product is (not "may be") dangerous to their health. Sixty million men and women are condemned to be the unalerted, high-risk candidates for cancer.

Illiterates do not buy "no-name" products in the supermarkets. They must depend on photographs or the familiar logos that are printed on the packages of brand-name groceries. The poorest people, therefore, are denied the benefits of the least costly products.

Illiterates depend almost entirely upon label recognition. Many labels, however, are not easy to distinguish. Dozens of different kinds of Campbell's soup appear identical to the nonreader. The purchaser who cannot read and does not dare to ask for help, out of the fear of being stigmatized (a fear which is unfortunately realistic), frequently comes home with something which she never wanted and her family never tasted.

Illiterates cannot read instructions on a pack of frozen food. Packages sometimes provide an illustration to explain the cooking preparations; but illustrations are of little help to someone who must "boil water, drop the food—*within* its plastic wrapper—in the boiling water, wait for it to simmer, instantly remove."

Even when labels are seemingly clear, they may be easily mistaken. A woman in Detroit brought home a gallon of Crisco for her children's dinner. She thought that she had bought the chicken that was pictured on the label. She had enough Crisco now to last a year—but no more money to go back and buy the food for dinner.

Illiterates cannot travel freely. When they attempt to do so, they encounter risks that few of us can dream of. They cannot read traffic signs and, while they often learn to recognize and to decipher symbols, they cannot manage street names which they haven't seen before. The same is true for bus and subway stops. While ingenuity can sometimes help a man or woman to discern directions from familiar landmarks, buildings, cemeteries, churches, and the like, most illiterates are virtually immobilized. They seldom wander past the streets and neighborhoods they know. Geographical paralysis becomes a bitter metaphor for their entire existence. They are immobilized in almost every sense we can imagine. They can't move up. They can't move out. They cannot see beyond. Illiterates may take an oral test for drivers' permits in most sections of America. It is a questionable concession. Where will they go? How will they get there? How will they get home? Could it be that some of us might like it better if they stayed where they belong?

Travel is only one of many instances of circumscribed existence. Choice, in almost all its facets, is diminished in the life of an illiterate adult. Even the printed TV schedule, which provides most people with the luxury of preselection, does not belong within the arsenal of options in illiterate existence. One consequence is that the viewer watches only what appears at moments when he happens to have time to turn the switch. Another consequence, a lot more common, is that the TV set remains in operation night and day. Whatever the program offered at the hour when he walks into the room will be the nutriment that he accepts and swallows. Thus, to passivity, is added frequency—indeed, almost uninterrupted continuity. Freedom to select is no more possible here than in the choice of home or surgery or food.

"You don't choose," said one illiterate woman. "You take your wishes from somebody else." Whether in perusal of a menu, selection of highways, purchase of groceries, or determination of affordable enjoyment, illiterate Americans must trust somebody else: a friend, a relative, a stranger on the street, a grocery clerk, a TV copywriter.

Billing agencies harass poor people for the payment of the bills for purchases that might have taken place six months before. Utility companies offer an agreement for a staggered payment schedule on a bill past due. "You have to trust them," one man said. Precisely for this reason, you end up by trusting no one and suspecting everyone of possible deceit. A submerged sense of distrust becomes the corollary to a constant need to trust. "They are cheating me . . . I have been tricked . . . I do not know. . . ."

Not knowing: This is a familiar theme. Not knowing the right word for the right thing at the right time is one form of subjugation. Not knowing the world that lies concealed behind those words is a more terrifying feeling. The longitude and latitude of one's existence are beyond all easy apprehension. Even the hard, cold stars within the firmament above one's head begin to mock the possibilities for self-location. Where am I? Where did I come from? Where will I go?

"I've lost a lot of jobs," one man explains. "Today, even if you're a janitor, there's still reading and writing. . . . They leave a note saying, 'Go to room so-and-so. . . .' You can't do it. You can't read it. You don't know."

"Reading directions, I suffer with. I work with chemicals. . . . That's scary to begin with. . . ."   26

"You sit down. They throw the menu in front of you. Where do you go from there? Nine times out of ten you say, 'Go ahead. Pick out something for the both of us.' I've eaten some weird things, let me tell you!"   27

A landlord tells a woman that her lease allows him to evict her if her baby cries and causes inconvenience to her neighbors. The consequence of challenging his words conveys a danger which appears, unlikely as it seems, even more alarming than the danger of eviction. Once she admits that she can't read, in the desire to maneuver for the time in which to call a friend, she will have defined herself in terms of an explicit importance that she cannot endure. Capitulation in this case is preferable to self-humiliation. Resisting the definition of oneself in terms of what one cannot do, what others take for granted, represents a need so great that other imperatives (even one so urgent as the need to keep one's home in winter's cold) evaporate and fall away in face of fear. Even the loss of home and shelter, in this case, is not so terrifying as the loss of self.   28

Another illiterate, looking back, believes she was not worthy of her teacher's time. She believes that it was wrong of her to take up space within her school. She believes that it was right to leave in order that somebody more deserving could receive her place.   29

People eat what others order, know what others tell them, struggle not to see themselves as they believe the world perceives them. A man in California spoke about his own loss of identity, self-location, definition: 30

"I stood at the bottom of the ramp. My car had broke down on the freeway. There was a phone. I asked for the police. They was nice. They said to tell them where I was. I looked up at the signs. There was one that I had seen before. I read it to them: ONE WAY STREET. They thought it was a joke. I told them I couldn't read. There was other signs above the ramp. They told me to try. I looked around for somebody to help. All the cars was going by real fast. I couldn't make them understand that I was lost. The cop was nice. He told me: 'Try once more.' I did my best. I couldn't read. I only knew the sign above my head. The cop was trying to be nice. He knew that I was trapped. 'I can't send out a car to you if you can't tell me where you are.' I felt afraid. I nearly cried. I'm forty-eight years old. I only said: 'I'm on a one-way street. . . .'"   31

Perhaps we might slow down a moment here and look at the   32
realities described above. This is the nation that we live in. This is
a society that most of us did not create but which our President
and other leaders have been willing to sustain by virtue of malign
neglect. Do we possess the character and courage to address a
problem which so many nations, poorer than our own, have found
it natural to correct?

The answers to these questions represent a reasonable test of   33
our belief in the democracy to which we have been asked in public school to swear allegiance.

READING FOR MEANING

This section presents three activities that will help you reread Kozol's essay
with a critical eye. Done in sequence, these activities lead you from a basic understanding of the selection to a more personal response to it and finally to an
analysis that deepens your understanding and critical thinking about what you
are reading.

Read to Comprehend

Reread the selection, and write a few sentences identifying the most serious effects of illiteracy and explaining Kozol's purpose for writing. Does
he seem to be simply describing a hopeless situation, hoping for reform, or
aiming for a specific response from readers? What in the text leads you to your
answer? Also make a list of any words you do not understand—for example,
mendacious (paragraph 4), *countenance* (4), *admonitions* (9), *capitulation* (28).
Look up their meanings in a dictionary to see which definition best fits the
context.

To expand your understanding of this reading, you might use one or more
of the following critical reading strategies that are explained and illustrated
in Appendix 1: *outlining, paraphrasing,* and *questioning to understand and
remember.*

Read to Respond

Write several paragraphs exploring your initial thoughts and feelings about
"The Human Cost of an Illiterate Society." Focus on anything that stands out for
you, perhaps because it resonates with your own experience or because you find
a statement puzzling.

You might consider writing about

- Kozol's claim that illiteracy undermines democracy, summarizing his main
  ideas (from paragraphs 2–4) and adding any ideas of your own.

- the connection made between morality and literacy in paragraph 1, explaining possible connections you see and speculating about whom Kozol seems to be accusing of immoral actions.

- "the power [that] knowledge gives" (2), using firsthand examples of how the knowledge you have gained from reading has contributed to your achievements, sense of identity, or privileges.

- your own experience with someone who is illiterate.

To develop your response to Kozol's essay, you might use the following critical reading strategy that is explained and illustrated in Appendix 1: *evaluating the logic of an argument.*

Read to Analyze Underlying Assumptions

Write several paragraphs exploring one or more of the assumptions, values, and beliefs underlying Kozol's essay. As you write, explain how the assumptions are reflected in the text, as well as what you now think of them (and perhaps of your own assumptions) after rereading the essay with a critical eye.

You might consider writing about

- the assumption that illiterate citizens are more likely than others to "vote for a face, a smile, or a style, not for a mind or character or body of beliefs" (paragraph 3).

- Kozol's assertion that if enough illiterates "could vote, and read enough and do sufficient math to vote in their self-interest, Ronald Reagan would not likely have been chosen president" (4).

- the assumptions underlying Kozol's comments about the "[g]eographical paralysis" of illiterate people, who "can't move up . . . can't move out . . . cannot see beyond. . . . Could it be that some of us might like it better if they stayed where they belong?" (20).

- Kozol's assumptions, in paragraph 32, that national leaders have shown a "malign neglect" of the problem of widespread illiteracy and that a nation as rich as the United States should find it "natural" to address the problem. (Note that "malign neglect" is a takeoff on "benign neglect," a phrase that caused controversy in the late 1960s when an adviser to President Richard Nixon used it in a memorandum recommending that the federal government become less active in promoting civil rights and other policies on behalf of African Americans.)

To probe assumptions more deeply, you might use one or both of the following critical reading strategies that are explained and illustrated in Appendix 1: *reflecting on challenges to your beliefs and values* and *recognizing emotional manipulation.*

READING LIKE A WRITER
SUPPORTING PROPOSED EFFECTS

Kozol proposes many effects of illiteracy. A mere list of possible effects would be interesting, but to convince readers to take all of these effects seriously, Kozol must argue for—or support—them in ways that enhance their plausibility. To do so, all writers speculating about effects have many resources available to them to support their proposed effects: examples, statistics, quotations from authorities, personal anecdotes, analogies, scenarios, quotes from interviews, and more. As a writer speculating about causes or effects, you will need to support your speculations in these ways in order to make them plausible. You can learn more about supporting speculations by analyzing how Kozol does it.

Analyze

1. *Choose* one of Kozol's proposed effects of illiteracy: helplessness in financial affairs (paragraphs 11 and 12), confusion about supermarket purchases (16–19), limited travel (20), or loss of self (28–31).

2. *Examine* the support carefully. What kind of support do you find? More than one kind? Does the support seem to come from many or few sources?

3. *Evaluate* the support. Does it seem appropriate for the proposed effect? Does it seem believable and trustworthy? Does it seem consistent with the other support for the effect? If so, how does it complement the other support?

Write

Write several sentences explaining how Kozol supports the effect you have chosen. Also *evaluate* the plausibility of the support he offers. *Give details* from the paragraphs you have analyzed. As one of Kozol's intended readers, *explain* how convincing you find the support.

CONSIDERING IDEAS FOR YOUR OWN WRITING

Consider speculating, like Kozol does, about the effects of a significant social problem. List several major social problems (local or national) that concern you. Your list might include, for example, the high pregnancy rate among unmarried teenagers, high-school dropout rates, high costs of a college education, unsafe working conditions at your job, shortages of adequate day-care facilities for working parents, growth in the number of people without health insurance, or uncontrolled development in your community. Choose one problem, and consider how you can speculate about its effects. What effects can you argue for? As a writer, how could you convince readers that your proposed effects are plausible? Will you need to research the problem to write about it authoritatively? Remember, your purpose is not to propose a solution to the problem but to speculate about its possible effects.

Alternatively, you could recall a recent controversial decision by college or community leaders that concerns you, such as a decision about campus life (safety, recreation, tutoring, or other special services) or about the future of your community (growth, transportation, safety). List several such decisions, and then choose one you would like to write about. Consider how you would write a letter to your college or community newspaper speculating about the effects or consequences of the decision. What short-term and long-term consequences would you propose? How would you convince readers to take your ideas seriously?

SARAH WEST

The Rise in Reported Incidents of Workplace Sexual Harassment

Sarah West wrote this essay for an assignment in her first-year college writing course.

Like Natalie Angier, West speculates about a trend: a sharp increase in reported incidents of workplace sexual harassment over a four-year period. She begins by establishing that the trend exists. Notice that her concern is not whether workplace sexual harassment was increasing but whether reported incidents of it were increasing. She no doubt recognizes that it would be difficult to demonstrate that actual acts of harassment were increasing or decreasing; she may also recognize that such acts were very likely decreasing as reported incidents increased and received wide publicity. West then launches her speculations about the causes for the increasing number of reports.

As you read, keep in mind that the U.S. Supreme Court has defined illegal sexual harassment as "sufficiently severe or pervasive to alter the conditions of the victim's employment." In other words, it is not a casual or unthreatening one-time incident, but several incidents that create a hostile work environment and undermine victims' trust and ability to do their jobs.

To those students who recently graduated from high school, it may sound like the Dark Ages, but it wasn't: Until 1964, an employee who refused to give in to his or her employer's sexual advances could be fired—legally. An employee being constantly humiliated by a co-worker could be forced either to deal with the lewd comments, the stares, and the touching or to just quit his or her job. It is truly strange to think that sexual harassment was perfectly legal in the United States until Congress passed the Civil Rights Act of 1964.

But even after 1964, sexual harassment still persisted. It was not widely known exactly what sexual harassment was or that federal laws against it existed. Often when an employee was sexually harassed on the job, he or she felt too alienated and humiliated to speak out against it (Martell and Sullivan 6). During the 1970s and 1980s, however, sexual-harassment victims began coming forward to challenge their harassers. Then suddenly in the 1990s, the number of sexual-harassment complaints and lawsuits sharply rose. According to a 1994 survey conducted by the Society for Human Resource Management, the percentage of human resource professionals who have reported that their departments handled at least one sexual-harassment complaint rose from 35 percent in 1991 to

65 percent in 1994 (*Sexual*). Why did this large increase occur in such a short amount of time? Possible answers to this question surely would include growing awareness of the nature of workplace sexual harassment, government action, efforts of companies to establish anti-harassment policies and encourage harassed employees to come forward, and prominence given by the media to many cases of workplace harassment.

One significant cause of the rise in reported incidents of sexual harassment was most likely the increased awareness of what constitutes sexual harassment. There are two distinct types of sexual harassment, and although their formal names may be unfamiliar, the situations they describe will most certainly ring a bell. *Hostile environment* sexual harassment occurs when a supervisor or co-worker gives the victim "unwelcome sexual attention" that "interferes with (his or her) ability to work or creates an intimidating or offensive atmosphere" (Stanko and Werner 15). *Quid pro quo* sexual harassment occurs when "a workplace superior demands some degree of sexual favor" and either threatens to or does retaliate in a way that "has a tangible effect on the working conditions of the harassment victim" if he or she refuses to comply (Stanko and Werner 15).

A fundamental cause of the rise in reports of workplace harassment was government action in 1964 and again in 1991. After the passage of the Civil Rights Act of 1991, which allowed, among other things, larger damage awards for sexually harassed employees, many more employees began coming forward with complaints. They realized that sexual harassment was not legal and they could do something about it. Suddenly, it became possible for a company to lose millions in a single sexual-harassment case. For example, Rena Weeks, a legal secretary in San Francisco, sued the law firm of Baker & McKenzie for $3.5 million after an employee, Martin Greenstein, "dumped candy down the breast pocket of her blouse, groped her, pressed her from behind and pulled her arms back to 'see which one (breast) is bigger' " ("Workplace"). The jury awarded Weeks $7.1 million in punitive damages, twice what she sought in her lawsuit ("Workplace"). In addition, research revealed that the mere existence of sexual harassment in a company could lead to "hidden costs" such as absenteeism, lower productivity, and loss of valuable employees (Stanko and Werner 16). These "hidden costs" could add up to $6 or $7 million a year for a typical large company, according to one survey of Fortune 500 companies (Stanko and Werner 16).

Concerned about these costs, most companies decided to develop and publicize sexual-harassment policies, making every employee aware of the problem and more likely to come forward as early as possible so that employers have a chance to remedy the situation before it gets out of hand (Martell and Sullivan 8). Prior to 1991, sexual-harassment victims were often asked by their employers simply to remain silent (Martell and Sullivan 8). These new policies and procedures, along with training sessions, made it much more likely that employees would report incidents of sexual harassment. And we should not be surprised that the Internet has provided independent information to employees about dealing with workplace sexual harassment ("Handling"; "Sexual").

The media have also contributed to the rise of reports of workplace sexual harassment by giving great attention to a few prominent cases. In 1991, Supreme Court Justice Clarence Thomas in Senate hearings on his nomination had to defend himself from sexual-harassment charges by his former colleague Anita Hill. Later that same year, U.S. male navy officers were accused of sexually harassing female navy officers at the infamous Tailhook Convention, a yearly gathering of navy aviators (Nelton 24). Highly publicized cases like these made sexual harassment a much-discussed public issue that sparked debate and encouraged victims to come forward.

Not everyone believes that there has been an increase in reports of workplace sexual harassment. One journalist has argued that the rise in reported sexual-harassment complaints is actually a sort of illusion caused by insufficient research, since "research on this topic has only been undertaken since the 1970s" (Burke 23). Although this statement is largely true, it is only true because the Civil Rights Act did not exist until 1964. How could sexual harassment be measured and researched if it was not even acknowledged yet by society?

It has also been suggested that the trend is the result of a greater percentage of women in the workplace (Martell and Sullivan 5). This may be a sufficient argument since women report sexual harassment in a significantly greater number of cases than men do (men report roughly one-tenth of what women report). It has been noted, however, that there has been a rise in sexual-harassment complaints reported by male victims as well recently. According to the Equal Employment Opportunity Commission, the number of sexual-harassment complaints filed annually by men has more than doubled from 1989 to 1993 (Corey). Sexual harassment is by no means a new occurrence. It has most likely existed since workplace environments have existed. Yet, that there are more women in the workplace today has likely increased the percentage of women workers being sexually harassed, but it is also very plausible that the rise in reported incidents of sexual harassment is

because of increased awareness of sexual harassment and the steps
that one can legally take to stop it.

It has taken thirty years, but American society seems to be mak-   9
ing significant progress in bringing a halt to a serious problem.
Sexual harassment, a phrase that was unfamiliar to most of us only
a few years ago, is now mentioned almost daily on television and
in newspapers. We can only hope that the problem will end if we
continue to hear about, to read about, and, most importantly, to
talk about sexual harassment and its negative consequences as we
educate each other about sexual harassment. Then, perhaps some-
day, sexual harassment can be stopped altogether.

Works Cited

Burke, Ronald J. "Incidence and Consequences of Sexual Harassment in a Professional
   Services Firm." *Employee Counselling Today* Feb. 1995: 23–29.
Corey, Mary. "On-the-Job Sexism Isn't Just a Man's Sin Anymore." *Houston Chronicle*
   30 Aug. 1993: D1.
"Handling Sexual Harassment Complaints." *Employer and Employee.* 1997. 8 Jan. 1998
   <http://www.employer-employee.com/sexhar1.html>.
Martell, Kathryn, and George Sullivan. "Strategies for Managers to Recognize and
   Remedy Sexual Harassment." *Industrial Management* May–June 1994: 5–8.
Nelton, Sharon. "Sexual Harassment: Reducing the Risks." *Nation's Business* Mar.
   1995: 24–26.
"Sexual Harassment: FAQ." *Employment: Workplace Rights and Responsibilities.* 1998.
   8 Jan. 1998 <http://www.nolo.com/ChunkEMP/emp7.html>.
*Sexual Harassment Remains a Workplace Problem, but Most Employers Have Policies in
   Place, SHRM Survey Finds.* Alexandria: Society for Human Resource Management.
   1994.
Stanko, Brian B., and Charles A. Werner. "Sexual Harassment: What Is It? How to Pre-
   vent It." *National Public Accountant* June 1995: 14–16.
"Workplace Bias Lawsuits." *USA Today* 30 Nov. 1994: B2.

READING FOR MEANING

This section presents three activities that will help you reread West's causal
argument with a critical eye. Done in sequence, these activities lead you from a
basic understanding of the selection to a more personal response to it and finally
to an analysis that deepens your understanding and critical thinking about what
you are reading.

Read to Comprehend

Reread the selection, and write a few sentences briefly restating the four
causes West proposes to explain the increase in reports of sexual harassment.
Also make a list of any words you do not understand—for example, *alienated*

(paragraph 2), *punitive* (4), *absenteeism* (4). Look up their meanings in a dictionary to see which definition best fits the context.

To expand your understanding of this reading, you might want to use one or more of the following critical reading strategies that are explained and illustrated in Appendix 1: *annotating, outlining, paraphrasing,* and *questioning to understand and remember.*

Read to Respond

Write several paragraphs exploring your initial thoughts and feelings about West's causal argument. Focus on anything that stands out for you, perhaps because it resonates with your own experience or because you find a statement puzzling.

You might consider writing about

- what you know about the Civil Rights Acts of 1964 and of 1991.

- a time when you or someone you know was sexually harassed (or accused of harassment) at work, explaining what happened, and what—if anything—was done about it.

- the difference, if any, in your view, between sexual harassment of women versus men.

- sexual-harassment policies or incidents at your college.

To develop your response to West's essay, you might use one or both of the following critical reading strategies that are explained and illustrated in Appendix 1: *contextualizing* and *evaluating the logic of an argument.*

Read to Analyze Underlying Assumptions

Write several paragraphs exploring one or more of the assumptions, values, and beliefs underlying West's causal argument. As you write, explain how the assumptions are reflected in the text, as well as what you now think of them (and perhaps of your own assumptions) after rereading the selection with a critical eye.

You might consider writing about

- the values reflected in the idea that a company will change its policies if doing so will keep costs down (paragraph 4).

- the assumption that the federal government should have a role in protecting people from sexual harassment and other workplace hazards, such as unsafe physical conditions or punishment for whistle-blowing about illegal actions.

- the assumptions that sexual harassment is a "serious problem," that "American society seems to be making significant progress in bringing a halt to" it, and that it might be possible to eliminate it completely (9).

- the shift in cultural values or assumptions from the early 1960s, when employees experiencing sexual harassment often "felt too alienated and humiliated to speak out against it" (2) and could legally be fired for resisting it, to the early 1990s (the period West is writing about) or the present day.

To probe assumptions more deeply, you might use one or more of the following critical reading strategies that are explained and illustrated in Appendix 1: *reflecting on challenges to your beliefs and values, recognizing emotional manipulation,* and *judging the writer's credibility.*

READING LIKE A WRITER
ESTABLISHING CREDIBILITY

To be credible is to be believable. When you write an essay speculating about the causes or effects of something, readers will find your argument believable when they sense that you are able to see the various complexities of your subject. Therefore, if you do not oversimplify, trivialize, or stereotype your subject, if you do not overlook possible alternative causes or effects that will occur to readers, and if you convey more than casual knowledge of your subject and show that you have thought about it deeply and seriously, you will establish your credibility with readers.

Before you attempt your own essay speculating about causes or effects, it will be helpful for you to consider carefully how West establishes her credibility to speculate about the rise in reported incidents of workplace sexual harassment.

Analyze

1. *Reread* this brief essay, and *annotate* it for evidence of credibility or lack of it. (Because you cannot know West personally, you must look closely at the words, evidence, and arguments of her essay to decide whether she constructs a credible argument.) *Examine closely* how knowledgeable she seems about the subject. Where does her knowledge assure or even impress you as one of her intended readers? Where does her knowledge seem thin? *Consider* especially how she presents the subject and trend (paragraphs 1–3). *Assess* also the sources she relies on and how effectively she uses them.

2. *Look* for evidence that West has not trivialized a complex subject. Keeping in mind that she appropriately limits herself to speculating about possible causes, *note* how her argument reflects the complexity of her subject or fails to do so.

3. *Consider* how West's counterarguments (7 and 8) influence your judgment of her credibility.

4. *Examine* her approach to readers. What assumptions does she make about their knowledge and beliefs? What attitude does she have toward her readers? *Note* evidence of the writer's assumptions and attitude toward readers.

Write

Write several sentences presenting evidence of West's attempts to establish her credibility. Then *write a few more sentences* evaluating how credible her essay is to you as one of her intended readers. To explain your judgment, *point to* parts of the essay and *comment on* the influence of your own attitudes about and knowledge of workplace sexual harassment.

CONSIDERING IDEAS FOR YOUR OWN WRITING

West speculates about the causes of a trend (the rise in reported incidents of workplace sexual harassment), but she could have speculated about the phenomenon of sexual harassment itself—asking, for example, why there seems to be so much of it in the workplace. Following her lead, you could speculate about the causes of a trend or a phenomenon that influences how people live and work. Here are some examples: the increase in the number of students working part-time or full-time while in college; the increase in standardized testing requirements in public schools; the increase in the cost of a college education; the decline of neighborhood or community cohesion; the rising or declining influence of the political right; the growing gap in income and wealth between rich Americans and the rest of the population; or the increasing reliance by technology companies on workers trained in other countries.

LA DONNA BEATY

What Makes a Serial Killer?

> *La Donna Beaty was a college student when she wrote this essay*
> *speculating about what produces serial killers. Like Natalie Angier*
> *and Sarah West, Beaty relies in large part on speculations from a wide*
> *range of published research to put together her argument. She is in*
> *control of the argument because she selects certain speculations (and*
> *not others) and weaves them into her own design.*
>
> *As you read, notice the wide range of speculations she brings into*
> *her argument.*
>
> *The other readings in this chapter are followed by reading and*
> *writing activities. Following this reading, however, you are on your*
> *own to decide how to read for meaning and read like a writer.*

Jeffrey Dahmer, John Wayne Gacy, Mark Allen Smith, Richard   1
Chase, Ted Bundy—the list goes on and on. These five men alone
have been responsible for at least ninety deaths, and many suspect
that their victims may total twice that number. They are serial
killers, the most feared and hated of criminals. What deep, hidden
secret makes them lust for blood? What can possibly motivate a
person to kill over and over again with no guilt, no remorse, no
hint of human compassion? What makes a serial killer?

Serial killings are not a new phenomenon. In 1798, for example,   2
Micajah and Wiley Harpe traveled the backwoods of Kentucky
and Tennessee in a violent, year-long killing spree that left at least
twenty—and possibly as many as thirty-eight—men, women, and
children dead. Their crimes were especially chilling as they seemed
particularly to enjoy grabbing small children by the ankles and
smashing their heads against trees (Holmes and DeBurger 28). In
modern society, however, serial killings have grown to near epidemic proportions. Ann Rule, a respected author and expert on
serial murders, stated in a seminar at the University of Louisville
on serial murder that between 3,500 and 5,000 people become victims of serial murder each year in the United States alone (qtd. in
Holmes and DeBurger 21). Many others estimate that there are
close to 350 serial killers currently at large in our society (Holmes
and DeBurger 22).

Fascination with murder and murderers is not new, but re-   3
searchers in recent years have made great strides in determining
the characteristics of criminals. Looking back, we can see how
naive early experts were in their evaluations: in 1911, for example,
Italian criminologist Cesare Lombrosco concluded that "murderers as a group [are] biologically degenerate [with] blood-shot eyes,

aquiline noses, curly black hair, strong jaws, big ears, thin lips, and menacing grins" (qtd. in Lunde 84). Today, however, we don't expect killers to have fangs that drip human blood, and many realize that the boy-next-door may be doing more than woodworking in his basement. While there are no specific physical characteristics shared by all serial killers, they are almost always male and 92 percent are white. Most are between the ages of twenty-five and thirty-five and often physically attractive. While they may hold a job, many switch employment frequently as they become easily frustrated when advancement does not come as quickly as expected. They tend to believe that they are entitled to whatever they desire but feel that they should have to exert no effort to attain their goals (Samenow 88, 96). What could possibly turn attractive, ambitious human beings into cold-blooded monsters?

One popular theory suggests that many murderers are the product of our violent society. Our culture tends to approve of violence and find it acceptable, even preferable, in many circumstances (Holmes and DeBurger 27). According to research done in 1970, one out of every four men and one out of every six women believed that it was appropriate for a husband to hit his wife under certain conditions (Holmes and DeBurger 33). This emphasis on violence is especially prevalent in television programs. Violence occurs in 80 percent of all prime-time shows, while cartoons, presumably made for children, average eighteen violent acts per hour. It is estimated that by the age of eighteen, the average child will have viewed more than 16,000 television murders (Holmes and DeBurger 34). Some experts feel that children demonstrate increasingly aggressive behavior with each violent act they view (Lunde 15) and become so accustomed to violence that these acts seem normal (Lunde 35). In fact, most serial killers do begin to show patterns of aggressive behavior at a young age. It is, therefore, possible that after viewing increasing amounts of violence, such children determine that this is acceptable behavior; when they are then punished for similar actions, they may become confused and angry and eventually lash out by committing horrible, violent acts.

Another theory concentrates on the family atmosphere into which the serial killer is born. Most killers state that they experienced psychological abuse as children and never established good relationships with the male figures in their lives (Ressler, Burgess, and Douglas 19). As children, they were often rejected by their parents and received little nurturing (Lunde 94; Holmes and DeBurger 64–70). It has also been established that the families of serial killers often move repeatedly, never allowing the child to feel a sense of stability; in many cases, they are also forced to live out-side the family home before reaching the age of eighteen (Ressler, Burgess, and Douglas 19–20). Our culture's tolerance for violence may overlap with such family dynamics: with 79 percent of the population believing that slapping a twelve-year-old is either nec-essary, normal, or good, it is no wonder that serial killers relate tales of physical abuse (Holmes and DeBurger 30; Ressler, Burgess, and Douglas 19–20) and view themselves as the "black sheep" of the family. They may even, perhaps unconsciously, assume this same role in society.

While the foregoing analysis portrays the serial killer as a lost, lonely, abused little child, another theory, based on the same infor-mation, gives an entirely different view. In this analysis, the killer is indeed rejected by his family but only after being repeatedly defiant, sneaky, and threatening. As verbal lies and destructiveness increase, the parents give the child the distance he seems to want in order to maintain a small amount of domestic peace (Samenow 13). This interpretation suggests that the killer shapes his parents much more than his parents shape him. It also denies that the media can influence a child's mind and turn him into something that he doesn't already long to be. Since most children view similar amounts of violence, the argument goes, a responsible child filters what he sees and will not resort to criminal activity no matter how acceptable it seems to be (Samenow 15–18). In 1930, the noted psychologist Alfred Adler seemed to find this true of any criminal. As he put it, "With criminals it is different: they have a private logic, a private intelligence. They are suffering from a wrong out-look upon the world, a wrong estimate of their own importance and the importance of other people" (qtd. in Samenow 20). 6

Most people agree that Jeffrey Dahmer or Ted Bundy had to be "crazy" to commit horrendous multiple murders, and scientists have long maintained that serial killers are indeed mentally dis-turbed (Lunde 48). While the percentage of murders committed by mental hospital patients is much lower than that among the general population (Lunde 35), it cannot be ignored that the rise in serial killings happened at almost the same time as the deinsti-tutionalization movement in the mental health care system during the 1960s (Markman and Bosco 266). While reform was greatly needed in the mental health care system, it has now become nearly impossible to hospitalize those with severe problems. In the United States, people have a constitutional right to remain mentally ill. Involuntary commitment can only be accomplished if the person is deemed dangerous to self, dangerous to others, or gravely disabled. However, in the words of Ronald Markman, "According to the way 7 that the law is interpreted, if you can go to the mailbox to pick up your social security check, you're not gravely disabled even if you think you're living on Mars"; even if a patient is thought to be dangerous, he or she cannot be held longer than ninety days unless it can be proved that the patient actually committed dangerous acts while in the hospital (Markman and Bosco 267). Many of the most heinous criminals have had long histories of mental illness but could not be hospitalized due to these stringent requirements. Richard Chase, the notorious Vampire of Sacramento, believed that he needed blood in order to survive, and while in the care of a psychiatric hospital, he often killed birds and other small animals in order to quench this desire. When he was released, he went on to kill eight people, one of them an eighteen-month-old baby (Biondi and Hecox 206). Edmund Kemper was equally insane. At the age of fifteen, he killed both of his grandparents and spent five years in a psychiatric facility. Doctors determined that he was "cured" and released him into an unsuspecting society. He killed eight women, including his own mother (Lunde 53–56). The world was soon to be disturbed by a cataclysmic earthquake, and Herbert Mullin knew that he had been appointed by God to prevent the catastrophe. The fervor of his religious delusion resulted in a death toll of thirteen (Lunde 63–81). All of these men had been treated for their mental disorders, and all were released by doctors who did not have enough proof to hold them against their will.

Studies have given increasing consideration to the genetic makeup of serial killers. The connection between biology and behavior is strengthened by research in which scientists have been able to develop a violently aggressive strain of mice simply through selective inbreeding (Taylor 23). These studies have caused scientists to become increasingly interested in the limbic system of the brain, which houses the amygdala, an almond-shaped structure located in the front of the temporal lobe. It has long been known that surgically altering that portion of the brain, in an operation known as a lobotomy, is one way of controlling behavior. This surgery was used frequently in the 1960s but has since been discontinued as it also erases most of a person's personality. More recent developments, however, have shown that temporal lobe epilepsy causes electrical impulses to be discharged directly into the amygdala. When this electronic stimulation is re-created in the laboratory, it causes violent behavior in lab animals. Additionally, other forms of epilepsy do not cause abnormalities in behavior, except during seizure activity. Temporal lobe epilepsy is linked with a wide range of antisocial behavior, including anger, paranoia,

8

and aggression. It is also interesting to note that this form of epilepsy produces extremely unusual brain waves. These waves have been found in only 10 to 15 percent of the general population, but over 79 percent of known serial killers test positive for these waves (Taylor 28–33).

The look at biological factors that control human behavior is by   9
no means limited to brain waves or other brain abnormalities. Much work is also being done with neurotransmitters, levels of testosterone, and patterns of trace minerals. While none of these studies is conclusive, they all show a high correlation between anti-social behavior and chemical interactions within the body (Taylor 63–69).

One of the most common traits that all researchers have noted   10
among serial killers is heavy use of alcohol. Whether this correlation is brought about by external factors or whether alcohol is an actual stimulus that causes certain behavior is still unclear, but the idea deserves consideration. Lunde found that the majority of those who commit murder had been drinking beforehand and commonly had a urine alcohol level of between .20 and .29, nearly twice the legal level of intoxication (31–32). Additionally, 70 percent of the families that reared serial killers had verifiable records of alcohol abuse (Ressler, Burgess, and Douglas 17). Jeffrey Dahmer had been arrested in 1981 on charges of drunkenness, and before his release from prison on sexual assault charges, his father had written a heart-breaking letter pleading that Jeffrey be forced to undergo treatment for alcoholism—a plea that, if heeded, might have changed the course of future events (Davis 70, 103). Whether alcoholism is a learned behavior or an inherited predisposition is still hotly debated, but a report issued by Harvard Medical School stated that "[a]lcoholism in the biological parent appears to be a more reliable predictor of alcoholism in the children than any other environmental factor examined" (qtd. in Taylor 117). While alcohol was once thought to alleviate anxiety and depression, we now know that it can aggravate and intensify such moods (Taylor 110); for the serial killers this may lead to irrational feelings of powerlessness that are brought under control only when the killer proves he has the ultimate power to control life and death.

"Man's inhumanity to man" began when Cain killed Abel,   11
but this legacy has grown to frightening proportions, as evidenced by the vast number of books that line the shelves of modern bookstores—row after row of titles dealing with death, anger, and blood. We may never know what causes a serial killer to exact his revenge on an unsuspecting society, but we need to

continue to probe the interior of the human brain to discover the delicate balance of chemicals that controls behavior; we need to be able to fix what goes wrong. We must also work harder to protect our children. Their cries must not go unheard; their pain must not become so intense that it demands bloody revenge. As today becomes tomorrow, we must remember the words of Ted Bundy, one of the most ruthless serial killers of our time: "Most serial killers are people who kill for the pure pleasure of killing and cannot be rehabilitated. Some of the killers themselves would even say so" (qtd. in Holmes and DeBurger 150).

Works Cited

Biondi, Ray, and Walt Hecox. *The Dracula Killer*. New York: Simon, 1992.

Davis, Ron. *The Milwaukee Murders*. New York: St. Martin's, 1991.

Holmes, Ronald M., and James DeBurger. *Serial Murder*. Newbury Park: Sage, 1988.

Lunde, Donald T. *Murder and Madness*. San Francisco: San Francisco Book, 1976.

Markman, Ronald, and Dominick Bosco. *Alone with the Devil*. New York: Doubleday, 1989.

Ressler, Robert K., Ann W. Burgess, and John E. Douglas. *Sexual Homicide—Patterns and Motives*. Lexington: Heath, 1988.

Samenow, Stanton E. *Inside the Criminal Mind*. New York: Times, 1984.

Taylor, Lawrence. *Born to Crime*. Westport: Greenwood, 1984.

READING FOR MEANING

Reading for meaning involves three activities:

- reading to comprehend
- reading to respond
- reading to analyze underlying assumptions

Reread Beaty's essay, and then write a page or so explaining your understanding of its basic meaning or main point, a personal response you have to it, and what you see as one of its underlying assumptions.

READING LIKE A WRITER

Writers of essays speculating about causes or effects

- present the subject.
- make a logical, step-by-step cause or effect argument.
- support—or argue for—each cause or effect.

- take into account readers' likely objections to the proposed causes or effects as well as readers' alternative or preferred causes or effects.

- establish their credibility.

Focus on one of these strategies in Beaty's essay, and analyze it carefully through close rereading and annotating. Then write several sentences explaining what you have learned, giving specific examples from the reading to support your explanation. Add a few sentences evaluating how successfully Beaty uses the strategy to argue convincingly for what makes a serial killer.

REVIEWING WHAT MAKES ESSAYS SPECULATING ABOUT CAUSES OR EFFECTS EFFECTIVE

In this chapter, you have been learning how to read cause or effect arguments for meaning and how to read them like a writer. Before going on to write an essay speculating about causes or effects, pause here to review and contemplate what you have learned about the elements of effective cause or effect essays.

Analyze

Choose one reading from this chapter that seems to you especially effective. Before rereading the selection, *jot down* one or two reasons you remember it as an example of effective cause or effect writing.

Reread your chosen selection, adding further annotations about what makes it particularly effective. *Consider* the selection's purpose and how well it achieves that purpose for its readers. (You can make an informed guess about the intended readers and their expectations by noting the publication source of the essay.) Then *focus* on how well the essay

- presents the subject.

- makes a logical, step-by-step cause or effect argument.

- supports—or argues for—each cause or effect.

- handles readers' likely objections to the proposed causes or effects.

- evaluates readers' alternative or preferred causes or effects.

- establishes the writer's credibility.

You can review all of these basic features in the Guide to Reading Essays Speculating about Causes or Effects (p. 404).

Your instructor may ask you to complete this activity on your own or to work with a small group of other students who have chosen the same reading. If you work with others, allow enough time initially for all group members to reread the selection thoughtfully and to add their annotations. Then *discuss* as a group what makes the essay effective. *Take notes* on your discussion. One student in your group should then report to the class what the group has learned about the effectiveness of cause or effect argument. If you are working individually, write up what you have learned from your analysis.

Write

Write at least a page, justifying your choice of this essay as an example of effective cause or effect argument. *Assume* that your readers—your instructor and classmates—have read the selection but will not remember many details about it. They also might not remember it as especially successful. Therefore, you will need to *refer* to details and specific parts of the essay as you explain how it works and as you justify your evaluation of its effectiveness. You need not argue that it is the best essay in the chapter or that it is flawless, only that it is, in your view, a strong example of the genre.

■ A Guide to Writing Essays Speculating about Causes or Effects

The readings in this chapter have helped you learn a great deal about writing that speculates about causes or effects. Now that you have seen how writers present their subjects to particular readers, propose causes or effects readers may not think of, support those causes or effects so as to make them plausible to readers, and anticipate readers' questions and objections, you can approach this type of writing confidently. The readings remain an important resource for you as you develop your own essay. Use them to review how other writers have solved the problems you face and to rethink the strategies that help writers achieve their purposes.

This Guide to Writing is designed to assist you in writing your essay. Here you will find activities to help you identify a subject and discover what to say about it, organize your ideas and draft the essay, read the draft critically, revise the draft to strengthen your argument, and edit and proofread the essay to improve its readability.

INVENTION AND RESEARCH

The following activities will help you find a subject and begin developing your argument. A few minutes spent completing each writing activity will improve your chances of producing a detailed and convincing first draft. You can decide on a subject for your essay, explore what you presently know about it and gather additional information, think about possible causes or effects, and develop a plausible argument.

Choosing a Subject

The subject of an essay speculating about causes or effects may be a trend, an event, or a phenomenon, as the readings in this chapter illustrate. List the most promising subjects you can think of, beginning with any you listed for the Considering Ideas for Your Own Writing activities following the readings in this chapter. These varied possibilities for analyzing causes or effects may suggest a subject you would like to explore, or you may still need to find an appropriate subject for your essay. Continue listing possible topics. Making such a list often generates ideas: As you list subjects, you will think of new ideas you cannot imagine now.

Even if you feel confident about a subject you have selected, continue listing other possibilities to test your choice. Try to list specific subjects, and make separate lists for trends, events, and phenomena. Here are some other ideas to consider:

Trends

- Changes in men's or women's roles and opportunities in marriage, education, or work

- Changing patterns in leisure, entertainment, life-style, religious life, health, or technology

- Completed artistic or historical trends (various art movements or historical changes)

- Long-term changes in economic conditions or political behavior or attitudes

- Increasing reliance on the Internet for research, entertainment, shopping, and conversation

Events

- A recent college, community, national, or international event that is surrounded by confusion or controversy

- A recent surprising event at your college, such as the closing of a tutorial or health service, the cancellation of popular classes, a change in library hours or dormitory regulations, the loss of a game by a favored team, or some hateful or violent act by one student against another

- A recent puzzling or controversial event in your community, such as the abrupt resignation of a public official, a public protest by an activist group, a change in traffic laws, a zoning decision, or the banning of a book from school libraries

- A historical event about which there is still some dispute as to its causes or effects

Phenomena

- A social problem, such as discrimination, homelessness, child abuse, illiteracy, high-school dropout rates, youth suicides, or teenage pregnancy

- One or more aspects of college life, such as libraries too noisy to study in, large classes, lack of financial aid, difficulties in scheduling classes, shortcomings in student health services, or insufficient availability of housing (in this essay you would not need to solve the problems, only to speculate about their causes or effects)

- A human trait, such as anxiety, selfishness, fear of success or failure, leadership, jealousy, insecurity, envy, opportunism, curiosity, or restlessness

After you have completed your lists, reflect on the possible topics you have compiled. Because an authoritative essay analyzing causes or effects requires sustained thinking, drafting, revising, and possibly even research, you will want to choose a subject to which you can commit yourself enthusiastically for a week or two. Above all, choose a topic that interests you, even if you feel uncertain about how to approach it. Then consider carefully whether you are more interested in the causes or the effects of the event, trend, or phenomenon. Consider, as well, whether the subject in which you are interested invites speculation about its causes or effects or perhaps even precludes speculation about one or the other. For example, you could speculate about the causes for increasing membership in your church, whereas the effects (the results or consequences) of the increase might for now be so uncertain as to discourage plausible speculation. Some subjects invite speculation about both their causes and effects. For this assignment, however, you need not do both.

Developing Your Subject

The writing and research activities that follow will enable you to test your subject choice and to discover what you have to say about it. These activities, most of which take only a few minutes to complete, will help you produce a fuller, more focused draft.

Exploring Your Subject.   *You may discover that you know more about your subject than you suspect if you write about it for a few minutes without stopping.* This brief sustained writing will stimulate your memory, help you probe your interest in the subject, and enable you to test your subject choice. As you write, consider the following questions:

- What interests me in this subject? What about it will interest my readers?

- What do I already know about the subject?

- Why does the trend, event, or phenomenon not already have an accepted explanation for its causes or effects? What causes or effects have others already suggested for this subject?

- How can I learn more about the subject?

Considering Causes or Effects.   *Before you research your subject (should you need to), you want to discover which causes or effects you can already imagine. Make a list of possible causes or effects.* For *causes* consider underlying or background causes, immediate or instigating causes, and ongoing causes. For example, if you lost your job delivering pizzas, an underlying cause could be that years ago a plant-closing in your town devastated the local economy, which has never recovered; an immediate cause could be that the pizza-chain outlet you worked for has been hit hard by the recent arrival of a new pizza-chain outlet; an ongoing cause could be that for several years some health-conscious residents regularly eat salad, rather than pizza, for dinner. For *effects,* consider both short-term and long-term consequences, as well as how one effect may lead to another in a kind of chain reaction. Try to think not only of obvious causes or effects but also of ones that are likely to be overlooked in a superficial analysis of your subject.

Identify the most convincing causes or effects in your list. Do you have enough to make a strong argument? Imagine how you might convince readers of the plausibility of some of these causes or effects.

Researching Your Subject.   *When developing an essay analyzing causes or effects, you can often gain great advantage by researching your subject.* (See Appendix 2, Strategies for Research and Documentation.) You can gain a greater understanding of the event, trend, or phenomenon, and you can review and evaluate others' proposed causes or effects in case you want to present any of these alternatives in your own essay. Reviewing others' causes or effects may suggest to you plausible causes or effects you have overlooked. You may also find support for your own counterarguments to readers' objections.

If you are speculating about the causes of a trend, you will also need to do some research to confirm that it actually is a trend and not just a short-term fluctuation or a fad. To do so, you will need to find examples and probably statistics that show an increase or a decrease in the trend over time and that indicate the date when this change began. (For example, recall that Sarah West cites dates and statistics to demonstrate that reported incidents of sexual harassment on the job actually increased.) If you are unable to find evidence to confirm that a trend exists, you will have to choose a different subject for your essay.

RESEARCHING YOUR SUBJECT ONLINE

Searching the Web may help you establish the existence of the phenomenon or trend and provide information you can use in presenting it to your readers. Enter a key term describing your subject in a search engine such as Google <google.com> or Yahoo! Directory <dir.yahoo.com>. Adding the word *trend* to your key term may help— for example, *religion trends* or *dieting trends.*

If you are interested in trends in education, you might find information at the National Center for Education Statistics Web site <http://nces.ed.gov/ssbr/pages/trends.asp>. For other national trends, look for the relevant statistics link on the U.S. government Web site <http://firstgov.gov>.

Bookmark or keep a record of promising sites. Download any materials you might wish to cite in your evaluation, remembering to record the source information required to document them.

Analyzing Your Readers. *Write for a few minutes, identifying who your readers are, what they know about your subject, and how they can be convinced by your proposed causes or effects.* Describe your readers briefly. Mention anything you know about them as a group that might influence the way they would read your essay. Estimate how much they know about your subject, how extensively you will have to present it to them, and what is required to demonstrate to them the importance of the subject. Speculate about how they will respond to your argument.

Rehearsing Part of Your Argument. *Select one of your causes or effects and write several sentences about it, trying out an argument for your readers.* The heart of your essay will be the argument you make for the plausibility of your proposed causes or effects. Like a ballet dancer or baseball pitcher warming up for a performance, you can prepare for your first draft by rehearsing part of the argument you will make. How will you convince readers to take this cause or effect seriously? This writing activity will focus your thinking and encourage you to keep discovering new arguments until you start drafting. It may also lead you to search for additional support for your speculations.

Testing Your Choice. *Pause now to decide whether you have chosen a subject about which you will be able to make a convincing argument.* At this point you have probed your subject in several ways and have some insights into how you would attempt to present and argue for it with particular readers. If your interest in the subject is growing and you are gaining confidence in the argument you want to make, you have probably made a good choice. However, if your interest in the subject is waning or you have been unable to come up with several plausible causes or effects beyond the simply obvious ones, you may want to consider choosing another subject. If your subject does not seem promising, return to your list of possible subjects to select another.

Considering Visuals. *Consider whether visuals—drawings, photographs, tables, or graphs—would strengthen your argument.* You could construct your own visuals, scan materials from books and magazines, or download them from the Internet. If you submit your essay electronically to other students and your instructor, or if you post it on a Web site, consider including photographs as well as snippets of film or sound. Visual and audio materials are not at all a requirement of an effective speculative essay, as you can tell from the readings in this chapter, but they could add a new dimension to your writing. If you want to use photographs or recordings of people, be sure to obtain their permission. If you want to post a visual on the Web, ask permission from the source. Also, be sure to document the sources of visuals just as you would for written texts.

Considering Your Purpose.   *Write for several minutes about your purpose for writing this essay.* The following questions will help you think about your purpose:

- What do I hope to accomplish with my readers? What one big idea do I want them to grasp and remember?

- How can I interest them in my subject? How can I help them see its importance or significance? How can I convince them to take my speculations seriously?

- How much resistance should I expect from readers to each of the causes or effects I propose? Will my readers be largely receptive? Skeptical but convinceable? Resistant and perhaps even antagonistic?

Formulating a Working Thesis.   *Draft a thesis statement.* A working—as opposed to final—*thesis* enables you to bring your invention work into focus and begin your draft with a clearer purpose. At some point during the drafting of your essay, however, you will likely decide to revise your working thesis or even try out a new one. A thesis for an essay speculating about causes or effects nearly always announces the subject; it may also mention the proposed causes or effects and suggest the direction the argument will take. Here are two sample thesis statements from the readings in this chapter:

- "Today, the world is no longer safe for boys. A boy being a shade too boyish risks finding himself under the scrutiny of parents, teachers, guidance counselors, child therapists—all of them on watch for the early glimmerings of a medical syndrome, a bone fide behavioral disorder" (Angier, paragraph 3).

- "According to a 1994 survey conducted by the Society for Human Resource Management, the percentage of human resource professionals who have reported that their departments handled at least one sexual-harassment complaint rose from 35 percent in 1991 to 65 percent in 1994 (*Sexual*). Why did this large increase occur in such a short amount of time? Possible answers to this question surely would include growing awareness of the nature of workplace sexual harassment, government action, efforts of companies to establish anti-harassment policies and encourage harassed employees to come forward, and prominence given by the media to many cases of workplace harassment" (West, paragraph 2).

Notice, for instance, that West's thesis clearly announces her subject—workplace sexual harassment—as well as how she will approach the subject: by focusing on the increase in reported incidents and speculating about the causes of the increase. Her thesis also forecasts her speculations, identifying the causes and the order in which she will argue for them in the essay.

DRAFTING

The following guidelines will help you set goals for your draft, plan its organization, and think about a useful sentence strategy.

Setting Goals

Establishing goals for your draft before you begin writing will enable you to make decisions and work more confidently. Consider the following questions now, and keep them in mind as you draft. They will help you set goals for drafting as well as recall how the writers you have read in this chapter tried to achieve similar goals.

- *How can I convince my readers that my proposed causes or effects are plausible?* Should I give many examples, as Kozol does, or quote authorities and published research, as Angier, Ramachandran and Hubbard, West, and Beaty all do? Can I, like Kozol, include personal anecdotes and cases or, like King and Angier, introduce analogies?

- *How should I anticipate readers' objections to my argument?* What should I do about alternative causes or effects? Should I anticipate readers' objections and questions, like Angier does, or answer readers' likely questions, like Konner? Can I refute alternative causes, as West does? How can I find common ground—shared attitudes, values, and beliefs—with my readers, even with those whose objections or alternative causes I must refute?

- *How much do my readers need to know about my subject?* Do I need to describe my subject in some detail, in the way that Ramachandran and Hubbard describe synesthesia or in the way that West describes the legal context for the rise in reported incidents of workplace sexual harassment? Or can I assume that my readers have personal experience with my subject, as King seems to assume? If my subject is a trend, how can I demonstrate that the trend exists?

- *How can I begin engagingly and end conclusively?* Should I begin, as Angier and Beaty do, by emphasizing the importance or timeliness of my subject? Might I begin with an event like Konner's, or with an unusual statement like King's? How can I conclude by returning to an idea in the opening paragraph (as Kozol does), restating the urgency of the problem (West and Beaty), or repeating the main cause (Konner)?

- *How can I establish my authority and credibility to argue the causes or effects of my subject?* Can I do this by showing a comprehensive understanding of the likely effects of the phenomenon, as Kozol does, or by showing a willingness to consider a wide range of causes, like Ramachandran and Hubbard and Konner? Or can I do this by displaying my research (Beaty), by counter-arguing responsibly (West), or by relying on what I have learned through research and interviews (Angier)?

Organizing Your Draft

With goals in mind and invention notes at hand, you are ready to make a tentative outline of your draft. The sequence of proposed causes or effects will be at the center of your outline, but you may also want to plan where you will consider alternatives or counterargue objections. Notice that some writers who conjecture about causes consider alternative causes—evaluating, refuting, or accepting them—before they present their own. Much of an essay analyzing causes may be devoted to considering alternatives. Both writers who conjecture about causes and writers who speculate about effects usually consider readers' possible objections to their causes or effects along with the argument for each cause or effect. If you must provide readers with a great deal of information about your subject as context for your argument, you may want to outline this information carefully. For your essay, this part of the outline may be a major consideration. Your plan should make the information readily accessible to your readers. This outline is tentative; you may decide to change it after you start drafting.

Considering a Useful Sentence Strategy

As you draft your essay, you will want to help your readers recognize the stages of your argument and the support you offer for each proposed cause or effect. One effective way to do so is to use clear topic sentences, especially ones that are grammatically parallel. Topic sentences usually open the paragraph or are placed early in the paragraph.

They can announce a new cause or effect, introduce counterargument (the writer's response to readers' likely questions or alternative causes or effects), or identify different parts of the support for a cause, effect, or counterargument. Topic sentences may also include key terms that the writer introduced in a thesis statement at the beginning of the essay, and they may take identical or similar sentence forms so that readers can recognize them more easily. The following topic sentences from King's essay identify what King believes to be the three main causes for many moviegoers' attraction to horror movies:

> Why? Some of the reasons are simple and obvious. To show that we can, that we are not afraid, that we can ride this roller coaster. (paragraph 3)

> We also go to re-establish our feelings of essential normality. (4)

> And we go to have fun. . . . The fun comes from seeing others menaced—sometimes killed. (5–6)

King assists readers in identifying each new stage of his argument by introducing the grammatical subject *we* in the first topic sentence and then repeating it to signal the next two stages: "we can," "We also go," "And we go."

While King relies on topic sentences within paragraphs to signal the stages in his argument, as do all the writers in this chapter, Kozol signals his topic sentences of support for his argument by writing them in parallel grammatical form, reinforcing his point about the harmful effects of illiteracy on people:

> **Illiterates cannot** read the menu in a restaurant. (paragraph 6)

> **Illiterates cannot** read the letters that their children bring home from their teachers. (8)

> **Illiterates cannot** read instructions on a bottle of prescription medicine. (9)

> **Illiterates cannot** read instructions on a pack of frozen food. (18)

> **Illiterates cannot** travel freely. (20)

Although Angier does not use exact parallel structure, she does signal the causes of intolerance of boyish behavior with clear topic sentences that use common terminology for a causal essay: *reason* and *cause.*

> Perhaps part of the **reason** why boyish behavior is suspect these days is Americans' obsessive fear of crime. (paragraph 11)

> Another **cause** for the intolerance of boyish behavior is the current school system. (12)

In addition to using topic sentences that help readers follow the stages of your argument and using parallel grammatical form to present related examples, you can strengthen your causal argument by using other sentence strategies as well. You may want to look at the information about using appositives (pp. 319–21) and sentences that combine concession and refutation (pp. 639–40).

READING A DRAFT CRITICALLY

Getting a critical reading of your draft will help you see how to improve it. Your instructor may schedule class time for reading drafts, or you may want to ask a classmate or a tutor in the writing center to read your draft. Ask your reader to use the following guidelines and to write out a response for you to consult during your revision.

Read for a First Impression

1. Read the draft without stopping to annotate or comment, and then write two or three sentences giving your general impression.

2. Identify one aspect of the draft that seems particularly effective.

Read Again to Suggest Improvements

1. Recommend ways to make the presentation of the subject more effective.

   - Read the opening paragraphs that present the subject to be speculated about, and then tell the writer what you find most interesting and useful.

   - Point out one or two places where a reader unfamiliar with the subject might need more information.

   - Suggest ways the writer could make the subject seem more interesting or significant.

   - If the subject is a trend, explain what you understand to be the increase or decrease and let the writer know whether you think further evidence is required to demonstrate conclusively that the subject is indeed a trend.

   - If the beginning seems unlikely to engage readers, suggest at least one other way of beginning.

2. Suggest ways to strengthen the cause or effect argument.

   - List the causes or effects. Tell the writer whether there seem to be too many, too few, or just about the right number. Point to one cause or effect that seems especially imaginative or surprising and to one that seems too obvious. Make suggestions for dropping or adding causes or effects.

   - Evaluate the support for each cause or effect separately. To help the writer make every cause or effect plausible to the intended readers, point out where the support seems thin or inadequate. Point to any support that seems irrelevant to the argument, hard to believe, or inconsistent with other support. Consider whether the writer has overlooked important resources of support: anecdotes, examples, statistics, analogies, or quotations from publications or interviews.

3. Suggest ways to strengthen the counterargument.

   - Locate every instance of counterargument—places where the writer anticipates readers' objections or questions or evaluates readers' preferred alternative causes or effects. Mark these in the margin of the draft. Review these as a set, and then suggest objections, questions, and alternative causes or effects the writer seems to have overlooked.

   - Identify counterarguments that seem weakly supported, and suggest ways the writer might strengthen the support.

   - If any of the refutations attack or ridicule readers, suggest ways the writer could refute without insulting or unduly irritating readers.

4. Suggest how credibility can be enhanced.

- Tell the writer whether the intended readers are likely to find the essay knowledgeable and authoritative. Point to places where it seems most and least authoritative.

- Identify places where the writer seeks common ground—shared values, beliefs, and attitudes—with readers. Try to identify other places where the writer might do so.

5. Suggest how the organizational plan could be improved.

- Consider the overall plan, perhaps by making a scratch outline (see Appendix 1). Analyze closely the progression of the causes or effects. Decide whether the causes or effects follow a logical step-by-step sequence.

- Suggest ways the causes or effects might be more logically sequenced.

- Review the places where counterarguments appear and consider whether they are smoothly woven into the argument. Give advice on the best places for the counterarguments.

- Indicate where new or better transitions might cue the steps in the argument and keep readers on track.

6. Evaluate the effectiveness of visuals.

- Look at any visuals in the essay, and tell the writer what they contribute to your understanding of the writer's speculations.

- If any visuals do not seem relevant, or if there seem to be too many visuals, identify the ones that the writer could consider dropping, explaining your thinking.

- If a visual does not seem appropriately placed, suggest a better place for it.

REVISING

This section offers suggestions for revising your draft. Revising means reenvisioning your draft, trying to see it in a new way, given your purpose and readers, in order to strengthen your cause or effect argument.

The biggest mistake you can make while revising is to focus initially on words or sentences. Instead, first try to see your draft as a whole in order to assess its likely impact on your readers. Think imaginatively and boldly about cutting unconvincing material, adding new material, and moving material around. Your computer makes even drastic revisions physically easy, but you still need to make the mental effort and decisions that will improve your draft.

You may have received help with this challenge from a classmate or tutor who gave your draft a critical reading. If so, keep this valuable feedback in mind as you decide which parts of your draft need revising and what specific changes you could make. The following suggestions will help you solve problems and strengthen your essay.

To Present the Subject More Effectively

- If readers unfamiliar with the subject may not understand it readily, provide more information.

- If the importance or significance of the subject is not clear, dramatize it with an anecdote or highlight its social or cultural implications.

- If the subject is a trend, show evidence of a significant increase or decrease over an extended period of time.

To Strengthen the Cause or Effect Argument

- If you propose what seem like too many causes or effects, clarify the role of each one or drop one or more that seem too obvious, obscure, or minor.

- If a cause or effect lacks adequate support, come up with further examples, anecdotes, statistics, or quotes from authorities.

To Strengthen the Counterargument

- If you do not anticipate readers' likely questions about your argument and objections to it, do so now. Remember that you can either accommodate these objections and questions in your argument, conceding their value by making them part of your own argument, or refute them, arguing that they need not be taken seriously.

- If you do not anticipate readers' likely alternative causes or effects, do so now, conceding or refuting each one.

- If you attack or ridicule readers in your refutations, seek ways to refute their ideas decisively while showing respect for them as people.

- If you neglect to establish common ground with your readers, especially those who may think about your subject quite differently from the way you do, attempt to show them that you share some common values, attitudes, and beliefs.

To Enhance Credibility

- If readers of your draft question your credibility as a writer of cause or effect argument, learn more about your subject, support your argument more fully, anticipate a wider range of readers' likely objections, or talk with others who can help you think more imaginatively about your speculations.

- If your choice of words or your approach to readers weakens your credibility, consider your word choices throughout the essay and look for ways to show readers respect and to establish common ground with them.

To Organize More Logically and Coherently

- If readers question the logical sequence of your causes or effects, consider strengthening your plan by adding or dropping causes or effects or changing their sequence. Ensure that one cause or effect leads to the next in a logically linked chain of reasoning.

- If your logic seems sound but the links are not clear to your readers, provide clearer transitions from one step in the argument to the next. Use clear topic sentences to signal the stages of your argument and the support you provide for each cause or effect.

- If your various counterarguments are not smoothly integrated into your argument, move them around to make the connections clearer.

EDITING AND PROOFREADING

After you have revised your essay, be sure to spend some time checking for errors in usage, punctuation, and mechanics and considering matters of style. If you keep a list of errors you typically make, begin by checking your draft against this list. Ask someone else to proofread your essay before you print out a copy for your instructor or send it electronically.

From our research on student writing, we know that essays speculating about causes or effects have a high percentage of errors in the use of numbers and "reason is because" sentences. Because you must usually rely on numbers to present statistics when you support your argument or demonstrate the existence of a trend, you will need to learn and follow the conventions for presenting different kinds of numbers. Because you are usually drawn into "reason is because" sentences when you make a causal argument, you will need to know options for revising such sentences. Refer to a writer's handbook for help with these potential problems.

REFLECTING ON WHAT YOU HAVE LEARNED

Speculating about Causes or Effects

In this chapter, you have read critically several essays that speculate about causes or effects and have written one of your own. To better remember what you have learned, pause now to reflect on the reading and writing activities you completed in this chapter.

1. *Write* a page or so reflecting on what you have learned. *Begin* by describing what you are most pleased with in your essay. Then *explain* what you think contributed to your achievement. *Be specific* about this contribution.

   - If it was something you learned from the readings, *indicate* which readings and specifically what you learned from them.

   - If it came from your invention writing, *point out* the section or sections that helped you most.

   - If you got good advice from a critical reader, *explain* exactly how the person helped you—perhaps by helping you understand a particular problem in your draft or by adding a new dimension to your writing.

   - *Try to write* about your achievement in terms of what you have learned about the genre.

2. Now *reflect* more generally on speculation about causes or effects, a genre of writing that plays an important role in social life and public policy in the United States. *Consider* some of the following questions: Do you tend to adopt a tentative or an assertive stance when making speculations? Why do you think you generally adopt this stance over the other? How might your personal preferences and values influence your speculations? How might your gender, ethnicity, religious beliefs, age, or social class influence your ideas about a subject? What contribution might essays speculating about causes or effects make to our society that other genres cannot make?

CHAPTER 8

Proposal to Solve a Problem

Proposals are vital to democratic institutions. By reading and writing proposals, citizens and colleagues learn about problems affecting their well-being and explore possible actions that could be taken to remedy these problems. People read and write proposals every day in government, business, education, and the professions.

Many proposals address social problems and attempt to influence the direction of public policy. For example, a student activist group writes a proposal advocating that all campus food services be restricted from using genetically manufactured foods until the potential health hazards of such foods have been fully researched. A special United Nations task force recommends ways to eliminate acid rain worldwide. The College Entrance Examination Board commissions a report proposing strategies for reversing the decline in Scholastic Assessment Test (SAT) scores. A specialist in children's television writes a book suggesting that the federal government fund the development of new educational programming for preschool and elementary school students.

Proposals are also a basic ingredient of the world's work. A team of engineers and technical writers in a transportation firm, for example, might write a proposal to compete for a contract to build a new subway system. The manager of a fashion outlet might write a memo to a company executive proposing an upgrading of the computer system to include networking within the chain of stores. Seeking funding to support her research on a new cancer treatment, a university professor might write a proposal to the National Institutes of Health.

Still other proposals are written by individuals who want to solve problems involving groups or communities to which they belong. A college student irritated by long waits to see a nurse at the campus health clinic writes the clinic director, proposing a more efficient way to schedule and accommodate students. After funding for dance classes has been cut by their school board, students and parents interested in dance write a proposal to the school principal, asking her help in arranging after-school classes taught by a popular high-school teacher who would be paid with community funds. The board of directors of a historical society in a small ranching community proposes to the county board of supervisors that it donate an unused county building to the society so it can display historical records, photographs, and artifacts.

Proposal writing requires a critical questioning attitude—wondering about alternative approaches to bringing about change, puzzling over how a goal might be achieved, questioning why a process unfolds in a particular way, posing challenges to the status quo. In addition, it demands imagination and creativity. To solve a problem, you need to see it anew, to look at it from new perspectives and in new contexts.

Because a proposal tries to convince readers that its way of analyzing and creatively solving the problem makes sense, proposal writers must be sensitive to readers' needs and different perspectives. Readers need to know details of the solution and to be convinced that it will solve the problem and can be implemented. If readers initially favor a different solution, knowing why the writer rejects it will help them decide whether to support or reject the writer's proposed solution. Readers may be wary of costs, demands on their time, superficial changes, and grand schemes.

As you plan and draft a proposal, you will want to determine whether your readers know about the problem and whether they recognize its seriousness. In addition, you will want to consider how your readers might rate other possible solutions. Knowing what your readers know, what their assumptions and biases are, and what kinds of arguments appeal to them is crucial to proposal writing, as it is to all good argumentative writing.

Reading the proposal essays in this chapter will help you discover why the genre is so important and how it works. From the readings and from the suggestions for writing that follow each reading, you will get ideas for your own proposal essay. As you read and write about the selections, keep in mind the following assignment, which sets out the goals for writing a proposal. To support your writing of this assignment, the chapter concludes with a Guide to Writing Proposals.

THE WRITING ASSIGNMENT

Proposal

Write an essay proposing a solution to a problem affecting a community or group to which you belong. Your tasks are to analyze the problem and establish that it is serious enough to need solving, to offer a solution that will remedy the problem or at least help solve it, and to lay out the particulars by which your proposed solution would be put into effect. Address your proposal to one or more members of the group or to outsiders who could help solve the problem, being sure to take into account readers' likely objections to your proposed solution as well as their alternative solutions.

WRITING SITUATIONS FOR PROPOSALS

Writing that proposes solutions to problems plays a significant role in college and professional life, as the following examples indicate:

- Frustrated by what they see as the failure of high schools to prepare students for the workplace, managers of a pharmaceuticals company decide to develop a proposal to move vocational and technical training out of an ill-equipped high-school system and onto the plant's floor. Seven divisional managers plus the firm's technical writers meet weekly to plan the proposal. They read about other on-the-job training programs and interview selected high-school teachers and current employees who attended the high-school program they want to replace. After several months' research, they present to the company CEO and to the school board a proposal that includes a timetable for implementing their solution and a detailed budget.

- For a political science class, a college student analyzes the question of presidential term limits. Citing examples from recent history, she argues that U.S. presidents spend the first year of each term getting organized and the fourth year either running for reelection or weakened by their status as a lame duck. Consequently, they are fully productive for only half of their four-year terms. She proposes limiting presidents to one six-year term, claiming that this change would remedy the problem by giving presidents four or five years to put their programs into effect. She acknowledges that it could make presidents less responsive to the public will, but insists that the system of legislative checks and balances would make that problem unlikely.

- For an economics class, a student looks into the many problems arising from *maquiladoras,* industries in Mexico near the border with the United States that provide foreign exchange for the Mexican government, low-paying jobs for Mexican workers, and profits for American manufacturers. Among these problems are inadequate housing and health care for workers, frequent injuries on the job, and environmental damage. His instructor encourages him to select one of the problems, research it more thoroughly, and propose a solution. Taking injuries on the job as the problem most immediately within the control of American manufacturers, he proposes that they observe standards established by the U.S. Occupational Safety and Health Administration.

THINKING ABOUT YOUR EXPERIENCE WITH PROPOSALS

Before studying a type of writing, it is useful to spend some time thinking about what you already know about it. You may have discussed with friends an idea of yours or theirs that you hoped would solve a problem or make changes for the better. You might have written essays for classes examining the proposals of experts in a field such as sociology or political science, or you might have written a proposal of your own to solve a social or political problem. Mathematicians, astronomers, anthropologists, physicists, philosophers—people in these and other disciplines are called upon to make proposals to solve problems in their fields.

To analyze your experience with proposal arguments, try to recall a time when you argued—orally or in writing—for a plan or an action that interested or concerned you. What problem existed that made you think of a proposal to solve it? Who was the audience for your argument? What did you hope to achieve with your proposal? What interested you about it or made you think it was significant? Did you need to explain in detail the problem that prompted your solution, or was the problem already understood by your audience?

Consider also the proposal arguments you have read, heard, or seen on television. If you recall someone else's argument in detail, try to identify what made it interesting to you. Was it the problem itself, or did the author's solution seem uniquely imaginative or practical to you? Did the author make the argument for the proposal convincing? If so, how? Were there illuminating details or unusual points of view?

Write at least a page about your experience with proposal arguments.

■ A Guide to Reading Proposals

This guide introduces you to proposal writing. By completing all the activities in it, you will prepare yourself to learn a great deal from the other readings in this chapter about how to read and write a proposal. The guide focuses on a proposal by Robert J. Samuelson, a well-known writer on social and economic issues. You will read Samuelson's essay twice. First, you will read it for meaning, seeking to understand Samuelson's argument and the meaning it holds for you. Then, you will reread the essay like a writer, analyzing the parts to see how Samuelson constructs his argument and to learn the strategies he uses to make his proposal effective. These two activities—reading for meaning and reading like a writer—follow every reading in this chapter.

ROBERT J. SAMUELSON

Reforming Schools through a Federal Test for College Aid

Robert J. Samuelson (b. 1945) began his journalism career at the Washington Post *in 1969, after earning a B.A. in government from Harvard, and became a contributing editor for* Newsweek *in 1984. For his syndicated column on economic and social issues, Samuelson has won numerous journalism awards. In addition, he has published two books,* The Good Life and Its Discontents: The American Dream and the Age of Entitlement 1945–1995 *(1996) and* Untruth: Why the Conventional Wisdom Is (Almost Always) Wrong *(2001).*

The following proposal, "Reforming Schools through a Federal Test for College Aid," was first published in Newsweek *in 1991, but the problem it addresses continues today. When Samuelson refers to "the Bush plan," know that he means President George H. W. Bush, not his son, George W. Bush. Seeking to encourage individual states to voluntarily participate in the National Assessment of Educational Progress (NAEP), the elder Bush proposed a federally funded system of testing students in relation to national standards established for such disciplines as mathematics, reading, science, writing, U.S. history, and geography. This voluntary school testing program was implemented during the Clinton administration, and in 2001 the younger Bush sponsored legislation requiring states and school districts receiving federal Title I funds to participate in the fourth- and eighth-grade reading and mathematics tests administered every two years. You may remember taking these exams periodically when you were in school. The NAEP tests do not grade students individually; they report grades for the entire school so that school boards, parents, and legislators can assess which schools excel or need improvement. Samuelson argues that such tests do little to improve schools because they fail to motivate students. Instead, he proposes a federal test for college financial aid, which he argues would both motivate students and put pressure on high schools to better prepare students for college.*

Like most of Samuelson's original Newsweek *readers, you have experience with high-school testing that puts you in an excellent position to judge his proposal. As you read, write your reactions to and questions about his argument in the margins of the text.*

We are not yet serious about school reform. The latest plan   1
from the Bush administration mixes lofty rhetoric (a pledge to
"invent new schools") with vague proposals to rate our schools
with national tests. It doesn't address the most dreary—and
important—fact about American education: our students don't
work very hard. The typical high-school senior does less than an

hour of homework an evening. No school reform can succeed unless this changes. What's depressing is that we could change it, but probably won't.

We could require students receiving federal college aid to pass a qualifying test. This is a huge potential lever. Nearly two-thirds of high-school graduates go to college (including community colleges and vocational schools), and roughly two-fifths—6 million students—get federal aid. In fiscal 1991, government grants and guaranteed loans totaled $18.1 billion. As a practical matter any federal test would also affect many unaided students; most colleges couldn't easily maintain a lower entrance requirement for the rich. The message would be: anyone wanting to go to college can't glide through high school.

Just how well our schools perform depends heavily on student attitudes. This is one reason why the Bush plan, which proposes tests to evaluate schools, is so empty. The tests hold no practical consequences for students and, therefore, lack the power to motivate them. When students aren't motivated, they don't treat school seriously. Without serious students, it's hard to attract good people into teaching no matter how much we pay them. And bad teachers ensure educational failure. This is the vicious circle we must break.

Unfortunately, we don't now expect much of our students. For most high-school students, it doesn't pay to work hard. Their goal is college, and almost anyone can go to some college. There are perhaps 50 truly selective colleges and universities in the country, Chester Finn Jr., professor of education at Vanderbilt University, writes in his new book, *We Must Take Charge: Our Schools and Our Future.* To survive, the other 3,400 institutions of "higher learning" eagerly recruit students. Entrance requirements are meager and financial assistance from states and the federal government is abundant.

"Coast and get into college and have the same opportunities as someone who worked hard," says one senior quoted by Finn. "That is the system." It's this sort of silly rationalization that hurts American students, precisely because they can't always make up what they've missed in the past. Opportunities go only to those who have real skills—not paper credentials or many years spent on campus. The college dropout rate is staggering. After six years, less than half of students at four-year colleges have earned a degree. The graduation rate is even lower for community colleges.

Every other advanced society does it differently. "The United States is the only industrial country that doesn't have some (testing) system external to the schools to assess educational achievement," says Max Eckstein, an expert on international education.

Their tests, unlike ours, typically determine whether students can continue in school. As the lone holdout, we can compare our system with everyone else's. Well, we rank near the bottom on most international comparisons.

In the media, the school "crisis" is often pictured as mainly a problem of providing a better education for the poor and minorities. Stories focus on immigrants and inner-city schools. Almost everyone else is (by omission) presumed to be getting an adequate education. Forget it. In fact, the test scores of our poorest students, though still abysmally low, have improved. Likewise, high-school dropout rates have declined. What we minimize is the slippage of our average schools.

COMMON SENSE

When mediocrity is the norm, even good students suffer. In international comparisons, our top students often fare poorly against other countries' top students, notes economist John Bishop of Cornell University. Grade inflation is widespread. In 1990 1.1 million high-school students took the college board exams. These are the best students: 28 percent had A averages, 53 percent B's and the rest C's. Yet, two-fifths of these students scored less than 390 on the verbal SAT.

The idea that college-bound students should be required (by test) to demonstrate the ability to do college-level work is common sense. It's hard to see how anyone could object, especially with so much public money at stake. But almost no educators or political leaders advocate it. The American belief in "equality" and "fairness" makes it hard for us to create barriers that block some students. Our approach is more indirect and dishonest: first, we give them meaningless high-school degrees; then we let them drop out of college.

The same spirit of self-deception pervades much of the school debate. We skirt the obvious—students will work if there's a good reason—and pursue painless and largely fictitious cures. There's a constant search for new teaching methods and technologies that will, somehow, miraculously mesmerize students and automatically educate them. Computers are a continuing fad. Liberals blame educational failure on inadequate spending; conservatives lambaste public schools as rigid bureaucracies. These familiar critiques are largely irrelevant.

Low spending isn't the main problem. Between 1970 and 1990, "real" (inflation adjusted) spending per student in public schools rose 63 percent. In 1989, U.S. educational spending totaled 6.9 percent of gross national product, which equals or exceeds most nations'. As for "vouchers" and "choice"—conservatives' current cure—the experiment has already been tried in higher education. It failed. Government loans and grants are vouchers that allow students choice. The perverse result is that colleges compete by reducing entrance requirements in order to increase enrollments and maximize revenues.

A test for college aid would stem this corrosive process. The number of college freshmen would decline, but not—given the high dropout rates—the number of college graduates. Because high-school standards are so lax, the passing grade of any meaningful test would flunk many of today's seniors. Tests are available, because a few state college systems, such as New Jersey's and Tennessee's, give them to freshmen. Failing students must take remedial courses. In 1990, 37 percent of New Jersey freshmen flunked a verbal-skills test and 58 percent an algebra test.   12

AN UPROAR

Who would be hurt? Not students who can pass the test today: that's perhaps 40 to 60 percent of college freshmen. Not students who might pass the test with more study: that's another big fraction. (In New Jersey and Tennessee, most students pass remedial courses. If they can do it at 18 or 19, they can do it at 17.) Some students who now go to college wouldn't. Often, these students drop out after saddling themselves with a hefty student loan. Would they be worse off? On college loans, default rates range as high as 25 percent.   13

But let's be candid. None of this is about to happen soon. Requiring tests for college aid would cause an uproar. There would be charges of elitism, maybe racism. Colleges and universities would resist. They depend on the current open-ended flow of students and, without it, some would have to shut down. This wouldn't be bad for the country, because we now overinvest in higher education. With one-fifth the students, colleges and universities account for two-fifths of all educational spending. But today's waste has spawned a huge constituency.   14

Little wonder that President Bush—and all politicians—steer clear of this sort of reform. It's too direct. It wouldn't cure all our educational problems, but it would make a start. It would jolt students, parents and teachers. It would foster a climate that rewards effort. It would create pressures for real achievement, not just inflated grades. It would force schools to pay more attention to non-college-bound students, rather than assuming everyone can go somewhere. It would strip away our illusions, which, sadly, are precisely what we cherish most.   15

READING FOR MEANING

This section presents three activities that will help you reread Samuelson's proposal with a critical eye. Done in sequence, these activities lead you from a basic understanding of the selection to a more personal response to it and finally to an analysis that deepens your understanding and critical thinking about what you are reading.

Read to Comprehend

Reread the selection, and write a few sentences briefly explaining in your own words Samuelson's proposal as well as the major problem he aims to solve. Also make a list of any words you do not understand—for example, *lofty* (paragraph 1), *rationalization* (5), *elitism* (14), *spawned* (14). Look up their meanings in a dictionary to see which definition best fits the context.

To expand your understanding of this reading, you might use one or more of the following critical reading strategies that are explained and illustrated in Appendix 1: *annotating, previewing, summarizing,* and *contextualizing.*

Read to Respond

Write several paragraphs exploring your initial thoughts and feelings about "Reforming Schools through a Federal Test for College Aid." Focus on anything that stands out for you, perhaps because it resonates with your own experience or because you find a statement puzzling.

You might consider writing about

- the "vicious circle" (paragraph 3), explaining what Samuelson means to convey with that phrase and evaluating it from your perspective as a former high-school student.

- one or two of the alternative solutions Samuelson refutes in paragraphs 10 and 11, explaining why you agree or disagree with him about their potential value in improving high-school students' preparation for college.

- what you think of Samuelson's predictions that an "uproar" would result from his proposal and that "charges of elitism, maybe racism" would ensue (14).

To develop your response to Samuelson's proposal, you might use one or both of the following critical reading strategies that are explained and illustrated in Appendix 1: *summarizing* and *reflecting on challenges to your beliefs and values.*

Read to Analyze Underlying Assumptions

Write several paragraphs exploring one or more of the assumptions, values, and beliefs underlying Samuelson's proposal. As you write, explain how the assumptions are reflected in the text, as well as what you now think of them (and perhaps of your own assumptions) after rereading the selection with a critical eye.

Notice that Samuelson makes explicit a number of his assumptions—such as "our students don't work very hard" (paragraph 1) and "[w]hen students aren't motivated, they don't treat school seriously" (3). But like any other text, this one also contains assumptions, values, and beliefs—either of the author or of others—that are not stated but only implied. For example, consider his assertion that the current tests, which evaluate schools but not individual students, "hold no practical consequences for students and, therefore, lack the power to motivate them" (3). He seems to believe that students will be motivated by personal financial gain—federal college aid—but not by other factors such as pride in their own personal achievement or satisfaction in a job well done. In its most general terms, his underlying assumption is that people are most motivated to work hard by the possibility of their own financial gain—not a surprising assumption by a writer whose work focuses on economics. Interestingly, though, Samuelson seems to think differently about the motivation of teachers: the underlying assumption in paragraph 3 is that some people will choose teaching over higher-paying careers if they can teach students who take school seriously. How do these assumptions agree or conflict with your own beliefs about what motivates students and teachers? The purpose of examining underlying assumptions in a reading is to give us an opportunity to think critically about unexamined assumptions—those of others as well as our own, many of which may be ingrained in our culture, our education, and even our language.

You might consider writing about

- the assumption underlying Samuelson's statement that the message behind a federal test for college aid would be "anyone wanting to go to college can't glide through high school" (paragraph 2), perhaps considering whether you think college-bound students "glide" through high school now or whether some students do so because of reasons that Samuelson does not explore.

- the beliefs and values underlying the statement, "When mediocrity is the norm, even good students suffer" (8).

- "the American belief in 'equality' and 'fairness' " that Samuelson says "makes it hard for us to create barriers that block some students" (9), or his own assumptions and values that are reflected in this assertion.

- the assumptions about what the goal of attending college should be that lead Samuelson to support his proposal with this assertion: "The number of college freshmen would decline, but not—given the high dropout rates—the number of college graduates" (12).

To probe assumptions more deeply, you might use one or more of the following critical reading strategies that are explained and illustrated in Appendix 1: *reflecting on challenges to your beliefs and values, looking for patterns of opposition,* and *recognizing emotional manipulation.*

READING LIKE A WRITER

This section guides you through an analysis of Samuelson's argumentative strategies: *introducing the problem; presenting the solution; arguing directly for the proposed solution; counterarguing readers' objections, questions, and alternative solutions;* and *establishing credibility*. For each strategy you will be asked to reread and annotate part of Samuelson's essay to see how he uses the strategy in "Reforming Schools through a Federal Test for College Aid."

When you study the selections later in this chapter, you will see how different writers use these same strategies. The Guide to Writing Proposals near the end of the chapter suggests ways you can use these strategies in writing your own proposal.

Introducing the Problem

Every proposal begins with a problem. Depending on what their readers know about the problem, writers may explain how it came to be or what attempts have been made to solve it. Sometimes, readers are already aware of a problem, especially if it affects them directly. In such cases, the writer can merely identify the problem and move directly to presenting a solution. At other times, readers will be unaware that the problem exists or have difficulty imagining it. In these situations, the writer may have to describe the problem in detail, helping readers recognize its importance and the consequences of failing to solve it.

Writers may also believe that readers misunderstand the problem, failing to recognize it for what it really is. They may then decide that their first task is to redefine the problem in a way that helps readers see it in a different way. Samuelson does precisely that. Because he believes that efforts to reform American schools are doomed because they fail to recognize the real problem, his opening strategy must be to redefine the problem.

Analyze

1. *Reread* paragraphs 3–6, noting in the margin which kinds of support Samuelson uses to convince readers that the problem should be redefined as one of student motivation. Where does he point to causes of the problem and to its consequences, rely on comparisons, quote authorities, give examples, make use of statistics, or make judgments?

2. *Consider* how effectively Samuelson redefines the problem. As one of his intended readers, *explain* why you are or are not convinced of his redefinition. In what ways might he have made his argument more convincing?

Write

Write several sentences explaining Samuelson's strategy for introducing the problem and evaluating how convincing you find his argument. *Give details* from the reading.

Presenting the Solution

The proposal writer's primary purposes are to convince readers of the wisdom of the proposal solution and to take action on its implementation. In order to achieve these purposes, the writer must ensure that readers can imagine the solution being implemented.

Some proposals have little chance of success unless every small step for implementing them is detailed for readers. For this reason, a proposed solution to a highly technical engineering problem might run many pages in length. In contrast, a more general proposal, such as Samuelson's idea for encouraging greater student preparedness for college through federal testing and incentives, could be brief. This type of proposal seeks to gain readers' adherence to the principle of testing and defers the implementation—the types of tests, when they would be offered, how they would be evaluated, and so forth—to specialists who would work out the details later. Although the writer may think that detailing the implementation is premature, some critical readers might be skeptical that the tests Samuelson proposes would escape the problems that already exist for similar national tests such as the SAT. As you look closely at the way Samuelson presents his solution, you will want to consider how well he handles the question of implementation given his purpose, his space limitations, and his *Newsweek* readers' expectations.

Analyze

1. *Reread* paragraph 12, and *underline* the few details Samuelson gives about his proposed solution.

2. Keeping in mind his space constraints, *list* two or three additional key details Samuelson might have included to help readers more easily imagine how his proposed solution would be implemented.

Write

List the details Samuelson gives about his proposed federal test for financial aid. Then *add a few sentences* evaluating whether Samuelson gives enough details for you to imagine how the solution might be implemented, even though it is not spelled out.

Arguing Directly for the Proposed Solution

In arguing for solutions, writers rely on two interrelated strategies: arguing directly for the proposed solution and counterarguing readers' likely objections, questions, and alternative solutions. (We take up the second strategy, counterargument, in the next section.)

Whatever else proposal writers do, they must argue energetically, imaginatively, and sensitively for their proposed solutions. A proposal may describe a problem well or complain with great feeling about it; if it goes no further, however, it cannot be a proposal. Writers must try to convince readers that the solution presented will actually alleviate the problem. The solution should also appear feasible, cost-effective, and more promising than alternative solutions.

In thinking about how to support their argument, proposal writers should ask themselves why their solution would work. Such support may include personal experience, hypothetical cases and scenarios, statistics, facts, assertions, examples, speculations about causes or consequences, and quotations from authorities. The most convincing support surprises readers: They see it and think, "I never thought of it that way."

Although Samuelson describes his solution only briefly and says almost nothing about how it might be implemented, he does argue energetically for it, relying on a variety of strategies.

Analyze

1. *Reread* paragraphs 8, 12, 13, and 15, where Samuelson argues directly for his solution. In each of these paragraphs, *underline* the one main reason Samuelson gives for advocating his solution.

2. *Review* these paragraphs, this time noting in the margin the kinds of support Samuelson offers.

3. *Consider* the strengths of Samuelson's direct argument for his solution. What do you find most and least convincing in his reasons and support?

Write

Write several sentences describing and evaluating Samuelson's argument in the paragraphs you analyzed. What kinds of reasons and support does he use? *Give examples* from the reading. *Conclude with a few more sentences* that evaluate the effectiveness of Samuelson's argument.

Counterarguing Readers' Objections, Questions, and Alternative Solutions

As they argue for their solutions, experienced writers are continually aware of readers' objections to the argument or questions about it. Writers may *accommodate* readers' likely objections and questions by modifying their own arguments, perhaps even pointing out how they have done so. What better way to disarm a skeptical or antagonistic reader? Or writers may *refute* readers' objections and questions; that is, try to show them to be wrong. Experienced arguers bring their readers' questions and objections right into their arguments. They do not ignore their readers' concerns or conveniently assume that readers are on their side.

Experienced proposal writers may also acknowledge other solutions. When a writer knows or suspects readers may have alternative solutions in mind, it is best to discuss them directly in the argument. If Samuelson had failed to acknowledge obvious alternative solutions, readers would have regarded him as ill-informed about the problem. As with questions and objections, a writer can either accommodate an alternative solution by integrating all or part of it into his or her own solution, or refute the alternative as unworkable.

Analyze

1. *Reread* paragraphs 7 and 13, where Samuelson anticipates readers' likely objections and questions. *Underline* the specific objections or questions against which Samuelson seems to be counterarguing. Then *note in the margin* whether he accommodates or refutes the objections and the strategies he uses to do so.

2. *Reread* paragraphs 10 and 11, where Samuelson opposes some popular alternative solutions. *Identify* the alternative solutions. Then *consider* whether Samuelson accommodates or refutes the alternatives and how he goes about doing so.

Write

Write a few sentences explaining how Samuelson counterargues. *Give examples* of both objections or questions and alternative solutions. Then *write a few more sentences* evaluating Samuelson's counterarguments. How successfully do you think he handles readers' likely objections or questions? How do you think advocates of the alternative solutions Samuelson evaluates would respond to his counterarguments?

Establishing Credibility

For an argument to be considered credible by readers, they must find it authoritative, believable, or trustworthy. Readers have many ways of deciding whether an argument is credible. They may already know the writer by reputation. They may have confidence in the magazine, book, or Web site where the argument is published. They may learn information about the writer—jobs held, degrees earned, books published, awards won, and so on—from a biographical note published with the reading. The most important basis for readers' judgments about credibility, however, is the argument itself—the attitudes toward readers revealed in the writer's choice of wording and use of sources, the ring of truth in interview quotes and personal experience stories, the step-by-step logic of the argument, the plausibility of reasons, the adequacy of support, and the sensitivity in handling readers' likely questions, objections, and alternative solutions.

Analyze

1. *Reread* the biographical note introducing Samuelson's essay. How do the facts given there contribute to the credibility of his argument? What do you know about the publications he has worked for and published in? What more might you want to know?

2. Keeping in mind that you are among the intended readers of Samuelson's argument, *skim the essay* with a focus on assessing the credibility of the writer and his argument. *Note in the margin* your impressions and judgments.

Write

Write several sentences describing the impression you have of Samuelson from both the biographical note and his essay. What makes you trust or distrust his argument? *Give examples* from his argument to support your answer.

■ Readings

KAREN KORNBLUH

The Parent Trap

> *Karen Kornbluh is a graduate of Bryn Mawr College and earned a master's degree at Harvard's Kennedy School of Government. As director of the Work and Family Program of the New America Foundation, she leads an effort to allow Americans more control over their work and family lives through increased flexibility in the scheduling of work hours, the amount of time spent working, and the availability of entry and exit points over the course of a career. Kornbluh has advised elected leaders across the political spectrum on work and family issues. She is also a recognized expert on telecommunications policy. Her articles on work and family issues have appeared in the* Atlantic Monthly, Washington Post, *and* Washington Monthly. *She has also written on technology policy for the* New York Times, Harvard Journal of Law and Technology, *and* Los Angeles Times.
>
> *Kornbluh joined New America's Work and Family Program after ten years of public service. She served as deputy chief of staff to U.S. Treasury Secretary Robert Rubin in the Clinton administration, director of the Office of Legislative and Intergovernmental Affairs at the Federal Communications Commission, and a legislative assistant to U.S. Senator John F. Kerry. She had previously worked as an economist at the economic forecasting firm Townsend-Greenspan and as a management consultant advising manufacturing firms on business strategy.*
>
> *"The Parent Trap" was first published in a 2003 issue of the* Atlantic Monthly, *a magazine whose audience is interested in in-depth coverage of current events and social and political issues. Kornbluh argues for changes in the workplace that will help parents adapt to changes in the American family, especially in the amount of time they spend with their children given that in most families both parents now work outside the home. Because we cannot simply return to "the way things used to be" decades ago, she argues, we must change policies at work and in government to help the new "juggler family."*
>
> *As you read, think about your experiences as a child, a parent, or both and how they may affect your response to Kornbluh's proposal. Do you still think of the ideal family as one where the father works outside the home and the mother inside the home? Have you or your parents had to juggle parenting responsibilities with work responsibilities—and if so, how did you feel about it?*

The American family changed dramatically over the last decades of the twentieth century. In the postwar years up to the early 1970s a single breadwinner—working forty hours a week, often for the same employer, until retirement—generally earned enough to support children and a spouse. Today fully 70 percent of families with children are headed by two working parents or by an unmarried working parent. The traditional family—one breadwinner and one homemaker—has been replaced by the "juggler family," and American parents have twenty-two fewer hours a week to spend with their kids than they did in 1969. As a result, millions of children are left in unlicensed day care or at home with the TV as a babysitter.

Yet the nation clings to the ideal of the 1950s family; many of our policies for and cultural attitudes toward families are relics of a time when Father worked and Mother was home to mind the children. Every time a working parent has to risk a job to take a sick child to the doctor, and every time parents have to leave their children home alone or entrust them to inadequate supervision, families are paying the price for our outdated policies.

The 1950s family is not coming back anytime soon, however, in part because the economic conditions that supported it no longer exist. Starting in the 1970s de-industrialization, corporate restructuring, and globalization led to stagnating wages and greater economic insecurity. Many women went to work to help make ends meet. Indeed, conservatives who lament that feminism undermined the traditional family model overlook the fact that the changing economic environment made that model financially impossible for most American families.

These days most women and men—across all income levels—expect to remain in the workplace after having children. Thus to be decent parents, workers now need greater flexibility than they once did. Yet good part-time or flex-time jobs remain rare. Whereas companies have embraced flexibility in virtually every other aspect of their businesses (inventory control, production schedules, financing), full-time workers' schedules remain inflexible. Employers often demand that high-level workers be available around the clock, and hourly workers can be fired for refusing overtime. Moreover, many employees have no right to a minimum number of sick or vacation days: more than a third of all working parents—and an even larger percentage of low-income parents—lack both sick and vacation leave. Though the Family and Medical Leave Act of 1993 finally guaranteed that workers at large companies could take a leave of absence for the birth or adoption of a baby, or for the illness of a family member, that leave is unpaid. This means that the United States is one of only two countries in the Organization for Economic Cooperation and Development without paid maternity leave—and the other country, Australia, is actively considering providing it.

Many parents who need flexibility find themselves shunted into   5
part-time, temporary, on-call, or contract jobs with reduced wages
and career opportunities and, often, no benefits. A full quarter of
American workers are in these jobs. Only 15 percent of women
and 12 percent of men in such jobs receive health insurance from
their employers. In other developed countries health benefits are
often government-provided, and therefore not contingent on full-
time employment. The United States is the only advanced industrial nation that relies on a voluntary employer-based system to
provide health insurance and retirement benefits to its citizens.

Our nation has also failed to respond to the need for affordable,   6
high-quality child care. Schools still operate on an agrarian schedule, closing at three every day and for more than two months in
the summer. After-school-care programs are relatively scarce, and
day-care standards are uneven. (Training requirements for hair-
dressers and manicurists are currently more stringent than those
for child-care workers.) And the expense of day care—which is
often more than the tuition at a state college—is borne almost
entirely by parents alone. In stark contrast, most European nations
view child care as a national responsibility and publicly subsidize
it. In France, for instance, day-care centers and preschools are
heavily subsidized—and staffed by qualified child-care workers
whose education is financed by the government.

A sensible modern family policy—that supports rather than   7
undermines today's juggler family—would have three components. The first is paid leave. No American worker should have to
fear losing a job or suffering a reduction in pay because he or she
needs to care for a child or a parent. Every worker should be entitled to at least a minimum number of days of paid leave for personal illness or that of a family member, or to care for a new child.
In September, California adopted the first law in the country that
provides workers with paid family and medical leave, up to six
weeks' worth.

The second component of a smart family policy is high-quality   8
child care. The United States is practically alone among developed
countries in leaving day care almost entirely to the private market.
At a minimum, U.S. day-care facilities must be held to higher standards than they are now, and parents should be eligible for subsidies, so that they do not have to shoulder the cost of this care all
on their own. In addition, preschool and after-school programs
should be universally available.

The third and most important component is more fundamen-   9
tal: we should sever the link between employers and basic benefits.
In today's labor market, when working parents need maximum

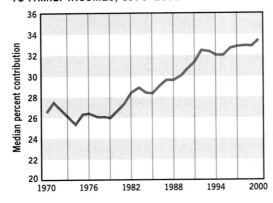

CONTRIBUTION OF WIVES' EARNINGS
TO FAMILY INCOMES, 1970–2000

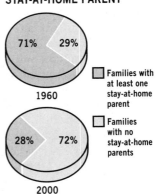

DECLINE OF THE
STAY-AT-HOME PARENT

flexibility and people move frequently from job to job, it no longer makes sense to rely on employers for the provision of health insurance and pensions. The link between them is an industrial-era relic that often denies benefits and tax subsidies to parents who require nonstandard working arrangements. We need a new approach to our social-insurance system, one in which control and responsibility lie with individuals, not their employers, and in which government subsidies are granted based on an individual's ability to pay, rather than on whether he or she works full time, part time, or flex time. Unlinking benefits from employment could do wonders for the American family: parents could have the flexibility of part-time work with the benefits that today accompany full-time work.

Unlinking health care from employment could be accomplished in a number of ways. One way would be to expand Medicare to cover all citizens, not just the elderly, thus creating a single-payer system. But a better approach would be to create a system of mandatory self-insurance, with government subsidies for low-income workers and for people taking time off to care for family members. Creating such a system—one that ensures that everyone is covered while keeping costs low—could not be done easily or quickly, of course, but there are precedents. Switzerland, for instance, provides universal health-care coverage without relying on a single-payer system. Another model can be found closer to home: auto insurance, which almost all American states require car owners to have. In the health-care

10

version of this model everyone would either choose a plan from a regional insurance exchange or be enrolled in a default plan by the government. Participating health-insurance providers would be required to offer a "basic" plan—with a minimum level of coverage—and to cover anyone who applied. Federal subsidies would ensure that no one spent more than a fixed percentage of income on basic health insurance.

Though the government would have to subsidize those who cannot afford to pay for a basic plan on their own, this cost could be largely offset by redirecting both the funds currently spent on Medicaid and the nearly $100 billion that workers get in tax breaks through their employer-provided health insurance. Employers should welcome the change, because although they would likely continue to provide employees with the same level of total compensation they do now (for instance, by increasing wages), they would be relieved of the administrative burdens and the restrictions on flexibility imposed by the current social-insurance system.

For the past few decades both Democrats and Republicans have tried to lay claim to the "pro-family" mantle. Neither party, however, has offered a coherent plan for giving American parents the security and the flexibility they need. A plan that offers both would appeal powerfully to the many voters who are having such difficulty balancing their work and family obligations.

READING FOR MEANING

This section presents three activities that will help you reread Kornbluh's essay with a critical eye. Done in sequence, these activities lead you from a basic understanding of the selection to a more personal response to it and finally to an analysis that deepens your understanding and critical thinking about what you are reading.

Read to Comprehend

Reread the selection, and write a few sentences briefly explaining the problems that Kornbluh's proposal is designed to solve. Then list the three components of her proposal, giving a brief explanation of how she says they would solve the problems. Also make a list of any words you do not understand—for example, *stagnating* (paragraph 3), *agrarian* (6), *subsidize* and *subsidies* (6 and 8–11), *mandatory* (10). Look up the words in a dictionary and see which definition best fits the context.

To expand your understanding of this reading, you might use one or more of the following critical reading strategies that are explained and illustrated in Appendix 1: *annotating, summarizing,* and *contextualizing.*

Read to Respond

Write several paragraphs exploring your initial thoughts and feelings about Kornbluh's proposal. Focus on anything that stands out for you, perhaps because it resonates with your own experience or because you find a statement puzzling. You might consider writing about

- Kornbluh's statement that as a result of parents having "twenty-two fewer hours a week to spend with their kids than they did in 1969 . . . millions of children are left in unlicensed day care or at home with the TV as a babysitter" (paragraph 1), perhaps in relation to your own experience, either as a parent or a child, with the conditions that Kornbluh laments.

- the effect created by Kornbluh's repetition of the words "flexibility" and "subsidies" throughout her article, tracing them through the text to see how they are used.

- Kornbluh's statement that "conservatives who lament that feminism undermined the traditional family model overlook the fact that the changing economic environment made that model financially impossible for most American families" (3).

- Kornbluh's assertion that "to be decent parents, workers now need greater flexibility than they once did" (4).

- whether the analogy Kornbluh draws between "mandatory self-insurance" and state-mandated auto insurance (10) makes sense, allowing you to see the connection and believe in the similarities.

- why Kornbluh entitles her proposal "The Parent Trap," and whether she "earns" her title in the body of her essay.

- what the graph and the pie charts add to your understanding or appreciation of Kornbluh's proposal.

To develop your response to Kornbluh's proposal, you might use one or more of the following critical reading strategies that are explained and illustrated in Appendix 1: *evaluating the logic of an argument, recognizing emotional manipulation,* and *judging the writer's credibility.*

Read to Analyze Underlying Assumptions

Write several paragraphs exploring one or more of the assumptions, values, and beliefs underlying Kornbluh's proposal. As you write, explain how the assumptions are reflected in the text, as well as what you now think of them (and perhaps of your own assumptions) after rereading the selection with a critical eye. You might consider writing about

- the "cultural attitudes toward families" that Kornbluh says are "relics of a time when Father worked and Mother was home to mind the children" (paragraph 2).

- what Kornbluh seems to assume about her audience and about the United States when she cites examples of how other industrialized nations handle "the parent trap."

- what Kornbluh believes about the role of the government in the United States, especially regarding social programs, judging from her reference to "unlicensed day care" (1) and her statements in several places that the government will need to subsidize the programs in her proposal.

To probe assumptions more deeply, you might use one or both of the following critical reading strategies that are explained and illustrated in Appendix 1: *reflecting on challenges to your beliefs and values* and *looking for patterns of opposition.*

READING LIKE A WRITER
INTRODUCING THE PROBLEM

In introducing the problem, proposal writers may define or describe it as well as argue for its seriousness. Depending on their purpose and readers, writers must decide whether they need to identify the problem briefly, as Samuelson does, or introduce it at some length, as Kornbluh does in the first half of her essay.

Analyze

1. *Reread* paragraphs 1–6, where Kornbluh explains the significant changes in the American family since the 1950s. *Annotate* the information, highlighting where she mentions these changes as well as where she points out the disadvantages facing U.S. parents compared to parents in other countries.

2. *Evaluate* how well Kornbluh presents the problem in paragraphs 1–6. Does she appeal to readers who may themselves be clinging to the notion of the 1950s family or who haven't even realized there is a problem? Where does her argument that there is a problem seem most successful? Least successful?

Write

Write several sentences describing how Kornbluh introduces the problem and emphasizes its importance in paragraphs 1–6. What strategies and kinds of evidence does she use? *Give details* from the reading to support your answer. *Conclude with a few sentences* evaluating Kornbluh's presentation of the problem. Given her purpose and readers, how successful do you find her argument? Which parts do you find most convincing? Least convincing?

CONSIDERING IDEAS FOR YOUR OWN WRITING

Consider writing about a problem that seems to be national but might be solvable on a local scale for your community or college. For example, you might have your own ideas to add to Kornbluh's about how to solve the problem of getting adequate local child care for working parents. Or you might want to investigate whether local companies have policies about flex-time for working parents. Other national problems are binge drinking and hazing in college fraternities or other social groups that sometimes lead to serious injury or even death. Perhaps you could propose a solution for groups in your college that are experiencing problems. Or you might consider the growing problem of lack of health insurance and how it affects children, thinking of proposals to ease the crisis in your local community that no one else has yet thought of. "Suburban sprawl" is another national issue that might be affecting your area; do some research on planned growth to see if you could make a proposal to solve this or a similar problem.

MATTHEW MILLER

A New Deal for Teachers

Matthew Miller (b. 1963) received a B.A. in economics from Brown University in 1983 and a law degree from Columbia University in 1986. A nationally syndicated columnist and an award-winning contributor to the New York Times, Wall Street Journal, Atlantic Monthly, Fortune, Slate, *and other national newspapers and magazines, Miller is also a commentator for National Public Radio's* Morning Edition, *the host of the political week-in-review program* Left, Right, and Center, *and a frequent commentator on such television programs as* Crossfire, Nightline, 20/20, *and* Conversations with Charlie Rose. *As a consultant to corporations, nonprofit organizations, and government on issues of strategy, policy, and communications, he specializes in projects in the fields of education, health care, and the economy. His first book,* The Two Percent Solution: Fixing America's Problems in Ways Liberals and Conservatives Can Love, *was published in 2003.*

The following proposal, "A New Deal for Teachers," was published in the July–August 2003 issue of the Atlantic Monthly. *Miller is responding to recently published information about the problems of schools in poor districts, where test scores are low and teachers tend to leave in discouragement. He is also responding to the fact that two-thirds of U.S. public school teachers would be retiring in the next ten years, offering an opportunity for the nation to make new policies to recruit new, well-qualified teachers who might bring about improvements in poor schools. Following his proposal are several letters (published in the October 2003 issue) from readers responding to Miller's ideas. These letters illustrate a broad range of views about the role of teaching, ways to recruit and evaluate teachers, and teachers' salaries.*

As you read, think about your experiences with the teachers you had before college. What do you think motivated them to teach? How do you feel about teaching as a career? How would you feel if the salaries were considerably higher?

No one should need convincing that schools in the nation's poor districts are in crisis. A recent Department of Education study found that fourth-grade students in low-income areas tested three grade levels behind students in higher-income areas. "Most 4th graders who live in U.S. cities can't read and understand a simple children's book," a special report in *Education Week* concluded a few years ago, "and most 8th graders can't use arithmetic to solve a practical problem." 1

There are probably a hundred things these schools need, and ten things that could make a very big difference, but if we had to focus on only one thing, the most important would be improving 2 teacher quality. Owing to rising enrollments and a coming wave of retirements, more than two million teachers must be recruited over the next decade—700,000 of them in poor districts. That means fully two thirds of the teacher corps will be new to the job. Finding top talent and not simply warm bodies is a tall order, especially in urban districts, where half of new teachers quit within three years (and studies suggest that it's the smarter half). Research shows that much of the achievement gap facing poor and minority students comes not from poverty or family conditions but from systemic differences in teacher quality; thus recruiting better teachers for poor schools is not only the biggest issue in education but the next great frontier for social justice.

The obstacles to improving teacher quality are great. Good teachers in urban schools have told me with dismay of the incompetence of many of their colleagues. The state competency requirements that aspiring teachers must meet are appallingly low. The late Albert Shanker, the legendary president of the American Federation of Teachers, once said that most of the state tests are so easy to pass that they keep only "illiterates" out of teaching. Yet even these minimal standards are routinely waived so that districts can issue "emergency credentials"; in our biggest cities as many as half of new hires, and up to a quarter of city teachers overall, aren't properly trained or credentialed.

The situation may soon get even worse, because many of the teachers now reaching retirement age are among the best in the system. Until the 1960s and 1970s schools attracted talented women and minority members to whom most higher-paying careers weren't open. Now people who might once have taught science or social studies become doctors, lawyers, and engineers. Salaries that start, on average, at $29,000 simply can't compete with the pay in other professions. In 1970 in New York City a lawyer starting out at a prestigious firm and a teacher going into public education had a difference in their salaries of about $2,000. Today that lawyer makes $145,000 (including bonus), whereas the teacher earns roughly $40,000. Sandra Feldman, the president of the American Federation of Teachers, is quite open about the problem. "You have in the schools right now, among the teachers who are going to be retiring, *very* smart people," she told me. "We're not getting in the same kinds of people. In some places it's disastrous."

How should we address this crisis? Most discussion so far has revolved around improving the skills of the teachers we already have. But upgrading the skills of current teachers can get us only so far when so many new teachers will be needed. Although changing the kind of person who goes into teaching may be hopelessly beyond the power of local school budgets and policies, we need to seize this moment of generational turnover in the teaching ranks to lure top college graduates to our toughest classrooms.

How to do this? Let's stipulate first that pay isn't everything.   6
Teachers are the only category of people I've ever met who routinely say, without irony, that their jobs are so fulfilling they hardly care how little they make. For many of them, too, job security, good health benefits and pensions, and free summers offset the low income. But fulfillment and fringe benefits will never suffice to attract and retain hundreds of thousands of talented new teachers for poor districts.

There's no way to get large numbers of top people without pay-   7
ing up. Conservatives rightly worry that pouring more money into the system will subsidize mediocrity rather than lure new talent—especially when union rules make it next to impossible to fire bad teachers. "Dismissing a tenured teacher is not a process," one California official has said. "It's a career." The effort can take years and involve hundreds of thousands of dollars. Rather than being fired, bad teachers are shuffled from school to school. In a recent five-year period only sixty-two of the 220,000 tenured teachers in California were dismissed.

A grand bargain could be struck between unions and conserva-   8
tives: make more money available for teachers' salaries in exchange for flexibility in how it is spent. For instance, the standard "lockstep" union pay scale, whereby a teacher with a degree in biochemistry has to be paid the same as one with a degree in physical education if both have the same number of years in the classroom (even though the biochemist has lucrative options outside teaching), should be scrapped. Better-performing teachers should make more than worse ones. And dismissing poor performers—who, even union leaders agree, make up perhaps 10 percent of urban teachers—should be made much easier.

If the quality of urban schools is to be improved, teaching poor   9
children must become the career of choice for talented young Americans who want to make a difference with their lives and earn a good living too. To achieve that the federal government should raise the salary of every teacher in a poor school by at least *50 percent*. But this increase would be contingent on two fundamental reforms: teachers' unions would have to abandon the lockstep pay schedules, so that the top-performing half of the teacher corps could be paid significantly more; and the dismissal process for poor-performing teachers would have to be condensed to four to six months.

In Los Angeles teachers currently earn about $40,000 to start   10
and top out, after thirty years and a Ph.D., at about $70,000. Under
this new deal those teachers would start at $60,000, and the top-
performing half of teachers would make $85,000 to $90,000 a year,
on average. A number of the best teachers could earn close to
$150,000 a year. The plan is designed to pay America's best teach-
ers of poor students salaries high enough to allow them to put
aside a million dollars in savings by the end of their careers.

How much would this plan cost? Roughly $30 billion a year,   11
which would lift the federal share of K–12 spending from seven
percent to 14 percent of the total nationwide—only right, given
that on their own poor districts can't afford the skilled teachers
they need. This federal investment looks modest beside the
$80 billion a year that some representatives of corporate America
say they spend training ill-prepared high school graduates to work
in modern industry. The plan could be administered through a
program similar to Title I, which provides supplementary federal
funds to poor schools. We might call it Title I for Teachers.

To find out whether this basic plan is politically feasible, I pre-   12
sented it to big-city superintendents, high-ranking union leaders,
and assorted education experts and teachers.

"I'd endorse something like that in a hot minute," said Day   13
Higuchi, the president of the Los Angeles teachers' union from
1996 to 2002. "Right now L.A. Unified is the employer of last resort.
People who can't get jobs elsewhere come here. If we did this, we'd
become the employer of first resort. High-powered college students
will be taking the job." Arne Duncan, the CEO of the Chicago Public Schools, told me that now there's "very little incentive outside of
pure altruism" to get someone into teaching. This proposal "would
dramatically change the face of the teacher profession," he said.

To gauge the conservative reaction, I spoke with Chester E. Finn   14
Jr., a longtime school reformer on the right. Finn is the president
of the Thomas B. Fordham Foundation, and served as an assistant
secretary of education in the Reagan Administration. He expressed
several concerns. "The troubling part of this proposal," he said, "is
a 50 percent boost for just showing up for work, without any reference to whether anybody you teach learns a damned thing."

I replied that the offer was designed to make it worthwhile for   15
the unions to accept real reform in pay and dismissal practices.
And the pay increase would subsidize mediocrity only briefly,
because under the new dismissal rules bad teachers could much
more easily be fired.

Finn had his own variation to offer. "If you wanted to make this   16
plan really interesting," he told me, "job security and tenure would

be traded for this raise. The swap here ought to be that you take a risk with your employment and you don't have to be retained if you're not good at what you do. If you are good and you get retained, you get paid a whole lot more money. If current teachers can't swallow that tradeoff, make this a parallel personnel system for new ones coming in and for the existing ones who want to do it."

How might that work? I asked.

"Any current teacher is free to join this new system on its terms," Finn said, "or to stick with the old arrangement, in which they have high security and low pay. That's just a political accommodation to an existing work force for whom this might be too abrupt a shift. Over time you'll get a very different kind of person into teaching."

"It sounds tempting from a union point of view," Sandra Feldman told me of Finn's parallel approach. "The more voluntary you can make a system like this, the easier it is to sell. But I worry that something like that could create resentment between the people in the different tracks." Other union and district leaders, however, told me they thought that virtually every new hire would opt for the new system, as would perhaps a quarter of the senior teachers—meaning that most of the urban teacher corps would be on the plan within five years.

That union leaders think it makes sense to move toward serious pay differentials for teachers is important. But educators are concerned about two related questions. In determining pay rates, who will decide which teachers are better performers? And what standards will be used to assess teachers?

I asked Sandra Feldman if there was a consensus in the faculty lounges at most schools about who the best teachers were. "Absolutely," she said. The question is how to evaluate performance in a way that is objective and untainted by cronyism.

The superintendents and conservative reformers I spoke to agreed that serious weight should be given to students' test scores. In theory, so-called "value-added analysis"—the effort to track the impact of teachers on student achievement each year—is the holy grail of accountability, and thus the ideal basis for performance pay. But in reality, many people think it has serious limits. "There's just no reliable way of doing that right now," Feldman told me. This isn't only a union view. Joseph Olchefske, the superintendent of schools in Seattle, has studied the issue; he believes it would be hard to measure the value added by individual teachers. Others, however, think individual value-added analysis may soon be practical. Day Higuchi, the former L.A. union leader, argues that in elementary school, where each child has essentially one teacher, the right testing could constructively measure that teacher's impact.

23   Finn and others suggested a blended approach to teacher assessment. "You could have value-added analysis at the school level, which is clearly going to be done," Finn said, "combined with some other kind of performance reviews." Adam Urbanski, the president of the Rochester Teachers Association, who has spearheaded union-reform efforts for two decades, said, "It would be a fatal mistake not to include student learning outcomes as the ultimate test of this. It would be equally fatal to use only test scores, because you would have a huge invitation to cheating and manipulation." He and others proposed that various indicators regarded as germane to teacher assessment by educators and the public—such as dropout rates, graduation rates, peer review, specialized training, teaching technique, and student work—be considered along with test scores.

24   The superintendents all told me that principals should be the final arbiters of teacher performance. This is a sticking point with the unions. The problem with giving principals control is that many teachers think principals don't know the first thing about good teaching. Jene Galvin, a teacher who has worked in the Cincinnati school system for twenty-seven years, told me, "We don't really believe that the principals are the experts on pedagogy or classroom teaching or classroom management. The reason is they just didn't do it very long." The solution might be to have peer evaluators—mentor and master teachers—do the evaluations along with principals.

25   Experts I spoke with, including Finn, thought that all these challenges ultimately seemed surmountable. Finn said that a key to his supporting such a plan would be "that it included the ability for managers of schools to have a whole lot of control over who is working in their school."

26   If this agenda were presented as a federal challenge, in which the President or congressional leaders said, "We're putting this pot of money on the table for those communities that can come together around a plan that meets its conditions and make it work," school districts would almost surely step forward. If unions declined to come to the table, local media and business leaders could ask why they were balking at billions of dollars. Rank-and-file teachers, who might earn an extra $20,000 to $50,000 a year, would obviously have a huge stake in the plan's adoption. They might tell union leaders they supported finding ways of speedily dismissing poor performers.

27   Some Republicans may resist. After all, teachers' unions are big Democratic donors and the chief foes of Republican efforts to

introduce school vouchers. The last thing we need, these Republicans might say, is a bunch of teachers with more money to spend on making sure that Republicans never get elected.

But some savvy Republicans think the time for a plan like this is ripe. Rick Davis, a political adviser to Senator John McCain, believes that such a plan may be inevitable. "Anybody who has looked at teacher pay as an element of the overall problem in education realizes that money matters," Davis told me. "Other than the voucher debate, we've exhausted the Republican position on education. So sooner or later we're going to get to teacher pay, because we can't be against teachers making money. The American public is going to figure out that their teachers make less than their garbage collectors, and they're not going to be for that."

28

READERS' RESPONSE LETTERS

Miller discusses the use of "emergency credentials" and implies a connection between teacher quality and teacher credentialing. The most prestigious independent schools, where the rich send their sons and daughters, have very few credentialed teachers, and those teachers are paid less than their public school peers. Having worked in such schools, I know that many of these "unqualified" teachers are highly talented and highly qualified. In fact, not having to waste a year of their lives in a terrible teacher-credentialing program may explain why they are teaching in a private school in the first place. One might wonder why our urban poor are not allowed to benefit from those who are teaching the nation's wealthiest students.

1

Paying urban teachers a higher salary would unquestionably bring more talented people into urban school systems. However, there is a larger issue, unaddressed by Miller. As he notes, half of new teachers in urban schools quit within the first three years. And by and large they are the stronger half. But why are these teachers leaving? Surely they knew what the salary schedule was when they signed on for the job. In my view, the top college graduates who enter urban schools leave because of the appalling work conditions in these schools, where teachers are not given the freedom to teach what they believe is right (unlike their counterparts in independent schools) but, rather, are forced to march through a standardized, "teacher-proof" curriculum to prepare students for multiple-choice tests. Professionals, be they lawyers, doctors, or consultants, are given autonomy and are expected to achieve results. Until we treat teachers like intelligent, thoughtful professionals, we will be unable to recruit enough people deserving of such expectations. Even if we do recruit some by paying them

2

drastically higher salaries, they will surely quit in disgust when they experience the mind-numbing bureaucracy as it exists today.

I remember well my frustration (as one of the "top college graduates" that Miller refers to) with the public school hiring process, and despite having obtained a teaching credential (in physics and math, no less), I eschewed the higher salaries in the public schools for the autonomy that independent schools allowed. Some teachers may work in private schools because of the perception of "easier" students—but I believe that the professionalization of the teaching position in these schools is a greater draw.

Ben Daley

Associate Principal, High Tech High, San Diego

While proposing higher pay and noting that women and members of minorities no longer form a ready pool of talented teachers-to-be, Matthew Miller misses the point as to why teachers leave the profession. For the past thirty years teachers have consistently been portrayed as lazy, unprofessional, stupid, and incapable of performing their duties. People enter the profession believing in the cliché that they can make a difference. But making a difference is not that easy. Here is where Miller errs when he talks about "poor" schools. No amount of training or salary can compensate for the array of problems that students in such schools present. Typically, these students come from chaotic backgrounds. They may attend two or three or more schools in one year. Even if a school system has an absolutely rigid curriculum, with every teacher in every grade teaching the same lesson on the same day, children who move from school to school cannot keep up. Similarly, these students often have terrible attendance, making it virtually impossible for them to achieve even basic skills. Coupled with these problems is another issue that Miller completely ignores—the real lack of respect that teachers in "poor" schools get from students and the adults in their lives.

The violence rampant in some areas of our country spills over into every institution in those communities. Teachers are ill prepared to deal with gang-related problems, students with guns, students who act out by cursing and swearing and throwing things. No amount of motivation on the part of the teacher can bring the "teachable moment" to students whose lives are consumed by anger fomented by a society that pays them and their needs no attention.

Chester E. Finn, of the Thomas B. Fordham Foundation, can say all he wants that teachers should "take a risk with [their] employment," trading job security and benefits for a salary based on what Adam Urbanski, of the Rochester Teachers Association, calls "student learning outcomes." As a teacher for more than thirty years, I would challenge Finn to be held accountable for students whose lives away from school make it impossible for them to learn in school. Students who do well in school are those whose families support the entire education process. This is not to say that students in underperforming schools learn nothing. Many of them actually perform quite well, considering the distress of their environment (even if their performance will never match that of children whose fortune it has been to be born into the middle or upper class). Teaching is a wonderful career, one that I have thoroughly enjoyed. In my most recent permutation as a teacher, I have moved from a working-class high school to a university. The difference between teaching when classroom management is a part of the job and teaching when communication of information is the primary function is astonishing. Does that mean I wish I had taught college for my whole career? In no way. I consistently run into students I taught, and I see each as a success in his or her own way. That's what teaching really is, actually—meeting children at their level of development and helping them. Teachers in "poor" and underperforming schools try their hardest, against great odds, to do that. When they are held to impossible standards, they quit. How many doctors or lawyers or CEOs would like to be held accountable for their performance based on only the sickliest patients, the most criminal clients, or the worst-performing organizations?

Barbara M. Simon
Teacher, Baltimore

"A New Deal for Teachers" highlighted some creative approaches to improving our education system. Why not provide parents with the opportunity to grade teachers? Those teachers who get high marks from parents should receive bonuses on top of their pay. This approach will motivate teachers to work hard to communicate with parents, and will also promote more parental involvement in education.

Paul Feiner
Parent, Greenburgh, New York

READING FOR MEANING

This section presents three activities that will help you reread Miller's proposal with a critical eye. Done in sequence, these activities lead you from a basic understanding of the selection to a more personal response to it and finally to an analysis that deepens your understanding and critical thinking about what you are reading.

Read to Comprehend

Reread the selection, and write a few sentences briefly explaining the problem, its causes, and the proposed solution. What bargain would teachers have to make for Miller's proposal to work? Also make a list of any words you do not understand—for example, *systemic* (paragraph 2), *"lockstep"* (8), *contingent* (9), *altruism* (13), *cronyism* (21), *arbiters* (24), *surmountable* (25). Look up their meanings in a dictionary to see which definition best fits the context.

To expand your understanding of this reading, you might use one or more of the following critical reading strategies that are explained and illustrated in Appendix 1: *previewing, outlining,* and *questioning to understand and remember.*

Read to Respond

Write several paragraphs exploring your initial thoughts and feelings about "A New Deal for Teachers." Focus on anything that stands out for you, perhaps because it resonates with your own experience or because you find a statement puzzling.

You might consider writing about

- Miller's assertion that "recruiting better teachers for poor schools is not only the biggest issue in education but the next great frontier for social justice" (paragraph 2).

- the fact that the gap between starting salaries for lawyers and for public school teachers in New York City has widened from $2,000 in 1970 to more than $100,000 today (4).

- the effect of Miller's use of questions at the beginnings of paragraphs 5 and 6.

- the teaching practices or personal qualities that made your favorite or best (or least favorite or worst) teacher in high school stand out in your mind.

- what you think of one of the alternative solutions proposed in the letters.

To develop your response to Miller's proposal, you might use the following critical reading strategy that is explained and illustrated in Appendix 1: *looking for patterns of opposition.*

Read to Analyze Underlying Assumptions

Write several paragraphs exploring one or more of the assumptions, values, and beliefs underlying Miller's proposal. As you write, explain how the assumptions are reflected in the text, as well as what you now think of them (and perhaps of your own assumptions) after rereading the selection with a critical eye.

You might consider writing about

- the values and the assumptions about his audience that Miller reveals in this assertion: "recruiting better teachers for poor schools is . . . the next great frontier for social justice" (paragraph 2).

- the assumptions that teachers' unions and conservatives could agree on the "grand bargain" Miller presents in paragraph 8 and that a president and congressional leaders would set aside a "pot of money" (26) to finance the proposal.

- the assumptions and beliefs—about Republicans, teachers, Americans, or garbage collectors—that lie behind the statements by Rick Davis that Republicans "can't be against teachers making money" and that Americans are "not going to be for" having "their teachers make less than their garbage collectors" (28).

- Miller's assumptions about what motivates people to become teachers and how his proposed changes might draw more teachers into the field.

- the assumption that standardized tests, either of students or of teachers themselves, are an effective method of evaluating teachers' performance.

To probe assumptions more deeply, you might use one or both of the following critical reading strategies that are explained and illustrated in Appendix 1: *evaluating the logic of an argument* and *judging the writer's credibility*.

READING LIKE A WRITER
COUNTERARGUING READERS' OBJECTIONS, QUESTIONS, AND ALTERNATIVE SOLUTIONS

Because proposal writers want their readers to accept their proposed solution and sometimes even take action to help implement it, they must make an extraordinary effort to anticipate their readers' objections and questions. This task is a major part of what is known as *counterargument*. Miller knows he faces tough opposition because change in something as entrenched and widely accepted as our public education system calls for a significant change in thinking. His proposal also involves money, and people don't usually like to spend money on something they can't see, something that isn't directly theirs. Miller therefore devotes a large part of his proposal to counterargument: Throughout his essay, he raises the questions, objections, and preferred solutions of authorities in the field, addressing each of them one by one. The following activity will guide you in analyzing his approach. It will also prepare you for counterarguing convincingly in your own proposal.

Analyze

1. *Reread* paragraphs 14–18, and *summarize* the conservative reaction to Miller's basic proposal and suggested variation of it. Then *reread* paragraphs 19–21, and *summarize* the union's view of the conservative suggestion. Finally, *synthesize* the approaches presented for teacher assessment. *Notice* that Miller takes the advice of his "readers" and incorporates their suggestions into his own proposal.

2. *Evaluate* how successfully Miller addresses both conservative and union points of view about raising teacher pay. Does his argument present enough evidence to convince you that his proposal might be workable? Do you have questions that Miller overlooked?

Write

Write several sentences explaining how Miller counterargues. *Cite examples* from the reading. Then *add a few sentences* describing how successful you find his counterarguments.

A SPECIAL READING STRATEGY

Comparing and Contrasting Related Readings: Miller's "A New Deal for Teachers" and Readers' Responses

Comparing and contrasting related readings is a special critical reading strategy useful both in reading for meaning and in reading like a writer. This strategy is particularly applicable when writers deal with precisely the same subject, as is the case in the proposal by Matthew Miller and the letters from readers responding to his proposal. To strengthen his counterargument, Miller consulted with experts in education and politics to understand different points of view about attracting and keeping good teachers in inner-city (and other) public schools, and he discusses some of these other perspectives in his essay. In the letters are represented still other points of view. To compare and contrast Miller's proposal with the objections or alternative proposals of the letter writers, think about issues such as these:

- Compare Miller's essay and the letters in terms of their understanding of the issues faced by teachers. How do the letters—written by a teacher and others who have actually experienced and had to try to solve the problem Miller is writing about—contribute to your knowledge of the problems teachers must address? What do these perspectives add to Miller's more distanced point of view as an outside observer?

- Compare the assumptions, values, and beliefs of one or more of the letter writers with those of Miller. What similarities or differences exist that made the letter writer(s) agree or disagree with Miller?

- Compare and contrast the treatment of one of the issues in Miller's "new deal" and the treatment of the same issue by one or more of the letter writers, noting similarities and differences in approaches to the material. Consider, for example, organization, point of view, and kinds of support.

See Appendix 1 for detailed guidelines on using the comparing and contrasting related readings strategy.

CONSIDERING IDEAS FOR YOUR OWN WRITING

Miller takes on a national problem when he proposes changing the pay structure for teachers. The problem of poor schools, though, has local implications. Consider writing about the local implications of a large social problem, either a school-related one like school violence or overcrowding or a more general problem such as juvenile crime, homelessness, or the lack of affordable child care for children of college students or working parents. Although problems like these often are national in scope, you may be able to propose a practical solution for your campus community or neighborhood. You would want to start by talking with people who experience the problem in order to enlarge your understanding of it. For example, you might interview some homeless people as well as someone who works for an agency or shelter for the homeless. Through interviews and observations, you can learn about the practical difficulties that homeless people encounter, discover alternative solutions and assess their strengths and weaknesses, and identify the individuals or groups to whom you might address your proposal.

MARK HERTSGAARD

A Global Green Deal

A freelance journalist and political commentator for National Public Radio, Mark Hertsgaard (b. 1956) contributes articles to numerous newspapers and magazines such as the New York Times, New Yorker, Atlantic Monthly, Outside, Rolling Stone, *and* Nation. *He also teaches nonfiction writing at Johns Hopkins University and has written five books, including* Nuclear, Inc.: The Men and Money behind Nuclear Energy *(1983),* On Bended Knee: The Press and the Reagan Presidency *(1988), and* A Day in the Life: The Music and Artistry of the Beatles *(1995). For* Earth Odyssey: Around the World in Search of Our Environmental Future *(1999), Hertsgaard traveled to nineteen countries around the world to conduct extensive research on their environmental problems and how these are being solved or addressed by local communities and businesses. The terrorist attacks of September 11, 2001, prompted him to use the impressions formed during those travels to write his most recent book,* The Eagle's Shadow: Why America Fascinates and Infuriates the World *(2002).*

"A Global Green Deal," which was published in Time *magazine's Special Earth Day edition in April–May 2000, also reflects extensive research. Hertsgaard's title indicates that he wants readers to see his proposal as similar to President Franklin Roosevelt's "New Deal," which aimed to help the United States recover from the depression of the 1930s. Hertsgaard proposes that governments of wealthy countries like the United States should encourage businesses to develop and use new technologies that are both economically profitable and environmentally safe.*

As you read the essay, notice that Hertsgaard addresses his argument to the business community as well as to voters generally. He tries to convince businesspeople that solving environmental problems is in their best interests and can be done with existing technologies. At the same time, he tries to convince the voting public that government can and should play a role.

The bad news is that we have to change our ways—and fast. 1
Here's the good news: it could be a hugely profitable enterprise.

So what do we do? Everyone knows the planet is in bad shape, 2
but most people are resigned to passivity. Changing course, they reason, would require economic sacrifice and provoke stiff resistance from corporations and consumers alike, so why bother? It's easier to ignore the gathering storm clouds and hope the problem magically takes care of itself.

Such fatalism is not only dangerous but mistaken. For much 3
of the 1990s I traveled the world to write a book about our

environmental predicament. I returned home sobered by the extent of the damage we are causing and by the speed at which it is occurring. But there is nothing inevitable about our self-destructive behavior. Not only could we dramatically reduce our burden on the air, water and other natural systems, we could make money doing so. If we're smart, we could make restoring the environment the biggest economic enterprise of our time, a huge source of jobs, profits and poverty alleviation.

What we need is a Global Green Deal: a program to renovate our civilization environmentally from top to bottom in rich and poor countries alike. Making use of both market incentives and government leadership, a 21st century Global Green Deal would do for environmental technologies what government and industry have recently done so well for computer and Internet technologies: launch their commercial takeoff.

Getting it done will take work, and before we begin we need to understand three facts about the reality facing us. First, we have no time to lose. While we've made progress in certain areas—air pollution is down in the U.S.—big environmental problems like climate change, water scarcity and species extinction are getting worse, and faster than ever. Thus we have to change our ways profoundly—and very soon.

Second, poverty is central to the problem. Four billion of the planet's 6 billion people face deprivation inconceivable to the wealthiest 1 billion. To paraphrase Thomas Jefferson, nothing is more certainly written in the book of fate than that the bottom two-thirds of humanity will strive to improve their lot. As they demand adequate heat and food, not to mention cars and CD players, humanity's environmental footprint will grow. Our challenge is to accommodate this mass ascent from poverty without wrecking the natural systems that make life possible.

Third, some good news: we have in hand most of the technologies needed to chart a new course. We know how to use oil, wood, water and other resources much more efficiently than we do now. Increased efficiency—doing more with less—will enable us to use fewer resources and produce less pollution per capita, buying us the time to bring solar power, hydrogen fuel cells and other futuristic technologies on line.

Efficiency may not sound like a rallying cry for environmental revolution, but it packs a financial punch. As Joseph J. Romm reports in his book *Cool Companies*, Xerox, Compaq and 3M are among many firms that have recognized they can cut their greenhouse-gas emissions in half—and enjoy 50% and higher returns on investment through improved efficiency, better lighting and insulation and smarter motors and building design. The rest of us (small businesses, homeowners, city governments, schools) can reap the same benefits.

Super-refrigerators use 87% less electricity than older, standard   9
models while costing the same (assuming mass production) and performing better, as Paul Hawken, L. Hunter Lovins, and Amory Lovins explain in their book *Natural Capitalism*. In Amsterdam the headquarters of ING Bank, one of Holland's largest banks, uses one-fifth as much energy per square meter as a nearby bank, even though the buildings cost the same to construct. The ING center boasts efficient windows and insulation and a design that enables solar energy to provide much of the building's needs, even in cloudy Northern Europe.

Examples like these lead even such mainstream voices as AT&T   10
and Japan's energy planning agency, NEDO, to predict that environmental restoration could be a source of virtually limitless profit. The idea is to retrofit our farms, factories, shops, houses, offices and everything inside them. The economic activity generated would be enormous. Better yet, it would be labor intensive; investments in energy efficiency yield two to ten times more jobs than investments in fossil fuel and nuclear power. In a world where 1 billion people lack gainful employment, creating jobs is essential to fighting the poverty that retards environmental progress.

But this transition will not happen by itself—too many   11
entrenched interests stand in the way. Automakers often talk green but make only token efforts to develop green cars because gas-guzzling sport-utility vehicles are hugely profitable. But every year the U.S. government buys 56,000 new vehicles for official use from Detroit. Under the Global Green Deal, Washington would tell Detroit that from now on the cars have to be hybrid-electric or hydrogen-fuel-cell cars. Detroit might scream and holler, but if Washington stood firm, carmakers soon would be climbing the learning curve and offering the competitively priced green cars that consumers say they want.

We know such government pump-priming works; it's why so   12
many of us have computers today. America's computer companies began learning to produce today's affordable systems during the 1960s while benefiting from subsidies and guaranteed markets under contracts with the Pentagon and the space program. And the cyberboom has fueled the biggest economic expansion in history.

The Global Green Deal must not be solely an American project,   13
however. China and India, with their gigantic populations and ambitious development plans, could by themselves doom everyone else to severe global warming. Already, China is the world's second

largest producer of greenhouse gases (after the U.S.). But China would use 50% less coal if it simply installed today's energy-efficient technologies. Under the Global Green Deal, Europe, America and Japan would help China buy these technologies, not only because that would reduce global warming but also because it would create jobs and profits for workers and companies back home.

Governments would not have to spend more money, only shift existing subsidies away from environmentally dead-end technologies like coal and nuclear power. If even half the $500 billion to $900 billion in environmentally destructive subsidies now offered by the world's governments were redirected, the Global Green Deal would be off to a roaring start. Governments need to establish "rules of the road" so that market prices reflect the real social costs of clear-cut forests and other environmental abominations. Again, such a shift could be revenue neutral. Higher taxes on, say, coal burning would be offset by cuts in payroll and profits taxes, thus encouraging jobs and investment while discouraging pollution. A portion of the revenues should be set aside to assure a just transition for workers and companies now engaged in inherently anti-environmental activities like coal mining.

All this sounds easy enough on paper, but in the real world it is not so simple. Beneficiaries of the current system—be they U.S. corporate-welfare recipients, redundant German coal miners, or cut-throat Asian logging interests—will resist. Which is why progress is unlikely absent a broader agenda of change, including real democracy: assuring the human rights of environmental activists and neutralizing the power of Big Money through campaign-finance reform.

The Global Green Deal is no silver bullet. It can, however, buy us time to make the more deep-seated changes—in our often excessive appetites, in our curious belief that humans are the center of the universe, in our sheer numbers—that will be necessary to repair our relationship with our environment.

None of this will happen without an aroused citizenry. But a Global Green Deal is in the common interest, and it is a slogan easily grasped by the media and the public. Moreover, it should appeal across political, class and national boundaries, for it would stimulate both jobs and business throughout the world in the name of a universal value: leaving our children a livable planet. The history of environmentalism is largely the story of ordinary people pushing for change while governments, corporations and other established interests reluctantly follow behind. It's time to repeat that history on behalf of a Global Green Deal.

READING FOR MEANING

This section presents three activities that will help you reread Hertsgaard's proposal with a critical eye. Done in sequence, these activities lead you from a basic understanding of the selection to a more personal response to it and finally to an analysis that deepens your understanding and critical thinking about what you are reading.

Read to Comprehend

Reread the selection, and list the three key elements of Hertsgaard's Global Green Deal. Then explain briefly how he would implement them. Also make a list of any words you do not understand—for example, *renovate* (paragraph 4), *incentives* (4), *ascent* (6), *subsidies* (12), *abominations* (14). Look up their meanings in a dictionary to see which definition best fits the context.

To expand your understanding of this reading, you might use one or more of the following critical reading strategies that are explained and illustrated in Appendix 1: *previewing, outlining,* and *questioning to understand and remember.*

Read to Respond

Write several paragraphs exploring your initial thoughts and feelings about "A Global Green Deal." Focus on anything that stands out for you, perhaps because it resonates with your own experience or because you find a statement puzzling.

You might consider writing about

- what you know of environmental problems in this country and around the world, and how your knowledge influences your response to Hertsgaard's proposal.

- how willing you are as a consumer to make "buying green" a priority.

- Hertsgaard's assertion that we need to make "deep-seated changes . . . in our curious belief that [we] are the center of the universe" and "in our sheer numbers" (paragraph 16).

- some specific ways that Hertsgaard's proposal could be implemented in your community.

To develop your response to Hertsgaard's essay, you might use one or more of the following critical reading strategies that are explained and illustrated in Appendix 1: *paraphrasing, contextualizing,* and *evaluating the logic of an argument.*

Read to Analyze Underlying Assumptions

Write several paragraphs exploring one or more of the assumptions, values, and beliefs underlying Hertsgaard's proposal. As you write, explain how the assumptions are reflected in the text, as well as what you now think of them (and perhaps of your own assumptions) after rereading the essay with a critical eye.

You might consider writing about

- the assumptions Hertsgaard makes about his readers in starting his proposal by saying that "it could be a hugely profitable enterprise" (paragraph 1) and citing examples from businesses and "mainstream voices" (8–10).

- the "curious belief that humans are the center of the universe," which Hertsgaard claims is in need of "deep-seated change" (16).

- Hertsgaard's assumption in the conclusion that "leaving our children a livable planet" is a "universal value" (17), perhaps in relation to his statement in the introduction that "[e]veryone knows the planet is in bad shape, but most people are resigned to passivity" (2).

To probe assumptions more deeply, you might use one or both of the following critical reading strategies that are explained and illustrated in Appendix 1: *reflecting on challenges to your beliefs and values* and *looking for patterns of opposition.*

READING LIKE A WRITER
ESTABLISHING CREDIBILITY

To be taken seriously, a proposal must demonstrate to readers that the writer fully understands the problem and has seriously considered possible objections and alternative solutions. One way Hertsgaard tries to establish credibility is by telling readers that his proposal is based on his extensive research. He announces in paragraph 3 that he has spent "much of the 1990s" studying environmental problems throughout the world. In addition to this firsthand observation, Hertsgaard shows that he is well read on the subject; for example, in paragraphs 8 and 9, he refers to two related books by other authors. Readers' trust is likely to be enhanced by the fact that Hertsgaard's research has been published in a book as well as in this article in *Time,* a respected newsmagazine. Finally, knowing that Hertsgaard has written other books and other articles for prestigious journals further bolsters his credibility. The following activity invites you to analyze still other ways that Hertsgaard tries to establish credibility: by challenging readers to see the seriousness of the problem and by attempting to convince them that something can be done about the problem.

Analyze

1. *Reread* paragraphs 1–3, and *underline* words like *passivity* (paragraph 2) and *fatalism* (3) that Hertsgaard uses to characterize the attitude he assumes his readers have about "our environmental predicament" (3).

2. *Look for* and *mark* places elsewhere in the essay where Hertsgaard shifts into more positive language (for example, in paragraphs 5 and 6, he describes the problem as a "challenge" requiring effort and hard work).

3. *Examine* the concluding paragraphs (16 and 17) to see how Hertsgaard represents his own proposal as "no silver bullet."

Write

Write several sentences describing what you have learned about Hertsgaard's representation of readers' negative attitude as well as his own more positive attitude. *Explain* the effect you think this shift in tone might have on his credibility with readers. *Conclude with a few sentences* describing the writer's tone at the end of the essay and speculating about its possible effects on readers.

CONSIDERING IDEAS FOR YOUR OWN WRITING

Hertsgaard's admittedly limited proposal might suggest to you other ideas that might help in even a small way to solve environmental problems. For example, you might consider writing a proposal for increasing the use of carpools on campus, reducing energy consumption in dormitories, or instituting a campus recycling program. You might interview people in your community about the feasibility of subsidizing alternative energy sources, such as solar-heating panels that could be installed in public buildings and parks. You might also research new technologies for a proposal addressed to your college administration encouraging use of promising technologies.

KATHERINE S. NEWMAN

Dead-End Jobs: A Way Out

> *Katherine S. Newman (b. 1953) is the dean of social science at Harvard University's Radcliffe Institute and Malcolm Wiener Professor of Urban Studies in Harvard's John F. Kennedy School of Government. She has written several books on middle-class economic insecurity, including* Falling from Grace: Downward Mobility in the Age of Affluence *(1988) and* Declining Fortunes: The Withering of the American Dream *(1993). Her 1999 book,* No Shame in My Game: The Working Poor in the Inner City, *which focuses on the job-search strategies, work experiences, and family lives of African American and Latino youths and adults in the Harlem neighborhood of New York City, won several awards. Her most recent book,* A Different Shade of Gray: Mid-Life and beyond in the Inner City *(2003), examines the experience of aging among inner-city residents.*
>
> *The following proposal comes out of Newman's study of inner-city fast-food workers, in which she learned that many such workers experience great difficulty finding better, higher-paying jobs because the "social networks"—the connections they depend on for job information and referrals—help them make only lateral moves or lead them into industries that were economically vital a generation ago but are now shrinking. In this proposal, originally published in 1995 in the* Brookings Review, *a journal concerned with public policy, Newman proposes that managers of inner-city fast-food businesses form an "employer consortium" to give their most successful employees "upward mobility."*
>
> *As you read the proposal, think about your own experience job hunting and whether you have been helped by knowing someone who could serve as a reference or give you useful inside information about a job. Do you think a system that depends so much on who you know is beneficial and fair? What would you suggest to replace it?*

Millions of Americans work full-time, year-round in jobs that 1
still leave them stranded in poverty. Though they pound the pavement looking for better jobs, they consistently come up empty-handed. Many of these workers are in our nation's inner cities.

I know, because I have spent two years finding out what working 2
life is like for 200 employees—about half African-American, half Latino—at fast food restaurants in Harlem. Many work only part-time, though they would happily take longer hours if they could get them. Those who do work full-time earn about $8,840 (before taxes)—well below the poverty threshold for a family of four.

These fast food workers make persistent efforts to get better jobs, 3
particularly in retail and higher-paid service-sector occupations.

They take civil service examinations and apply for jobs with the electric company or the phone company. Sometimes their efforts bear fruit. More often they don't.

A few workers make their way into the lower managerial ranks of the fast food industry, where wages are marginally better. An even smaller number graduate into higher management, a path made possible by the internal promotion patterns long practiced by these firms. As in any industry, however, senior management opportunities are limited. Hence most workers, even those with track records as reliable employees, are locked inside a low-wage environment. Contrary to those who preach the benefits of work and persistence, the human capital these workers build up—experience in food production, inventory management, cash register operation, customer relations, minor machinery repair, and cleaning—does not pay off. These workers are often unable to move upward out of poverty. And their experience is not unusual. Hundreds of thousands of low-wage workers in American cities run into the same brick wall. Why? And what can we do about it?   4

STAGNATION IN THE INNER CITY

Harlem, like many inner-city communities, has lost the manufacturing job base that once sustained its neighborhoods. Service industries that cater to neighborhood consumers, coupled with now dwindling government jobs, largely make up the local economy. With official jobless rates hovering around 18 percent (114 people apply for every minimum wage fast food job in Harlem), employers can select from the very top of the preference "queue." Once hired, even experienced workers have virtually nowhere to go.   5

One reason for their lack of mobility is that many employers in the primary labor market outside Harlem consider "hamburger flipper" jobs worthless. At most, employers credit the fast food industry with training people to turn up for work on time and to fill out job applications. The real skills these workers have developed go unrecognized. However inaccurate the unflattering stereotypes, they help keep experienced workers from "graduating" out of low-wage work to more remunerative employment. . . .   6

As Harry Holzer, an economist at Michigan State University, has shown, "central city" employers insist on specific work experience, references, and particular kinds of formal training in addition to literacy and numeracy skills, even for jobs that do not require a college degree. Demands of this kind, more stringent in the big-city labor markets than in the surrounding suburbs, clearly limit the upward mobility of the working poor in urban areas. If   7 the only kind of job available does not provide the "right" work experience or formal training, many better jobs will be foreclosed.

Racial stereotypes also weaken mobility prospects. Employers view ghetto blacks, especially men, as a bad risk or a troublesome element in the workplace. They prefer immigrants or nonblack minorities, of which there are many in the Harlem labor force, who appear to them more deferential and willing to work harder for low wages. As Joleen Kirshenman and Kathryn Neckerman found in their study of Chicago workplaces, stereotypes abound among employers who have become wary of the "underclass." Primary employers exercise these preferences by discriminating against black applicants, particularly those who live in housing projects, on the grounds of perceived group characteristics. The "losers" are not given an opportunity to prove themselves. . . . 8

SOCIAL NETWORKS

Social networks are crucial in finding work. Friends and acquaintances are far more useful sources of information than are want ads. The literature on the urban underclass suggests that inner-city neighborhoods are bereft of these critical links to the work world. My work, however, suggests a different picture: the working poor in Harlem have access to two types of occupational social networks, but neither provides upward mobility. The first is a homogeneous *lateral* network of age mates and acquaintances, employed and unemployed. It provides contacts that allow workers to move sideways in the labor market—from Kentucky Fried Chicken to Burger King or McDonald's—but not to move to jobs of higher quality. Lateral networks are useful, particularly for poor people who have to move frequently, for they help ensure a certain amount of portability in the low-wage labor market. But they do not lift workers out of poverty; they merely facilitate "churning" laterally in the low-wage world. 9

Young workers in Harlem also participate in more heterogeneous *vertical* networks with their older family members who long ago moved to suburban communities or better urban neighborhoods to become homeowners on the strength of jobs that were more widely available 20 and 30 years ago. Successful grandparents, great-aunts and uncles, and distant cousins, relatives now in their 50s and 60s, often have (or have retired from) jobs in the post office, the public sector, the transportation system, public utilities, the military, hospitals, and factories that pay union wages. But these industries are now shedding workers, not hiring them. As a result, older generations are typically unable to help job-hunting young relatives. 10

Although little is known about the social and business networks   11
of minority business owners and managers in the inner city, it seems
that Harlem's business community, particularly its small business
sector, is also walled off from the wider economy of midtown. Fast
food owners know the other people in their franchise system. They
do business with banks and security firms inside the inner city. But
they appear less likely to interact with firms outside the ghetto.

For that reason, a good recommendation from a McDonald's   12
owner may represent a calling card that extends no farther than
the general reputation of the firm and a prospective employer's
perception—poor, as I have noted—of the skills that such work
represents. It can move someone from an entry-level job in one
restaurant to the same kind of job in another, but not into a good
job elsewhere in the city.

Lacking personal or business-based ties that facilitate upward   13
mobility, workers in Harlem's fast food market find themselves on
the outside looking in when it comes to the world of "good jobs."
They search diligently for them, they complete many job applications, but it is the rare individual who finds a job that pays a family wage. Those who do are either workers who have been selected
for internal promotion or men and women who have had the luxury of devoting their earnings solely to improving their own educational or craft credentials. Since most low-wage service workers
are under pressure to support their families or contribute to the
support of their parents' households, this kind of human capital
investment is often difficult. As a result, the best most can do is to
churn from one low-wage job to another.

THE EMPLOYER CONSORTIUM

Some of the social ills that keep Harlem's fast food workers at   14
the bottom of a short job ladder—a poor urban job base, increasing downward mobility, discrimination, structural problems in
the inner-city business sector—are too complex to solve quickly
enough to help most of the workers I've followed. But the problem
of poor social networks may be amenable to solution if formal
organizations linking primary and secondary labor market
employers can be developed. An "employer consortium" could
help to move hardworking inner-city employees into richer job
markets by providing the job information and precious referrals
that "come naturally" to middle-class Americans.

How would an employer consortium function? It would   15
include both inner-city employers of the working poor and downtown businesses or nonprofit institutions with higher-paid

employees. Employers in the inner city would periodically select employees they consider reliable, punctual, hard-working, and motivated. Workers who have successfully completed at least one year of work would be placed in a pool of workers eligible for hiring by a set of linked employers who have better jobs to offer. Entry-level employers would, in essence, put their own good name behind successful workers as they pass them on to their consortium partners in the primary sector.

Primary-sector employers, for their part, would agree to hire   16
from the pool and meet periodically with their partners in the low-wage industries to review applications and follow up on the performance of those hired through the consortium. Employers "up the line" would provide training or educational opportunities to enhance the employee's skills. These training investments would make it more likely that hirees would continue to move up the new job ladders.

As they move up, the new hirees would clear the way for others   17
to follow. First, their performance would reinforce the reputation of the employers who recommended them. Second, their achievements on the job might begin to lessen the stigma or fear their new employers may feel toward the inner-city workforce. On both counts, other consortium-based workers from the inner city would be more likely to get the same opportunities, following in a form of managed chain migration out of the inner-city labor market. Meanwhile, the attractiveness of fast food jobs, now no better reputed among inner-city residents than among the rest of society, would grow as they became, at least potentially, a gateway to something better.

ADVANTAGES FOR EMPLOYERS

Fast food employers in Harlem run businesses in highly com-   18
petitive markets. Constant pressure on prices and profit discourage them from paying wages high enough to keep a steady workforce. In fact, most such employers regard the jobs they fill as temporary placements: they *expect* successful employees to leave. And despite the simple production processes used within the fast food industry to minimize the damage of turnover, sudden departures of knowledgeable workers still disrupt business and cause considerable frustration and exhaustion.

An employer consortium gives these employers—who *can't* raise   19
wages if they hope to stay in business—a way to compete for workers who will stay with them longer than usual. In lieu of higher pay, employers can offer access to the consortium hiring pool and the

prospect of a more skilled and ultimately better-paying job upon graduation from this real world "boot camp." . . .

Consortiums would also appeal to the civic spirit of minority business owners, who often choose to locate in places like Harlem rather than in less risky neighborhoods because they want to provide job opportunities for their own community. The big franchise operations mandate some attention to civic responsibility as well. Some fast food firms have licensing requirements for franchisees that require demonstrated community involvement.

20

At a time when much of the public is voicing opposition to heavy-handed government efforts to prevent employment discrimination, employer consortiums have the advantage of encouraging minority hiring based on private-sector relationships. Institutional employers in particular—for example, universities and hospitals, often among the larger employers in East Coast cities—should find the consortiums especially valuable. These employers typically retain a strong commitment to workforce diversity but are often put off by the reputation of secondary-sector workers as unskilled, unmotivated, and less worthy of consideration.

21

The practical advantages for primary-sector managers are clear. Hirees have been vetted and tested. Skills have been assessed and certified in the most real world of settings. A valuable base of experience and skills stands ready for further training and advancement. The consortium assures that the employers making and receiving recommendations would come to know one another, thus reinforcing the value of recommendations—a cost-effective strategy for primary-sector managers who must make significant training investments in their workers.

22

MINIMAL GOVERNMENT INVOLVEMENT

Despite the evident advantages for both primary and secondary labor market employers, it may be necessary for governments to provide modest incentives to encourage wide participation. Secondary-sector business owners in the inner city, for example, might be deterred from participating by the prospect of losing some of their best employees at the end of a year. Guaranteeing these employers a lump sum or a tax break for every worker they promote into management internally or successfully place with a consortium participant could help break down such reluctance.

23

Primary-sector employers, who would have to provide support for training and possibly for schooling of their consortium employees, may also require some kind of tax break to subsidize

24

their efforts at skill enhancement. Demonstration projects could experiment with various sorts of financial incentives for both sets of employers by providing grants to underwrite the costs of training new workers.

Local governments could also help publicize the efforts of par- 25 ticipating employers. Most big-city mayors, for example, would be happy to shower credit on business people looking to boost the prospects of the deserving (read working) poor.

Government involvement, however, would be minimal. Employer 26 consortiums could probably be assembled out of the existing economic development offices of U.S. cities, or with the help of the Chamber of Commerce and other local institutions that encourage private-sector activity. Industry- or sector-specific consortiums could probably be put together with the aid of local industry councils.

Moreover, some of the negative effects of prior experiments 27 with wage subsidies for the "hard to employ"—efforts that foundered on the stigma assigned to these workers and the paperwork irritants to employers—would be reversed here. Consortium employees would be singled out for doing well, for being the cream of the crop. And the private sector domination of employer consortiums would augur against extensive paperwork burdens.

BUILDING BRIDGES

The inner-city fast food workers that I have been following in 28 Harlem have proven themselves in difficult jobs. They have shown that they are reliable, they clearly relish their economic independence, and they are willing to work hard. Still, work offers them no escape from poverty. Trapped in a minimum-wage job market, they lack bridges to the kind of work that can enable them to support their families and begin to move out of poverty. For reasons I have discussed, those bridges have not evolved naturally in our inner cities. But where they are lacking, they must be created and fostered. And we can begin with employer consortiums, to the benefit of everyone, workers and employers alike.

READING FOR MEANING

This section presents three activities that will help you reread Newman's essay with a critical eye. Done in sequence, these activities lead you from a basic understanding of the selection to a more personal response to it and finally to an analysis that deepens your understanding and critical thinking about what you are reading.

Read to Comprehend

Reread the selection, and write a few sentences briefly explaining the problems that prompted Newman to write her proposal. Then write a few more sentences explaining in your own words the proposal she makes to solve the problems. Also make a list of any words you do not understand—for example, *remunerative* (paragraph 6), *deferential* (8), *homogeneous* (9), *heterogeneous* (10), *incentives* (23). Look up their meanings in a dictionary to see which definition best fits the context.

To expand your understanding of this reading, you might want to use one or more of the following critical reading strategies that are explained and illustrated in Appendix 1: *previewing, outlining,* and *questioning to understand and remember.*

Read to Respond

Write several paragraphs exploring your initial thoughts and feelings about Newman's proposal. Focus on anything that stands out for you, perhaps because it resonates with your own experience or because you find a statement puzzling. You might consider writing about

- the "unflattering stereotypes" of "'hamburger flipper' jobs" (paragraph 6) and whether you think fast-food workers learn useful and marketable skills, as Newman suggests in paragraph 4, perhaps in relation to your own experience with such jobs.

- the idea that people in "dead-end" fast-food jobs would be willing to forgo the immediate gratification of "higher pay" for the future "prospect of a more skilled and ultimately better-paying job" (19).

- Newman's assertion about the importance of "social networks" in job hunting and the distinction she makes between "lateral" and "vertical" networks (9 and 10), perhaps in relation to your own experience with such networks.

- the amount that a full-time worker at a Harlem fast-food restaurant earned in the mid-1990s (2) or the number of people who apply for every job in such a restaurant (5).

To develop your response to Newman's proposal, you might use one or both of the following critical reading strategies that are explained and illustrated in Appendix 1: *contextualizing* and *evaluating the logic of an argument.*

Read to Analyze Underlying Assumptions

Write several paragraphs exploring one or more of the assumptions, values, and beliefs underlying Newman's proposal. As you write, explain how the assumptions are reflected in the text, as well as what you now think of them (and perhaps of your own assumptions) after rereading the selection with a critical eye.

You might consider writing about

- the values and beliefs underlying Newman's statement that Harlem's fast-food workers cannot find a job that pays a "family wage" (paragraph 13).

- the cultural assumptions, values, and beliefs of "those who preach the benefits of work and persistence" (4) to inner-city job seekers, or of employers that impose higher standards for employees in the inner city than in the suburbs and discriminate against "ghetto blacks," especially men and people living in housing projects, in favor of "immigrants and nonblack minorities" (8).

- the underlying assumption Newman makes about her readers in using the heading "Minimal Government Involvement" (23).

To probe assumptions more deeply, you might use one or more of the following critical reading strategies that are explained and illustrated in Appendix 1: *recognizing emotional manipulation, judging the writer's credibility,* and *comparing and contrasting related readings.*

READING LIKE A WRITER
PRESENTING THE SOLUTION

Proposal writers often go into detail explaining how the proposed solution would work and arguing that the changes would be beneficial. Presenting the solution in an attractive way becomes especially difficult when the chief beneficiary is a third party and not the readers who are being addressed in the proposal. This is the case in Newman's proposal to form an employer consortium. She is writing to employers about her proposal to help employees move into better jobs. Convincing managers of any organization—including fast-food businesses—to make fundamental changes in their policies or practices is a daunting task for any proposal writer. It is especially challenging to convince managers that making changes designed primarily to help their employees get other jobs will benefit and not harm their businesses. The following activity will help you see how Newman tries to present her proposed solution in a way that reduces the concerns of her intended readers—inner-city employers.

Analyze

1. *Reread* paragraphs 14–22, where Newman provides many details about how an employer consortium would function. *Annotate* the information she presents on how the solution would be implemented—the different roles that would be played by "entry-level employers" who would recommend their best employees for advancement and by "primary-sector

employers" who would hire successful employees. Also *annotate* the "advantages" Newman argues her proposal would have for both sets of employers, particularly for "entry-level employers" who are being asked to give up their best workers.

2. *Evaluate* Newman's success, in paragraphs 14–22, in presenting the solution to inner-city employers at entry and advanced levels. Where does Newman's argument seem most successful? Least successful?

Write

Write several sentences explaining how Newman presents the solution in paragraphs 14–22. *Include specific examples* from these paragraphs. Also briefly *evaluate* the success of Newman's presentation.

CONSIDERING IDEAS FOR YOUR OWN WRITING

Newman's topic suggests a type of proposal you might want to consider for your essay—a proposal to improve the living or working conditions of a group of people. You could focus on a particular category of people and a problem they face. For example, you might think of ways to help elderly and infirm people in your community who need transportation, or you might want to help elementary school kids who have no after-school programs to organize their time. Newman's proposal might also suggest the possibility of other kinds of job-training and referral programs to help college students find work to support their education. You could find out what resources are available on your campus and check the Internet to discover if there are any services other campuses provide that might be useful on your campus. You might also interview students as well as employers in the community to see whether a new campus job-referral service could be developed or an existing one could be improved.

You might also consider writing a proposal to improve the functioning of a goal-directed organization such as a sports team, business, or public institution (small-claims court, traffic offenders' school, welfare office, recreation center, or school). You could propose a solution to a problem in an institution in which you participated regularly or one in which you had a single disappointing experience. Your goal is not to ridicule or complain, but to attempt to bring about change that would make the organization more humane, efficient, productive, or successful in fulfilling its goals. Do not limit yourself to your own experience. Seek out former and current members who experienced the problem; they can help you understand the problem in a deeper way, refine your presentation of a solution, and strengthen your argument for the solution.

PATRICK O'MALLEY

More Testing, More Learning

Patrick O'Malley wrote the following proposal while he was a first-year college student. He proposes that college professors give students frequent brief examinations in addition to the usual midterm and final exams. After discussing his unusual rhetorical situation—a student advising teachers on how to plan their courses—with his instructor, O'Malley decided to revise the essay into the form of an open letter to professors on his campus, a letter that might appear in the campus newspaper.

O'Malley's essay may strike you as unusually authoritative. This air of authority is due in large part to what O'Malley learned from interviewing two professors (his writing instructor and the writing program director) and several students in his classes. As you read, notice particularly how O'Malley responds to the objections to his proposal that he expects many professors to raise as well as their preferred solutions to the problem he identifies.

It's late at night. The final's tomorrow. You got a *C* on the midterm, so this one will make or break you. Will it be like the midterm? Did you study enough? Did you study the right things? It's too late to drop the course. So what happens if you fail? No time to worry about that now—you've got a ton of notes to go over.

Although this last-minute anxiety about midterm and final exams is only too familiar to most college students, many professors may not realize how such major, infrequent, high-stakes exams work against the best interests of students both psychologically and intellectually. They cause unnecessary amounts of stress, placing too much importance on one or two days in the students' entire term, judging ability on a single or dual performance. They don't encourage frequent study and they fail to inspire students' best performance. If professors gave additional brief exams at frequent intervals, students would learn more, study more regularly, worry less, and perform better on midterms, finals, and other papers and projects.

Ideally, a professor would give an in-class test or quiz after each unit, chapter, or focus of study, depending on the type of class and course material. A physics class might require a test on concepts after every chapter covered, while a history class could necessitate quizzes covering certain time periods or major events. These exams should be given weekly, or at least twice monthly. Whenever possible, they should consist of two or three essay questions rather than many multiple-choice or short-answer questions. To preserve class time for lecture and discussion, exams should take no more than 15 or 20 minutes.

The main reason professors should give frequent exams is that when they do, and when they provide feedback to students on how well they are doing, students learn more in the course and perform better on major exams, projects, and papers. It makes sense that in a challenging course containing a great deal of material, students will learn more of it and put it to better use if they have to apply or "practice" it frequently on exams, which also helps them find out how much they are learning and what they need to go over again. A recent Harvard study notes students' "strong preference for frequent evaluation in a course." Harvard students feel they learn least in courses that have "only a midterm and a final exam, with no other personal evaluation." They believe they learn most in courses with "many opportunities to see how they are doing" (Light, 1990, p. 32). In a review of a number of studies of student learning, Frederiksen (1984) reports that students who take weekly quizzes achieve higher scores on final exams than students who take only a midterm exam and that testing increases retention of material tested.

Another, closely related argument in favor of multiple exams is that they encourage students to improve their study habits. Greater frequency in test taking means greater frequency in studying for tests. Students prone to cramming will be required—or at least strongly motivated—to open their textbooks and notebooks more often, making them less likely to resort to long, kamikaze nights of studying for major exams. Since there is so much to be learned in the typical course, it makes sense that frequent, careful study and review are highly beneficial. But students need motivation to study regularly, and nothing works like an exam. If students had frequent exams in all their courses, they would have to schedule study time each week and gradually would develop a habit of frequent study. It might be argued that students are adults who have to learn how to manage their own lives, but learning history or physics is more complicated than learning to drive a car or balance a checkbook. Students need coaching and practice in learning. The right way to learn new material needs to become a habit, and I believe that frequent exams are key to developing good habits of study and learning. The Harvard study concludes that "tying regular evaluations to good course organization enables students to plan their work more than a few days in advance. If quizzes and homework are scheduled on specific days, students plan their work to capitalize on them" (Light, 1990, p. 33).

By encouraging regular study habits, frequent exams would also decrease anxiety by reducing the procrastination that produces anxiety. Students would benefit psychologically if they were not subjected to the emotional ups and downs caused by major exams, when after being virtually worry-free for weeks they are suddenly ready to check into the psychiatric ward. Researchers at the University of Vermont found a strong relationship among procrastination, anxiety, and achievement. Students who regularly put off studying for exams had continuing high anxiety and lower grades than students who procrastinated less. The researchers found that even "low" procrastinators did not study regularly and recommended that professors give frequent assignments and exams to reduce procrastination and increase achievement (Rothblum, Solomon, & Murakami, 1986, pp. 393, 394).

Research supports my proposed solution to the problems I have described. Common sense as well as my experience and that of many of my friends support it. Why, then, do so few professors give frequent brief exams? Some believe that such exams take up too much of the limited class time available to cover the material in the course. Most courses meet 150 minutes a week—three times a week for 50 minutes each time. A 20-minute weekly exam might take 30 minutes to administer, and that is one-fifth of each week's class time. From the student's perspective, however, this time is well spent. Better learning and greater confidence about the course seem a good trade-off for another 30 minutes of lecture. Moreover, time lost to lecturing or discussion could easily be made up in students' learning on their own through careful regular study for the weekly exams. If weekly exams still seem too time-consuming to some professors, their frequency could be reduced to every other week or their length to 5 or 10 minutes. In courses where multiple-choice exams are appropriate, several questions could be designed to take only a few minutes to answer.

Another objection professors have to frequent exams is that they take too much time to read and grade. In a 20-minute essay exam, a well-prepared student can easily write two pages. A relatively small class of 30 students might then produce 60 pages, no small amount of material to read each week. A large class of 100 or more students would produce an insurmountable pile of material. There are a number of responses to this objection. Again, professors could give exams every other week or make them very short. Instead of reading them closely they could skim them quickly to see whether students understand an idea or can apply it to an unfamiliar problem; and instead of numerical or letter grades they could give a plus, check, or minus. Exams could be collected and responded to only every third or fourth week. Professors who have readers or teaching assistants could rely on them to grade or check

7

8

exams. And the Scantron machine is always available for instant grading of multiple-choice exams. Finally, frequent exams could be given *in place of* a midterm exam or out-of-class essay assignment.

Since frequent exams seem to some professors to create many problems, however, it is reasonable to consider alternative ways to achieve the same goals. One alternative solution is to implement a program that would improve study skills. While such a program might teach students to study for exams, it cannot prevent procrastination or reduce "large test anxiety" by a substantial amount. One research team studying anxiety and test performance found that study skills training was "not effective in reducing anxiety or improving performance" (Dendato & Diener, 1986, p. 134). This team, which also reviewed other research that reached the same conclusion, did find that a combination of "cognitive/relaxation therapy" and study skills training was effective. This possible solution seems complicated, however, not to mention time-consuming and expensive. It seems much easier and more effective to change the cause of the bad habit than treat the habit itself. That is, it would make more sense to solve the problem at its root: the method of learning and evaluation.

Still another solution might be to provide frequent study questions for students to answer. These would no doubt be helpful in focusing students' time studying, but students would probably not actually write out the answers unless they were required to. To get students to complete the questions in a timely way, professors would have to collect and check the answers. In that case, however, they might as well devote the time to grading an exam. Even if it asks the same questions, a scheduled exam is preferable to a set of study questions because it takes far less time to write in class, compared to the time students would devote to responding to questions at home. In-class exams also ensure that each student produces his or her own work.

Another possible solution would be to help students prepare for midterm and final exams by providing sets of questions from which the exam questions will be selected or announcing possible exam topics at the beginning of the course. This solution would have the advantage of reducing students' anxiety about learning every fact in the textbook, and it would clarify the course goals, but it would not motivate students to study carefully each new unit, concept, or text chapter in the course. I see this as a way of complementing frequent exams, not as substituting for them.

From the evidence and from my talks with professors and students, I see frequent, brief in-class exams as the only way to improve students' study habits and learning, reduce their anxiety and procrastination, and increase their satisfaction with college. These exams are not a panacea, but only more parking spaces and a winning football team would do as much to improve college life. Professors can't do much about parking or football, but they can give more frequent exams. Campus administrators should get behind this effort, and professors should get together to consider giving exams more frequently. It would make a difference. 12

References

Dendato, K. M., & Diener, D. (1986). Effectiveness of cognitive/relaxation therapy and study-skills training in reducing self-reported anxiety and improving the academic performance of test-anxious students. *Journal of Counseling Psychology, 33,* 131–135.

Frederiksen, N. (1984). The real test bias: Influences of testing on teaching and learning. *American Psychologist, 39,* 193–202.

Light, R. J. (1990). *Explorations with students and faculty about teaching, learning, and student life.* Cambridge, MA: Harvard University Graduate School of Education and Kennedy School of Government.

Rothblum, E. D., Solomon, L., & Murakami, J. (1986). Affective, cognitive, and behavioral differences between high and low procrastinators. *Journal of Counseling Psychology, 33,* 387–394.

READING FOR MEANING

This section presents three activities that will help you reread O'Malley's proposal with a critical eye. Done in sequence, these activities lead you from a basic understanding of the selection to a more personal response to it and finally to an analysis that deepens your understanding and critical thinking about what you are reading.

Read to Comprehend

Reread the selection, and write a few sentences briefly explaining the problem O'Malley sees and the solution he proposes. Then list the alternative solutions that O'Malley counterargues. Also make a list of any terms you do not understand—for example, *retention* (paragraph 4), *kamikaze* (5), *capitalize on* (5), *procrastination* (6). Look up their meanings in a dictionary to see which definition best fits the context.

To expand your understanding of this reading, you might use one or more of the following critical reading strategies that are explained and illustrated in Appendix 1: *annotating, summarizing, paraphrasing,* and *contextualizing.*

Read to Respond

Write several paragraphs exploring your initial thoughts and feelings about "More Testing, More Learning." Focus on anything that stands out for you, perhaps because it resonates with your own experience or because you find a statement puzzling.

You might consider writing about

- whether O'Malley's proposal, if it were adopted by professors, would make a difference in your own study habits or address any problems that you have with studying.

- how successfully O'Malley addresses the concerns of busy professors who might not want to give frequent exams, perhaps in relation to whether you think your professors would be willing to change their ways.

- the relation O'Malley attempts to establish between high-pressure exams and poor performance (paragraph 2), testing it against your own experience.

- which classes, in your experience, are and are not suited to frequent brief exams.

- your own experience preparing for major exams such as midterms and finals, comparing it with the scenario O'Malley describes in paragraph 1.

To develop your response to O'Malley's proposal, you might use one or both of the following critical reading strategies that are explained and illustrated in Appendix 1: *looking for patterns of opposition* and *judging the writer's credibility*.

Read to Analyze Underlying Assumptions

Write several paragraphs exploring one or more of the assumptions, values, and beliefs underlying O'Malley's proposal. As you write, explain how the assumptions are reflected in the text, as well as what you now think of them (and perhaps of your own assumptions) after rereading the selection with a critical eye.

You might consider writing about

- why O'Malley mentions the psychological as well as the intellectual drawbacks of infrequent testing.

- the assumptions and beliefs underlying professors' objections to frequent testing and O'Malley's response to them (paragraphs 7 and 8).

- the assumptions underlying O'Malley's assertions in the conclusion that students will be more satisfied with college if professors follow his proposal and that "only more parking spaces and a winning football team would do as much to improve college life" (12).

To probe assumptions more deeply, you might use one or more of the following critical reading strategies that are explained and illustrated in Appendix 1:

reflecting on challenges to your beliefs and values, exploring the significance of figurative language, and *looking for patterns of opposition.*

READING LIKE A WRITER
ARGUING DIRECTLY FOR THE PROPOSED SOLUTION

Arguing directly for the proposed solution, like counterarguing readers' likely questions and alternative solutions, is especially important in proposals. Writers argue directly for a proposed solution by explaining the reasons it should be implemented and then supporting those reasons with evidence or examples. Many types of support are available: personal experience, assertions, research, reviews of research, quotes from authorities, effects or consequences, benefits, contrasts, analogies, and causes. O'Malley makes use of all of these types of support.

Analyze

1. *Skim* paragraphs 4–6. In each paragraph, *underline* the sentence that announces the reason for the solution.

2. *Note in the margin* the kinds of support O'Malley relies on. *Categorize* all of his support.

3. *Evaluate* how effectively O'Malley argues to support his solution. Do the reasons seem plausible? Is one reason more convincing to you than the others? How believable do you find the support?

Write

Write several sentences explaining what you have learned about O'Malley's attempt to convince readers to take his proposed solution seriously. *Give examples* from the reading. Then *add a few sentences* evaluating how convincing you find his argument. Which parts do you find most convincing? Least convincing? *Explain* your choices.

CONSIDERING IDEAS FOR YOUR OWN WRITING

Much of what happens in high school and college is predictable and conventional. Examples of conventional practices that have changed very little over the years are exams, classroom lectures, graduation ceremonies, required courses, and lower admission requirements for athletes. Think of additional examples of established practices in high school or college; then select one that you believe needs to be improved or refined in some way. What changes would you propose? What individual or group might be convinced to take action on your proposal for improvement? What questions or objections should you anticipate? How could you discover whether others have previously proposed improvements in the practice you are concerned with? Whom might you interview to learn more about the practice and the likelihood of changing it?

SHANNON LONG

Wheelchair Hell: A Look at Campus Accessibility

> *Shannon Long wrote this essay for a first-year composition course at the University of Kentucky and later sent her proposal to campus administrators. In it, she tries to convince readers that there is a serious accessibility problem for wheelchair-bound students on campus. She painstakingly documents the problem and offers a simple but practical solution. As you read Long's essay, think about how accessible your own campus is for students in wheelchairs.*
>
> *The other readings in this chapter are followed by reading and writing activities. Following this reading, however, you are on your own to decide how to read for meaning and read like a writer.*

It was my first week of college, and I was on my way to the third floor of the library to meet up with someone to study. After entering the library, I went to the elevator and hit the button calling it. A few seconds later, the elevator door opened, and I rolled inside. The doors closed behind me. Expecting the buttons to be down in front of me, I suddenly noticed that they were behind me—and too high to reach. There I was stuck in the elevator with no way to call for help. Finally, someone got on at the fourth floor. I'd been waiting fifteen minutes.

I'm not the only one who has been a victim of inaccessibility on campus. The University of Kentucky (UK) currently has twelve buildings that are inaccessible to students in wheelchairs (Karnes). Many other UK buildings, like the library, are accessible, but have elevators that are inoperable by handicapped students. Yet, Section 504 of the Rehabilitation Act of 1973 states that

> No qualified handicapped person shall, because a recipient's facilities are inaccessible to or unusable by handicapped persons, be denied the benefits of, be excluded from participation in, or otherwise be subjected to discrimination under any program or activity receiving Federal financial assistance. (qtd. in *Federal Register* 22681)

When this law went into effect in 1977, the University of Kentucky started a renovation process in which close to $1 million was spent on handicap modifications (Karnes). Even though that much money has been spent, there are still many more modifications needed. Many buildings remain inaccessible to wheelchair-bound students: the Administration building, Alumni House, Barker Hall, Bowman Hall, Bradley Hall, Engineering Quadrangle,

Gillis building, Kinkead Hall, Miller Hall, Safety and Security building, Scovell Hall, and several residence halls.

The inaccessibility of so many buildings on campus creates many unnecessary problems for UK students in wheelchairs. For example, handicapped students who want to meet with an administrator must make an appointment for somewhere else on campus because the Administration building is not accessible. Making appointments is usually not a problem, but there is still the fact that able-bodied students have no problem entering the Administration building while handicapped students cannot. Although handicapped students can enter the Gillis building, they cannot go beyond the ground floor and even have to push a button to get someone to come downstairs to help them. Finally, for handicapped students to get counseling from the Career Planning Center, they must set up an appointment to meet with someone at another place. Some of these students might not use the center's counseling services because of the extra effort and inconvenience involved (Croucher).

4

Even many of the buildings that are accessible have elevators, water fountains, and door handles that are inoperable by handicapped students, forcing them to ask somebody for assistance. If there is nobody around to ask, the handicapped student simply has to wait. In the Chemistry and Physics building, for example, a key is needed to operate the elevator, forcing wheelchair-bound students to ride up and down the hall to find somebody to help them. Many water fountains are inaccessible to people in wheelchairs, and some buildings have only one accessible water fountain. Finally, hardly any buildings have doorknobs that students with hand and arm impairments can operate independently.

5

In addition, many residence halls, such as Boyd, Donovan, Patterson, and Keenland, are completely inaccessible. When handicapped students want to drop by and see friends or attend a party in one of these dorms, they have to be carried up the steps. Kirivan Tower and Blanding Tower have no accessible bathrooms. Also, in Kirivan Tower the elevators are so small that someone has to lift the back of the wheelchair into the elevator. The complex low-rises—Shawneetown, Commonwealth Village, and Cooperstown Apartments—are also inaccessible. Cooperstown has some accessible first-floor apartments, but a handicapped student couldn't very well live there because the bathrooms are inaccessible. All eleven sorority houses are inaccessible, and only five of the sixteen fraternity houses are accessible. Since the land that these sorority and fraternity houses are on is owned by the university, Section 504 of the Rehabilitation Act requires that the houses be accessible to handicapped students (University 14, 15).

6

With so many places on campus still inaccessible to wheelchair-   7
bound UK students, it is obvious that hundreds of modifications
need to be done. According to Jake Karnes, assistant dean of students and director of Handicap Student Services, "it will probably
take close to $1 million to make UK totally accessible." UK's cur-
rent budget allows for just $10,000 per year to go toward handicap
modifications (Karnes). If no other source of funds is sought, the
renovation process could be strung out for many years.

A possible solution could be the use of tuition. If only $2 were   8
collected from each UK student's tuition, there would be almost
$50,000 extra per semester for handicap modifications. Tuition is
already used to pay for things ranging from teacher salaries to the
funding of the campus radio station. This plan could be started
with the upcoming fall semester. The money could be taken from
each of the existing programs the tuition now pays for, so there
would be no need for an increase in tuition. Also, this would not
be a permanent expense because with an extra $50,000 a semester,
all of the needed modifications could be completed within ten
years. After that, the amount taken from the tuition could be lowered to fifty cents to help cover the upkeep costs of the campus
improvements. This plan is practical—and more importantly, it is
ethical. Surely if part of our tuition already goes to fund a radio
station, some of it can be used to make UK a more accessible place.
Which is more important, having a radio station to play alternative music or having a campus that is accessible to all students?

June 1980 was the deadline for meeting the requirements of Sec-   9
tion 504 (Robinson 28). In compliance with the law, the University
of Kentucky has spent almost $1 million making its campus more
accessible. But there are still many more changes needed. These
changes will take a lot of money, but if $2 could be used out of
each student's tuition, the money would be there. Handicapped
students often work to overachieve to prove their abilities. All they
ask for is a chance, and that chance should not be blocked by high
buttons, heavy doors, or steps.

Works Cited

Croucher, Lisa. "Accountability at UK for Handicapped Still Can Be Better." *Kentucky Kernal* n.d.: n. pag.

Karnes, Jake. Personal interview. 17 Oct. 1989.

Rehabilitation Act of 1973. Title 5 of Pub. L. 93–112. 26 Sept. 1973. 87 stat. 355; 24 USC 794 as amended. *Federal Register* 24 (4 May 1977): 22681.

Robinson, Rita. "For the Handicapped: Renovation Report Card." *American School and University* Apr. 1980: 28.

University of Kentucky. Transition Plan. Report. N.d.

READING FOR MEANING

Reading for meaning involves three activities:

- reading to comprehend

- reading to respond

- reading to analyze underlying assumptions

Reread Long's essay, and then write a page or so explaining your understanding of its basic meaning or main point, a personal response you have to it, and what you see as one of its underlying assumptions.

READING LIKE A WRITER

Writers of proposals

- introduce the problem.

- present the solution.

- argue directly for the proposed solution.

- counterargue readers' objections, questions, and alternative solutions.

- establish credibility.

Focus on one of these strategies in Long's essay, and analyze it carefully through close rereading and annotating. Then write several sentences explaining what you have learned about the strategy, giving specific examples from the reading to support your explanation. Add a few sentences evaluating how successfully Long uses the strategy to construct a persuasive argument.

REVIEWING WHAT MAKES PROPOSALS EFFECTIVE

In this chapter, you have been learning how to read proposals for meaning and how to read them like a writer. Before going on to write a proposal of your own, pause here to review and contemplate what you have learned about the elements of effective proposal writing.

Analyze

Choose one reading from this chapter that seems to you especially effective. Before rereading the selection, *jot down* one or two reasons you remember it as an example of good proposal writing.

Reread your chosen selection, adding further annotations about what makes it a particularly successful example of proposal writing.

Consider the selection's purpose and how well it achieves that purpose for its intended readers. (You can make an informed guess about the intended readers and their expectations by noting the publication source of the essay.) Then *focus* on how well the essay

- introduces the problem.

- presents the solution.

- argues directly for the proposed solution.

- counterargues readers' objections, questions, and alternative solutions.

- establishes credibility.

You can review all of these basic features in the Guide to Reading Proposals (p. 495).

Your instructor may ask you to complete this activity on your own or to work with a small group of other students who have chosen the same reading. If you work with others, allow enough time initially for all group members to reread the selection thoughtfully and to add their annotations. Then *discuss* as a group what makes the essay effective. *Take notes* on your discussion. One student in your group should then report to the class what the group has learned about the effectiveness of proposal writing. If you are working individually, write up what you have learned from your analysis.

Write

Write at least a page explaining your choice of this reading as an example of effective proposal writing. *Assume* that your readers—your instructor and classmates—have read the selection but will not remember many details about it. They also may not remember it as especially successful. Therefore, you will need to *refer* to details and specific parts of the reading as you explain how it works and as you justify your evaluation of its effectiveness. You need not argue that it is the best essay in the chapter or that it is flawless, only that it is, in your view, a strong example of the genre.

■ A Guide to Writing Proposals

The readings in this chapter have helped you learn a great deal about proposal writing. A proposal has two basic features: the problem and the solution. Now that you have seen how writers establish that the problem exists and is serious, offer a detailed analysis of the problem, attempt to convince readers to accept the solution offered, and demonstrate how the proposed solution can be implemented, you can approach this type of writing confidently. Using these strategies will help you develop a convincing proposal of your own.

This Guide to Writing is designed to assist you in writing your essay. Here you will find activities to help you identify a subject and discover what to say about it, organize your ideas and draft the essay, read the draft critically, revise the draft to strengthen your argument, and edit and proofread the essay to improve readability.

INVENTION AND RESEARCH

Invention is a process of discovery and planning by which you generate something to say. The following activities will help you choose a problem for study, analyze the problem and identify a solution, consider your readers, develop an argument for your proposed solution, and research your proposal. A few minutes spent completing each writing activity will improve your chances of producing a detailed and convincing first draft.

Choosing a Problem

Begin the selection process by reviewing what you wrote for the Considering Ideas for Your Own Writing activities following the readings in this chapter. Then try listing several groups or organizations to which you currently belong—for instance, a neighborhood or town, film society, dormitory, sports team, biology class. For each group, list as many problems facing it as you can. If you cannot think of any problems for a particular organization, consult with other members. Reflect on your list of problems, and choose the one for which you would most like to find a solution. It can be a problem that everyone already knows about or one about which only you are aware.

Proposing to solve a problem in a group or community to which you belong gives you an important advantage: You can write as an expert, an insider. You know about the history of the problem, have felt the urgency to solve it, and perhaps have already thought of possible solutions. Equally important, you know precisely where to send the proposal and who would most benefit from it. You have the access needed to interview others in the group, people who can contribute different, even dissenting viewpoints about the problem and solution. You are in a position of knowledge and authority—from which comes confident, convincing writing. If you choose a problem that affects a wider group, concentrate on one with which you have direct experience and for which you can suggest a detailed plan of action.

Developing Your Proposal

The writing and research activities that follow will enable you to test your problem and proposal and develop an argument that your readers will take seriously.

Analyzing the Problem. Write a few sentences in response to each of these questions:

- Does the problem really exist? How can you tell?
- What caused this problem? Consider immediate and deeper causes.
- What is the history of the problem?
- What are the negative consequences of the problem?
- Who in the community or group is affected by the problem?
- Does anyone benefit from the existence of the problem?

Considering Your Readers. *With your understanding of the problem in mind, write for a few minutes about your intended readers.* Will you be writing to all members of your group or to only some of them? To an outside committee that might supervise or evaluate the group, or to an individual in a position of authority inside or outside the group? Briefly justify your choice of readers. Then gauge how much they already know about the problem and what solutions they might prefer. Consider the problem's direct or indirect impact on them. Comment on what values and attitudes you share with your readers and how they have responded to similar problems in the past.

Finding a Tentative Solution. *List at least three possible solutions to the problem.* Think about solutions that have already been tried as well as solutions that have been proposed for related problems. Find, if you can, solutions that eliminate causes of the problem. Also consider solutions that reduce the symptoms of the problem. If the problem seems too complex to be solved all at once, list solutions for one or more parts of the problem. Maybe a series of solutions is required and a key solution should be proposed first. From your list, choose the solution that seems to you most timely and practicable and write two or three sentences describing it.

Anticipating Readers' Objections.   *Write a few sentences defending your solution against each of the following predictable objections.* For your proposal to succeed, readers must be convinced to take the solution seriously. Try to imagine how your prospective readers will respond.

- It won't really solve the problem.
- I'm comfortable with things as they are.
- We can't afford it.
- It will take too long.
- People won't do it.
- Too few people will benefit.
- I don't see how to get started on your solution.
- It's already been tried, with unsatisfactory results.
- You're making this proposal because it will benefit you personally.

Counterarguing Alternative Solutions.   *Identify two or three likely solutions to the problem that your readers may prefer, solutions different from your own.* Choose the one that poses the most serious challenge to your solution. Then write a few sentences comparing your solution with the alternative solution, weighing the strengths and weaknesses of each. Explain how you might demonstrate to readers that your solution has more advantages and fewer disadvantages than the alternative solution.

RESEARCHING YOUR SUBJECT ONLINE

Searching the Web can be a productive way of learning about solutions other people have proposed or tried out. Here are some specific suggestions for finding information about solutions:

- Enter keywords—words or brief phrases related to the problem or a solution—into a search tool such as Google <www.google.com> or Yahoo! <www.yahoo.com>. For example, if you are concerned that many children in your neighborhood have no adult supervision after school, you could try keywords associated with the problem such as *latchkey kids* or keywords associated with possible solutions such as *after-school programs.*

- If you think solutions to your problem may have been proposed by a government agency, you could try adding the word *government* to your keywords or searching on <FirstGov.gov>, the U.S. govern-ment's official Web portal. For example, you might explore the problem of latchkey children by following links at the Web site of the U.S. Department of Health and Human Services <www.hhs.gov>. If you want to see whether the problem has been addressed by your state or local government, you can go to the Library of Congress Internet Resource Page on State and Local Governments <www.loc .gov/global/state> and follow the links.

Bookmark or keep a record of promising sites. You may want to download or copy information you could use in your essay, including visuals; if so, remember to record documentation information.

Supporting Your Solution.   *Write down every plausible reason your solution should be heard or tried.* Then review your list and highlight the strongest rea-sons, the ones most likely to persuade your readers. Write for a few minutes about the single most convincing reason for your solution. Support this reason in any way you can. You want to build an argument that readers will take seri-ously.

Researching Your Proposal.   *Try out your proposal on members of the group, or go to the library to research a larger social or political problem.* If you are writing about a problem affecting a group to which you belong, talk with other members of the group to learn more about their understanding of the problem. Try out your solution on one or two people; their objections and questions will help you counterargue and support your argument more successfully.

If you are writing about a larger social or political problem, you should do research to confirm what you remember and to learn more about the problem. You can probably locate all the information you need in a good research library or on the Internet; you could also interview an expert on the problem. Readers will not take you seriously unless you are well informed.

Formulating a Working Thesis.   *Draft a working thesis statement.* A working thesis helps you begin drafting your essay purposefully. The thesis statement in a proposal is simply a statement of the solution you propose. Keep in mind that you may need to revise your working thesis as you learn more about your sub-ject and as you draft your essay.

Here are three examples of thesis statements from the readings in this chap-ter. Notice that because a proposal often involves complex problems and solu-tions with multiple parts, the writer will often use more than one sentence or even more than one paragraph to express the thesis, as in the first two examples.

In the first example, Kornbluh introduces the idea of a three-part solution at the beginning of a paragraph, then uses the rest of that paragraph and the next two paragraphs to present each of the three parts in turn. In the second example, Hertsgaard introduces the central idea of the thesis in two sentences at the end of a paragraph, and then develops and explains it further in the two-sentence paragraph that follows.

- "A sensible modern family policy—that supports rather than undermines today's juggler family—would have three components. The first is paid leave. . . . The second component of a smart family policy is high-quality child care. . . . The third and most important component is more fundamental: we should sever the link between employers and basic benefits" (Kornbluh, paragraphs 7–9).

- "Not only could we dramatically reduce our burden on the air, water and other natural systems, we could make money doing so. If we're smart, we could make restoring the environment the biggest economic enterprise of our time, a huge source of jobs, profits and poverty alleviation.

  What we need is a Global Green Deal: a program to renovate our civilization environmentally from top to bottom in rich and poor countries alike. Making use of both market incentives and government leadership, a 21st century Global Green Deal would do for environmental technologies what government and industry have recently done so well for computer and Internet technologies: launch their commercial takeoff" (Hertsgaard, paragraphs 3 and 4).

- "If professors gave additional brief exams at frequent intervals, students would learn more, study more regularly, worry less, and perform better on midterms, finals, and other papers and projects" (O'Malley, paragraph 2).

Notice that each of these thesis statements makes clear what the writer is proposing. Each thesis also mentions or implies the problem to be solved, even though it has already been described in the essay. In addition, O'Malley's thesis statement forecasts the specific benefits of solving the problem, a strategy that helps readers anticipate how the argument is sequenced.

Considering Visuals.   *Consider whether visuals—drawings, photographs, tables, or graphs—would strengthen your proposal.* You could construct your own visuals, scan materials from books and magazines, or download them from the Internet. If you submit your essay electronically to other students and your instructor, or if you post it on a Web site, consider including photographs as well as snippets of film or sound. Visual and auditory materials are not at all a requirement of a successful proposal, as you can tell from the readings in this chapter, but they could add a new dimension to your writing. If you want to use photographs or recordings of people, though, be sure to obtain their permission.

DRAFTING

The following guidelines will help you set goals for your draft, plan its organization, and consider a useful sentence strategy for it.

Setting Goals

Establishing goals for your draft before you begin writing will enable you to make decisions and work more confidently. Consider the following questions now, and keep them in mind as you draft. They will help you set goals for drafting as well as recall how the writers you have read in this chapter tried to achieve similar goals.

- *How can I introduce the problem in a way that interests my readers and convinces them that it needs to be solved?* Like Kornbluh, do I have to convince my readers that there really is a problem? Like Newman, should I draw on my authority from having observed the group carefully for some time? Must I describe the problem at length, as Kornbluh does, or merely identify it, as O'Malley does?

- *How should I present the solution?* Should I describe in detail how the solution might be implemented, as do Kornbluh, Miller, and Newman? Or need I describe the solution only briefly, like Samuelson and O'Malley do, letting other interested parties work out the details and take action?

- *How can I argue convincingly for my proposed solution?* Should I give examples of similar solutions that have proven successful, as Hertsgaard does? Describe the benefits of my solution, as Newman and O'Malley do? Offer statistics, like Kornbluh, Miller, and Long? Provide scenarios for what the solution could look like, as Miller does? Or, like O'Malley and Kornbluh, refer to research?

- *How should I anticipate readers' objections and their alternative solutions?* Should I refute readers' likely objections to the argument for my solution, as O'Malley and Samuelson do? Should I attempt to answer readers' questions, as Miller does? Should I accommodate objections from my readers, as Hertsgaard does when he acknowledges that his proposal is not a "silver bullet"? Should I consider and refute alternative solutions, as O'Malley and Samuelson do?

- *How can I establish my credibility so that my readers will want to join me in taking action to solve the problem?* Should I feature my firsthand experience with the problem, as O'Malley and Long do? Should I set up a logical step-by-step argument, as all the writers in this chapter do? Should I show my respect for and knowledge of my readers by counterarguing at length, as Miller and O'Malley do? Can I reveal my efforts to learn about the problem by quoting some of the people I interviewed (as Miller and Long do) or by showing what I learned from published sources (as O'Malley and Hertsgaard do)?

Organizing Your Draft

With goals in mind and invention notes at hand, you are ready to make a first outline of your draft. The basic parts are quite simple: the problem, the solution, and the reasons in support of the solution. This simple plan is nearly always complicated by other factors, however. In outlining your material, you must take into consideration many other details, such as whether readers already recognize the problem, how much agreement exists on the need to solve the problem, how much attention should be given to alternative solutions, and how many objections and questions by readers should be expected.

Your outline should reflect your own writing situation. You should not hesitate to change this outline after you start drafting. For example, you might discover a more convincing way to order the reasons for adopting your proposal, or you might realize that counterargument must play a larger role than you first imagined. The purpose of an outline is to identify the basic features of your proposal, not to lock you in to a particular structure.

Considering a Useful Sentence Strategy

As you draft your essay proposing a solution to a problem, you will want to connect with your readers. You will also want readers to become concerned with the seriousness of the problem and thoughtful about the challenge of solving it. Sentences that take the form of rhetorical questions can help you achieve these goals. A *rhetorical question* is conventionally defined as a sentence posing a question to which the writer expects no answer from the reader. (Of course, not being face to face with the writer, a reader could not possibly answer.) In proposals, however, rhetorical questions do important rhetorical work—that is, they assist writers in realizing a particular purpose and they influence readers in certain ways. In particular, you can use rhetorical questions to engage your readers, orient them to reading your proposal, and forecast the plan of your proposal or introduce parts of it.

Here are examples of rhetorical questions from Newman's proposal:

Why? And what can we do about it? (paragraph 4)

How would an employer consortium function? (15)

These questions help readers understand that they will be reading a proposal: Newman implies through the questions that she will explain why inner-city workers are trapped in low-wage jobs and outline a proposal to solve the problem. In addition, she engages readers by sharing with them the questions behind her research project and voicing one of the specific questions they are likely to have about her proposed solution. Consequently, readers have confidence that Newman will answer the questions she has posed so boldly.

Other writers in this chapter use different kinds of rhetorical questions to achieve the same effects.

- To orient readers to the proposal:

  How should we address this crisis? (Miller, paragraph 5)

  So what do we do? (Hertsgaard, paragraph 2)

- To forecast the plan of the argument or introduce parts of it:

  How much would this plan cost? (Miller, paragraph 11)

  Why, then, do so few professors give frequent brief exams? (O'Malley, paragraph 7)

  Who would be hurt? (Samuelson, paragraph 13)

- To engage readers, such as by showing how important it is to solve the problem or how much better the solution would be than the situation that now exists:

  Which is more important, having a radio station to play alternative music or having a campus that is accessible to all students? (Long, paragraph 8)

Almost all of the authors in this chapter use at least one rhetorical question. Nevertheless, rhetorical questions are not a requirement for a successful proposal—and when they are used, they appear only occasionally. For another sentence strategy that can strengthen your proposal, using sentences that introduce concession and refutation, see Chapter 9 (pp. 639–40).

READING A DRAFT CRITICALLY

Getting a critical reading of your draft will help you see how to improve it. Your instructor may schedule class time for reading drafts, or you may want to ask a classmate or a tutor in the writing center to read your draft. Ask your reader to use the following guidelines and to write out a response for you to consult during your revision.

Read for a First Impression

1. Read the draft without stopping to annotate or comment, and then write two or three sentences giving your general impression.

2. Identify one aspect of the draft that seems to you particularly effective.

Read Again to Suggest Improvements

1. Recommend ways to present the problem more effectively.

   - Locate places in the draft where the problem is defined and described. Point to places where you believe the intended readers will need more explanation or where the presentation seems unclear or confusing.

- Consider whether readers might want to know more about the causes or effects of the problem. Suggest ways the writer might do more to establish the seriousness of the problem, creating a sense of urgency to gain readers' support and to excite their curiosity about solutions.

2. Suggest ways to present the solution more effectively.

   - Find the solution, and notice whether it is immediately clear and readable. Point to places where it could be made clearer and more readable.

   - Advise the writer whether it would help to lay out steps for implementation.

   - Tell the writer how to make the solution seem more practical, workable, and cost-effective.

3. Recommend ways to strengthen the argument for the solution.

   - List the reasons the writer gives for adopting the solution or considering it seriously. Point out the reasons most and least likely to be convincing. Let the writer know whether there are too many or too few reasons. If the reasons are not sequenced in a logical, step-by-step sequence, suggest a new order.

   - Evaluate the support for each reason. Point out any passages where the support seems insufficient, and recommend further kinds of support.

4. Suggest ways to extend and improve the counterargument.

   - Locate places where the writer anticipates readers' objections to and questions about the proposal. Keeping in mind that the writer can accommodate or refute each objection or question, evaluate how successfully the writer does so. Recommend ways to make the response to each question or objection more convincing.

   - Suggest any likely objections and questions the writer has overlooked.

   - Identify any alternative solutions the writer mentions. Give advice on how the writer can present these alternative solutions more clearly and responsibly, and suggest ways to accommodate or refute them more convincingly.

5. Suggest ways to make the argument more credible.

   - Tell the writer whether the intended readers are likely to find the proposal knowledgeable and authoritative. Point to places where it seems most and least authoritative.

   - Identify places where the writer seems most insightful in anticipating what readers need to know, what questions and objections they may have, and what alternative solutions they may prefer. Note whether the writer responds to readers' concerns responsibly and respectfully.

6. Suggest how the organization might be improved.

- Consider the overall plan, perhaps by making a scratch outline (see Appendix 1 for advice on scratch outlining). Decide whether the reasons and counterarguments follow a logical, step-by-step sequence. Suggest a more logical sequence, if necessary.

- Indicate where new or better transitions might help identify steps in the argument and keep readers on track.

7. Evaluate the effectiveness of visuals.

- Look at any visuals in the essay, and tell the writer what they contribute to your understanding of the writer's argument.

- If any visuals do not seem relevant, or if there seem to be too many visuals, identify the ones that the writer could consider dropping, explaining your thinking.

- If a visual does not seem to be appropriately placed, suggest a better place for it.

REVISING

This section offers suggestions for revising your draft. Revising means reenvisioning your draft, trying to see it in a new way, given your purpose and readers, in order to develop a convincing proposal.

The biggest mistake you can make while revising is to focus initially on words or sentences. Instead, first try to see your draft as a whole in order to assess its likely impact on readers. Think imaginatively and boldly about cutting unconvincing material, adding new material, and moving material around to improve readability and strengthen your argument. Your computer makes even drastic revisions physically easy, but you still need to make the mental effort and decisions that will improve your draft.

You may have received help with this challenge from a classmate or tutor who gave your draft a critical reading. If so, keep this valuable feedback in mind as you decide which parts of your draft need revising and what specific changes you could make. The following suggestions will help you solve problems and strengthen your essay.

To Introduce the Problem More Effectively

- If readers are unfamiliar with the problem or doubt that it exists, briefly address its history or describe it in some detail to make its impact seem real.

- If readers know about the problem but believe it is insignificant, argue for its seriousness, perhaps by dramatizing its current and long-term effects or by adding a dramatic rhetorical question. Or speculate about the complications that might arise in the future if the problem is not solved.

To Present the Solution More Effectively

- If readers cannot see how to implement your proposed solution, outline the steps of its implementation. Lead them through it chronologically, perhaps with the help of rhetorical questions. Demonstrate that the first step is easy to take; or, if it is unavoidably challenging, propose ways to ease the difficulty.

- If a solution is beyond your expertise, explain where the experts can be found and how they can be put to use.

- If all readers can readily imagine how the solution would be implemented and how it would look once in place, reduce the amount of space you give to presenting the solution.

To Strengthen the Argument for the Proposed Solution

- If you have not given adequate reasons for proposing the solution, give more reasons.

- If your reasons are hidden among other material, move them to the foreground. Consider announcing them explicitly at the beginnings of paragraphs (the first reason why, the second, the third; the main reason why; the chief reason for; and so on).

- If your argument seems unconvincing, support your reasoning and argument with examples, anecdotes, statistics, quotes from authorities or members of the group, or any other appropriate support.

To Strengthen the Counterarguments

- If you have not anticipated all of your readers' weighty objections and questions, do so now. (You may want to use a rhetorical question or two for this purpose.) Consider carefully whether you can accommodate some objections by either granting their wisdom or adapting your solution in response to them. If you refute objections or dismiss questions, do so in a spirit of continuing collaboration with members of your group; there is no need to be adversarial. You want readers to support your solution and perhaps even to join with you in implementing it.

- If you have neglected to mention alternative solutions that are popular with readers, do so now. (You may want to use a rhetorical question or two for this purpose.) You may accommodate or reject these alternatives, or— a compromise—incorporate some of their better points. If you must reject all aspects of an alternative, do so through reasoned argument, without questioning the character or intelligence of those who prefer the alternative. You may be able to convince some of them that your solution is the better one.

To Enhance Credibility

- If critical readers of your draft questioned your credibility, learn more about the problem, seek advice on presenting the solution in a more compelling way, make the feasibility of the solution clearer, and talk with more members of the group so that you can incorporate or address more viewpoints.

- If your attitude toward readers weakens your credibility, look for ways to show readers more respect and to establish a common ground with them.

To Organize More Logically and Coherently

- If your argument lacks logical progression, reorganize the reasons supporting your proposed solution.

- If your various counterarguments are not smoothly integrated into your argument, try another sequence or add better transitions.

- If your critical reader had trouble following the logical progression of your proposal, consider adding one or two rhetorical questions to forecast your plan of argument or introduce parts of it.

EDITING AND PROOFREADING

After you have revised the essay, be sure to spend some time checking for errors in usage, punctuation, and mechanics and considering matters of style. If you keep a list of errors you typically make, begin by checking your draft against this list. Ask someone else to proofread your essay before you print out a copy for your instructor or send it electronically.

From our research on student writing, we know that proposal writers tend to refer to the problem or solution by using the pronoun *this* or *that* ambiguously. Edit carefully any sentences with *this* or *that* to ensure that a noun immediately follows the pronoun to make the reference clear. Check a writer's handbook for help with avoiding ambiguous pronoun reference.

Proposal to Solve a Problem

In this chapter, you have read critically several proposals and have written one of your own. To better remember what you have learned, pause now to reflect on the reading and writing activities you completed in this chapter.

1. *Write* a page or so reflecting on what you have learned. *Begin* by describing what you are most pleased with in your essay. Then *explain* what you think contributed to your achievement. *Be specific* about this contribution.

   - If it was something you learned from the readings, *indicate* which readings and specifically what you learned from them.

   - If it came from your invention writing, *point out* the section or sections that helped you most.

   - If you got good advice from a critical reader, *explain* exactly how the person helped you—perhaps by helping you understand a particular problem in your draft or by adding a new dimension to your writing.

   - *Try to write* about your achievement in terms of what you have learned about the genre.

2. Now *reflect* more generally on proposals, a genre of writing that plays an important role in our society. *Consider* some of the following questions: How confident do you feel about making a proposal that might lead to improvements in the functioning of an entire group or community? Does your proposal attempt fundamental or minor change in the group? How necessary is your proposed change in the scheme of things? Whose interest would be served by the solution you propose? Who else might be affected? In what ways does your proposal challenge the status quo in the group? What contribution might essays proposing solutions to problems make to our society that other genres of writing cannot make?

CHAPTER 9

Position Paper

Y ou may associate arguing with quarreling or with the in-your-face debating we hear so often on radio and television talk shows. These ways of arguing may let us vent strong feelings, but they seldom lead us to consider seriously other points of view, let alone to look critically at our own thinking or learn anything new.

This chapter presents a more deliberative way of arguing that we call *reasoned argument* because it depends on giving reasons rather than raising voices. It demands that positions be supported rather than merely asserted. It also commands respect for the right of others to disagree with you as you may disagree with them. Reasoned argument requires more thought than quarreling, but no less passion or commitment, as you will see when you read the position papers in this chapter.

Controversial issues are, by definition, issues about which people have strong feelings and sometimes disagree vehemently. The issue may involve a practice that has been accepted for some time, like naming sports teams for Native American tribes, or it may concern a newly proposed or recently instituted policy, like federal limits on embryonic stem cell research. People may agree about goals but disagree about the best way to achieve them, as in the perennial debate over how to guarantee adequate health care for all citizens. Or they may disagree about fundamental values and beliefs, as in the debate over affirmative action in college admissions.

As these examples suggest, position papers take on controversial issues that have no obvious "right" answer, no truth everyone accepts, no single authority everyone trusts. Consequently, simply gathering information—finding the facts or learning from experts—will not settle these disputes because ultimately they are matters of opinion and judgment.

Although it is not possible to prove that a position on a controversial issue is right or wrong, it is possible through argument to convince others to consider a particular position seriously or to accept or reject a position. To be convincing, a position paper must argue for its position by giving readers strong reasons and solid support. It also must anticipate opposing arguments.

As you read and discuss the selections in this chapter, you will discover why position papers play such an important role in college, the workplace, and civic life. You will also learn how position papers work. From the essays and from the ideas for writing that follow each selection, you will get many ideas for taking a position on an issue that you care about. As you read and write about the selections, keep in mind the following assignment, which sets out the goals for writing a position paper. The Guide to Writing Position Papers, which follows the readings, supports your writing of this assignment.

THE WRITING ASSIGNMENT

Arguing a Position on an Issue

Choose an issue about which you have strong feelings. Write an essay arguing your position on this issue. Your purpose is to try to convince your readers to take your argument seriously. Therefore, you will want to acknowledge readers' opposing views as well as any objections or questions they might have.

WRITING SITUATIONS FOR POSITION PAPERS

Writing that takes a position on a controversial issue plays a significant role in college work and professional life, as the following examples indicate:

- A committee made up of business and community leaders investigates the issue of regulating urban growth. After reviewing the arguments for and against government regulation, committee members argue against it on the grounds that supply and demand alone will regulate development, that landowners should be permitted to sell their property to the highest bidder, and that developers are guided by the needs of the market and thus serve the people.

- For a sociology class, a student writes a term paper on surrogate mothering. She first learns about the subject from television news, but she knows that she needs more information to write a paper on the topic. In the library, she finds several newspaper and magazine articles that help her understand better the debate over the issue. In her paper, she presents the strongest arguments on each side but concludes that, from a sociological perspective, surrogate mothering should not be allowed because it exploits poor women by creating a class of professional breeders.

- For a political science class, a student is assigned to write an essay on public employees' right to strike. Having no well-defined position herself, she discusses the issue with her mother, a nurse in a county hospital, and her uncle, a firefighter. Her mother believes that public employees like hospital workers and teachers should have the right to strike, but that police officers and firefighters should not because public safety would be endangered. The uncle disagrees, arguing that allowing hospital workers to strike would jeopardize public safety as much as allowing firefighters to strike. He insists that the central issue is not public safety, but individual rights. In her essay, the student supports the right of public employees to strike, but she argues that the timing of a strike should be arbitrated whenever a strike might jeopardize public safety.

THINKING ABOUT YOUR EXPERIENCE WITH POSITION ARGUMENTS

Before studying a type of writing, it is useful to spend some time thinking about what you already know about it. You may have discussed with friends or family your position on a controversial issue, trying to help them see why you think the way you do. You also may have written essays for classes examining the positions of experts in fields where controversial issues abound, such as in science, social science, business, education, and even your writing class. People in all fields, ranging from medicine and government to corporations and small businesses, deal with controversial issues every day, taking positions based on their knowledge at the time.

To analyze your experience with position arguments, you might recall a time when you argued orally or in writing about a controversial issue that captured your interest: What did you already know about the issue when you took your position? What was at stake for you? What prompted your original interest in the issue, and what made you care strongly enough about it to take a position to begin with? Who was your audience for your argument? What did you hope to achieve by taking your position? What made you think it was significant? Did you need to present the issue in detail, or was your audience already familiar with it?

Consider also the position arguments you have read, heard, or seen in the media. If you recall someone's argument in detail, try to identify what made it interesting and memorable. Was it the issue itself, or did the person's position seem powerful and well supported? How did the person make the argument convincing? Were there illuminating details or unusual points of view?

Write at least a page about your experience with position arguments.

■ A Guide to Reading Position Papers

This guide introduces you to essays that take a position on controversial issues. By completing all the activities in it, you will prepare yourself to learn a great deal from the other readings in this chapter about how to read and write a position paper. The guide focuses on a brief but forceful argument by Richard Estrada against the practice of naming sports teams and mascots after Native Americans. You will read Estrada's essay twice. First, you will read it for meaning, seeking to understand and respond to Estrada's argument. Then, you will read the essay like a writer, analyzing the parts to see how Estrada crafts his essay and to learn the strategies he uses to make his argument convincing. These two activities—reading for meaning and reading like a writer—follow every reading in this chapter.

RICHARD ESTRADA

Sticks and Stones and Sports Team Names

Richard Estrada (1951–1999) wrote a nationally syndicated newspaper column. This essay was first published in the Dallas Morning News *on October 29, 1995, during the baseball World Series in which the Atlanta Braves played the Cleveland Indians. The series between these teams drew attention to a long-standing debate in the United States over sports teams using names associated with Native Americans, as well as dressing team mascots like Native Americans on the warpath and encouraging fans to rally their teams with gestures like the "tomahawk chop" and pep yells like the "Indian chant." Various high schools and at least one university, Stanford, have changed the names of their sports teams in recent years because of this ongoing controversy.*

The title of the essay, as you may know, refers to a children's chant: "Sticks and stones will break my bones, but words will never hurt me." As you read, consider why Estrada thought this title was appropriate.

When I was a kid living in Baltimore in the late 1950s, there was only one professional sports team worth following. Anyone who ever saw the movie *Diner* knows which one it was. Back when we liked Ike, the Colts were the gods of the grid-iron and Memorial Stadium was their Mount Olympus.   1

Ah, yes: The Colts. The Lions. Da Bears. Back when defensive tackle Big Daddy Lipscomb was letting running backs know exactly   2 what time it was, a young fan could easily forget that in a game where men were men, the teams they played on were not invariably named after animals. Among others, the Packers, the Steelers and the distant 49ers were cases in point. But in the roll call of pro teams, one name in particular always discomfited me: the Washington Redskins. Still, however willing I may have been to go along with the name as a kid, as an adult I have concluded that using an ethnic group essentially as a sports mascot is wrong.

The Redskins, along with baseball teams like the Atlanta Braves, the Cleveland Indians and the Kansas City Chiefs, should find other names that avoid highlighting ethnicity.   3

By no means were such names originally meant to disparage Native Americans. The noble symbols of the Redskins or college football's Florida Seminoles or the Illinois Illini are meant to be strong and proud. Yet, ultimately, the practice of using a people as mascots is dehumanizing. It sets them apart from the rest of society. It promotes the politics of racial aggrievement at a moment when our storehouse is running over with it.   4

The World Series between the Cleveland Indians and the Atlanta Braves reignited the debate. In the chill night air of October, tomahawk chops and war chants suddenly became far more familiar to millions of fans, along with the ridiculous and offensive cartoon logo of Cleveland's "Chief Wahoo."   5

The defenders of team names that use variations on the Indian theme argue that tradition should not be sacrificed at the altar of political correctness. In truth, the nation's No. 1 P.C. [politically correct] school, Stanford University, helped matters some when it changed its team nickname from "the Indians" to "the Cardinals." To be sure, Stanford did the right thing, but the school's status as P.C. without peer tainted the decision for those who still need to do the right thing.   6

Another argument is that ethnic group leaders are too inclined to cry wolf in alleging racial insensitivity. Often, this is the case. But no one should overlook genuine cases of political insensitivity in an attempt to avoid accusations of hypersensitivity and political correctness.   7

The real world is different from the world of sports entertainment. I recently heard a father who happened to be a Native American complain on the radio that his child was being pressured into participating in celebrations of Braves baseball. At his kid's school, certain days are set aside on which all children are told to dress in Indian garb and celebrate with tomahawk chops and the like.   8

That father should be forgiven for not wanting his family to serve as somebody's mascot. The desire to avoid ridicule is legitimate and   9 understandable. Nobody likes to be trivialized or deprived of their dignity. This has nothing to do with political correctness and the provocations of militant leaders.

Against this backdrop, the decision by newspapers in Min-   10
neapolis, Seattle and Portland to ban references to Native American nicknames is more reasonable than some might think.

What makes naming teams after ethnic groups, particularly   11
minorities, reprehensible is that politically impotent groups continue to be targeted, while politically powerful ones who bite back are left alone. How long does anyone think the name "Washington Blackskins" would last? Or how about "the New York Jews"?

With no fewer than 10 Latino ballplayers on the Cleveland Indi-   12
ans' roster, the team could change its name to "the Banditos." The trouble is, they would be missing the point: Latinos would correctly object to that stereotype, just as they rightly protested against Frito-Lay's use of the "Frito Bandito" character years ago.

It seems to me that what Native Americans are saying is that   13
what would be intolerable for Jews, blacks, Latinos and others is no less offensive to them. Theirs is a request not only for dignified treatment, but for fair treatment as well. For America to ignore the complaints of a numerically small segment of the population because it is small is neither dignified nor fair.

READING FOR MEANING

This section presents three activities that will help you reread Estrada's position paper with a critical eye. Done in sequence, these activities lead you from a basic understanding of the selection to a more personal response to it and finally to an analysis that deepens your understanding and critical thinking about what you are reading.

Read to Comprehend

Reread the selection, and write a few sentences briefly explaining Estrada's position on using Native American names for sports teams. Then list the main reasons for his position (look in paragraphs 4 and 11). Also make a list of any words you do not understand—for example, *dehumanizing* (paragraph 4), *alleging* (7), *hypersensitivity* (7), *trivialized* (9). Look up their meanings in a dictionary to see which definition best fits the context.

To expand your understanding of this reading, you might use one or both of the following critical reading strategies that are explained and illustrated in Appendix 1: *annotating* and *summarizing*.

Read to Respond

Write several paragraphs exploring your initial thoughts and feelings about "Sticks and Stones and Sports Team Names." Focus on anything that stands out for you, perhaps because it resonates with your own experience or because you find a statement puzzling.

You might consider writing about

- the power of words to hurt, especially words that make people feel different or inferior, perhaps in relation to your own experience with being called demeaning names (or calling names yourself).

- a question you would like to ask Estrada, an addition you would make to his argument, or an alternative position you would argue for.

- how you feel about Estrada's examples of outrageous team names such as "Washington Blackskins," "New York Jews" (paragraph 11), and "Cleveland Banditos" (12).

- what Estrada means when he asserts that "[t]he real world is different from the world of sports entertainment" (8) or that Native Americans are subjected to this treatment only because they are "politically impotent" (11).

To develop your response to Estrada's position argument, you might use one or both of the following critical reading strategies that are explained and illustrated in Appendix 1: *questioning to understand and remember* and *contextualizing*.

Read to Analyze Underlying Assumptions

Write several paragraphs exploring one or more of the assumptions, values, and beliefs underlying Estrada's position paper. As you write, explain how the assumptions are reflected in the text, as well as what you now think of them (and perhaps of your own assumptions) after rereading the selection with a critical eye.

Analyzing underlying assumptions in a text is important because it gives us an opportunity to think critically about unexamined values and beliefs—those of others as well as our own, many of which may be ingrained in our culture, our education, and even our language. This task is particularly important for position papers because they deal with controversial issues—matters of opinion and judgment that have no generally accepted "right" or "wrong" answers. You will need to support your position with solid evidence. But in order to persuade your readers to consider your position, you will also need to find common ground with them. One good way to establish common ground is to find shared beliefs and values—that is, common assumptions.

Consider, for example, Estrada's last line: "For America to ignore the complaints of a numerically small segment of the population because it is small is neither dignified nor fair" (13). Earlier he gives several speculative examples of how more politically powerful minority groups would object strongly to having names associated with their ethnicities given to sports teams (such as "Washington Blackskins" and "New York Jews" in paragraph 11). When he then asserts that similar names are no less offensive to Native Americans just because they are a "small" minority, he is counting on his audience to share his assumption that the size of an ethnic group should make no difference in its right to dignity, fair treatment, and equality—all widely supported values in American society.

You might consider writing about

- the apparent contradiction between Estrada's assumption that naming a sports team "the Redskins" was originally intended to be admiring and not disparaging, and his assertion that "ultimately, the practice of using a people as mascots is dehumanizing" (paragraph 4).

- the assumptions and values underlying Estrada's statement that "[n]obody likes to be trivialized or deprived of their dignity" (9).

- the assumptions and values of those who "argue that tradition should not be sacrificed at the altar of political correctness"(6).

To probe assumptions more deeply, you might use one or more of the following critical reading strategies that are explained and illustrated in Appendix 1: *reflecting on challenges to your beliefs and values, evaluating the logic of an argument,* and *recognizing emotional manipulation.*

READING LIKE A WRITER

This section guides you through an analysis of Estrada's argumentative writing strategies: *presenting the issue; asserting a clear, unequivocal position; arguing directly for the position; counterarguing objections and opposing positions;* and *establishing credibility.* For each strategy you will be asked to reread and annotate part of Estrada's essay to see how he uses the strategy in "Sticks and Stones and Sports Team Names."

When you study the selections later in this chapter, you will see how different writers use the same strategies to develop a position paper. The Guide to Writing Position Papers near the end of this chapter suggests ways you can use these strategies in your own writing.

Presenting the Issue

For position papers published in the midst of an ongoing public debate, writers may need only to mention the issue. In most cases, however, writers need to identify the issue as well as explain it to readers. To present the issue, writers may provide several kinds of information. They may, for example, place the issue in its historical or cultural context, cite specific instances to make the issue seem less abstract, show their personal interest in the debate, or establish or redefine the terms of the debate.

Analyze

1. *Reread* paragraphs 1 and 2, where Estrada introduces the issue, and *make notes* about the approach he takes.

2. Then *reread* paragraph 5, where Estrada describes the events at the World Series that "reignited the debate." *Look closely* at his description of the television images, and *underline* any words that might lead readers to take his argument seriously.

Write

Write several sentences describing how Estrada presents the issue. Specifically, how does he introduce the issue and connect it to his readers' experiences and interests? Then *add a few sentences* evaluating how successfully Estrada presents the issue and prepares readers for his argument.

Asserting a Clear, Unequivocal Position

Writers of position papers always take sides. Their primary purposes are to assert a position of their own and to influence readers' thinking. The assertion is the main point of the essay, its thesis. Writers try to state the thesis simply and directly, although they may qualify the thesis by limiting its applicability. For example, a thesis in favor of the death penalty might limit capital punishment to certain kinds of crimes. The thesis statement often forecasts the stages of the argument as well, identifying the main reason or reasons that will be developed and supported in the essay.

Where the thesis is placed depends on various factors. Most likely, you will want to place the thesis early in the essay to let readers know right away where you stand. But when you need to spend more time presenting the issue or defining the terms of the debate, you might postpone introducing your own position. Restating the thesis at various points in the body of the essay and at the end can also help keep readers oriented.

Analyze

1. *Find* the first place where Estrada explicitly asserts his position (at the end of paragraph 2), and *underline* the sentence that states the thesis.

2. *Skim* paragraphs 3, 4, 9, and 13, and *put brackets around* the sentences in these paragraphs that restate the thesis.

3. *Examine* the context for each of these restatements. *Look closely* at the language he uses to see whether he repeats key words, uses synonyms, or adds new words.

Write

Write a few sentences explaining what you have learned about how Estrada states and restates his position. *Describe* the different contexts in which he restates the thesis and how the wording changes. *Cite examples* from the reading. Then *add a few sentences* speculating about the possible reasons for reasserting a thesis so often in a brief essay like this one.

Arguing Directly for the Position

Not only do writers of position papers explicitly assert their positions, but they also give reasons for them. Moreover, they usually support their reasons with facts, statistics, examples, anecdotes, quotes from authorities, and analogies.

Facts are statements that can be proven objectively to be true; but readers may need to be reassured that the facts indeed come from trustworthy sources. Although *statistics* may be mistaken for facts, they often are only interpretations or correlations of numerical data. Their reliability depends on how and by whom the information was collected and interpreted. *Examples* and *anecdotes,* in contrast, are not usually even claimed to be proof of the writer's position or evidence that it applies in every case. Instead, they present particular stories and vivid images that work by appealing to readers' emotions. Somewhere in between these two extremes are expert opinions and analogies. Readers must decide whether to regard *quotes from experts* as credible and authoritative. They must also decide how much weight to give *analogies,* comparisons that encourage readers to assume that what is true about one thing is also true about something to which it is compared. As a critical reader, you should look skeptically at analogies to determine whether they are logical as well as persuasive.

Analyze

1. *Reread* paragraphs 11–13, where Estrada develops his final reason for opposing the use of Native American names for sports teams. *Find* the first place where Estrada explicitly asserts his reason, and *put brackets around* the sentence or sentences that state the topic sentence of this part of his argument.

2. *Look closely* at how Estrada supports this reason with analogy. *Underline* the three sports team names that he facetiously proposes in paragraphs 11 and 12, and then *compare* them to the actual teams named after Native Americans that he mentions in paragraphs 2–4.

3. *Consider* how persuasive his analogies are in paragraphs 11 and 12.

Write

Write several sentences briefly describing Estrada's strategy of argument by analogy. *Cite examples* of his analogies. Then *add a few sentences* speculating about the persuasiveness of his strategy. Why do you think some readers would find the argument in this part of the essay compelling and other readers would not?

Counterarguing Objections and Opposing Positions

Writers of position papers often try to anticipate likely objections and questions readers might raise as well as opposing positions. Writers may concede points with which they agree and may even modify a thesis to accommodate valid objections. But when they think the criticism is groundless or opposing arguments are flawed, writers counterargue aggressively. They refute the challenges to their argument by poking holes in their opponents' reasoning and support.

Analyze

1. *Reread* paragraphs 6 and 7, where Estrada introduces two opposing arguments to his position. *Underline* the sentence in each paragraph that best states an opposing position.

2. *Examine* paragraphs 6–9 to see how Estrada counterargues these two predictable opposing arguments. For example, *notice* that he both concedes and refutes, and *consider* why he would attempt to do both. What seems to be his attitude toward those who disagree with him or, at least, object to parts of his argument?

3. *Consider* how well the anecdote about a Native American father (paragraphs 8 and 9) supports Estrada's counterargument, particularly why the anecdote might appeal to his *Dallas Morning News* readers.

Write

Write several sentences briefly explaining Estrada's counterargument. Then *add a few sentences* evaluating the probable success of this strategy with his newspaper readers.

Establishing Credibility

Readers judge the credibility of a position paper about a controversial issue by the way it presents the issue, argues for the position, and counterargues objections and opposing positions. Critical readers expect writers to advocate forcefully for their position, but at the same time they expect writers to avoid misrepresenting other points of view, attacking opponents personally, or manipulating readers' emotions. To establish credibility, writers thus aim instead to support their position responsibly with the help of authoritative sources and a well-reasoned, well-supported argument.

Another factor that can influence readers' judgment of an argument's credibility is whether the writer seems to share at least some of their values, beliefs, attitudes, and ideals. Readers often are more willing to trust a writer who expresses concerns they also have about an issue. Many readers respect arguments based on strong values even if they do not share those particular values or hold to them as strictly. Yet readers also tend to dislike moralizing and resent a condescending or belittling tone as much as a shrill or lecturing one. Instead, readers usually appreciate a tone that acknowledges legitimate differences of opinion, while seeking to establish common ground where possible.

Analyze

1. Quickly *reread* Estrada's entire essay. As you read, *put a question mark* in the margin next to any passages where you doubt Estrada's credibility, and *put a checkmark* next to any passages where he seems especially trustworthy.

2. *Review* the passages you marked. Where possible, *note in the margin* a word or phrase that describes the dominant tone of each marked passage.

3. Then *consider* what language, information, or other element in the marked passages contributes to your judgment of Estrada's credibility.

Write

Write several sentences describing your impression of Estrada's credibility. *Cite examples* from the reading to support your view.

■ Readings

MICHAEL SANDEL

Bad Bet

> *Michael Sandel (b. 1953) is a professor of government at Harvard University. A Rhodes Scholar, he earned a doctorate from Oxford University. He writes frequently for general publications such as the* Atlantic Monthly, New York Times, *and* New Republic. *His books include* Liberalism and Its Critics *(1984),* Democracy's Discontent: America in Search of a Public Philosophy *(1996), and* Liberalism and the Limits of Justice *(1999). Sandel currently serves on the President's Council on Bioethics, a national body appointed by the president to examine the ethical implications of new biomedical technologies.*
>
> *In this essay published in the* New Republic *in 1997, Sandel takes a position on state-sponsored lotteries: He opposes such lotteries, defining them as a form of civic corruption that undermines democracy. By "civic" he means those activities available to all citizens of a democracy regardless of their religious or political affiliations—activities like voting, going to school, joining various organizations, seeking information about local or national problems and issues, exercising rights of speech or assembly, and supporting an admired public official or working to defeat a disliked one.*
>
> *Before you read, think about your own experiences with gambling—perhaps with friends, on the Internet, or in clubs and casinos—or with state lotteries. Have you or members of your family purchased lottery tickets? With what result? What do you know about how your state's lottery operates? What programs does it offer, and how does it advertise them? What are your personal views about gambling and lotteries?*
>
> *As you read, notice how Sandel presents the opposing views of lottery proponents or defenders while arguing energetically for his own position.*

Political corruption comes in two forms. Most familiar is the hand-in-the-till variety: bribes, payoffs, influence-peddling, lobbyists lining the pockets of public officials in exchange for access and favors. This corruption thrives in secrecy, and is usually condemned when exposed.

But another kind of corruption arises, by degree, in full public view. It involves no theft or fraud, but rather a change in the habits of citizens, a turning away from public responsibilities. This second, civic corruption, is more insidious than the first. It violates no law, but enervates the spirit on which good laws depend. And by the time it becomes apparent, the new habits may be too pervasive to reverse.

Consider the most fateful change in public finance since the income tax: the rampant proliferation of state lotteries. Illegal in every state for most of the century, lotteries have suddenly become the fastest-growing source of state revenue. In 1970, two states ran lotteries; today, thirty-seven states and the District of Columbia run them. Nationwide, lottery sales exceed $34 billion a year, up from $9 billion in 1985.

The traditional objection to lotteries is that gambling is a vice. This objection has lost force in recent decades, partly because notions of sin have changed but also because Americans are more reluctant than they once were to legislate morality. Even people who find gambling morally objectionable shy away from banning it on that ground alone, absent some harmful effect on society as a whole.

Freed from the traditional, paternalistic objections to gambling, proponents of state lotteries advance three seemingly attractive arguments: first, lotteries are a painless way of raising revenue for important public services without raising taxes; unlike taxes, lotteries are a matter of choice, not coercion. Second, they are a popular form of entertainment. Third, they generate business for the retail outlets that sell lottery tickets (such as convenience stores, gas stations and supermarkets) and for the advertising firms and media outlets that promote them.

What, then, is wrong with state-run lotteries? For one thing, they rely, hypocritically, on a residual moral disapproval of gambling that their defenders officially reject. State lotteries generate enormous profits because they are monopolies, and they are monopolies because privately operated numbers games are prohibited, on traditional moral grounds. (In Las Vegas, where casinos compete with one another, the slot machines and blackjack tables pay out around 90 percent of their take in winnings. State lotteries, being monopolies, only pay out about 50 percent.) Libertarian defenders of state lotteries can't have it both ways. If a lottery is, like dry cleaning, a morally legitimate business, then why should it not be open to private enterprise? If a lottery is, like prostitution, a morally objectionable business, then why should the state be engaged in it?

Lottery defenders usually reply that people should be free to decide the moral status of gambling for themselves. No one is forced to play, they point out, and those who object can simply abstain. To those troubled by the thought that the state derives revenue from sin, advocates reply that government often imposes "sin taxes" on products (like liquor and tobacco) that many regard as undesirable. Lotteries are better than taxes, the argument goes, because they are wholly voluntary, a matter of choice.

But the actual conduct of lotteries departs sharply from this laissez-faire ideal. States do not simply provide their citizens the opportunity to gamble; they actively promote and encourage them to do so. The nearly $400 million spent on lottery advertising each year puts lotteries among the largest advertisers in the country. If lotteries are a form of "sin tax," they are the only kind in which the state spends huge sums to encourage its citizens to commit the sin.

Not surprisingly, lotteries direct their most aggressive advertising at their best customers—the working class, minorities and the poor. A billboard touting the Illinois lottery in a Chicago ghetto declared, "This could be your ticket out." Ads often evoke the fantasy of winning the big jackpot and never having to work again. Lottery advertising floods the airwaves around the first of each month, when Social Security and welfare payments swell the checking accounts of recipients. In sharp contrast to most other government amenities (say, police protection), lottery ticket outlets saturate poor and blue-collar neighborhoods and offer less service to affluent ones.

Massachusetts, with the highest grossing per capita lottery sales in the country, offers stark evidence of the blue-collar bias. A recent series in *The Boston Globe* found that Chelsea, one of the poorest towns in the state, has one lottery agent for every 363 residents; upscale Wellesley, by contrast, has one agent for every 3,063 residents. In Massachusetts, as elsewhere, this "painless" alternative to taxation is a sharply regressive way of raising revenue. Residents of Chelsea spent a staggering $915 per capita on lottery tickets last year, almost 8 percent of their income. Residents of Lincoln, an affluent suburb, spent only $30 per person, one-tenth of 1 percent of their income.

For growing numbers of people, playing the lottery is not the free, voluntary choice its promoters claim. Instant games such as scratch tickets and Keno (a video numbers game with drawings every five minutes), now the biggest money-makers for the lottery, are a leading cause of compulsive gambling, rivaling casinos and racetracks. Swelling the ranks of Gamblers Anonymous are lottery addicts, like the man who scratched $1,500 worth of tickets per day, exhausted his retirement savings and ran up debt on eleven credit cards.

Meanwhile, the state has grown as addicted to the lottery as its problem gamblers. Lottery proceeds now account for 13 percent of state revenues in Massachusetts, making radical change all but unthinkable. No politician, however troubled by the lottery's harmful effects, would dare raise taxes or cut spending sufficiently to offset the revenue the lottery brings in.

With states hooked on the money, they have no choice but to   13
continue to bombard their citizens, especially the most vulnerable
ones, with a message at odds with the ethic of work, sacrifice and
moral responsibility that sustains democratic life. This civic corruption is the gravest harm that lotteries bring. It degrades the
public realm by casting the government as the purveyor of a perverse civic education. To keep the money flowing, state governments across America must now use their authority and influence
not to cultivate civic virtue but to peddle false hope. They must
persuade their citizens that with a little luck they can escape the
world of work to which only misfortune consigns them.

READING FOR MEANING

This section presents three activities that will help you reread Sandel's position paper with a critical eye. Done in sequence, these activities lead you from a
basic understanding of the selection to a more personal response to it and finally
to an analysis that deepens your understanding and critical thinking about what
you are reading.

Read to Comprehend

Reread the selection, and write a few sentences briefly explaining what you
think Sandel's purpose is for writing this essay. What does he seem to want to
accomplish with his readers? Then list the main reasons he gives to support his
position (look especially in paragraphs 6, 8, 9, and 11–13). Also make a list of any
words you do not understand—for example, *insidious* (paragraph 2), *enervates* (2),
proliferation (3), *degrades* (13), *consigns* (13). Look up their meanings in a dictionary
to see which definition best fits the context.

To expand your understanding of this reading, you might use one or more
of the following critical reading strategies that are explained and illustrated in
Appendix 1: *annotating, previewing, outlining,* and *summarizing.*

Read to Respond

Write several paragraphs exploring your initial thoughts and feelings about
"Bad Bet." Focus on anything that stands out for you, perhaps because it resonates with your own experience or because you find a statement puzzling.

You might consider writing about

- Sandel's charge of hypocrisy in paragraphs 6–8, defining *hypocrisy* and
  explaining who is being hypocritical and in what ways.

- how you feel about the government's role in legislating morality, whether it
  be lotteries or other forms of "sin."

- your own or your friends' or family's participation in a state lottery, in light of Sandel's argument.

- Sandel's charge that lotteries deliberately target the working class, the poor, and minorities.

To develop your response to Sandel's position argument, you might use one or more of the following critical reading strategies that are explained and illustrated in Appendix 1: *questioning to understand and remember, contextualizing, and looking for patterns of opposition.*

Reading to Analyze Underlying Assumptions

Write several paragraphs exploring one or more of the assumptions, values, and beliefs underlying Sandel's position paper. As you write, explain how the assumptions are reflected in the text, as well as what you now think of them (and perhaps of your own assumptions) after rereading the selection with a critical eye.

You might consider writing about

- the assumption underlying the Chicago billboard's claim, "This could be your ticket out" (paragraph 9).

- the belief about the role of government implied in Sandel's assertion that state governments should attempt to define civic virtue and sustain democratic life by encouraging an "ethic of work, sacrifice and moral responsibility" (13).

- the belief about "civic corruption" and citizens' habits implied by the statement, "the new habits may be too pervasive to reverse" (2).

- the implications of some of Sandel's more "loaded" words, such as *secrecy* (1), *vice* (4), *morality* (4), *sin* (7), *addicts* (11), and *corruption* (13).

To probe assumptions more deeply, you might use one or more of the following critical reading strategies that are explained and illustrated in Appendix 1: *reflecting on challenges to your beliefs and values, evaluating the logic of an argument, recognizing emotional manipulation,* and *judging the writer's credibility.*

READING LIKE A WRITER
PRESENTING THE ISSUE

Every position paper begins with an issue. Consequently, in planning and drafting a position paper, one of the first questions a writer must answer is how much readers know about the issue. If they are very familiar with the issue, the writer may need to tell them very little about it. If they are unfamiliar with the issue, however, the writer may need to present it in great detail. Whether they are familiar or unfamiliar with the issue, readers may benefit from knowing about its history. They may also appreciate the writer's speculations about the larger social significance of the issue and even the likely immediate personal importance of it to themselves. Writers need not—and probably should not—assume that readers will find an issue immediately engaging and worth their time to learn more about. Writers may therefore open a position paper not with a straightforward description of the issue, but with an interesting anecdote, arresting quotation, troubling fact, doomsday scenario, rhetorical question, or something else that is likely to engage readers' interest.

In addition, writers must address another important question: how to define the issue. Often, writers seek to redefine a familiar issue in order to convince readers to look at it in a new way. If they succeed, then they can argue to support the issue in their own terms, as they have redefined it. Sandel's position paper offers a good example of this strategy. Before he presents his own position or counterargues others' positions, he begins by defining the issue under debate in his own terms. In this case, Sandel wants the reader to see his argument against state lotteries in a very broad context, one that will bring in issues not only of morality and politics but also of the role of government in a democracy.

Analyze

1. *Reread* paragraphs 1 and 2, and *underline* key words connected to "political corruption" and "civic corruption." *Notice* the differences between these terms.

2. Then skim the essay noting ways Sandel develops the argument that lotteries promote or reflect "civic corruption."

Write

Write several sentences describing how Sandel defines the two kinds of corruption in paragraphs 1 and 2. Then *add a few sentences* explaining how, in subsequent paragraphs, Sandel develops his argument about "civic corruption." What issues do you expect Sandel to address, based on what he presents in these four paragraphs?

CONSIDERING IDEAS FOR YOUR OWN WRITING

Consider writing about a local civic issue related to Sandel's concern about "a turning away from public responsibilities" (2). Here are some possibilities: Should communities provide homeless people with free food and shelter? Should community growth be limited? Should height and design restrictions be placed on new commercial buildings? Should there be a police review board to handle complaints against the police? Should skateboarding be banned from all sidewalks? Should parents be held responsible legally and financially for crimes committed by their children under age eighteen? One major advantage of writing a position paper on a local civic issue is that you can gather information by researching the issue in local newspapers and talking with community leaders and residents.

STANLEY KURTZ

Point of No Return

> *Stanley Kurtz has a Ph.D. in social anthropology and has taught in the "great books" program at Harvard University and been a Dewey Prize Lecturer in the social sciences at the University of Chicago. A prominent conservative intellectual, he was formerly affiliated with the Hudson Institute and is currently a research fellow at Stanford University's Hoover Institution and a contributing editor at* National Review Online. *Kurtz's essays have also appeared in many other periodicals, including the* Wall Street Journal, *the* Weekly Standard, Commentary, *and the* Chronicle of Higher Education.
>
> *This essay was first published as part of an online debate about same-sex marriage that Kurtz conducted with Jonathan Rauch and others over a two-week period in 2001 at* National Review Online. *Dated August 3, 2001, it is the fourth exchange in the debate. (The online version available at < www.nationalreview.com/full _coverage/gay-marriage.shtml > contains links to the other exchanges by Rauch and Kurtz.) Rauch's response of August 6, 2001, "Who's More Worthy?" follows as the next reading in this chapter (p. 600). Note that this debate took place after Vermont became the first state to establish an official civil union policy for same-sex couples, a policy adopted by the legislature in response to a decision by the state supreme court. But the debate took place well before the events of 2003 and 2004, including the Massachusetts Supreme Court decision that led to the establishment of full marriage rights for gay and lesbian couples in that state, the efforts by San Francisco officials and other city governments to institute same-sex marriage on the local level, and the concerted attempts by opponents of same-sex marriage to amend the U.S. Constitution and a number of state constitutions (including that of Massachusetts) to limit marriage to male-female couples.*
>
> *As you read, notice that Kurtz refers several times to articles that others besides himself and Rauch have written on the topic of same-sex marriage. Think about Kurtz's values and beliefs about marriage as they are revealed in this essay. Do you share them, in part or in whole?*

I thank Jonathan Rauch for his thoughtful and courteous reply   1
to my two earlier pieces, "Love and Marriage," and "The Right Balance." I have long admired Rauch's command of this issue (and of other issues) and value this opportunity for an exchange.

Rauch, it seems to me, has missed my central point in "Love and   2
Marriage." It is true that marriage itself, and not merely women and children, domesticates men. But my point is that marriage is only able to do so by building upon the underlying dynamic of

male-female sexuality. Marriage does indeed invoke public expectations of fidelity and mutual support through ritual gestures like
weddings. But wedding or no, the public will not condemn a man
who sleeps around on another man, or who fails to support his
male partner financially. A wedding embodies and reinforces already
existing public sentiments about a man's responsibilities to a
woman; it cannot create such sentiments out of thin air.

In an elegant little essay, "I Do?," David Blankenhorn shows us   3
why weddings don't always do what they used to do. Blankenhorn
focuses on the vogue for ceremonies in which couples create their
own vows. In the old view, the vow existed prior to the couple, and
therefore embodied a set of public standards to which the couple
could be held accountable. But in a world of self-created vows, the
couple is prior to the promise, which can be made (or withdrawn)
at will.

Rauch wants to invent, not merely some vows, but a whole new   4
form of marriage (two actually—gay and lesbian), all the while
assuming that the standards and expectations of the most traditional
forms of heterosexual marriage will trail along for the ride. But
those expectations have been attenuated, even for many heterosexual marriages. And the very same people who now see marriage as
a subjective projection, rather than a shared social standard to
which to aspire, are the people who favor gay marriage, the idea of
which appeals to them precisely as a symbol of the infinite flexibility of social life. Rauch seems to be depending on the Left half of
the country to enact gay marriage, while assuming that the Right
half will enforce the traditional social expectations on gay couples.
Rauch's intentions are admirable, but this simply will not happen.

Supporters of gay marriage keep telling us that the sky will not   5
fall. What they do not understand is that, when it comes to marriage, the sky has already fallen. It is lying about our feet, and considerable effort will be required even to hoist it back a few yards
over our heads. The trouble with gay marriage is that it forecloses
that possibility. Personally, I neither seek, nor think possible, a
complete restoration of the traditional system—when the expectations for marriage were so powerful that homosexuals felt compelled to wed heterosexually.

But gay marriage is a surpassingly radical attack on the very   6
foundations of marriage itself. It detaches marriage from the distinctive dynamics of heterosexual sexuality, divorces marriage from
its intimate connection to the rearing of children, and opens the
way to the replacement of marriage by a series of infinitely flexible
contractual arrangements. (For more on this last point, see my
piece in the September 2000 issue of *Commentary*.) All this can

only destroy the finely woven web of social expectations upon which Rauch wishes to depend. As I argued in "Love and Marriage," for example, once marriage has been divorced from heterosexuality, it will be impossible to induce even a partial restoration of traditional courtship. (And by the way, this subversive effect on the sexual complementarity so integral to marriage will derive every bit as much from lesbian marriages as from gay male marriages.)

For Rauch, our increased tolerance for homosexuality is of but trivial significance—in comparison with the cultural changes of the sixties and seventies—in bringing about the current weakening of marriage. But the point is, our increased tolerance for homosexuality is inextricably bound up with the cultural changes of the sixties—and is by no means trivial in its effects. As the ultimate symbol of the detachment of sexuality from reproduction, homosexuality embodies the sixties ethos of sexual self-fulfillment. That, after all, is why it is such a hot-button issue in the culture wars. So changing social attitudes toward homosexuality cannot help but have a profound effect upon the social and moral significance of sexuality itself.

In the mainstream press, we hear often (and rightly so) from brilliant moderates like Jonathan Rauch. Yet radical gays—the writer Michael Bronski, for example—have argued at length (and correctly) that complete social equivalence between homosexuality and heterosexuality cannot help but undermine social restraints upon sexuality, thus ushering in the final triumph of the sixties ethos. Like Bronski, vast sections of the gay community support gay marriage, not on Rauch's "conservative" grounds, and not even simply as a road to social acceptance, but out of the entirely justified conviction that gay marriage will be a critical step in the undoing of marriage itself. These writings seldom find their way into the *Wall Street Journal,* yet they merit our attention.

Rauch claims that the effect of gay marriage on the larger institution is an empirical question. As it happens, we have some very important empirical evidence on the matter—all the more powerful because it was collected by a lesbian sociologist who writes as an advocate of gay marriage. That evidence paints a picture of gay marriage greatly at variance with Rauch's assurances.

Gretchen Stiers's 1999 study, *From This Day Forward,* makes it clear that while exceedingly few of even the most committed gay and lesbian couples believe that marriage will strengthen and stabilize their personal relationships, nearly half of those gays and lesbians who actually disdain traditional marriage (and even gay commitment ceremonies) will nonetheless get married. Why? For "the bennies"—the financial and legal benefits of marriage.

And as Stiers shows, many radical gays and lesbians who actually   11
yearn to see marriage abolished (and multiple sexual unions legit-
imized) intend to marry, not only as a way of securing benefits, but
as part of a self-conscious attempt to subvert the institution of
marriage from within.

Stiers's study was focused on the very most committed gay cou-   12
ples. Yet even in a sample artificially weighted with nearly every gay
male couple in Massachusetts who had gone through a commitment ceremony (and Stiers had to go out of her research protocol
just to find enough male couples to balance out the committed lesbian couples) nearly 20 percent of the men questioned did not
practice monogamy. Obviously, in a truly representative sample of
gay male couples, that number would be vastly higher. More significantly, a mere 10 percent of even these most committed gay men
mentioned monogamy as an important aspect of commitment
(necessarily meaning that even many of those men in the sample
who had undergone "union ceremonies" failed to identify fidelity
with commitment). And these, the very most committed gay male
couples, are theoretically the people who will be enforcing marital
norms on their gay male peers, and exemplifying modern marriage
for the nation. So concerns about the effects of gay marriage on the
social ideal of marital monogamy seem more than justified.

Rauch seems to think that if his cost-free portrait of gay marriage   13
turns out to be mistaken, we can simply call off the experiment. But
by then it will surely be too late. Such effects take years to play out,
decades more to measure, and even when measured, agreement on
the meaning of such data is nearly impossible to achieve. Just think
of the battle over the effects of day care. There is no such thing as an
experiment in gay marriage. Once legalized, the damage will have
been done, and reversal, if possible at all, would take decades.

Rauch persists in identifying federalism with variable practices   14
among the states. But federalism is actually a careful balancing of
national unity with state diversity. And as I argued in "The Right
Balance," federalism has always demanded national commonality
in the fundamental definition of marriage. The legal history of
marriage demonstrates what should in any case be obvious, that
traveling across country and finding out that you are no longer
married is an entirely different matter than working up a will or
taking a state bar exam. Imagine a married couple, where one
spouse is hospitalized after a car accident in another state, losing
visiting rights or the right to make medical decisions, because their
marriage isn't recognized in that state. If even what was once experienced as the horror of miscegenation could not stand against
that, how can we expect judges to sit still for it now?

Rauch appears to have abandoned his own and Andrew Sulli-   15
van's[1] legal arguments and now rests his assurances on the matter
of nationally imposed gay marriage upon a strictly political judgment. Naturally, at the moment, the Supreme Court would be
loathe to impose gay marriage. But just wait until the practice is
legalized in some state, or states, and the social and political chaos
begins. At that point, the Court will take the case, and could easily
go either way. (And that's just this Supreme Court. Remember,
we're talking about future Supreme Courts as well.) At the time,
the conventional wisdom was that the Supreme Court would turn
Bush v. Gore back to Florida. But the specter of a national crisis
goaded the Court into action.

So far as I can tell, Jonathan Rauch and Andrew Sullivan have   16
welcomed the imposition of civil unions upon the Vermont state
legislature by the Vermont state supreme court. Yet that action,
which pretended to find a mandate for gay marriage buried in the
state's constitution, was surely one of the most egregious viola-
tions of the principles of judicial restraint in this country's history.

The Federal Marriage Amendment not only guards against the   17
nationalization of gay marriage by judicial fiat, it also guards
against a state judiciary that has cast all democratic restraint to the
wind and has taken the right to define and regulate marriage out
of the hands of the people. Having broken faith with the principles
of democracy, the nation's judiciary has left the public with little
recourse.

The decision in Vermont was a direct result of a national cam-   18
paign by gay rights activists to make an end run around legislatures and impose gay marriage upon the country through the
courts. So far as I can tell, "conservative" advocates of gay marriage have been acting in concert with that campaign, not calling
it to account for its undemocratic excesses. And now we are told
to make DOMA[2] constitutional, which would do nothing to prevent judicial usurpations of democracy such as we saw in Vermont.

Anyone awake to this issue understands that there is already a   19
national culture war over the issue of gay marriage. The Federal

---

[1] *Andrew Sullivan* (b. 1963): a political and social commentator who is gay
and has written widely in support of same-sex marriage.

[2] *DOMA:* the Defense of Marriage Act, a federal law enacted in 1996 that
defines marriage as the union of a man and a woman and allows states to
refuse to recognize same-sex marriages performed in other states.

Marriage Amendment did not start this war. Judicial arrogance in Vermont did that. But as I have argued, the Federal Marriage Amendment, by balancing a national definition of marriage with at least the possibility of differential state-by-state benefits packages, might lead to a workable, if imperfect, solution to this intractable problem.

Despite my differences with both Jonathan Rauch and Andrew   20
Sullivan, I greatly admire them both for the brilliance, honor, and tenacity of their fight to legalize same-sex marriage. As I have said publicly, I personally do not see homosexuality as sinful, and do not wish to see a return to the fifties. This battle has an element of tragedy about it, for while I do not believe gay marriage will succeed in domesticating gay men, or even in entirely removing the stigma of homosexuality, I do believe that gay marriage would be received by a stigmatized group as a welcome sign of social approval. But I also believe that the price of that sign is too high—that gay marriage will be a major step in the further unstringing of our most fundamental—and most fundamentally threatened—social institution. And in the end, because we are all children first, gay marriage will hurt all of us far more than it will help.

READING FOR MEANING

This section presents three activities that will help you reread Kurtz's position paper with a critical eye. Done in sequence, these activities lead you from a basic understanding of the selection to a more personal response to it and finally to an analysis that deepens your understanding and critical thinking about what you are reading.

Read to Comprehend

Reread the selection, and write a few sentences briefly explaining Kurtz's position on gay marriage. Then list the main reasons he provides for opposing gay marriage (see, especially, paragraphs 2–5, 13, and 14). Also make a list of any words you do not understand—for example, *attenuated* (paragraph 4), *commonality* (14), *miscegenation* (14), *mandate* (16), *egregious* (16). Look up their meanings in a dictionary to see which definition best fits the context.

To expand your understanding of this reading, you might use one or more of the following critical reading strategies that are explained and illustrated in Appendix 1: *annotating, summarizing,* and *questioning to understand and remember.*

Read to Respond

Write several paragraphs exploring your initial thoughts and feelings about "Point of No Return." Focus on anything that stands out for you, perhaps because it resonates with your own experience or because you find a statement puzzling.

You might consider writing about

- your own definition of marriage and how it affects your response to this essay.

- your feelings about the role of a constitutional amendment to mandate that marriage can be only between a man and a woman.

- your own view of same-sex marriage.

- whether you agree with Kurtz that "when it comes to marriage, the sky has already fallen" (paragraph 5).

- Kurtz's assertion that the motive of "vast sections of the gay community" (8) and "many radical gays and lesbians" (11) in supporting same-sex marriage is actually to try to destroy marriage.

- Kurtz's assertion that the motive of the U.S. Supreme Court in overturning the Florida Supreme Court in *Bush v. Gore* was to prevent "a national crisis" (15).

To develop your response to Kurtz's position argument, you might use one or more of the following critical reading strategies that are explained and illustrated in Appendix 1: *contextualizing, looking for patterns of opposition,* and *recognizing emotional manipulation.*

Read to Analyze Underlying Assumptions

Write several paragraphs exploring one or more of the assumptions, values, and beliefs underlying Kurtz's position paper. As you write, explain how the assumptions are reflected in the text, as well as what you now think of them (and perhaps of your own assumptions) after rereading the selection with a critical eye.

You might consider writing about

- the assumption underlying Kurtz's assertion that "marriage itself, and not merely women and children, domesticates men" (paragraph 2).

- the assumption underlying Kurtz's belief that marriage is built on "the underlying dynamic of male-female sexuality" (2) and "the distinctive dynamics of heterosexual sexuality" (6).

- the value system implied by Kurtz's distress that gay couples—even those who ostensibly oppose marriage—would nevertheless marry to obtain "the financial and legal benefits of marriage" (10).

- Kurtz's assumption that even if same-sex marriage gains public acceptance, "the public will not condemn a man who sleeps around on another man" (2).

- the values underlying Kurtz's assertion that "once marriage has been divorced from heterosexuality, it will be impossible to induce even a partial restoration of traditional courtship" (6), perhaps following the link provided in the headnote to his "Love and Marriage" article to see how he defines "traditional courtship."

To probe assumptions more deeply, you might use one or more of the following critical reading strategies that are explained and illustrated in Appendix 1: *reflecting on challenges to your beliefs and values, evaluating the logic of an argument, performing a Toulmin analysis,* and *judging the writer's credibility.*

READING LIKE A WRITER
ESTABLISHING CREDIBILITY

To establish their credibility, writers of position papers try to show how knowledgeable they are about their subject. More importantly, they need to show that they share values and beliefs with their readers, thus finding common ground on which to build their argument. In the case of issues as controversial and emotional as gay marriage and an amendment to the Constitution, it is particularly important to project fairness and an unprejudiced approach. Kurtz makes several efforts to establish his credibility in "Point of No Return"—and as you reread the essay, you can judge whether or not he is successful.

Analyze

1. *Reread* the first and last paragraphs, and *notice* the language Kurtz uses to characterize his opponents.

2. Then *reread* paragraphs 9–12, where Kurtz uses the authority of another writer to buttress his position.

3. *Evaluate* the success of Kurtz's use of this particular authority to provide evidence for his position that gay and lesbian marriage would undermine the values he sees in heterosexual marriage.

Write

Write several sentences explaining what you have learned about establishing credibility from this activity. *Cite examples* from the reading. Then *add a few sentences* explaining whether you think Kurtz is successful in establishing his credibility and why.

A SPECIAL READING STRATEGY

Comparing and Contrasting Related Readings: Kurtz's "Point of No Return" and Rauch's "Who's More Worthy?"

Comparing and contrasting related readings is a special critical reading strategy useful both in reading for meaning and in reading like a writer. This strategy is particularly applicable when writers deal with exactly the same subject, as is the case in the position papers written by Stanley Kurtz (p. 590) and Jonathan Rauch (p. 600) on the debate over same-sex marriage. Although the debate between Kurtz and Rauch takes place in an online forum that includes other authors, they address each other's positions directly. As you compare and contrast the positions of Kurtz and Rauch, think about issues such as these:

- Compare and contrast the general rhetorical approach and tone each writer takes to the other. In considering tone, you might look at the way each writer deploys the sentence strategies for counterarguing discussed on pages 639–40. Highlight these strategies to see whether they are effective in making the writer appear fair and reasonable. Also think about how your opinion of the credibility of the authors is affected by these strategies and the way Kurtz and Rauch address each other directly.

- Compare and contrast the fundamental beliefs about the function and purpose of marriage explored by Kurtz and Rauch. How do their beliefs help you understand the positions they take on same-sex marriage?

- Compare and contrast any differences you may find between Rauch's attitude toward same-sex marriage as a homosexual man and Kurtz's point of view as a heterosexual man.

- Compare and contrast the authors' different points of view on federalism. (You may want to do some research on federalism.)

See Appendix 1 for detailed guidelines on using the comparing and contrasting related readings strategy.

CONSIDERING IDEAS FOR YOUR OWN WRITING

In addition to the following essay by Rauch, "Who's More Worthy?" you might read some of the other exchanges at the Web site mentioned in the headnote, and then join the conversation on same-sex marriage by writing your own position paper. Or you might choose another gender- or sex-related subject, such as whether it is desirable to live together before marriage or save yourself for marriage; whether parental permission or a judge's consent should be required before a doctor treating minors can prescribe the "abortion pill" (such as RU-486) or perform an abortion; whether residents should be informed when a sex offender moves into their neighborhood; whether prostitution should be legalized or decriminalized; and whether the victim's name and sexual history should be kept secret by the media in cases of rape. You might also choose to write on other issues that have a legal or moral dimension, such as stem cell research, genetic engineering, cloning, medical marijuana, or the legalization or decriminalization of "recreational" drugs.

JONATHAN RAUCH

Who's More Worthy?

Jonathan Rauch (b. 1960) has been a local newspaper reporter for the Winston-Salem Journal, *a national correspondent for the* Economist, *and a columnist for the* National Journal. *His writings have appeared in the* Wall Street Journal, New Republic, Reason Online, Atlantic Monthly, *and* Slate. *Rauch has published several books, including* The Outnation: A Search for the Soul of Japan *(1992),* Kindly Inquisitors: The New Attacks on Free Thought *(1993),* Demosclerosis: The Silent Killer of American Government *(1994),* Government's End: Why Washington Stopped Working *(1999), and* Gay Marriage: Why It Is Good for Gays, Good for Straights, and Good for America *(2004). A writer-in-residence at the Brookings Institution, a Poynter Fellow, and a Japan Society Fellow, Rauch also received an award for his coverage of the European Parliament in the* Economist.

Rauch's essay "Who's More Worthy?" was first published on August 6, 2001, as part of an online debate about same-sex marriage conducted at National Review Online *<www.nationalreview.com/full_coverage/gay-marriage.shtml>. It is the fifth exchange in the debate. Rauch is responding to Stanley Kurtz's "Point of No Return" (p. 590), posted three days earlier. In the final paragraphs of his essay, Rauch refers to various ways same-sex marriage could be made legal: by congressional legislation, by "plebiscite" (a vote of state legislatures on a proposed amendment to the U.S. Constitution), or by "judicial fiat" (a Supreme Court decision in which the justices would rule that nothing in the Constitution prohibits same-sex marriage). Rauch also refers to a proposed constitutional amendment that Kurtz favors, the Federal Marriage Amendment, which defines marriage as a union between a man and a woman. In July 2004, another proposed constitutional amendment that would have prohibited same-sex marriage was defeated in the U.S. Senate.*

As you read, note how Rauch addresses Kurtz's points one by one, redefining and reshaping the argument according to his own values and beliefs.

Thanks to Stanley Kurtz for another provocative and richly argued article. Shall we drill a little deeper? If I read him correctly, his argument boils down to something like this: 1

1. Marriage is rooted essentially in "the underlying dynamic of male-female sexuality." Nothing else can sustain marriage.

2. As a result, it is simply impossible for same-sex (especially male-male) couples to be good marital citizens. They may get married, but they won't act married, and society won't treat them as married.

3. Because homosexuals will do a bad job of "exemplifying modern marriage for the nation" and marriage is in bad enough shape already, homosexuals should not be allowed to marry.

4. Allowing same-sex marriage anywhere in America at any time is effectively the same as mandating it everywhere forever. So same-sex marriage must never be tried anywhere, ever.

Or, to put it a bit coarsely: "I don't believe homosexuals can handle marriage responsibly. And they should never be allowed a chance to prove me wrong. Sorry, gay people, but that's life."

Kurtzism, as I'll take the liberty of calling this approach, gets four things wrong. It misanalyzes marriage. It misunderstands homosexuality. It sits crosswise with liberalism. And it traduces federalism. Other than that, no problem.

Start with Proposition 1. Kurtz argues that, whatever else marriage is about, ultimately and indispensably it's about "the underlying dynamic of male-female sexuality." I'm not sure exactly what this means beyond saying that marriage must be between a man and a woman, so I'm not sure how to address it specifically. Here is what I think marriage is indispensably about: the commitment to care for another person, for better or worse, in sickness and in health, till death do you part.

A marriage can and often does flourish long after the passion has faded, long after the children have gone, and (yes) long after infidelity; it can flourish without children and even without sex. A marriage is a real marriage as long as the spouses continue to affirm that caring for and supporting and comforting each other is the most important task in their lives. A golden anniversary is not a great event because both spouses have held up their end of a "dynamic of male-female sexuality" but because 50 years of devotion is just about the noblest thing that human beings can achieve.

I can't prove I'm right and Kurtz is wrong. But I think my view is much closer to what people actually think their marriages are fundamentally about, and also, by the way, to what marriage should be fundamentally about. Most married people I know regard themselves as more or less equal partners in an intricate relationship whose essential ingredient is the lifelong caregiving contract. Obviously, they'd agree that male-female sexual dynamics play an important role in their marriage; but then, they're male-female couples, so they *would* say that. If you told them that marriage is fundamentally about (in Kurtz's words) "a man's responsibilities to a woman," rather than a person's responsibilities to a person, they'd look at you funny.

Why is Kurtz so reluctant to put commitment instead of sex roles at the center of marriage? Because, I suspect, he knows homosexuals can form commitments. To cut off this pass, he claims that in practice homosexuals too often won't form commitments (Proposition 2). Same-sex couples, or in any case male same-sex couples, won't act married, and society won't be bothered if they don't, so marriage will become a hollow shell.

I've explained why I believe that a world where everyone, straight and gay, can grow up aspiring to marry will be a world where gays and straights and marriage are all better off. Kurtz has explained why he thinks otherwise. All of that is well and good, but it only gets us so far, because the key questions are all empirical. How would married gay couples behave? How would married heterosexuals react? Unfortunately, we have no direct evidence. One can say that in Vermont, which has a civil-union law, "the institution of marriage has not collapsed," as the governor recently said. One can say that gay men (no one seems worried about lesbians not taking marriage seriously) represent probably 3 percent of the population, and that it seems a stretch to insist that the 97 percent will emulate the 3 percent. But none of that proves anything. Absent some actual experience with same-sex marriage, everything is conjecture.

Still, I think Kurtz's conjecture is based on a view of homosexuality that is both misguided and at least unintentionally demeaning. His article contains this arresting phrase: "As the ultimate symbol of the detachment of sexuality from reproduction, homosexuality embodies the sixties ethos of sexual self-fulfillment." So there you are. My relationship with my partner Michael is about "sexual self-fulfillment," because, I guess, we can't have children. Let me gently but passionately say to Kurtz that this is an affront. It implies that a straight man's life partner is his wife, while a gay man's life partner is just his squeeze. Let me also gently but firmly instruct Kurtz on a point that I and other homosexuals are in a position to know something about. Our partners are not walking dildos and vibrators. Our partners are our companions, our soulmates, *our loves*.

I'm not familiar with the Stiers book he cites and I couldn't get it on deadline, so I can't comment on it. I can say, though, that I wouldn't be the least surprised if right now, in 2001, grown gay men and women often regard marriage as a novelty or a convenient benefits package. What does Kurtz expect? These are people who grew up knowing they could never marry, who have structured their whole lives outside of marriage, and who have of necessity built their relationships as alternatives to marriage.

I don't expect that homosexuals will all flock to the altar the day after marriage is legalized. You don't take a culture that has been defined forever by exclusion from marriage and expect it to

7

8

9

10

change overnight. I do think that, a few years after legalization, we'll see something new: A whole generation of homosexuals growing up knowing that they can marry, seeing successfully married gay couples out and about, and often being encouraged to marry by their parents and mentors. Making the closet culture the exception rather than the rule for young gay people was the work of one or maybe two generations. The shift to a normative marriage culture may happen just as fast.

I know, I know. Kurtz will simply insist that real, committed marriage will never be normative for homosexuals; gays just don't have that "dynamic of male-female sexuality" thing. Unfortunately, I don't think I can persuade him by telling him about all the gay people I know who have committed their enduring love and care to each other. I doubt I could persuade him even by telling him about all the men I know who have fed and comforted and carried their dying partners, and covered their partners with their bodies to keep them warm, and held their hands at the end and then sobbed and sobbed. Who is more fit to marry, the homosexual who comes home every night to wipe the vomit from the chin of his wasting partner, or the heterosexual who serves his first wife with divorce papers while she is in the hospital with cancer so that he can get on with marrying his second wife? Alas, I think I know what Kurtz would say.

Kurtz cites figures on gay men's fidelity and attitudes toward monogamy. There are lots of problems with these kinds of numbers, but the more interesting question is: Just what does Kurtz think this kind of data proves? Exactly how monogamous do homosexuals have to be in order to earn the right to marry? I'd have thought that being better than 80 percent faithful would be pretty darn good. Would 90 percent satisfy him? Maybe 98.2 percent? And if a group's average fidelity is the qualification for marriage, shouldn't Kurtz let lesbians marry right now? And why are homosexuals the only class of people who are not allowed to marry until they prove, in advance, that they'll be good marital citizens? Last time I checked, heterosexual men were allowed to take a fifth wife, no questions asked, even if they beat their first, abandoned their second, cheated on their third, and attended orgies with their fourth.

For centuries, homosexuals have been barred from marrying and even from having open relationships. The message has been: Furtive, underground sex is all homosexuals deserve. And now Kurtz is insisting (Proposition 3) that homosexuals can't wed because we're not as sexually well-behaved as married heterosexuals? While also insisting that, no matter how badly heterosexuals behave, their right to marry will go unquestioned? Really, the gall!

11

12

13

Forgive my ill temper on that point. I understand that, to Kurtz   14
and many other Americans, same-sex marriage seems a radical
concept, an abuse of the term "marriage." What I think Kurtz and
too many other opponents of gay marriage fail to appreciate is the
radicalism of telling millions of Americans that they can never
marry anybody they love. To be prohibited from taking a spouse is
not a minor inconvenience. It is a lacerating deprivation. Marriage, probably more even than voting and owning property and
having children, is *the* core element of aspiration to the good life.
Kurtz would deprive all homosexuals of any shot at it lest some of
them set a poor example. I think this is both inhumane and cuts
against liberalism's core principle, which is that people are to be
treated ends in themselves, not as means to some utilitarian social
end. I am grateful to Kurtz for leaving the door open to domestic-
partnership programs as a consolation prize; this is a good-
hearted gesture, and I accept it as such. But surely he recognizes
that domestic partnership is no substitute for matrimony. Surely,
indeed, that is his point in offering it.

Same-sex marriage is too important to be approached thought-   15
lessly. I'm glad that Kurtz is thinking as strenuously about the possible downsides as I am about the possible upsides. Where he veers
toward something like extremism is in his demand that homosexuals be denied any chance to prove his conjectures wrong (Proposition 4). "There is no such thing as an experiment in gay marriage,"
he says. "Rauch seems to think that if his cost-free portrait of gay
marriage turns out to be mistaken, we can simply call off the experiment. But by then it will surely be too late. Such effects take years to
play out, decades more to measure, and even when measured, agreement on the meaning of such data is nearly impossible to achieve."

But pretty nearly all major social-policy reforms play out over   16
years and decades, and agreement on how to measure the results is
never complete; Kurtz might just as well say that no state should
be allowed to try welfare reform or charter schools or a "living
wage" because the effects take years to play out, decades to measure, etc. The whole point of federalism is to allow states to try
reforms that *might not work,* and to allow states' voters—not me or
Stanley Kurtz—to decide for themselves what counts as working.
In rejecting this principle root and branch, Kurtz emerges as a radical enemy not just of same-sex marriage but of federalism itself.

I don't have much new to say about his peculiar claim that, once   17
any state adopts same-sex marriage, every other state will have to
follow, because Kurtz doesn't have anything new to say defending
it. He simply re-asserts it. "Imagine a married couple, where one
spouse is hospitalized after a car accident in another state, losing

visiting rights or the right to make medical decisions, because their marriage isn't recognized in that state," he says, as if the situation is obviously untenable. OK, I've imagined it. That kind of arrangement would be perfectly manageable. Gay spouses in a state with same-sex marriage would understand that they will need a medical power of attorney that's valid out-of-state. None of these complexities is remotely thorny enough to force any state to recognize same-sex marriage against its will. It seems to me that what Kurtz really fears is that one state will adopt same-sex marriage and others will look at it and say, "Actually, that doesn't seem so bad—pretty good, even. We don't mind recognizing it even if we don't adopt it ourselves." What he really fears, in other words, is not a disastrous state experiment but a successful one.

Again Kurtz asserts that federal judges will high-handedly impose one state's same-sex marriages on all the others. Again I say that there is—just as he says—plenty of room in the law for determined judges to decide this legal issue either way, but that any sane Supreme Court will be determined not to impose same-sex marriage on an unwilling nation. And if undemocratic judicial fiat is what worries Kurtz, why does he greet with silence my suggestion that a simple constitutional amendment—far easier to pass than the one he supports—would solve the problem?

18

But all of this stuff about states' being "forced" to accept same-sex marriage is a red herring. Kurtz makes it clear that he is no happier if a state adopts same-sex marriage by legislation or plebiscite than by judicial fiat. His proposed constitutional amendment accordingly strips states, and not just judges, of the power to permit same-sex marriage, even if everybody in some state wants to try it. What I suspect Kurtz really knows and fears is that as more homosexuals form devoted and visible unions, and as more of the public accepts and honors those unions, same-sex marriage will seem ever less strange and radical, and ever more in harmony with Americans' core values—which it is. Although he fears that same-sex marriage will come to pass over the public's objections, he fears even more that it will come to pass with the public's assent.

19

READING FOR MEANING

This section presents three activities that will help you reread Rauch's position paper with a critical eye. Done in sequence, these activities lead you from a basic understanding of the selection to a more personal response to it and finally to an analysis that deepens your understanding and critical thinking about what you are reading.

Read to Comprehend

Reread the selection, and write a few sentences briefly explaining how Rauch addresses each of the issues introduced in paragraph 2, issues he believes Kurtz gets "wrong." Also make a list of any words you do not understand—for example, *traduces* (paragraph 2), *federalism* (2), *emulate* (7), *conjecture* (7), *demeaning* (8), *affront* (8), *lacerating* (14). Look up their meanings in a dictionary to see which definition best fits the context.

To expand your understanding of this reading, you might use one or more of the following critical reading strategies that are explained and illustrated in Appendix 1: *annotating, outlining, summarizing,* and *synthesizing.*

Read to Respond

Write several paragraphs exploring your initial thoughts and feelings about "Who's More Worthy?" Focus on anything that stands out for you, perhaps because it resonates with your own experience or because you find a statement puzzling.

You might consider writing about

- the effect on you of the tone of Rauch's argument, as exemplified in such statements as "Shall we drill a little deeper?" (paragraph 1), "Kurtzism, as I'll take the liberty of calling this approach, gets four things wrong" (2), "this is an affront" (8), "Really, the gall!" (13), and "Forgive my ill temper on that point" (14).

- your response to the idea that marriage is "indispensably" about *either* " 'the underlying dynamic of male-female sexuality' " *or* "the commitment to care for another person, for better or worse, in sickness and in health, till death do you part" (3).

- your response to Rauch's argument that giving gay marriage a try is similar to doing so for other innovations such as welfare reform or charter schools.

To develop your response to Rauch's position argument, you might use one or both of the following critical reading strategies that are explained and illustrated in Appendix 1: *contextualizing* and *looking for patterns of opposition.*

Read to Analyze Underlying Assumptions

Write several paragraphs exploring one or more of the assumptions, values, and beliefs underlying Rauch's position paper. As you write, explain how the assumptions are reflected in the text, as well as what you now think of them (and perhaps of your own assumptions) after rereading the selection with a critical eye.

You might consider writing about

- the assumption underlying the notion that "marriage is fundamentally about (in Kurtz's words) 'a man's responsibilities to a woman' " (paragraph 5).

- the assumption of both authors that underlies Kurtz's statement, quoted by Rauch: " 'As the ultimate symbol of the detachment of sexuality from reproduction, homosexuality embodies the sixties ethos of sexual self-fulfillment' " (8).

- the fundamental differences in the two writers' value systems that Rauch says is the reason he will never be able to persuade Kurtz "by telling him about all the gay people I know who have committed their enduring love and care to each other" (11).

- the values implicit in Rauch's assertions that "be[ing] prohibited from taking a spouse is not a minor inconvenience. It is a lacerating deprivation" and that "[m]arriage, probably more even than voting and owning property and having children, is *the* core element of aspiration to the good life" (14).

- Rauch's assumption that if same-sex marriage is legalized, within one or two generations it will become the norm for young gay people and something "encouraged . . . by their parents and mentors" (10).

- Rauch's assumption that what Kurtz really fears is not that gay marriage will be a failure as a social experiment but that it will be a success (17–19).

To probe assumptions more deeply, you might use one or more of the following critical reading strategies that are explained and illustrated in Appendix 1: *reflecting on challenges to your beliefs and values, evaluating the logic of an argument, recognizing emotional manipulation,* and *judging the writer's credibility.*

READING LIKE A WRITER
ARGUING DIRECTLY FOR THE POSITION

Central to creating a successful position paper is the development of a strong argument in support of the writer's position on the issue. The writer may effectively counterargue readers' or opponents' questions, objections, and opposing positions, but that does not complete the argument. Readers also want to know in positive terms why the writer holds his or her particular position and what sort of reasoned argument the writer can devise. In brief, readers expect reasons and support.

Rauch's essay shows how writers of position papers make use of several strategies to support their reasons. Although he bases his argument on the points Kurtz makes, addressing each of them in turn, Rauch also uses strategies to support his own argument.

Analyze

1. *Reread* the following groups of paragraphs, looking for examples of the strategies Rauch uses to support his reasons: defining key terms (paragraphs

3, 5, and 13), reporting on or speculating about results (4, 8–10, 14, 17, and 18), citing statistics (7 and 12), citing authorities (7), giving examples (8, 10–12, and 17), setting up comparisons or contrasts (3–8, 10–12, 14, 17, and 19), and creating analogies (8 and 9).

2. *Select two* of these strategies to analyze and evaluate, and *look closely* at the relevant paragraphs to see how Rauch uses each strategy. *Make notes* in the margin about how he develops the strategy. What kinds of details does he include, and what sorts of sentences does he rely on?

3. *Evaluate* how effectively Rauch uses each strategy to support his reasons. What is most and least convincing about the support? What does it contribute to the overall argument?

Write

Write several sentences explaining Rauch's use of the two strategies you analyzed. *Support* your explanation with details from the paragraphs. Then *add a few sentences* evaluating how successfully Rauch uses the strategies.

CONSIDERING IDEAS FOR YOUR OWN WRITING

Consider responding, as Rauch does, to an argument with which you disagree. The argument could be on almost any subject covered in a magazine, newspaper, book, or Web site. First research the topic to make sure you have enough information to argue credibly. Then carefully deconstruct your opponent's argument and address each point with which you disagree, making sure to support your own points with reasons and evidence.

RANDALL KENNEDY

You Can't Judge a Crook by His Color

Randall Kennedy (b. 1954) is a law professor at Harvard University Law School. In 1983 and 1984, he was a law clerk for Supreme Court Justice Thurgood Marshall. Kennedy writes occasionally for general publications such as Time, *the* New Republic, Boston Globe, *and* Wall Street Journal. *He has also written* Race, Crime, and the Law *(1997), which won the 1998 Robert F. Kennedy Book Award, and* Interracial Intimacies: Sex, Marriage, Identity, and Adoption *(2002). His latest book* Nigger: The Strange Career of a Troublesome Word *(2002) "deconstructs" this charged word in American culture. His honors include election to the American Academy of Arts and Sciences and an honorary degree from Haverford College.*

Kennedy wrote the following position paper for the New Republic *in 1999. In it he addresses the controversial issue of racial profiling, a law-enforcement strategy that relies on a suspect's race as a reason to question, search, or arrest that person. A lawyer, Kennedy is interested in the legal as well as the social and moral implications of racial profiling, and he fully reviews the opposing position on this important current issue. In fact, readers must wait for several paragraphs to discover Kennedy's position, which may come as something of a surprise following his respectful presentation of the opposing position.*

Before you read, reflect on whether you have ever been stopped by the police when you were not doing anything illegal. If so, why do you think you were stopped? What happened? What was your reaction at the time? How did it influence your attitude toward police officers and toward law enforcement in general?

As you read, be patient with Kennedy's careful, unhurried consideration of many aspects of this explosive issue. Because he has thought and written about racial profiling for several years, you are in the hands of a respected expert who is not going to oversimplify a complex issue. Be assured that he is writing not for fellow legal scholars but for readers like you.

In Kansas City, a Drug Enforcement Administration officer stops and questions a young man who has just stepped off a flight from Los Angeles. The officer has focused on this man because intelligence reports indicate that black gangs in L.A. are flooding the Kansas City area with illegal drugs. Young, toughly dressed, and appearing nervous, he paid for his ticket in cash, checked no luggage, brought two carry-on bags, and made a beeline for a taxi when he arrived. Oh, and one other thing: The young man is black. When asked why he decided to question this man, the officer declares that he considered race, along with other factors, because doing so helps him allocate limited time and resources efficiently.

Should we applaud the officer's conduct? Permit it? Prohibit it? This is not a hypothetical example. Encounters like this take place every day, all over the country, as police battle street crime, drug trafficking, and illegal immigration. And this particular case study happens to be the real-life scenario presented in a federal lawsuit of the early '90s, *United States v. Weaver,* in which the 8th U.S. Circuit Court of Appeals upheld the constitutionality of the officer's action.

"Large groups of our citizens," the court declared, "should not be regarded by law enforcement officers as presumptively criminal based upon their race." The court went on to say, however, that "facts are not to be ignored simply because they may be unpleasant." According to the court, the circumstances were such that the young man's race, considered in conjunction with other signals, was a legitimate factor in the decision to approach and ultimately detain him. "We wish it were otherwise," the court maintained, "but we take the facts as they are presented to us, not as we would like them to be." Other courts have agreed that the Constitution does not prohibit police from considering race, as long as they do so for bona fide purposes of law enforcement (not racial harassment) and as long as it is only one of several factors.

These decisions have been welcome news to the many law enforcement officials who consider what has come to be known as racial profiling an essential weapon in the war on crime. They maintain that, in areas where young African American males commit a disproportionate number of the street crimes, the cops are justified in scrutinizing that sector of the population more closely than others—just as they are generally justified in scrutinizing men more closely than they do women.

As Bernard Parks, chief of the Los Angeles Police Department, explained to Jeffrey Goldberg of *The New York Times Magazine:* "We have an issue of violent crime against jewelry salespeople. . . . The predominant suspects are Colombians. We don't find Mexican Americans, or blacks, or other immigrants. It's a collection of several hundred Colombians who commit this crime. If you see six in a car in front of the Jewelry Mart, and they're waiting and watching people with briefcases, should we play the percentages and follow them? It's common sense."

Cops like Parks say that racial profiling is a sensible, statistically based tool. Profiling lowers the cost of obtaining and processing crime information, which in turn lowers the overall cost of doing the business of policing. And the fact that a number of cops who support racial profiling are black, including Parks, buttresses claims

that the practice isn't motivated by bigotry. Indeed, these police officers note that racial profiling is race-*neutral* in that it can be applied to persons of all races, depending on the circumstances. In predominantly black neighborhoods in which white people stick out (as potential drug customers or racist hooligans, for example), whiteness can become part of a profile. In the southwestern United States, where Latinos often traffic in illegal immigrants, apparent Latin American ancestry can become part of a profile.

But the defenders of racial profiling are wrong. Ever since the Black and Latino Caucus of the New Jersey Legislature held a series of hearings, complete with testimony from victims of what they claimed was the New Jersey state police force's overly aggressive racial profiling, the air has been thick with public denunciations of the practice. In June 1999, at a forum organized by the Justice Department on racial problems in law enforcement, President Clinton condemned racial profiling as a "morally indefensible, deeply corrosive practice." Vice President Al Gore has promised that, if he is elected president, he will see to it that the first civil rights act of the new century would end racial profiling. His rival for the Democratic nomination, Bill Bradley, has countered that Gore should prepare an executive order and ask the president to sign it *now*.   7

Unfortunately, though, many who condemn racial profiling do so without really thinking the issue through. One common complaint is that using race (say, blackness) as one factor in selecting surveillance targets is fundamentally racist. But selectivity of this sort can be defended on nonracist grounds. "There is nothing more painful to me at this stage in my life," Jesse Jackson said in 1993, "than to walk down the street and hear footsteps and start to think about robbery and then look around and see somebody white and feel relieved." Jackson was relieved not because he dislikes black people, but because he estimated that he stood a somewhat greater risk of being robbed by a black person than by a white person. Statistics confirm that African Americans—particularly young black men—commit a dramatically disproportionate share of street crime in the United States. This is a sociological fact, not a figment of a racist media (or police) imagination. In recent years, victims report blacks as perpetrators of around 25 percent of violent crimes, although blacks constitute only about 12 percent of the nation's population.   8

So, if racial profiling isn't bigoted, and if the empirical claim upon which the practice rests is sound, why is it wrong?   9

Racial distinctions are and should be different from other lines of social stratification. That is why, since the civil rights revolution of the 1960s, courts have typically ruled—based on the 14th Amendment's equal protection clause—that mere reasonableness   10 is an insufficient justification for officials to discriminate on racial grounds. In such cases, courts have generally insisted on applying "strict scrutiny"—the most intense level of judicial review—to government actions. Under this tough standard, the use of race in governmental decision making may be upheld only if it serves a compelling government objective and only if it is "narrowly tailored" to advance that objective.

A disturbing feature of this debate is that many people, includ- 11 ing judges, are suggesting that decisions based on racial distinctions do not constitute unlawful racial discrimination—as long as race is not the only reason a person was treated objectionably. The court that upheld the DEA agent's action at the Kansas City airport, for instance, declined to describe it as racially discriminatory and thus evaded strict scrutiny.

But racially discriminatory decisions typically stem from mixed 12 motives. For example, an employer who prefers white candidates to black candidates—except for those black candidates with supe- rior experience and test scores—is engaging in racial discrimina- tion, even though race is not the only factor he considers (since he selects black superstars). In some cases, race is a marginal factor; in others it is the only factor. The distinction may have a bearing on the moral or logical justification, but taking race into account at all means engaging in discrimination.

Because both law and morality discourage racial discrimina- 13 tion, proponents should persuade the public that racial profiling is justifiable. Instead, they frequently neglect its costs and mini- mize the extent to which it adds to the resentment blacks feel toward the law enforcement establishment. When O. J. Simpson was acquitted, many recognized the danger of a large sector of Americans feeling cynical and angry toward the system. Such alienation creates witnesses who fail to cooperate with police, cit- izens who view prosecutors as the enemy, lawyers who disdain the rules they have sworn to uphold, and jurors who yearn to get even with a system that has, in their eyes, consistently mistreated them. Racial profiling helps keep this pool of accumulated rage filled to the brim.

The courts have not been sufficiently mindful of this risk. In 14 rejecting a 1976 constitutional challenge that accused U.S. Border Patrol officers in California of selecting cars for inspection partly on the basis of drivers' apparent Mexican ancestry, the Supreme Court noted in part that, of the motorists passing the checkpoint, fewer than 1 percent were stopped. It also noted that, of the 820 vehicles inspected during the period in question, roughly 20 percent contained illegal aliens.

Justice William J. Brennan dissented, however, saying the Court   15
did not indicate the ancestral makeup of *all* the persons the Border Patrol stopped. It is likely that many of the innocent people
who were questioned were of apparent Mexican ancestry who then
had to prove their obedience to the law just because others of the
same ethnic background have broken laws in the past.

The practice of racial profiling undercuts a good idea that needs   16
more support from both society and the law: Individuals should
be judged by public authorities on the basis of their own conduct
and not on the basis of racial generalization. Race-dependent
policing retards the development of bias-free thinking; indeed, it
encourages the opposite.

What about the fact that in some communities people associated   17
with a given racial group commit a disproportionately large number of crimes? Our commitment to a just social order should
prompt us to end racial profiling even if the generalizations on
which the technique is based are supported by empirical evidence.
This is not as risky as it may sound. There are actually many contexts in which the law properly enjoins us to forswear playing
racial odds even when doing so would advance legitimate goals.

For example, public opinion surveys have established that   18
blacks distrust law enforcement more than whites. Thus, it would
be rational—and not necessarily racist—for a prosecutor to use
ethnic origin as a factor in excluding black potential jurors. Fortunately, the Supreme Court has outlawed racial discrimination of
this sort. And because demographics show that in the United
States, whites tend to live longer than blacks, it would be perfectly
rational for insurers to charge blacks higher life-insurance premiums. Fortunately, the law forbids that, too.

The point here is that racial equality, like all good things in life,   19
costs something. Politicians suggest that all Americans need to do
in order to attain racial justice is forswear bigotry. But they must
also demand equal treatment before the law even when unequal
treatment is defensible in the name of nonracist goals—and even
when their effort will be costly.

Since abandoning racial profiling would make policing more   20
expensive and perhaps less effective, those of us who oppose it
must advocate a responsible alternative. Mine is simply to spend
more money on other means of enforcement—and then spread
the cost on some nonracial basis. One way to do that would be to
hire more police officers. Another way would be to subject everyone to closer surveillance. A benefit of the second option would
be to acquaint more whites with the burden of police intrusion,
which might prompt more of them to insist on limiting police

power. As it stands now, the burden is unfairly placed on minorities—imposing on Mexican Americans, blacks, and others a special kind of tax for the war against illegal immigration, drugs, and other crimes. The racial element of that tax should be repealed.

I'm not saying that police should never be able to use race as a guideline. If a young white man with blue hair robs me, the police should certainly be able to use a description of the perpetrator's race. In this situation, though, whiteness is a trait linked to a particular person with respect to a particular incident. It is not a free-floating accusation that hovers over young white men practically all the time—which is the predicament young black men currently face. Nor am I saying that race could never be legitimately relied upon as a signal of increased danger. In an extraordinary circumstance in which plausible alternatives appear to be absent, officials might need to resort to racial profiling. This is a far cry from routine profiling that is subjected to little scrutiny.

Now that racial profiling is a hot issue, the prospects for policy change have improved. President Clinton directed federal law enforcement agencies to determine the extent to which their officers focus on individuals on the basis of race. The Customs Service is rethinking its practice of using ethnicity or nationality as a basis for selecting subjects for investigation. The Federal Aviation Administration has been re-evaluating its recommended security procedures; it wants the airlines to combat terrorism with computer profiling, which is purportedly less race-based than random checks by airport personnel. Unfortunately, though, a minefield of complexity lies beneath these options. Unless we understand the complexities, this opportunity will be wasted.

To protect ourselves against race-based policing requires no real confrontation with the status quo, because hardly anyone defends police surveillance triggered *solely* by race. Much of the talk about police "targeting" suspects on the basis of race is, in this sense, misguided and harmful. It diverts attention to a side issue. Another danger is the threat of demagoguery through oversimplification. When politicians talk about "racial profiling," we must insist that they define precisely what they mean. Evasion—putting off hard decisions under the guise of needing more information—is also a danger.

Even if routine racial profiling is prohibited, the practice will not cease quickly. An officer who makes a given decision partly on a racial basis is unlikely to acknowledge having done so, and supervisors and judges are loath to reject officers' statements. Nevertheless, it would be helpful for President Clinton to initiate a strict

21

22

23

24

anti-discrimination directive to send a signal to conscientious, law-abiding officers that there are certain criteria they ought not use.

To be sure, creating a norm that can't be fully enforced isn't 25 ideal, but it might encourage us all to work toward closing the gap between our laws and the conduct of public authorities. A new rule prohibiting racial profiling might be made to be broken, but it could set a new standard for legitimate government.

READING FOR MEANING

This section presents three activities that will help you reread Kennedy's position paper with a critical eye. Done in sequence, these activities lead you from a basic understanding of the selection to a more personal response to it and finally to an analysis that deepens your understanding and critical thinking about what you are reading.

Read to Comprehend

Reread the selection, and write a few sentences briefly explaining what you think Kennedy hopes to accomplish with his readers, well-informed citizens and policymakers. How does he want to influence their thinking about racial profiling? Then list the main reasons he opposes racial profiling (in paragraphs 10, 12, 13, and 16). Also make a list of any words you do not understand—for example, *hypothetical* (paragraph 2), *bona fide* (3), *surveillance* (8), *stratification* (10), *alienation* (13), *demagoguery* (23). Look up their meanings in a dictionary to see which definition best fits the context.

To expand your understanding of this reading, you might use one or more of the following critical reading strategies that are explained and illustrated in Appendix 1: *annotating, previewing, outlining,* and *summarizing.*

Read to Respond

Write several paragraphs exploring your initial thoughts and feelings about "You Can't Judge a Crook by His Color." Focus on anything that stands out for you, perhaps because it resonates with your own experience or because you find a statement puzzling.

You might consider writing about

- how the events of September 11, 2001, affect your reading of Kennedy's essay.

- a time when you were questioned by police or denied a job, speculating about why it happened in light of Kennedy's essay.

- how the drawing that accompanies the essay adds to your understanding or appreciation of Kennedy's argument.

To develop your response to Kennedy's position argument, you might use one or more of the following critical reading strategies that are explained and illustrated in Appendix 1: *paraphrasing, synthesizing, questioning to understand and remember,* and *contextualizing.*

Read to Analyze Underlying Assumptions

Write several paragraphs exploring one or more of the assumptions, values, and beliefs underlying Kennedy's position paper. As you write, explain how the assumptions are reflected in the text, as well as what you now think of them (and perhaps of your own assumptions) after rereading the selection with a critical eye.
You might consider writing about

- the values underlying the argument of some law enforcers that racial profiling is acceptable because it helps them "allocate limited time and resources efficiently" (paragraph 1), "is a sensible, statistically based tool," and "lowers the cost of obtaining and processing crime information, which in turn lowers the overall cost of doing the business of policing" (6).

- the assumptions and values underlying Kennedy's assertion that one reason to avoid racial profiling is that it creates resentment and alienation of witnesses, citizens, lawyers, and jurors (13).

- Kennedy's assumption that "racial equality, like all good things in life, costs something" (19).

- the assumptions and values underlying Kennedy's distinction between "an extraordinary circumstance" and "routine profiling" (21).

To probe assumptions more deeply, you might use one or more of the following critical reading strategies that are explained and illustrated in Appendix 1: *reflecting on challenges to your beliefs and values, looking for patterns of opposition,* and *evaluating the logic of an argument.*

READING LIKE A WRITER
ASSERTING A CLEAR, UNEQUIVOCAL POSITION

The writer's statement of position is the one sentence (or two or three) that lights up a position paper. Like moons and planets, the other sentences reflect the light of this position statement. Without it, the essay would be only a faint explanation of the debate on an issue, not a luminous argument for a position on it. Writers usually (but not always) assert their positions early in the argument. To keep readers in focus, they may reassert the position later in the essay and nearly always in the conclusion. Because readers must be able to understand readily and unambiguously just what the writer's position is, it should be stated clearly and without equivocation or waffling. That is not to say, however, that the position cannot be carefully qualified. Key terms must be precisely defined unless there is little likelihood that readers will differ over what the key terms mean. (As noted earlier in this chapter, the position statement is also the thesis statement in a position paper.)

Analyze

1. *Underline* Kennedy's statement, restatements, and qualifications of his position (you will find these sentences at the beginnings of paragraphs 7, 9, and 21 and in the third-from-last sentence of paragraph 21).

2. *Consider* whether the writer's position statements are clear and unequivocal. *Think about* where they are located in relation to the other parts of his argument.

Write

Write several sentences reporting what you have learned about how Kennedy asserts his position on the issue of racial profiling. Point to places where he restates and/or qualifies his position. What does each statement add to the others? Then *add a few sentences* evaluating how effectively Kennedy asserts his position for his particular readers. *Make judgments* about the clarity of the statements. What does Kennedy gain or lose by waiting so long to assert and reassert his position and to qualify it?

CONSIDERING IDEAS FOR YOUR OWN WRITING

Consider writing a position paper on a current law that you consider unfair or unjust. Here are some examples: Should the "three strikes" law that sends a criminal to jail for life on his or her third felony conviction remain in force or be modified? Should cancer patients be able to purchase marijuana legally for use in reducing their nausea and pain? Should term limits for elected officials be maintained or eliminated? Should motor vehicle laws be changed to make it more difficult for older drivers to renew their licenses?

BRENT KNUTSON

Auto Liberation

> *Brent Knutson wrote this position paper for his first-year college composition course. In it he addresses the issue of whether national speed limits are necessary on U.S. interstate highways and argues that, on the basis of his experience driving German autobahns, the speed limits are unnecessary. You will discover that Knutson asserts his position boldly and seems confident that he has a convincing argument to support it. Yet he applies much of his argument to counterarguing two particular objections he expects his readers will raise.*
>
> *Because Knutson's instructor asked him to cite sources formally, Knutson does so within the text of his position paper. These in-text citations refer to the published sources in the works-cited list at the end of his essay. Previous position papers in this chapter refer to sources informally within the text of the argument. They need not adopt a formal citation style like the one Knutson relies on because the conventions of newspaper and magazine publishing usually do not require it.*
>
> *Before you read, consider whether interstate highways in your part of the country could accommodate cars traveling at unlimited speeds. What problems do you see? What advantages might there be?*

The driver of a late-model Japanese sports car grins as he downshifts into third gear, blips the throttle with his heel, and releases the clutch. The car's rear end abruptly steps out in the wide, sweeping corner. He cranks the wheel, gathering the tail while eagerly stabbing the accelerator. The engine emits a metallic wail and barks angrily as the driver pulls the gearshift into fourth. Controlled pandemonium ensues as the secondary turbocharger engages and slams the driver's cranium against the headrest. With adrenaline thumping in his temples, he watches the needle on the speedometer sweep urgently toward the end of the scale. The driver then flicks the turn signal and blasts onto the interstate like a guided missile launching from a fighter jet. Today, he will not be late for work.

This scenario may seem a bit far-fetched, enough so that one might conclude that the driver is unnecessarily risking his life and the lives of other people on the road. But, on Germany's autobahns, people normally drive in excess of 80 miles per hour. Yet, these German superhighways are the safest in the world, filled with German drivers who are skilled, competent, and courteous. Using the autobahn system as a model, it is possible to examine whether national speed limits in the United States are necessary.

In fact, there is solid reasoning to support the claim that the   3
speed limits on U.S. interstate highways should be repealed. Not
only are American speed limits unnecessarily restrictive, but also
they infringe on the personal freedoms of American citizens.
Although there are locations where speed limits are appropriate, in
most cases these limits are arbitrarily imposed and sporadically
enforced. Modern automobiles are capable of traveling safely at
high speeds, and despite what the auto-insurance companies
would have us believe, speed does not kill. With proper training,
American drivers could be capable of driving "at speed" responsibly. Perhaps the most compelling reason to lift the national speed
limit is the simplest: driving fast is enjoyable.

Those opposed to lifting the national speed limit argue that   4
removing such restrictions would result in mayhem on the free-
ways; they're convinced that the countryside would be littered with
the carcasses of people who achieved terminal velocity only to
career off the road and explode into flames. Speed limit advocates
also argue that American drivers do not possess the skill or capacity
to drive at autobahn speeds. They contend that our driver-
education programs do not sufficiently prepare drivers to operate
vehicles and that obtaining a driver's license in most states is com-
ically easy; therefore, lifting the speed limit would be irresponsible.

The belief that a "no speed limit" highway system would result   5
in widespread carnage appears to be based more on fear than fact.
In 1987, Idaho Senator Steve Symms introduced legislation allowing states to raise speed limits on rural interstates to 65 miles
per hour (Csere, "Free"). Auto-insurance industry advocates responded that the accident rates would skyrocket and the number
of fatalities caused by auto accidents would increase accordingly.
Ironically, the Insurance Institute for Highway Safety (IIHS)
reported in July 1994 that "[o]nly 39,235 deaths resulting from
auto-related accidents were reported during 1992, the lowest
number since 1961. The institute found that 1992 was the fourth
year in which automotive deaths consistently declined" (qtd. in
"Highways" 51). Coincidentally, that decline in fatalities began two
years after many states raised interstate speed limits. Unfortunately,
the insurance industry has made it a habit to manipulate statistics
to suit its purposes. Later in the essay, I'll discuss evidence of this
propensity to deceive.

The contention that American drivers are not capable of dri-   6
ving safely at higher speeds has some merit. During a drive around
any city in this country, one is bound to witness numerous displays of behind-the-wheel carelessness. Because of poor driver-
education programs, as well as general apathy, Americans have

earned their high standing among the worst drivers in the world. Regarding our poor driving habits, automotive journalist Csaba Csere wrote in the April 1994 issue of *Car and Driver* that "American drivers choose their lanes randomly, much in the way cows inexplicably pick a patch of grass on which to graze" ("Drivers"). Fortunately, Americans' poor driving habits can be remedied. Through intensive driver-education programs, stringent licensing criteria, and public-service announcement campaigns, we can learn to drive more proficiently.

I recently returned from a four-year stay in Kaiserslautern, Germany. While there, I learned the pleasure of high-speed motoring. I was particularly impressed by the skill and discipline demonstrated by virtually all drivers traveling on the network of superhighways that make up the autobahn system. Germany's automobile regulatory laws are efficient, practical, and serve as an example for all countries to follow. It is striking that automobiles and driving fast are such integral components of German culture. Germans possess a passion for cars that is so contagious I didn't want to leave the country. German Chancellor Helmut Kohl summed up the German attitude regarding speed limits quite concisely: "For millions of people, a car is part of their personal freedom" (qtd. in Cote 12). 7

It is apparent in the United States that there are not many old, junky cars left on the road. The majority of vehicles operating in the United States are newer cars that have benefited from automotive engineering technology designed to increase the performance of the average vehicle. With the advent of independent suspension, electronic engine-management systems, passive restraints, and other technological improvements, modern automobiles are more capable than ever of traveling at high speeds safely. Indeed, the stringent safety requirements imposed by the Department of Transportation for vehicles sold in the United States ensure that our cars and trucks are the safest in the world. 8

One of the biggest fallacies perpetrated by the auto-insurance industry and car-fearing legislators is that "speed kills." Driving fast in itself, however, is not a hazard; speed combined with incompetence, alcohol, or hazardous conditions is dangerous. A skilled motor-vehicle operator traveling at 90 miles per hour, in light traffic, on a divided highway does not present a significant risk. Psychologist and compensation theorist G. J. Wilde "developed the RHT (risk homeostasis theory) to account for the apparent propensity of drivers to maintain a constant level of experienced accident risk" (qtd. in Jackson and Blackman 950). During a driving-simulation experiment in which he changed "non-motivational factors," Wilde determined that "[n]either speed 9 limit nor speeding fine had a significant impact on accident loss" (qtd. in Jackson and Blackman 956). Wilde's theory is convincing because he emphasizes the human tendency toward self-preservation. The impact of RHT could be far-reaching. As Wilde says, "The notion that drivers compensate fully for non-motivational safety countermeasures is significant because it is tantamount to the claim that most legislated safety measures will not permanently reduce the total population traffic accident loss" (qtd. in Jackson and Blackman 951). What this means is that drivers would not increase their personal risk by driving faster than their capabilities dictate, regardless of the speed limit.

Unfortunately, the IIHS doesn't see things this way. It has been busy manipulating statistics in an attempt to convince people that raising the interstate speed limits to 65 miles per hour has resulted in a veritable bloodbath. A headline in an edition of the IIHS status report states, "For Sixth Year in a Row, Deaths on U.S. Rural Interstates Are Much Higher Than Before Speed Limits Were Raised to 65 mph" (qtd. in Bedard 20). That claim is more than a little misleading because it does not compensate for the increased number of drivers on the road. Patrick Bedard explains: "What's the real conclusion? Rural interstate fatalities over the whole United States increased 19 percent between 1982 and 1992. But driving increased 44 percent. So the fatality rate is on a definite downward trend from 1.5 to 1.2 [percent]" (21). 10

One might ask what the insurance industry stands to gain by misrepresenting auto-fatality statistics. The real issue is what it stands to lose if speed limits are deregulated. The lifting of speed limits translates into fewer traffic citations issued by police. Fewer tickets means fewer points assessed on Americans' driving records, which would remove the insurance industry's primary tool for raising premiums. Needless to say, auto-insurance companies aren't thrilled about the prospect of less money in their coffers. 11

There is one lucid and persuasive argument for abolishing interstate speed limits: Driving fast is pure, unadulterated, rip-snortin' fun. I experienced the thrill of a lifetime behind the wheel of a 1992 Ford Mustang while chasing a BMW 525i on the Frankfurt–Mainz Autobahn. I remember my heart racing as I glanced at my speedometer, which read 120 mph. When I looked up, I saw the high-beam flash of headlights in my rearview mirror. Moments after I pulled into the right lane, a bloodred Ferrari F-40 passed in a surreal symphony of sound, color, and power, marked by the enraged howl of a finely tuned Italian motor running fullout. At that moment, I was acutely aware of every nerve ending in my body, as I experienced the automotive equivalent of Zen consciousness. It was 12 a sort of convergence of psyche and body that left me light-headed and giddy for ten minutes afterward. I was glad to discover that my reaction to driving fast was not unique:

> Few people can describe in words the mixture of sensations they experience, but for some the effect is so psychologically intense that no other experience can match it. . . . For some people the psychological effects are experienced as pure fear. For others, however, this basic emotional state is modified to give a sharply tingling experience which is perceived as intensely pleasurable. The fear, and the state of alertness are still there—but they have been mastered. (Marsh and Collett 179)

Repealing interstate speed limits is an objective that every driver should carefully consider. At a time when our elected officials are striving to control virtually every aspect of our lives, it is imperative that we fight to regain our freedom behind the wheel. Like Germans, Americans have a rich automotive culture and heritage. The automobile represents our ingenuity, determination, and independence. It is time to return control of the automobile to the driver, and "free us from our speed slavery once and for all" (Csere, "Free").

13

Works Cited

Bedard, Patrick. "Auto Insurance Figures Don't Lie, but Liars Figure." Editorial. *Car and Driver* Mar. 1994: 20–21.

Cote, Kevin. "Heartbrake on Autobahn." *Advertising Age* 26 Sept. 1994: 1+.

Csere, Csaba. "Drivers We Love to Hate." Editorial. *Car and Driver* Apr. 1994: 9.

———. "Free the Speed Slaves." Editorial. *Car and Driver* Nov. 1993: 9.

"Highways Become Safer." *Futurist* Jan.–Feb. 1994: 51–52.

Jackson, Jeremy S. H., and Roger Blackman. "A Driving Simulator Test of Wilde's Risk Homeostasis Theory." *Journal of Applied Psychology* 79.6 (1994): 950–58.

Marsh, Peter, and Peter Collett. *Driving Passion.* Winchester: Faber, 1987.

READING FOR MEANING

This section presents three activities that will help you reread Knutson's position paper with a critical eye. Done in sequence, these activities lead you from a basic understanding of the selection to a more personal response to it and finally to an analysis that deepens your understanding and critical thinking about what you are reading.

Read to Comprehend

Reread the selection, and write a few sentences briefly explaining Knutson's purpose for writing this position paper. What does he seem to assume about his readers, and how does he hope to influence them? Then list the main reasons he gives for his position (in paragraphs 8, 9, and 12). Also make a list of any words you do not understand—for example, *pandemonium* (paragraph 1), *adrenaline* (1), *carcasses* (4), *carnage* (5), *propensity* (5), *tantamount* (9). Look up their meanings in a dictionary to see which definition best fits the context.

To expand your understanding of this reading, you might use one or more of the following critical reading strategies that are explained and illustrated in Appendix 1: *annotating, outlining, summarizing,* and *synthesizing.*

Read to Respond

Write several paragraphs exploring your initial thoughts and feelings about "Auto Liberation." Focus on anything that stands out for you, perhaps because it resonates with your own experience or because you find a statement puzzling.

You might consider writing about

- how Knutson's account of a personal experience in paragraph 12 affects your response to his argument.

- an objection you have to Knutson's position, explaining your thinking and connecting it to some aspect of his argument.

- the driving conditions on highways in your area, considering whether highways could accommodate unlimited speeds and whether drivers could adjust to them.

- a particular driving experience of your own that supports or challenges Knutson's advocacy of unlimited speed limits on U.S. interstate highways.

To develop your response to Knutson's position argument, you might use one or more of the following critical reading strategies that are explained and illustrated in Appendix 1: *questioning to understand and remember, contextualizing,* and *exploring the significance of figurative language.*

Read to Analyze Underlying Assumptions

Write several paragraphs exploring one or more of the assumptions, values, and beliefs underlying Knutson's position paper. As you write, explain how the assumptions are reflected in the text, as well as what you now think of them (and perhaps of your own assumptions) after rereading the selection with a critical eye.

You might consider writing about

- the assumption underlying Knutson's main reason for increasing or banning speed limits: because driving fast is fun (paragraphs 3 and 12, especially).

- the assumption underlying Knutson's repeated use of the word "freedom" in paragraphs 3, 7, and 13, and the kind of freedom he is writing about.

- Knutson's assumptions about the motives of the auto-insurance industry.

To probe assumptions more deeply, you might use one or both of the following critical reading strategies that are explained and illustrated in Appendix 1: *recognizing emotional manipulation* and *judging the writer's credibility*.

READING LIKE A WRITER
COUNTERARGUING OBJECTIONS AND OPPOSING POSITIONS

One of the challenges—and pleasures—of writing position papers is that in nearly every writing situation writers recognize that some or many or even all of their readers will hold opposing positions or, if they have no position, will question or object to some part of the argument. Therefore, one of the special challenges of the position paper is to counterargue readers' positions, objections, or questions. To do so convincingly, writers must succeed with two basic moves: (1) demonstrate that they understand their readers' opposing positions and recognize their readers' objections or questions, and (2) concede or refute those positions, objections, or questions without exasperating, insulting, or harassing readers. To *concede* is to admit the usefulness or wisdom of readers' views. To *refute* is to attempt to argue that readers' views are limited or flawed. (For more on counterarguing, turn to the Reading like a Writer section following the Estrada selection, p. 578, and to Considering a Useful Sentence Strategy on p. 639.)

Knutson counterargues extensively. In fact, he organizes his entire argument around two particular objections he anticipates his readers will raise.

Analyze

1. In paragraph 4, *underline* the first sentence (up to the semicolon) and the second sentence. These sentences introduce the two (interrelated) reader objections that Knutson counterargues throughout his essay. In thinking about his readers, he seems to assume that his argument cannot succeed unless he convincingly refutes these two objections.

2. *Reread* paragraphs 5, 8, 10, and 11, where Knutson attempts to counterargue the "mayhem" objection (*mayhem* can mean both "permanent crippling or disfigurement" and "disorder or violence"). *Make notes* in the margins about what strategies Knutson deploys, whether he only refutes and never concedes, and what his attitude seems to be toward the Insurance Institute for Highway Safety.

3. *Reread* paragraphs 6, 7, and 9, where Knutson attempts to counterargue the "lack of skill" objection. *Make notes* in the margins about what strategies Knutson deploys, noticing where he refutes and where he concedes.

Write

Write several sentences explaining what you have learned about how Knutson counterargues. *Give examples* from the reading. Then *add a few sentences* evaluating how convincingly Knutson counterargues. What do you find most or least convincing in his counterargument—and why?

A SPECIAL READING STRATEGY

Evaluating the Logic of an Argument

To evaluate the logic of an argument, apply the ABC test by asking yourself three basic questions:

A. How *appropriate* is the support for each reason offered?

B. How *believable* is the support?

C. How *consistent and complete* is the overall argument?

Such an evaluation requires a comprehensive and thoughtful critical reading, but your efforts will help you understand more fully what makes a position paper successful. Follow the detailed guidelines for evaluating the logic of an argument in Appendix 1. There you will find definitions and explanations (pp. 675–79) as well as an illustration based on an excerpt from a famous essay by Martin Luther King Jr. (p. 678).

CONSIDERING IDEAS FOR YOUR OWN WRITING

Consider the cultural and economic practices of other countries that might be adopted in the United States. Here are some examples: Should we legislate national health care, as in Germany, Canada, and England? Should we have a national curriculum in all schools or ban students from wearing head scarves, as in France? Should we follow Sweden's lead and give new parents a paid year off from work immediately following the birth of a child? Should we have a nationwide system of preschool education based on the one in France? Should required secondary education end at our current grade 10, as in Germany? Should competitive sports programs be transferred from public schools to voluntary programs sponsored by town or city sports organizations, as in Italy? Should the price of gasoline more closely reflect the costs of maintaining and policing roads and highways and cleaning the air from smog created by cars and trucks, as in England and Japan? Should our tax system be more progressive, as in Germany? Should all public school students study one other language for at least ten years, as in Norway and Sweden?

JESSICA STATSKY

Children Need to Play, Not Compete

> *Jessica Statsky was a college student when she wrote this position paper in which she takes the position that organized sports are not good for children between the ages of six and twelve. Before you read, recall your own experiences as an elementary school student playing competitive sports, either in or out of school. If you were not actively involved yourself, did you know anyone who was? Looking back, do you recall whether winning was unduly emphasized? What value was placed on having a good time? On learning to get along with others? On developing athletic skills and confidence?*
>
> *As you read, notice how Statsky supports the reasons for her position and how she handles readers' likely objections to her argument. Also pay attention to the visible cues Statsky provides to guide you through her argument step by step.*
>
> *The other readings in this chapter are followed by reading and writing activities. Following this reading, however, you are on your own to decide how to read for meaning and read like a writer.*

Over the past several decades, organized sports for children have increased dramatically in the United States. And though many adults regard Little League Baseball and Peewee Football as a basic part of childhood, the games are not always joyous ones. When overzealous parents and coaches impose adult standards on children's sports, the result can be activities that are neither satisfying nor beneficial to children.

I am concerned about all organized sports activities for children between the ages of six and twelve. The damage I see results from noncontact as well as contact sports, from sports organized locally to those organized nationally. Highly organized competitive sports such as Peewee Football and Little League Baseball are too often played to adult standards, which are developmentally inappropriate for children and can be both physically and psychologically harmful. Furthermore, because they eliminate many children from organized sports before they are ready to compete, they are actually counterproductive for developing either future players or fans. Finally, because they emphasize competition and winning, they unfortunately provide occasions for some parents and coaches to place their own fantasies and needs ahead of children's welfare.

One readily understandable danger of overly competitive sports is that they entice children into physical actions that are bad for growing bodies. Although the official *Little League Online* Web site acknowledges that children do risk injury playing baseball, the league insists that severe injuries are infrequent, "far less than the risk of riding a skateboard, a bicycle, or even the school bus" ("What about My Child"). Nevertheless, Leonard Koppett in *Sports Illusion, Sports Reality* claims that a twelve-year-old trying to throw a curve ball, for example, may put abnormal strain on developing arm and shoulder muscles, sometimes resulting in life-long injuries (294). Contact sports like football can be even more hazardous. Thomas Tutko, a psychology professor at San Jose State University and coauthor of the book *Winning Is Everything and Other American Myths,* writes:

> I am strongly opposed to young kids playing tackle foot-ball. It is not the right stage of development for them to be taught to crash into other kids. Kids under the age of four-teen are not by nature physical. Their main concern is self-preservation. They don't want to meet head on and slam into each other. But tackle football absolutely requires that they try to hit each other as hard as they can. And it is too trau-matic for young kids. (qtd. in Tosches A1)

As Tutko indicates, even when children are not injured, fear of being hurt detracts from their enjoyment of the sport. *Little League Online* ranks fear of injury as the seventh of seven reasons children quit ("What about My Child"). One mother of an eight-year-old Peewee Football player explained, "The kids get so scared. They get hit once and they don't want anything to do with football anymore. They'll sit on the bench and pretend their leg hurts . . ." (qtd. in Tosches A1). Some children are driven to even more desperate mea-sures. For example, in one Peewee Football game, a reporter watched the following scene as a player took himself out of the game:

> "Coach, my tummy hurts. I can't play," he said. The coach told the player to get back onto the field. "There's nothing wrong with your stomach," he said. When the coach turned his head the seven-year-old stuck a finger down his throat and made himself vomit. When the coach turned back, the boy pointed to the ground and told him, "Yes there is, coach. See?" (Tosches A33)

Besides physical hazards and anxieties, competitive sports pose psychological dangers for children. Martin Rablovsky, a former sports editor for the *New York Times,* says that in all his years of watching young children play organized sports, he has noticed very few of them smiling. "I've seen children enjoying a spontaneous pre-practice scrimmage become somber and serious when the coach's whistle blows," Rablovsky says. "The spirit of play suddenly disappears, and sport becomes joblike" (qtd. in Coakley 94). The primary goal of a professional athlete—winning—is not appropriate for children. Their goals should be having fun, learning, and being with friends. Although winning does add to the fun, too many adults lose sight of what matters and make winning the most important goal. Several studies have shown that when children are asked whether they would rather be warming the bench on a winning team or playing regularly on a losing team, about 90 percent choose the latter (Smith, Smith, and Smoll 11).

Winning and losing may be an inevitable part of adult life, but they should not be part of childhood. Too much competition too early in life can affect a child's development. Children are easily influenced, and when they sense that their competence and worth are based on their ability to live up to their parents' and coaches' high expectations—and on their ability to win—they can become discouraged and depressed. Little League advises parents to "keep winning in perspective" (*Little League Online,* "Your Role"), noting that the most common reasons children give for quitting, aside from change in interest, are lack of playing time, failure and fear of failure, disapproval by significant others, and psychological stress (*Little League Online,* "What about My Child"). According to Dr. Glyn C. Roberts, a professor of kinesiology at the Institute of Child Behavior and Development at the University of Illinois, 80 to 90 percent of children who play competitive sports at a young age drop out by sixteen (Kutner C8).

This statistic illustrates another reason I oppose competitive sports for children: because they are so highly selective, very few children get to participate. Far too soon, a few children are singled out for their athletic promise, while many others, who may be on the verge of developing the necessary strength and ability, are screened out and discouraged from trying out again. Like adults, children fear failure, and so even those with good physical skills may stay away because they lack self-confidence. Consequently, teams lose many promising players who with some encouragement and experience might have become stars. The problem is that many parent-sponsored, out-of-school programs give more importance to having a winning team than to developing children's physical skills and self-esteem.

Indeed, it is no secret that too often scorekeeping, league standings, and the drive to win bring out the worst in adults who are more absorbed in living out their own fantasies than in enhancing the quality of the experience for children (Smith, Smith, and Smoll 9). The news provides plenty of horror stories. *Los Angeles Times* reporter Rich Tosches, for example, tells the story of a brawl among seventy-five parents following a Peewee Football game, which began when a parent from one team confronted a player from the other team (A33). Another example is provided by an *L.A. Times* editorial about a Little League manager who intimidated the opposing team by setting fire to one of its jerseys on the pitching mound before the game began. As the editorial writer commented, the manager showed his young team that "intimidation could substitute for playing well" ("The Bad News" B6). In addition, the Web site of the National Association of Sports Officials lists an appalling number of incidences of attacks on referees and field supervisors, including Thomas Juntas's fatal beating of a Massachusetts man who had been supervising a pick-up hockey game in which Juntas's son was playing.

Although not all parents or coaches behave so inappropriately, 9 the seriousness of the problem is illustrated by the fact that Adelphi University in Garden City, New York, offers a sports psychology workshop for Little League coaches, designed to balance their "animal instincts" with "educational theory" in hopes of reducing the "screaming and hollering," in the words of Harold Weisman, manager of sixteen Little Leagues in New York City (Schmitt B2). In a three-and-one-half-hour Sunday morning workshop, coaches learn how to make practices more fun, treat injuries, deal with irate parents, and be "more sensitive to their young players' fears, emotional frailties, and need for recognition." Little League is to be credited with recognizing the need for such workshops.

Some parents would no doubt argue that children cannot start 10 too soon preparing to live in a competitive free-market economy. After all, secondary schools and colleges require students to compete for grades, and college admission is extremely competitive. And it is perfectly obvious how important competitive skills are in finding a job. Yet the ability to cooperate is also important for success in life. Before children are psychologically ready for competition, maybe we should emphasize cooperation and individual performance in team sports rather than winning.

Many people are ready for such an emphasis. One New York 11 Little League official who had attended the Adelphi workshop tried to ban scoring from six- to eight-year-olds' games—but parents wouldn't support him (Schmitt B2). An innovative children's sports program in New York City, City Sports for Kids, emphasizes fitness, self-esteem, and sportsmanship. In this program's basketball games, every member on a team plays at least two of six eight-minute periods. The basket is seven feet from the floor, rather than ten feet, and a player can score a point just by hitting the rim (Bloch C12). I believe this kind of local program should replace overly competitive programs like Peewee Football and Little League Baseball. For example, childhood-fitness expert Stephen Virgilio of Adelphi University recommends "positive competition," which encourages children to strive to do their best without comparing themselves to an opponent. Virgilio also suggests that improvements can come from a few simple rule changes, such as rotating players to different positions several times during each game to show that "you're more interested in skill development than just trying to win a game" (qtd. in Rosenstock).

Authorities have clearly documented the excesses and dangers   12
of many competitive sports programs for children. It would seem that few children benefit from these programs and that those who do would benefit even more from programs emphasizing fitness, cooperation, sportsmanship, and individual performance. Thirteen- and fourteen-year-olds may be eager for competition, but few younger children are. These younger children deserve sports programs designed specifically for their needs and abilities.

Works Cited

"The Bad News Pyromaniacs?" Editorial. *Los Angeles Times* 16 June 1990: B6.

Bloch, Gordon B. "Thrill of Victory Is Secondary to Fun." *New York Times* 2 Apr. 1990, late ed.: C12.

Coakley, Jay J. *Sport in Society: Issues and Controversies.* St. Louis: Mosby, 1982.

Koppett, Leonard. *Sports Illusion, Sports Reality.* Boston: Houghton, 1981.

Kutner, Lawrence. "Athletics, through a Child's Eyes." *New York Times* 23 Mar. 1989, late ed.: C8.

Little League Online. "What about My Child." 2003. Little League Baseball, Inc. 30 June 2004 < http://www.littleleague.org/guide/parents/yourchild.asp >.

————. "Your Role as a Little League Parent." 2003. Little League Baseball, Inc. 30 June 2004 < http://www.littleleague.org/guide/parents/yourrole.asp >.

National Association of Sports Officials. "Poor Sporting Behavior Reported to NASO." Feb. 2004. 29 June 2004 < http://www.naso.org/sportsmanship/badsports.html >.

Rosenstock, Bonnie. "Competitive Sports for Kids: When Winning Becomes Cumbersome Instead of Fun." June 2002. Parentsknow.com database. 28 June 2004 < http://www.parentsknow.com/articles/june02-sports_comp.php >.

Schmitt, Eric. "Psychologists Take Seat on Little League Bench." *New York Times* 14 Mar. 1988, late ed.: B2.

Smith, Nathan, Ronald Smith, and Frank Smoll. *Kidsports: A Survival Guide for Parents.* Reading: Addison, 1983.

Tosches, Rich. "Peewee Football: Is It Time to Blow the Whistle?" *Los Angeles Times* 3 Dec. 1988: A1+.

READING FOR MEANING

Reading for meaning involves three activities:

- reading to comprehend
- reading to respond
- reading to analyze underlying assumptions

Reread Statsky's essay, and then write a page or so explaining your understanding of its basic meaning or main point, a personal response you have to it, and what you see as one of its underlying assumptions.

READING LIKE A WRITER

Writers of position papers

- present the issue.
- assert a clear, unequivocal position.
- argue directly for the position.
- counterargue objections and opposing positions.
- establish credibility.

Focus on one of these strategies in Statsky's essay, and analyze it carefully through close rereading and annotating. Then write several sentences explaining what you have learned about the strategy, giving specific examples from the reading to support your explanation. Add a few sentences evaluating how successfully Statsky uses the strategy to argue convincingly for her position.

REVIEWING WHAT MAKES POSITION PAPERS EFFECTIVE

In this chapter, you have been learning how to read position papers for meaning and how to read them like a writer. Before going on to write a position paper, pause here to review and contemplate what you have learned about the elements of effective position arguments.

Analyze
Choose one reading from this chapter that seems to you especially effective. Before rereading the selection, *jot down* one or two reasons you remember it as an example of an effective position paper.

Reread your chosen selection, adding further annotations about what makes it a particularly effective example of the genre. *Consider* the selection's purpose and how well it achieves that purpose for its intended readers. (You can make an informed guess about the intended readers and their expectations by noting the publication source of the essay.) Then *focus* on how well the essay

- presents the issue.

- asserts a clear, unequivocal position.

- argues directly for the position.

- counterargues objections and opposing positions.

- establishes credibility.

You can review all of these basic features in the Guide to Reading Position Papers (p. 574).

Your instructor may ask you to complete this activity on your own or to work with a small group of other students who have chosen the same reading. If you work with others, allow enough time initially for all group members to reread the selection thoughtfully and to add their annotations. Then *discuss* as a group what makes the essay effective. *Take notes* on your discussion. One student in your group should then report to the class what the group has learned about the effectiveness of position papers. If you are working individually, write up what you have learned from your analysis.

Write

Write at least a page supporting your choice of this reading as an example of an effective position paper. *Assume* that your readers—your instructor and classmates—have read the selection but will not remember many details about it. They also might not remember it as especially successful. Therefore, you will need to *refer* to details and specific parts of the essay as you explain how it works and as you justify your evaluation of its effectiveness. You need not argue that it is the best essay in the chapter or that it is flawless, only that it is, in your view, a strong example of the genre.

■ A Guide to Writing Position Papers

The readings in this chapter have helped you learn a great deal about position papers. Now that you have seen how writers construct arguments supporting their position on issues for their particular readers, you can approach this type of writing confidently. The readings will remain an important resource for you as you develop your own position paper. Use them to review how other writers solved the types of problems you will encounter in your writing.

This Guide to Writing is designed to assist you in writing your position paper. Here you will find activities to help you choose an issue and discover what to say about it, organize your ideas and draft the essay, read the draft critically, revise the draft to strengthen your argument, and edit and proofread the essay to improve readability.

INVENTION AND RESEARCH

The following activities will help you choose an issue to write about and develop an argument to support your position on the issue. You will also explore what you already know about the issue and determine whether you need to learn more about it through extended research. A few minutes spent completing each writing activity will improve your chances of producing a detailed and convincing first draft.

Choosing an Issue

Rather than limiting yourself to the first issue that comes to mind, widen your options by making a list of the issues that interest you. List the most promising issues you can think of, beginning with any you listed for the Considering Ideas for Your Own Writing activities following the readings in this chapter. Continue listing other possible issues. Making such a list often generates still other ideas: As you list ideas, you will think of new issues you cannot imagine now.

List the issues in the form of questions like these:

- Should local school boards have the power to ban such books as *The Adventures of Huckleberry Finn* and *Of Mice and Men* from school libraries?

- Should teenagers be required to get their parents' permission to obtain birth-control information and contraceptives?

- Should businesses remain loyal to their communities, or should they move to wherever labor costs, taxes, and other conditions are more favorable?

After you have completed your list, reflect on the possible issues you have compiled. Choose an arguable issue, one about which people disagree but that cannot be resolved simply with facts or by authorities. Your choice also may be influenced by whether you have time for research and whether your instructor requires it. Issues that have been written about extensively—such as whether weapon searches should be conducted on high-school campuses or affirmative action should be continued in college admissions—make excellent topics for extended research. Other issues—such as whether students should be required to perform community service or discouraged from taking part-time jobs that interfere with their studies—may be confidently based on personal experience.

Developing Your Argument

The writing and research activities that follow will enable you to test your choice of an issue and discover good ways to argue for your position on the issue.

Defining the Issue. *To see how you can define the issue, write nonstop for a few minutes.* This brief but intensive writing will help stimulate your memory, letting you see what you already know about the issue and whether you will need to do research to discover more about it.

Considering Your Own Position and Reasons for It. *Briefly state your current position on the issue and give a few reasons you take this position.* You may change your position as you develop your ideas and learn more about the issue, but for now say as directly as you can where you stand and why.

Researching the Issue. *If your instructor requires you to research the issue, or if you decide your essay would benefit from research, consult Appendix 2, Strategies for Research and Documentation, for guidelines on finding library and Internet sources.* Research can help you look critically at your own thinking and help you anticipate your readers' arguments and possible objections to your argument.

RESEARCHING YOUR SUBJECT ONLINE

To learn more about opposing positions, search for your issue online. To do so, enter a key term—a word or brief phrase—of your issue into a search tool such as Google <http://www.google.com> or Yahoo! Directory <http://dir.yahoo.com>. If possible, identify at least two positions different from your own. No matter how well argued, they need not weaken your confidence in your position. Your purpose is to understand opposing positions so well that you can represent one or more of them accurately and counterargue them effectively.

Bookmark or keep a record of promising sites. Download any materials that may help you represent and counterargue opposing positions.

Analyzing Your Readers. *Write for a few minutes identifying who your readers are, what they know about the issue, and how they can be convinced that your position may be plausible.* Describe your readers briefly. Mention anything you know about them as a group that might influence the way they would read your position paper. Speculate about how they will respond to your argument.

Rehearsing the Argument for Your Position. *Consider the reasons you could give for your position, and then write for a few minutes about the one reason you think would be most convincing to your readers.* Which reason do you think is the strongest? Which is most likely to appeal to your readers? As you write, try to show your readers why they should take this reason seriously.

Rehearsing Your Counterargument. *List what will likely be the one or two strongest opposing arguments or objections to your argument, and then write for a few minutes either conceding or refuting each one.* Try to think of arguments or objections your readers will expect you to know about and respond to, especially any criticism that could seriously undermine your argument.

Testing Your Choice. *Pause now to decide whether you have chosen an issue about which you will be able to make a convincing argument.* At this point you have some insights into how you will attempt to present the issue and argue to support your position on it for your particular readers. If your interest in the issue is growing and you are gaining confidence in the argument you want to make, you have probably made a good choice. However, if your interest in the issue is waning and you have been unable to come up with at least two or three plausible reasons why you take the position you do, you may want to consider choosing another issue. If your issue does not seem promising, return to your list of possible subjects to select another.

Considering Visuals. *Consider whether visuals—drawings, photographs, tables, or graphs—would strengthen your argument.* You could construct your own visuals, scan materials from books and magazines, or download them from the Internet. If you submit your essay electronically to other students and your instructor, or if you post it on a Web site, consider including photographs as well as snippets of film or sound. Visual and auditory materials are not at all a requirement of a successful position paper, as you can tell from the readings in this chapter, but they could add a new dimension to your writing. If you want to use photographs or recordings of people, though, be sure to obtain their permission.

Considering Your Purpose. *Write for several minutes about your purpose for writing this position paper.* The following questions will help you think about your purpose:

- What do I hope to accomplish with my readers? How do I want to influence their thinking? What one big idea do I want them to grasp and remember?

- How much resistance to my argument should I expect from my readers? Will they be largely receptive? Skeptical but convincible? Resistant and perhaps even antagonistic?

- How can I interest my readers in the issue? How can I help my readers see its significance—both to society at large and to them personally?

Formulating a Working Thesis. *Draft a thesis, or position, statement.* A working thesis—as opposed to a final or revised thesis—will help you bring your invention writing into focus and begin your draft with a clear purpose. As you draft and revise your essay, you may decide to modify your position and reformulate your thesis. Remember that the thesis for a position paper should assert your position on the issue and may define or qualify that position. In addition, the thesis usually forecasts your argument; it might also forecast your counter-argument. The thesis and forecasting statements, therefore, may occupy several sentences. Here are three examples from the readings:

- "Still, however willing I may have been to go along with the name [Washington Redskins] as a kid, as an adult I have concluded that using an ethnic group essentially as a sports mascot is wrong" (Estrada, paragraph 2).

- "But gay marriage is a surpassingly radical attack on the very foundations of marriage itself. It detaches marriage from the distinctive dynamics of heterosexual sexuality, divorces marriage from its intimate connection to the rearing of children, and opens the way to the replacement of marriage by a series of infinitely flexible contractual arrangements" (Kurtz, paragraph 6).

- "When overzealous parents and coaches impose adult standards on children's sports, the result can be activities that are neither satisfying nor beneficial to children.

   I am concerned about all organized sports activities for children between the ages of six and twelve. The damage I see results from non-contact as well as contact sports, from sports organized locally to those organized nationally. Highly organized competitive sports such as Peewee Football and Little League Baseball are too often played to adult standards, which are developmentally inappropriate for children and can be both physically and psychologically harmful. Furthermore, because they eliminate many children from organized sports before they are ready to compete, they are actually counterproductive for developing either future players or fans. Finally, because they emphasize competition and winning, they unfortunately provide occasions for some parents and coaches to place their own fantasies and needs ahead of children's welfare" (Statsky, paragraphs 1 and 2).

DRAFTING

The following guidelines will help you set goals for your draft, plan its organization, and consider a useful sentence strategy.

Setting Goals

Establishing goals for your draft before you begin writing will enable you to make decisions and work more confidently. Consider the following questions now, and keep them in mind as you draft. They will help you set goals for drafting as well as recall how the writers you have read in this chapter tried to achieve similar goals.

- *How can I present the issue in a way that will interest my readers?* Should I open with an anecdote (as Kennedy does), a scenario (as Knutson does), a response to a debate under way (as Kurtz and Rauch do), or a connection to my personal experience (as Estrada does)? Do I need to define the issue explicitly, perhaps by distinguishing between terms (like Sandel)? Should I present the issue in a historical context, as Kennedy and Statsky do? Or should I start with alarming statistics, as Sandel does?

- *How can I support my argument in a way that will win the respect of my readers?* Should I quote authorities or offer statistics from research studies, as Sandel, Kurtz, Knutson, and Statsky do? Should I argue that my position is based on shared values, as all the writers in this chapter do? Should I create analogies, as Sandel and Kennedy do? Should I provide examples or speculate about consequences, like all the writers? Should I support my argument with personal experience, as Rauch and Knutson do?

- *How can I counterargue effectively?* Should I introduce my argument by reviewing readers' opposing positions and likely objections, as Sandel, Kurtz, Rauch, Kennedy, and Knutson do? Should I concede the wisdom of readers' views, as Sandel and Knutson do? Or should I attempt to refute readers' views, as all the writers do?

- *How can I establish my authority and credibility on the issue?* Should I support my argument through research, as all the writers in this chapter do? Should I risk bringing in my personal experience, as Estrada, Rauch, and Knutson do? How can I refute readers' views without attacking them, as Sandel and Kennedy manage to do? Should I make an appeal to possible shared moral values with readers, as Estrada and Sandel do?

Organizing Your Draft

With goals in mind and invention notes in hand, you are ready to make a tentative outline of your draft. First list the reasons you plan to use as support for your argument. Decide how you will sequence these reasons. Writers of position papers often end with the strongest reasons because this organization gives the best reasons the greatest emphasis. Then add to your outline the opposing positions or objections that you plan to counterargue.

Considering a Useful Sentence Strategy

As you draft your essay, you will need to move back and forth smoothly between direct arguments for your position and counterarguments for your readers' likely objections, questions, and preferred positions. One useful strategy for making this move is to concede the value of a likely criticism and then attempt to refute it immediately, either in the same sentence or in the next one. Here are two examples from Statsky's essay that illustrate ways to use concessions (shown in italics) and refutations (shown in bold):

> The primary goal of a professional athlete—winning—is not appropriate for children. Their goals should be having fun, learning, and being with friends. *Although winning does add to the fun,* **too many adults lose sight of what matters and make winning the most important goal.** (paragraph 5)

> *And it is perfectly obvious how important competitive skills are in finding a job.* **Yet the ability to cooperate is also important for success in life.** (10)

In these examples from different stages in her argument, Statsky concedes the importance or value of some of her readers' likely objections, but then firmly refutes them. (Because these illustrations are woven into an extended argument, you may better appreciate them if you look at them in context by turning to the paragraphs where they appear.)

Here are two examples from other readings in the chapter:

> *I'm glad that Kurtz is thinking as strenuously about the possible downsides as I am about the possible upsides.* **Where he veers toward something like extremism is in his demand that homosexuals be denied any chance to prove his conjectures wrong.** (Rauch, paragraph 15)

> Another argument is that ethnic group leaders are too inclined to cry wolf in alleging racial insensitivity. *Often, this is the case.* **But no one should overlook genuine cases of political insensitivity in an attempt to avoid accusations of hypersensitivity and political correctness.** (Estrada, paragraph 7)

This important counterargument strategy sometimes begins not with concession but with acknowledgment; that is, the writer simply restates part of an opponent's argument without conceding the wisdom of it. Here are some examples:

> *Supporters of gay marriage keep telling us that the sky will not fall.* **What they do not understand is that, when it comes to marriage, the sky has already fallen.** (Kurtz, paragraph 5)

> *Lotteries are better than taxes, the argument goes, because they are wholly voluntary, a matter of choice.*
> **But the actual conduct of lotteries departs sharply from this laissez-faire ideal.** (Sandel, paragraphs 7 and 8)

> *Politicians suggest that all Americans need to do in order to attain racial justice is forswear bigotry.* **But they must also demand equal treatment before the law even when unequal treatment is defensible in the name of nonracist goals—and even when their effort will be costly.** (Kennedy, paragraph 19)

The concession-refutation move, sometimes called the "yes-but" strategy, is important in most arguments; in fact, it usually recurs, as it does in all the readings in this chapter. Following is a list of some of the other language this chapter's authors rely on to introduce their concession-refutation moves:

Introducing the Concession	*Introducing the Refutation That Follows*
It is true that . . .	But my point is . . .
In the old view . . .	But in a world of . . .
Rauch's intentions are admirable . . .	But this simply will not happen if . . .
I do believe . . .	But I also believe . . .
I can't prove I'm right . . .	But I think my view . . .
I understand that . . .	What I think is . . .
I'm not saying that . . .	This is a far cry from . . .
One might ask . . .	The real issue is . . .
Although not all . . .	The seriousness of the problem is illustrated by . . .

In addition to using concession and refutation, you can strengthen your position paper with other rhetorical strategies. You may want to review the section on using appositives to identify or establish the authority of a source in Chapter 5 (pp. 319–21).

READING A DRAFT CRITICALLY

Getting a critical reading of your draft will help you see how to improve it. Your instructor may schedule class time for reading drafts, or you may want to ask a class-mate or a tutor in the writing center to read your draft. Ask your reader to use the following guidelines and to write out a response for you to consult during revision.

Read for a First Impression

1. Read the draft without stopping to annotate or comment, and then write two or three sentences giving your general impression.

2. Identify one aspect of the draft that seems particularly effective.

Read Again to Suggest Improvements

1. Suggest ways of presenting the issue more effectively.

   - Read the paragraphs that present the issue, and tell the writer how they help you understand the issue or fail to help you.

   - Point to any key terms used to present the issue that seem surprising, con-fusing, antagonizing, or unnecessarily loaded.

2. Recommend ways of asserting the position more clearly and unequivocally.

   - Find the writer's thesis, or position statement, and underline it. If you can-not find a clear thesis, let the writer know.

   - If you find several restatements of the thesis, examine them closely for consistency.

   - If the position seems extreme or overstated, suggest how it might be qual-ified and made more reasonable.

3. Help the writer argue more directly for the position and strengthen the ar-gument.

   - Indicate any reasons that seem unconvincing, and explain briefly why you think so.

   - Look at the support the writer provides for each reason. If you find any of it ineffective, briefly explain why you think so and how it could be strengthened.

   - If you find places in the draft where support is lacking, suggest what kinds of support (facts, statistics, quotations, anecdotes, examples, or analogies) the writer might consider adding—and why.

4. Suggest ways of improving the counterargument.

- If any part of the refutation could be strengthened, suggest what the writer could add or change.

- If only the weakest objections or opposing positions have been acknowledged, remind the writer of the stronger ones that should be taken into account.

5. Suggest how credibility can be enhanced.

- Tell the writer whether the intended readers are likely to find the essay authoritative and trustworthy. Point to places where the argument seems most and least trustworthy.

- Identify places where the writer seeks to establish a common ground of shared values, beliefs, and attitudes with readers. Point to other places where the writer might attempt to do so without undermining the position being argued.

6. Suggest ways of improving readability.

- Consider whether the beginning adequately sets the stage for the argument, perhaps by establishing the tone or forecasting the argument.

- If the organization does not seem to follow a logical plan, suggest how it might be rearranged or where transitions could be inserted to clarify logical connections.

- Note whether the ending gives the argument a satisfactory sense of closure.

7. Evaluate the effectiveness of visuals.

- Look at any visuals in the essay, and tell the writer what they contribute to your understanding of the argument.

- If any visuals do not seem relevant, or if there seem to be too many visuals, identify the ones that the writer could consider dropping, explaining your thinking.

- If a visual does not seem appropriately placed, suggest a better place for it.

REVISING

This section offers suggestions for revising your draft. Revising means reenvisioning your draft, trying to see it in a new way, given your purpose and readers, in order to develop a well-argued position paper.

The biggest mistake you can make while revising is to focus initially on words or sentences. Instead, first try to see your draft as a whole in order to assess its likely impact on your readers. Think imaginatively and boldly about cutting unconvincing material, adding new material, and moving material around to enhance clarity and strengthen your argument. Your computer makes even drastic revisions physically easy, but you still need to make the mental effort and decisions that will improve your draft.

You may have received help with this challenge from a classmate or tutor who gave your draft a critical reading. If so, keep this valuable feedback in mind as you decide which parts of your draft need revising and what specific changes you could make. The following suggestions will help you solve problems and strengthen your essay.

To Present the Issue More Effectively

- If readers do not fully understand what is at stake in the issue, consider adding anecdotes, examples, or facts to make the issue more specific and vivid, or try explaining more systematically why you see the issue as you do.

- If the terms you use to present the issue are surprising, antagonizing, or unnecessarily loaded, consider revising your presentation of the issue in more familiar or neutral terms, perhaps by using the sentence strategy of concession and refutation or acknowledgment and refutation.

To Assert the Position More Clearly and Unequivocally

- If your position on the issue seems unclear to readers, try reformulating it or spelling it out in more detail.

- If your thesis statement is not easy for readers to find, try stating it more directly to avoid misunderstanding.

- If your thesis is not appropriately qualified to account for valid opposing arguments or objections, modify it by limiting its scope.

To Argue More Directly for the Position and Strengthen the Argument

- If a reason seems unconvincing, try clarifying its relevance to the argument.

- If you need better support, review your invention notes or do more research to find facts, statistics, quotations, examples, or other types of support that will help bolster your argument.

To Improve the Counterargument

- If your refutation seems unconvincing, provide more or better support (such as facts and statistics from reputable sources) to convince readers that your counterargument is not idiosyncratic or personal. Avoid attacking your opponents on a personal level; refute only their ideas.

- If your counterargument ignores any strong, opposing positions or reasonable objections, revise your essay to address them directly, perhaps using the sentence strategy of concession and refutation. If you cannot refute an opposing position, acknowledge its validity—and, if necessary, modify your position to accommodate it.

- If you can make any concessions without doing injustice to your own views, consider doing so now.

To Enhance Credibility

- If readers find any of your sources questionable, either establish these sources' credibility or choose more reliable sources to back up your argument.

- If readers think you ignore any opposing arguments, demonstrate to readers that you know and understand, even if you do not accept, these different points of view on the issue. Consider using the sentence strategy of concession and refutation or acknowledgment and refutation.

- If readers find your tone harsh or off-putting, consider the implications and potential offensiveness of your word choices; then look for ways to show respect for and establish common ground with readers, revising your essay to achieve a more accommodating tone. Again, consider using the concession-refutation strategy.

To Improve Readability

- If the beginning seems dull or unfocused, rewrite it, perhaps by adding a surprising or vivid anecdote.

- If readers have trouble following your argument, consider adding a brief forecast of your main points at the beginning of your essay.

- If the reasons and counterarguments are not logically arranged, reorder them. Consider announcing each reason more explicitly or adding transitions to make the connections clearer.

- If the ending seems weak, search your invention and research notes for a memorable quotation or a vivid example that will strengthen your ending.

EDITING AND PROOFREADING

After you have revised the essay, be sure to spend some time checking for errors in usage, punctuation, and mechanics and considering matters of style. If you keep a list of errors you typically make, begin by checking your draft against this list. Ask someone else to proofread your essay before you print out a copy for your instructor or send it electronically.

From our research on student writing, we know that essays arguing positions have a high percentage of sentence fragment errors involving subordinating conjunctions as well as punctuation errors involving conjunctive adverbs. Because arguing a position often requires you to use subordinating conjunctions (such as *because, although,* and *since*) and conjunctive adverbs (such as *therefore, however,* and *thus*), you want to be sure you know the conventions for punctuating sentences that include these types of words. Check a writer's handbook for help with avoiding sentence fragments and using punctuation correctly in sentences with subordinating conjunctions and conjunctive adverbs.

REFLECTING ON WHAT YOU HAVE LEARNED

Position Paper

In this chapter, you have read critically several position papers and have written one of your own. To better remember what you have learned, pause now to reflect on the reading and writing activities you completed in this chapter.

1. *Write* a page or so reflecting on what you have learned. *Begin* by describing what you are most pleased with in your essay. Then *explain* what you think contributed to your achievement. *Be specific* about this contribution.

   - If it was something you learned from the readings, *indicate* which readings and specifically what you learned from them.

   - If it came from your invention writing, *point out* the section or sections that helped you most.

   - If you got good advice from a critical reader, *explain* exactly how the person helped you—perhaps by helping you understand a particular problem in your draft or by adding a new dimension to your writing.

   - *Try to write* about your achievement in terms of what you have learned about the genre.

2. Now *reflect* more generally on position papers, a genre of writing that plays an important role in our society. *Consider* some of the following questions: As a reader and writer of position papers, how important are reasons and supporting evidence? When people argue their positions on television, on radio talk shows, and in online discussion forums like blogs, do they tend to emphasize reasons and support? If not, what do they emphasize? How do you think their purpose differs from the purpose of the writers you read in this chapter and from your own purpose in writing a position paper? What contribution might position papers make to our society that other genres of writing cannot make?

A Catalog of Critical Reading Strategies

Serious study of a text requires a pencil in hand—
how much pride that pencil carries.

IRVING HOWE

Here we present seventeen specific strategies for reading critically, strategies that you can learn readily and then apply not only to the selections in this book but also to your other college reading. Mastering these strategies may not make the critical reading process any easier, but it can make reading much more satisfying and productive and thus help you handle difficult material with confidence. These strategies are:

- *Annotating:* recording your reactions to and questions about a text directly on the page

- *Previewing:* learning about a text before reading it closely

- *Outlining:* listing the main idea of each paragraph to see the organization of a text

- *Summarizing:* briefly presenting the main ideas of a text

- *Paraphrasing:* restating and clarifying the meaning of a few sentences from a text

- *Synthesizing:* combining ideas and information selected from different texts

- *Questioning to understand and remember:* inquiring about the content

- *Contextualizing:* placing a text within an appropriate historical and cultural framework

- *Reflecting on challenges to your beliefs and values:* examining your responses to reveal your own unexamined assumptions and attitudes

- *Exploring the significance of figurative language:* seeing how metaphors, similes, and symbols enhance meaning

- *Looking for patterns of opposition:* discovering what a text values by analyzing its system of binaries/contrasts

- *Evaluating the logic of an argument:* testing the argument of a text to see whether it makes sense

- *Using a Toulmin analysis:* evaluating the underlying assumptions of an argument

- *Recognizing logical fallacies:* looking for errors in reasoning

- *Recognizing emotional manipulation:* looking for false or exaggerated appeals

- *Judging the writer's credibility:* determining whether a text can be trusted

- *Comparing and contrasting related readings:* exploring likenesses and differences between texts to understand them better

ANNOTATING

For each of these strategies, annotating directly on the page is fundamental. *Annotating* means underlining key words, phrases, or sentences; writing comments or questions in the margins; bracketing important sections of the text; connecting ideas with lines or arrows; numbering related points in sequence; and making note of anything that strikes you as interesting, important, or questionable. (If writing on the text itself is impossible or undesirable, you can annotate a photocopy.)

Most readers annotate in layers, adding further annotations on second and third readings. Annotations can be light or heavy, depending on a reader's purpose and the difficulty of the material.

For several of the strategies in this appendix, you will need to build on and extend annotating by *taking inventory:* analyzing and classifying your annotations, searching systematically for patterns in the text, and interpreting their significance. An inventory is basically a list. When you take inventory, you make various kinds of lists in order to find meaning in a text. As you inventory your annotations on a particular reading, you may discover that the language and ideas cluster in various ways.

Inventorying annotations is a three-step process:

1. Examine your annotations for patterns or repetitions of any kind, such as recurring images or stylistic features, related words and phrases, similar examples, or reliance on authorities.

2. Try out different ways of grouping the items.

3. Consider what the patterns you have found suggest about the writer's meaning or rhetorical choices.

The patterns you discover will depend on the kind of reading you are analyzing and on the purpose of your analysis. (See Exploring the Significance of Figurative Language, p. 669, and Looking for Patterns of Opposition, p. 672, for examples of inventorying annotations.) These patterns can help you reach a deeper understanding of the text.

The following selection has been annotated to demonstrate the processes required by the critical reading strategies we describe in the remainder of Appendix 1. As you read about each strategy, you will refer back to this annotated example.

MARTIN LUTHER KING JR.

An Annotated Sample from "Letter from Birmingham Jail"

Martin Luther King Jr. (1929–1968) first came to national notice in 1955, when he led a successful boycott against back-of-the-bus seating of African Americans in Montgomery, Alabama, where he was minister of a Baptist church. He subsequently formed a national organization, the Southern Christian Leadership Conference, that brought people of all races from across the country to the South to fight nonviolently for racial integration. In 1963, King led demonstrations in Birmingham that were met with violence: A black church was bombed, killing four little girls. King was arrested and, while in prison, wrote this famous "Letter from Birmingham Jail" to answer local clergy's criticism. King begins by discussing his disappointment with the lack of support he received from white moderates, such as the group of clergymen who published their criticism in the local newspaper (the complete text of the clergymen's published criticism appears at the end of this appendix).

The following brief excerpt from King's "Letter" is annotated to illustrate some of the ways you can annotate as you read. Since annotating is the first step for all critical reading strategies in this catalog, these annotations are referred to throughout this appendix. As you read, add your own annotations in the right-hand margin.

¶1 White moderates block progress

. . . I must confess that over the past few years I have been gravely disappointed with the white moderate. I have almost reached the regrettable conclusion that the Negro's [great stumbling block in his stride toward freedom] is not the White Citizen's Counciler or the Ku Klux Klanner, but the white moderate, who is more devoted to "order" than to justice; who prefers a negative peace which is the absence of tension to a positive peace which is the presence of justice;

Order vs. justice

Negative vs. positive

1

Ends vs. means
Treating others like children

who constantly says: "I agree with you in the goal you seek, but I cannot agree with your methods of direct action"; who (paternalistically) believes he can set the timetable for another man's freedom; who lives by a mythical concept of time and who constantly advises the Negro to wait for a "more convenient season." Shallow understanding from people of good will is more frustrating than absolute misunderstanding from people of ill will. [Lukewarm acceptance is much more bewildering than outright rejection.]

¶12 Tension necessary for progress

Tension already exists

Simile: hidden tension is "like a boil"

True?

I had hoped that the white moderate would understand that law and order exist for the purpose of establishing justice and that when they fail in this purpose they become the [dangerously structured dams that block the flow of social progress.] I had hoped that the white moderate would understand that the present tension in the South is a necessary phase of the transition from an [obnoxious negative peace,] in which the Negro passively accepted his unjust plight, to a [substantive and positive peace,] in which all men will respect the dignity and worth of human personality. Actually, we who engage in nonviolent direct action are not the creators of tension. We merely bring to the surface the hidden tension that is already alive. We bring it out in the open, where it can be seen and dealt with. [Like a boil that can never be cured so long as it is covered up but must be opened with all its ugliness to the natural medicines of air and light, injustice must be exposed, with all the tension its exposure creates, to the light of human conscience and the air of national opinion before it can be cured.]

¶13 King questions clergymen's logic of blaming the victim

Yes!

In your statement you assert that our actions, even though peaceful, must be condemned because they precipitate violence. But is this a logical assertion? Isn't this like condemning [a robbed man] because his possession of money precipitated the evil act of robbery? Isn't this like condemning [Socrates] because his unswerving commitment to truth and his philosophical inquiries precipitated the act by the misguided populace in which they made him drink hemlock? Isn't this like condemning [Jesus] because his unique God-consciousness and never-ceasing devotion to God's will precipitated the evil act of crucifixion? We must come to see that, as the federal courts have consistently affirmed, it is wrong to urge an individual to cease his efforts to gain his basic constitutional rights because the question may precipitate violence. [Society must protect the robbed and punish the robber.]

2

3

¶4 Justifies
urgency

I had also hoped that the white moderate would reject the myth concerning time in relation to the struggle for freedom. I have just received a letter from a white brother in Texas. He writes: "All Christians know that the colored people will receive equal rights eventually, but it is possible that you are in too great a religious hurry. It has taken Christianity almost two thousand years to accomplish what it has. The teachings of Christ take time to come to earth." Such an attitude stems from a tragic misconception of time, from the strangely irrational notion that there is something in the very flow of time that will inevitably cure all ills. [Actually, time itself is neutral; it can be used either destructively or constructively.] More and more I feel that the people of ill will have used time much more effectively than have the people of good will. We will have to repent in this generation not merely for the [hateful words and actions of the bad people] but for the [appalling silence of the good people.] Human progress never rolls in on [wheels of inevitability;] it comes through the tireless efforts of men willing to be co-workers with God, and without this hard work, time itself becomes an ally of the forces of social (stagnation.) [We must use time creatively, in the knowledge that the time is always ripe to do right.] Now is the time to make real the promise of democracy and transform our pending [national (elegy)] into a creative [(psalm) of brotherhood.] Now is the time to lift our national policy from the [quicksand of racial injustice] to the [solid rock of human dignity.]

Quotes white
moderate as
example

Critiques
assumptions

Silence is as
bad as hateful
words and
actions

Not moving

Elegy = death;
psalm =
celebration
Metaphors:
quicksand, rock

¶5 Refutes
criticism, King
not an
extremist

You speak of our activity in Birmingham as extreme. At first I was rather disappointed that fellow clergymen would see my nonviolent efforts as those of an extremist. I began thinking about the fact that I stand in the middle of two opposing forces in the Negro community. One is a [force of complacency,] made up in part of Negroes who, as a result of long years of oppression, are so drained of self-respect and a sense of "somebodiness" that they have adjusted to segregation; and in part of a few middle-class Negroes, who because of a degree of academic and economic security and because in some ways they profit by segregation, have become insensitive to the problems of the masses. The other [force is one of bitterness and hatred,] and it comes perilously close to advocating violence. It is expressed in the various black nationalist [groups that are springing up] across the nation, the largest and best-known being Elijah Muhammad's Muslim movement. Nourished by the Negro's frustration over the

Complacency
vs. hatred

Malcolm X?

4

5

continued existence of racial discrimination, this movement is made up of people who have lost faith in America, who have absolutely repudiated Christianity, and who have concluded that the white man is an incorrigible "devil."

¶6 Claims to offer better choice

I have tried to stand between these two forces, saying that we need emulate neither the "do-nothingism" of the complacent nor the hatred and despair of the black nationalist. For there is the more excellent way of love and nonviolent protest. I am grateful to God that, through the influence of the Negro church, the way of nonviolence became an integral part of our struggle.

6

¶7 Claims his movement prevents racial violence

If...then... Veiled threat?

If this philosophy had not emerged, by now many streets of the South would, I am convinced, be flowing with blood. And I am further convinced that if our white brothers dismiss as "rabble-rousers" and "outside agitators" those of us who employ nonviolent direct action, and if they refuse to support our nonviolent efforts, millions of Negroes will, out of frustration and despair, seek solace and security in black-nationalist ideologies—a development that would inevitably lead to a frightening racial nightmare.

7

¶8 Change inevitable: evolution or revolution?

Spirit of the times Worldwide uprising against injustice

[Oppressed people cannot remain oppressed forever.] The yearning for freedom eventually manifests itself, and that is what has happened to the American Negro. Something within has reminded him of his birthright of freedom, and something without has reminded him that it can be gained. Consciously or unconsciously, he has been caught up by the (Zeitgeist,) and with his black brothers of Africa and his brown and yellow brothers of Asia, South America and the Caribbean, the United States Negro is moving with a sense of great urgency toward the [promised land of racial justice.] If one recognizes this [vital urge that has engulfed the Negro community,] one should readily understand why public demonstrations are taking place. The Negro has many [pent-up resentments] and latent frustrations, and he must release them. So let him march; let him make prayer pilgrimages to the city hall; let him go on freedom rides—and try to understand why he must do so. If his repressed emotions are not released in nonviolent ways, they will seek expression through violence; this is not a threat but a fact of history. So I have not said to my people: "Get rid of your discontent." Rather, I have tried to say that this normal and healthy discontent can be [channeled into the creative outlet of nonviolent direct action.] And now this approach is being termed extremist.

8

Why "he," not "I"?

Repeats "let him"

Not a threat?

"I" channel discontent

¶9 Justifies extremism for righteous ends

Hebrew prophet

Christ's disciple

Founded Protestantism
English preacher
Freed slaves
Wrote Declaration of Independence

No choice but to be extremists, but what kind?

But though I was initially disappointed at being categorized as an extremist, as I continued to think about the matter I gradually gained a measure of satisfaction from the label. Was not Jesus an extremist for love: "Love your enemies, bless them that curse you, do good to them that hate you, and pray for them which despitefully use you, and persecute you." Was not (Amos) an extremist for justice: "Let justice roll down like waters and righteousness like an ever-flowing stream." Was not (Paul) an extremist for the Christian gospel: "I bear in my body the marks of the Lord Jesus." Was not (Martin Luther) an extremist: "Here I stand; I cannot do otherwise, so help me God." And (John Bunyan:) "I will stay in jail to the end of my days before I make a butchery of my conscience." And (Abraham Lincoln:) "This nation cannot survive half slave and half free." And (Thomas Jefferson:) "We hold these truths to be self-evident, that all men are created equal. . . ." [So the question is not whether we will be extremists, but what kind of extremists we will be.] Will we be extremists for hate or for love? Will we be extremists for the preservation of injustice or for the extension of justice? In that dramatic scene on Calvary's hill three men were crucified. We must never forget that all three were crucified for the same crime—the crime of extremism. Two were extremists for immorality, and thus fell below their environment. The other, (Jesus Christ,) was an extremist for love, truth and goodness, and thereby rose above his environment. Perhaps the South, [the nation and the world are in dire need of creative extremists.]

¶10 Disappointed in white moderate critics; thanks supporters

Who are they?

Left unaided

I had hoped that the white moderate would see this need. Perhaps I was too optimistic; perhaps I expected too much. I suppose I should have realized that few members of the oppressor race can understand the deep groans and passionate yearnings of the oppressed race, and still fewer have the vision to see that [injustice must be rooted out] by strong, persistent and determined action. I am thankful, however, that some of our white brothers in the South have grasped the meaning of this social revolution and committed themselves to it. They are still all too few in quantity, but they are big in quality. Some—such as Ralph McGill, Lillian Smith, Harry Golden, James McBride Dabbs, Ann Braden and Sarah Patton Boyle—have written about our struggle in eloquent and prophetic terms. Others have marched with us down nameless streets of the South. They have (languished) in filthy, roach-infested jails, suffering the abuse and brutality

9

10

of policemen who view them as "dirty nigger-lovers." Unlike so many of their moderate brothers and sisters, they have recognized the urgency of the movement and sensed the need for powerful ["action" antidotes] to combat the [disease of segregation.]

Framing—recalls boil simile

CHECKLIST

Annotating

To annotate a reading:

1. Mark the text using notations.
   - Circle words to be defined in the margin.
   - Underline key words and phrases.
   - Bracket important sentences and passages.
   - Use lines or arrows to connect ideas or words.
   - Use question marks to note any confusion or disagreement.
2. Write marginal comments.
   - Number each paragraph for future reference.
   - State the main idea of each paragraph.
   - Define unfamiliar words.
   - Note responses and questions.
   - Identify interesting writing strategies.
   - Point out patterns.
3. Layer additional markings on the text and comments in the margins as you reread for different purposes.

PREVIEWING

Previewing enables you to get a sense of what the text is about and how it is organized before reading it closely. This simple critical reading strategy includes seeing what you can learn from headnotes, biographical notes about the author, or other introductory material; skimming to get an overview of the content and organization; and identifying the genre and rhetorical situation.

Learning from Headnotes

Many texts provide some introductory material to orient readers. Books often have brief blurbs on the cover describing the content and author, as well as a preface, an introduction, and a table of contents. Articles in professional and academic journals usually provide some background information. Scientific articles, for example, typically begin with an abstract summarizing the main points. In this book, as in many textbooks, headnotes introducing the author and identifying the circumstances under which the selection was originally published precede the reading selections.

Because Martin Luther King Jr. is a well-known figure, the headnote might not tell you anything you do not already know. If you know something else about the author that could help you better understand the selection, you might want to make a note of it. As a critical reader, you should think about whether the writer has authority and credibility on the subject. Information about the writer's education, professional experience, and other publications can help. If you need to know more about a particular author, you could consult a biographical dictionary or encyclopedia in the library, such as *Who's Who, Biography Index, Current Biography, American National Biography,* or *Contemporary Authors.*

Some of these print indexes have Web-based equivalents that you can access either from your school's library or from home, using your library's Web site as a portal. Or try one of the Web sites that offer annotated lists of the best biographical sites on the Web, such as *Lives, the Biography Resource* <http://amillionlives.com>. Google is another source for author information.

Skimming for an Overview

When you *skim* a text, you give it a quick, selective, superficial reading. For most explanations and arguments, a good strategy is to read the opening and closing paragraphs; the first usually introduces the subject and may forecast the main points, while the last typically summarizes what is most important in the essay. You should also glance at the first sentence of every internal paragraph because it may serve as a topic sentence, introducing the point discussed in the paragraph. Because narrative writing is usually organized chronologically rather than logically, often you can get a sense of the progression by skimming for time markers such as *then, after,* and *later.* Heads and subheads, figures, charts, and the like also provide clues for skimming.

To illustrate, turn back to the King excerpt and skim it. Notice that the opening paragraph establishes the subject: the white moderate's criticism of Dr. King's efforts. It also forecasts many of the main points that are taken up in subsequent paragraphs; for example, the moderate's greater devotion to order than to justice (paragraph 2), the moderate's criticism that King's methods, though nonviolent, precipitate violence (3), and the moderate's "paternalistic" timetable (4).

Identifying the Genre and Rhetorical Situation

Reading an unfamiliar text is like traveling in unknown territory: You can use a map to check what you see against what you expect to find. In much the same way, previewing for genre equips you with a set of expectations to guide your reading. *Genre,* meaning "kind" or "type," is generally used to classify pieces of writing according to their particular social function. Nonfiction prose genres include autobiography, observation, reflection, explanations of concepts, and various forms of argument, such as evaluation, analysis of causes or effects, proposals to solve a problem, and position papers on controversial issues. These genres are illustrated in Chapters 2 through 9 with guidelines to help you analyze and evaluate their effectiveness. After working through these chapters, you will be able to identify the genre of most unfamiliar pieces of writing you encounter.

You can make a tentative decision about the genre of a text by first looking at why the piece was written and to whom it was addressed. These two elements—purpose and audience—constitute the rhetorical or writing situation. Consider the writing of "Letter from Birmingham Jail." The title explicitly identifies this particular selection as a letter. We know that letters are usually written with a particular reader in mind, but can also be written for the reading public (as in a letter to the editor of a magazine); that they may be part of an ongoing correspondence; and that they may be informal or formal.

Read the clergymen's statement at the end of this appendix (pp. 696–98) to gain some insight into the situation in which King wrote his letter and some understanding of his specific purpose for writing. As a public letter written in response to a public statement, "Letter from Birmingham Jail" may be classified as a position paper, one that argues for a particular point of view on a controversial issue.

Even without reading the clergymen's statement, you can get a sense of the rhetorical situation from the opening paragraph of the King excerpt. You would not be able to identify the "white moderate" with the clergymen who criticized King, but you would see clearly that he is referring to people he had hoped would support his cause but who, instead, have become an obstacle. King's feelings about the white moderate's lack of support are evident in the first paragraph, where he uses such words as "gravely disappointed," "regrettable conclusion," "frustrating," and "bewildering." The opening paragraph, as noted earlier, also identifies the white moderate's specific objections to King's methods. Therefore, you not only learn very quickly that this is a position paper, but you also learn the points of disagreement between the two sides and the writer's attitude toward those with whom he disagrees.

Knowing that this is an excerpt from a position paper allows you to appreciate the controversiality of the subject King is writing about and the sensitivity of the rhetorical situation. You can see how he asserts his own position at the same time that he tries to bridge the gap separating him from his critics. You can then evaluate the kinds of points King makes and the persuasiveness of his argument.

> **CHECKLIST**
>
> *Previewing*
>
> To orient yourself before reading closely:
>
> 1. See what you can learn from headnotes or other introductory material.
> 2. Skim the text to get an overview of the content and organization.
> 3. Identify the genre and rhetorical situation.

OUTLINING

Outlining is an especially helpful critical reading strategy for understanding the content and structure of a reading. Outlining, which identifies and organizes the text's main ideas, may be done as part of the annotating process, or it may be done separately. Writing an outline in the margins of the text as you read and annotate makes it easier to find information later. Writing an outline on a separate piece of paper gives you more space to work with and thus usually includes more detail.

The key to effective outlining is distinguishing between the main ideas and the supporting material, such as examples, factual evidence, and explanations. The main ideas form the backbone that holds the various parts and pieces of the text together. Outlining the main ideas helps you uncover this structure.

Making an outline, however, is not simple. The reader must exercise judgment in deciding which are the most important ideas. Reading is never a passive or neutral act; the process of outlining shows how active reading can be.

You may make either a *formal, multileveled outline* with roman (I, II) and arabic (1, 2) numerals together with capital and lowercase letters, or you can make an *informal, scratch outline* that lists the main idea of each paragraph. A formal outline is harder and more time-consuming to create than a scratch outline. You might choose to make a formal outline of a reading about which you are writing an in-depth analysis or evaluation. For example, on the next page is a formal outline that a student wrote for a paper evaluating the logic of the King excerpt. Notice the student's use of roman numerals for the main ideas or claims, capital letters for the reasons, and arabic numerals for supporting evidence and explanation.

Making a scratch outline, in contrast to a formal outline, takes less time but still requires careful reading. A scratch outline will not record as much information as a formal outline, but it is sufficient for most critical reading purposes. To make a scratch outline, you need to locate the topic of each paragraph. The topic is usually stated in a word or phrase, and it may be repeated or referred to

Formal Outline

I. The Negro's great stumbling block in his stride toward freedom is . . . the white moderate
  A. *Because* the white moderate is more devoted to "order" than to justice (paragraph 2)
    1. Law and order should exist to establish justice
    2. Law and order compare to dangerously structured dams that block the flow of social progress
  B. *Because* the white moderate prefers a negative peace (absence of tension) to a positive peace (justice) (paragraph 2)
    1. The tension already exists
    2. It is not created by nonviolent direct action
    3. Society that does not eliminate injustice compares to a boil that hides its infections. Both can be cured only by exposure (boil simile)
  C. *Because* even though the white moderates agree with the goals, they do not support the means to achieve them (paragraph 3)
    1. The argument that the means—nonviolent direct action—are wrong because they precipitate violence is flawed
    2. Analogy of the robbed man condemned because he had money
    3. Comparison with Socrates and Jesus
  D. *Because* the white moderates paternalistically believe they can set a timetable for another man's freedom (paragraph 4)
    1. Rebuts the white moderate's argument that Christianity will cure man's ills and man must wait patiently for that to happen
    2. Argues that time is neutral and that man must use time creatively for constructive rather than destructive ends
II. Creative extremism is preferable to moderation
  A. Classifies himself as a moderate (paragraphs 5–8)
    1. I stand between two forces: the white moderate's complacency and the black Muslim's rage
    2. If nonviolent direct action were stopped, more violence, not less, would result
    3. "Millions of Negroes will, out of frustration and despair, seek solace and security in black-nationalist ideologies" (paragraph 7)
    4. Repressed emotions will be expressed—if not in nonviolent ways, then through violence (paragraph 8)
  B. Redefines himself as a "creative extremist" (paragraph 9)
    1. Extremism for love, truth, and goodness is creative extremism
    2. Identifies himself with the creative extremists Jesus, Amos, Paul, Martin Luther, John Bunyan, Abraham Lincoln, and Thomas Jefferson
  C. Not all whites are moderates; many are creative extremists (paragraph 10)
    1. Lists names of white writers
    2. Refers to white activists

throughout the paragraph. For example, the opening paragraph of the King excerpt (pp. 649–50) makes clear that its topic is the white moderate.

After you have found the topic of the paragraph, figure out what is being said about it. To return to our example: If the white moderate is the topic of the opening paragraph, then what King says about the topic can be found in the second sentence, where he announces the conclusion he has come to—namely, that the white moderate is "the Negro's great stumbling block in his stride toward freedom." The rest of the paragraph specifies the ways the white moderate blocks progress.

When you make an outline, you can use the writer's words, your own words, or a combination of the two. A paragraph-by-paragraph outline appears in the margins of the selection, with numbers for each paragraph (see pp. 649–54). Here is the same outline as it might appear on a separate piece of paper, slightly expanded and reworded:

Paragraph Scratch Outline

¶1 White moderates block progress in the struggle for racial justice
¶2 Tension is necessary for progress
¶3 The clergymen's criticism is not logical
¶4 King justifies urgent use of time
¶5 Clergymen accuse King of being extreme, but he claims to stand between two extreme forces in the black community
¶6 King offers a better choice
¶7 King's movement has prevented racial violence by blacks
¶8 Discontent is normal and healthy but must be channeled creatively rather than destructively
¶9 Creative extremists are needed
¶10 Some whites have supported King

CHECKLIST

Outlining

To make a scratch outline of a text:

1. Reread each paragraph systematically, identifying the topic and what is being said about it. Do not include examples, specific details, quotations, or other explanatory and supporting material.

2. List the main ideas in the margin of the text or on a separate piece of paper.

SUMMARIZING

Summarizing is one of the most widely used strategies for critical reading because it helps you understand and remember what is most important in a text. Another advantage of summarizing is that it creates a condensed version of the reading's ideas and information, which you can refer to later or insert into your own written text. Along with quoting and paraphrasing, summarizing enables you to refer to and integrate other writers' ideas into your own writing.

Relatively brief restatements of the reading's main ideas, summaries have many functions, depending on context. When you search for sources through your college library's online catalog, summaries help you decide whether you want to read the complete source. You may also notice summaries at key points in your textbooks, points where the author wants you to review information covered in previous pages. When you begin using journal articles in your field of study, brief summaries called abstracts can help you tell right away whether the report is relevant to your research.

Summaries also vary in length. Some summaries are very brief—a sentence or even a subordinate clause. For example, if you were referring to the excerpt from "Letter from Birmingham Jail" and simply needed to indicate how it relates to your other sources, your summary might focus on only one aspect of the reading. It might look something like this:

> There have always been advocates of extremism in politics. Martin Luther King Jr., in "Letter from Birmingham Jail," for instance, defends nonviolent civil disobedience as an extreme but necessary means of bringing about racial justice.

If, however, you were surveying the important texts of the civil rights movement, you might write a longer, more detailed summary, one that not only identifies the reading's main ideas but also shows how the ideas relate to one another.

Many writers find it useful to outline the reading as a preliminary to writing a summary. A paragraph-by-paragraph scratch outline (like the one illustrated in the preceding section) lists the reading's main ideas following the sequence in which they appear in the original. But writing a summary requires more than merely stringing together the entries in an outline. A summary has to make explicit the logical connections between the ideas. Writing a summary shows how reading critically is a truly constructive process of interpretation involving both close analysis and creative synthesis.

To summarize, you need to segregate the main ideas from the supporting material, usually by making an outline of the reading. You want to use your own words for the most part because doing so confirms that you understand the material you have read, but you may also use key words and phrases from the reading. You may also want to cite the title and refer to the author by name, using verbs like *expresses, acknowledges,* and *explains* to indicate the writer's purpose and strategy at each point in the argument.

Following is a sample summary of the King excerpt. It is based on the outline on pages 657–58, but is much more detailed. Most important, it fills in connections between the ideas that King left for readers to make.

> King expresses his disappointment with white moderates who, by opposing his program of nonviolent direct action, have blocked progress toward racial justice. He acknowledges that his program has raised tension in the South, but he explains that tension is necessary to bring about change. Furthermore, he argues that tension already exists. But because it has been unexpressed, it is unhealthy and potentially dangerous.
>
> He defends his actions against the clergymen's criticisms, particularly their argument that he is in too much of a hurry. Responding to charges of extremism, King claims that he has actually prevented racial violence by channeling the natural frustrations of oppressed blacks into nonviolent protest. He asserts that extremism is precisely what is needed now—but it must be creative, rather than destructive, extremism. He concludes by again expressing disappointment with white moderates for not joining his effort as many other whites have.

CHECKLIST

Summarizing

To restate briefly the main ideas in a text:

1. Make an outline.

2. Write one or more paragraphs that present the main ideas largely in your own words. Use the outline as a guide, but reread parts of the original text as necessary.

3. To make the summary coherent, fill in connections between ideas.

PARAPHRASING

Unlike a summary, which is much briefer than the original text, a *paraphrase* is generally as long as the original and often longer. Whereas summarizing seeks to present the gist or essence of the reading and leave out everything else, paraphrasing tries to be comprehensive and leave out nothing that contributes to the meaning. (For more on summarizing, see the preceding section.)

Paraphrasing works as a critical reading strategy for especially complex and obscure passages. Because it requires a word-for-word or phrase-by-phrase rewording of the original text, paraphrasing is too time-consuming and labor intensive to use with long texts. But it is perfect for making sure you understand the important passages of a difficult reading. To paraphrase, you need to work systematically through the text, looking up in a good college dictionary many of the key words, even those you are somewhat familiar with. You can quote the author's words, but if you do, put quotation marks around them and be sure to define them.

Following are two passages. The first is excerpted from paragraph 2 of "Letter from Birmingham Jail." The second passage paraphrases the first.

Original

I had hoped that the white moderate would understand that law and order exist for the purpose of establishing justice and that when they fail in this purpose they become the dangerously structured dams that block the flow of social progress. I had hoped that the white moderate would understand that the present tension in the South is a necessary phase of the transition from an obnoxious negative peace, in which the Negro passively accepted his unjust plight, to a substantive and positive peace, in which all men will respect the dignity and worth of human personality.

Paraphrase

King writes that he had hoped for more understanding from the white moderates—specifically that they would recognize that law and order are not ends in themselves but means to the greater end of establishing justice. When law and order do not serve this greater end, they stand in the way of progress. King expected the white moderates to recognize that the current tense situation in the South is part of a transition that is necessary for progress. The current situation is bad because although there is peace, it is an "obnoxious" and "negative" kind of peace based on blacks passively accepting the injustice of the status quo. A better kind of peace, one that is "substantive," real and not imaginary, as well as "positive," requires that all people, regardless of race, be valued.

When you compare the paraphrase to the original, you can see that the paraphrase tries to remain true to the original by including *all* the important information and ideas. It also tries to be neutral, to avoid inserting the reader's opinions or distorting the original writer's ideas. But because paraphrasing requires the use of different words and putting those words together into different sentences, the resulting paraphrase will be different from the original. The paraphrase always, intentionally or not, expresses the reader's interpretation of the original text's meaning.

Paraphrasing

To paraphrase information in a text:

1. Reread the passage to be paraphrased, looking up unfamiliar words in a college dictionary.

2. Relying on key words in the passage, translate the information into your own sentences.

3. Revise to ensure coherence.

SYNTHESIZING

Synthesizing involves combining ideas and information gleaned from different sources. As a critical reading strategy, synthesizing can help you see how different sources relate to one another—for example, by offering supporting details or opposing arguments.

When you synthesize material from different sources, you construct a conversation among your sources, a conversation in which you also participate. Synthesizing contributes most to critical thinking when writers use sources not only to support their ideas but to challenge and extend them as well.

In the following example, the reader uses a variety of sources related to the King passage (pp. 649–54). The synthesis brings the sources together around a central idea. Notice how quotation, paraphrase, and summary are all used to present King's and the other sources' ideas.

When King defends his campaign of nonviolent direct action against the clergymen's criticism that "our actions, even though peaceful, must be condemned because they precipitate violence" (King excerpt, paragraph 3), he is using what Vinit Haksar calls Mohandas Gandhi's "safety-valve argument" ("Civil Disobedience and Non-Cooperation" 117). According to Haksar, Gandhi gave a "non-threatening warning of worse things to come" if his demands were not met. King similarly makes clear that advocates of actions more extreme than those he advocates are waiting in the wings: "The other force is one of bitterness and hatred, and it comes perilously close to advocating violence" (King excerpt, paragraph 5). King identifies this force with Elijah Muhammad, and although he does not name him, King's contemporary readers would have known that he was referring also to Malcolm X who, according to Herbert J. Storing, "urged that Negroes take seriously the idea of revolution" ("The Case against Civil Disobedience" 90). In fact, Malcolm X accused King of being a modern-day Uncle Tom, trying "to keep us under control, to keep us passive and peaceful and nonviolent" (*Malcolm X Speaks* 12).

CHECKLIST

Synthesizing

To synthesize ideas and information:

1. Find and read a variety of sources on your topic, annotating the passages that give you ideas about the topic.

2. Look for patterns among your sources, possibly supporting or refuting your ideas or those of other sources.

3. Write one or more paragraphs synthesizing your sources, using quotation, paraphrase, and summary to present what they say on the topic.

QUESTIONING TO UNDERSTAND AND REMEMBER

As a student, you are accustomed to teachers asking you questions about your reading. These questions are designed to help you understand a reading and respond to it more fully. However, when you need to understand and use new information, it may be more beneficial for *you* to write the questions. This strategy, *questioning to understand and remember,* involves writing questions while you read a text the first time. In difficult academic reading, you will understand the material better and remember it longer if you write a question for every paragraph or brief section.

We can demonstrate how this strategy works by returning to the excerpt from "Letter from Birmingham Jail" and examining, paragraph by paragraph, some questions that might be written about it. Reread the King selection (pp. 649–54). When you finish each paragraph, look at the question numbered to match that paragraph in the following list. Assume for this rereading that your goal is to comprehend the information and ideas. Notice that each question in the list asks about the content of a paragraph and that you can answer the question with information from that paragraph.

Paragraph	*Question*
1	How can white moderates be more of a barrier to racial equality than the Ku Klux Klan?
2	How can community tension resulting from nonviolent direct action benefit the civil rights movement?
3	How can peaceful actions be justified even if they cause violence?
4	Why should civil rights activists take action now instead of waiting for white moderates to support them?
5	How are complacent members of the community different from black nationalist groups?
6	What is King's position in relation to these two forces of complacency and anger?
7	What would have happened if King's nonviolent direct action movement had not started?
8	What is the focus of the protest, and what do King and others who are protesting hope to achieve?
9	What other creative extremists does King associate himself with?
10	Who are the whites who have supported King, and what has happened to some of them?

Each question focuses on the main idea in the paragraph, not on illustrations or details. Note, too, that each question is expressed partly in the reader's own words, not just copied from parts of the paragraph.

How can writing questions during reading help you understand and remember the content—the ideas and information—of the reading? Researchers studying the ways people learn from their reading have found that writing questions during reading enables readers to remember more than they would by reading the selection twice. Researchers who have compared the results of readers who write brief summary sentences for a paragraph with readers who write questions have found that readers who write questions learn more and remember the information longer. These researchers conjecture that writing a question involves reviewing or rehearsing information in a way that allows it to enter long-term memory, where it is more easily recalled. The result is that you clarify and "file" the information as you go along. You can then read more confidently because you have more of a base on which to build your understanding, a base that allows meaning to develop and that enables you to predict what is coming next and add it readily to what you have already learned.

This way of reading informational material is very slow, and at first it may seem inefficient. In those reading situations where you must use the information in an exam or a class discussion, it can be very efficient, however. Because this reading strategy is relatively time-consuming, you will, of course, want to use it selectively.

Questioning to Understand and Remember

To use questioning to understand and remember a reading, especially one that is unfamiliar or difficult:

1. Pause at the end of each paragraph to review the information.

2. Try to identify the most important information—the main ideas or gist of the discussion.

3. Write a question that can be answered by the main idea or ideas in the paragraph.

4. Move on to the next paragraph, repeating the process.

CONTEXTUALIZING

The texts you read were all written sometime in the past and often embody historical and cultural assumptions, values, and attitudes different from your own. To read critically, you need to become aware of these differences. *Contextualizing* is a critical reading strategy that involves making inferences about a reading's historical and cultural contexts and examining the differences between those contexts and your own.

We can divide the process of contextualizing into two steps:

1. Reread the text to see how it represents the historical and cultural situation. Compare the way the text presents the situation with what you know about the situation from other sources—such as what you have read in other books and articles, seen on television or in the movies, and learned in school or from talking with people who were directly involved.

   Write a few sentences describing your understanding of what it was like at that particular time and place. Note how the representation of the time and place in the text differs in significant ways from the other representations with which you are familiar.

2. Consider how much and in what ways the situation has changed. Write another sentence or two exploring the historical and cultural differences.

The excerpt from "Letter from Birmingham Jail" is a good example of a text that benefits from being read contextually. If you knew little about the history of slavery and segregation in the United States, Martin Luther King Jr., or the civil rights movement, it would be very difficult to understand the passion for justice and the impatience with delay expressed in the King selection. Most Americans, however, have read about Martin Luther King Jr. and the civil rights movement, or they have seen television histories such as *Eyes on the Prize* or films such as Spike Lee's *Malcolm X*.

Here is how one reader contextualized the excerpt from "Letter from Birmingham Jail":

> 1. I am not old enough to remember what it was like in the early 1960s when Dr. King was leading marches and sit-ins, but I have seen television documentaries of newsclips showing demonstrators being attacked by dogs, doused by fire hoses, beaten and dragged by helmeted police. Such images give me a sense of the violence, fear, and hatred that King was responding to.
>
> The tension King writes about comes across in his writing. He uses his anger and frustration creatively to inspire his critics. He also threatens them, although he denies it. I saw a film on Malcolm X, so I could see that King was giving white people a choice between his nonviolent way and Malcolm's more confrontational way.
>
> 2. Things have certainly changed since the sixties. Legal segregation has ended. The term *Negro* is no longer used, but there still are racists like the detective in the O. J. Simpson case. African Americans like Oprah Winfrey and Barack Obama are highly respected and powerful. The civil rights movement is over. So when I'm reading King, I'm reading history.
>
> But then again, police officers still beat black men like Rodney King, and extremists like Ice T still threaten violence. I don't know who's playing Dr. King's role today.

CHECKLIST

Contextualizing

To contextualize:

1. Describe the historical and cultural situation as it is represented in the reading and in other sources with which you are familiar.

2. Compare the text's historical and cultural contexts to your own historical and cultural situations.

REFLECTING ON CHALLENGES TO YOUR BELIEFS AND VALUES

Reading often challenges our attitudes, our unconsciously held beliefs, or our positions on current issues. We may feel anxious, irritable, or disturbed; threatened or vulnerable; ashamed or combative. We may feel suddenly wary or alert. When we experience these feelings as we read, we are reacting in terms of our personal or family values, religious beliefs, racial or ethnic group, gender, sexual orientation, social class, or regional experience.

You can grow intellectually, emotionally, and in social understanding if you are willing (at least occasionally) to *reflect on challenges to your beliefs and values* instead of simply resisting them. Learning to question your unexamined assumptions and attitudes is an important part of becoming a critical thinker.

This reading strategy involves marking the text where you feel challenged, and then reflecting on why you feel challenged. As you read a text for the first time, simply mark an *X* in the margin at each point where you sense a challenge to your attitudes, beliefs, or values. Make a brief note in the margin about what you feel at that point or about what in the text seems to create the challenge. The challenge you feel may be mild or strong. It may come frequently or only occasionally.

Review the places you have marked in the text where you felt challenged in some way. Consider what connections you can make among these places or among the feelings you experienced at each place. For example, you might notice that you object to only a limited part of a writer's argument, resist nearly all of an authority's quoted statements, or dispute implied judgments about your gender or social class.

Write about what you have learned. Begin by describing briefly the part or parts of the text that make you feel challenged. Then write several sentences, reflecting on your responses. Keep the focus on your feelings. You need not defend or justify your feelings. Instead, try to give them a voice. Where do they come from? Why are they important to you? Although the purpose is to explore why you feel as you do, you may find that thinking about your values, attitudes, and beliefs sends you back to the text for help with defining your own position.

Here, for example, is how one writer responded to the excerpt from "Letter from Birmingham Jail":

> I'm troubled and confused by the way King uses the labels *moderate* and *extremist*. He says he doesn't like being labeled an extremist but he labels the clergymen moderate. How could it be okay for King to be moderate and not okay for the clergymen? What does *moderate* mean anyway? My dictionary defines *moderate* as "keeping within reasonable or proper limits; not extreme, excessive, or intense." Being a moderate sounds a lot better than being an extremist. I was taught not to act rashly or to go off the deep end. I'm also troubled that King makes a threat (although he says he does not).

> ▉ CHECKLIST
>
> ## *Reflecting on Challenges to Your Beliefs and Values*
>
> To reflect on challenges to your beliefs and values:
>
> 1. Identify the challenges by marking where in the text you feel your beliefs and values are being opposed, criticized, or unfairly characterized.
>
> 2. Select one or two of the most troubling challenges you have identified, and write a few sentences describing why you feel as you do. Do not attempt to defend your feelings; instead, analyze them to see where they come from.

EXPLORING THE SIGNIFICANCE OF FIGURATIVE LANGUAGE

Figurative language—metaphors, similes, and symbols—takes words literally associated with one object or idea and applies them to another object or idea. Because it embodies abstract ideas in vivid images, figurative language can often communicate more dramatically than direct statement. Figurative language also enriches meaning by drawing on a complex of feeling and association, indicating relations of resemblance and likeness. Here are definitions and examples of the most common figures of speech.

Metaphor implicitly compares two things by identifying them with each other. For instance, when King calls the white moderate "the Negro's great stumbling block in his stride toward freedom" (paragraph 1), he does not mean that the white moderate literally trips the Negro who is attempting to walk toward freedom. The sentence makes sense only when it is understood figuratively: The white moderate trips up the Negro by frustrating every effort to eliminate injustice. Similarly, King uses the image of a dam to express the abstract idea of the blockage of justice (paragraph 2).

Simile, a more explicit form of comparison, uses *like* or *as* to signal the relation of two seemingly unrelated things. King uses simile when he says that injustice is "like a boil that can never be cured so long as it is covered up" (paragraph 2). This simile makes several points of comparison between injustice and a boil. It suggests that injustice is a disease of society, just as a boil is a disease of the body, and that injustice, like a boil, must be exposed or it will fester and worsen. A simile with many points of comparison is called an *extended simile* or *conceit.*

A *symbol* is something that stands for or represents something else. Critics do not agree about the differences between a metaphor and a symbol, but one popular line of thought is that a symbol relates two or more items that already have a strong recognized alliance or affinity, whereas metaphor involves a more general association of two related or unrelated items. By this definition, King uses the white moderate as a symbol for supposed liberals and would-be supporters of civil rights who are actually frustrating the cause.

How these figures of speech are used in a text reveals something of the writer's feelings about the subject and attitude toward prospective readers, and may even suggest the writer's feelings about the act of writing. Annotating and taking inventory of patterns of figurative language can thus provide insight into the tone and intended emotional effect of the writing.

Exploring the significance of figurative language involves (1) annotating and then listing all the metaphors, similes, and symbols you find in the reading; (2) grouping the figures of speech that appear to express similar feelings and attitudes, and labeling each group; and (3) writing to explore the meaning of the patterns you have found.

The following sample inventory and analysis of the King excerpt demonstrate the process of exploring the significance of figurative language.

Listing Figures of Speech

Step 1 produced the following inventory:

order is a dangerously structured dam that blocks the flow

social progress should flow

stumbling block in the stride toward freedom

injustice is like a boil that can never be cured

the light of human conscience and air of national opinion

time is something to be used, neutral, an ally, ripe

quicksand of racial injustice

the solid rock of human dignity

human progress never rolls in on wheels of inevitability

men are co-workers with God

groups springing up

promised land of racial justice

vital urge engulfed

pent-up resentments

normal and healthy discontent can be channeled into the creative outlet of nonviolent direct action

root out injustice

powerful action is an antidote

disease of segregation

Grouping Figures of Speech

Step 2 yielded three common themes:

Sickness: segregation is a disease; action is healthy, the only antidote; injustice is like a boil

Underground: tension is hidden; injustice must be rooted out; extremist groups are springing up; discontent can be channeled into a creative outlet

Blockage: forward movement is impeded by obstacles—the dam, stumbling block; human progress never rolls in on wheels of inevitability; social progress should flow

Exploring Patterns

Step 3 entailed about ten minutes of writing to explore the themes listed in step 2:

The patterns of *blockage* and *underground* suggest a feeling of frustration. Inertia is a problem; movement forward toward progress or upward toward the promised land is stalled. There seems to be a strong need to break through the resistance, the passivity, the discontent, and to be creative, active, vital. These are probably King's feelings both about his attempt to lead purposeful, effective demonstrations and his effort to write a convincing letter.

The simile of injustice being like a boil links the two patterns of *underground* and *sickness,* suggesting something bad, a disease, is inside the people or the society. The cure is to expose, to root out, the blocked hatred and injustice and to release the tension or emotion that has so long been repressed. This implies that repression itself is the evil, not simply what is repressed.

CHECKLIST

Exploring the Significance of Figurative Language

To understand how figurative language—metaphors, similes, and symbols—contributes to a reading's meaning:

1. Annotate and then list all the figures of speech you find.

2. Group them, and label each group.

3. Write to explore the meaning of the patterns you have found.

LOOKING FOR PATTERNS OF OPPOSITION

All texts contain *voices* or *patterns of opposition*. These voices may echo the views and values of critical readers the writer anticipates or predecessors to which the writer is responding; they may even reflect the writer's own conflicting values. You may need to look closely for such a dialogue of opposing voices within the text.

When we think of oppositions, we ordinarily think of polarities such as *yes* and *no, up* and *down, black* and *white, new* and *old*. Some oppositions, however, may be more subtle. The excerpt from "Letter from Birmingham Jail" is rich in such oppositions: *moderate* versus *extremist, order* versus *justice, direct action* versus *passive acceptance, expression* versus *repression*. These oppositions are not accidental; they form a significant pattern that gives a critical reader important information about King's letter.

A careful reading shows that one of the two terms in an opposition is nearly always valued over the other. In the King excerpt, for example, *extremist* is valued over *moderate* (paragraph 9). This preference for extremism is surprising. The critical reader should ask why, when white extremists like the Ku Klux Klan have committed so many outrages against black southerners, King would prefer extremism. If King is trying to convince his readers to accept his point of view, why would he represent himself as an extremist? Moreover, why would a clergyman advocate extremism instead of moderation?

By studying the patterns of opposition, you can answer these questions more fully. You can see that King sets up this opposition to force his readers to examine their own values and realize that they are in fact misplaced. Instead of working toward justice, he says, those who support law and order maintain the unjust status quo. Getting his readers to think of the white moderate as blocking rather than facilitating peaceful change brings them to align themselves with King and perhaps even embrace his strategy of nonviolent resistance.

Looking for patterns of opposition is a four-step method of analysis:

1. Divide a piece of paper in half lengthwise or select two column formatting in your word-processing program. In the left-hand column, list those words and phrases from the text that you have annotated as indicating oppositions. Enter in the right-hand column the word or phrase that seems, according to this writer, the opposite of each word or phrase in the left-hand column. You may have to paraphrase or even supply this opposite word or phrase if it is not stated directly in the text.

2. For each pair of words or phrases, put an asterisk next to the one that seems to be preferred by the writer.

3. Study the list of preferred words or phrases, and identify what you think is the predominant system of values put forth by the text. Do the same for the other list, identifying the alternative system or systems of values implied in the text. Take about ten minutes to describe the oppositions in writing.

4. To explore these conflicting points of view, write a few sentences presenting one side, and then write a few more sentences presenting the other side. Use as many of the words or phrases from the list as you can—explaining, extending, and justifying the values they imply. You may also, if you wish, quarrel with the choice of words or phrases on the grounds that they are loaded or oversimplify the issue.

The following sample inventory and analysis of the King excerpt demonstrate the method for exploring patterns of opposition in a text.

Listing Oppositions

Steps 1 and 2: This list of oppositions uses asterisks to identify King's preferred word or phrase in each pair:

white moderate	*extremist
order	*justice
negative peace	*positive peace
absence of justice	*presence of justice
goals	*methods
*direct action	passive acceptance
*exposed tension	hidden tension
*robbed	robber
*individual	society
*words	silence
*expression	repression
*extension of justice	preservation of injustice
*extremist for love, truth, and justice	extremist for immorality

Analyzing Oppositions

Step 3 produced the following description of the conflicting points of view:

> In this reading, King addresses as "white moderates" the clergymen who criticized him. He sees the moderate position in essentially negative terms, whereas extremism can be either negative or positive. Moderation is equated with passivity, acceptance of the status quo, fear of disorder, perhaps even fear of any change. The moderates believe justice can wait, whereas law and order cannot. Yet, as King points out, there is no law and order for blacks who are victimized and denied their constitutional rights.
>
> The argument King has with the white moderates is basically over means and ends. Both agree on the ends but disagree on the means that should be taken to secure those ends. What means are justified to achieve one's goals? How does one decide? King is willing to risk a certain amount of tension and disorder to bring about justice; he suggests that if progress is not made, more disorder, not less, is bound to result. In a sense, King represents himself as a moderate caught between the two extremes—the white moderates' "do-nothingism" and the black extremists' radicalism.
>
> At the same time, King substitutes the opposition between moderation and extremism with an opposition between two kinds of extremism, one for love and the other for hate. In fact, he represents himself as an extremist willing to make whatever sacrifices—and perhaps even to take whatever means—are necessary to reach his goal of justice.

Considering Alternative Points of View

Step 4 entailed a few minutes of exploratory writing about the opposing point of view, and then several more minutes of writing about King's possible response to the opposition's argument:

> *The moderates' side:* I can sympathize with the moderates' fear of further disorder and violence. Even though King advocates nonviolence, violence does result. He may not cause it, but it does occur because of him. Moderates do not really advocate passive acceptance of injustice, but want to pursue justice through legal means. These methods may be slow, but, since ours is a system of law, the only way to make change is through that system. King wants to shake up the system, to force it to move quickly for fear of violence. That strikes me as blackmail, as bad as if he were committing violence himself. Couldn't public opinion be brought to bear on the legal system to move more quickly? Can't we elect officials who will change unjust laws and see that the just ones are obeyed? The *vote* should be the weapon in a democracy, shouldn't it?

King's possible response: He would probably have argued that the opposing viewpoint was naive. One of the major injustices at that time was that blacks were prevented from voting, and no elected official would risk going against those who voted for him or her. King would probably have agreed that public opinion needed to be changed, that people needed to be educated, but he would also have argued that education was not enough when people were being systematically deprived of their legal rights. The very system of law that should have protected people was being used as a weapon against blacks in the South. The only way to get something done was to shake people up, make them aware of the injustice they were allowing to continue. Seeing their own police officers committing violence should have made people question their own values and begin to take action to right the wrongs.

CHECKLIST

Looking for Patterns of Opposition

To explore and analyze the patterns of opposition in a reading:

1. Annotate the selection to identify the oppositions, and list the pairs on a separate page.

2. Put an asterisk next to the writer's preferred word or phrase in each pair of opposing terms.

3. Examine the pattern of preferred terms to discover the system of values the pattern implies; then do the same for the unpreferred terms.

4. Write to analyze and evaluate the opposing points of view or, in the case of a reading that does not take a position, the alternative systems of value.

EVALUATING THE LOGIC OF AN ARGUMENT

An *argument* has two essential parts: the claim and the support. The *claim* asserts a conclusion—an idea, an opinion, a judgment, or a point of view—that the writer wants readers to accept. The *support* includes *reasons* (shared beliefs, assumptions, and values) and *evidence* (facts, examples, statistics, and authorities) that give readers the basis for accepting the writer's conclusion.

When you *evaluate the logic of an argument,* you are concerned about the process of reasoning as well as the argument's truthfulness. Three conditions must be met for an argument to be considered logically acceptable—what we call the ABC test:

A. The support must be *appropriate* to the claim.
B. All of the statements must be *believable.*
C. The argument must be *consistent* and *complete.*

In addition to the ABC test, you can also use other ways to evaluate the logic of an argument. The next two sections of this appendix explain how to use a specific method called a Toulmin analysis to determine the underlying assumptions in an argument (p. 679) and how to recognize specific kinds of errors in reasoning, or logical fallacies (p. 683).

A. Testing for Appropriateness

To assess whether a writer's reasoning is *appropriate,* you look to see if all of the evidence is relevant to the claim it supports. For example, if a writer claims that children must be allowed certain legal rights, readers could readily accept as appropriate support quotations from Supreme Court justices' decisions but might question quotations from a writer of popular children's books. Readers could probably accept the reasoning that if women have certain legal rights then so should children, but few readers would agree that all human rights under the law should be extended to animals.

As these examples illustrate, appropriateness of support comes most often into question when the writer is invoking authority or arguing by analogy. For example, in the excerpt from "Letter from Birmingham Jail," King argues by analogy and, at the same time, invokes authority: "Isn't this like condemning Socrates because his unswerving commitment to truth and his philosophical inquiries precipitated the act by the misguided populace in which they made him drink hemlock?" (paragraph 3). Readers not only must judge the appropriateness of comparing the Greek populace's condemnation of Socrates to the white moderates' condemnation of King's action, but also must judge whether it is appropriate to accept Socrates as an authority on this subject. Because Socrates is generally respected for his teaching on justice, his words and actions are likely to be considered appropriate to King's situation in Birmingham.

In paragraph 2, King argues that if law and order fail to establish justice, "they become the dangerously structured dams that block the flow of social progress." The analogy asserts a logical relationship: that law and order are to social justice what a dam is to water. If readers do not accept this analogy, then the argument fails the test of appropriateness. Arguing by analogy is usually considered a weak kind of argument because most analogies are parallel only up to a point, beyond which they may fail.

B. Testing for Believability

Believability is a measure of the degree to which readers are willing to accept the assertions supporting the claim. Whereas some assertions are obviously true, most depend on the readers' sharing certain values, beliefs, and assumptions with the writer. Readers who agree with the white moderate that maintaining law and order is more important than establishing justice are not going to accept King's claim that the white moderate is blocking progress.

Other statements, such as those asserting facts, statistics, examples, and authorities, present evidence to support a claim. Readers must put all of these kinds of evidence to the test of believability.

Facts are statements that can be proven objectively to be true. The believability of facts depends on their *accuracy* (they should not distort or misrepresent reality), their *completeness* (they should not omit important details), and the *trustworthiness* of their sources (sources should be qualified and unbiased). In the excerpt from "Letter from Birmingham Jail," for instance, King asserts as fact that African Americans will not wait much longer for racial justice (paragraph 8). His critics might question the factuality of this assertion by asking: Is it true of all African Americans? How much longer will they wait? How does King know what African Americans will and will not do?

Statistics are often assumed to be factual, but they are really only interpretations of numerical data. The believability of statistics depends on the *accuracy* of the methods of gathering and analyzing data (representative samples should be used and variables accounted for), the *trustworthiness* of the sources (sources should be qualified and unbiased), and often on the *comparability* of the data (are apples being compared to oranges?).

Examples and *anecdotes* are particular instances that if accepted as believable lead readers to accept the general claim. The power of examples depends on their *representativeness* (whether they are truly typical and thus generalizable) and their *specificity* (whether particular details make them seem true to life). Even if a vivid example or gripping anecdote does not convince readers, it strengthens argumentative writing by bringing home the point dramatically. In paragraph 5, for example, King supports his generalization that there are black nationalist extremists motivated by bitterness and hatred by citing the specific example of Elijah Muhammad's Muslim movement. Conversely, in paragraph 9, he refers to Jesus, Paul, Luther, and others as examples of extremists motivated by love. These examples support his assertion that extremism is not in itself wrong, that any judgment must depend on the cause for which one is an extremist.

Authorities are people whom the writer consults for expertise on a given subject. Such authorities not only must be appropriate, as mentioned earlier, but must be believable as well. The believability of authorities, their *credibility,* depends on whether the reader accepts them as experts on the topic. King cites authorities repeatedly throughout the essay, referring not only to religious leaders such as Jesus and Luther, but also to American political leaders such as Lincoln and Jefferson. These figures are certain to have a high degree of credibility among King's readers.

C. Testing for Consistency and Completeness

Be sure that all the support works together, that no supporting statement contradicts any of the others, and that no important objection or opposing argument is unacknowledged. To test for *consistency* and *completeness,* ask yourself: Are any of the supporting statements contradictory? Are there any objections or opposing arguments that are not refuted?

In his essay, a potential contradiction is King's characterizing himself first as a moderate between the forces of complacency and violence, and later as an extremist opposed to the forces of violence. King attempts to reconcile this apparent contradiction by explicitly redefining extremism in paragraph 9. Similarly, the fact that King fails to examine and refute every legal recourse available to his cause might allow a critical reader to question the sufficiency of his supporting arguments.

Following is one student's evaluation of the logic of King's argument. The student wrote these paragraphs after applying the ABC test, evaluating the appropriateness, believability, consistency, and completeness of King's supporting reasons and evidence.

> King writes both to the ministers who published the letter in the Birmingham newspaper and to the people of Birmingham. He seems to want to justify his group's actions. He challenges white moderates, but he also tries to avoid antagonizing them. Given this purpose and his readers, his supporting statements are generally appropriate. He relies mainly on assertions of shared belief with his readers and on memorable analogies. For example, he knows his readers will accept assertions like "law and order exist for the purpose of establishing justice"; it is good to be an extremist for "love, truth, and goodness"; and progress is not inevitable, but results from tireless work and creativity. His analogies also seem acceptable and are based on appropriate comparisons. For example, he compares injustice to a boil that nonviolent action must expose to the air if it is to be healed.
>
> Likewise, his support is believable in terms of the well-known authorities he cites (Socrates, Jesus, Amos, Paul, Luther, Bunyan, Lincoln, Jefferson), the facts he asserts (for example, that racial tension results from injustice, not from nonviolent action), and the examples he offers (such as his assertion that extremism is not in itself wrong— as exemplified by Jesus, Paul, and Luther). If there is an inconsistency in the argument, it is the contradiction between King's portraits of himself both as a moderating force and as an "extremist for love"; but

his redefinition of extremism as a positive value for any social change is central to the overall persuasiveness of his logical appeal to white moderates.

Evaluating the Logic of an Argument

To determine whether an argument makes sense, apply the ABC test:

1. *Test for appropriateness* by checking to be sure that each piece of evidence is clearly and directly related to the claim it is supposed to support.

2. *Test for believability* by deciding whether you can accept as true the writer's facts, statistics, and expert testimony, and whether you can accept the generalizations based on the examples given.

3. *Test for consistency and completeness* by ascertaining whether there are any contradictions in the argument and whether any important objections or opposing arguments have been ignored.

Then write a few sentences exploring the appropriateness, believability, consistency, and completeness of the argument.

USING A TOULMIN ANALYSIS

In addition to the ways of evaluating the logic of an argument that are discussed in the previous section, scholars have developed various formal systems for doing so. In *The Uses of Argument* (1964), Stephen Toulmin sets out a popular approach to reading, writing, and critical thinking that is widely used to discover and assess the logical structure of arguments. Students of legal writing frequently use Toulmin analysis, and you may find it helpful in your own reading and writing. As a user of this book, you may find that the most useful part of Toulmin's analysis is uncovering the underlying assumptions in an argument (or in any piece of writing)—the focus of the third part of the Reading for Meaning activities that follow the readings in Chapters 2 through 9.

Toulmin's specialized terms—*claim, data* and *grounds,* and *warrant*—are defined as follows:

- *Claim:* the thesis or main point of the argument.

- *Data* and *grounds:* the reasons and evidence that support the claim.

- *Warrant:* the beliefs, values, and assumptions that "warrant" or justify the claim based on the evidence. Often the warrant is unstated or implicit.

In order to find the warrant, you must figure out the belief or value system that enables the author to make the claim or draw the conclusion from the reasons and evidence set forth. The following strategies will help you identify the warrant underlying the argument. Once you uncover the warrant or assumption, you can determine whether the evidence—in Toulmin's words—"authorizes, entitles, or justifies the writer to make the claim based on the data," which basically means that the warrant helps you judge whether the writer's claim is justified by the evidence provided.

Identifying the Warrant

Let's look again at the beginning of the excerpt from King's "Letter from Birmingham Jail":

> . . . I must confess that over the past few years I have been gravely disappointed with the white moderate. I have almost reached the regrettable conclusion that the Negro's great stumbling block in his stride toward freedom is not the White Citizen's Counciler or the Ku Klux Klanner, but the white moderate, who is more devoted to "order" than to justice; who prefers a negative peace which is the absence of tension to a positive peace which is the presence of justice; who constantly says: "I agree with you in the goal you seek, but I cannot agree with your methods of direct action"; who paternalistically believes he can set the timetable for another man's freedom; who lives by a mythical concept of time and who constantly advises the Negro to wait for a "more convenient season." Shallow understanding from people of good will is more frustrating than absolute misunderstanding from people of ill will. Lukewarm acceptance is much more bewildering than outright rejection.
>
> I had hoped that the white moderate would understand that law and order exist for the purpose of establishing justice and that when they fail in this purpose they become the dangerously structured dams that block the flow of social progress. I had hoped that the white moderate would understand that the present tension in the South is a necessary phase of the transition from an obnoxious negative peace, in which the Negro passively accepted his unjust plight, to a substantive and positive peace, in which all men will respect the dignity and worth of human personality.

STEP 1. To apply a Toulmin analysis to King's argument, you first need to *find the claim and reasons* in the passage. What is the author's assertion? What point is the author trying to make? The answer to these questions is the claim. Then ask why the author thinks this claim is true: What reasons are offered to support it? Often you can paraphrase the passage as a *because* statement that is completed by those reasons: This claim is true because of reason one, reason two, and so on. It is helpful to use as much of the writer's own language as possible because the writer's choice of words will be important when you try to analyze the assumptions and discover the warrant. It is also helpful to underline or highlight words and phrases that seem to have a great deal of importance to the author.

A Toulmin analysis of the preceding passage might look like this:

- *Claim:* White moderates impede the African American's progress toward freedom

- *Reason 1:* because they care more for *order* than *justice*

- *Reason 2:* because they prefer "a *negative peace* which is the *absence of tension* to a *positive peace* which is the *presence of justice*"

STEP 2. *Uncover the warrant* by discovering the assumptions of the writer. Write a few sentences exploring the values and beliefs implied by each key term or phrase. Ask yourself these questions: What are the connotations of these words? What do they mean beyond their literal meaning? How does their context in this passage affect my understanding of their meaning?

Let's look first at the argument based on reason 1. King apparently assumes his readers believe, as he does, that justice is more important than order. Readers would have to ask themselves what these two key terms, *order* and *justice,* mean to King. How would you define these terms as King uses them? After you identify key terms, look up their dictionary meanings (*denotations*). Then write out the emotional or cultural associations (*connotations*) the words carry within the context of the passage. For example, the <www.dictionary.com> definition of *order* is "a state of public peace or conformity to law." Clearly King believes that a state of public peace exists at the expense of African Americans' march toward freedom. He is troubled that white moderates prefer "a negative peace which is the absence of tension to a positive peace which is the presence of justice." An *order* that does not include justice, then, leads to his connotative definition: that the current *order* means a state of stagnation and a force for inertia (or not making any change or progress). However, in the next few lines, King adds to his connotative definition by criticizing white moderates for "prefer[ring] a negative peace," for "paternalistically believ[ing they] can set the timetable for another man's freedom," for suffering from a "shallow understanding" of the problem, and for not understanding "that law and order exist for the purpose of establishing justice and that when they fail in this purpose they become the dangerously structured dams that block the flow of social progress."

The <www.dictionary.com> definition for *justice* is "the quality of conforming to principles of reason, to generally accepted standards of right and wrong, and to the stated terms of laws, rules, agreements, etc. in matters affecting persons who could be wronged or unduly favored." Here King's connotative meaning is complex: He questions the laws that keep order, if the laws are not just.

(That is why he later so carefully defines just and unjust laws.) When he writes that "law and order exist for the purpose of establishing justice and . . . when they fail in this purpose they become the dangerously structured dams that block the flow of social progress," he is adding to the connotations of the word *justice* (as well as *order*) by arguing how tightly linked order must be to justice—that order for its own sake can prevent society from changing in ways that it needs to change.

Once you define the denotative and connotative meanings of key terms in a passage, write a few sentences summarizing the beliefs and values you have discovered in these meanings. For example, King believes that justice can be achieved only by disturbing the current order or, to put it another way, that a preference for order keeps people from making progress. Order means the status quo, as opposed to change or "progress towards freedom." By uncovering this warrant, you know that King believes that a disturbance of order is necessary to foster African Americans' progress. He does not believe that order is what is most important; rather, he believes a disturbance of order is justified by the goal of progress toward freedom. King also believes that justice cannot be achieved without disturbing order and that justice is more important than order.

STEP 3. *Consider alternative assumptions* readers might have about the key terms in King's argument. If you know anything about the context of the period when the passage was written, or if the author gives you any clues or direct information about the audience, you will be able to figure out these assumptions from the text. For example, whereas King values justice over order, he clearly assumes that white moderates and other readers in 1963 would think the opposite. Write a few sentences exploring the meanings of *order* and *justice* that might lead someone to value order more than justice. King's readers may not feel quite the same way about the concepts embodied in these terms: *Order* could mean "safety"; or, if justice can come only at the price of social chaos, perhaps (as King worries) readers might conclude that it is better to wait for justice than to risk social upheaval.

STEP 4. *Restate the warrants underlying the argument (the claim and the reasons)* using the denotations and connotations of the key terms. One way to do this is to phrase the beliefs of the author in *that* clauses:

King expects his readers to believe as he does:

—that justice for African Americans in the 1960s requires progress toward freedom

—that anyone who stops or slows this progress is a stumbling block

—that peace is less important than justice

—that order is less important than justice

—that safety is less important than justice

—that progress is more important than maintaining the status quo

—that social unrest and disorder are necessary to achieve justice

—that although breaking the law (what King calls "direct action" and we know as "civil disobedience") disrupts order, peace, and safety, it is necessary to achieve justice

STEP 5. *Explore your own values and beliefs* in relation to those uncovered in your Toulmin analysis. How do you feel about the warrants you identified, given your own experience? Given the difference (if any) between the time the passage was written and the present?

CHECKLIST

Using a Toulmin Analysis

To perform a Toulmin analysis:

1. Identify the author's claim. Identify the reasons and evidence that support that claim.

2. Consider how key terms reflect the author's beliefs and values by defining those terms denotatively and connotatively.

3. Consider alternative assumptions readers might have about the key terms.

4. Restate the author's warrants—the beliefs, values, and assumptions that "warrant" the claim.

5. Compare your own values and beliefs with the author's.

RECOGNIZING LOGICAL FALLACIES

A *logical fallacy* is an error or distortion in the reasoning process. Sometimes writers are unaware that they have committed a logical fallacy: They believe their logic is correct and don't understand why it is faulty. In many cases, however, writers use a fallacy deliberately because they want to avoid reasoning that might undermine their argument or because they want to divert the reader into a different line of reasoning. As you learn to spot logical fallacies in your reading (and in what you hear on radio and television), you will learn also to avoid them in your writing. Students who study formal debate in a speech course or debate club often learn fallacies so they can call attention to and refute the false logic in an opponent's argument. Ethical writers should beware of using fallacies, but they should know how to recognize them and how to refute them.

Identifying fallacies can be tricky, however. Many of them involve subtle and complex issues of reasoning that require careful thought and analysis. In addition, in many cases reasoning becomes fallacious or false only when it is taken too far—when it has become extreme—and reasonable people can disagree about when that point is reached. In logic, as in life, the line between truth and falsehood is often not clearly defined. In fact, one of the most common logical fallacies is the belief that there are only two choices in particular situations.

In general, though, you should suspect that you might be reading a logical fallacy when you stop to think "wait a minute—that doesn't make sense" or when you believe the writer has "gone too far." Recognizing the following common fallacies is an important step in learning to be a critical reader.

Slippery Slope

A *slippery-slope* fallacy occurs when someone asserts that if one thing happens, a series of bad related consequences will *necessarily* follow. The name comes from the idea that if a person takes one step down a slippery slope, he or she cannot help sliding all the way to the bottom. Here are a few examples of this type of faulty reasoning:

- Often when people start making improvements to their homes, the work leads to the need for more improvements. If you paint one room, it makes the rest of the rooms look dingy, so you have to paint them, too; and then the windows need replacing; and so on. This is a valid slippery-slope argument because a particular chain of events does often or usually result from the initial action (though not necessarily in every case).

- Antidrug campaigns often claim that if someone smokes marijuana, he or she will likely become addicted to other illegal drugs. While there is some evidence that marijuana use may lead to additional drug use, this is not true of most people.

- A common argument against euthanasia is that if we allow people to take their own lives (or allow doctors or relatives to help them do so) in order to avoid extraordinary misery in their final days, then down the line we will allow or encourage assisted suicide for matters that might not be devastating or fatal. Given the relatively brief time in which euthanasia has been practiced legally anywhere in the world, it seems too early to judge whether this argument is based on sound reasoning or is a slippery-slope fallacy.

Post hoc, ergo propter hoc

One of the most common fallacies has the Latin name *post hoc, ergo propter hoc,* which means "after this, therefore because of this." A *post hoc* fallacy wrongly assumes that just because an event occurs *after* another event, the second event is caused by the first. In many cases, there is no connection at all between the events; in others, a connection does exist, but it is more complicated than the person making it realizes or admits. This fallacy in causal analysis often occurs when writers try to attribute to one cause something that has several or many causes. When complex issues are made to seem simple, look for this fallacy. Here are some examples:

- If you took medicine prescribed by your doctor for a cold and then broke out in hives, you might assume the medicine caused the hives. However, if you took the medicine with a drink you had never had before, it could have been the drink or the combination of the drink and the medicine that caused the hives. Or the hives might be from a case of nerves or another cause completely unrelated to the medicine, the drink, or anything else you ingested.

- Some people argue that depictions of violence on television and in films cause teenagers to act violently. But most teenagers do not become violent even if they watch a great deal of violence on the screen. To avoid the *post hoc* fallacy, someone making this argument would have to show a clear statistical connection between the amount of violence teenagers watch and the likelihood that they will become violent themselves. The person would also need to consider other possible causes, such as membership in gangs, alienation at school, parental abuse, and so on.

False Dilemma (Either/or Reasoning)

One of the most common fallacies, the *false dilemma,* or *either/or reasoning,* puts readers in the position of having to choose one of two options as if there were no other choices—but rarely in life are options narrowed down to only two. Writers who employ the false dilemma fallacy are usually trying to make the reader choose an option they favor by making the reader believe there are only two choices. Their reasoning avoids the complexities of most issues. Here are some examples:

- Martin Luther King Jr., in paragraph 5 of the excerpt from "Letter from Birmingham Jail" (p. 651), refutes an either/or argument made by others. Arguing that the choice between a "force of complacency" or a force "of bitterness and hatred" is a false dilemma, King points out that there are other alternatives, among them the option of nonviolent protest that he represents.

- Since the terrorist attacks of September 11, 2001, there has been considerable debate about whether the United States should combat terrorism with military force or with intelligence operations and diplomacy. This is a false dilemma: The United States can certainly afford and could well pursue both strategies, depending on the circumstances in particular situations.

Mistaking the Part for the Whole
(Nonrepresentative Sample)

The *nonrepresentative sample* fallacy occurs when a writer assumes that if something is true of a part of a larger whole, it is true of the whole, or vice versa. Sometimes this is indeed the case, but often it is not because the part is not representative—it does not have the typical characteristics—of the whole. This fallacy often occurs in connection with public opinion polls, especially online polls, when no effort is made to ensure that respondents accurately represent the characteristics of the larger group whose opinion they are said to reflect. Here are some examples of this fallacy:

- One of the best-known examples of a nonrepresentative sample in political polling occurred in the 1936 presidential election, when *Literary Digest* magazine conducted a telephone poll that predicted President Franklin D. Roosevelt would be defeated for reelection by his Republican opponent, Alfred P. Landon. On Election Day, Roosevelt won reelection in a landslide. The main explanation for this faulty forecast was the way in which the poll was conducted: Because Republican voters tended to be wealthier than Democratic ones, and because during the depression of the 1930s many Democratic voters could not afford telephones, there was a disproportionate number of Republicans among those the magazine had surveyed.

- Suppose that your school has the best football team in its conference. That does not necessarily mean that the quarterback, the kicker, or the defensive line is the best in the conference, because putting the various members of the team together gives the team as a whole qualities that are different from those of the individuals involved.

Hasty Generalization

A *hasty generalization* leaps to a conclusion without providing enough evidence to support the leap. Here are some examples:

- Government leaders think that the appearance of troop maneuvers in a border town of a neighboring country signals an immediate invasion of the nearby territory. However, in the absence of other, confirming information, it could be just as likely that a leader decided the border town was a good place to practice troop maneuvers, especially if the goal was to impress the neighbor with their military might, with no invasion planned at all.

- "Crime in this city is getting worse and worse. Just yesterday, two people were held up at ATMs downtown." Two crimes, no matter how serious, do not indicate that the overall *rate* of crime is rising. This may indeed be the case, but proving it would require statistics, not just a couple of examples.

Bandwagon Appeal

This fallacy can be recognized when someone is appealing to the notion that "since everyone else does it, you should too." *Bandwagon appeals* are probably most common in advertising and political rhetoric. Here are some examples:

- "Join the thousands who've found relief from arthritis pain with Ache-No-More."

- "A powerful new political tide is surging through America. Want to come together with millions of your fellow citizens in a movement to change our nation's priorities? Volunteer for Americans for National Renewal."

Ad hominem (or *ad personam*) Attack

These Latin names mean "to the man" or "to the person." An *ad hominem* or *ad personam attack* occurs when writers succumb to attacking the person who propounds the ideas with which they disagree, rather than the ideas themselves. Certainly the character and credibility of the writer making the argument affect how persuasive a reader finds it, but they do not affect the underlying soundness of the argument. Here are some examples:

- Whenever a writer attacks a person, be alert for a logical fallacy. Martin Luther King Jr. could have attacked the clergy who wrote the letter he is addressing in "Letter from Birmingham Jail"—he could have called them intolerant or foolish, for example. Instead, he carefully addresses their arguments step by step and shows how his logic is superior to theirs. Some readers might think King does fall victim to this fallacy when he says that the white moderate has only a "shallow understanding" (paragraph 1) of the problem, but he goes on to show how complex the problem is and how the white moderate needs to become more engaged and active in implementing change.

- "My opponent, one of the richest men in the state, wants to cut taxes for himself and his rich friends." "Of course my opponent favors raising corporate taxes. He's just a political hack who's never had to meet a payroll." Whether or not a proposal is a good idea does not depend on whether the person making it will personally benefit from it or has personal experience with the issue involved. Something that benefits the person who proposes it may well (although not necessarily) benefit society in general, and someone with an outsider's perspective on an issue may well (although not necessarily) have better ideas about it than someone with experience. Again, note that sound reasoning is not the same as credibility: Those with nothing personal to gain from a proposal or with experience in the issue may carry more credibility with the people they are trying to persuade, but that does not mean that their views are any more logical. An important part of becoming a critical reader is learning to disregard personal attacks on (or ridicule of) the person making an argument and to focus on the logic of the argument.

Straw Man (or Straw Person)

In a straw-man fallacy, the writer portrays an opponent's position as more extreme than it actually is so that it can be refuted more easily, as one would be able to knock down a straw scarecrow more easily than a live human being. As with many other fallacies, however, the line between what is and is not a straw-man argument is not always clear. Sometimes the writer claims that the opponent's position is part of a plan to achieve a more extreme position—and this claim could be considered either a straw-man argument (which would be fallacious) or a slippery-slope argument (which might be fallacious or might not). Here is an example:

- If a political candidate supports partial privatization of Social Security, an opponent who simply claims that the candidate "proposes doing away with Social Security" is creating a straw-man fallacy. If the opponent simply claims that "partial privatization would be a first step toward doing away with Social Security," this would be a slippery-slope argument—which may or may not be fallacious in itself, but is not a straw-man argument because it does not actually misrepresent the candidate's position. Finally, if the opponent argues that the candidate "supports partial privatization as a first step toward doing away with Social Security," the reader would have to consider other evidence (such as other positions the candidate has taken or his or her voting record) to judge whether this is a fallacious straw-man argument or a sound slippery-slope one.

Begging the Question (Circular Reasoning)

In *begging the question,* the writer makes an argument that assumes the truth of what is theoretically the point at issue. In other words, in order to believe what the argument is trying to prove, the reader has to already believe it. Here are some examples:

- "We shouldn't do that because it's a bad idea." This statement essentially just says, "That's a bad idea because it's a bad idea."

- "God created the world in seven days; this has to be true because the Bible says so, and the Bible is the word of God." This example shows why this fallacy is often called *circular reasoning:* The reasoning simply circles back to the original underlying claim that God is all-powerful. If the reader already believes that the Bible is the word of God and therefore is sufficient evidence for God's creation of the world in seven days, then there is no need to make this claim. If not, then he or she will not be convinced by this argument for it.

- When the U.S. Supreme Court was deciding whether to hear the case of *Bush v. Gore,* an appeal of a decision by the Florida Supreme Court after the disputed presidential election of 2000, Justice Anton Scalia argued that the Court should accept the case to avoid "casting a cloud" over the election of George W. Bush as president. But the point at issue in the case—the claim that was being argued—was whether Bush had indeed been elected president. Gore supporters pointed out that Scalia's argument, based on the assumption that the claim had already been established, was an example of circular reasoning.

Red Herring

You can remember this fallacy by the picture it presents—dragging a dead fish across a trail to distract dogs from pursuing the scent of their real target. In this case, writers use irrelevant arguments to distract readers from the real issue, perhaps because their own argument is weak and they don't want the reader to notice. Red herrings often occur in political debates when one debater does not really want to address an issue raised by the other debater. Here are some examples:

- "My opponent tries to blame my administration for the high price of prescription drugs, but he supports a government takeover of health care." That the opponent supports a government takeover of health care (whether true or false) has nothing to do with whether the policies of the speaker's administration are responsible for the high price of prescription drugs.

- In a U.S. Senate race in 2004, a candidate argued that gay people should not be allowed to adopt children because incest may result if adopted siblings unknowingly marry each other. The risk the candidate mentions is real (if remote), but it is no more likely for children adopted by gay people than for those adopted by heterosexuals. In trying to make an argument against gay adoption, the candidate was making an argument against adoption in general (also implying another kind of incest is likely to occur—between parent and child).

CHECKLIST

Recognizing Logical Fallacies

To determine whether the writer succumbs to any logical fallacies:

1. Annotate places in the text where you stop to think "wait a minute—that doesn't make sense" or where you think the writer has "gone too far."

2. Analyze these places to see if they represent any of the fallacies discussed in this section.

3. Write a few sentences exploring what you discover.

RECOGNIZING EMOTIONAL MANIPULATION

Writers often try to arouse emotions in readers—to excite their interest, make them care, move them to action. Although nothing is wrong with appealing to readers' emotions, it is wrong to manipulate readers with false or exaggerated emotional appeals.

Many words have connotations, associations that enrich their meaning and give words much of their emotional power. For example, we use the word *manipulation* in naming this particular critical reading strategy to arouse an emotional response in readers like you. No one wants to be manipulated. Everyone wants to feel in control of his or her attitudes and opinions. This is especially true in reading arguments: We want to be convinced, not tricked.

Emotional manipulation often works by distracting readers from relevant reasons and evidence. To keep from being distracted, you want to pay close attention as you read and try to distinguish between emotional appeals that are acceptable and those that you consider manipulative or excessive.

Here is an example of one student's reaction to the emotional appeal of the excerpt from "Letter from Birmingham Jail":

> As someone King would probably identify as a white moderate, I can't help reacting negatively to some of the language he uses in this reading. For example, in the first paragraph, he equates white moderates with members of the Ku Klux Klan even though he admits that white moderates were in favor of racial equality and justice. He also puts down white moderates for being paternalistic. Finally, he uses scare tactics when he threatens "a frightening racial nightmare."

CHECKLIST

Recognizing Emotional Manipulation

To assess whether emotional appeals are unfair and manipulative:

1. Annotate places in the text where you sense emotional appeals are being used.

2. Write a few sentences identifying the kinds of appeals you have found and exploring your responses to them.

JUDGING THE WRITER'S CREDIBILITY

Writers often try to persuade readers to respect and believe them. Because readers may not know them personally or even by reputation, writers must present an image of themselves in their writing that will gain their readers' confidence. This image cannot be made directly but must be made indirectly, through the arguments, language, and the system of values and beliefs implied in the writing. Writers establish *credibility* in several ways:

- By showing their knowledge of the subject

- By building common ground with readers

- By responding fairly to objections and opposing arguments

Testing for Knowledge

Writers demonstrate their knowledge of the subject through the facts and statistics they marshal, the sources they rely on for information, and the scope and depth of their understanding. As a critical reader, you may not be sufficiently expert on the subject yourself to know whether the facts are accurate, the sources reliable, and the understanding sufficient. You may need to do some research to see what others are saying about the subject. You can also check credentials—the writer's educational and professional qualifications, the respectability of the publication in which the selection first appeared, any reviews of the writer's work— to determine whether the writer is a respected authority in the field. King brings with him the authority that comes from being a member of the clergy and a respected leader of the Southern Christian Leadership Conference.

Testing for Common Ground

One way writers can establish common ground with their readers is by basing their reasoning on shared values, beliefs, and attitudes. They use language that includes their readers (*we*) rather than excludes them (*they*). They qualify their assertions to keep them from being too extreme. Above all, they acknowledge differences of opinion and try to make room in their argument to accommodate reasonable differences. As a reader, you will be affected by such appeals.

King creates common ground with readers by using the inclusive pronoun *we,* suggesting shared concerns between himself and his audience. Notice, however, his use of masculine pronouns and other references ("the Negro . . . he," "our brothers"). Although King intended this letter to be published in the local newspaper, where it would be read by an audience of both men and women, he addressed it to male clergy. By using language that excludes women, King missed the opportunity to build common ground with half his readers.

Testing for Fairness

Writers display their character by how they handle objections to their arguments. As a critical reader, you want to pay particular attention to how writers treat possible differences of opinion. Be suspicious of those who ignore differences and pretend everyone agrees with their viewpoints. When objections or opposing views are represented, you should consider whether they have been distorted in any way; if they are refuted, you want to be sure they are challenged fairly—with sound reasoning and solid evidence.

One way to gauge an author's credibility is to identify the tone of the argument. *Tone,* the writer's attitude toward the subject and toward the reader, is concerned not so much with what is said as with how it is said. By reading sensitively, you should be able to detect the writer's tone. To identify the tone, list whatever descriptive adjectives come to mind in response to either of these questions: How would you characterize the attitude of this selection? What sort of emotion does the writer bring to his or her writing? Judging from this piece of writing, what kind of person does the author seem to be?

Here is one student's answer to the second question, based on the excerpt from "Letter from Birmingham Jail":

> I know something about King from television programs on the civil rights movement. But if I were to talk about my impression of him from this passage, I'd use words like *patient, thoughtful, well educated, moral, confident.* He doesn't lose his temper but tries to convince his readers by making a case that is reasoned carefully and painstakingly. He's trying to change people's attitudes; no matter how annoyed he might be with them, he treats them with respect. It's as if he believes that their hearts are right, but they're just confused. If he can just set them straight, everything will be fine. Of course, he also sounds a little pompous when he compares himself to Jesus and Socrates, and the threat he appears to make in paragraph 8 seems out of character. Maybe he's losing control of his self-image at those moments.

CHECKLIST

Judging the Writer's Credibility

To decide whether you can trust the writer:

1. As you read and annotate, consider the writer's knowledge of the subject, how well the writer establishes common ground with readers, and whether the writer deals fairly with objections and opposing arguments.

2. Write a few sentences exploring what you discover.

COMPARING AND CONTRASTING RELATED READINGS

When you *compare* two reading selections, you look for similarities. When you *contrast* them, you look for differences. As critical reading strategies, comparing and contrasting enable you to see both texts more clearly.

Both strategies depend on how imaginative you are in preparing the grounds or basis for comparison. We often hear that it is fruitless, so to speak, to compare apples and oranges. It is true that you cannot add or multiply them, but you can put one against the other and come up with some interesting similarities and differences. For example, comparing apples and oranges in terms of their roles as symbols in Western culture (say, the apple of Adam and Eve compared to the symbol for Apple computers) could be quite productive. The grounds or basis for comparison, like a camera lens, brings some things into focus while blurring others.

To demonstrate how this strategy works, we compare and contrast the excerpt from "Letter from Birmingham Jail" (pp. 649–54) with the following selection by Lewis H. Van Dusen Jr.

LEWIS H. VAN DUSEN JR.

Legitimate Pressures and Illegitimate Results

A respected attorney and legal scholar, Lewis H. Van Dusen Jr. has served as chair of the American Bar Association Committee on Ethics and Professional Responsibility. This selection comes from the essay "Civil Disobedience: Destroyer of Democracy," which first appeared in the American Bar Association Journal *in 1969. As you read, notice the annotations we made comparing this essay to the one by King.*

There are many civil rights leaders who show impatience with the process of democracy. They rely on the sit-in, boycott, or mass picketing to gain speedier solutions to the problems that face every citizen. But we must realize that the legitimate pressures that [won concessions in the past] can easily escalate into the illegitimate power plays that might [(extort) demands in the future.] The victories of these civil rights leaders must not shake our confidence in the democratic procedures, as the pressures of demonstration are desirable only if they take place within the limits allowed by law. Civil rights gains should continue to be won by the persuasion of Congress and other legislative bodies and by the

To get something by force or intimidation

1

decision of courts. Any illegal entreaty for the [rights of some] can be an injury to the [rights of others,] for <u>mass demonstrations often trigger violence.</u>

Those who advocate [taking the law into their own hands] should reflect that when they are disobeying what they consider to be an immoral law, they are deciding on a possibly immoral course. <u>Their answer is that the process for</u> democratic relief is <u>too slow,</u> that only mass confrontation can bring immediate action, and that any injuries are the inevitable cost of the pursuit of justice. Their answer is, simply put, that <u>the end justifies the means.</u> It is this justification of <u>any form of demonstration</u> as a form of dissent that threatens to destroy a society built on the rule of law.

2

Our Bill of Rights guarantees wide opportunities to use <u>mass meetings, public parades and organized demonstrations</u> to stimulate sentiment, to dramatize issues and to cause change. The Washington freedom march of 1963 was such a call for action. <u>But the rights of free expression cannot be mere force cloaked in the garb of free speech.</u> As the courts have decreed in labor cases, free assembly does not mean mass picketing or sit-down strikes. These <u>rights are subject to limitations</u> of time and place so as to secure the rights of others. When militant students storm a college president's office to achieve demands, when certain groups plan rush-hour car stalling to protest discrimination in employment, these are not dissent, but a <u>denial of rights to others.</u> Neither is it the lawful use of mass protest, but rather the unlawful use of mob power.

3

Justice Black, one of the foremost advocates and defenders of the right of protest and dissent, has said:

4

> . . . Experience demonstrates that it is not a far step from what to many seems to be the earnest, honest, patriotic, kind-spirited multitude of today, to the fanatical, threatening, lawless mob of tomorrow. And the crowds that press in the streets for noble goals today can be supplanted tomorrow by street mobs pressuring the courts for precisely opposite ends.

Society must censure those demonstrators who would trespass on the public peace, as it must condemn those rioters whose pillage would destroy the public peace. But more ambivalent is society's posture toward the civil disobedient. Unlike the rioter, <u>the true civil disobedient commits no violence.</u> Unlike the mob demonstrator, <u>he commits no trespass on others' rights.</u> The civil disobedient, while deliberately violating a law, <u>shows an oblique respect for the law</u> by

5

King's concern with time

Ends vs. means debate
Any form?

These are legal

Right to demonstrate is limited

Can't deny others' rights

voluntarily submitting to its sanctions. He neither resists arrest nor evades punishment. Thus, he breaches the law but not the peace.

Isn't he contradicting himself?

But civil disobedience, whatever the ethical rationalization, is still an assault on our democratic society, an affront to our legal order and an attack on our constitutional government. To indulge civil disobedience is to invite anarchy, and the permissive arbitrariness of anarchy is hardly less tolerable than the repressive arbitrariness of tyranny. Too often the license of liberty is followed by the loss of liberty, because into the desert of anarchy comes the man on horseback, a Mussolini or a Hitler.

Threatens repression as retaliation

6

We had already read and annotated the King excerpt, so we read the Van Dusen selection looking for a basis for comparison. We decided to base our contrast on the writers' different views of nonviolent direct action. We carefully reread the Van Dusen selection, annotating aspects of his argument against the use of nonviolent direct action. These annotations led directly to the first paragraph of our contrast, which summarizes Van Dusen's argument. Then we reread the King excerpt, looking for how he justifies nonviolent direct action. The second paragraph of our contrast presents King's defense, plus some of our own ideas on how he could have responded to Van Dusen.

King and Van Dusen present radically different views of legal, nonviolent direct action, such as parades, demonstrations, boycotts, sit-ins, or pickets. Although Van Dusen acknowledges that direct action is legal, he nevertheless fears it; and he challenges it energetically in these paragraphs. He seems most concerned about the ways direct action disturbs the peace, infringes on others' rights, and threatens violence. He worries that, even though some groups make gains through direct action, the end result is that everyone else begins to doubt the validity of the usual democratic procedures of relying on legislation and the courts. He condemns advocates of direct action like King for believing that the end (in this case, racial justice) justifies the means (direct action). Van Dusen argues that demonstrations often end violently and that an organized movement like King's can in the beginning win concessions through direct action but then end up extorting demands through threats and illegal uses of power.

In contrast, King argues that nonviolent direct action preserves the peace by bringing hidden tensions and prejudices to the surface where they can be acknowledged and addressed. Direct action enhances democracy by changing its unjust laws and thereby strengthening it. Since direct action is entirely legal, to forgo it as a strategy for change would be to turn one's back on a basic democratic principle. Although it may inconvenience people, its end (a more just social order) is entirely justified by its means (direct action). King would no doubt insist that the occasional violence that follows direct action results always from aggressive, unlawful interference with demonstrations, interference sometimes led by police officers. He might also argue that neither anarchy nor extortion followed from his group's actions.

Notice that these paragraphs address each writer's argument separately. An alternative plan would have been to compare and contrast the two writers' arguments point by point.

CHECKLIST

Comparing and Contrasting Related Readings

To compare and contrast two related readings:

1. Read them both to decide on a basis or grounds for comparison or contrast.

2. Reread and annotate one selection to identify points of comparison or contrast.

3. Reread the second selection, annotating for the points you have already identified.

4. Write up your analyses of the two selections, revising your analysis of the first selection to reflect any new insights you have gained. Or write a point-by-point comparison or contrast of the two selections.

Martin Luther King Jr. wrote "Letter from Birmingham Jail" in response to the following public statement by eight Alabama clergymen.

Public Statement by Eight Alabama Clergymen

April 12, 1963

We the undersigned clergymen are among those who, in January, issued "An Appeal for Law and Order and Common Sense," in dealing with racial problems in Alabama. We expressed understanding that honest convictions in racial matters could properly

1

be pursued in the courts, but urged that decisions of those courts should in the meantime be peacefully obeyed.

Since that time there has been some evidence of increased forebearance and a willingness to face facts. Responsible citizens have undertaken to work on various problems which cause racial friction and unrest. In Birmingham, recent public events have given indication that we all have opportunity for a new constructive and realistic approach to racial problems.

However, we are now confronted by a series of demonstrations by some of our Negro citizens, directed and led in part by outsiders. We recognize the natural impatience of people who feel that their hopes are slow in being realized. But we are convinced that these demonstrations are unwise and untimely.

We agree rather with certain local Negro leadership which has called for honest and open negotiation of racial issues in our area. And we believe this kind of facing of issues can best be accomplished by citizens of our own metropolitan area, white and Negro, meeting with their knowledge and experience of the local situation. All of us need to face that responsibility and find proper channels for its accomplishment.

Just as we formerly pointed out that "hatred and violence have no sanction in our religious and political traditions," we also point out that such actions as incite to hatred and violence, however technically peaceful those actions may be, have not contributed to the resolution of our local problems. We do not believe that these days of new hope are days when extreme measures are justified in Birmingham.

We commend the community as a whole, and the local news media and law enforcement officials in particular, on the calm manner in which these demonstrations have been handled. We urge the public to continue to show restraint should the demonstrations continue, and the law enforcement officials to remain calm and continue to protect our city from violence.

We further strongly urge our own Negro community to withdraw support from these demonstrations, and to unite locally in working peacefully for a better Birmingham. When rights are consistently denied, a cause should be pressed in the courts and in negotiations among local leaders, and not in the streets. We appeal to both our white and Negro citizenry to observe the principles of law and order and common sense.

Signed by:
C. C. J. CARPENTER, D.D., LL.D., *Bishop of Alabama*
JOSEPH A. DURICK, D.D., *Auxiliary Bishop, Diocese of Mobile-Birmingham*

Rabbi MILTON L. GRAFMAN, *Temple Emanu-El, Birmingham, Alabama*

Bishop PAUL HARDIN, *Bishop of the Alabama-West Florida Conference of the Methodist Church*

Bishop NOLAN B. HARMON, *Bishop of the North Alabama Conference of the Methodist Church*

GEORGE M. MURRAY, D.D., LL.D., *Bishop Coadjutor, Episcopal Diocese of Alabama*

EDWARD V. RAMAGE, *Moderator, Synod of the Alabama Presbyterian Church in the United States*

EARL STALLINGS, *Pastor, First Baptist Church, Birmingham, Alabama*

Strategies for Research and Documentation

As many of the essays in *Reading Critically, Writing Well* show, writers often rely on research to expand and test their own ideas about a topic. This appendix offers advice on conducting research, evaluating potential sources, integrating source material you decide to use with your own writing, and documenting this material in an acceptable way.

CONDUCTING RESEARCH

In your college career, you may have opportunities to do many different kinds of research, including laboratory experiments and statistical surveys. Here we introduce the three basic types of research you are most likely to use to satisfy the assignments in *Reading Critically, Writing Well* and to fulfill requirements of other lower-division courses: field research using observation and interview, library research, and Internet research.

Field Research

Observation and *interview* are the two major kinds of *field* or *ethnographic research.* The observational essays in Chapter 3 illustrate some of the ways you might use field research. You might also use these research techniques when proposing a solution to a problem (Chapter 8) or when arguing a position on a controversial issue (Chapter 9). You may be asked to read and write essays based on field research in other courses as well, such as in sociology, political science, anthropology, psychology, communication, or business.

Observation

Following are guidelines for planning an observational visit, taking notes on your observations, and reflecting on what you observed.

PLANNING THE VISIT

To ensure that you use your time productively during observational visits, you must plan them carefully.

GETTING ACCESS. If the place you propose to visit is public, you probably will have easy access to it. Ask yourself whether everything you need to see is within casual view. If not, you have encountered a potential problem of access. If you require special access or permission, you will need to call ahead or make a get-acquainted visit to introduce yourself and explain your purpose.

ANNOUNCING YOUR INTENTIONS. Explain politely who you are, where you are from, and why you would like access. You may be surprised at how receptive people can be to a student on assignment from a college course. Not every place you wish to visit will welcome you, however. A variety of constraints on outside visitors exist in private businesses as well as public institutions. But generally, if people know your intentions, they may be able to tell you about aspects of a place or an activity you would not have thought to observe.

BRINGING TOOLS. Take a notebook with a firm back so that you will have a steady writing surface, perhaps a small stenographer's pad with a spiral binding across the top. Take a few pens or pencils. If you prefer to use a tape recorder to record your observations, bring along extra tapes and batteries. Also take a notebook in case something goes wrong with the tape recorder.

OBSERVING AND TAKING NOTES

Here are some practical suggestions for making observations and taking notes.

OBSERVING. Some activities invite multiple vantage points, whereas others seem to limit the observer to a single perspective. Explore the space as much as possible, taking advantage of every vantage point available to you. Consider it from different angles, both literally and figuratively. Since your purposes are to analyze as well as to describe your subject, look for its typical and atypical features, how it is like and unlike similar subjects. Think also about what would make the subject interesting to your readers.

NOTETAKING. You undoubtedly will find your own style of notetaking, but here are a few pointers:

- Write only on one side of the page. Later, when you organize your notes, you may want to cut up the pages and file notes under different headings.
- Along with writing words, phrases, or sentences, draw diagrams and sketches that will help you see and recall the place later on.

- Use abbreviations as much as you like, but use them consistently and clearly.

- Note any ideas or questions that occur to you.

- Use quotation marks around any overheard conversation you take down.

Because you can later reorganize your observational notes easily, you do not need to record them in any planned or systematic way. Your notes should include information about the place, the people, and your personal reactions to both.

The Place. Begin by listing objects you see. Then add details of some of these objects—color, shape, size, texture, function, relation to similar or dissimilar objects. Although visual details will probably dominate your notes, you might also want to note sounds and smells. Be sure to include some notes about the shape, dimensions, and layout of the place. How big is it? How is it organized?

The People. Note the number of people and their activities, movements, and behavior. Describe their appearance or dress. Record parts of overheard conversations. Note whether you see more men than women, more people of one racial group than of another, more older than younger people. Most important, note anything surprising or unusual about people in the scene and how they interact with one another.

Your Impressions. Include in your notes the feelings, ideas, or insights you have about what you observe.

REFLECTING ON YOUR OBSERVATIONS

Immediately after your visit (within a few minutes, if possible), find a quiet place to reflect on what you saw, review your notes, and add any images, details, insights, or questions you now recall. Give yourself at least a half hour for quiet thought. Finally, review all your notes, and write a few sentences about your main impressions of the place. What did you learn? How did this visit change or confirm your preconceptions? What impression of the place and people would you like to convey to readers?

Interview

Here are guidelines for planning and setting up an interview, conducting an interview, and reflecting on what you learned.

PLANNING THE INTERVIEW

CHOOSING AN INTERVIEW SUBJECT. If you will be interviewing a person who is the focus of your research, consider beginning with one or two background interviews with other people. If several people play important roles, be sure to interview as many of them as possible. Try to be flexible, however, because you may be unable to speak with the people you targeted initially and may wind up interviewing someone else—an assistant, perhaps. You might even learn more from an assistant than you would from the person in charge.

ARRANGING AN INTERVIEW. You may be nervous about phoning a busy person and asking for some of his or her time. Indeed, you may get turned down. If so, do ask if someone else might talk with you: Many people are genuinely flattered to be asked about themselves and their work. Moreover, because you are a college student on assignment, some people may feel that they are doing a public service by allowing you to interview them. When arranging the interview, introduce yourself with a short, simple, and enthusiastic description of your project.

Keep in mind that the person you want to interview will be donating time to you. When you call ahead to arrange a specific time for the interview, be sure to ask what time is most convenient. Arrive at the appointed time and bring all the materials you will need to conduct the interview. Remember, too, to express your thanks when the interview has ended.

PREPARING FOR THE INTERVIEW. Make any necessary observational visits and do any essential background reading before the interview. Consider your objectives: For example, do you want the "big picture," answers to specific questions, or clarification of something you observed, read, or heard about in another interview?

The key to good interviewing is flexibility. You may be looking for facts, but your interview subject may not have any to offer. In that case, you should be willing to shift gears and go after whatever insight your subject does have to offer.

COMPOSING INTERVIEW QUESTIONS. You probably will want to mix *specific questions* requesting factual information with *open-ended questions,* which are likely to generate anecdotes and reveal attitudes that could lead to other, more penetrating questions. In interviewing a small-business owner, for example, you might begin with a specific question about when the business was established and then follow up with an open-ended question, such as "Could you take a few minutes to tell me something about your early days in the business? I'd be interested to hear about how you got started, what your hopes were, and what problems you had to face." Also consider asking directly for an anecdote ("What happened when your employees threatened to strike?"), encouraging reflection ("What do you think has helped you most? What has hampered you?"), or soliciting advice ("What advice would you give someone trying to start a new business today?").

The best questions encourage the interview subject to talk freely but to the point. If the answer strays too far from the point, a follow-up question may be necessary to refocus the talk. Another way to direct the conversation is to rephrase the subject's answer, saying something like "Let me see if I have this right . . ." or "Am I correct in saying that you feel . . . ?" Often, the interview subject will take this opportunity to amplify the original response by adding just the anecdote or quotation you have been looking for.

One type of question to avoid during interviewing is the *leading question.* Such questions assume too much. Consider, for example, this question: "Do you think the increase in the occurrence of rape is due to the fact that women are perceived as competitors in a severely depressed economy?" The question makes several assumptions, including that there is an increase in the occurrence of rape, that women are perceived (apparently by rapists) as competitors, and that the economy is severely depressed. A better way of asking the question might be to make the assumptions more explicit by dividing the question into its parts: "Do you think there is an increase in the occurrence of rape? What could have caused it? I've heard some people argue that the economy has something to do with it. Do you think so? Do you think rapists perceive women as competitors? Could the current economic situation have made this competition more severe?" This form of questioning allows you to voice what others have said without bullying your subject into echoing your terms.

BRINGING TOOLS. You will need several pencils or pens and a notebook with a firm back so you can write without a table. We recommend dividing the page into two columns. Use the left-hand column (one-third of the page) to note your impressions and descriptions of the scene, the person, and the mood of the interview. Title this column *Impressions.* Title the wider right-hand column *Information.* Before the interview, write down a few basic questions to jog your memory. During the interview, however, listen and ask questions based on what your interview subject says. Do not mechanically go through your list of questions.

TAKING NOTES DURING THE INTERVIEW

Your interview notes might include a few full quotations, key words, and phrases to jog your memory, as well as descriptive jottings about the scene, the person, and the mood of the interview. Remember that how something is said may be as important as what is said. Do not try to record everything your subject says during the interview. Except for the occasional quotation that you will cite directly, you do not want to make a verbatim transcript of the interview. You may not have much confidence in your memory, but if you pay close attention to your subject you are likely to recall a good deal of the conversation immediately after the interview, when you should take the time to add to your notes.

REFLECTING ON THE INTERVIEW

Soon after the interview has concluded, find a quiet place to review your notes. Spend at least half an hour adding to your notes and thinking about what you learned. At the end of this time, write a few sentences about your main impressions from the interview:

- What were the highlights of the interview for you?

- Which questions did not get as much of a response as you anticipated or seem less important to you now?

- How did the interview change your attitude toward or understanding of the subject?

- How has this experience influenced your plans to interview others or to reinterview this person?

Integrating Library and Internet Research

Although this appendix includes separate sections on library and Internet research, these two methods of researching information are closely intertwined. You can often use the Internet to access your library's resources—the catalog of books and other items, indexes to periodical articles, and other kinds of electronic databases—from your own computer in your home or dorm room. On the other hand, you will need or want to go through the library's computers rather than your own to access many Web-based resources, including those that charge fees for subscriptions or for downloading and printing documents.

For most research topics, finding source materials will entail both library and Internet research because each offers material not available from the other. The vast majority of books and articles published in print are not available online, and so you will almost certainly need to consult some of these print sources to avoid getting a skewed perspective on your topic, especially if it deals with events that occurred more than a few years ago. Keep in mind that print sources also tend to offer more reliable information than online sources (for the reasons listed on pp. 716–18). Likewise, though, very little online material ever appears in print, and especially for current topics, you will almost certainly want to check the Web as well as the electronic sources to which your campus library subscribes for the latest developments or research findings. In addition, compared with print sources, online sources usually take less time and effort both to find and to integrate into your own writing. While in these ways online sources can help you do a more thorough job of research within a limited period of time, be careful not to rely too heavily on the Web just because it is easy to use.

Library Research

Library research involves a variety of activities: checking the library catalog, browsing in the stacks, consulting bibliographical indexes, and evaluating sources. Although librarians are there to help, all college students should learn basic library research skills. You should familiarize yourself with your college library's resources and keep careful notes as you research so that you will not have to go back over the same ground later on.

Library research can be useful at various stages of the writing process, depending on the kind of essay you are writing and the special needs of your subject. You may, for example, need to do research immediately to choose a subject. Or you may choose a topic without the benefit of research, and then use the library to find specific information to develop and support your thesis. But no matter when you enter the stacks, you need to follow a systematic strategy: Keep a working bibliography; prepare to search for sources by determining the appropriate subject headings or other criteria; consult standard reference works, such as bibliographical indexes and computer databases; and search for books, articles, and other sources on your topic. Later in this appendix, in Evaluating Sources Critically (pp. 721–24), you will find guidelines to help you evaluate the relevancy and credibility of these and other sources.

Keep a Working Bibliography

A *working bibliography* is a preliminary, ongoing record of all the references you consult as you research, even including those that you do not plan to cite in your essay. Encyclopedias, bibliographies, and indexes, for example, should go into the working bibliography, though you will not list these resources in your final bibliography. The working bibliography is a record of the *research process* as a whole; the final bibliography is a record of the *research paper* that you ultimately write.

Since the working bibliography is a first draft of your final list of sources, it is a good idea to use the same documentation style from the start. In Acknowledging Sources (pp. 735–60), later in this appendix, two styles of documentation are discussed and illustrated: the style adopted by the Modern Language Association (MLA) and widely used in the humanities, and the style advocated by the American Psychological Association (APA) for use in the social sciences. Individual disciplines often have their own preferred styles of documentation, which your instructor may wish you to use.

You can keep your working bibliography on index cards, in a notebook, or in a computer file. Whatever method you choose, make your entries accurate and complete. If the call number for a book is missing a single digit, for example, you might not be able to find the book in the stacks.

Consult Standard Reference Works

To get an overview of your topic, look up your subject headings in *standard reference works*. Usually, these resources are found in the reference section of the library and cannot be checked out, so budget your library time for consulting reference works accordingly.

The most useful standard reference works include *specialized encyclopedias, disciplinary guides, government publications,* and *bibliographies.* In addition, a general encyclopedia such as *Encyclopedia Americana* might help provide a very general overview of your topic, while almanacs, atlases, and dictionaries are sometimes useful as well.

SPECIALIZED ENCYCLOPEDIAS

A specialized encyclopedia, such as *Encyclopedia of Crime and Justice,* or a disciplinary guide, such as *Social Sciences: A Cross-Disciplinary Guide to Selected Sources,* can offer background on your subject and starting points for further research. Specialized encyclopedias often include an explanation of issues related to the topic, definitions of specialized terminology, and selective bibliographies naming additional sources. Specialized encyclopedias can be found in the catalog under the subject heading for the discipline, such as "psychology," and the subheading "dictionaries and encyclopedias." Three particular reference sources can help you identify specialized encyclopedias covering your topic:

- *ARBA Guide to Subject Encyclopedias and Dictionaries* (1997). Lists specialized encyclopedias by broad subject category, with descriptions of coverage, focus, and any special features. Also available online through library portals.

- *Subject Encyclopedias: User Guide, Review Citations, and Keyword Index* (1999). Lists specialized encyclopedias by broad subject category and provides access to individual articles within them. By looking under the key terms that describe a topic, you can find references to specific articles in any of over four hundred specialized encyclopedias.

- *Kister's Best Encyclopedias: A Comparative Guide to General and Specialized Encyclopedias* (1994). Describes over a thousand encyclopedias, both print and electronic. Includes major foreign-language encyclopedias.

DISCIPLINARY GUIDES

Disciplinary guides can help you locate the major handbooks, encyclopedias, bibliographies, journals, periodical indexes, and computer databases in various academic fields. These types of works are published rarely and are not known for their currency. However, they can be valuable references, if you take the time to check dates and supplement your sources as needed. Here is a sample of disciplinary guides:

- *The Humanities: A Selective Guide to Information Sources,* 5th ed. (2000). By Ron Blazek and Elizabeth S. Aversa. Also available online through library portals.

- *Introduction to Library Research in Anthropology,* 2nd ed. (1998). By John M. Weeks.

- *The American Historical Association's Guide to Historical Literature,* 3rd ed. (1995). Edited by Mary Beth Norton and Pamela Gerardi.

- *Political Science: A Guide to Reference and Information Sources* (1990). By Henry E. York.

- *Literary Research Guide: A Guide to Reference Sources for the Study of Literatures in English and Related Topics,* 4th ed. (2002). By James L. Harner.

GOVERNMENT RESOURCES

Some government publications and statistical reports may be found in the reference section or in a special government documents section of your college library. If you are researching current issues, for example, you might want to consult *Congressional Quarterly Almanac* or *CQ Weekly.* On the Internet, try the home page of the U.S. Congress for the *Congressional Record* <http://thomas .loc.gov/home/thomas2.html>. For compilations of statistics, try *Statistical Abstract of the United States, Statistical Reference Index,* and *The Gallup Poll: Public Opinion.* The Gallup Web site <http://www.gallup.com> provides descriptions of some of its most recent polls.

BIBLIOGRAPHIES

A bibliography is simply a list of books on a given topic, which can be more or less exhaustive depending on its purpose. (To discover how selections were made, check the bibliography's preface or introduction.) A good way to locate a comprehensive, up-to-date bibliography on your subject is to look in the *Bibliographic Index.* A master list of bibliographies that contain fifty or more titles, the *Bibliographic Index* draws from articles, books, and government publications. The index, published yearly, is not cumulative, so check the most recent volume for current information.

Identify Subject Headings and Keywords

To extend your research beyond standard reference works, you need to find appropriate subject headings and keywords. *Subject headings* are specific words and phrases used in library catalogs, periodical indexes, and other databases to categorize the contents of books and articles so that people can look for materials about a particular topic. One way to begin your search for subject headings is to consult the *Library of Congress Subject Headings* (LCSH), which your library probably makes available both in print and online. This work lists the standard subject headings used in library catalogs. Here is an example from the LCSH:

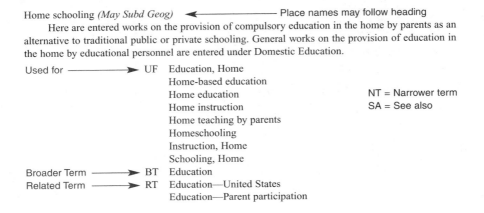

Home schooling *(May Subd Geog)* ◄─────────────── Place names may follow heading
    Here are entered works on the provision of compulsory education in the home by parents as an alternative to traditional public or private schooling. General works on the provision of education in the home by educational personnel are entered under Domestic Education.

Used for ────────► UF   Education, Home
                                Home-based education
                                Home education   NT = Narrower term
                                Home instruction   SA = See also
                                Home teaching by parents
                                Homeschooling
                                Instruction, Home
                                Schooling, Home
Broader Term ────────► BT   Education
Related Term ────────► RT   Education—United States
                                Education—Parent participation

This sample entry proved particularly useful because when the student researching this topic found nothing listed in the library catalog under "Home schooling," she tried the other headings until "Education—Parent participation" and "Education—United States" yielded information on three books. Note, too, that this entry explains the types of books that would be found under these headings and those that would be found elsewhere.

Instead of looking for likely headings in the LCSH, however, you can usually locate useful subject headings faster by searching the catalog or other database using *keywords,* words or phrases that you think describe your topic. As you read about your subject in an encyclopedia or other reference book, you should keep a list of keywords that may be useful. (Make sure you spell your keywords correctly. Computers are unforgiving of spelling errors.) As you review the results of a keyword search, look for the titles that seem to match most closely the topics that you are looking for. When you call up the detailed information for these titles, look for the section labeled "Subject" or "Subject Heading," which will show the headings under which the book or article is classified. (In the example that follows, this section is abbreviated as "Subj-lcsh.") In many computerized catalogs and databases, these subject headings are links that you can click on to get a list of other materials on the same subject. Keep a list in your working bibliography of all the subject headings you find that relate to your topic, so that you can refer to them each time you start looking for information. Here is an example of an online catalog listing for a book on home schooling:

Title: Pathways to privatization in education / by Joseph Murphy . . . [et al.]
Imprint: Greenwich, Conn.: Ablex Pub. Corp., c1998

LOCATION	CALL NO	STATUS
MAIN	LB2806.36 .P38 1998	NOT CHCKD OUT

Description: xiii, 244 p.; 24 cm
Series: Contemporary studies in social and policy issues in education

Subj-lcsh   **Privatization in education — United States**
                 Educational vouchers — United States
                 Home schooling — United States

Add author: Murphy, Joseph, 1949–
Note(s):   Includes bibliographical references (p. 209–236) and index
ISBN: 1567503632 (cloth)
             1567503640 (pbk.)

DETERMINING THE MOST PROMISING SOURCES

As you follow a subject heading into the library catalog and periodical indexes, you will discover many seemingly relevant books and articles. How do you decide which ones to track down and examine? You may have little to go on but author, title, date, and publisher or periodical name, but these details actually provide useful clues. Look again, for example, at the online catalog reference to a book on home schooling. The title, *Pathways to Privatization in Education,* is the first clue to the subject coverage of the book. Note that the publication date, 1998, is fairly recent. From the subject headings, you can see that this book focuses on various aspects of the privatization of education, which includes home schooling, and that the geographic focus of the book is the United States. Finally, from the notes, you can see that the book includes an extensive bibliography that could lead you to other sources.

Now look at the following entry from *Education Index,* a periodical index:

Home schooling
    Do children have to go to school? [Great Britain] C. Henson. *Child Educ (Engl)* v73 p68 Mr '96
    Homegrown learning [Twin Ridges Elementary School District combines homeschooling with regular classroom instruction] D. Hill. il *Teach Mag* v7 p40-5 Ap '96
    Should we open extracurriculars to home-schoolers? J. Watford; B. Dickinson. il *Am Teach* v80 p4 Mr '96

This entry lists articles that address different aspects of home schooling, briefly describing some of the articles. You can see that the first article deals with the issue from a British point of view, which might provide an interesting cross-cultural perspective for your essay. The title of the third article seems to indicate an argument on the issue; because it appears in a magazine for teachers, it might give you a sense of that profession's attitudes toward home schooling. Be careful, though, to stay focused on your specific research topic or thesis, especially if you are pressed for time and cannot afford to become distracted exploring sources that sound interesting but are unlikely to be useful.

In addition, each entry contains the information that you will need to locate it in a library. Going back to the first article, here is what each piece of information means:

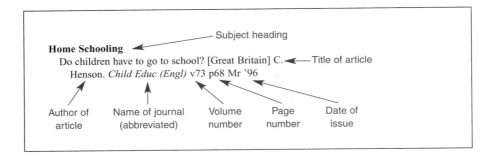

When you look in catalogs and indexes, consider the following points when deciding whether you should track down a particular source:

- *Relevance to your topic:* Do the title, subtitle, description, subject headings, and abstract help you determine how directly the particular source addresses your topic?

- *Publication date:* How recent is the source? For current controversies, emerging trends, and scientific or technological developments, you must consult recent material. For historical or biographical topics, you will want to start with present-day perspectives but eventually explore older sources that offer authoritative perspectives. You may also want or need to consult sources written at the time of the events or during the life of the person you are researching.

- *Description:* Does the length indicate a brief treatment of the topic or an extended treatment? Does the work include illustrations that may elaborate on concepts discussed in the text? Does it include a bibliography that could lead you to other works or an index that could give you an overview of what is discussed in the text? Does the abstract indicate the focus of the work?

From among the sources that look promising, select publications that seem by their titles to address different aspects of your topic or to approach it from different perspectives. Try to avoid selecting sources that are mostly by the same author, from the same publisher, or in the same journal. Common sense will lead you to an appropriate decision about diversity in source materials.

Search Online Library Catalogs and Databases

Computerized library catalogs and other databases consist of thousands or millions of records, each representing an individual item such as a book, an article, or a government publication. The record is made up of different fields describing the item and allowing users to search for it and retrieve it from the database. Here is a record for a book from a library's online catalog, with the searchable fields in bold:

Author:	Gordon, William MacGuire, 1935–
Title:	The law of home schooling / William M. Gordon, Charles J. Russo, Albert S. Miles. Topeka, Kan.: National Organization on Legal Problems of Education, c1994.
Location:	Main
Call No:	JLL 74-383 no. 52
Description:	74 p.; 23 cm.
Series:	NOLPE monograph series no. 52.
Notes:	Includes bibliographical references and index.
Subjects:	Home schooling — Law and legislation — United States. Educational law and legislation — United States. Education — Parent participation — United States.
Other entries:	Russo, Charles J.

USING DIFFERENT SEARCH TECHNIQUES

Basic search strategies include author, title, and subject searches. When you request an *author search,* the computer looks for a match between the name you type and the names listed in the author field of all the records in the online catalog or other database. When you request a *title search* or a *subject search,* the computer looks for a match in the title field or the subject field, respectively. Computers are very literal. They try to match only the exact terms you enter, and most do not recognize variant or incorrect spellings. That is an incentive to become a good speller and a good typist. However, because most library catalogs and databases also offer the option of searching for titles and subjects by keywords, you need not enter the full exact title or subject heading. In addition, you can be flexible where the computer cannot. For instance, if you were researching the topic of home schooling, you could do a subject search not only for "home schooling" but also for "homeschooling" and "home-schooling."

DOING ADVANCED SEARCHES AND USING BOOLEAN OPERATORS

The real power of using a computerized library catalog or other database is demonstrated when you need to look up books or articles using more than one keyword. For example, suppose you want information about home schooling in California. Rather than looking through an index listing all the articles on home schooling and picking out those that mention California, you can ask the computer to do the work for you by linking your two keywords. Many online catalogs and databases now offer the option of an *advanced search,* sometimes on a separate page from the main search page, that allows you to search for more than one keyword at a time, search for certain keywords while excluding others, or search for an exact phrase. Or you may be able to create this kind of advanced search yourself by using the *Boolean operators* AND, OR, and NOT along with quotation marks and parentheses.

To understand the operation of *Boolean logic* (developed by and named after George Boole, a nineteenth-century mathematician), picture one set of articles about home schooling and another set of articles about California. A third set is formed by articles that are about both home schooling and California. The diagrams on page 713 provide an illustration of how each Boolean operator works.

The search mechanisms for catalogs and databases usually require that the Boolean operators be typed in all capital letters. Some mechanisms use the plus sign (+) or the ampersand (&) instead of AND, the minus sign (−) instead of NOT, and the | sign instead of OR; check the help page or home page for instructions if necessary.

You can also use quotation marks around a group of words to search for a phrase (with the words in the same order). And you can use parentheses to combine the Boolean operators: for example, *home schooling* NOT (*California* OR *Texas*) will retrieve all articles about home schooling except ones that mention California and ones that mention Texas.

USING TRUNCATION

Another useful search strategy is *truncation.* With this technique, you drop the ending of a word or term and replace it with a symbol, which indicates you want to retrieve records containing any term that begins the same way as your term. For example, by entering the term "home school#" you would retrieve all the records that have terms such as "home school," "home schooling," "home schools," "home schooled," or "home schoolers." Truncation is useful when you want to retrieve both the plural and singular forms of a word or any word for which you are not sure of the ending. Truncation symbols vary with the catalog or database. The question mark (?), asterisk (*), and pound sign (#) are frequently used.

AND

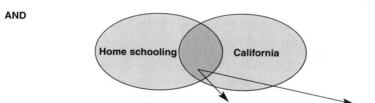

Returns references that contain both the term **home schooling** AND the term **California**

- Narrows the search
- Combines unrelated terms
- Is the default used by most online catalogs and databases

OR

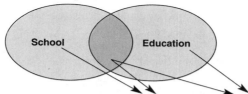

Returns all references that contain either the term **school** OR the term **education** OR both terms

- Broadens the search **("OR is more")**
- Is useful with synonyms and variant spellings: ("home schooling" and "homeschooling")

NOT

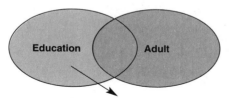

Returns references that include the term **education** but NOT the term **adult**

- Narrows the search
- May eliminate relevant material

The Boolean Operators: AND, OR, and NOT

Search for Books

The primary source of information on books is the library's *online catalog*. Until a decade or so ago a library's catalog consisted of small file cards organized alphabetically into rows of drawers, by subject, title, and author's name. Today the same type of information is organized electronically in an online catalog. The online catalog provides more flexibility in searching and often tells you whether the book is available or checked out. Another distinct advantage is that you can print out source information, making it unnecessary for you to copy it by hand. You should, however, check to make sure that the online catalog goes far enough back in time for your purposes. If the computerized records do not date far enough back, see whether your library has maintained its hard-copy card catalog for the period in question.

Each catalog or computer entry gives the same basic information: the name of the author, the title of the book, the subject heading(s) related to the book, and the call number you will need to find the book on the library shelves. Most libraries provide a map showing where the various call numbers are shelved. The accompanying example shows one college library's online catalog display of the author entry for a book on home schooling. Notice the call number in the middle of the bottom line. (On cards, look for the call number in the upper left-hand corner.)

Even if you attend a large research university, your library is unlikely to hold every book or journal article you might need. Remember that your library's online catalog and serial record (a list of the periodicals the library holds) include only records of the books and periodicals it holds. As you will learn in the following section on Internet research, you can access the online catalogs of other libraries to find sources not within your library's holdings. At that point, you can request an interlibrary loan from another college library, a procedure handled by email or in person at the reference desk. Keep in mind, however, that it may take up to a couple of weeks to obtain a source by way of interlibrary loan.

AUTHOR:	Guterson, David, 1951–
TITLE:	Family matters: Why homeschooling makes sense
EDITION:	1st Harvest ed.
PUBLISHER:	San Diego: Harcourt Brace & Co., c1992
PHYSICAL DESC:	x, 254 p.; 18 cm.
NOTES:	Includes bibliographical references and index.
SUBJECTS:	Education—United States
	Education—parent participation
	Teaching methods
LOCATION/CALL NUMBER	STATUS
UCSD Undergrad/649.68 g 1993	Available

Search for Articles

Articles published in periodicals (magazines, journals, and newspapers) usually are not listed in the library catalog. To find them, you will want to use *periodical indexes,* which originally appeared only in print form but today are likely to take the form of a CD-ROM, an online database, or a hybrid of the two. As computer technology becomes more sophisticated, some database services have begun to offer full-text articles along with the listings of articles. *Indexes* list citations of articles; *abstracts* summarize the articles as well. *Full-text retrieval* means you can view an entire article online and potentially download it (often excluding graphics) for reading offline.

Following is a list of some of the computer database services that your library might subscribe to or that provide free access to their contents:

- *Readers' Guide to Periodical Literature* (1900–; CD-ROM, 1983–; online). The classic index for periodicals, updated quarterly, offering about two hundred popular periodicals. <http://www.silverplatter.com/catalog/wipl.htm>

- *ERIC (Education Resources Information Center)* (1969–; online). Houses indexes, abstracts, and the full text of selected articles from 750 education journals. <http://www.eric.ed.gov>

- *Business Periodicals Ondisc* (1988–), and *ABI/INFORM* (1988–). Provide the full text of articles from business periodicals. If your library has a printer attached to a terminal, you can print out articles, including illustrations.

- *IngentaConnect* (1998–; online). An online document-delivery service that lists articles from more than 5,400 online journals and 26,000 other publications. For a fee, you can receive the full text of the article, online or by fax. <http://www.ingentaconnect.com>

- *Lexis-Nexis* (1973–; online and CD-ROM). An information service for journalists, lawyers, and financial analysts. <http://www.lexis-nexis.com>

- *InfoTrac* (online and CD-ROM). An information supplier that provides access to the following three indexes: (1) *General Periodicals Index,* which lists information an over twelve hundred general-interest publications; (2) *Academic Index,* which provides the full text of articles from five hundred popular and academic periodicals; and (3) *National Newspaper Index,* which covers the *Christian Science Monitor, Los Angeles Times, New York Times, Wall Street Journal,* and *Washington Post.* <http://www.infotrac-college.com/wadsworth/access.html>

Using *Academic Index* to do a search for "home schooling" would yield several listings, including the two examples shown here. Notice that the results specify whether an abstract is available and where the periodical can be found in the library.

```
Home Schooling
     Mommy, what's a classroom? (the merits of home
schooling are still being debated) Bill Roorback.
The New York Times Magazine, Feb 2, 1997 p30 col1
(112 col in).
     —Abstract Available—
     Holdings: 10/92—present Periodicals—1st Floor
Paper 01/66—present Microfilm (Room #162)

Microfilm
     The natural curriculum. (educating children at
home) Rosie Benson-Bunch. Times Education Supple-
ment, Dec 27, 1996 n4200 pA25(1).
     —Abstract Available—
```

While InfoTrac is intended for popular and academic reference purposes, *Business Periodicals Ondisc* and ERIC are designed for use within specific disciplines. Other discipline-specific databases include *Accounting and Tax Index, Art Index, Education Index, Historical Abstracts, MLA International Bibliography* (literature), *Psychological Abstracts,* and *Sociological Abstracts.* For current events and topics in the news, you can use news-specific databases, including *NewsBank, Newspaper Abstracts,* and *Alternative Press Index.* Most of these resources use the Library of Congress subject headings, but some have their own systems of classification. *Sociological Abstracts,* for example, has a separate volume for subject headings. To see how subjects are classified in the index or abstract you are using, check the opening page or screen.

When you look for the print periodicals in your library, you will typically find them arranged alphabetically by title in a particular section of the building. For previous years' collections of popular magazines and many scholarly journals, look for bound annual volumes rather than individual issues. Some older periodicals may be stored on microfilm (reels) or microfiche (cards) that must be read in viewing machines.

You might also want to check the Web sites of local or national newspapers whose coverage you respect. Here are some possibilities:

Chicago Tribune	http://www.chicagotribune.com
Los Angeles Times	http://www.latimes.com
New York Times	http://www.nytimes.com
San Francisco Chronicle	http://www.sfgate.com/chronicle
San Jose Mercury News	http://www.mercurynews.com
Washington Post	http://www.washingtonpost.com

Be warned, though, that some online news publishers now charge a fee for the full-text retrieval of articles. Finding the article is usually free of charge, but downloading the full text of an article to your computer will likely cost a small fee.

Internet Research

The Internet is a vast global computer network that enables users to store and share information quickly and easily. The World Wide Web is a network of sites on the Internet, each with its own electronic address (called a *URL,* or *uniform resource locator*). You can gain access to the Internet through your library or campus computer system or at home through a commercial Internet service provider (ISP). By now, most of you are familiar with searching the Internet. This section provides some basic background information about the Net and introduces you to some tools and strategies that will help you use it more efficiently to find information on a topic.

As you use the Internet for conducting research, keep the following concerns and guidelines in mind:

- *The Internet has no central system of organization.* On the Internet, a huge amount of information is stored on many different networks and servers and in many different formats, each with its own system of organization. The Internet has no central catalog, reference librarian, or standard classification system for the vast resources available there.

- *Many electronic sources are not part of the Internet or require a paid subscription or other fees.* Computerized library catalogs, electronic periodical indexes, full-text article databases, and other electronic resources are often stored on CD-ROMs or on campus computer networks rather than on the Internet and so are available to students only through the library or other campus computers. Furthermore, some databases on the Web charge for a subscription or for downloading or printing out content. For these reasons (as well as the one discussed below), you should plan to use the library or campus computer system for much of your electronic research, since it will give you access to more material at a lower cost. You will not need to pay for subscriptions, and you may be able to download or print out material for free as well.

- *Internet sources that you find on your own are generally less reliable than print sources or than electronic sources to which your library or campus subscribes.* Because it is relatively easy for anyone to publish on the Internet, judging the reliability of online information is a special concern. Depending on your topic, purpose, and audience, the sources you find on the Internet may not be as credible or authoritative as print sources or subscription electronic sources, which have usually been screened by publishers, editors, librarians, and authorities on the topic. For some topics, most of what you find on the Internet may be written by highly biased or amateur authors, so you will need to balance or supplement these sources with information from your library or campus and print sources. When in doubt about the reliability of an online source for a particular assignment, check with your instructor.

- *Internet sources are not as stable as print sources or as the electronic sources to which your library or campus subscribes.* A Web site that existed last week may no longer be available today, or its content may have changed.

- *Internet sources must be documented, and so you need to include them in your working bibliography.* A working bibliography is an ongoing record of all the possible sources you discover as you research your subject. The working bibliography becomes the draft for the list of references or works cited at the end of your essay, even if you do not include all these sources in your final list. You will need to follow appropriate conventions for quoting, paraphrasing, summarizing, and documenting the online sources you use, just as you do for print sources. Because an Internet source can change or disappear quickly, be sure to record the information for the working-bibliography entry when you first find the source. Whenever possible, download and print out the source to preserve it. Make sure your download or printout includes all the items of information required for the entry or at least all those you can find. Citation forms for Internet sources typically require more information than those for print sources, but the items are often harder (or impossible) to identify because Internet sources do not appear in the kinds of standard formats that print sources do.

Learn How to Navigate the Web

Most material on the Web is available twenty-four hours a day, as long as your server is up and running. For many academic users, an especially useful feature of the Web is that it allows *hypertext links* to other documents or files, so that with a simple click of the mouse a reader might find more detailed information on a subject or access a related document.

A *Web browser* is a software program that allows you to display and navigate Web pages on your computer. Web browsers have evolved from basic text-driven browsers such as Lynx (still used today) into graphical, point-and-click interfaces such as Netscape Navigator and Microsoft Internet Explorer, which support not only text and hypertext links but also images, sound, animation, and even video.

A browser lets you move around a *Web site,* a set of connected pages (programming files) made available to the public. The central or starting point for a Web site is often called its *home page.* Web sites may be sponsored by companies, institutions, government agencies, organizations, clubs, or individuals.

As noted earlier, each Web site has its own electronic address or uniform resource locator. The URL for the Library of Congress is typical:

http://www.loc.gov

The first part of a URL usually consists of the abbreviation *http://* that tells the sending and receiving computers the type of information being sent and how to transfer it. The second part usually includes the standard *www* (meaning "World Wide Web"), the name of the page, and a three-letter suffix that characterizes the site's sponsor. If the sponsor is an educational institution, for example, the name of the page is followed by *.edu.* Sites sponsored by government agencies use the suffix *.gov,* those sponsored by companies use *.com,* and those sponsored by nonprofit organizations use *.org.* If the sponsoring institution is outside the United States, the name of the page—or, in some cases, the three-letter suffix—is followed by a two-letter country suffix (*.uk* for sites whose sponsors are located in Britain, for example). For a page within a Web site, the first two parts of the URL are followed by the subdirectory name or names and the filename, as in this URL from a page on the Library of Congress site: <http://www.loc.gov/folklife/vets/stories>.

URLs can be rather long, so you may need to break them between lines when citing them in an essay or a reference list. In MLA-style documentation (see p. 736), a URL within a list of works cited should be broken only after a slash; in APA style (p. 750), the URL should be broken after a slash or before a period. Whatever documentation style you follow, do not use a hyphen to indicate the line break, and if your word-processing program adds a hyphen, delete it.

Many organizational and resource sites list the URLs of their home pages in print publications so that readers can access the Web sites for further information. Keep an eye out for such resources related to your research projects.

Search the Web

Because the World Wide Web does not have a central directory, *search tools* are important resources for finding relevant information on your topic. To use these tools effectively, you should understand their features, strengths, and limitations.

Many search tools now allow you to look for sources using both search engines and subject directories. *Search engines* are based on keywords. They are simply computer programs that scan the Web—or that part of the Web that is in the particular search engine's database—looking for the keywords you have entered. *Subject directories* are based on categories, like the subject headings in a library catalog or periodical index. Beginning with a menu of general subjects, you click on increasingly narrow subjects (for example, from "science" to "biology" to "genetics" to "DNA mapping") until you reach either a list of specific Web sites or a point where you have to do a keyword search within the narrowest subject you have chosen. Search engines are most useful when you have a good idea of the appropriate keywords for your topic or when you are not sure under what category the topic falls. But subject directories can help quickly narrow your search to those parts of the Web that are likely to be most productive, thereby avoiding keyword searches that produce hundreds or thousands of results.

You can access these common search tools directly via their URLs:

All the Web	http://www.alltheweb.com
AltaVista	http://www.altavista.com
Excite	http://www.excite.com
GO	http://www.go.com
Google	http://www.google.com
HotBot	http://www.hotbot.com
Lycos	http://www.lycos.com
Teoma	http://www.teoma.com
Yahoo!	http://www.yahoo.com

Several search tools can perform meta-searches, collecting the results from multiple search tools simultaneously. These include the following:

Ixquick	http://www.ixquick.com
ProFusion	http://www.profusion.com
WebCrawler	http://www.webcrawler.com

Two other search tools, the Internet Public Library <http://www.ipl.org> and the WWW Virtual Library <http://vlib.org>, provide extensive lists of subjects arranged according to the *Library of Congress Subject Headings.* An added advantage to the Internet Public Library site is that librarians are available to answer questions via email.

Always click on the help, hints, or tips link on a search tool's home page to find out more about its recognized commands and advanced-search techniques. Most search tools allow searches using Boolean operators (see pp. 712–13) or incorporate Boolean logic into an advanced-search page. Many also let you limit a search to specific dates, languages, or other criteria.

As with searches of library catalogs and databases, the success of a Web search depends to a great extent on the keywords you choose. Remember that many different words often describe the same topic. If your topic is ecology, for example, you may find information under the keywords *ecosystem, environment, pollution,* and *endangered species,* as well as a number of other related keywords, depending on the focus of your research. When you find a source that seems promising, be sure to create a bookmark for the Web page so that you can return to it easily later on.

Access Online Library Catalogs

Many library catalogs throughout the world can be accessed online, whether by a Web browser, a telnet connection, or direct modem-to-modem dialing. Contact your college library to see whether it offers Web-based, telnet, or modem access to the online catalogs of other libraries. Searches of the book catalogs of local and remote libraries may yield lists of valuable resources or, in some cases, complete articles. For more information, as well as a comprehensive list of links to searchable library catalogs, visit the Library of Congress site <http://catalog.loc.gov>.

Use Email and Online Discussion Forums

You may be able to contact other researchers and experts directly through *email* (electronic mail). Some authors include their email addresses with their articles, allowing you to write to them for further information. Web pages often include email links to individuals who have further information on specific topics.

Another important resource for some projects, *online discussion forums,* are interest groups in which people post messages in a public forum for discussion. The messages are usually posted on the Internet for anyone to read and respond to, much like a public bulletin board. An *email discussion list (listserv)* is like a discussion forum except that messages are not posted in a public forum but are sent automatically to all subscribers of the group by private email. In addition, the discussion that takes place through discussion lists tends to be more serious and focused than that of discussion forums. One student researching language acquisition, for instance, subscribed to a discussion list made up primarily of teachers of English as a second language. She read the group's email discussions for a while to determine whether her questions would be appropriate to the list rather than posting her message immediately. She decided to post a message with questions related to her research. In return, she received a great deal of useful information from professionals in the field.

Finally, note that most discussion forums and some discussion lists maintain searchable archives of previous postings. Contact a reference librarian for help in identifying these useful research tools, or start with a search engine that specializes in online groups, such as Google Groups <http://www.groups.google.com>. If all else fails, you can try a keyword search online combining the keyword *listserv* or *discussion forum* with your topic to see what you can find.

EVALUATING SOURCES CRITICALLY

From the very beginning of your search for sources, you should evaluate each potential source to determine whether it will be useful and relevant to your essay. Obviously, you must decide which sources provide information relevant to the topic, but you also must read sources with a critical eye to decide how credible or trustworthy they are. Just because a book or essay appears in print or an article is posted on a Web site does not necessarily mean the information or opinions within it are reliable.

Criteria for Evaluating Sources

To help you evaluate the sources you have found, try using the following criteria. Your goal is to determine the relevance, currency, range of viewpoints, and authoritativeness of each potential source. In addition, you want to take special care when evaluating sources gathered from the Internet.

Determine the Relevance of Potential Sources

Begin your evaluation of sources by narrowing your working bibliography to the most relevant works. To decide how relevant a particular source is to your topic, you need to examine the source in depth. Do not depend on title alone, for it may be misleading. If the source is a book, check its table of contents and index to see how many pages are devoted to the precise subject you are exploring. In most cases you will want an in-depth, not a superficial, treatment of the subject. Read the preface or introduction to a book, the abstract or opening paragraphs of an article, and any biographical information given about the author to determine the author's basic or distinctive approach to the subject. As you look at all these elements, consider the following questions:

- Does the source provide a general overview or a specialized point of view? General sources are helpful early in your research, but ultimately you will need the authoritative and up-to-date coverage of specialized sources (excluding those that are overly technical).

- Is the source long enough to provide adequate detail?

- Is the source written for general readers or specialists? Advocates or critics?

- Is the author an expert on the topic? Does the author's way of looking at the topic support or challenge other views?

- Is the information in the source substantiated elsewhere? Does its approach seem to be comparable to, or a significant challenge to, the approaches of other credible sources?

Determine the Currency of Potential Sources

Although you should always consult the most up-to-date sources available on your subject, older sources often establish the principles, theories, and data on which later work is based and may provide a useful perspective for evaluating it. If older works are considered authoritative, you may want to become familiar with them. To determine which sources are authoritative, note the ones that are cited most often in encyclopedia articles, bibliographies, and recent works on the subject. If your source is on the Web, consider whether it has been regularly updated.

Determine the Viewpoint of Potential Sources

Your sources should represent a variety of viewpoints on the topic. Just as you would not depend on a single author for all of your information, you would not want to use authors who all belong to the same school of thought. Authors come to their subjects with particular viewpoints derived from their philosophies, experiences, educational backgrounds, and affiliations. In evaluating your sources, then, consider carefully how these viewpoints are reflected in the writing and how they affect the way authors present their arguments.

Although the text of a source gives you the most precise indication of the author's viewpoint, you can often get a good idea of it by also looking at the preface or introduction or at the sources the author cites. You will want to determine whether the document fairly represents other views on the topic with which you are familiar. When you examine a reference, you can often determine the point of view it represents by considering the following elements:

- *Title:* Look closely at the title and subtitle to see if they use words that indicate a particular viewpoint. Keep in mind, however, that titles and subtitles are often determined by editors or publishers rather than authors, especially in the case of newspaper and magazine articles.

- *Author:* Consider how the author's professional affiliation might affect his or her perspective on the topic. Look at the tone of the writing and any biographical information provided about the author. Also try entering the author's name into a search engine to see what you can learn from online sources.

- *Editorial slant:* Notice where the selection was published. To determine the editorial slant of a newspaper or periodical, all you have to do is read some of its editorials, opinion columns, or letters to the editor. You can also check such sources as the *Gale Directory of Publications and Broadcast Media* (2003) and *Magazines for Libraries* (2003). For books, read the preface or introduction as well as the acknowledgments and sources cited to get an idea of how the authors position themselves in relation to other specialists in the field. For Internet sources, notice what organization, if any, stands behind the author's work.

Determine Whether the Sources Are Authoritative

To help determine whether a source is reliable and authoritative, check the author's professional credentials, background, and publication history to verify that he or she is an established voice in the field. To help determine which authors are established, note whether they are cited in encyclopedia articles, bibliographies, and recent works on the subject. For books, you can also look up reviews in newspapers or academic journals.

Experts will (and should) disagree on topics, and each author will naturally see the topic in his or her own way. Yet authoritative authors explain and support, not just assert, their opinions. They also cite their sources. Because articles published in most academic journals and books published by university presses are judged by other experts in the field, you can assume that these authors' views are respected even if they are controversial. Allowing for differences of viewpoint, information about the topic provided in the source should be consistent with information you have found on the topic in other sources.

Use Special Care in Evaluating Internet Sources

Unlike most published print resources, which have been selected and reviewed by editors in a "filtering" process to ensure their accuracy and credibility, most publications on the Internet have been through no comparable filtering process. Anyone who can upload material to a server can publish on the Internet. Web sites may be sponsored by academic institutions, government agencies, companies, organizations, clubs, or individuals—for recreational or professional use. This variety makes it essential that you take extra care in evaluating the credentials of the author and the credibility of the information before you use an Internet publication as a source.

The information needed to evaluate Internet sources is often more difficult to locate than it is for print sources. Books, for example, display the name of their publisher on the spine and the title page, include information about the author in the beginning or at the end of the book, and often make the purpose of the work clear in a preface or introduction. Determining the publisher, the purpose, and sometimes even the author of a Web page, however, can often be more difficult because of the technical differences between print and online media. For example, Web pages that are part of a larger Web site might—when they are accessed by a search engine—give few pointers to the rest of the site. These Web pages may carry little or no indication of who published or sponsored the site or of its overall purpose or author. In this situation, you should not use the source unless more information about the Web site can be tracked down.

The following techniques will help you evaluate Internet sources:

- *Look for the following information on online articles you retrieve:* the author's professional title, affiliation, and other credentials; the sponsor of the page and the Web site; a link to the site's home page; and the date the site was created or last revised. Check the title, headers, and footers of the Web page for this information. If it is provided, it may indicate a willingness to publish in a professional manner, and it will help you evaluate the source according to the criteria discussed earlier. Checking the home page of the Web site will help you discover, for example, if its purpose is commercial (a site published to sell radar detectors) or one of public safety (a site established by the Highway Patrol to give information on speed limits).

- *Try to contact the sponsoring institution.* By deleting all but the initial directory from a lengthy URL, you may be able to determine the sponsoring institution for the Web page. For example, in <http://loc.gov/z3950/gateway .html>, taking away the subdirectory name (z3950) and the filename (gateway.html) will reveal the sponsoring computer's address: <http:// loc.gov> (which in this case is the Library of Congress home page). Enter the abbreviated URL address in your browser to access the site and to determine where the information comes from.

- *Follow links out from the site to others.* Internet sources sometimes provide direct links to other sources so you can see the context from which a fact, statistic, or quotation has been taken. Many also link to Web site "consumer reports" that have rated the site favorably, but you need to consider whether the site doing the ratings is trustworthy.

- *Use any other evaluation techniques available.* Even if you cannot discover the author's credentials, you can check his or her facts, details, and presentation: Does the information make sense to you? Can you verify the facts? You may find that, even though the author is not a recognized expert in the field, he or she offers information valuable to your project. One advantage of the Web is that anyone, not just recognized experts, can express views and relate firsthand experiences that may be useful in developing your topic.

INTEGRATING SOURCES WITH YOUR OWN WRITING

Writers commonly use sources by quoting directly, by paraphrasing, and by summarizing. This section provides guidelines for deciding when to use each of these three methods and how to do so effectively.

Deciding Whether to Quote, Paraphrase, or Summarize

As a general rule, quote only in these situations: (1) when the wording of the source is particularly memorable or vivid or expresses a point so well that you cannot improve it without destroying the meaning, (2) when the words of reliable and respected authorities would lend support to your position, (3) when you wish to highlight the author's opinions, (4) when you wish to cite an author whose opinions challenge or vary greatly from those of other experts, or (5) when you are going to discuss the source's choice of words. Paraphrase passages whose details you wish to note completely but whose language is not particularly striking. Summarize any long passages whose main points you wish to record selectively as background or general support for a point you are making.

Quoting

A *quotation* duplicates the source exactly, word for word. If the source has an error, copy it and add the notation *sic* (Latin for "thus") in brackets immediately after the error to indicate that it is not your error but your source's:

```
According to a recent newspaper article, "Plagirism [sic] is
a problem among journalists and scholars as well as students"
(Berensen 62).
```

However, you can change quotations (1) to emphasize particular words by underlining or italicizing them, (2) to omit irrelevant information or to make the quotation conform grammatically to your sentence by using ellipsis marks, and (3) to make the quotation conform grammatically or to insert information by using brackets.

Use Underlining or Italicizing for Emphasis

You may underline or italicize any words in the quotation that you want to emphasize, and add the words *emphasis added* (in regular type, not italicized or underlined) in brackets immediately after the words you want to emphasize.

```
In his introduction, Studs Terkel (1972) claims that his
book is about a search for "daily meaning as well as daily
```

```
bread, for recognition as well as cash, for astonishment
rather than torpor [emphasis added]; in short, for a sort
of life rather than a Monday through Friday sort of dying"
(xi).
```

Use Ellipsis Marks for Omissions

A writer may decide to leave certain words out of a quotation because they are not relevant to the point being made or because they add information readers will not need in the context in which the quotation is being used. When you omit words from within a quotation, you must use ellipsis marks—three spaced periods (. . .)—in place of the missing words. When the omission occurs within the sentence, include a space before the first ellipsis mark and after the closing mark. There should also be spaces between the three marks.

```
Ellen Ruppel Shell claims in "Does Civilization Cause
Asthma?" that what asthma "lacks in lethality, it more than
makes up for in morbidity: it wears people down . . . and
threatens their livelihood" (90).
```

When the omission falls at the end of a sentence, place a sentence period *directly after* the final word of the sentence, followed by a space and three spaced ellipsis marks.

```
But Grimaldi's recent commentary on Aristotle contends that
for Aristotle, rhetoric, like dialectic, had "no limited and
unique subject matter upon which it must be exercised. . . .
Instead, rhetoric as an art transcends all specific
disciplines and may be brought into play in them" (6).
```

A period plus ellipsis marks can indicate the omission of the rest of the sentence as well as whole sentences, paragraphs, or even pages.

When a parenthetical reference follows the ellipsis marks at the end of a sentence, place the three spaced periods after the quotation, and place the sentence period after the final parenthesis:

```
But Grimaldi's recent commentary on Aristotle contends that
for Aristotle, rhetoric, like dialectic, had "no limited and
unique subject matter upon which it must be exercised . . . "
(6).
```

When you quote only single words or phrases, you do not need to use ellipsis marks because it will be obvious that you have left out some of the original.

```
According to Geoffrey Nunberg, many people believe that the
Web is "just one more route along which English will march on
an ineluctable course of world conquest" (40).
```

For the same reason, you need not use ellipsis marks if you omit the beginning of a quoted sentence unless the rest of the sentence begins with a capitalized word and still appears to be a complete sentence.

Use Brackets for Insertions or Changes

Use brackets around an insertion or other change needed to make a quotation conform grammatically to your sentence, such as a change in the form of a verb or pronoun or in the capitalization of the first word of the quotation. In this example from an essay on James Joyce's "Araby," the writer adapts Joyce's phrases "we played till our bodies glowed" and "shook music from the buckled harness" to fit the grammar of her sentences:

```
In the dark, cold streets during the "short days of winter,"
the boys must generate their own heat by "play[ing] till
[their] bodies glowed." Music is "[shaken] from the buckled
harness" as if it were unnatural, and the singers in the
market chant nasally of "the troubles in our native
land" (30).
```

You may also use brackets to add or substitute explanatory material in a quotation:

```
Guterson notes that among Native Americans in Florida,
"education was in the home; learning by doing was reinforced
by the myths and legends which repeated the basic value
system of their [the Seminoles'] way of life" (159).
```

Some changes that make a quotation conform grammatically to another sentence may be made without any signal to readers: (1) A period at the end of a quotation may be changed to a comma if you are using the quotation within your own sentence, and (2) double quotation marks enclosing a quotation are changed to single quotation marks when the quotation is enclosed within a longer quotation.

Integrating Quotations

Depending on its length, a quotation may be incorporated into your text by being enclosed in quotation marks or set off from your text in a block without quotation marks. In either case, be sure to blend the quotation into your essay rather than dropping it in without appropriate integration.

In-Text Quotations

Incorporate brief quotations (no more than four typed lines of prose or three lines of poetry) into your text. You may place the quotation virtually anywhere in your sentence:

At the Beginning

```
"To live a life is not to cross a field," Sutherland quotes
Pasternak at the beginning of her narrative (11).
```

In the Middle

```
Anna Quindlen argues that "booze and beer are not the same as
illegal drugs. They're worse" (88)--a claim that meets much
resistance from students and parents alike.
```

At the End

```
In The Second Sex, Simone de Beauvoir describes such an
experience as one in which the girl "becomes as object, and
she sees herself as object" (378).
```

Divided by Your Own Words

```
"Science usually prefers the literal to the nonliteral term,"
Kinneavy writes, "--that is, figures of speech are often out
of place in science" (177).
```

When you quote poetry within your text, use a slash (/) with spaces before and after to signal the end of each line of verse:

```
Alluding to St. Augustine's distinction between the City of
God and the Earthly City, Lowell writes that "much against my
will / I left the City of God where it belongs" (4-5).
```

Block Quotations

In MLA documentation style, use block form for prose quotations of five or more typed lines and poetry quotations of four or more lines. Indent the quotation an inch (ten character spaces) from the left margin, as shown in the following example. In APA style, use block form for quotations of forty words or more. Indent the block quotation five to seven spaces, keeping your indents consistent throughout your paper.

In a block quotation, double-space between lines just as you do in your text. *Do not* enclose the passage within quotation marks. Use a colon to introduce a block quotation, unless the context calls for another punctuation mark or none at all. When quoting a single paragraph or part of one in MLA style, do not indent the first line of the quotation more than the rest. In quoting two or more paragraphs, indent the first line of each paragraph an extra quarter inch (three spaces). If you are using APA style, the first line of subsequent paragraphs in the block quotation indents an additional five to seven spaces from the block quotation indent.

```
In "A Literary Legacy from Dunbar to Baraka," Margaret Walker
says of Paul Lawrence Dunbar's dialect poems:
            He realized that the white world in the United
            States tolerated his literary genius only because
            of his "jingles in a broken tongue," and they found
            the old "darky" tales and speech amusing and within
            the vein of folklore into which they wished to
            classify all Negro life. This troubled Dunbar
            because he realized that white America was
            denigrating him as a writer and as a man. (70)
```

Introducing Quotations

Statements that introduce quotations take a range of punctuation marks and lead-in words. Here are some examples of ways writers typically introduce quotations.

INTRODUCING A QUOTATION USING A COLON

A colon usually follows an independent clause that introduces a quotation.

```
Richard Dyer argues that racism will disappear only when
whites stop thinking of themselves as raceless: "White people
need to learn to see themselves as white, to see their
particularity" (12).
```

INTRODUCING A QUOTATION USING A COMMA

A comma usually follows an introduction that incorporates the quotation in its sentence structure (an introduction that could not stand on its own as a sentence).

```
Similarly, Duncan Turner asserts, "As matters now stand, it
is unwise to talk about communication without some
understanding of Burke" (259).
```

INTRODUCING A QUOTATION USING *THAT*

No punctuation is generally needed with *that,* and no capital letter is used to begin the quotation.

```
Noting this failure, Alice Miller asserts that "the reason
for her despair was not her suffering but the impossibility
of communicating her suffering to another person" (255).
```

Punctuating within Quotations

Although punctuation within a quotation should reproduce the original, some adaptations may be necessary. Use single quotation marks for quotations within the quotation:

Original from Guterson (16–17)

E. D. Hirsch recognizes the connection between family and learning, suggesting in his discussion of family background and academic achievement "that the significant part of our children's education has been going on outside rather than inside the schools."

Quoted Version

```
Guterson claims that E. D. Hirsch "recognizes the connection
between family and learning, suggesting in his discussion of
family background and academic achievement 'that the
significant part of our children's education has been going
on outside rather than inside the schools'" (16-17).
```

If the quotation ends with a question mark or an exclamation point, retain the original punctuation:

```
"Did you think I loved you?" Edith later asks Dombey (566).
```

If a quotation ending with a question mark or an exclamation point concludes your sentence, retain the question mark or exclamation point, and put the parenthetical reference and sentence period outside the quotation marks:

```
Edith later asks Dombey, "Did you think I loved you?" (566).
```

Avoiding Grammatical Tangles

When you incorporate quotations into your writing, and especially when you omit words from quotations, you run the risk of creating ungrammatical sentences. Three common errors you should try to avoid are *verb incompatibility, ungrammatical omissions,* and *sentence fragments.*

Verb Incompatibility

When this error occurs, the verb form in the introductory statement is grammatically incompatible with the verb form in the quotation. When your quotation has a verb form that does not fit in with your text, it is usually possible to use just part of the quotation, thus avoiding verb incompatibility.

The narrator suggests his bitter disappointment when ^*he describes seeing himself* ~~"I saw~~ ~~myself~~ "as a creature driven and derided by vanity" (35).

As this sentence illustrates, use the present tense when you refer to events in a literary work.

Ungrammatical Omission

Sometimes omitting text from a quotation leaves you with an ungrammatical sentence. Two ways of correcting the grammar are (1) to adapt the quotation (with brackets) so that its parts fit together grammatically and (2) to use only one part of the quotation.

From the moment of the boy's arrival in Araby, the bazaar is presented as a commercial enterprise: "I could not find any sixpenny entrance and . . . ^*hand[ed]* ~~handing~~ a shilling to a weary-looking man" (34).

From the moment of the boy's arrival in Araby, the bazaar is presented as a commercial enterprise: ^*He* ~~"I~~ "could not find any sixpenny entrance *"* and ~~. . . handing a shilling to a weary-~~ ^*so had to pay a shilling to get in (34).* ~~looking man" (34).~~

Sentence Fragment

Sometimes when a quotation is a complete sentence, writers neglect the sentence that introduces the quote—for example, by forgetting to include a verb. It is important to make sure that the quotation is introduced by a complete sentence.

The girl's interest in the bazaar ^*leads* ~~leading~~ the narrator to make what amounts to a sacred oath: "If I go . . . I will bring you something" (32).

Paraphrasing and Summarizing

In addition to quoting sources, writers have the option of paraphrasing or summarizing what others have written.

Paraphrasing

In a *paraphrase,* the writer restates primarily in his or her own words all the relevant information from a passage, without offering any additional comments or any suggestion of agreement or disagreement with the source's ideas. Paraphrasing is useful for recording details of the passage when the order of the details is important but the source's wording is not. It also allows you to avoid quoting too much—or at all when the author's choice of words is not worth special attention. Because all the details of the passage are included in a paraphrase, it is often about the same length as the original passage.

Here are a passage from a book on home schooling and an example of an acceptable paraphrase of it:

Original Passage

Bruner and the discovery theorists have also illuminated conditions that apparently pave the way for learning. It is significant that these conditions are unique to each learner, so unique, in fact, that in many cases classrooms can't provide them. Bruner also contends that the more one discovers information in a great variety of circumstances, the more likely one is to develop the inner categories required to organize that information. Yet life at school, which is for the most part generic and predictable, daily keeps many children from the great variety of circumstances they need to learn well.

—David Guterson, *Family Matters: Why Homeschooling Makes Sense,* p. 172

Acceptable Paraphrase

According to Guterson, the "discovery theorists," particularly Bruner, have found that there seem to be certain conditions that help learning to take place. Because each individual requires different conditions, many children are not able to learn in the classroom. When people can explore information in many different situations, Bruner's argument goes on, they learn to classify and order what they discover. The general routine of the school day, however, does not provide children with the diverse activities and situations that would allow them to learn these skills (172).

Readers assume that some words in a paraphrase are taken from the source. Indeed, it would be nearly impossible for paraphrasers to avoid using any key terms from the source, and it would be counterproductive to try to do so because the original and paraphrase necessarily share the same information and concepts. Notice, though, that of the total of eighty-seven words in the paraphrase, the paraphraser uses only a name ("Bruner") and a few key nouns and verbs ("discovery theorists," "conditions," "children," "learn[ing]," "information," "situations") for which it would be awkward to substitute other words or phrases. If the paraphraser had wanted to use other kinds of language from the source, such as the description of life at school as "generic and predictable," these adjectives should have been enclosed in quotation marks. In fact, the paraphraser does put quotation marks around the term "discovery theorists," a technical term likely to be unfamiliar to readers.

The source of all the material in the paraphrase is identified by the author's name in the first sentence and by the page number in the last sentence, which indicates where the paraphrased material appears in David Guterson's book. This source citation follows the style of the Modern Language Association (MLA). Notice that placing the citation information in this way indicates clearly to readers where the paraphrase begins and ends, so that they understand where the text is expressing ideas taken from a source and where it is expressing the writer's own ideas (or ideas from a different source). Should readers want to check the accuracy or completeness of the paraphrase, they could turn to the alphabetically arranged list of works cited at the end of the essay, look for Guterson's name, and find there all the information they would need to locate the book and check the source.

Although it is acceptable and often necessary to reuse a few key terms or to quote striking or technical language from a source, paraphrasers must avoid borrowing too many words or repeating the same sentence structure. Notice in the following paraphrase of Guterson's first sentence that the paraphraser repeats too many of the author's own words and phrases:

Unacceptable Paraphrase: Too Many Borrowed Words and Phrases

```
     Apparently, some conditions, which have been illuminated
by Bruner and other discovery theorists, pave the way for
people to learn.
```

By comparing the source's first sentence and this paraphrase of it, you can see that the paraphraser borrows almost all of the key terms from the original sentence, including the entire phrase "pave the way for." Even if you cite the source, this sort of heavy borrowing is an example of *plagiarism*—using the ideas and words of others as though they were your own (see p. 735).

The following paraphrase of the same sentence is unacceptable because it too closely resembles the structure of the original sentence:

Unacceptable Paraphrase: Sentence Structure Repeated Too Closely

```
     Bruner and other researchers have also identified
circumstances that seem to ease the path to learning.
```

Here the paraphraser borrows the phrases and clauses of the source and arranges them in an identical sequence, merely substituting synonyms for Guterson's key terms: "researchers" for "theorists," "identified" for "illuminated," "circumstances" for "conditions," "seem to" for "apparently," and "ease the path to" for "pave the way for." Even though most key terms have been changed, this paraphrase is also an example of plagiarism because it duplicates the source's sentence structure.

Summarizing

Like a paraphrase, a *summary* may use key terms from the source, but it is made up mainly of words supplied by the writer. A summary presents only the main ideas of the source, leaving out examples and details. Consequently, summaries allow you to bring concisely into your writing large amounts of information from source material.

Here is an example of a summary of five pages from Guterson's book. You can see at a glance how drastically some summaries condense information, in this case from five pages to five sentences. Depending on the summarizer's purpose, however, the same five pages could be summarized in one sentence or in two dozen sentences.

Summary

In looking at different theories of learning that discuss individual-based programs (such as home schooling) versus the public school system, Guterson describes the disagreements among "cognitivist theorists." One group, the "discovery theorists," believes that individual children learn by creating their own ways of sorting the information they take in from their experiences. Schools should help students develop better ways of organizing new material, not just present them with material that is already categorized, as traditional schools do. "Assimilationist theorists," by contrast, believe that children learn by linking what they don't know to information they already know. These theorists claim that traditional schools help students learn when they present information in ways that allow children to fit the new material into categories they have already developed (171–75).

Notice that the source of the summarized material is identified by the author's name in the first sentence and that the page numbers from the source are cited parenthetically in the last sentence, following MLA citation style. As with a paraphrase, putting the citation information at the beginning and the end of the summary in this way makes clear to the reader the boundaries between the ideas in the source and the writer's own ideas (or the ideas in a different source).

Although this summarizer encloses in quotation marks three technical terms from the original source, summaries usually do not include quotations: Their purpose is not to display the source's language but to present its main ideas. Even a lengthy summary is more than a dry list of main ideas from a source; it is a coherent, readable new text composed of the source's main ideas. An effective summary provides balanced coverage of the source, following the same sequence of ideas while avoiding any hint of agreement or disagreement.

ACKNOWLEDGING SOURCES

Notice in the preceding examples that the source is acknowledged by name. Even when you use your own words to present someone else's information, you must acknowledge that you borrowed the information. The only types of information that do not require acknowledgment are common knowledge (John F. Kennedy was assassinated in Dallas), facts widely available in many sources (before 1933, U.S. presidents were inaugurated on March 4 rather than on January 20), well-known quotations ("To be or not to be. That is the question"), and material you created or gathered yourself, such as your own photographs or survey data. Remember to acknowledge the source of visuals (photographs, tables, charts, graphs, diagrams, drawings, maps, screen shots) that you do not create yourself as well as the source of any information that you use to create your own visuals. (You should also request permission from the source of every visual you want to borrow if your essay will be posted on the Web.) When in doubt about the need to acknowledge a source, it is always safer to include a citation.

The documentation guidelines later in this appendix (pp. 736–60) present various styles for citing sources. Whichever style you use, the most important thing is that your readers be able to tell where words or ideas that are not your own begin and end. You can accomplish this most readily by taking and transcribing notes carefully, by placing parenthetical source citations correctly, and by separating your words from those of the source with *signal phrases,* such as "According to Smith," "Peters claims," and "As Olmos asserts." (When you cite a source for the first time in a signal phrase, you may use the author's full name; after that, use just the last name.)

Avoiding Plagiarism

Writers—students and professionals alike—occasionally fail to acknowledge sources properly. The word *plagiarism,* which derives from the Latin word for "kidnapping," refers to the unacknowledged use of another's words, ideas, sentence structure, or information. Students sometimes get into trouble because they mistakenly assume that plagiarizing occurs only when another writer's exact words are used without acknowledgment. In fact, plagiarism applies to such diverse forms of expression as musical compositions and visual images as well as ideas and statistics. So keep in mind that, with the exceptions listed above, you must indicate the source of any borrowed information or ideas you use in your essay, whether you have paraphrased, summarized, or quoted directly from the source or have reproduced it or referred to it in some other way.

Remember especially the need to document electronic sources fully and accurately. Perhaps because it is so easy to access and distribute text and visuals online and to copy material from one electronic document and paste it into another, many students do not realize or forget that information, ideas, and images from electronic sources require acknowledgment in even more detail than those from print sources do (and are often easier to detect if they are not acknowledged).

Some people plagiarize simply because they do not know the conventions for using and acknowledging sources. This appendix makes clear how to incorporate sources into your writing and how to acknowledge your use of those sources. Others plagiarize because they keep sloppy notes and thus fail to distinguish between their own and their sources' ideas. Either they neglect to enclose their sources' words in quotation marks, or they fail to indicate when they are paraphrasing or summarizing a source's ideas and information. If you keep a working bibliography and careful notes, you will not make this serious mistake.

Another reason some people plagiarize is that they doubt their ability to write the essay by themselves. They feel intimidated by the writing task or the deadline or their own and others' expectations. If you experience this same anxiety about your work, speak to your instructor. Do not run the risk of failing a course or being expelled because of plagiarism. If you are confused about what is and what is not plagiarism, be sure to ask your instructor.

Understanding Documentation Styles

Although there is no universally accepted system for acknowledging sources, most documentation styles use parenthetical in-text citations keyed to a separate list of works cited or references. The information required in the in-text citations and the order and content of the works-cited entries vary across academic disciplines. The following guidelines present the basic features of two styles: the *Modern Language Association (MLA)* system, which is widely used in the humanities, and the *American Psychological Association (APA)* system, which is widely used in the social sciences. Earlier in this book, you can find essays written by students that follow MLA style (Linh Kieu Ngo and Lyn Gutierrez, Chapter 5; Sarah West and La Donna Beaty, Chapter 7; Shannon Long, Chapter 8; and Brent Knutson and Jessica Statsky, Chapter 9) and APA style (Patrick O'Malley, Chapter 8).

Documenting Sources Using MLA Style

The following guidelines are sufficient for most college research assignments in English and other humanities courses that call for MLA-style documentation. For additional information, see the *MLA Handbook for Writers of Research Papers*, sixth edition (2003), or check the MLA Web site <http://www.mla.org>.

Use In-Text Citations to Show Where You Have Used Material from Sources

The MLA author-page system generally requires that in-text citations include the author's last name and the page number of the passage being cited. There is no punctuation between author and page. The parenthetical citation should follow the quoted, paraphrased, or summarized material as closely as possible without disrupting the flow of the sentence.

```
Dr. James is described as a "not-too-skeletal Ichabod Crane"
(Simon 68).
```

Note that the parenthetical citation comes before the final period. With block quotations, however, the citation comes after the final period, preceded by a space (see p. 729 for an example).

If you mention the author's name in your text, supply just the page reference in parentheses.

```
Simon describes Dr. James as a "not-too-skeletal Ichabod
Crane" (68).
```

USE THE FOLLOWING MODELS FOR IN-TEXT CITATIONS

1. When the source has more than one author

```
Dyal, Corning, and Willows identify several types of
students, including the "Authority-Rebel" (4).
```

```
Authority-rebels see themselves as "superior to other
students in the class" (Dyal, Corning, and Willows 4).
```

```
The drug AZT has been shown to reduce the risk of
transmission from HIV-positive mothers to their infants by as
much as two-thirds (Van de Perre et al. 4-5).
```

For four or more authors, use all the authors' names or only the first author's name followed by *et al.*, as in the example above.

2. When the author is not named

```
In 1992, five years after the Symms legislation, the number
of deaths from automobile accidents reached a thirty-year low
("Highways" 51).
```

3. When the source has a corporate or government author

```
A tuition increase has been proposed for community and
technical colleges to offset budget deficits from Initiative
601 (Washington State Board for Community and Technical
Colleges 4).
```

4. When two or more works by the same author are cited

```
When old paint becomes transparent, it sometimes shows the
artist's original plans: "A tree will show through a woman's
dress" (Hellman, Pentimento 1).
```

Because more than one of Hellman's works is included in the list of works cited, the title follows the author's name in the parentheses.

5. When two or more authors have the same last name

According to Edgar V. Roberts, Chaplin's <u>Modern Times</u>
provides a good example of montage used to make an editorial
statement (246).

Chaplin's <u>Modern Times</u> provides a good example of montage
used to make an editorial statement (E. V. Roberts 246).

Note that Roberts's first and middle initials are included in the parentheses because another author with the same last name is included in the list of works cited.

6. When a work without page numbers is cited

The average speed on Montana's interstate highways, for
example, has risen by only 2 miles per hour since the repeal
of the federal speed limit, with most drivers topping out at
75 (Schmid).

There is no page number available for this source because it comes from the Internet.

7. When a quotation is taken from a secondary source

Chancellor Helmut Kohl summed up the German attitude: "For
millions of people, a car is part of their personal freedom"
(qtd. in Cote 12).

Create a works-cited entry for the secondary source in which you found the quote, rather than for the original source (for this example, an entry for Cote, not Kohl, would appear in the list of works cited).

8. When a citation comes from a multivolume work

"Double meaning," according to Freud, "is one of the most
fertile sources for . . . jokes" (8: 56).

In the parentheses, the number *8* indicates the volume and *56* indicates the page. (For a works-cited entry for a single volume in a multivolume work, see p. 741, entry 8.)

9. When the source is a literary work

For a novel or other prose work available in various editions, provide the page numbers from the edition used. To help readers locate the quotation in another edition, add the part and/or chapter number.

In <u>Hard Times</u>, Tom reveals his utter narcissism by blaming
Louisa for his own failure: "'You have regularly given me up.
You never cared for me'" (Dickens 262; bk. 3, ch. 9).

For a play in verse, such as a Shakespearean play, indicate the act, scene, and
line numbers instead of the page numbers.

At the beginning, Regan's fawning rhetoric hides her true
attitude toward Lear: "I profess / Myself an enemy to all
other joys / . . . / And find I am alone felicitate / In
your dear highness' love" (<u>King Lear</u> I.i.74–75, 77–78).

For a poem, indicate the line numbers and stanzas (if they are numbered)
instead of the page numbers.

In "Song of Myself," Whitman finds poetic details in busy
urban settings, as when he describes "the blab of the pave,
tires of carts . . . / . . . the driver with his
interrogating thumb" (8.153–54).

If the source gives only line numbers, use the term *lines* in the first citation; in
subsequent citations, give only the numbers.

10. When the citation comes from a work in an anthology

In "Six Days: Some Rememberings," Grace Paley recalls that
when she was in jail for protesting the Vietnam War, her pen
and paper were taken away and she felt "a terrible pain in
the area of my heart--a nausea" (191).

If you are discussing the editor's *preface* or *introduction,* name the editor.

11. When two or more works are cited in the same parentheses

When two or more different sources are used in the same passage, it may be
necessary to cite them in the same parentheses. Separate the citations with a
semicolon.

A few studies have considered differences between oral and
written discourse production (Scardamalia, Bereiter, and
Goelman; Gould).

The scene registers conflicts in English law as well, for
while the medieval Westminster statutes also distinguish
between lawful and unlawful exchanges of women, sixteenth-
century statutes begin to redefine rape as a violent crime
against a woman rather than as a property crime against her
guardians (Maitland 2:490–91; Post; Bashar; Gossett).

12. When an entire work is cited

In <u>The Structure of Scientific Revolutions</u>, Thomas Kuhn
discusses how scientists change their thinking.

13. When material from the Internet is cited

In handling livestock, "many people attempt to restrain
animals with sheer force instead of using behavioral
principles" (Grandin).

If the author is not named, give the document title. Include page or paragraph numbers, if available.

Include All of Your Sources in a Works-Cited List at the End of Your Essay

The works-cited list provides information that enables readers to find the sources cited in the essay. Every source referred to in the text of your essay must have a corresponding entry in the list of works cited at the end of your essay. Conversely, every entry in the works-cited list must correspond to at least one in-text citation in the essay. The MLA recommends that the list of works cited be placed at the end of the paper, beginning on a new page with pages numbered consecutively; that the first line of each entry begins flush with the left margin; that subsequent lines of the same entry indent five character spaces; and that the entire list be double-spaced, between and within entries.

Do not worry about including information that is unavailable within the source, such as the author's middle initial or the issue number for a periodical. If your instructor permits, you may italicize rather than underline book titles and periodical names.

BASIC ENTRY FOR A BOOK

Author's last name, First name, Middle initial. <u>Book Title</u>.
    City of publication: Publisher's name, year published.

USE THE FOLLOWING MODELS FOR BOOKS

1. A book by a single author

Arnold, Marion I. <u>Women and Art in South Africa</u>. New York:
    St. Martin's, 1996.

2. Multiple works by the same author (or same group of authors)

Vidal, Gore. <u>Empire</u>. New York: Random, 1987.

---. <u>Lincoln</u>. New York: Random, 1984.

3. A book by an agency, organization, or corporation

Association for Research in Nervous and Mental Disease. <u>The Circulation of the Brain and Spinal Cord: A Symposium on Blood Supply</u>. New York: Hafner, 1966.

4. A book by two or more authors

For two or three authors:

Saba, Laura, and Julie Gattis. <u>The McGraw-Hill Homeschooling Companion</u>. New York: McGraw, 2002.

For three or more authors, name all the authors *or* only the first author followed by *et al.* ("and others"):

Belenky, Mary F., Blythe M. Clinchy, Nancy R. Goldberger, and Jill M. Tarule. <u>Women's Ways of Knowing: The Development of Self, Voice, and Mind</u>. New York: Basic, 1986.

Belenky, Mary F., et al. <u>Women's Ways of Knowing: The Development of Self, Voice, and Mind</u>. New York: Basic, 1986.

5. A book with an unlisted author

<u>Rand McNally Commercial Atlas and Marketing Guide</u>. Skokie: Rand, 2003.

6. A book with one or more editors

Axelrod, Steven Gould, and Helen Deese, eds. <u>Robert Lowell: Essays on the Poetry</u>. Cambridge: Cambridge UP, 1986.

7. A book with an author and an editor

If you refer to the work itself:

Arnold, Matthew. <u>Culture and Anarchy</u>. Ed. J. Dover Wilson. Cambridge: Cambridge UP, 1966.

If you discuss the editor's work in your essay:

Wilson, J. Dover, ed. <u>Culture and Anarchy</u>. By Matthew Arnold. Cambridge: Cambridge UP, 1966.

8. One volume of a multivolume work

If only one volume from a multivolume set is used, indicate the volume number after the title:

Freud, Sigmund. <u>The Complete Psychological Works of Sigmund Freud</u>. Vol. 8. Trans. James Strachey. London: Hogarth, 1962.

9. Two or more volumes of a multivolume work

```
Sandburg, Carl. Abraham Lincoln. 6 vols. New York: Scribner's,
    1939.
```

10. A book that is part of a series

Include the series name, without underlining or quotation marks, followed by the series number. If the word *Series* is part of the name, include the abbreviation *Ser.* before the number.

```
Zigova, Tanya, et al. Neural Stem Cells: Methods and
    Protocols. Methods in Molecular Biology 198. Totowa:
    Humana, 2002.
```

11. A republished book

Provide the original publication date after the title of the book, followed by normal publication information for the current edition:

```
Alcott, Louisa May. An Old-Fashioned Girl. 1870. New York:
    Puffin, 1995.
```

12. A later edition of a book

```
Rottenberg, Annette T. The Structure of Argument. 2nd ed.
    Boston: Bedford, 1997.
```

13. A book with a title in its title

Do not underline a title normally underlined when it appears within the title of a book or other work that is underlined:

```
Hertenstein, Mike. The Double Vision of Star Trek: Half-
    Humans, Evil Twins, and Science Fiction. Chicago:
    Cornerstone, 1998.

O'Neill, Terry, ed. Readings on To Kill a Mockingbird. San
    Diego: Greenhaven, 2000.
```

Use quotation marks around a work normally enclosed in quotation marks when it appears in the title of a book or other work that is underlined:

```
Miller, Edwin Haviland. Walt Whitman's "Song of Myself": A
    Mosaic of Interpretations. Iowa City: U of Iowa P, 1989.
```

14. A work in an anthology or a collection

```
Fairbairn-Dunlop, Peggy. "Women and Agriculture in Western
    Samoa." Different Places, Different Voices. Ed. Janet H.
```

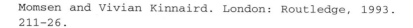

Momsen and Vivian Kinnaird. London: Routledge, 1993.
    211-26.

15. A translation

If you refer to the work itself:

Tolstoy, Leo. <u>War and Peace</u>. Trans. Constance Garnett.
    London: Pan, 1972.

If you discuss the translation in your essay:

Garnett, Constance, trans. <u>War and Peace</u>. By Leo Tolstoy.
    London: Pan, 1972.

16. An article in a reference book

Rowland, Lewis P. "Myasthenia Gravis." <u>The Encyclopedia
    Americana</u>. 2001 ed.

17. An introduction, preface, foreword, or afterword

Holt, John. Introduction. <u>Better than School</u>. By Nancy
    Wallace. Burnett: Larson, 1983. 9-14.

BASIC ENTRY FOR AN ARTICLE

Author's last name, First name, Middle initial. "Title of the
    Article." <u>Journal Name</u> Volume number. Issue number (year
    published): page range.

USE THE FOLLOWING MODELS FOR ARTICLES

18. An article from a newspaper

Peterson, Andrea. "Finding a Cure for Old Age." <u>Wall Street
    Journal</u> 20 May 2003: D1+.

19. An article from a weekly or biweekly magazine

Gross, Michael Joseph. "Family Life during Wartime." <u>Advocate</u>
    29 Apr. 2003: 42-48.

20. An article from a monthly or bimonthly magazine

Stacey, Patricia. "Floor Time." <u>Atlantic Monthly</u> Jan.-Feb.
    2003: 127-34.

21. An article in a scholarly journal with continuous annual pagination

Shan, Jordan Z., Alan G. Morris, and Fiona Sun. "Financial
    Development and Economic Growth: An Egg and Chicken
    Problem?" Review of International Economics 9 (2001):
    443-54.

22. An article in a scholarly journal that paginates each issue separately

Epstein, Alexandra. "Teen Parents: What They Need to Know."
    High/Scope Resource 1.2 (1982): 6.

23. An editorial

"The Future Is Now." Editorial. National Review 22 Apr. 2002:
    15-16.

24. A letter to the editor

Orent, Wendy, and Alan Zelicoff. Letter. New Republic 18 Nov.
    2002: 4-5.

25. A review

If the review is titled:

Cassidy, John. "Master of Disaster." Rev. of Globalization
    and Its Discontents, by Joseph Stiglitz. New Yorker 12
    July 2002: 82-86.

If the review is untitled:

Lane, Anthony. Rev. of The English Patient, dir. Anthony
    Minghella. New Yorker 25 Nov. 1996: 118-21.

If the review has no title and no named author, start with the words *Rev. of* and
the title of the work being reviewed.

26. An unsigned article

"A Shot of Reality." US News and World Report 1 July 2003: 13.

Alphabetize the entry according to the first word after any initial *A, An,* or *The.*

BASIC ENTRY FOR AN ELECTRONIC SOURCE

Although there are many varieties of works-cited entries for Internet
sources, the information generally follows this order:

Author's last name, First name, Middle initial. "Title of
    Short Work." Title of Book, Periodical, or Web Site.

```
Publication date or date of last revision. Page numbers
or number of paragraphs. Name of sponsoring institution
or organization. Date of access. <URL>.
```

USE THE FOLLOWING MODELS FOR ELECTRONIC SOURCES

Citations of electronic sources require information normally included in citations of print sources (author, document title, and publication date) as well as information specific to electronic sources, including the following:

- Version number of the site, if available, preceded by *Vers.*

- Date of electronic publication or most recent update.

- Name of any institution or organization that sponsors the site (usually found at the bottom of the home page).

- Date you most recently accessed the source.

- URL, in angle brackets. Try to give the URL for the specific part of the source you are citing, but if this URL is very long or not provided, give the URL for the search page of the site, so that readers can find the source using the author or title. (In still other situations, the best URL you can give will be a site's home page.) In MLA style, a URL that will not fit on one line should be broken only after a slash. Do not use a hyphen at the break, and delete any hyphen added by your word processor.

If you cannot locate all of this information, include what you do find. You can learn more about citing electronic sources at the MLA Web site <www.mla.org>.

27. An entire Web site

Professional Web site:

```
The International Virginia Woolf Society Web Page. 31 Aug.
     2002. International Virginia Woolf Society. 20 Jan. 2003
     <http://www.utoronto.ca/IVWS>.
```

Personal Web site:

```
Chesson, Frederick W. Home page. 1 Apr. 2003. 7 July 2003
     <http://pages.cthome.net/fwc>.
```

28. A book or short work within a scholarly project

Book:

```
Corelli, Marie. The Treasure of Heaven. London: Constable,
     1906. Victorian Women Writers Project. Ed. Percy
     Willett. 10 July 1999. Indiana U. 3 Dec. 2002
```

```
<http://www.indiana.edu/~letrs/vwwp/corelli/
treasure.html>.
```

Short work:

```
Heims, Marjorie. "The Strange Case of Sarah Jones." The Free
    Expression Policy Project. 24 Jan. 2003. FEPP. 18 Apr.
    2003 <http://www.fepproject.org/Commentaries/
    sarahjones.html>.
```

When listing the URL, give the address of the book or short work, not the project.

29. An article from an online journal

```
Lankshear, Colin, and Michele Knobel. "Mapping Postmodern
    Literacies: A Preliminary Chart." Journal of Literacy
    and Technology 1.1 (2000). 10 Jan. 2002
    <http://www.literacyandtechnology.org/v1n1/lk.html>.
```

30. An article from an online magazine

If you accessed the article through a personal subscription:

```
Weeks, W. William. "Beyond the Ark." Nature Conservancy. Mar.-
    Apr. 1999. America Online. 2 Apr. 1999. Keyword: Ecology.
```

If the service supplies no URL that someone else could use to retrieve the article, end with the word *Keyword,* a colon, and the keyword you used (as shown above) or with the word *Path,* a colon, and the sequence of links you followed, with semicolons between the links.

If you accessed the article through a library subscription:

```
Hillenbrand, Laura. "A Sudden Illness: Personal History." New
    Yorker 7 July 2003: 56. ProQuest. U of South Florida,
    Main Lib. 10 July 2003 <http://www.proquest.umi.com>.
```

31. A posting to a discussion group or listserv

A discussion group posting:

```
Rostrum, Rich. "Did Jefferson Really Wish for the Abolishment
    of Slavery?" Online posting. 6 July 2003. 14 July 2003
    <news:soc.hist.war.us-revolution>.
```

A listserv posting:

```
Martin, Francesca Alys. "Wait--Did Somebody Say 'Buffy'?"
    Online posting. 8 Mar. 2000. Cultstud-1. 16 Mar. 2000.
    <http://lists.accomp.usf.edu/cgi-bin/
    lyris.pl?visit=cultstud-1&id=111011221>.
```

32. An online scholarly project

The Darwin Correspondence Project. Ed. Duncan Porter. 2 June
    2003. Cambridge U Lib. 13 July 2003
    <http://www.lib.cam.ac.uk/Departments/Darwin/>.

33. Material from a periodically published database on CD-ROM

Braus, Patricia. "Sex and the Single Spender." American
    Demographics 15.11 (1993): 28–34. ABI/INFORM. CD-ROM.
    UMI-ProQuest. 1993.

If no print version is available, include the author, title, and date (if provided),
along with information about the electronic source.

34. A nonperiodical publication on CD-ROM, magnetic tape, or diskette

Picasso: The Man, His Works, the Legend. CD-ROM. Danbury:
    Grolier Interactive, 1996.

USE THE FOLLOWING MODELS FOR OTHER SOURCES

35. An interview

Published interview:

Lowell, Robert. "Robert Lowell." Interview with Frederick
    Seidel. Paris Review 25 (1975): 56–95.

Personal interview:

Franklin, Ann. Personal interview. 3 Sept. 2002.

Broadcast interview:

Calloway, Cab. Interview with Rich Conaty. The Big Broadcast.
    WFUV, New York. 10 Dec. 1990.

36. A lecture or public address

Birnbaum, Jack. "The Domestication of Computers." Keynote
    address. Conf. of the Usability Professionals
    Association. Hyatt Grand Cypress Resort, Orlando. 10
    July 2002.

37. A government document

United States. Dept. of Health and Human Services. Building
    Communities Together: Federal Programs Guide, 1999–2000.
    Washington: GPO, 1999.

If the author is known, the author's name may either come first or be placed after the title and introduced with the word *By*.

38. A pamphlet

Boat U.S. Foundation for Boating Safety and Clean Water.
    Hypothermia and Cold Water Survival. Alexandria: Boat
    U.S. Foundation, 2001.

39. A published doctoral dissertation

Hilfinger, Paul N. Abstraction Mechanisms and Language
    Design. Diss. Carnegie Mellon U, 1981. Cambridge: MIT P,
    1983.

40. An unpublished doctoral dissertation

Bullock, Barbara. "Basic Needs Fulfillment among Less
    Developed Countries: Social Progress over Two Decades of
    Growth." Diss. Vanderbilt U, 1986.

41. A dissertation abstract

Bernstein, Stephen David. "Fugitive Genre: Gothicism,
    Ideology, and Intertextuality." Diss. Yale U, 1991. DAI
    51 (1991): 3078-79A.

42. Published proceedings of a conference

Duffett, John, ed. Against the Crime of Silence. Proc. of the
    Intl. War Crimes Tribunal, Nov. 1967, Stockholm. New
    York: Clarion-Simon, 1970.

If the name of the conference is part of the title of the publication, it need not be repeated. Use the format for a work in an anthology (see entry 14 on p. 742) to cite an individual presentation.

43. A letter

Hamilton, Alexander. "To William Seton." 3 Dec. 1790. The
    Papers of Alexander Hamilton. Ed. Harold C. Syrett.
    Vol. 7. New York: Columbia UP, 1969. 190.

Rogers, Katherine. Letter to the author. 22 Mar. 2003.

44. A map or chart

Mineral King, California. Map. Berkeley: Wilderness P, 1979.

45. A cartoon or comic strip

Kaplan, Bruce Eric. Cartoon. <u>New Yorker</u> 8 July 2002: 36.

Provide the cartoon's title (if given) in quotes.

46. An advertisement

City Harvest Feed the Kids 2003. Advertisement. <u>New York</u> 26
    May 2003: 15.

47. A work of art or a musical composition

De Goya, Francisco. <u>The Sleep of Reason Produces Monsters</u>.
    Norton Simon Museum, Pasadena.

Beethoven, Ludwig van. Violin Concerto in D Major, op. 61.

Gershwin, George. <u>Porgy and Bess</u>.

48. A performance

<u>Proof</u>. By David Auburn. Dir. Daniel Sullivan. Perf. Mary-Louise
    Parker. Walter Kerr Theatre, New York. 9 Sept. 2001.

Include the names of any performers or other contributors who are relevant to
or cited in your essay.

49. A television or radio program

"Murder of the Century." <u>American Experience</u>. Narr. David
    Ogden Stiers. Writ. and prod. Carl Charlson. PBS. WEDU,
    Tampa. 14 July 2003.

Include the names of any contributors who are relevant to or cited in your
essay. If you are discussing the work of a particular person (for example, the
director or writer), begin the entry with that person's name.

50. A film or video recording

<u>Space Station</u>. Prod. and dir. Toni Myers. Narr. Tom Cruise.
    IMAX, 2002.

<u>Casablanca</u>. Dir. Michael Curtiz. Perf. Humphrey Bogart. 1942.
    Videocassette. MGM-UA Home Video, 1992.

Include the names of any performers or other contributors who are relevant to
or cited in your essay. If you are discussing the work of a particular person (for
example, an actor), begin the entry with that person's name:

Bogart, Humphrey, perf. <u>Casablanca</u>. Dir. Michael Curtiz.
    1942. Videocassette. MGM-UA Home Video, 1992.

51. A sound recording

Bach, Johann Sebastian. Italian Concerto in F, Partita no. 1,
    and Toccata in D. Dubravka Tomsic, piano. Polyband, 1987.

Jane's Addiction. "Been Caught Stealing." Ritual de lo
    Habitual. Audiocassette. Warner Brothers, 1990.

If the year of issue is not known, add *n.d.*

Documenting Sources Using APA Style

The following guidelines are sufficient for most college research reports that call for APA-style documentation. For additional information, see the *Publication Manual of the American Psychological Association,* fifth edition (2001), or check the APA Web site <http://www.apa.org>.

Use In-Text Citations to Show Where You Have Used Material from Sources

The APA author-year system calls for the last name of the author and the year of publication of the original work in the citation. If the cited material is a quotation, you also need to include the page number(s) of the original. If the cited material is not a quotation, the page reference is optional. Use commas to separate author, year, and page in a parenthetical citation. The page number is preceded by *p.* for a single page or *pp.* for a range. Use an ampersand (&) to join the names of multiple authors.

Dr. James is described as a "not-too-skeletal Ichabod Crane"
(Simon, 1982, p. 68).

Racial bias does not necessarily diminish merely through
exposure to individuals of other races (Johnson & Tyree,
2001).

If you are citing an electronic source without page numbers, give the paragraph number if it is provided, preceded by the paragraph symbol (¶) or the abbreviation *para.* If no paragraph number is given, give the heading of the section and the number of the paragraph within it where the material appears, if possible.

The subjects were tested for their responses to various
stimuli, both positive and negative (Simpson, 2002, para. 4).

If the author's name is mentioned in your text, cite the year in parentheses directly following the author's name, and place the page reference in parentheses before the final sentence period. Use *and* to join the names of multiple authors.

Simon (1982) describes Dr. James as a "not-too-skeletal
Ichabod Crane" (p. 68).

As Johnson and Tyree (2001) have found, racial bias does not diminish merely through exposure to individuals of other races.

USE THE FOLLOWING MODELS FOR IN-TEXT CITATIONS

1. When the source has two authors

Gallup and Elam (1988) show that lack of proper financial support ranked third on the list of the problems in public schools, while poor curriculum and poor standards ranked fifth on the list.

In a 1988 Gallup poll, lack of proper financial support ranked third on the list of the problems in public schools; poor curriculum and poor standards ranked fifth on the list (Gallup & Elam).

When a source with two or more authors is cited parenthetically, use an ampersand (&) instead of the word *and* before the last author's name, as shown in the preceding example.

2. When the source has three or more authors

First citation for a source with three to five authors:

Dyal, Corning, and Willows (1975) identify several types of students, including the "Authority-Rebel" (p. 4).

One type of student that can be identified is the "Authority-Rebel" (Dyal, Corning, & Willows, 1975, p. 4).

Subsequent citations for a source with three to five authors:

According to Dyal et al. (1975), Authority-Rebels "see themselves as superior to other students in the class" (p. 4).

Authority-Rebels "see themselves as superior to other students in the class" (Dyal et al., 1975, p. 4).

For a source with six or more authors, use the last name of the first author and *et al.* in all in-text citations. But in the list of references, give all the authors' names, regardless of the number.

3. When the author is not named

As reported in the 1994 *Economist* article "Classless Society," estimates as late as 1993 placed the number of home-schooled children in the 350,000 to 500,000 range.

An international pollution treaty still to be ratified would prohibit all plastic garbage from being dumped at sea ("Awash," 1987).

4. When the author is an agency or a corporation

First in-text or parenthetical citation:

According to the Washington State Board of Community and Technical Colleges ([WSBCTC], 1995), a tuition increase has been proposed to offset budget deficits from Initiative 601.

Tuition increases proposed for Washington community and technical colleges would help offset budget deficits brought about by Initiative 601 (Washington State Board of Community and Technical Colleges [WSBCTC], 1995).

Subsequent parenthetical citations for the same source:

The tuition increases would amount to about 3 percent and would still not cover the loss of revenue (WSBCTC, 1995).

5. When two or more authors have the same last name

"Women are more in the public world, the heretofore male world, than at any previous moment in history," transforming "the lives of women and men to an extent probably unparalleled by any other social or political movement" (W. Brown, 1988, pp. 1, 3).

If two or more primary authors with the same last name are listed in the references, include the authors' first initial in all text citations, even if the year of publication of the authors' works differs.

6. When two or more works are cited in the same parentheses

Through support organizations and programs offered by public schools, home-schooled children are also able to take part in social activities outside the home, such as field trips and sports (Guterson, 1992; Hahn & Hasson, 1996).

When citing two or more works by different authors, arrange them alphabetically by the authors' last names, as in the preceding example. However, when citing multiple works by the same author in the same parentheses, order the citations by date, with the oldest reference first: (*Postman, 1979, 1986*).

7. When two or more works by the same author share the same publication year

When old paint becomes transparent, it sometimes shows the artist's original plans: "A tree will show through a woman's dress" (Hellman, 1973b, p. 1).

When two or more works by the same author or authors are cited, the years of publication are usually enough to distinguish them. An exception occurs when the works share the same publication date. In this case, arrange the works alphabetically by title, and then add *a, b, c,* and so on after the year to distinguish works published in the same year by the same author(s).

8. **When a quotation is taken from a secondary source**

```
Forster says "the collapse of all civilization, so realistic
for us, sounded in Matthew Arnold's ears like a distant and
harmonious cataract" (as cited in Trilling, 1955, p. 11).
```

Create an entry in the list of references for the secondary source in which you found the quote, not for the original source.

9. **When material from the Internet is cited**

```
Each type of welfare recipient "requires specific services or
assistance to make the transition from welfare to work"
(Armato & Halpern, 1996, para. 7).
```

10. **When an email or other personal communication is cited**

```
According to L. Jones (personal communication, May 2, 2001),
some parents believe they must maximize their day-care value
and leave their children at day-care centers for up to ten
hours a day, even on their days off.
```

In addition to email messages, personal communications include letters, memos, personal interviews, telephone conversations, and online discussion group postings that are not archived. Give the initial(s) as well as the surname of the communicator, and provide as exact a date as possible. Personal communications are cited only in the text; do not include them in the list of references.

Include All of Your Sources in a References List at the End of Your Essay

This list, inserted on a separate page titled *References,* provides information that enables readers to find the sources cited in the essay. Every source referred to in the text of your essay (except personal communications) must have a corresponding entry in the list of references at the end of your essay. Likewise, every entry in the references list must correspond to at least one in-text citation in the essay. If you want to show the sources you consulted but did not cite in the essay, list them on a separate page titled *Bibliography.*

The APA recommends that all references be double-spaced and that students use a *hanging indent:* The first line of the entry is not indented, but subsequent lines are indented five to seven spaces. The examples in this section demonstrate the hanging-indent style. The APA encourages use of italics, as shown in the following model entries, but your instructor may permit or even prefer underlining instead.

Copy the author's name and the title from the first or title page of the source, but do not use first names, only initials. Do not worry about including information that is unavailable, such as the author's middle initial or the issue number for a journal article.

BASIC ENTRY FOR A BOOK

```
Author's last name, First initial. Middle initial. (year
    published). Book title. City of publication: Publisher's
    name.
```

USE THE FOLLOWING MODELS FOR BOOKS

1. A book by a single author

```
Ehrenreich, B. (2001). Nickel and dimed: On (not) getting by
    in America. New York: Metropolitan.
```

2. A book by more than one author

```
Saba, L., & Gattis, J. (2002). The McGraw-Hill homeschooling
    companion. New York: McGraw-Hill.
```

```
Hunt, L., Po-Chia Hsia, R., Martin, T. R., Rosenwein, B. H.,
    Rosenwein, H., & Smith, B. G. (2001). The making of the
    West: Peoples and cultures. Boston: Bedford/St.
    Martin's.
```

3. A book by an agency, organization, or corporation

```
Association for Research in Nervous and Mental Disease.
    (1966). The circulation of the brain and spinal cord: A
    symposium on blood supply. New York: Hafner.
```

4. A book with an unlisted author

```
Rand McNally commercial atlas and marketing guide. (2003).
    Skokie, IL: Rand McNally.
```

When the word *Anonymous* appears on the title page, cite the author as *Anonymous*.

5. A later edition of a book

```
Lewis, I. M. (1996). Religion in context: Cults and charisma
    (2nd ed.). New York: Cambridge University Press.
```

6. Multiple works by the same author (or same group of authors)

Ritzer, G. (1993). *The McDonaldization of society*. Newbury Park, CA: Pine Forge Press.

Ritzer, G. (1994). *Sociological beginnings: On the origins of key ideas in sociology*. New York: McGraw-Hill.

Two or more books published by the same author or authors are listed in chronological order, as shown above.

However, when the books also have the same publication date, arrange them alphabetically by title and add a lowercase letter after the date: *1996a, 1996b*. (See item 22 on p. 757 for examples.)

7. A multivolume work

Sandburg, C. (1939). *Abraham Lincoln: Vol. 2. The war years*. New York: Scribner's.

Sandburg, C. (1939). *Abraham Lincoln* (Vols. 1–6). New York: Scribner's.

8. A book with an author and an editor

Baum, L. F. (1996). *Our landlady* (N. T. Koupal, Ed.). Lincoln: University of Nebraska Press.

9. An edited collection

Waldman, D., & Walker, J. (Eds.). (1999). *Feminism and documentary*. Minneapolis: University of Minnesota Press.

10. A work in an anthology or a collection

Fairbairn-Dunlop, P. (1993). Women and agriculture in western Samoa. In J. H. Momsen & V. Kinnaird (Eds.), *Different places, different voices* (pp. 211–226). London: Routledge.

11. A republished book

Arnold, M. (1966). *Culture and anarchy* (J. D. Wilson, Ed.). New York: Cambridge University Press. (Original work published 1869)

Note: Both the original and the republished dates are included in the in-text citation, separated by a slash: *(Arnold, 1869/1966)*.

12. A translation

Tolstoy, L. (1972). *War and peace* (C. Garnett, Trans.).
    London: Pan Books. (Original work published 1869)

Note: Both the original publication date and the publication date for the translation are included in the in-text citation, separated by a slash: *(Tolstoy, 1869/1972).*

13. An article in a reference book

Rowland, R. P. (2001). Myasthenia gravis. In *Encyclopedia Americana* (Vol. 19, p. 683). Danbury, CT: Grolier.

14. An introduction, preface, foreword, or afterword

Holt, J. (1983). Introduction. In N. Wallace, *Better than school* (pp. 9–14). Burnett, NY: Larson.

BASIC ENTRY FOR AN ARTICLE

Author's last name, First initial. Middle initial.
    (publication date). Title of the article. *Journal Name, volume number*(issue number), page range.

USE THE FOLLOWING MODELS FOR ARTICLES

15. An article in a scholarly journal with continuous annual pagination

Shan, J. Z., Morris, A. G., & Sun, F. (2001). Financial development and economic growth: A chicken and egg problem? *Review of Economics, 9,* 443–454.

16. An article in a scholarly journal that paginates each issue separately

Tran, D. (2002). Personal income by state, second quarter 2002. *Current Business, 82*(11), 55–73.

17. An article from a newspaper

Peterson, A. (2003, May 20). Finding a cure for old age. *The Wall Street Journal,* pp. D1, D5.

18. An article from a magazine

Stacey, P. (2003, January/February). Floor time. *The Atlantic Monthly, 291,* 127–134.

19. An unsigned article

Communities blowing whistle on street basketball. (2003,
    November 9). *USA Today,* p. 20A.

20. A review

Cassidy, J. (2002, July 12). Master of disaster [Review of
    the book *Globalization and its discontents*]. *The New
    Yorker,* 82-86.

If the review is untitled, use the bracketed information as the title, retaining the brackets.

21. An editorial or a letter to the editor

Meader, R. (1997, May 11). Hard to see how consumers will
    benefit from deregulation [Letter to the editor].
    Seattle Post-Intelligencer, p. E3.

22. Two or more articles by the same author published in the same year

Selimuddin, A. K. (1989a, March 25). The selling of America.
    USA Today, pp. 12-14.

Selimuddin, A. K. (1989b, September). Will America become #2?
    USA Today Magazine, 14-16.

BASIC ENTRY FOR AN ELECTRONIC SOURCE

Author's last name, First initial. Middle initial.
    (Publication date). Title of document. *Title of complete
    document.* [Retrieved] date of retrieval [from] URL.

USE THE FOLLOWING MODELS FOR ELECTRONIC SOURCES

While the APA's guidelines for citing online resources are still something of a work in progress, a rule of thumb is that citation information must allow readers to access and retrieve the information cited. The APA also recommends that you check the URLs of your Internet sources frequently to make sure that they still provide access to the source, updating them as necessary.

23. An Internet article based on a print source

If you believe the Internet version is the same as the print version:

Banker, B. S., & Gaertner, S. L. (1998). Achieving stepfamily
    harmony: An intergroup relations approach. [Electronic
    version]. *Journal of Family Psychology, 12*(3), 310-325.

If you have reason to believe the Internet version is not the same as the print version:

Banker, B. S., & Gaertner, S. L. (1998). Achieving stepfamily
    harmony: An intergroup relations approach. *Journal of
    Family Psychology, 12*(3), 310–325. Retrieved October 4,
    2001, from http://www.apa.org/journals/fam/998ab.html

24. An article from a journal that appears only on the Internet

Kamradt, T. (2001, September 28). Lyme disease and current
    aspects of immunization. *Arthritis Research.* Retrieved
    October 4, 2001, from http://arthritis-research.com/
    content/AR-4-1-kamradt/abstract

25. A document on the Web site of a university program or department

Voigt, L. (1999, January). *Bridging the gap between language
    and literature.* Retrieved October 4, 2001, from Brown
    University, Harriet W. Sheridan Center for Teaching and
    Learning Web site: http://sheridan-center.stg.brown.edu/
    teachingexchange/TE_bridgegap.shtml

26. A Web document with no author or date identified

Begin the entry with the title of the document, and put *n.d.* in parentheses where the date of publication or update normally appears.

NUA Internet Survey: How many online? (n.d.). Retrieved
    October 4, 2001, from http://www.nua.ie/surveys/
    how_many_online

27. A U.S. government report available on a government agency Web site, no date

U.S. Department of Labor Bureau of Labor Statistics. (n.d.).
    Occupational outlook handbook 2000–01. Retrieved October
    4, 2001, from http://stats.bls.gov/ocohome.htm

28. A posting to a discussion forum or listserv

Postings to online discussion forums or email discussion lists (listservs) should be included in your reference list only if they are archived, so that readers can retrieve them. Otherwise, they should be cited only in the text, as personal communications. Include the author's name (use the screen name if the real name is not available), the date of the posting, its subject line, and any identifying number (in square brackets).

Sand, P. (1996, April 20). Java disabled by default in Linux
Netscape. Message posted to news://Keokuk.unh.edu

Crispen, P. (2001, September 2). The Hunger Site/Windows
RG/WebElements. Message posted to Internet Tourbus
electronic mailing list, archived at http://
www.tourbus.com/cgi-bin/archive.pl/2001/TB090201.HTM

29. An abstract retrieved from an electronic database

Natchez, G. (1987). Frida Kahlo and Diego Rivera: The
transformation of catastrophe to creativity.
Psychotherapy Patient, 8, 153-174. Abstract retrieved
October 4, 2001, from PsychLIT database.

30. A newspaper article retrieved from an electronic database

Chass, M. (1998, September 8). Big bang: McGwire breaks
Maris's home run record. *New York Times.* Retrieved
September 9, 1998, from http://www.nytimes.com

31. An email message

The APA's *Publication Manual* discourages including email messages in the list of references. Cite an email message only in the text as a personal communication (see entry 10 on p. 753).

USE THE FOLLOWING MODELS FOR OTHER SOURCES

32. A government document

U.S. Department of Health and Human Services. (1999).
*Building communities together: Federal programs
guide, 1999-2000.* Washington, DC: Government Printing
Office.

33. An unpublished doctoral dissertation

Bullock, B. (1986). *Basic needs fulfillment among less
developed countries: Social progress over two decades of
growth.* Unpublished doctoral dissertation, Vanderbilt
University, Nashville, TN.

34. A television program

Charlson, C. (Writer/Producer). (2003, July 14). Murder of the
century [Television series episode]. In M. Samels (Executive producer), *American experience.* Tampa, FL: WEDU.

35. A film or video recording

Myers, T. (Producer/Director). (2002). *Space station* [Motion
     picture]. New York: IMAX.

36. A music recording

Springsteen, B. (1984). Dancing in the dark. On *Born in the
     U.S.A.* [CD]. New York: Columbia.

Beethoven, L. van. (1806). Violin concerto in D major, op. 61
     [Recorded by USSR State Orchestra]. (Cassette Recording
     No. ACS 8044). New York: Allegro. (1980)

If the recording date differs from the copyright date, it should appear in parentheses after the name of the label. When it is necessary to include a number for the recording, use parentheses for the medium; otherwise, use brackets.

37. An interview

Do not list personal interviews in your APA-style references list. Simply cite the person's name (last name and initials) in your text, and in parentheses give the notation *personal communication* (in regular type, not italicized or underlined) followed by a comma and the date of the interview. For published interviews, use the appropriate format for an article.

Acknowledgments (continued from copyright page)

James Berardinelli. "This Ring Is Golden." From http://movie-reviews.colossus.net/movies/l/lotr3.html. Copyright © 2003 by James Berardinelli. Reprinted with the permission of the author.

David Brooks. "Merits of Meritocracy." From *The Atlantic Monthly,* May 2002. Copyright © 2002 by David Brooks. Reprinted with the permission of the author.

Ty Burr. "Hobbit Fatigue." From *The Boston Globe*, December 16, 2003. Copyright © 2003 by the Globe Newspaper Company. Reprinted with the permission of the Globe Newspaper Co. via the Copyright Clearance Center.

Leigh Christy. "Gehry's Disney Concert Hall." From *Architecture Week*, January 21, 2004. Copyright © 2004 by Artifice, Inc. Reprinted with the permission of the publishers.

Amanda Coyne. "The Long Good-Bye: Mother's Day in Federal Prison." From *Harper's,* May 1997. Copyright © 1997 by Harper's Magazine. Reprinted with the permission of Harper's.

Annie Dillard. Excerpt from *An American Childhood*, pp. 45–49. Copyright © 1987 by Annie Dillard. Reprinted with the permission of HarperCollins Publishers, Inc.

John T. Edge. "Hey There, Hot Lips." Originally titled "I'm Not Leaving Until I Eat This Thing." From *The Oxford American,* September/October 1999. Copyright © 1999 by John T. Edge. Reprinted with the permission of the author.

Mark Edmundson. "The Teacher Who Opened My Mind." From the *Utne Reader*, January/February 2003. Copyright © 2003 by Mark Edmundson. Reprinted with the permission of the author.

Barbara Ehrenreich. "Are Families Dangerous?" Originally titled "Oh, the Family Values." From *Time*, July 18, 1994. Copyright © 1994 by Time, Inc. Reprinted by permission.

Richard Estrada. "Sticks and Stones and Sports Team Names." From *The Los Angeles Times,* October 29, 1995. Copyright © 1995 by The Washington Post Writers Group. Reprinted with permission.

Amitai Etzioni. "Working at McDonald's." From *The Miami Herald*, August 24, 1986. Copyright © 1986 by Amitai Etzioni, author of *The Spirit of Community.* Director, George Washington University Center for Communitarian Policy Studies. Reprinted with the permission of the author.

Howard Gardner. "A Rounded Version: The Theory of Multiple Intelligences." From *Multiple Intelligences* by Howard Gardner. Copyright © 1993 by Howard Gardner. Reprinted by permission of Basic Books, a member of Perseus Books, L.L.C.

Nancy Gibbs. "Free the Children." From *Time*, July 14, 2003. Copyright © 2003 by Time, Inc. Reprinted with permission.

Daniel T. Gilbert and Timothy D. Wilson. "Miswanting: Some Problems in the Forecasting of Future Affective States." From *Feeling and Thinking: The Role of Affect in Social Cognition.* Copyright © 1999. Reprinted with the permission of Cambridge University Press.

Mark Hertsgaard. "A Global Green Deal." From *Time*, April/May 2000. Copyright © 2000 by Time, Inc. Reprinted by permission.

Virginia Holman. "Their First Patient." From *DoubleTake*, Winter 2000. Copyright © 2000. Reprinted with the permission of the author.

Randall Kennedy. "You Can't Judge a Crook by His Color." From *The New Republic,* September 13, 1999. Copyright © 1999 by The New Republic, Inc. Reprinted with the permission of The New Republic.

Brent Staples. "Black Men and Public Space." From *Harper's*, 1987. Copyright © 1987 by Brent Staples. Reprinted with the permission of the author.

Deborah Tannen. "Marked Women." Originally "Marked Women, Unmarked Men." From *The New York Times Magazine*, June 20, 1993. Copyright © 1993 by Deborah Tannen. Reprinted with the permission of the author.

Lewis H. Van Dusen, Jr. "Legitimate Pressures and Illegitimate Results." From "Civil Disobedience: Destroyer of Democracy" from *American Bar Association Journal*, 1969. Copyright © 1969 by Lewis H. Van Dusen, Jr. Reprinted with the permission of the American Bar Association.

Suzanne Winckler. "A Savage Life." From *The New York Times Magazine*, February 7, 1999. Copyright © 1999 Suzanne Winckler. Reprinted with the permission of the author.

Virginia Woolf. Excerpts from *Moments of Being* by Virginia Woolf. Copyright © by Quentin Bell and Angelica Garnett, 1976. Reprinted by permission of Harcourt, Inc.

Amy Wu. "A Different Kind of Mother." From *Chinese American Forum* 9. Reprinted with the permission of the author.

Photo Credits

2.1 & 2.3. Two illustrations by Arthur E. Giron. © 2004 Arthur E. Giron. Reproduced by permission of Gerald & Cullen Rapp, agents for the photographer.

3.1. Image of pig's "Hot Lips." © Shannon Brinkman. Reproduced by permission. www.shannonbrinkman.com.

4.1. Illustration of children going fishing and schoolbus. © Dan Yaccarino, Inc. Reproduced by permission. www.danyaccarino.com.

6.1, 6.2 & 6.3 a/b/c. Photos of Hy-wire car. © Tom Tavee. Reproduced by permission.

6.5–6.7a/b. Group of photos of interior and exterior of the Walt Disney Concert Hall. Originally featured in "Gehry's Disney Concert Hall" by Leigh Christy. As reproduced in *Architecture Week*, January 21, 2004. www.architectureweek.com. © Andrew Joseph/Bmotion Design. © Tom Bonner. © Gehry Partners. © David C. Miller. © Tim Street-Porter. © Federico Zignani. www.artdrive.org. Courtesy of the Los Angeles Philharmonic. Reprinted by permission.

David Emmite. Two illustrations accompanying "Hearing Colors, Tasting Shapes." From *Scientific American*, May 2003: 52, 56. © David Emmite. Reproduced by permission of David Emmite Photography, Inc.

8.3. Drawing of a teacher being offered an apple. © Barry Blitt. Reproduced by permission.

Index to Methods of Development

This index lists the readings in the text according to the methods of writing the authors used to develop their ideas. For readings relying predominantly on one method or strategy, we indicate the first page of the reading. If a method plays a minor role in a reading, we provide both the first page of the reading as well as the paragraph number(s) where the method is put to use.

Comparison and Contrast

Definition

Narration

Index of Authors, Titles, and Terms

Where can you find more help?
At bedfordstmartins.com.

We have a wide variety of Web sites designed to help students with their most common writing concerns. You'll find advice from experts, models you can rely on, and exercises that will tell you right away how you're doing. And it's all free and available any hour of the day.

Need help with tricky grammar problems?
Exercise Central
bedfordstmartins.com/exercisecentral

Want to see what other papers for your course look like?
Model Documents Gallery
bedfordstmartins.com/modeldocs

Stuck somewhere in the research process? (Maybe at the beginning?)
The English Research Room
bedfordstmartins.com/researchroom

Wondering whether a Web site is good enough to use in your paper?
Tutorial for Evaluating Online Sources
bedfordstmartins.com/onlinesourcetutorial

Having trouble figuring out how to cite a source?
Research and Documentation Online
bedfordstmartins.com/resdoc

Confused about plagiarism?
The St. Martin's Tutorial on Avoiding Plagiarism
bedfordstmartins.com/plagiarismtutorial

Want to learn more features of your word processor?
Using Your Word Processor
bedfordstmartins.com/wordprocessor

Trying to improve the look of your paper?
Using Your Word Processor to Design Documents
bedfordstmartins.com/docdesigntutorial

ate slides for a presentation?
ring Presentation Slide Tutorial
tmartins.com/presentationslidetutorial

a Web site?
orial
ns.com/webdesigntutorial